MOON

P9-CAD-756

NEW YORK STATE

JULIE SCHWIETERT COLLAZO

Contents

DISCOVER
New York State

New York. Just say the words and your imagination takes control of your senses. The scent of spicy brown mustard wafts from a Central Park hot dog cart. Heat and excitement rise from the masses crushed together in Times Square, waiting in jovial chaos for the ball to drop. Broadway's bright lights shimmer with glitter and glam. Frosty breezes whip through the scarves of Rockefeller Center ice-skaters.

Even those who have never had the chance to stroll the streets of the Big Apple can conjure up its magic in an instant, having long been fed the stories of the city that never sleeps through movies, novels, plays, and melodies that stick in your head for much longer than a New York minute.

As amazing as it is, though—and it *is* pretty amazing—it's only a small part of what New York is and what it offers to visitors.

No one can argue that Manhattan is the shiniest, glitziest, most faceted jewel in the crown, but the myriad gems hidden throughout the other 99 percent of the state are special, too. There are pockets of arts and culture in the Finger Lakes, for example, and culinary excellence to be found in the Hudson Valley. There is tangible history you can experience walking through Harriet Tubman's house in Auburn or the Indian Field cemetery in Montauk.

Many of these shining jewels are hidden away along the state's labyrinth of scenic highways. Looking past the City's bright reflection, you'll see a breathtaking landscape of rivers, lakes, and mountains. Explore the charming riverside towns of the Hudson Valley, the sublime falls of Niagara, and the Adirondacks, waiting amid the largest semi-wilderness east of the Mississippi.

All of this is New York. Turn the page to discover all the jewels of the Empire State's crown.

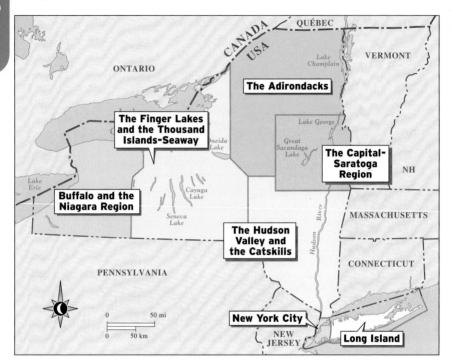

Planning Your Trip

Where to Go

NEW YORK CITY

This dazzling, shape-shifting metropolis belongs more to the world than it does to the state. Great art, theaters, restaurants, nightlife, shopping, hotels, people—and, therefore, people-watching—are all here. Movies have convinced most people that New York equals Manhattan, but the other boroughs, particularly Brooklyn and Queens, are worth a visit.

LONG ISLAND

This thin ribbon of land east of the City is home to popular beaches that stretch for miles along its southern coast. Jones Beach is the most popular, while Fire Island seashore may be the most unusual. The Hamptons is the summer playground of the rich and

famous while other seaside villages are filled with posh restaurants, inns, and B&Bs. The northern Gold Coast is lined with grand turn-of-the-19th-century mansions.

THE HUDSON VALLEY AND THE CATSKILLS

North of the City, the Hudson Valley is rich with historical, cultural, and scenic sites, including sumptuous Hudson River estates, world-class art and history museums, Revolutionary War sites, and plenty of farm-to-table restaurants, resorts, and B&Bs. To the west rise the romantic and mysterious Catskills, where you'll find the fabled villages of Woodstock, Saugerties, and Cooperstown, home to the National Baseball Hall of Fame.

New York City skyline

THE CAPITAL-SARATOGA REGION

Filled with tales of political intrigue, both historical and contemporary, the capital city of Albany is also host to the ambitious Empire State Plaza, as well as the Albany Institute of History & Art and the New York State Museum. This region is also famous for Victorian-era Saratoga Springs, host to the country's finest horse racing and home to natural springs. The small towns of central New York have interesting pasts matched by hopeful futures and robust revitalization movements.

THE ADIRONDACKS

North of Saratoga sprawls Adirondack Park, the East's greatest wilderness. Summer vacationers flock to its vast forests, rugged peaks, gleaming lakes and ponds, and rushing rivers and streams. Near the park's center is Lake Placid, site of the 1932 and 1980 Olympics. To the park's east is magnificent Lake Champlain.

THE FINGER LAKES AND THE THOUSAND ISLANDS-SEAWAY

The long, narrow Finger Lakes are flanked by vineyards, stately 19th-century towns, and a number of historical landmarks, many related to civil rights and women's history. Auburn was once home to abolitionists Harriet Tubman and William Seward; Seneca Falls was the site of the first women's rights convention. Northward are the isolated Thousand Islands, scattered over the St. Lawrence River.

BUFFALO AND THE NIAGARA REGION

Sublime Niagara Falls is the state's second most popular tourist attraction (after New York City). The Erie Canal winds its way west through tiny canal towns. Western New York is also home to Buffalo, the state's second largest city, once known for its steel industry. Today, it boasts robust arts and preservation movements.

The Best of New York State

Visit New York City for its cultural, historical, and commercial attractions. Travel to upstate New York for the outdoors—forests, mountains, rivers, and lakes—as well as historic sites and picturesque villages. Combine them to get the best of two very different worlds.

You could easily spend two weeks exploring this large, diverse state. With less time, you can combine a few days in New York City with another region: Long Island, the Hudson Valley, the Catskills, or the Adirondacks. More suggestions for spending time in New York City can be found on page 15.

The farthest reaches of the state, such as the Finger Lakes or the Niagara region, are more accessible from Rochester or Buffalo. They are best explored as standalone getaways focused on outdoor recreation.

New York City

DAY 1

Start your day early with a visit to the Statue of Liberty and Ellis Island. Grab a slice of pizza or a simple lunch from a food truck to enjoy on The High Line and take in the latest art installations at a gallery or two in Chelsea and the Meatpacking District. Browse in quirky boutiques or take a self-guided walking tour through Greenwich Village, SoHo, or other unique Lower Manhattan neighborhoods before having dinner at a popular local restaurant, such as upscale Eleven Madison Park or more affordable abc kitchen. Cap off the evening with a cocktail at one of the city's growing number of rooftop bars, such as the one at Hyatt Times Square, the tallest in the city, with views of both the Hudson and East Rivers.

DAY 2

Spend the morning at the Museum of Modern Art before dipping into beautiful Central Park. From there, walk south on 5th Avenue, shopping or window-shopping along the way. At night, brave the Times Square madness to take in a Broadway show

American Museum of Natural History in New York City

and dinner in the Theater District. Visit the Empire State Building, open until 2am, to end the day with the lights of the city laid out before you.

DAY 3

Start the day on the Upper West Side, paying a visit to the iconic blue whale at the American Museum of Natural History. Then, stock up on road-trip snacks at Zabar's, or swap sides of the park to fill your art tank at the Guggenheim Museum or Frick Collection, both on the Upper East Side. Check for free evening concerts at Manhattan School of Music; perhaps you'll luck out and catch a performance by the school's impressive 19-piece Afro-Cuban Jazz Orchestra.

The Hudson Valley
DAY 4

Let the city recede in your rearview mirror and head north on Route 9 to Tarrytown. Though it's just a 30-minute drive, you'll notice a dramatic transition between the throbbing energy of the city and the more pastoral, rural rhythms of the Hudson Valley. Here, you can tour the historic homes of Washington Irving at Sunnyside, John D. Rockefeller, Sr. at Kykuit, and Jay Gould at Lyndhurst. If time permits, take a late afternoon walk through Rockefeller State Park Preserve. At night, dine in one of the area's many excellent restaurants, such as the farm-to-table Blue Hill at Stone Barns. If your budget permits, overnight at one of the Hudson Valley's castles; Castle Hotel and Spa, looming large over the Hudson River in Tarrytown, is one grand choice.

DAY 5

Head north on Route 9 to Hyde Park, where The Culinary Institute of America offers a tasty lunch at one of its signature restaurants. Nearby, you'll also find FDR's Home, Library, and Museum and lovely, free paths overlooking the Hudson within the Vanderbilt Mansion property. Farther north is Rhinebeck, a town featuring indie bookshops, cafés, a lovely organic and sustainable

product farmers' market on Sundays, or the unique Aerodrome classic biplane show on summer weekends.

The Capital-Saratoga Region
DAY 6

Continue north another 40 miles or so to the historic town of Hudson, home to the Persian-style castle, Olana, the FASNY Museum of Firefighting, numerous antique shops, and plenty of restaurants for lunch. Afterward, head on to Albany, about a half hour farther north on I-87. Stop at Albany Heritage Area Visitor Center for a good introduction to this historic region or go straight to the New York State Museum at Empire State Plaza, admiring impressive art and architecture en route. For a free, bird's-eye view of Albany, take an elevator to the observation level of Corning Tower.

DAY 7

Continue another 40 minutes north on I-87 to Saratoga Springs. In the morning, hit the track for breakfast and enjoy a behind-the-scenes tram tour, or drop some belongings to secure your seats or picnic table for afternoon races. Head downtown to shop and eat lunch along quaint Broadway, admiring the street's historic buildings. If you're not returning to the races, take in a spa treatment or go for a dip in one of the pools at Saratoga Spa State Park, or drive out to nearby Yaddo and stroll its calm, pretty gardens.

DAY 8

Before leaving Saratoga, make a stop at Saratoga National Historical Park, where battles that turned the course of the American Revolution were fought. From there, continue on Route 9 another half hour to Glens Falls, home to the Hyde Collection, a mansion filled with Old Masters paintings. Alternately, head to the town of Cambridge and the nearby New Skete Monastery, famous for its onion-domed structures and pay-by-honor-system cheesecake made by New Skete nuns.

the Capitol building in Albany

The Adirondacks

DAY 9

Head back to Saratoga Springs and take I-87 north to Lake George. Along the way, stop at Grant Cottage to see the literal deathbed of the former U.S. president. Keep driving north along the shores of Lake George and Lake Champlain. In picturesque Westport, continue on Route 9N (which turns west), past the mountain villages of Elizabethtown and Keene, to Route 73, which leads to Lake Placid. Spend the rest of the day exploring Lake Placid; if time permits, observe feats performed year-round at the Olympic Ski Jump Complex or go snowless sledding with a bobsled experience on the Olympic track. You could choose to bring the adrenaline down a notch at John Brown Farm State Historic Site.

DAY 10

Drive eight miles south of Lake Placid and visit Adirondak Loj on the shores of Heart Lake. Set out from the lodge and spend the day hiking, snowshoeing, or cross-country skiing on Adirondack trails, depending on the season.

DAY 11

Start heading south again, taking leisurely, scenic Route 30 through the heart of the Adirondacks. You can stop at Adirondack Museum along the way, but budget 3-4 hours for driving; your destination is the Catskills. Overnight at The Graham & Co., a hip hotel in the town of Phoenicia.

Into the Catskills

DAY 12

Fuel up at one of Phoenicia's breakfast spots and then head east toward Woodstock and Saugerties. Along the way, you may want to stop for a ride on The Catskill Mountain Railroad or take a short detour to Mount Tremper to see the Kaatskill Kaleidoscope. Woodstock and Saugerties are both home to numerous restaurants, shops, and B&Bs. In Saugerties, be sure to visit outdoor sculpture park Opus 40.

DAY 13

From Woodstock and Saugerties, head south to explore the tiny canal town of High Falls. Along the way, take a break at one of the area's many organic farms to pick your own snacks of apples or raspberries, natural fuel to get you ready for climbing the Shawangunks to Mohonk Mountain House and Preserve. The Victorian mountaintop castle is more than 140 years old and is the region's loveliest resort. Purchase a day pass to enjoy miles of gorgeous hiking trails, dotted with hand-hewn wooden gazebos for rest stops. If visiting in winter, take a cocoa break by the massive stone ice-skating pavilion's bonfire.

Stay for the night and take time to enjoy afternoon tea and cookies, a wealth of unique activities, or the resort's excellent spa. If more rustic accommodations are preferred, continue down the south side of the mountain past New Paltz and historic Huguenot Street to Bear Mountain State Park.

DAY 14

Take Route 9W south to Bear Mountain State Park, where you can take a short hike or drive to the top of Bear Mountain, where a clear day reveals the NYC skyline. Continue, depending on your interests, to Washington's Headquarters, Storm King Art Center, or West Point.

Then head back to New York City to finish the trip with a walk across the Brooklyn Bridge. Toast to the Empire State at one of Brooklyn's or Manhattan's craft cocktail bars.

The Best of New York City

You could spend a lifetime in New York City and never run out of things to see. But here are some options if you only have one day. Combine them for a very active long weekend.

Classic NYC

The city's most impressive attractions are packed within a short distance, allowing you to enjoy a classic New York experience in one whirlwind day.

▸ Start your day with a bagel with cream cheese and smoked fish at Upper West Side institution Barney Greengrass.

▸ Cross Central Park in a pedicab or taxi to explore Frank Lloyd Wright's final masterpiece, the Guggenheim Museum.

▸ Take the subway—itself a New York must—to Lexington Avenue; you'll emerge just outside Bloomingdale's. Grab a hot dog or pretzel as you window-shop on 5th Avenue, the renowned stretch of high-end fashion retail.

▸ At 53rd Street, hang a right and head toward the Museum of Modern Art.

▸ It's just a few blocks to Rockefeller Center, which features ice-skating and the famed Christmas tree during the winter. Majestic St. Patrick's Cathedral is just across the street.

▸ Hail a taxi and travel down 5th Avenue to 34th Street, making sure to view every inch of the Empire State Building as you approach. Ride the elevators to the 86th-floor observatory to take in the majestic views at twilight.

▸ Now that you've worked up enough of an appetite, take a cab over to Gramercy Tavern for a classic New York City dining experience.

▸ Visit Times Square to gaze at the billboards, news tickers, and giant TV screens. They're so bright, you'll swear it's daytime.

▸ Top off the evening with a Broadway show, a must for a first-time visit to the city. Be sure to buy tickets ahead of time—you can scout out discount tickets to same-day performances at the TKTS booth.

▸ If you still have the energy, enjoy a nightcap at one of the bars in the elegant, wood-paneled Algonquin Hotel.

State of the Arts

You can easily lose yourself in the well-known wonders of New York City's art scene, but there are plenty of amazing arts institutions outside the city too.

LONG ISLAND

· **Parrish Art Museum** (page 160) is best known for its collection of paintings by northeast artists such as William Merritt Chase and Jackson Pollock. Speaking of Pollock...

· **Pollock-Krasner House and Study Center** (page 167) in East Hampton preserves Pollock's paint-splattered studio and the home that he shared with artist Lee Krasner.

THE HUDSON VALLEY AND THE CATSKILLS

· **Dia:Beacon** (page 194) is a huge contemporary art museum. Just 30 minutes away is **Storm King Art Center** (page 201), a 500-acre setting for world-famous sculptures.

· **Opus 40** (page 223), near Saugerties, is a six-acre, hand-chiseled, bluestone sculpture, framed by views of the Overlook Mountains.

· **Maverick Concerts** (page 226) take place in a hand-hewn music chapel in Woodstock, created by Hervey White's artist colony in 1916.

THE CAPITAL-SARATOGA REGION

· **New York State Museum** (page 251) and **Albany Institute of History & Art** (page 251), both in the state capital, house strong collections of arts and crafts.

· Saratoga Springs has national museums dedicated to **dance** (page 266) and **racing** (page 263), but don't miss the **Tang Teaching Museum and Art Gallery** (page 262) at Skidmore College.

THE ADIRONDACKS

· As its name suggests, **Adirondack Museum** (page 325) is a trove of local artifacts, while Glens Falls' **Hyde Collection** (page 297) is a robust collection of master works by the likes of Cezanne, Rembrandt, Picasso, and van Gogh.

THE FINGER LAKES AND THOUSAND ISLANDS-SEAWAY

· The **Corning Museum of Glass** (page 376) has the largest collection of glass in the world while the **Rockwell Museum of Western Art** (page 377) features multimedia from diverse periods, all about the American West.

BUFFALO AND THE NIAGARA REGION

· Buffalo's **Albright-Knox Art Gallery** (page 424) and Lewiston's **Castellani Art Museum** (page 440) both have fine contemporary art collections.

Corning Museum of Glass

The High Line

NYC Like a Local

You don't have to live in New York to experience the city like a local; you just need to know where to go.

▶ In the morning, head to foodie-complex Chelsea Market for a breakfast pastry. If you are in the mood for something sweet, order a cup of the popular, creamy hot chocolate at Sarabeth's. You can also pick up items for a picnic lunch to enjoy at the end of your next stop.

▶ From Chelsea Market, it's a quick walk to The High Line, an elevated park that runs along Manhattan's west side. It's a popular place to have a leisurely chat while enjoying the view from one of the many benches lining the walkways.

▶ Skip big-name museums and beat the crowds at a smaller venue. A good choice is Rubin Museum of Art, an interesting five-story gallery space dedicated to art of the Himalayas. The powerhouse art collector-philanthropist Rubins are also the couple behind the nearby gallery The 8th Floor. Admission to the small, intimate space,

which specializes in well-curated Cuban art, is free.

▶ Go shopping at New York's favorite thrift store, Housing Works, whose proceeds from selling gently-used name-brand fashions and accessories go to a nonprofit by the same name that provides social services to people with HIV.

▶ Join the chic crowd for a locavore lunch at Haven's Kitchen, combination café, retail shop, cooking class kitchen, and supper club site.

▶ Wander south into the charming West Village, window-shopping along the way. Turn east on Bleecker Street to browse through some favorite city shops, including Bookbook, Murray's Cheese Shop, and perfumier Bond No. 9. Bleecker Street will take you all the way to the East Village.

▶ Every New Yorker has a favorite place for cheap eats. The East Village is known for the inexpensive Indian restaurants lining 6th Street; a good option is Panna II. Or if you're headed to nearby Chinatown, stop at Joe's Shanghai for a memorable meal on a dime before you shop your way across Canal Street.

▶ If it feels like bedtime, it means the night is young. Join the hipsters for artisanal cocktails at The Tippler or Pegu Club, where you can earnestly discuss the merits of each drink.

Summer in the City

In summer, New York City is full of life. Restaurants open their windows, café tables fill the sidewalks, and picnickers crowd the parks. Long days and warm nights leave plenty of time to explore the city.

▶ Start your day at a sidewalk table at Epicerie Boulud, filling up on warm, fresh quiche or healthy bircher muesli.

▶ Before it gets too hot, walk a few blocks south to Columbus Circle, where you can rent a bike from Citi Bike, and explore Central Park. Zoom past famous vistas, like Bethesda Terrace and Strawberry Fields,

or hire a guide to give you an introduction to the park's myriad sights.

▶ Cool down with a few inspiring hours at American Folk Art Museum, where admission is always free.

▶ Hop the N train at 59th Street and 5th Avenue to Madison Square Park, just off the 23rd Street stop. Here, you can grab a bite at Shake Shack. If the outdoor tables are full, take your shackburger and fries to a shady bench nearby.

▶ Cross the street for an iced espresso or scoop of fresh gelato at Eataly, a massive Italy-themed food court and shopping center.

▶ Browse miles of books—literally—at Strand Book Store. Postcards and souvenirs featuring highlights of literary New York are also available here.

▶ Catch one of the city's many popular open-air events. You might find a concert in

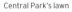
Central Park's lawn

the Empire State Building from Bryant Park

Madison Square Park or an outdoor movie playing in Bryant Park. There are also free outdoor concerts of top acts from around the world at Lincoln Center.

▶ After the show, treat yourself to a late dinner of salad and seafood at The Standard Grill, snagging a sidewalk table if it's a mild night.

▶ Finish off the evening with a cocktail alfresco on the outdoor terrace of Refinery Rooftop, with views of the city glowing against a darkened sky.

Day Trips from New York City

OYSTER BAY

A popular day trip on Long Island's North Shore is Oyster Bay, home to Sagamore Hill, Theodore Roosevelt's former summer home. After touring the estate and its adjoining visitors' center, have lunch in the village's Canterbury Ales Oyster Bar & Grill, or head east another six miles to Cold Spring Harbor. Here you'll find a number of other good lunch spots, along with attractive shops and art galleries, a fish hatchery, and The Whaling Museum—all interesting places to while away the afternoon.

TARRYTOWN

One of the best day trips in the Hudson Valley is Tarrytown, home to a collection of mansions that once belonged to famous men, among them Washington Irving (Sunnyside), John D. Rockefeller (Kykuit), and Jay Gould (Lyndhurst). Visit one of the mansion-museums in the morning and another in the afternoon, and have lunch in one of the village's many good restaurants. If time permits, make a stop at Old Dutch Burying Ground, where Washington Irving found inspiration for *The Legend of Sleepy Hollow*, or Union Church of Pocantico Hills, holding nine stunning stained glass windows by artist Marc Chagall. Splurge for dinner at Blue Hill at Stone Barns,

the region's favorite farm-to-table restaurant. Plan in advance, though; reservations are always needed.

WEST POINT AND STORM KING

Another good choice for a Hudson Valley day trip in the Hudson Valley is West Point, perched on a cliff at a bend in the Hudson River, and nearby Storm King Art Center. Spend the morning at The U.S. Military Academy, where you'll find a fascinating museum of military history, a visitors' center, and bus tours of the campus. Have lunch at the academy's Thayer Hotel. In the afternoon, take in Storm King Art Center, a stunning mountainside sculpture park featuring the work of world-famous artists spread out over 500 acres with great views. The center is open from early April to late November.

NEW PALTZ TO THE CATSKILLS

Fall is an especially good time to make a day trip to the Catskills; the foliage here is often spectacular. On your way north, stop in New Paltz, founded by French Huguenots in the late 1600s. The main sight here is Huguenot Street, known as "the oldest street in America with its original buildings." Official walking tours are offered May-October. New Paltz also holds many good lunch spots.

After lunch, continue north on Routes 213 and 209, past the scenic villages of High Falls, Stone Ridge, and Hurley. A bit farther north, pick up Route 28, which will bring you into Catskill Park. Take a scenic drive on Route 28A around Ashokan Reservoir, if time allows, and then head east to the artsy village of Woodstock, home to numerous shops, galleries, and good restaurants. From the village green, drive to the top of Overlook Mountain to explore the Tibetan monastery, Karma Triyana Dharmachakra (which has hosted the Dalai Lama), or take the steep but well-cleared carriage trail opposite the monastery to enjoy impressive views.

Following the Erie Canal

The Erie Canal cuts through several regions of the state, passing 234 towns on its 524-mile route. Tiny canal-side towns offer both natural beauty and a look back in time at the area's history. Hardcore paddlers can kayak 262 miles from Buffalo to Troy (or vice versa). A gentler route follows the exceptional 87-mile stretch of the canal between Rochester and Syracuse by car, cutting through the Finger Lakes' wine country, with water excursions along the way.

Day 1

Start your trip by flying into Greater Rochester International Airport and picking up a rental car. Before you hit the water, see the attractions on land. The George Eastman House has the largest collection of photographic equipment in the world and major collections of French and American photographs. History buffs might prefer the former home of suffragist Susan B. Anthony. Families shouldn't miss the National Museum of Play,

complete with indoor carousel. End the day in downtown Rochester's picturesque High Falls district, where you can enjoy dinner at Genesee Brew House. Overnight in downtown Rochester or head 20 minutes east to Woodcliff Hotel and Spa, which will put you in an ideal starting position for Day 2.

Day 2

Start your day in the bustling canal-side community of Fairport. Rent a kayak at Erie Canal Boat Company, which is right on the canal at the foot of the town's famous Lift Bridge. Paddle the always-calm water in either direction. Along the way, you'll see canal-side homes and plenty of flora and fauna, including herons and kingfishers, muskrats and mink.

When you're ready to rest and refuel, head back to Fairport to drop off your kayak. Make a pit stop at Donnelly's Public House, an excellent pub with good food and beer flowing from 33 taps. Then drive onward to Palmyra,

view of Fairport from the town's famous lift bridge

to overnight at Liberty House, a beautiful Victorian bed-and-breakfast.

Day 3

Spend the morning exploring Palmyra, which is packed with a surprising number of treasures, including Alling Coverlet Museum, William Phelps General Store, Palmyra Print Shop, and Palmyra Historical Museum, all conveniently clustered together. Nearby Hill Cumorah played a pivotal role in the Mormon faith; its visitor center focuses on the angel Moroni's appearance in Palmyra and the subsequent publication of *The Book of Mormon.*

Day 4

From Palmyra, head to Waterloo; the village sits on the Cayuga-Seneca Canal, which links two Finger Lakes—Cayuga and Seneca—to the Erie Canal. Start the day at Canal Side Experiences, where you can take a pontoon excursion on the canal, cruising right up to one of the lakes. Just up the road, you can experience the water in a totally different way: via human waterball, outfitted by Fuzzy Guppies. Climb inside a waterball and try to keep your balance as the ball spins and bounces on the water. When you've worked up an appetite, cruise next door for lunch at RiverPark Grille.

Spend the afternoon exploring the local vineyards. In the town of Geneva, Three Brothers, Zugibe, and Ventosa are clustered within a few miles. Overnight on a houseboat at Stivers Seneca Marina, docked in Geneva's marina. The large boat can be rented for multi-day trips on the canal, but if you prefer to stay docked, you'll be within a two-minute walk of local restaurants.

Day 5

A couple of miles to the east is Seneca Falls and its key attraction, Women's Rights National Historical Park. After touring the grounds and visitor center, drive south to the town of Auburn, where you can visit Seward House, former home of William Seward, abolitionist, 12th governor of New York, and Secretary of State under Presidents Lincoln and Johnson. Have lunch at favorite local grocery store, Wegmans, which has extensive hot and cold bars, before traveling on to Camillus. Explore Camillus Erie Canal Park with a canal boat tour, a museum visit, or a hike along 10 miles of trails. Then continue on to Syracuse and overnight in one of the city's downtown hotels or B&Bs.

Day 6

Spend your last full day in Syracuse. A must-stop is Erie Canal Museum, housed in the only remaining weighlock building in the United States, where boats were weighed as they traveled along the canal in the 19th century.

Be sure to visit Tipperary Hill, where you'll notice that something is just a bit odd at the intersection of Tompkins and Lowell Streets. Find out the history of the inverted stoplight—the only one in the United States—at the stone throwers monument before finishing your journey with lunch at Coleman's Authentic Irish Pub. Head for home via Syracuse's international airport.

Food and Wine Trails

In Vino Veritas: "In wine, truth."

New York restaurants get all the attention, but there's a whole crop of places throughout the state that are equally deserving. The state's culinary "trails" offer easy, organized access to a variety of experiences touring farms, orchards, vineyards, and breweries and sampling their ultra-fresh fare, often served by the folks who made it.

WINE

New York State is home to almost 1,500 family-owned vineyards. Most tastings are inexpensive (even free) and winemakers are accessible. Five areas (Long Island, Hudson Valley, Finger Lakes, the Lake Erie region, and Niagara) have formal **wine trails.** Passport programs offer **discounts** and **free tastings.** Get more information at www.newyorkwines.org.

CHEESE

Cheddars, goudas, and goat cheeses are just some of the varieties you'll find along the **Finger Lakes Cheese Trail** (www.flcheese-trail.com). Many of the farms are kid-friendly, with peeks into barns to see cows and goats. Every member cheese-maker is a family-owned

business, so days and times of operation change frequently.

BEER

New York State is poised to recover its title as the hops capital of the world. Nearly 70 breweries are registered members of the **New York State Brewery Trail** (www.thinknydrinkny.com), whose map and guide can help you plan a hoppy visit. Structured beer trails also exist in the **Hudson Valley** (www.hudsonvalleybeer-trail.com) and **Finger Lakes** (fingerlakesbeer-trail.com).

MAPLE SYRUP

New York is the second largest producer of maple syrup in the United States. Witnessing how syrup evolves from sap is a fun and tasty activity. The Adirondacks, the Capital-Saratoga region, and western New York all host special **"sugaring" season events,** ranging from tapping trees to pancake breakfasts. In recent years, warm weather has meant short sugaring seasons. Check **I Love NY's website** (www.iloveny.com) for dates and special events.

Wild New York

The Adirondacks, Catskills, and Finger Lakes are particularly well known for their wild places, but every region of the state offers something special.

The Hudson Valley and the Catskills

Nearest to New York City, find 5,000-acre Bear Mountain State Park and 46,000-acre Harriman State Park. Both offer excellent hiking.

Putnam County is home to Constitution Marsh Audubon Center Sanctuary, a 207-acre tidal marsh managed by the National Audubon Society, and 14,000-acre Clarence Fahnestock Memorial State Park, crisscrossed with hiking trails. Farther north, in Columbia County, are Taconic State Park and Lake Taghkanic State Park.

Another premier outdoors area is Catskill Park, a 900-square-mile preserve. Day hikes are plentiful, especially in Greene County, with the park's highest peaks. The Escarpment Trail stretches for 24 miles between Haines Falls and East Windham.

In Ulster County, the ancient Shawangunk Mountains are a mecca for rock-climbing enthusiasts. Minnewaska State Park holds two stunning glacial lakes, accessible by foot only.

The famous Appalachian Trail cuts through only a small section of New York in the Hudson Valley region for about 90 miles. The trail can most easily be picked up at Bear Mountain, Harriman, and Clarence Fahnestock State Parks.

The Adirondacks

Adirondack Park is a six-million-acre refuge with an unusual mixture of public and private lands. In the park's center tower the 46 High Peaks, most over 4,000 feet high. Skiing and other winter sports make the Lake Placid area a four-season option for nature lovers.

You can also enjoy magnificent beauty by driving its many scenic highways and byways.

sunrise in Letchworth State Park

Niagara Falls

Blue Mountain Lake, the northern part of Lake George, much of the western shores of Lake Champlain, and the High Peaks are especially scenic.

The Finger Lakes

Between Cayuga and Seneca Lakes lies Finger Lakes National Forest, a 16,212-acre preserve laced with over 30 miles of hiking trails. Though the terrain is largely flat, the forest contains some high hills with excellent vistas. The Finger Lakes Trail is a 557-mile route that begins at the Pennsylvania border and runs to the Catskills.

The town of Ithaca is surrounded by deep gorges and thundering waterfalls. Some of the most stunning can be found at wild, rugged Robert H. Treman State Park, spread over 1,025 acres.

At the Finger Lakes' western edge lies 17-mile-long Letchworth Gorge, dubbed the "Grand Canyon of the East." All around grows a dense, thicketed forest laced with about 20 miles of hiking trails.

Long Island

Most of 32-mile-long Fire Island belongs to Fire Island National Seashore and is accessible by ferry and boat taxi only. Exceptions are Robert Moses State Park and Smith Point County Park, located at either end of the island.

Orient Beach State Park is a favorite among bird-watchers. Hither Hills State Park is known for its so-called Walking Dunes; its trails wind through cranberry bogs, beach terrain, and pine forests. Montauk Point State Park, at the very tip of the island, is an excellent fishing and bird-watching spot.

The Capital-Saratoga Region

John Boyd Thacher State Park, near Albany, is where you'll find the unusual Indian Ladder Geologic Trail, one of the richest fossil-bearing formations in the world. Glimmerglass State Park, on the shore of Otsego Lake in Cooperstown, features a swimming beach, hiking trails, and a grand neoclassical mansion. Howe Caverns offers glimpses of an underground New York filled with stalactites and stalagmites.

Buffalo and the Niagara Region

There are myriad ways to experience the world-famous falls at Niagara Falls State Park. Even in urban Buffalo, you can find plenty of opportunities for recreation: kayak with BFLO Harbor Kayak or storm the tallest artificial climbing wall in the country at Silo City Rocks.

NEW YORK CITY

While you're walking through Times Square or gazing at the skyline from atop the Empire State Building, New York City feels like the center of the universe—and most New Yorkers would insist it is. Not a shy bunch, they'll reel off the numbers: 8.33 million people speaking more than 200 languages; 305 square miles (490 square kilometers) of everything you'd ever want, at any hour of the day or night.

Point out what an impossible place the city is, how all the concrete "would make a stone sick," as Nikita Khrushchev noted, and New Yorkers won't disagree. Instead, they'll regale you with stories of how bad it can be: the dirt, the heat, the humidity, the crowds! But there is pride in these stories, and more than a little wonder. The subtext is always that people prevail, and what's more, they do it in one of the most compelling places on earth.

New York is larger than life, a city of myth and legend. Still, much of what you've heard is true: The buildings are taller, the cab drivers feistier, the hipsters hipper, and the pace is either exhausting or exhilarating, depending on your energy level. It's the country's center of commerce—more than one billion shares are traded daily on the New York Stock Exchange—and its cultural heart. It draws people whose talent, ambition, and eccentricity are too big for any other place.

Much of what makes New York New York happens at street level, so the best way to see the city is on foot. Unless it's high summer, you can walk from the Empire State Building to Times Square and then to Central Park without

© DREAMSTIME.COM

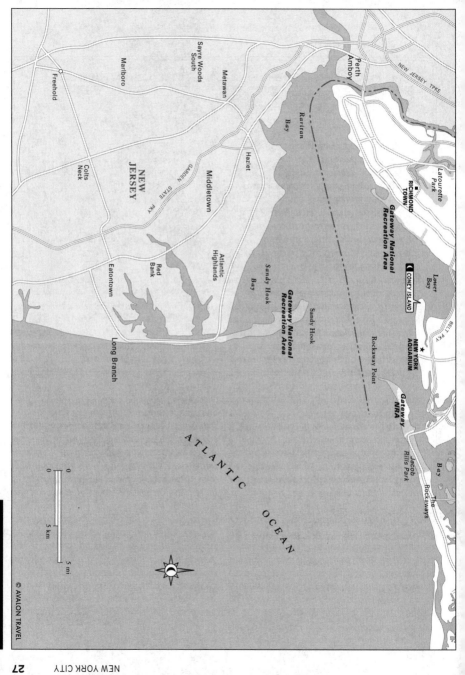

© AVALON TRAVEL

HIGHLIGHTS

◗ **Statue of Liberty and Ellis Island:** Between 1882 and 1924, 12 million immigrants beheld the sight of the statue while passing through Ellis Island (page 30).

◗ **Chinatown:** Mott Street is the bustling heart of Chinatown, lined with restaurants, bakeries, tiny food stores, and cheery souvenir shops (page 39).

◗ **SoHo Walking Tour:** Wander down the main shopping drags of Broadway, West Broadway, Prince, and Spring, where you'll find everything from street vendors to chic boutiques (page 42).

◗ **The High Line:** This park, constructed on an elevated railway, is a triumph of urban planning—and a magnet for tourists and locals alike (page 51).

◗ **Times Square:** This iconic square in the heart of the Theater District is a neon-splashed spectacle best taken in after the sun goes down (page 55).

◗ **Empire State Building:** The quintessential skyscraper was erected during the Depression in an astonishing 14 months (page 57).

◗ **Museum of Modern Art (MoMA):** One of the world's foremost museums showcases work by masters such as Van Gogh, Rousseau, and Picasso (page 59).

◗ **Central Park:** The 843-acre "lungs of New York" are entirely human-constructed, with every bush, tree, and rock planted by someone (page 60).

◗ **The Metropolitan Museum of Art:** The largest museum in the Western Hemisphere houses nearly three million works of art from all over the world (page 68).

◗ **Coney Island:** With a boardwalk, amusement rides, and carnival snack stands, Coney Island is quintessential old-time New York (page 110).

◗ **The Bronx Zoo and New York Botanical Garden:** One of the world's largest and most important zoos, housing over 4,000 animals, sits alongside well-tended gardens full of roses, orchids, ferns, and waterlilies (page 117).

© AVALON TRAVEL

LOOK FOR ◗ TO FIND RECOMMENDED SIGHTS, ACTIVITIES, DINING, AND LODGING.

breaking a sweat, and the spectacles you'll witness along the way will rival—and maybe even surpass—the city's famous sights. And it's on the street that you'll be swept up in New York's controlled chaos; it's a city of pedestrians who surge en masse across broad avenues, each alone in a crowd.

The city itself, with its renowned architecture and unique physical spaces, can be astounding. The experiences, however, are what go home with you, whether you're taking in a Broadway show or swirling a cocktail in a penthouse bar. As for New Yorkers themselves, collectively they are a phalanx of humanity, but a remarkably friendly and gregarious bunch, despite their reputation to the contrary. Talking to the cab driver from Pakistan, the Japanese student with orange hair, or the street vendor from Brazil, you'll find the mosaic of people is what makes New York City a truly unique place.

Whether it's your 1st visit or your 15th, any vacation in New York will quickly come to

resemble the city itself: densely packed, a little dizzying, and guaranteed to leave you wanting more. So go ahead—soak up some of the city's moxie and walk the New York walk. If your feet get tired, flag down one of the 13,237 yellow cabs, take a bus, or enter the 660-mile subway system, which is fairly clean and efficient. Bundle up in the winter, peel down in the summer, and enjoy the mild "shoulder season" months of May, June, September, and October. Revel in the Big Apple, and star in a few New York stories of your own.

PLANNING YOUR TIME

There's never enough time to explore New York City. That said, you can also see a lot in a few days. Manhattan, where most of the city's most famous attractions are located, is a compact place with an excellent public transportation system, not to mention it's the best place in the world for sightseeing on foot. First-time visitors will probably want to spend a day visiting the **Empire State Building** and **Metropolitan**

the fountain at Rockefeller Center in Manhattan

Sights

LOWER MANHATTAN

New York City began down here, on this tip of an island where the Hudson and East Rivers meet. This is where the Dutch West India Company established its first New World outpost, and where Peter Minuit "bought" Manhattan from the Algonquins for the grand sum of $24. This is where George Washington bade farewell to his troops at the end of the Revolutionary War, and where he was inaugurated as the first president of the United States. Here, the New York Stock Exchange was born beneath a buttonwood tree, and here more than 20 million immigrants entered the country on their way to new lives as Americans.

Whispers of this early history still echo throughout Lower Manhattan in sites tucked away among the glistening towers of corporate and financial America. In this most compressed of cities, this is the most compressed of neighborhoods. Everything here—the old and the new, the glitzy and the drab—is squeezed together on narrow, crooked streets that seem to belong more to the past than to the present.

Tragically, lower Manhattan is also the site of the former World Trade Center, destroyed in the terrorist attacks of September 11, 2001. Parts of the neighborhood retain a somber, solemn feel, particularly around the World Trade Center site, where new buildings are being constructed and a memorial stands as a permanent tribute to those who lost their lives. New Yorkers will never forget the tragedy of that day and those that followed, but more than a decade later, the area remains a vital nerve center for world commerce and people hurry through lower Manhattan's streets, going about their lives, busy as ever.

■ Statue of Liberty and Ellis Island

A gift from the people of France, the **Statue of Liberty** (www.nps.gov/stli) has become an indelible symbol of freedom and of the United States. Designed by sculptor Frédéric-Auguste Bartholdi, with internal structural engineering designed by Alexandre-Gustave Eiffel (of Eiffel Tower fame), the statue arrived in 1885 without a pedestal to support its 225-ton weight. Prompted by the urgings of newspaper magnate Joseph Pulitzer, thousands of Americans made donations to pay for the base's construction, and in 1886, the statue was assembled and dedicated in New York Harbor.

Across the water, **Ellis Island** (www.nps.gov/elis, daily 9:30am-5pm; closed Dec. 25) was once the nation's main immigration checkpoint. More than 12 million people passed through the site between 1892 and 1954, after which the number of immigrants dropped and the center ceased operation. After years of disuse, the main building of the former

Museum of Art, perhaps taking a wander through **Central Park** afterward. The next day could be devoted to the **Statue of Liberty**, **Ellis Island**, and a short walking tour of lower Manhattan, where highlights include **Wall Street** and **South Street Seaport**. On your third day, explore the streets of **Chinatown**, **SoHo**, and the **West Village**. At night, take in a **Broadway play**, visit a **jazz club**, and eat in one of the city's many ethnic restaurants.

If you have more time, spend a day at the **Museum of Modern Art** and take a stroll down 5th Avenue and across East 42nd Street, visiting **Rockefeller Center**, **St. Patrick's Cathedral**, the **New York Public Library**, and **Grand Central Terminal** along the way. Or, explore the **American Museum of Natural History** and take the A train up to revitalized 125th Street in **Harlem**. A fifth day could be spent shopping, visiting another museum, or visiting one of the outer boroughs' vibrant neighborhoods. On your sixth day, walk over the **Brooklyn Bridge** to **Brooklyn Heights** or take a day trip to **Coney Island**.

immigration complex was completely restored, reopening in 1986 as an interesting museum, displaying photos and artifacts from the island's past.

Parts of the museum were destroyed by Hurricane Sandy in 2012, and the island and its building were closed for a year. In fall 2013, Ellis Island reopened, though some exhibits and services remain closed while repairs are completed.

Statue Cruises is the official provider of transportation to Liberty and Ellis Islands. **Ferries** (877/523-9849, www.statuecruises. com, adults $17, seniors $14, children 4-12 $9) depart several times an hour from Battery Park and once or twice an hour from Liberty State Park in New Jersey, and include full access to both Liberty Island and Ellis Island, though access to the statue's pedestal and crown costs extra.

Castle Clinton

Though not much to look at now, this roofless, red sandstone ring called **Castle Clinton** (north end of Battery Park, 212/344-7220, daily 8:30am-5pm, free) was once an American fort protecting the city against the British. When it was built in 1807, it stood on an outcropping of land some 200 feet out in the harbor and could only be reached by drawbridge.

From 1855 to 1890, before the establishment of Ellis Island, Castle Clinton served as the Immigrant Landing Depot. In 1896, it was remodeled into the New York Aquarium. Today, it houses a small bookstore, tourist information center, and **ticket booth for the Statue of Liberty and Ellis Island ferries.** On the monument's east side, a small National Park Service museum chronicles the castle's history.

Staten Island Ferry

Few people—New Yorkers or tourists—ever get around to exploring Staten Island, but many ride **the Staten Island Ferry** (southern tip of Manhattan, 718/727-2508, www.siferry. com, daily 24 hours a day, free), one of the best deals in the city. The views of Manhattan from the ferry's trip across the harbor are spectacular,

especially at twilight when the sunset reflects off a hundred thousand windows, or at night, when the skyline lights up like a carnival midway.

On your right, as you head toward Staten Island, are Ellis Island and the Statue of Liberty. On your left are Governors Island and the Verrazano-Narrows Bridge. Governors Island, where 1,500 Confederate soldiers were imprisoned during the Civil War, became a U.S. Coast Guard Station in 1966. The Coast Guard left in 1998 and the federal government sold it to the city of New York for $1 in 2002. Governors Island is now open to the public on summer weekends and is accessed by ferry. From Manhattan, free ferries leave from the Battery Maritime Building at 10 South Street. Ferries from Brooklyn leave from Brooklyn Bridge Park's Pier 6. From Queens, take the East River Ferry, which imposes a fee each way. Check the island's website for the current season's ferry schedules.

National Museum of the American Indian

At State Street and Battery Place is the stunning former U.S. Custom House, a 1907 Beaux-Arts masterpiece designed by Cass Gilbert. Standing on the site of New York's first European settlement, the Custom House now houses the New York branch of the Smithsonian's **National Museum of the American Indian** (1 Bowling Green, 212/514-3700, www.americanindian. si.edu, daily 10am-5pm, Thurs. until 8pm, free). Inside the museum are displays holding some of the country's finest Native American art and artifacts, ranging in date of origin from 3200 BC to the present.

New Museum

Founded in 1977, **New Museum** (235 Bowery, 212/219-1222, www.newmuseum.org, Wed. and Fri.-Sun. 11am-6pm, Thurs. 11am-9pm, adults $16, seniors $14, students $10, children under 18 free; free Thurs. 7pm-9pm) is in the heart of the Bowery and offers frequent special events in addition to four ongoing exhibits focused on contemporary art by both U.S.

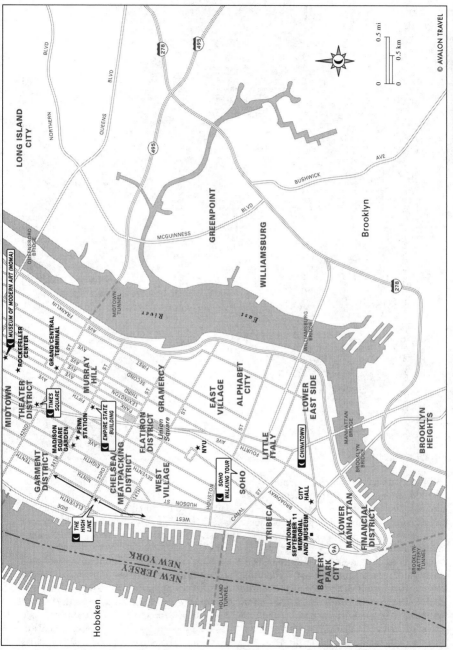

© AVALON TRAVEL

0.5 mi

0.5 km

LONG ISLAND CITY

NORTHERN

BLVD

BLVD

QUEENS

GREENPOINT

MCGUINNESS

BLVD

BUSHWICK

AVE

WILLIAMSBURG

Brooklyn

QUEENSBORO BRIDGE

★ MUSEUM OF MODERN ART (MOMA)

★ ROCKEFELLER CENTER

★ GRAND CENTRAL TERMINAL

FRANKLIN

MIDTOWN TUNNEL

East River

MIDTOWN

THEATER DISTRICT

★ TIMES SQUARE

MURRAY HILL

GRAMERCY

EAST VILLAGE

ALPHABET CITY

WILLIAMSBURG BRIDGE

LOWER EAST SIDE

MADISON SQUARE GARDEN

★ PENN STATION

★ EMPIRE STATE BUILDING

FLATIRON DISTRICT

Union Square

NYU

LITTLE ITALY

CHINATOWN

MANHATTAN BRIDGE

BROOKLYN HEIGHTS

GARMENT DISTRICT

CHELSEA

MEATPACKING DISTRICT

WEST VILLAGE

SOHO WALKING TOUR

SOHO

CITY HALL

BROOKLYN BRIDGE

★ THE HIGH LINE

HOUSTON ST

CANAL ST

BROADWAY

TRIBECA

LOWER MANHATTAN

FINANCIAL DISTRICT

WEST

HUDSON ST

NATIONAL SEPTEMBER 11 MEMORIAL AND MUSEUM

BATTERY PARK CITY

9A

HOLLAND TUNNEL

BROOKLYN BATTERY TUNNEL

NEW JERSEY
NEW YORK

Hoboken

278

495

495

495

278

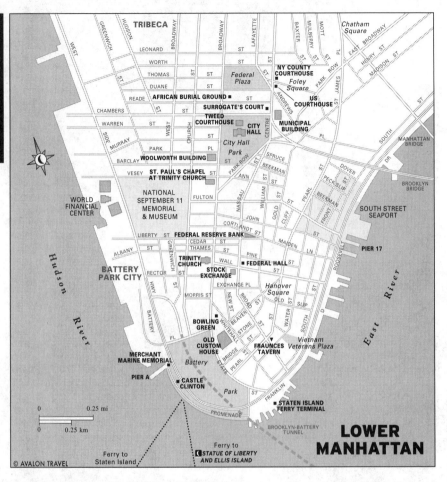

© AVALON TRAVEL

LOWER MANHATTAN

and international artists working in a variety of media. Its small cafe is the perfect place for a quick, sweet bite or a cup of tea or coffee before exploring the surrounding neighborhood.

Broad Street

About two blocks southeast of Bowling Green, off Broad Street, is **Stone Street,** a charming street closed to traffic and covered with outdoor seating for the chockablock restaurants and bars. The narrow lane became the first paved street in Manhattan in 1658. Legend has it that the street's resident brewer, Oloff

Stephensen Van Cortlandt, had the street paved at the urging of his wife and her friends, who hated the dust raised by the brewery's horses and carts. The job was completed in three years, with most of the work done by African slaves.

At the corner of Broad and Pearl Streets is the red-brick, yellow-shuttered **Fraunces Tavern** (54 Pearl St., 212/968-1776, www.fraunces-tavern.com), a 1907 renovation of the historic pub where George Washington bade goodbye to his troops in 1783. The tavern, which still serves food, is a lovely colonial setting and has

© FRANCISCO COLLAZO

the Statue of Liberty

a small **museum** (54 Pearl St., 212/425-1778, www.frauncestavernmuseum.org, daily noon-5pm, adults $7, seniors, students, and children 6-8 $4, children under 6 free) with exhibits on early American history.

Wall Street

One block north of Hanover Square, Pearl Street bumps into one of New York's most famous thoroughfares: Wall Street. Before heading west toward the canyon of financial buildings, look right, toward the East River, where the city's slave market once stood. Established by the British in the late 1600s to accommodate the Royal African Company's growing human cargo, this was once the busiest slave market outside of Charleston, South Carolina. In the early 1700s, nearly 20 percent of New York City's inhabitants were slaves, and it was here they were examined and sold to the highest bidder.

The wall for which Wall Street was named was erected by the Dutch in 1653 to defend the city against an expected attack by the British

(Britain and the Netherlands were at war at that time).

If you've never seen it before, Wall Street will seem surprisingly narrow, dark, and short. Surrounded by towering edifices that block out the sun most of the day, the street stretches only about a third of a mile before bumping into the lacy, Gothic spires of Trinity Church. At **55 Wall Street** is a landmark building with double tiers of Ionic and Corinthian columns; the Ionic ones were hauled here from Quincy, Massachusetts, by 40 teams of oxen. Morgan Guarantee Trust building, erected by J. P. Morgan in 1913, sits at **23 Wall Street.**

Federal Hall National Memorial (26 Wall St., 212/825-6990, www.nps.gov/feha), a fine Greek Revival building with a wide set of stairs that make a perfect perch for watching financial whizzes and fellow tourists go by, is near the western end of Wall Street. Beside the stairs is a bronze statue of George Washington, who took his inaugural oath of office here in 1789. Back then, the English City Hall stood on this site, and Washington, dressed in a plain brown suit, spoke to the crowds from the building's second-story balcony.

Just south of Federal Hall National Memorial is an enormous building resembling a Roman temple: the **New York Stock Exchange** (11 Wall St., 212/656-3000, www.nyse.com). As a plaque on the building reads, the exchange's origins can be traced to 1792, when a group of 24 brokers drew up a trading agreement beneath a buttonwood tree on Wall Street. The Exchange has been closed to visitors since 9/11; barricades and security personnel guard its entrance.

Trinity Church (Wall St. and Broadway, 212/602-0800, www.trinitywallstreet.org, Mon.-Fri. 7am-6pm, Sat. 8am-4pm, Sun. 7am-4pm) is one of the oldest and wealthiest churches in Manhattan. Its small museum (free admission), documenting Trinity's history, is open to the public. Some of New York's most illustrious early residents, among them Alexander Hamilton, are buried in the church's cemetery.

The **Federal Reserve Bank of New York** (33 Liberty St., 212/720-6130, www.newyorkfed.org) is a massive, fortress-like structure of dark limestone that fills an entire city block and safeguards a huge pile of gold—over 10,000 tons, worth about $140 billion. Built in the style of an Italian Renaissance palace, the Federal Reserve is a "bank for banks," where cash reserves are stored. Nearly 80 foreign countries also keep gold bullion here, in vaults five stories underground. As international fortunes change, the bars are simply moved from one country's pile to the next.

The Federal Reserve's free tours are offered six times a day, Monday-Friday, and include an informative video and a look at the vaults. No one has ever attempted to rob the Fed, but if someone should, the entire building shuts down in 31 seconds.

National September 11 Memorial and Museum

Ten years after the September 11, 2001 tragedy, the former World Trade Center site was reopened as the **National September 11 Memorial and Museum** (World Trade Center, 212/312-8800, www.911memorial.org, daily 10am-6pm, last entry at 5pm, free). The eight-acre memorial site sits in the footprints of the original World Trade Center towers, which were destroyed in the 9/11 attacks. The somber memorial features two reflecting pools with the largest artificially-constructed waterfalls in North America and bronze panels etched with the names of those who were killed in the 2011 terrorist attacks, as well as the earlier attack on the World Trade Center in 1993.

Admission is free, but passes are required and advance reservation is suggested. Passes can be obtained through the memorial's website (www.911memorial.org). Keep in mind that security in and around the memorial is tight. You'll need to have a photo ID and leave large bags and backpacks in your hotel room.

Surrounding the plaza, construction on skyscrapers for the new World Trade Center complex is ongoing. In addition to the shimmering exterior of One World Trade to the north, several other World Trade addresses are already in process, with at least five new buildings planned for the site. The plaza also includes a major transportation hub, with service for both subway and commuter rail.

Battery Park

To the immediate west of the World Trade Center Site is the **World Financial Center.** Though badly damaged during the September 11 attacks, it has since been restored to its former self: ultramodern office towers of glass and chrome, complete with shops and restaurants, an outdoor plaza, and **Winter Garden** (220 Vesey St., 212/945-0505, www.brookfieldplaceny.com)—a glass-domed public space with enormous palm trees imported from the Mojave Desert. Both the plaza and Winter Garden overlook the Hudson River, and Winter Garden is the site of frequent free concerts.

At Manhattan's tip, breezy 25-acre **Battery Park** (State St. at Battery Place, 212/344-3491, www.thebattery.org) stretches south and north of the World Financial Center. Built on landfill, it's lined by the wide **Admiral George Dewey Promenade,** a walkway within the park. Wooden benches along the promenade make great places to relax in the sun and enjoy superb harbor views. Along the way are Castle Clinton, playful sculptures, and playgrounds. The park also serves as the jumping-off point for visitors headed to Liberty and Ellis Islands. **Battery Park City Esplanade** (Battery Park City, 212/267-9700, www.bpcparks.org) is where weary Wall Streeters work off stress by jogging along the Hudson River. Benches provide rest spots with vistas of Lady Liberty and Ellis Island.

Battery Park is part of "The Battery," the term used for the whole downtown tip of Manhattan. The name comes from the battery of cannons that once stood along Battery Place, on the park's north side.

The Museum of Jewish Heritage (36 Battery Pl., at First Pl., 646/437-4202, www.mjhnyc.org, Sun.-Tues. and Thurs. 10am-5:45pm, Wed. 10am-8pm, Fri. hours vary, adults $12, seniors $10, students $7) overlooking the Hudson River is a freestanding, hexagonal building symbolic of the Star of David. Opened in 1997, the museum features thousands of moving photographs, cultural artifacts, and archival films documenting both the inconceivable inhumanity of the Holocaust and the resilience of the Jewish community.

South Street Seaport

Fulton Street meets the East River at **South Street Seaport** (www.southstreetseaport.com), one of the city's oldest and most historic areas. A thriving port during the 19th century, the seaport went into steep decline in the 20th century. In the early 1980s, the Rouse Company took over the site and filled it with commercial enterprises, restaurants, and shops.

The Seaport's historic sites are scattered throughout the 12-block district. Many of the sites are free, but to access the Seaport's galleries and 19th-century sailing ships or to join a walking tour, you'll need to purchase a ticket.

Much of South Street Seaport was affected by Hurricane Sandy in 2012 and continues to struggle to recover.

Around City Hall

The busy, though lovely, **City Hall Park** was first a cow pasture, then a gathering place for Revolutionary-era political meetings. Now it's the site of **City Hall** (212/788-3000, www.nyc.gov), one of the finest Federal-style buildings in New York. The City Hall area is full of impressive buildings and a visit to City Hall Park is rewarding in itself. The very interested may take a tour of City Hall (call 311 or visit www.nyc.gov to make reservations).

The **Woolworth Building** (233 Broadway, between Barclay St. and Park Pl.) stands at the edge of City Hall Park. Its glistening white walls and green copper roofs are best seen from a distance, where they can be appreciated in all their glory, but up close, the 1913 Cass Gilbert extravaganza is also a visual feast. Craggy-faced gargoyles peer down from a detailed Gothic exterior, while mosaic-covered ceilings grace the lobby. One lobby caricature shows Frank Woolworth, king of the discount stores, counting out his nickels and dimes. A farmer's son, Woolworth began as a salesman earning $8 a week. By the time he built his $13.5 million headquarters, however, he was able to pay for it *in cash*.

Behind City Hall is **Tweed Courthouse** (52 Chambers St.). William Marcy "Boss" Tweed and the Tammany Hall machine oversaw the building of the courthouse, which ultimately cost the city millions of dollars. The courthouse is now home to the city's Board of Education. In the building's lobby is a notable WPA mural.

Other landmarks in the area include **Park Row,** the diagonal street across from the Woolworth Building that was once the center of New York's newspaper industry; **Surrogate's Court and Hall of Records** (31 Chambers St.), at the north end of City Hall Park, a glorious, ostentatious building in the traditional Beaux-Arts style; and to its east, the skyscraping 1913 **Municipal Building,** designed by McKim, Mead & White. The Municipal Building houses many city offices, including

© MILO DEMARTILE

the Brooklyn Bridge's pedestrian walkway

nearly a quarter of existing bridges ultimately collapsed.

Today, the bridge remains a triumph of human ingenuity and it has been declared a National Historic Landmark by the National Park Service. Its elevated pedestrian walkway offers exceptional views of the New York skyline. It also affords an up-close look at the bridge's construction, including the narrow gaps in the path that show the cars passing below. For a great view of the bridge itself, head to Pier 17 at Manhattan's South Street Seaport.

LOWER EAST SIDE

No region of New York has been home to more immigrants than the East Side between the Brooklyn Bridge and Houston Street. Various ethnic groups have lived here over the years, including the Irish, Germans, and freed blacks in the mid-1800s and the Italians and especially the Jews in the late 1800s and early 1900s. Around the turn of the 20th century, more than 700 people per acre lived on the Lower East Side, making it the second most crowded place in the world, after Mumbai.

Today, the district is still home to small enclaves of Jews and Italians, as well as Puerto Ricans who arrived in the late 1900s, but it is the Chinese population that has exploded. On an island quickly becoming homogenized by white-collar professionals, this is one of the few remaining districts where you can see and feel the immigrant vibrancy that once characterized much of Manhattan. The Chinese began arriving in New York in the late 1870s. Many were former transcontinental railroad workers who came to escape the violent persecution they were encountering on the West Coast. But they weren't exactly welcomed on the East Coast either. Pushed out of a wide variety of occupations, they were forced to enter low-status service work, part of the reason they established so many laundries. Manhattan's Chinese population has grown to an estimated 90,000.

Chinatown, Little Italy, and parts of the Lower East Side are the sorts of neighborhoods where you can have a great time wandering haphazardly about, going nowhere in

those of the justice of the peace, where as many as 14,000 couples are married every year.

Brooklyn Bridge

Until this celebrated link between Brooklyn and Manhattan was built, New Yorkers had to brave a perilous ferry to cross the East River. German-born engineer John Roebling designed the revolutionary suspension bridge using pressurized underwater chambers, or caissons, and twisted steel cable, a new invention that Roebling produced and later made popular throughout the world. Unfortunately, the bridge's creation was not without sacrifices. Approximately 20 workers died during its construction, including Roebling himself. After 14 years, the Brooklyn Bridge was completed in 1883, its opening attended by more than 150,000 people. At the time, the bridge's 1,595-foot span was the longest in the world, and the towers anchoring it were taller than any other structure in North America. The bridge's completion—and permanence—is all the more fantastic considering it was built in a time when

THE LOWER EAST SIDE

© AVALON TRAVEL

particular. Especially in Chinatown, streets teem with jostling crowds and exotic markets. Chinatown's central street is Mott, just below Canal. What's left of Little Italy is centered on Mulberry Street just north of Canal. Orchard Street was once the heart of the Lower East Side.

Many New Yorkers visit Chinatown for lunch or dinner, and then head to Little Italy for dessert in one of its pastry shops. Orchard Street is at its liveliest on Sunday afternoons.

◖ Chinatown

Crowded with restaurants and festive shops, **Mott Street** (at Canal Street) is a great spot for catching the flavor of Chinatown. Mott Street is the oldest Chinese-inhabited street in the city, and has many of Chinatown's oldest restaurants as well as a plethora of Chinese stores.

One store of note is **Yunhong** (50 Mott St., 212/566-8828, www.happychopsticks.com), a tiny store dedicated to chopsticks. Be sure to explore the side streets off Mott Street, and take a walk into Columbus Park (at Mulberry and Bayard Sts.) to feel like you have left the streets of New York behind as clusters of men play Xiangqi (Chinese chess) and children play on the courts.

Museum of Chinese in America

The **Museum of Chinese in America** (215 Centre St., 212/619-4785 www.mocanyc.org, Tues.-Wed. and Fri-Sun. 11am-6pm, Thurs. 11am-9pm, adults $10, seniors and students $5, children under 12 free) examines the Chinese American experience in this nation of immigrants. Be sure to check out the museum's core exhibit With a Single Step: Stories in the

Making of America. On sale in the museum's bookstore is an excellent *Chinatown Historical Map & Guide,* which provides insight into the neighborhood's history, as well as tips on what to order in Chinese restaurants, where to shop, and what to buy. The bookstore also carries many other titles by or about Asian Americans.

Canal Street

You'll find it all on this remarkable street: fruits and vegetables, plastic toys, burglar alarms, car stereos, art supplies, knock-off perfumes and handbags, Asian banks, and hordes and hordes of people. It's easy to spend hours here just meandering about, soaking it all in.

Most overwhelming at first are the fish stores near Baxter Street where huge piles of fish seem to stare balefully at you as you pass by. Next, you'll notice the large number of banks. Some say that banks in Chinatown now outnumber restaurants, and although that seems hard to believe, the banks' presence is indicative of the enormous investments from Hong Kong, Taiwan, and China that have flooded New York in recent years.

Once located on the heart of Canal Street but now a few blocks farther north is **Pearl River** (477 Broadway, 212/431-4770, www. pearlriver.com), Chinatown's largest department store. On sale are Chinese musical instruments, kites, paper lanterns and parasols, chopsticks, ceramic bowls, clothing, slippers, stationery, gifts, and housewares.

Little Italy

In contrast to Chinatown, Little Italy—at its zenith between 1890 and 1924—is a shadow of its former self. Only about 10 percent of the neighborhood's residents are of Italian ancestry, and the heart of its dining and shopping district has shrunk to just three short blocks along **Mulberry Street** just above Canal Street. Here, Italian restaurants and cafés line the street, with tables and striped umbrellas set out in warm weather. It's all very touristy, but it's also a lot of fun, with mustachioed waiters gesticulating wildly like caricatures of themselves, and lots of bright, garish colors.

At the intersection of Mulberry and Grand Streets is a mother lode of great Italian food stores, including **Alleva Dairy** (188 Grand St., 212/226-7990, www.allevadairy.com), which claims to be the oldest Italian cheese store in the United States, and **Piemonte Homemade Ravioli** (190 Grand St., 212/226-0475, www. piemonteravioli.com), which has been turning out the pillows of pasta since 1920.

Lower East Side Tenement Museum

Visit this museum to get a taste of what immigrant life was like in the 19th and early 20th century. Start at the **Visitor Center and Museum Shop** (103 Orchard St., 212/982-8420, www.tenement.org, days, times, and prices vary by tour, call for details), then depart for a neighborhood walking tour or a guided visit through one of the immigrant apartments in a Lower East Side tenement building. The building, at 97 Orchard Street, is a deliberately dark and oppressive place; it originally had no windows, except in front, and no indoor plumbing. Declared illegal in 1935, it was sealed up and forgotten about until 1988, when historians looking for a structurally unaltered tenement building stumbled upon it.

Eldridge Street Synagogue

About four blocks south of the Tenement Museum is the 1886 **Eldridge Street Synagogue** (12 Eldridge St., between Division and Canal Sts.). The first synagogue in New York built by Eastern European Jews, it's a large and startlingly elaborate building with beautifully carved wooden doors. Due to a dwindling congregation, the main sanctuary was sealed in the 1930s and not entered again for 40 years. In the early 1990s, restoration work began, and the synagogue now houses **Museum at Eldridge Street** (12 Eldridge St., 212/219-0302, www.eldridgestreet.org, tours Sun.-Thurs. 10am-5pm and Fri. 10am-3pm, adults $10, seniors and students $8, children $6, free on Mon.). The museum can only be seen by guided tour; the tour tells the story of the synagogue and the Jewish immigrants of the area.

SOHO AND TRIBECA

Early in New York City history, SoHo (short for *So*uth of *Ho*uston) was a quiet residential suburb. By the 1870s, however, it had metamorphosed into an industrial center, home to foundries, factories, warehouses, and sweatshops. Frequent fires started by machinery sparks garnered the district the nickname, "Hell's Hundred Acres."

By the 1960s, most of the factories were gone and artists began moving in. Attracted to the area by its low rents and high-ceilinged spaces—perfect for studios—they illegally converted the commercial buildings into living spaces. Soon thereafter, art galleries arrived, and then the shops and restaurants. Almost overnight, SoHo became fashionable, so much so that artists could no longer afford high rents. Gallery owners held on until the mid-1990s,

but more recently, they, too, have largely moved on. Many have resettled in Chelsea.

SoHo is now primarily an upscale shopping and dining center. Within its 25 glittering blocks, bounded by Houston and Canal Streets, Lafayette Street and West Broadway, beckon dozens of restaurants, bars, hotels, and, especially, shops.

Heading south out of SoHo and crossing over Canal Street, you'll enter TriBeCa, short for *Tri*angle *Be*low *Ca*nal. Home to many of the city's toniest restaurants, encompassing about 40 blocks between Canal, Chambers, West, and Church Streets, the district is often referred to as another SoHo. Yet large sections of TriBeCa remain quiet and residential, with a 19th-century feel. Like SoHo, TriBeCa's main thoroughfares are Broadway and West Broadway, though some of its best cast-iron buildings are on side streets, especially White Street.

SoHo Walking Tour

SoHo is a compact neighborhood, perfect for just wandering about. **Broadway and West Broadway** are the main thoroughfares; **Prince and Spring Streets** hold an enormous array of shops. The intersections of Prince and Spring Streets with West Broadway are the heart of the district.

As you walk through the neighborhood, check out the architecture. SoHo's cast-iron buildings remain its greatest treasure. Originally envisioned as a cheap way to imitate elaborate stone buildings, the cast-iron facades were prefabricated in a variety of styles—including Italian Renaissance, French Second Empire, and Classical Greek—and bolted onto iron-frame structures. An American invention, the cast-iron building was erected primarily in New York, with SoHo boasting the largest collection.

Many of SoHo's finest cast-iron buildings can be found along Broadway. Foremost among them is Italianate **Haughwout Building** (488 Broadway). The magnificent edifice is five stories tall and nine bays wide on the Broadway side, and sports 92 windows, all flanked by Corinthian columns. Built for a merchant who once provided china to the White House, the store was the first in the city to install a passenger elevator.

Farther north is the **Singer Building** (561 Broadway), designed by the innovative architect Ernest Flagg in 1902. It's decked out with red terra-cotta panels, delicate wrought-iron detailing, and large plate-glass windows. Even farther north, note the maroon-and-white facade of **575 Broadway.**

Farther south, below Grand Street, is the so-called **"Queen of Greene Street"** (28-30 Greene St.), built in ornate Second Empire style.

New York City Fire Museum

Technically outside of SoHo to the west is the **New York City Fire Museum** (278 Spring St.,

212/691-1303, www.nycfiremuseum.org, daily 10am-5pm, adults $8, children under 12 $5). Housed in an actual firehouse that was active until 1959, the museum is staffed by ex-firefighters who enliven tours with personal anecdotes on request. It's filled with intriguing historical items, including a lifesaving net (which "caught you 75 percent of the time"), gorgeous 19th-century fire carriages, and an exhibit that honors the fire department's courageous work following the World Trade Center attacks.

Art Spaces

Not all of SoHo's art galleries have left the neighborhood. **Ronald Feldman Fine Arts** (31 Mercer St., 212/226-3232, www.feldmangallery.com, Tues.-Sat. 10am-6pm), for one, has long been a mainstay in SoHo, with a focus on avant-garde installations. Another top art attraction is **The Drawing Center** (35 Wooster St., 212/219-2166, www.drawingcenter.org, Wed.-Sun. noon-6pm, Thurs. noon-8pm, adults $5, seniors and students $3, children under 12 free), the only non-profit museum in the country to focus exclusively on historical and contemporary drawings. It was established in 1977. For a complete list of which galleries are still around, pick up a copy of the *Gallery Guide,* a free listings guide, available at many bookstores. *Time Out New York* and *The New Yorker* also have good listings.

EAST VILLAGE

For much of its existence, the East Village was simply an extension of the Lower East Side. At the turn of the 20th century, most of its residents were German Lutheran immigrants. By World War I, most were Poles, Ukrainians, Greeks, Jews, and Russians—some of whom still live in the neighborhood. Not long thereafter, a sizable Puerto Rican population moved in, settling in the easternmost stretches. They, too, are still here.

Then, in the 1950s, artists, writers, radicals, and counterculturists began arriving. Many were fleeing rising rents in the West Village and they transformed the East Village into a

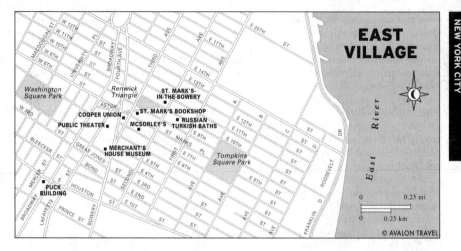

distinct neighborhood with a character all its own. First on the scene were artists such as Willem de Kooning, Paul Georges, and Joan Mitchell, followed quickly by writers such as Norman Mailer, W. H. Auden, and Allen Ginsberg. Next came the beatniks, and then the hippies and yippies, rock groups and punk musicians, artists and fashion designers.

Only in the 1980s did the East Village begin to gentrify. Young professionals moved in, bringing with them upscale restaurants and shops. Still, the East Village has not completely succumbed and offers a thriving mix of artists and careerists, students and tourists. Owners of hip boutiques share sidewalk space with the homeless.

Nightlife is a key component of East Village character. The neighborhood is home to scores of restaurants and bars, along with fly-by-night clubs, which in recent years have pushed as far east as Avenue D in the once notorious Alphabet City (Avenues A, B, C, and D).

St. Mark's-in-the-Bowery

Historic **St. Mark's-in-the-Bowery** (131 E. 10th St., 212/674-6377, www.stmarksbowery.org, Mon.-Fri. 9am-4pm, Sun. 9am-1pm) stands near the former site of Peter Stuyvesant's farm. The church is a hodgepodge of architectural styles, made up of a 1799 base, an 1828 Greek Revival steeple, and an 1854 cast-iron Italianate porch. Buried in the bricked-in graveyard surrounding the church is "Petrus Stuyvesant" himself, the last and most colorful of the Dutch governors.

Today, St. Mark's is known primarily for its **poetry readings** (212/674-0910, www.poetryproject.org), **dance presentations** (212/674-8112, www.danspaceproject.org), and leftist politics.

St. Mark's Place

Raucous and run-down in spots, outrageously entertaining in others, St. Mark's Place is the heart of the East Village. Artists and musicians, students and tourists, and drug dealers and the down-and-out all jostle each other, while the stores on either side sell everything from gourmet pretzels to frightening-looking leather goods. To get the full effect of the craziness, come after 10pm on a weekend night. The area today is leaning a bit toward touristy, so a better feel for the East Village might be found walking along 2nd Avenue.

Merchant's House Museum

The classic Greek Revival **Merchant's House Museum** (29 E. 4th St., 212/777-1089, www.merchantshouse.org, Thurs.-Mon. noon-5pm, adults $10, seniors and students $5) is furnished exactly as it was in 1835 when merchant Seabury Tredwell and his family lived here. It's the only remaining intact 19th-century family home in New York City, providing a rare glimpse into the lives of an affluent family of that period.

The Public Theater

Roughly two blocks north of the Merchant's House Museum is an imposing, columned building with colorful banners beckoning out front. Once the Astor Library, this is now **The Public Theater** (425 Lafayette St., 212/539-8500, www.publictheater.org), founded by Joseph Papp.

Until his death in 1991, Papp was one of America's most important theater producers. Best known as founder of the New York Shakespeare Festival, he was also the man who first produced *Hair, A Chorus Line,* and 15 other plays that moved to Broadway. Today, the Public is home to five stages, which produce Shakespeare and new works, as well as a bar-restaurant called The Library at The Public (www.thelibraryatthepublic.com) and a cabaret space called Joe's Pub (www.joespub.com).

Astor Place and Cooper Union

Adjoining the Public Theater is Astor Place, anchored by *Alamo,* a big black cube by artist Tony Rosenthal. Precariously balanced on one corner, the cube is supposed to rotate when pushed, but that's easier said than done. A visual counterpoint to the contemporary cube is the cast-iron reproduction of one of the original subway kiosks that once stood all over the city. Modeled after subway entrances of Budapest's metro system, the world's second oldest subway, the ornate entrance evokes lavish Hungarian garden houses known as *kushks.*

The largest brownstone in New York City is **Cooper Union** (located in the triangle between Astor Pl. and 3rd and 4th Aves.). The 1859 building was financed by Peter Cooper, a remarkable engineer who, among many other things, made a fortune in the iron industry, designed the first American locomotive, invented gelatin and a self-rocking cradle, and helped develop Morse's telegraph. The son of a poor storekeeper, Cooper built his Union to house a free school of practical arts and sciences. Still in operation today, Cooper Union was also the first coeducational, racially integrated school in the country.

Downstairs inside Cooper Union is the Great Hall, where Abraham Lincoln made his famous "Right makes might" speech that won him the Republican presidential nomination in 1860. Abolitionists Henry Ward Beecher, Frederick Douglass, and William Cullen Bryant also spoke here, as did every president following Lincoln up through Woodrow Wilson, and Bill Clinton.

WEST VILLAGE

Once a hotbed of radical and artistic activity, the narrow winding streets of the West Village now sometimes seem too tame, its restored buildings too cute, its shops and boutiques too name-brand rather than mom-and-pop. Only the well-to-do (or those lucky enough to have a rent-controlled apartment) can afford to live here now, and nearly all the dingy old dives have gone safely commercial and mainstream.

And yet, the West Village cannot be dismissed that easily; it still has a bohemian soul lurking somewhere underneath. You can feel it sometimes in the old jazz clubs, or in Washington Square on a windy afternoon, or in the faces of some of the older residents, who saw it all happen, not so long ago.

Once an Algonquin village, the West Village was settled by Dutch tobacco farmers in the late 1600s and by English landowners in the early 1700s. By the 1790s, however, large estates were breaking up as New Yorkers fled north to escape yellow fever epidemics in lower Manhattan. During the epidemics, the city erected barricades along Chambers Street to prevent people from returning to the infected areas, and the West Village started filling up with stores, banks, and other businesses.

Over the next few decades, the West Village turned into a low-rent backwater that attracted immigrants. First came the Irish in the 1850s,

WEST VILLAGE

then African Americans after the Civil War, and Italians in the 1890s.

Around 1910, artists and writers also discovered the low rents, and soon the area was teeming with artistic and political activity. Max Eastman founded his radical paper, *The Masses;* tea rooms, literary bars, and basement poetry clubs sprouted up; and theater groups flourished. Among the Village residents during this period were Eugene O'Neill, Edna St. Vincent Millay, Bette Davis, Sherwood Anderson, Theodore Dreiser, John Dos Passos, and e. e. cummings. The neighborhood's tolerance of "the third sex," as gays and lesbians were discreetly called, also dates from this period.

In the 1960s, folk clubs, antiwar rallies, and the civil rights movement brought to the Village another wave of new settlers, including Bob Dylan and Jimi Hendrix, Abbie Hoffman and Jerry Rubin. In 1969, the Village's Stonewall Riots marked the beginning of the national gay-rights movement.

Nearly every street in the West Village has something interesting to offer, and you can't go wrong just wandering about. But be sure to bring a map—there's no grid system here.

Washington Square

Washington Square Park is the heart of the Village. On a sunny day you'll find everyone here, from kids on skateboards and students strumming guitars, to committed Hare Krishnas spreading the word and old men taking in the sun. At the park's southwest corner are stone chess tables where the click-clack of the pieces never seems to stop; near the center is the dog run, where dogs of every conceivable shape and size dash madly to and fro.

Once marshland, the eight-acre park was purchased by the city near the end of the 18th century to be used as a potter's field. From 1797-1825, at least 20,000 people were buried here.

The square was turned into a park in the late 1820s. Elegant townhouses went up all around, including the still-standing, beautiful, red-brick Greek Revival townhouses on the north side of the square. By the 1830s, Washington Square was considered to be the city's most fashionable residential neighborhood.

New York University (NYU) erected its first building on the park in 1837, and now occupies much of the park's periphery. Most of the old townhouses have been replaced by institutional buildings, and the genteel old families replaced by students.

The park's biggest landmark is the marble **Washington Square Arch,** marking the north entrance. Eighty-six feet tall, the arch replaced a temporary wooden one erected in 1889 to commemorate the centennial of George Washington's inauguration. Citizens liked the wooden arch so much that they decided to have it remade in marble. The designer was architect Stanford White, and the sculptor was A. Stirling Calder (father of famous mobile sculptor Alexander Calder).

Forbes Magazine Galleries

On the ground floor of the Forbes Building are the **Forbes Magazine Galleries** (62 5th Ave., 212/206-5549, www.forbesgalleries. com, Tues.-Sat. 10am-4pm, free). The museum was once famous for its fabulous collection of Fabergé eggs, perfect in their miniature beauty. In fact, many visitors still arrive expecting to see the eggs, which were auctioned off in 2004.

Though the eggs are no longer on display, you'll find much else of interest. Rotating exhibits show how diverse the collecting interests of the Forbes family are; in any given season, you'll see American jewelry, photography, or part of the Forbes' extensive wooden boat collection.

Christopher Park and Sheridan Square

At Christopher Street and 7th Avenue South is Christopher Park, often mistaken for Sheridan Square. The latter is just southeast of Christopher Park at the triangle where Washington Place, Barrow, Grove, and West 4th Streets meet. The confusion is understandable as a statue of General Philip Sheridan stands in Christopher Park. Sheridan was a Union general best remembered for the unfortunate, often misquoted, line, "The only good Indians I saw were dead."

Next to the general is a George Segal sculpture depicting two gay couples—one male, the other female. Erected in 1991, the statue commemorates the Stonewall Riots, which took place across the street at Stonewall Inn on June 27, 1969. (The original Stonewall was at 51 Christopher Street and is now gone; the bar called Stonewall at 53 Christopher is a namesake.)

Across the street from Christopher Park is the former **home of Thomas Paine** (59 Grove St.), the Revolutionary War-era author of *Common Sense, The Crisis,* and *The Rights of Man.* It was Paine who wrote the famous words, "These are the times that try men's souls." Paine's house, marked with a plaque, is now the venerable gay piano bar **Marie's Crisis Cafe,** named partly as a tribute to Paine.

Children's Museum of the Arts

The **Children's Museum of the Arts** (103 Charlton St., 212/274-0986, www.cmany.org, Mon. and Wed. noon-5pm, Thurs.-Fri. noon-6pm, Sat.-Sun. 10am-5pm, adults $11, seniors and children under one free) is an experimental museum designed to expose kids to visual and performing arts by connecting them with working NYC artists. In the "Artist's Studio," youngsters can try their hand at sand painting, origami, and sculpture in a number of artist-monitored stations.

UNION SQUARE AND MADISON SQUARE PARK

The East Side between 14th and 42nd Streets is mostly residential, and lacks both the history of Lower Manhattan and the energy of the Villages. But it does have a considerable

UNION SQUARE AND MADISON SQUARE PARK

© AVALON TRAVEL

quiet charm and a number of quirky attractions sandwiched between brownstones and apartment buildings.

Various neighborhoods make up this section of the East Side. **Union Square** begins at 14th Street and Broadway. **Madison Square** begins at 23rd Street and Broadway. Farther east is **Gramercy Park,** a residential square centered at 20th Street and Irving Place.

Union Square

Built over a central subway station, **Union Square** is a bustling urban center complete with sleek megastores, upscale restaurants, fashionable bars, and what may be the city's most popular **Greenmarket** (212/788-7476, www.grownyc.org), open Monday, Wednesday, Friday, and Saturday.

Laid out as a park in 1815, Union Square was originally the province of prominent local families, such as the Roosevelts, who lived nearby. Then, in the mid-1800s, the city's entertainment and commercial industries moved in. The famous Academy of Music started on 14th Street, and department stores went up all along Broadway from 8th to 23rd Streets. This commercialism was short lived, however. By 1900, the theaters and shops had moved uptown to Madison Square at 23rd Street, and Union Square was home to garment factories and immigrants.

From the 1910s until after WWII, Union Square was a center for political demonstrations. Socialists, communists, and the Wobblies (members of the Industrial Workers of the World) protested here, while many left-wing organizations had headquarters on or near the square. One of the most dramatic protests took place on August 22, 1927, the night anarchists Nicola Sacco and Bartolomeo Vanzetti were executed. The police had machine guns mounted on a roof overlooking the square, but the demonstration remained peaceful. In recent years, the centrality of Union Square has again attracted protesters, especially during the Occupy Wall Street movement.

The sixth floor of the narrow Moorish-accented building at 33 Union Square West (between 16th and 17th Sts.) was once home to **Andy Warhol's Factory,** frequented by the likes of Lou Reed, John Cale, Nico of the Velvet Underground, Truman Capote, and John Lennon. Here, Warhol made many of his underground films, including *Blow Job, Flesh,* and *I, Man.*

Gramercy Park

Gramercy Park (between Park Ave. S. and 3rd Ave. and 20th and 21st Sts.) was bought and laid out in 1831 by lawyer and real estate developer Samuel Ruggles. As fashionable today as it was back then, the park consists of both stately buildings and an enclosed green to which only residents have access. Outsiders have to content themselves with peering in through an eight-foot-high iron fence.

Broadway and Lower 5th Avenue

During the late 1800s, Broadway between 8th and 23rd Streets was known as **Ladies' Mile** because of the many fashionable department stores located there. The original stores are long gone, but their elaborate cast-iron facades remain.

Theodore Roosevelt Birthplace National Historic Site (28 E. 20th St., 212/260-1616, www.nps.gov/thrb, Tues.-Sat. 9am-5pm, free) is a handsome, four-story brownstone and exact replica of Theodore Roosevelt's birthplace. It was rebuilt by Roosevelt's family and friends just after his death in 1919 and only a few years after the original building was torn down. The museum is filled with thousands of engrossing photographs and the world's largest collection of Roosevelt memorabilia, including TR's christening dress and his parents' wedding clothes.

Where 5th Avenue and Ladies' Mile meet at 23rd Street is one of Manhattan's most famous and idiosyncratic landmarks: The **Flatiron Building** was designed by Chicago architect Daniel H. Burnham in 1902. Its nickname comes from its narrow triangular shape, only six feet wide at the northern end. H. G. Wells once described it as a "prow...ploughing up through the traffic of Broadway and 5th Avenue in the late-afternoon light."

Madison Square

Between 23rd and 26th Streets and 5th and Madison Avenues is Madison Square. Once a marsh, potter's field, and parade ground, the square became fashionable in the mid-1800s. In those days, expensive hotels stood along its west side, the old Madison Square Garden stood to the north, and the Statue of Liberty's torch-bearing right arm stood in the center of the square, awaiting funding for the monument's base. Today all those buildings and the arm are gone, but other graceful structures have taken their place.

Madison Square Park (E. 23rd-26th Sts., between 5th and Madison Aves., 212/538-1884, www.madisonsquarepark.org) is known for its ambitious public art exhibits. In summer months, the park hosts free concerts for children and families. At the southeast corner of the park, New Yorkers line up at **Shake Shack** (At E. 23rd St., 212/889-6600, www.shakeshack.com), which brings a fresh, locavore angle to fast food. You can also buy snacks or a full picnic across the street at **Eataly** (200 5th Ave., 212/229-2560, www.eatalyny.com).

On the park's east side between 23rd and 25th Streets is the 1932 **Metropolitan Life Insurance Company,** an enormous Art Deco building made of limestone that seems to change color with the day. On the north corner of 25th Street is the 1900 **Appellate Division of the New York State Supreme Court,** covered with an impossible number of marble sculptures. Taking up the whole block between 26th and 27th Streets is **New York Life Insurance Company,** an 1898 wedding cake extravaganza designed by Cass Gilbert.

A recent addition to the neighborhood is **Museum of Mathematics** (11 E. 26th St., 212/542-0566, www.momath.org, daily 10am-5pm, adults $15 online or $16 at museum, seniors, students, and children over 2 $9 online or $10 at museum). Opened in late 2012, the hands-on museum tries to inspire even the most entrenched math-phobe to fall in love with numbers. The museum is especially child- and teen-friendly as every exhibit is interactive.

CHELSEA AND THE MEATPACKING DISTRICT

Heading north from the Village along Manhattan's west side, the buildings get taller and the landscape becomes more urban. Along the Hudson River, the pleasant, industrial-chic Meatpacking District straddles 14th Street, giving way to cosmopolitan Chelsea. Roughly stretching between 14th and 28th Streets, 6th Avenue and the Hudson River, Chelsea is made up of dozens of brownstones, row houses, tenements, and apartment buildings. Most of the area was once owned by Captain Thomas Clarke, whose grandson, Clement Charles Clarke, wrote the famous poem that begins, "'Twas the night before Christmas."

West of 10th Avenue, former warehouses turned contemporary galleries comprise the largest commercial arts district in the city. This corner of Chelsea is also home to The High Line, a unique public space built atop an elevated rail bed, which offers fantastic views of Midtown's skyline. Like the Meatpacking District, Chelsea is a renowned destination for nightlife, with many of New York's massive dance clubs and exclusive lounges clustered just north of the galleries around 27th and 28th Streets. Part residential, part industrial, this section of the city has a solid, gritty feel and its share of one-of-a-kind attractions, including cutting-edge arts organizations and galleries.

West Chelsea Galleries

Over the last decade, West Chelsea has metamorphosed into the new SoHo. Dozens of galleries have moved into the neighborhood, turning it from a rather nondescript area into one of New York's most exciting places. Even if you have little interest in contemporary art, it's worth visiting some of the exhibition spaces for their architectural exuberance alone.

Most of the galleries are in the West 20s between 10th and 11th Avenues, with an especially large collection located along West 22nd, 25th, 26th and 29th Streets. Among them are such major names in the New York art world as **Pace** (508, 510, and 534 W. 25th St., 212/929-7000, www.pacegallery.com, Tues.-Sat. 10am-6pm), exhibiting works by the likes of Sol LeWitt and Julian Schnabel; the **Paula Cooper Gallery** (521 and 534 W. 21st St., 212/255-1105, www.paulacoopergallery.com, Tues.-Sat. 10am-6pm), representing such heavyweights as Carl Andre and Claes Oldenburg; and the **Barbara Gladstone Gallery** (530 W. 21st St. and 515 W. 24th St., 212/206-9300, www.gladstonegallery.com, Tues.-Sat. 10am-6pm), specializing in painting, sculpture, and photography by established artists. The enormous **Gagosian Gallery** (555 W. 24th St. and other locations in the city, 212/741-1111, www.gagosian.com, Tues.-Sat. 10am-6pm) is dedicated to artists such as Andy Warhol, Richard Serra, and David Salle. If you're interested in mixed media, installation, video, or conceptual

© FRANCISCO COLLAZO

typical Manhattan brownstones

sculpture, stop by **MagnanMetz Gallery** (521 W. 26th St., 212/244-2344, www.magnanmetz.com, Tues.-Sat. 10am-6pm), which often introduces artists from Cuba and elsewhere to New York audiences.

If you're short on time or tired of walking, maximize your gallery visits by going to some of the larger buildings that house multiple galleries. Two good bets include 547 W. 27th Street, home to, among others, **Aperture Foundation Gallery** (547 W. 27th St., 212/505-5555, www.aperture.org/gallery), featuring classic and contemporary photography, and **Ceres Gallery** (547 W. 27th St., 212/947-6100, www.ceresgallery.org), a non-profit, artist-run gallery featuring contemporary work by women; and 210 11th Avenue, home to **Cavin-Morris Gallery** (210 11th Ave., 212/226-3768, www.cavinmorris.com), dedicated to eclectic global art, and **Kent Fine Art** (210 11th Ave., 212/365-9500, www.kentfineart.net), which represents a carefully-selected handful of international artists.

To find out more about galleries, or about who's exhibiting where, pick up a copy of *Gallery Guide,* available in many bookstores and galleries. Or, check listings in *Time Out New York* or *The New Yorker.*

Hotel Chelsea

Though **Hotel Chelsea** (222 W. 23rd St., www.hotelchelsea.com) is currently closed, it's worth a stroll past this beautiful, historic building that holds so many New York stories. With its deep maroon paint job, black gables, chimneys, and ornate cast-iron balconies, the hotel is a West Side landmark. One of the city's first cooperative apartment buildings when it opened in 1884, the Chelsea became a hotel in 1905 and almost immediately began attracting writers, many of whom took up residence. Plaques at the door, visible from the sidewalk, honor Dylan Thomas, Thomas Wolfe, Brendan Behan, Arthur Miller, and Mark Twain. Others who've lived here include Tennessee Williams, Vladimir Nabokov, Mary McCarthy, and Nelson Algren. Arthur C. Clarke wrote *2001: A Space Odyssey* here. William S. Burroughs wrote *Naked Lunch* here.

The hotel has also attracted an extraordinary number of actors, painters, photographers, musicians, and film producers over the years, among them Sarah Bernhardt, Jackson Pollock, Willem de Kooning, Jane Fonda, Robert Mapplethorpe, and Milos Forman. Andy Warhol filmed part of his movie *Chelsea Girls* here. Musician Virgil Thompson lived on the ninth floor for over 40 years.

In the late 1960s, the Chelsea became a favorite stopover for rock stars passing through town, including Janis Joplin, Jimi Hendrix, the Grateful Dead, The Mamas and the Papas, Leonard Cohen, and Patti Smith. Bob Dylan wrote "Sad-Eyed Lady of the Lowlands" while staying at the Chelsea.

The hotel's most notorious residents were Sid Vicious, lead singer for the Sex Pistols, and his girlfriend Nancy Spungen. The two were living here in 1978 when Nancy was found in her negligee beneath the bathroom sink, stabbed to death with a hunting knife. Vicious was indicted for the murder but died of a heroin overdose before he could stand trial. The hotel has since gotten rid of Room 100, where the murder was committed.

Rubin Museum of Art

Rubin Museum of Art (150 W. 17th St., 212/620-5000, www.rmanyc.org, Mon. and Thurs. 11am-5pm, Wed. 11am-7pm, Fri. 11am-10pm, Sat.-Sun. 11am-6pm, adults $10, seniors and students $5, children under 12 free) is a quiet, peaceful place that bills itself as the only museum in the world dedicated to Himalayan art. Opened in 2004, the Rubin was founded by private collectors reluctant to donate their work to a larger institution that might let it gather dust in storage. The museum's stunning permanent collection includes paintings, sculpture, textiles, and prints ranging in age from the 2nd to the 19th centuries, and in origin from Nepal to southern Siberia. Housed in the former Barney's department store, the museum also offers films, lectures, concerts, and dance events in its state-of-the-art auditorium.

The same family that lent its name and its collection to Rubin Museum of Art established **The 8th Floor** (17 W. 17th St., 646/839-5908, www.the8thfloor.org, free), a smaller, more intimate gallery nearby dedicated primarily to contemporary Cuban art.

◖ The High Line

A triumph in innovative urban planning, **The High Line** (Gansevoort St. to West 34th St., between 10th Ave. and 11th Ave., 212/500-6035, www.thehighline.org, daily 7am-11pm summer, daily 7am-10pm fall and spring, daily 7am-7pm winter) is a picturesque, 1.45-mile stretch of public walkways, sundecks, and gardens built atop an elevated rail bed that runs along Manhattan's west side. Cutting through the Chelsea gallery district and offering views of Midtown skyscrapers on one side and the Hudson River on the other, the park is open year-round (and fully accessible by wheelchair) and, on warm days, is often packed with locals and tourists alike. A vestige of the neighborhood's industrial past, the elevated railway was built in the 1930s, replacing the street-level freight trains that carried goods from the Meatpacking District to the warehouses and docks farther north. After falling into disuse in the 1980s, the structure was threatened with demolition (most of the original 13 miles of track were demolished in the 1960s). In response, a local community-based organization, Friends of the High Line, launched a campaign for the structure's preservation.

Together with the City of New York, Friends of the High Line began long-term planning for a new public park atop the structure. The first segment of The High Line was opened to the public in 2009, with an additional northern stretch opening in June 2011. Since then, The High Line has become a focal point of the neighborhood, with a crop of trendy hotels, great restaurants, and shops opening along its route, in addition to ongoing public art projects sponsored by Friends of the High Line. In 2015, the Whitney Museum of American Art will reopen in a new facility at the park's southern entrance.

© LUCIE ERICKSEN

The High Line

MIDTOWN AND TIMES SQUARE

Rush, rush, rush. Sometimes all the people in the world seem to be elbowing their way through here. Most of Manhattan's skyscrapers are in Midtown, along with most of its offices, major hotels, theaters, famous department stores and restaurants, and many visitor attractions.

Fifth Avenue is the heart of Midtown, the artery to which all other addresses relate. Though nothing more than a line on a map as late as 1811, Fifth Avenue was the city's most fashionable address by the time of the Civil War. The Astors, Vanderbilts, and many other wealthy families all had homes along it.

Fifth Avenue began to turn commercial in the early 1900s. Today, its Midtown stretch is almost entirely lined with shops and office buildings. Shops in the upper 30s and lower 40s tend to be tourist traps selling discounted electronic gadgetry and souvenirs; in the upper 40s and 50s stand upscale boutiques and department stores for which the avenue is famous.

To see Midtown at its frenzied best, come on a weekday. Most visitor attractions are also open on weekends. With the exception of Times Square and the Theater District, much of Midtown shuts up tight after business hours.

Morgan Library

Morgan Library (226 Madison Ave. at 36th St., 212/685-0008, www.themorgan.org, Tues.-Thurs. 10:30am-5pm, Fri. 10:30am-9pm, Sat. 10am-6pm, Sun. 11am-6pm, adults $18, seniors, students, and children 13-16 $12, children 12 and under free, free Fri. 7pm-9pm), built between 1902 and 1906, began its life as the personal library of financier Pierpont Morgan, who spent a portion of his great fortune on illuminated, literary, and historical manuscripts, early printed books, as well as some drawings and prints. Designed by famed architectural team McKim, Mead, & White, the Italian Renaissance-style palazzo is considered among their finest work. In 1924, Morgan's son decided the collection was too fine and too important to remain restricted

MIDTOWN AND TIMES SQUARE

solely to the family's enjoyment, and it was opened as a public institution.

Over the years, Morgan Library has expanded its physical structure, incorporating Morgan's brownstone residence and its collections. Its exhibits are always significant and ambitious, with recent shows featuring original manuscripts and ephemera of authors like Mark Twain, Edgar Allan Poe, and Charles Dickens.

Grand Central Terminal

Every day, roughly 750,000 people pass through **Grand Central Terminal** (42nd St., between Vanderbilt and Lexington Aves.), home to the city's busiest subway station

(seven lines pass through underground) and Metro North commuter trains. Completed in 1913 under the auspices of transportation magnate Cornelius Vanderbilt, the station is full of classical grandeur. The Beaux-Arts facade on 42nd Street looks more like the entrance to a Roman coliseum than a rail station, with its pair of Corinthian columns supporting sculptures of Hercules, Minerva, and Mercury, the Roman god of speed and commerce. With its towering ceilings and famous four-sided Tiffany clock (rumored to be worth $10-20 million) at the center, the station's Main Concourse is one of the most spectacular public spaces in the world. It's almost always alive with activity—especially during

© FRANCISCO COLLAZO

Grand Central Terminal

rush hour, when commuters make a dash to catch the train. Above it all, the cerulean blue ceiling depicts zodiac constellations with fiber-optic lights that really twinkle.

Not long ago, Grand Central was considered an eyesore; years of wear and neglect had slowly robbed it of its splendor and significance. A decade of renovations brought the station back to its former glory—perhaps even surpassing it. Since the restoration was completed in 1998, Grand Central has become a destination unto itself, with an impressive food hall and a range of shops along the lower concourse. Many locals stop in, even if they aren't commuting, to eat at beloved **Grand Central Oyster Bar** or **Junior's Cheesecake,** or to have a drink at The Campbell Apartment. Grand Central is also home to the world's largest Apple store, which opened in 2011.

To get the best view of Grand Central's busy lobby, ascend to the mezzanines on either the east or west side of the lobby. You can't loiter here, but you can stand here long enough to take in the scene and snap a photo.

The Chrysler Building

What the Empire State Building has in stature, the **Chrysler Building** (42nd St. and Lexington Ave., 212/682-3070, Mon.-Fri. 8am-6pm), the quintessential Art Deco skyscraper, achieves in style. At the time of its construction, between 1928 and 1930, another building at 40 Wall Street was vying for the title of tallest in the city. To keep his competitors guessing, the building's architect, William Van Alen, hid his final plans for the top of the structure, which included a seven-story spire. At the last minute, workers raised the spire right through what spectators had assumed was the roof and riveted it into place. It was the first manmade structure to reach over 1,000 feet. However, its run at the top lasted only for about 40 days: When the Empire State Building was completed it usurped its title as the highest building in the world.

From the outside, the 1,046-foot granite-and-glass structure, with its protruding gargoyles (designed to resemble the hood ornaments of Plymouth cars), is topped by distinctive crown ornamentation of stainless steel cladding. The luxurious lobby (once a car showroom) is the only interior space open to the public, giving visitors a chance to peek past the security gates at the marble walls, the polished nickel chrome decorations that embellish the stairway railings, the très Deco light fixtures, and the mural by Edward Trumbull, which depicts early 20th-century technological triumphs.

United Nations

In **United Nations Plaza** (extending from 42nd to 48th Sts. and from 1st Ave. to FDR Dr.) flags of 193 member states—each posted at equal height—flap in the breeze. Legally, the United Nations isn't part of New York at all, but is international territory. The United Nations has its own post office, postage stamps, and uniformed security force.

Reflecting the peace and serenity its organization seeks to promote, the U.N. headquarters stands on the banks of the East River, on a 17-acre plot donated by John D. Rockefeller in the mid-20th century. Built between 1950 and 1952, the complex is comprised of four structures: the 550-foot glass Secretariat Building, the domed General Assembly, the Conference Building, and Dag Hammarskjöld Library. The buildings are in the final phase of a $1.8 million-plus massive renovation, slated for completion in 2015.

Outdoors, visitors can enjoy the United Nations sculpture garden, the highlight of which is the Japanese peace bell, rung at the start of each new session in September. If you want to look inside the United Nations, take the 45-minute **tour** (www.visit.un.org., adults $18, seniors and students $11, children 5-12 $9, children under 5 not allowed on tour), led by an international team of guides. Not all of the chambers are open to visitors, due to renovations; however, tour groups do visit the General Assembly Hall, an 1,800-capacity room designed by 11 architects, where member nations meet. Along the way are donated objects and artwork from around the world, as well as displays that explain and document some of the missions of the United Nations.

◖ Times Square

Simultaneously New York's glitziest and seediest symbol, **Times Square** encompasses the intersection of Broadway and 7th Avenue between 42nd and 48th Streets. Not really a square at all, but rather two elongated triangles, it is named after *The New York Times,* once located in the white Times Tower building where Broadway, 7th Avenue, and 42nd Street meet. (Since 2007, *The Times* has occupied its eponymous building, constructed for the newspaper, at 620 8th Avenue.)

Before 1904, when *The New York Times* moved in, Times Square was known as Longacre Square. The center of the horse business in a city then largely dependent upon four-footed transportation, the square was lined with horse exchanges, carriage factories, stables, and blacksmith shops. Not until the 1910s did Times Square become a bona fide theater district; not until the 1960s did it become known for its thriving sex industry.

After a cleanup effort in the 1990s, the area became far more tourist-friendly, with places like the Hard Rock Café and the Disney Store opening. Today, there's even free Wi-Fi and public restrooms at **Times Square Museum and Visitors' Center** (1560 Broadway, entrance on 7th Ave. between 46th and 47th Sts., 212/452-5283, www.timessquarenyc.org, daily 8am-8pm). Police and private security officers patrol the streets 24 hours a day.

Times Square is best visited after sundown. That's when street performers—each one more inventive than the next—come out in droves, and neon signs start to burn. By night, streets are ablaze with huge panels of red, green, yellow, blue, and white. Except for the Las Vegas Strip, no other place in America boasts more neon lights. A recent change in the landscape has led to a designated pedestrian plaza bizarrely filled with chairs plunked onto the formerly busy road and New Yorkers shaking their heads at tourists stretched out, rubbernecking at the glowing chaos where taxis once cruised.

© DREAMSTIME.COM

Times Square

An estimated one million revelers gather for Times Square's annual New Year's Eve celebration, at which the famous crystal-covered ball drops from the flagpole at One Times Square. If you're considering rockin' with the crowds, be prepared: People start grabbing the best spots in the early afternoon, and, around 3pm, police start closing streets to traffic. There are no public restrooms available during the event and no bags are allowed past the barricades.

Theater District

Most Broadway theaters are not on Broadway at all, but on side streets surrounding Times Square. The area is home to 37 legitimate theaters, 22 of which are city landmarks. West 44th and 45th Streets between 7th and 8th Avenues are especially rich blocks; here, you'll find the **Shubert, Helen Hayes, Booth, Majestic,** and **Minskoff** theaters, among others.

Next to the Shubert, connecting 44th and 45th Streets, is **Shubert Alley,** where unemployed performers once waited, hoping for a part. Today, a souvenir shop selling theater memorabilia is located here. Across from the Shubert is legendary **Sardi's Restaurant** (234 W. 44th St., 212/221-8440, www.sardis.com, Tues.-Sun. lunch and dinner, $30), its walls lined with caricatures. Once frequented by theater folks, Sardi's now attracts mostly tourists, but is still a fun, lively spot serving varied international cuisine.

West 42nd Street

During the last decade, big changes have come to West 42nd Street, especially between 7th and 8th Avenues. For years a center for porn, this most historic of theatrical streets has regained some of its former glory.

Most of the block's nine historic theaters have been restored. The Victory, opened by Oscar Hammerstein in 1900, is now **The New Victory** (209 W. 42nd St., 646/223-3010, www.newvictory.org), specializing in programming for young people. **The New Amsterdam** (214 W. 42nd St., www.disneytheatricalsales. com/new_amsterdam_theatre), once home to the Ziegfeld Follies, is now owned by Disney. Movies and plays are on its docket.

Also on 42nd Street is **Madame Tussaud's New York** (234 W. 42nd St., 212/512-9600, www.nycwax.com, Sun.-Thurs. 10am-8pm, Fri.-Sat. 10am-10pm, adults $36, children 4-12 $29, tickets bought online are several dollars cheaper), where you'll find waxy renditions of famous New Yorkers, past and present.

Intrepid Sea, Air, and Space Museum Complex

The Intrepid (W. 46th St. at 12th Ave., 212/245-0072, www.intrepidmuseum.org, spring and summer Mon.-Fri. 10am-5pm, Sat. 10am-6pm, winter daily 10am-5pm, adults $22, seniors and college students $18, children 7-17 $17, children 3-6 $10), docked at Pier 86, is a former World War II aircraft carrier now serving as a military history museum housing lots of hands-on exhibits, most designed to appeal to kids. Decks feature small aircraft and space capsules. Permanent exhibits explore mysteries of satellite communication and ship design; special exhibits focus on such subjects as women pilots and Charles Lindbergh. Highlights are the Concorde and space shuttle *Enterprise.*

◖ Empire State Building

One of the world's most famous buildings and an Art Deco landmark, the **Empire State Building** (350 5th Ave. at 34th St., 212/736-3100, www.esbnyc.com, daily 8am-2am, last elevator up at 1:15am, adults $27, seniors $24, children 6-12 $21) was built during the Depression in an astonishing 14 months, at the rate of four stories a week. For years, it stood as the world's tallest building. That's no longer true, yet the Empire State remains the quintessential skyscraper and its stats remain impressive: 102 floors, 73 elevators, 6,500 windows, thousands of miles of telephone wire, and 1,860 steps. Visits to the two observation decks, one on the 86th floor, the other on the 102nd (additional fee), are so popular the lines are legendary, though a new express ticket at double the cost offers front-of-line access if time is tight.

Another way to decrease the wait is to buy tickets online before your visit.

In 1933, Irma Eberhardt became the first person to commit suicide by jumping off the Empire State. That same year, the original classic film *King Kong* was made, showing a giant ape climbing the skyscraper. In 1945, a B-25 bomber struck the building's 79th floor, killing 14 people. And in 1986, two parachutists jumped from the 86th floor, but with a happier ending: They landed safely on 5th Avenue. Also, in case you're wondering, pennies thrown off the Empire State *cannot* kill pedestrians below, but they can cause severe burns.

New York Public Library

The lavish, 1911 Beaux-Arts **New York Public Library–Stephen A. Schwarzman Building** (5th Ave., between 40th and 42nd Sts., 917/275-6975, www.nypl.org, Mon. and Thurs.-Sat. 10am-6pm, Tues.-Wed. 10am-8pm, Sun. 1pm-5pm), designed by Carrere & Hastings, houses one of the world's top five research libraries. The library's collection of over 15 million items—books, maps, and all manner of historical ephemera in more than 1,200 languages and dialects—occupies some 88 miles of shelves above ground and 84 miles below.

The library's grand entrance lobby, Astor Hall, is flanked by sweeping staircases; just beyond lies **Gottesman Hall,** where exhibits on subjects as diverse as Charles Dickens, New York City's culinary history, and Beat poets have been displayed. The third floor is home to the library's **Main Reading Room,** big as a football field and sumptuous as the lobby of a luxury hotel. Books are ordered via a pneumatic tube system that sucks call slips down into the bowels of the stacks. It was in the library's Map Room that the U.S. Army planned the invasion of North Africa during World War II, and in the library's Science and Technology Room that Chester Carlson invented Xerox and Edwin Land invented the Polaroid camera.

The stone lions lounging outside the library were originally named "Leo Astor" and "Leo Lenox," after the library's founders, John Jacob

Astor and James Lenox. In the 1930s, Mayor La Guardia dubbed the felines "Patience" and "Fortitude"—qualities he felt New York would need to survive the Depression.

Building tours (Mon.-Sat. 11am and 2pm, Sun. 2pm) and docent-led tours of **Gottesman Hall exhibits** (Mon.-Sat. 12:30pm and 2:30pm, Sun. 3:30pm) are free and no reservations are needed. Meet at the main information desk in the lobby.

Bryant Park

Just behind the library is **Bryant Park** (www.bryantpark.org), filled with pretty flower beds, gravel paths, a stylish indoor-outdoor restaurant, and lots of benches that are usually packed with office workers at lunchtime. There's a reading room and a lovely carousel for children, as well as a variety of recreational games in spring, summer, and fall, including chess and table tennis.

The park is named after poet and journalist William Cullen Bryant, a great proponent of parks and one of the people most responsible for the creation of Central Park. Outdoor movies in the summer, free evening open-air concerts in spring and fall, and a scenic winter market featuring holiday shopping stalls and a free ice-skating rink make this a nice four-season park.

International Center of Photography

Just one block north of the library and Bryant Park is the **International Center of Photography** (1133 6th Ave., 212/857-0000, www.icp.org, Tues.-Thurs. and Sat.-Sun. 10am-6pm, Fri. 10am-8pm, adults $14, seniors and students $10, children under 12 free). The Center includes spacious exhibit areas, a school, library, and bookshop. Founded in 1974 by Cornell Capa, Robert Capa's brother (Robert Capa was a photojournalist killed in Vietnam), the center presents many of the city's most important contemporary photography exhibits.

Diamond District

Continuing north, you'll come to the **Diamond**

Bryant Park

© LUCIE ERICKSEN

District (W. 47th St. between 5th and 6th Aves.), where an estimated $400 million in gems are exchanged daily. Many of the dealers and cutters of the 2,500 companies crammed into this block are Hasidic Jews, identifiable by their long beards, earlocks, and black frock coats. As has long been their tradition, the Hasidim often negotiate their biggest deals in back rooms or on the sidewalk.

Rockefeller Center

The area between 48th and 51st Streets and 5th and 6th Avenues was once a notorious red-light district. Today, it's occupied by **Rockefeller Center,** New York's most famous city within a city. Built by John D. Rockefeller during the height of the Depression, the magnificent Art Deco complex is comprised of 19 buildings, connected by plazas and underground passageways.

At the heart of the complex is the sunken **Lower Plaza,** home to an outdoor restaurant in summer, an ice-skating rink in winter, great people-watching year-round, and

© FRANCISCO COLLAZO

Rockefeller Center

a gilded Prometheus watching over it all. At Christmastime, the famous Rockefeller tree is erected directly behind him.

NBC Studios (49th St. between 5th and 6th Aves., 212/664-3700, www.nbcstudiotour. com) are in Top of the Rock at 30 Rockefeller Plaza, where you can peer into the *Today* show studio window or take a tour. One-hour tours leave from **The NBC Experience Store** (every 15 minutes Mon.-Sat. 8:30am-5:30pm, Sun. 9:30am-4:30pm, adults $24, seniors and children 6-12 $21, children under 6 not permitted, reservations recommended). **Top of the Rock Observation Deck** (212/698-2000, www. topoftherocknyc.com, daily 8am-midnight, adults and seniors $27, seniors $25, children 6-12 $17, children under 6 free) on the 70th floor has the advantage of seeing the Empire State building.

Radio City Music Hall

Despite, or perhaps because of, its dated feel, **Radio City Music Hall** (6th Ave. and 50th St., www.radiocity.com) has been bringing families back for generations. An over-the-top creation with a stage as wide as a city block, it's the world's largest indoor theater.

Though the Music Hall has hosted many unusual performers over the years—including elephants and horses—its most famous are the Rockettes. Chorus girls—all between five feet four inches and five feet seven inches in height—once appeared nightly. Now, the Rockettes kick and strut their stuff only during the Music Hall's two-month-long annual Christmas show.

One-hour **backstage tours** (6th Ave. and 50th St., 212/247-4777, www.radiocity.com, daily 11am-3pm, adults $19.95, seniors and children under 12 $15) are offered.

◖ Museum of Modern Art (MoMA)

Holding the largest collection of modern art in the world, **MoMA** (11 W. 53rd St., between 5th and 6th Aves., 212/708-9400, www.moma. org, Wed.-Thurs. and Sat.-Mon. 10:30am-5:30pm, Fri. 10:30am-8pm; late June-late

Sept. also open Tues. 10:30am-5:30pm, adults $20, seniors $16, students $12, children under 16 free) has a cool, elegant exterior that belies the many vibrant works on display inside. Founded during the Great Depression in 1929, the museum moved to this location on 53rd Street in 1939. The current 1939 building has gone through many alterations; the most recent redesign is by Japanese architect Yoshio Taniguchi. Completed in 2004, the renovation resulted in expanded exhibition space and a luminous six-story atrium that gives the signature sculpture garden, designed by Philip Johnson, even more prominence than before. The glass-sided walkways on the upper floors offer dramatic, sometimes vertigo-inducing views of the art and galleries below. The museum's 620,000 square feet include a bustling promenade, 110-foot atrium, sky-lit galleries, and a fine-dining restaurant, The Modern.

The museum's collection includes over 150,000 paintings, sculptures, drawings, prints, photographs, and architectural models, and some 22,000 films, videos, and media works. To view the museum's permanent collection, head to the 4th and 5th floors' Painting and Sculpture galleries, where you'll find such iconic works as Van Gogh's *Starry Night,* Rousseau's *The Sleeping Gypsy,* Monet's *Water Lilies,* and Picasso's *Les Demoiselles d'Avignon,* among works by other modern masters. The museum continues to acquire works by art superstars, such as Cindy Sherman and Richard Serra, as well as up-and-coming artists. Its temporary exhibitions are almost always worth the trip in themselves.

Fifth Avenue

St. Patrick's Cathedral (5th Ave. between 50th and 51st Sts.), the largest Roman Catholic cathedral in the United States, sits across from Rockefeller Center. Designed by James Renwick, this elaborate Gothic creation with its soaring towers and lovely rose window took 21 years to build, replacing the old St. Pat's in Little Italy in 1879. Its grandeur attests to the success of New York's Irish Catholics who, at

that time, were largely shunned by the city's predominantly Protestant upper classes.

Kitty-corner to St. Pat's, at the corner of 53rd Street, is another famous New York house of worship, **St. Thomas,** an Episcopal church completed in 1914. A French Gothic gem known for its lovely stonework and stained glass, the church has long been a favorite site for society weddings.

[C] CENTRAL PARK

Between the Upper East and the Upper West Sides lies that most glorious of New York spaces: **Central Park** (between 5th and 8th Aves., 59th to 110th Sts., 212/310-6600, www.centralparknyc.org). Without this vast, rolling green estate—the lungs of the city—life in New York would probably become unbearable. Central Park is where New Yorkers go to escape cramped apartments, roaring traffic, and the cityscape of concrete and steel that makes one forget Manhattan is an island.

The Central Park, as it was once known, was the brainchild of poet-turned-newspaper editor William Cullen Bryant. Worried that the city was being smothered by block after block of relentless building, Bryant first called for the park's creation in the July 3, 1844, edition of his *Evening Post.* Landscape architect Andrew Jackson Downing and a number of politicians soon added their voices to Bryant's plea. Together, they hammered away at city government for 12 years until finally, in 1856, the city bought most of the land now comprising the park for five million dollars.

Frederick Law Olmsted and Calvert Vaux were the visionary landscape architects who turned Bryant's Central Park dream into reality. As Olmsted saw it, the park had two functions. One was to provide a place for the contemplation of nature. The other was to create a social tableau where the haves and have-nots could pass each other every day, providing an opportunity for the poor to become inspired by the rich.

Entirely manmade, with every bush, tree, and rock planned, the park took 20 years to complete. By the time it was finished, workers

CENTRAL PARK

had shifted 10 million cartloads of dirt, imported a half-million cubic yards of topsoil, and planted 4-5 million trees. Central Park was an immediate success that led to a park movement across the United States and the world.

Central Park is 2.5 miles long and a 0.5 miles wide, covers 843 acres, and hosts 15-20 million visitors annually. Walking through it is like walking through a gigantic carnival site. You'll see scantily clad New Yorkers going running, biking, or rollerblading; oblivious lovers; stroller-pushing nannies; students lounging with textbooks; cough-racked beggars; cashmere-clad matrons; professional dog-walkers; and musicians playing everything from concertos to rap. Every size, shape, color, and make of humanity is here.

Generally speaking, the park is safe, but it's always advisable to stick to well-populated areas, especially during the week, when fewer people use the park. Avoid the park completely at night.

59th Street to 65th Street

Central Park South (59th Street) on the Plaza's north side is a gathering place for horse-drawn carriages and, farther west on 59th Street, pedicabs. **Carriage rides** (347/298-7927, $50 for 20 min.) can be reserved through Manhattan Carriage Company, though it's also easy to simply walk along 59th Street and contract a carriage directly. **NYC Pedicab Co.** (917/405-1303, www.centralparkpedicabs.com) offers one-hour and two-hour tours for $60 and $120, though a 25-percent discount is offered when you make reservations on the company's website.

An excellent way to tour the park is by bike. Several vendors can be found on the west side of 59th Street, at the park's entrance off Columbus Circle, including **Bike and Roll** (212/260-0400, www.bikenewyorkcity.com), which offers rentals as well as bike tours. If you're keen to try a **Citi Bike** (www.citibikenyc. com), the city's bike share program launched in 2013, there are several docking stations on the park's periphery, including 59th Street, where you can purchase a 24-hour or 7-day pass.

If you're on foot, enter Central Park at

© MARIO SAVOIA/123RF

the Great Lawn, Central Park

5th Avenue and 64th Street and you'll soon come to **Central Park Zoo** (830 5th Ave., 212/439-6500, www.centralparkzoo.com, early Apr.-early Nov. Mon.-Fri. 10am-5pm, Sat.-Sun. 10am-5:30pm, early Nov.-early Apr. daily 10am-4:30pm, adults $12, seniors $9, children 3-12 $7). The small zoo groups its animals by climatic zones; polar bears cavort and swim, while penguins promenade in a snowy clime behind thick underwater viewing glass. An excellent open-air rain forest environment with netted walkways and tucked-away reptile tanks for various creepy crawlies tops the list. Crowds gather to watch the staff feed the sea lions, while the behavior presentation mimics *Madagascar* movie moments. At the zoo's northeast end is Delacorte Clock, where every half-hour a parade of bronze animals marches around playing nursery tunes.

Nearby is **Wollman Rink** (212/439-6900, www.wollmanskatingrink.com, Mon.-Tues. 10am-2:30pm, Wed.-Thurs. 10am-10pm, Fri.-Sat. 10am-11pm, Sun. 10am-9pm, prices vary by day; check website for current cost), packed in winter with exuberant ice-skaters.

North of the rink is the octagonal **Chess and Checkers House,** complete with 24 concrete game boards outside and 10 inside. Visitors can borrow pieces or bring their own and play for free.

The nearby **Dairy** houses a **Visitor Center and Gift Shop** (212/794-6564, daily 10am-5pm). Never a working dairy, the Victorian cottage was built to provide fresh milk and snacks for children and their caregivers visiting the park.

West of the Dairy is the 1908 **Carousel** (mid-park at 64th St., Apr.-Oct. daily 10am-6pm, call for hours in Nov.-Mar., $3), where 57 carved horses go round. Other amusement rides are here as well.

The sunken transverse road running from East 65th Street to West 66th Street is one of four such roads in the park (others are at 79th, 85th, and 97th Sts.). These roads were one of Olmsted's most brilliant innovations. Dynamited out of bedrock, they allow cars and

© FRANCISCO COLLAZO

a Citi Bike station in Manhattan

buses to pass below the level of the park, while pedestrians pass on bridges above.

65th Street to 72nd Street

Heading a bit farther north and west, you'll come to **Sheep Meadow,** a huge expanse of lawn covered with thousands of semi-clad sun-worshippers in warm weather. Real sheep grazed here until 1934. By then, the sheep were so inbred that many were malformed.

East of Sheep Meadow is **The Mall,** a promenade lined with trees and busts of famous men. This quarter-mile avenue was once a parade ground for the elite, who cruised up and down in the late afternoons, courting and showing off their fancy carriages. Today, The Mall is frequented by rollerbladers, sidewalk artists, skateboarders trying to perfect their tricks, couples taking advantage of the romantic atmosphere to sit on the benches for heartfelt chats, and retirees working on their *New York Times* crosswords.

North of The Mall is the bandshell at **Rumsey Playfield,** where a first-rate series of

free outdoor concerts is presented every summer by **SummerStage** (212/360-1399, www.summerstage.org). Past performers have ranged from Patti LaBelle to Lila Downs to Youssou N'Dour.

72nd Street to 79th Street

Bethesda Terrace, just north of the bandshell and the 72nd Street Transverse, is one of the park's grandest sights. The wide, brick-paved plaza centers on an ornate fountain; a semicircle of tiered steps cups the plaza's southern side. Lapping at the north end is **The Lake,** usually crowded with splish-splashing rowboats. These boats can be rented at the nearby **Loeb Boathouse** (212/517-2233, www.thecentralparkboathouse.com, daily 10am-dusk, $12 per hour, with a $20 cash deposit). You can also take a half-hour gondola ride here for $30.

West of Bethesda Terrace is **Strawberry Fields,** which Yoko Ono had landscaped into a Garden of Peace as a memorial to her husband, John Lennon, who was murdered outside The Dakota apartment building in 1980. Just inside the garden at 72nd Street is a circular marble mosaic spelling out the word *Imagine;* flowers brought by fans in tribute to Lennon often cover the mosaic, one of the park's most photographed landmarks.

East of Bethesda Terrace is **Conservatory Water,** a.k.a. the "model-boat pond." The pond is often dotted with miniature boats, most radio-controlled. During warm weather, model-boat regattas are held Saturday mornings. If you want to pilot a boat, you can rent one from **Sail the Park** (www.sailthepark.com, $11 for 30 minutes).

Two of the park's most famous statues are near Conservatory Water. *Alice in Wonderland,* by Jose de Creefts, perches on a mushroom to the north, while *Hans Christian Andersen,* by Georg Lober, sits with his *Ugly Duckling* to the west. Both statues are usually covered with adoring children.

West of the pond and north of The Lake is the 38-acre **Ramble,** a near wild place crisscrossed with meandering paths. Far removed from city life, the Ramble is a favorite spot among bird-watchers; on a typical morning, about 15 kinds of warblers and 35 other species can be seen.

79th Street to 97th Street

North of the Ramble is the Gothic Revival **Belvedere Castle,** designed in 1858 by Calvert Vaux. Situated atop Vista Rock, one of the park's highest spots, the castle offers bird's-eye views of the Great Lawn and the Ramble. Downstairs is **Henry Luce Nature Observatory at Belvedere Castle** (mid-park at 79th St., 212/772-0210, daily 10am-5pm, free).

Nearby are **Shakespeare Garden,** filled with plants and flowers mentioned in the playwright's work; **Swedish Cottage** (performances Sat.-Sun. 1pm, call for price), one of the last public marionette companies in the United States; and **Delacorte Theater,** where New York Public Theater has presented free **Shakespeare in the Park** performances (212/967-7555, www.shakespeareinthepark. org) each summer for more than 50 years. Two

plays are usually featured, each running about a month. The free tickets for each day's show are handed out beginning at 6:15pm the same day; people start lining up in the early afternoon.

Abutting Delacorte Theater is the often dusty **Great Lawn.** Tens of thousands of New Yorkers spread out their blankets and picnic baskets on the lawn when the New York Philharmonic and the Metropolitan Opera Company perform here. The Lawn is often host to major personalities providing free concerts, lectures, or events. The Dalai Lama has spoken here several times and Simon and Garfunkel, Diana Ross, and Jon Bon Jovi have all played on the 55-acre lawn.

North of the Great Lawn is Central Park Reservoir, which holds about a billion gallons of water, most of which comes via aqueduct from the Catskills. Now known as **Jacqueline Onassis Reservoir** because the former first lady used to jog around its 1.58-mile perimeter, it is one of the city's most popular jogging courses.

97th to 110th Street

As Frederick Law Olmsted originally intended, the northernmost section of Central Park, between 97th and 110th Streets, becomes more rugged and wild, filled with secret waterfalls and craggy cliffs. But at 105th Street near 5th Avenue is the lovely, formal **Conservatory Garden.** Actually three gardens in one, the Conservatory blooms from late spring through early fall. Its most popular spot is the Secret Garden, named after Frances Hodgson Burnett's classic children's book.

Just above the Conservatory is 11-acre **Harlem Meer.** Up until the mid 1990s, this lake—like much of the park above 97th Street—was avoided by New Yorkers fearful of crime. But since then, Central Park Conservancy has poured millions of dollars into the area, and it's been vastly improved. Harlem Meer is now stocked with some 50,000 bluegill, largemouth bass, and catfish, and is a favorite fishing ground for youngsters who can borrow free poles at **Charles A. Dana Discovery Center** (212/860-1370, daily 10am-5pm, free), which also houses natural history exhibits and hosts hands-on science programs.

UPPER EAST SIDE

Since the turn of the century, the Upper East Side has been associated with wealth. Everyone from Andrew Carnegie to Gloria Vanderbilt has resided in this hushed, exclusive neighborhood. Here you'll find so many brownstones, clubs, and penthouses that at times the neighborhood resembles an open-air museum.

The wealthy began arriving on the Upper East Side in the late 1800s as an ever-encroaching business tide forced them off the Midtown stretches of 5th Avenue. But the real turning point came in 1905, when steel magnate Andrew Carnegie built his mansion on 5th Avenue at 91st Street. Soon thereafter, one industrialist after another followed suit, until the stretch of 5th Avenue facing Central Park became known as "Millionaire's Row." Many of these mansions have since been converted into museums and cultural institutions. One particularly notable Upper East Side home—though it's not part of Millionaire's Row—is the mayor's residence, **Gracie Mansion** (Carl Schurz Park, east end of 88th St., 212/570-4773, www.historichousetrust.org). The 18th-century Federal-style manor house has been the New York City mayor's official residence since 1942. Wednesday-only tours require reservations, but just walking the grounds, which overlook the Hell Gate Strait, is also pleasant.

But the Upper East Side is not only about the wealthy. It's also about more ordinary folk, who, as elsewhere in Manhattan, settled closer to the river. At one time, Madison, Park, and Lexington Avenues were basically middle class, while the area east of Lexington was working-class and home to recent immigrants. Yorkville, a hamlet established in the 1790s between what are now 83rd and 88th Streets, had an especially large German population.

Stretching roughly from 59th Street to 100th Street and 5th Avenue to the East River, the Upper East Side's long residential blocks are pleasant for strolling. Most of the sights and shops are along the north-south avenues rather than the east-west side streets. Madison Avenue is famed for its upscale shops and 5th Avenue is dubbed "Museum Mile" for the 10 museums within its 82nd Street to 104th Street length.

The Frick Collection

The Frick Collection (1 E. 70th St., 212/288-0700, www.frick.org, Tues.-Sat. 10am-6pm, Sun. 11am-5pm, adults $20, seniors $15, students $10, children under 10 not admitted), like so many other New York cultural institutions, owes its creation to a wealthy robber baron hoping to whitewash questionable behavior with a hefty endowment to the arts. In this case, it was steel tycoon Henry Clay Frick who broke up strikes with Pinkerton guards and narrowly avoided several assassination attempts. Upon Frick's demise (of natural causes) in 1919, a $15 million endowment and his posh 5th Avenue townhouse were donated to establish a museum displaying the primarily European artwork and furnishings he spent 40 years collecting; since then, the collection has grown to over 1,100 works, comprising one of the world's greatest private museums.

One of the Frick's most glorious rooms is West Gallery, a naturally lit hall that houses landscapes by Constable, Turner, and Corot, as well as portraits by Rembrandt, El Greco, and Velázquez. It is also the home of *Mistress and Maid,* one of three works by Vermeer in the collection. The indoor Garden Court, with a Romanesque fountain at its center, invites quiet reflection. Amid the palm fronds and stone frogs are Whistler's *Symphony in Grey and Green: The Ocean* and Corot's *The Boatman of Mortefontaine.*

Whitney Museum of American Art

The boxy gray building with the wedge-shaped front at the corner of Madison Avenue and 75th Street is **Whitney Museum of American Art** (945 Madison Ave., 212/570-3676, www.whitney.org, Wed.-Thurs. and Sat.-Sun. 11am-6pm, Fri. 11am-9pm, adults $20, seniors, students, youth 19-25 $16, visitors under 18 free). Designed by Marcel Breuer

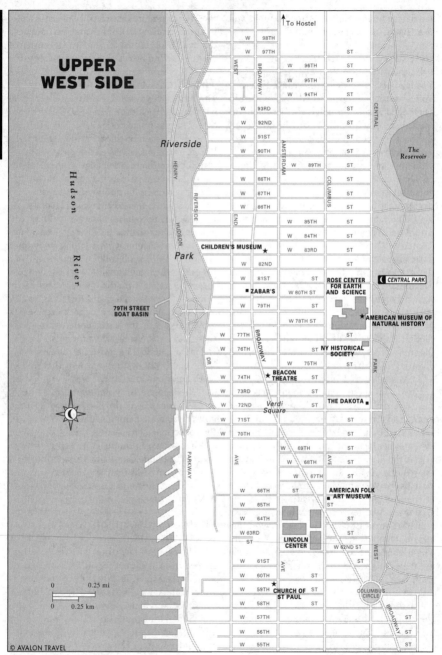

UPPER WEST SIDE

Hudson River

Riverside Park

79TH STREET BOAT BASIN

CHILDREN'S MUSEUM

ZABAR'S

ROSE CENTER FOR EARTH AND SCIENCE

AMERICAN MUSEUM OF NATURAL HISTORY

NY HISTORICAL SOCIETY

BEACON THEATRE

THE DAKOTA

Verdi Square

CENTRAL PARK

The Reservoir

AMERICAN FOLK ART MUSEUM

LINCOLN CENTER

CHURCH OF ST PAUL

COLUMBUS CIRCLE

To Hostel

0   0.25 mi

0   0.25 km

© AVALON TRAVEL

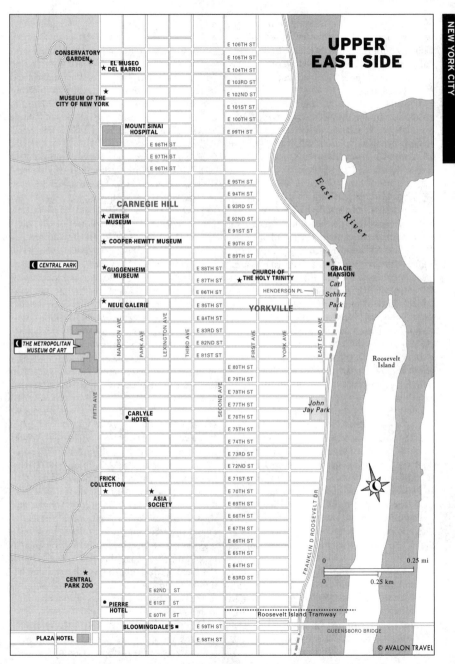

UPPER EAST SIDE

CONSERVATORY GARDEN

★ EL MUSEO DEL BARRIO

★ MUSEUM OF THE CITY OF NEW YORK

MOUNT SINAI HOSPITAL

E 106TH ST
E 105TH ST
E 104TH ST
E 103RD ST
E 102ND ST
E 101ST ST
E 100TH ST
E 99TH ST
E 98TH ST
E 97TH ST
E 96TH ST
E 95TH ST
E 94TH ST

CARNEGIE HILL

★ JEWISH MUSEUM

★ COOPER-HEWITT MUSEUM

★ GUGGENHEIM MUSEUM

C CENTRAL PARK

★ NEUE GALERIE

C THE METROPOLITAN MUSEUM OF ART

E 93RD ST
E 92ND ST
E 91ST ST
E 90TH ST
E 89TH ST
E 88TH ST
E 87TH ST
E 86TH ST
E 85TH ST
E 84TH ST
E 83RD ST
E 82ND ST
E 81ST ST
E 80TH ST
E 79TH ST
E 78TH ST
E 77TH ST
E 76TH ST
E 75TH ST
E 74TH ST
E 73RD ST
E 72ND ST
E 71ST ST
E 70TH ST
E 69TH ST
E 68TH ST
E 67TH ST
E 66TH ST
E 65TH ST
E 64TH ST
E 63RD ST
E 62ND ST
E 61ST ST
E 60TH ST
E 59TH ST
E 58TH ST

CHURCH OF ★ THE HOLY TRINITY

■ GRACIE MANSION

HENDERSON PL —

Carl Schurz Park

YORKVILLE

East River

Roosevelt Island

John Jay Park

MADISON AVE
PARK AVE
LEXINGTON AVE
THIRD AVE
SECOND AVE
FIRST AVE
YORK AVE
EAST END AVE
FIFTH AVE

FRANKLIN D ROOSEVELT DR

● CARLYLE HOTEL

FRICK COLLECTION ★

★ ASIA SOCIETY

★ CENTRAL PARK ZOO

● PIERRE HOTEL

BLOOMINGDALE'S ■

PLAZA HOTEL

0   0.25 mi
0   0.25 km

Roosevelt Island Tramway

QUEENSBORO BRIDGE

© AVALON TRAVEL

in 1966, the museum offers plenty to see from its collection of 20th-century American art. The museum is also known for its controversial Biennial, a show presented every two years to showcase the latest works of contemporary American artists.

The museum is currently building a new location downtown, near The High Line. When completed in late 2014, the Whitney will turn its uptown space over to The Metropolitan Museum of Art for exhibitions for a period of at least eight years.

(The Metropolitan Museum of Art

One of the world's greatest museums is **The Metropolitan Museum of Art** (1000 5th Ave., 212/535-7710, www.metmuseum.org, Sun.-Thurs. 10am-5:30pm, Fri.-Sat. 10am-9pm, recommended admission adults $25, seniors $17, students $12, children under 12 free), on the east side of Central Park at 5th Avenue and 82nd Street. Housed behind an imposing Beaux-Arts facade designed by Robert Morris Hunt, the museum spreads out over about 1.5 million square feet, holding nearly three million works of art in collections of everything from Egyptian sarcophagi to modern American paintings.

Directly up the staircase from the Great Hall is one of the Met's most stunning collections, **European paintings,** filling some 20-odd galleries. One room is filled with Rembrandts only; others house Vermeer, Van Dyck, Breughel, Rubens, Botticelli, El Greco, and Goya...and that's just for starters.

To the right of the Great Hall is the museum's famed **Egyptian collection,** displaying items as old as 4,000 years. The Met houses the largest collection of Egyptian art outside Egypt.

Three sides of the Met's original building are flanked by modern glass wings. At the back is the Robert Lehman Collection, housing an impressive collection of Old Masters and 19th-century French painters. On the south side are the Rockefeller and Acheson Wings. The Lila Acheson Wing is devoted to 20th-century art;

on its roof is a sculpture garden with great views of Central Park.

On the Met's north side are the Sackler and American Wings. The Sackler Wing houses 15th-century-BC Temple of Dendur, carved in faded hieroglyphics. The American Wing contains exhaustive galleries of decorative arts, and many fine paintings by the likes of Gilbert Stuart, Thomas Eakins, John Singer Sargent, and Mary Cassatt.

If possible, come on a weekday morning, or on a Friday or Saturday evening when the candlelit Great Hall Balcony Bar is open and a jazz or classical quintet performs.

Neue Galerie

Nearby is **Neue Galerie** (1048 5th Ave., at 86th St., 212/628-6200, www.neuegalerie. org, Thurs.-Mon. 11am-6pm, adults $20, seniors and students $10, children under 12 not admitted), devoted solely to fine and decorative arts of Germany and Austria from the first half of the 20th century. Housed in a renovated Beaux-Arts mansion, the museum holds a large permanent collection of works by Gustav Klimt and Egon Schiele, a bookstore, design shop, and the smart Cafe Sabarsky, where you can indulge in Viennese coffee and a piece of Sacher torte.

Guggenheim Museum

Guggenheim Museum (1071 5th Ave., 212/423-3500, www.guggenheim.org, Sun.-Wed. and Fri. 10am-5:45pm, Sat. 10am-7:45pm, adults $22, seniors and students $18, children 12 and under free) was the final masterpiece of architect Frank Lloyd Wright, and the building makes as strong an impression as any of the artwork it houses. Its smooth plastered-concrete exterior has been compared to everything from a nautilus shell to a toilet bowl, but there's little doubt that the daring spiral design interrupted Manhattan's rectangular uniformity and has reshaped perceptions of art and architecture.

Designed to house Solomon R. Guggenheim's collection of non-objective painting, the building was completed six months after Wright's death in 1959. The Guggenheim was the brainchild of mining magnate Solomon Guggenheim and Baroness Hilla Rebay von Ehrenwiesen, who dreamed of a new kind of museum that would suit the changing face of art. The collection began with works of 19th-century masters such as Cézanne and Van Gogh, but it is 20th-century artists like Marc Chagall, Paul Klee, Pablo Picasso, and Wassily Kandinsky for whom the Guggenheim is known. Today, the museum also champions contemporary artists, including Matthew Barney and Julie Mehretu.

Unlike many other New York museums, the Guggenheim does not overwhelm with the volume of its collections. A curved and continuous ramp connects a series of rooms that display works in the spare, minimalist way you would expect in a gallery. Several times a year, the entire museum is given over to an exhibition that surveys the work of single artists. In 2011, for example, the museum hung the entire collected work of contemporary artist Maurizio Cattelan from the ceiling of the central atrium.

Cooper-Hewitt National Design Museum

A branch of the Smithsonian Institution dedicated to design and the decorative arts, **Cooper-Hewitt** (2 E. 91st St., 212/849-8400, www.si.edu/ndm, Mon.-Fri. 10am-5pm, Sat. 10am-6pm, Sun. noon-5pm, adults $10, seniors and students $5, free to children under 12) focuses on such areas as textiles, metalwork, wallpaper, ceramics, furniture, and architectural design. But half the story is the building itself; the museum occupies a 64-room mansion built by industrialist Andrew Carnegie. The museum is currently undergoing renovation and is expected to reopen in late 2014, with gallery space expanded by 60 percent.

The Jewish Museum

Housed in a magnificent French Gothic mansion once belonging to businessman Felix Warburg, **The Jewish Museum** (1109 5th Ave., at 92nd St., 212/423-3200, www.the-jewishmuseum.org, Sat.-Tues. 11am-5:45pm, Thurs. 11am-8pm, Fri. 11am-4pm, adults $15, seniors $12, students $7.50, children under 18 free, free on Sat. and pay-what-you-wish on Thurs. 5pm-8pm) is the nation's largest Jewish culture museum. Changing, top-notch exhibits by famed Jewish artists such as Marc Chagall, as well as an outstanding permanent collection of ceremonial objects and cultural artifacts, are spread over three floors and a basement.

Museum of the City of New York

The renovated, neo-Georgian building on 5th Avenue between 103rd and 104th Streets houses the one-of-a-kind **Museum of the City of New York** (1220 5th Ave., 212/534-1672, www.mcny.org, daily 10am-6pm, suggested donation adults $10, students, seniors and students $6, families $20, children under 12 free). As its name suggests, the museum features "only in New York" exhibits, on topics both historical (Activist New York and The Gilded City: Beaux-Arts New York) and contemporary (Rising Waters: Photographs of Hurricane Sandy and From Bicycle Advocacy to Citi Bike: A Recent History of Bicycling in NYC). A strong emphasis on urban design has defined many recent exhibits.

El Museo del Barrio

Dedicated to the art and culture of Puerto Rico and Latin America, **El Museo del Barrio** (1230 5th Ave., 212/831-7272, www.elmuseo. org, Wed.-Sat. 11am-6pm, adults $9, students and seniors $5, children under 12 free) presents both contemporary and historical exhibits. Just a few blocks from Spanish Harlem, the museum was founded in an elementary school classroom over 25 years ago and continues to work closely with local residents. Most of its exhibits are temporary; on permanent display is a superb collection of *santos de palo* (carved wooden saints).

One block north of El Museo del Barrio at 105th Street is Central Park's truly lovely **Conservatory Garden,** most easily entered from 5th Avenue.

Asia Society

First-rate temporary exhibits, concerts, films, and lectures on various aspects of Asian culture and history are always on the calendar at **Asia Society** (725 Park Ave., 212/288-6400, www. asiasociety.org, Tues.-Sun. 11am-6pm, adults $12, seniors $10, students $7, children under 16 free). The museum is noted for its extensive collection of both traditional and contemporary work by Asian and Asian American artists, as well as a growing repository of video and new media work.

UPPER WEST SIDE

The Upper West Side is a mix of ornate 19th-century landmarks, solid pre-WWII apartment buildings, well-worn tenements, and some outstanding cultural institutions, including Lincoln Center and The American Museum of Natural History. The neighborhood is also known for its feisty liberal politics, love of culture, and upper-middle class population, including an especially large quotient of doctors, lawyers, writers, actors, musicians, dancers, and intellectuals.

The best streets for wandering are Broadway and Columbus Avenue, both lined with a multitude of shops. Streets running from east to west tend to be quiet and primarily residential.

Lincoln Center

The famed **Lincoln Center for the Performing Arts** (212/546-2656, www.lincolncenter.org) is actually a complex of buildings running from 60th to 66th Streets along Broadway, Columbus, and Amsterdam Avenues. As the home of The New York City Ballet, School of American Ballet, The New York Philharmonic, The Metropolitan Opera, and a host of other organizations and institutions, including Juilliard School of Music and Jazz at Lincoln Center, it's little wonder the center presents about 3,000 performances each year.

The fulcrum of Lincoln Center is a wide marble plaza featuring a circular fountain. The **Metropolitan Opera House,** on the plaza's west side, is the center's most ornate building, graced with sparkling multistoried windows, brilliant chandeliers, and two vivid murals by Marc Chagall. **The David H. Koch Theater** (formerly known as The New York State Theater), on the plaza's south side, is home to the New York City Ballet.

The center's renovation, a massive, six-year project completed in 2012, cost more than one billion dollars. It made an already vital institution even more inviting and dynamic, uniting West 65th Street between Broadway and Amsterdam Avenue with the surrounding cityscape. The David Rubenstein Atrium at Lincoln Center became a public community and cultural space offering free performances, shady seating with free Wi-Fi, information kiosks, a café, and discount ticket services. The renovation also created welcoming outdoor spaces in and around the main plaza, where in warmer weather, locals and visitors enjoy sitting and reading or sunning.

American Folk Art Museum

The **American Folk Art Museum** (2 Lincoln Sq./Columbus Ave. at 66th St., 212/595-9533, www.folkartmuseum.org, Tues.-Sat. noon-7:30pm, Sun. noon-6pm, free) sits just across from Lincoln Center, and exhibits a wide range of folk art, including quilts, toys, weather vanes, paintings, sculpture, handmade furniture, and the like. Temporary exhibits often focus on the work of individual self-taught artists.

The Dakota

Impressive buildings stand sentinel along Central Park West (CPW), the extension of 8th Avenue that borders Central Park. Most famous among them is **The Dakota** (northwest corner of 72nd St. and Central Park West). Built in 1884, the Dakota was financed by Edward Clark, heir to the Singer Sewing Machine fortune. At that time, the building stood so far north of the rest of Manhattan that it was said to be as remote as Dakota. Clark liked that idea, and had the architect add ears of corn and an Indian's head above the entrance.

The Dakota's roster of famous tenants is long and includes Lauren Bacall, Roberta Flack, Jose Ferrer, Rosemary Clooney, John Lennon (who was murdered outside the Dakota), Yoko Ono, Gilda Radner, and William Henry Pratt, a.k.a. Boris Karloff, among many others.

New-York Historical Society

The **New-York Historical Society** (170 Central Park West, 212/873-3400, www.nyhistory.org, Tues.-Thurs. and Sat. 10am-6pm, Fri. 10am-8pm, Sun. 11am-5pm, adults $18, seniors $14, students $12, children 5-13 $6, children under 5 free), founded in 1806, was one of the country's first cultural institutions. Today, it boasts a 17,000-square-foot gallery space featuring temporary exhibits that focus on all aspects of the city's history, from immigrants to board games, and a children's "museum within a museum," with interactive exhibits.

American Museum of Natural History

One of the city's greatest museums is the sprawling **American Museum of Natural History** (Central Park West at 79th St., 212/769-5100, www.amnh.org, daily 10am-5:45pm, adults $22, seniors and students $17, children 2-12 $12.50, shows cost extra). Behind its stone facade, the vast museum explores the wonders of Earth—its life, geology, and surroundings. Founded in 1869, the museum originally consisted of a few hundred mounted birds and mammals, but it quickly outgrew its first home, steadily acquiring an astonishing collection of rare gems; cultural artifacts from Asia, Africa, and the Americas; and the largest collection of dinosaur fossils in the world.

Among the many marvels in the Hall of Saurischian Dinosaurs is the fossilized skeleton of a Tyrannosaurus rex with a four-foot-long jaw, while the Hall of Ornithischian Dinosaurs features a stegosaurus and 65-million-year-old triceratops. The skeletons of extinct mammals, such as the woolly mammoth and saber-toothed tiger, have also been reconstructed and erected.

Inside Hayden Planetarium, an 87-foot globe housed within the glass casing of the Rose Center for Earth and Space, you can take a three-dimensional tour of our galaxy and beyond (for an additional $6). The museum's most-guarded attraction is the famed Star of India—a two-billion-year-old, 563-carat star sapphire that is part of the extensive gem and mineral collection; it was stolen in 1964 but recovered several months later. The Hall of Ocean Life, with its enormous fiberglass replica of a blue whale and exhibits of mammals from various continents, shows Earth's wildlife. Rooms dedicated to the cultures of the world add the human experience. With so much to see, it's impossible to fit it all into a single trip; explore the website to plan your visit.

Children's Museum of Manhattan

The bright and cheery **Children's Museum** (212 W. 83rd St., 212/721-1223, www.cmom. org, Tues.-Fri. and Sun. 10am-5pm, Sat. 10am-7pm, adults and children $11, seniors $7, free to children up to age one) is full of hands-on exhibits for kids ages 2-10. Here, children can draw and paint, learn crafts, drive a FDNY fire truck, listen to stories, or just explore one of the always-changing play areas.

Riverside Park and the Boat Basin

Riverside Drive abuts **Riverside Park** (stretching from 72nd to 153rd St. along the Hudson River), a long, narrow, sloping slice of green. Designed in the 1870s by Frederick Law Olmsted and Calvert Vaux, the park is a pleasant place with glorious views of the Hudson. Near the park's south end is **79th Street Boat Basin,** where houseboats dock. One important attraction in the park is **General Grant National Memorial** (Riverside Dr. at 122nd St., 212/666-1640, www.nps.gov/gegr, free), a Greco-Roman-style mausoleum honoring the country's 18th president and his wife, Julia. Mosaics in the tomb portray some of Grant's historic battles.

Columbia University Area

The world's largest Gothic cathedral, **Cathedral of St. John the Divine** (1047 Amsterdam Ave., 212/316-7540, www.stjohndivine.org, daily 7:30am-6pm) is said to be large enough to fit both Notre Dame and Chartres inside. The church can accommodate some 10,000 people and is still under construction. Scheduled completion date, *if* enough money becomes available: 2050, 158 years after the first stone was laid. Three different **tours** (212/316-7540, call for days, times, and prices) meet at the Visitor's Center and allow guests to walk through the bustling nave and serene chapels, including the unique **vertical tour,** involving a 124-foot climb through spiral stone staircases to reach a view of the Morningside Heights neighborhood from the upper buttresses atop the Cathedral.

Another lovely, historic house of worship in the neighborhood is **The Riverside Church** (490 Riverside Dr., 212/870-6700, www.theriversidechurchny.org), modeled on the 13th-century cathedral in Chartres, France, and partially financed by John D. Rockefeller Jr. The Gothic-style landmark, with its soaring 24-story tower, is one of New York's most architecturally striking churches.

Columbia University (2960 Broadway, 212/854-1754, www.columbia.edu) stretches from West 114th Street to West 120th Street, between Amsterdam Avenue and Broadway. Founded as King's College in 1754, it educated some of the country's earliest leaders, including Alexander Hamilton and John Jay (first chief justice of the U.S. Supreme Court). **tours** (212/854-4900, Mon.-Fri. 1pm-2pm) are given year-round. Maps and other materials for self-guided tours are available in the **Visitors Center** (Room 213 of Low Memorial Library).

HARLEM

Stretching roughly from 110th to 168th Streets, between the Harlem and Hudson Rivers, Harlem is one of the city's most historic and least understood neighborhoods. Once written off as a crime-infested no-man's-land, it's actually always been quite a diverse place, with many streets that are well-worn rather than raw, and a landscape studded with an impressive number of elegant brownstones and churches.

The area is divided into West and Central Harlem, comprised mostly of African Americans, and East Harlem, home to many Latinos, hence its nickname: El Barrio (or "The Neighborhood" in Spanish).

Harlem is currently in the midst of what some are calling the Second Harlem Renaissance. Much of Harlem can safely be explored on foot. The areas around 116th Street, 125th Street, and Schomburg Center, especially, are always crowded with people. It's best to stick to these main streets, however, and avoid parks.

In Harlem, many numbered avenues take on proper names. Sixth Avenue is Lenox Avenue or Malcolm X Boulevard; 7th Avenue is Adam Clayton Powell Jr. Boulevard (ACP Blvd.); and 8th Avenue is Frederick Douglass Boulevard.

Established as Nieuw Haarlem in 1658, Harlem remained a quiet farming community until 1837. Then, Harlem Railroad arrived, bringing with it hundreds of new settlers. In 1873, the village was annexed to the city; by the early 1900s, it was an affluent white suburb.

In 1901, the IRT subway was extended along Lenox Avenue and wealthy speculators, seeing the chance to make millions, built row after row of attractive townhouses. But they overextended themselves, and sales were slow. When a black realtor offered to fill the empty buildings with black tenants, the developers jumped at the chance. Fearing racial changes, the neighborhood's white residents fled.

During the 1920s and 1930s, Harlem was the country's African American cultural center. The Harlem Renaissance attracted writers and intellectuals such as Langston Hughes and W. E. B. DuBois, while streets were jammed with jazz clubs, theaters, dance halls, and speakeasies. Duke Ellington played at Cotton Club, Chick Webb at The Savoy.

Harlem lost much of this vibrancy during and after the Depression, when poverty began taking a stronger hold. In the 1960s, civil rights leaders Malcolm X, Stokely Carmichael, and others turned the neighborhood into a mecca for black consciousness.

Today, the area is transforming yet again. While it remains a vital center for the city's African American communities, and has absorbed a considerable number of African

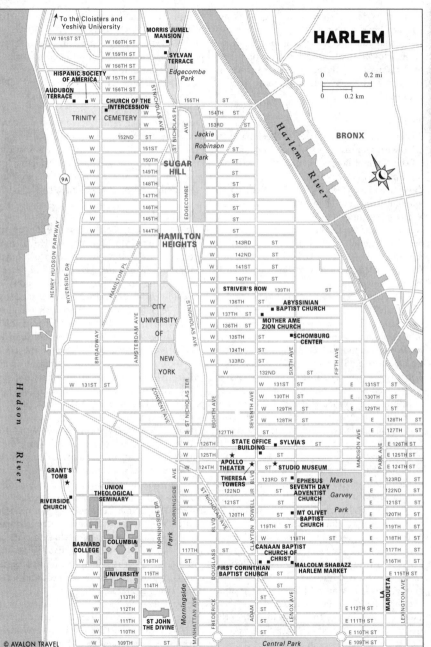

HARLEM

To the Cloisters and Yeshiva University

W 161ST ST
W 160TH ST
W 159TH ST
W 158TH ST

MORRIS JUMEL MANSION

SYLVAN TERRACE

W 157TH ST

Edgecombe Park

HISPANIC SOCIETY OF AMERICA

W 156TH ST

AUDUBON TERRACE

CHURCH OF THE INTERCESSION

155TH ST

154TH ST
153RD ST

TRINITY CEMETERY

BRONX

Harlem River

0   0.2 mi
0   0.2 km

Jackie Robinson Park

W 152ND ST
151ST ST
150TH ST
149TH ST
148TH ST
147TH ST
146TH ST
145TH ST
144TH ST

SUGAR HILL

Edgecombe

9A

HAMILTON HEIGHTS

HENRY HUDSON PARKWAY
RIVERSIDE DR
HAMILTON PL

143RD ST
142ND ST
141ST ST
140TH ST

STRIVER'S ROW   139TH ST

138TH ST   ABYSSINIAN BAPTIST CHURCH
137TH ST
136TH ST   MOTHER AME ZION CHURCH
135TH ST   SCHOMBURG CENTER
134TH ST
133RD ST
132ND ST

CITY UNIVERSITY OF NEW YORK

BROADWAY
AMSTERDAM AVE
CONVENT AVE
ST NICHOLAS TER
EIGHTH AVE
SEVENTH AVE
SIXTH AVE
FIFTH AVE

W 131ST ST

Hudson River

131ST ST
130TH ST
129TH ST
128TH ST
127TH ST

GRANT'S TOMB

RIVERSIDE CHURCH

UNION THEOLOGICAL SEMINARY

STATE OFFICE BUILDING   SYLVIA'S
126TH ST
125TH ST
APOLLO THEATER   STUDIO MUSEUM
124TH ST

E 126TH ST
E 125TH ST
E 124TH ST
E 123RD ST
E 122ND ST
E 121ST ST
E 120TH ST
E 119TH ST
E 118TH ST
E 117TH ST
E 116TH ST
E 115TH ST

THERESA TOWERS   123RD ST   EPHESUS SEVENTH DAY ADVENTIST CHURCH
122ND ST
121ST ST
120TH ST   MT OLIVET BAPTIST CHURCH
119TH ST
118TH ST

Marcus Garvey Park

MORNINGSIDE DR
MORNINGSIDE AVE
ST NICHOLAS AVE
FREDERICK DOUGLASS BLVD
ADAM CLAYTON POWELL JR BLVD
MADISON AVE
PARK AVE
LENOX AVE
LEXINGTON AVE

CANAAN BAPTIST CHURCH OF CHRIST

FIRST CORINTHIAN BAPTIST CHURCH

MALCOLM SHABAZZ HARLEM MARKET

BARNARD COLLEGE

COLUMBIA UNIVERSITY

Morningside Park

117TH ST
116TH ST
115TH ST
114TH ST
113TH ST
112TH ST
111TH ST
110TH ST
109TH ST

ST JOHN THE DIVINE

LA MARQUETA

E 112TH ST
E 111TH ST
E 110TH ST
E 109TH ST

Central Park

© AVALON TRAVEL

immigrants, Harlem is also rapidly gentrifying. The neighborhood's newest transition is due to residential and retail storefront rents skyrocketing below 96th Street. Prices have risen here to the point that beloved Harlem institutions, like Lenox Lounge, have had to move or close completely in recent years.

125th Street

The heart of Harlem is 125th Street, always alive with vibrant colors, sights, and sounds. As the neighborhood's main commercial drag for decades, 125th Street has had many ups and downs. Today, it's riding an optimistic wave, with more businesses in operation now than at any other time in recent history. The street is home to two major cultural landmarks: the Studio Museum in Harlem and The Apollo Theater. Just south of 125th Street, on 5th Avenue, is **Marcus Garvey Park,** lined with elegant brownstones.

The Studio Museum in Harlem (144 W. 125th St., 212/864-4500, www.studiomuseum. org, Thurs.-Fri. noon-9pm, Sat. 10am-6pm, Sun. noon-6pm, suggested admission adults $7, students and seniors $3, children under 12 free) was founded in 1968 in a small factory loft. Today, it's a first-class institution spread over several well-lit floors of a turn-of-the-century building. The "principal center for the study of Black art in America," the museum offers a permanent display of works by such masters as Romare Bearden, James VanDerZee, and Jacob Lawrence.

Perhaps the single most important landmark in the history of African American music, **The Apollo Theater** (253 W. 125th St., 212/531-5300, www.apollotheater.org) has hosted nearly every major jazz, blues, R&B, and soul artist to come along since the 1930s. Bessie Smith, Ella Fitzgerald, Billie Holiday, Duke Ellington, Louis Armstrong, Count Basie, Ray Charles, James Brown, Aretha Franklin, Diana Ross, and Michael Jackson all played The Apollo, and the list goes on and on. It is said that when a teenage Elvis Presley first came to New York, the one place he wanted to see was The Apollo. The same was later said of the Beatles.

Built in 1913, The Apollo was once Hurtig & Seamon's New Burlesque Theatre, which presented vaudeville to a Harlem that was then predominantly white. But by 1935, the neighborhood's racial mix had shifted, and the two-balconied theater, capable of seating 2,000, became famous for its Amateur Nights.

Now a nonprofit enterprise, The Apollo continues to present a variety of entertainment, including a Wednesday amateur night. A small exhibit on the theater's early history is in the lobby. **Tours** (212/531-5337) are available for groups of 20 or more; otherwise, you may be able to join a group that has already booked.

Central Harlem

The Schomburg Center for Research in Black Culture (515 Malcolm X Blvd./Lenox Ave. 212/491-2200, www.nypl.org/locations/ schomburg, Mon. and Fri.-Sat. 10am-6pm, Tues.-Thurs. noon-8pm, free admission) is a world-renowned institution founded by Arthur A. Schomburg, an Afro-Puerto Rican who as a child was told that blacks had no history. A respected research center and branch of The New York Public Library, the center's most interesting visitor attraction is its **gallery,** where a wide array of changing exhibits about African and diaspora cultures are presented. The center also has a small gift and bookshop upstairs.

Mother A.M.E. Zion Church (140 W. 137th St., 212/234-1544), a neo-Gothic building, was New York City's first church organized by and for blacks. It was founded in 1796—originally downtown at 156 Church Street—with money donated by a former slave. Also known as "Freedom Church" because of its connection to the Underground Railroad, the church has had many famous members, including Harriet Tubman, Frederick Douglass, Paul Robeson, and Sojourner Truth. The church welcomes visitors to participate in their music and worship services at 11am on Sundays.

One of Harlem's most famous addresses is the impressive **Abyssinian Baptist Church** (132 W. 138th St., 212/862-7474, www.abyssinian.org). It was founded in 1801 when a few members of the First Baptist Church refused to accept that church's racially segregated seating policy. The Abyssinian now has one of the country's largest black congregations. The Reverend Dr. Calvin Butts III is Abyssinian's current pastor, and he continues the church's activist tradition. Sunday services, complete with gospel music, are held at 9am and 11am. Visitors are welcome at the latter service on a first-come, first-seated basis, and must enter at a specially designated tourist entrance on the southeast corner of West 138th Street and Adam Clayton Powell Jr. Boulevard. The church has specific policies regarding dress and behavior during the service, all of which are detailed on the church's website.

East Harlem–El Barrio

Heading south and east to 116th Street, you'll come to Spanish Harlem, or El Barrio (meaning "The Neighborhood" in Spanish), filled with discount clothing stores, toy shops, beauty and wig salons, storefront churches, bakeries selling towering wedding cakes, pet stores selling homing pigeons, botanicas, and the sounds of salsa. Most of the residents here are of Puerto Rican, Cuban, and Dominican ancestry.

Morris-Jumel Mansion

Morris-Jumel Mansion (65 Jumel Terrace, 212/923-8008, www.morrisjumel.org, Wed.-Sun. 10am-4pm, adults $5, seniors and students $4, children under 12 free) sits high over the city in a small, lush park. Manhattan's last remaining Colonial residence, it was built in 1765 as a country home for British colonel Roger Morris and served as temporary headquarters for George Washington during the Revolutionary War.

Audubon Terrace

This monumental marble terrace is lined with impressive Beaux-Arts buildings to the south and friezes and statuary to the north. All of the land once belonged to ornithologist John James Audubon; the terrace was built later, in 1904.

One of the Beaux-Arts buildings houses **The Hispanic Society of America Museum and Library** (on Audubon Terrace, Broadway between 155th and 156th Sts., 212/926-2234, www.hispanicsociety.org, Tues.-Sat. 10am-4:30pm, Sun. 1pm-4pm, free), one of the city's hidden treasures. Dark, somber, and mansion-like in feel and oddly big and hollow, it houses exquisite paintings by Goya, Velásquez, and El Greco, along with heavy Spanish furnishings, porcelain, and mosaics. Curators offer free 45-minute tours of the building and collections on Saturdays at 2pm.

The Cloisters and Fort Tryon Park

High on a hill at the northern tip of Manhattan is a surprising sight: a magical "medieval monastery," with wonderful views of the Hudson, called **The Cloisters** (99 Margaret Corbin Dr., inside Fort Tryon Park, 212/923-3700, www.metmuseum.org, Sun.-Thurs. 10am-5:30pm, Fri.-Sat. 10am-9pm, suggested admission, which includes admission to The Met, adults $25, seniors $17, students $12, children under 12 free). Financed in 1938 by John D. Rockefeller, The Cloisters house The Metropolitan Museum of Art's medieval collections. Incorporated into the building are the actual remains of four medieval cloisters, transported here from Europe, and the museum's most prized possessions, its 16th-century unicorn tapestries.

Entertainment and Events

Comprehensive entertainment listings can be found in *The New Yorker, New York, Village Voice,* and the Friday and Sunday editions of *The New York Times. Time Out New York,* which includes hundreds upon hundreds of listings, is especially useful. *Village Voice* and *Time Out* do a very good job of covering downtown; *The New Yorker* is the best source for capsule theater reviews; it also has a "Goings on about Town" app for smart phones that's good for information on the go, with search by location, dates, critics' picks, and event listings. For information on the ever-changing club scene, *Time Out* is again the most useful.

POPULAR VENUES

New York's largest venue is **Madison Square Garden** (7th Ave. between 31st and 33rd Sts., 212/465-6741, www.thegarden.com), home to a packed schedule of concerts and other entertainment events, including the annual **Westminster Kennel Club Dog Show** (www.westminsterkennelclub.org), as well as the city's basketball and hockey teams.

Grand **Radio City Music Hall** (1260 6th Ave., at 50th St., 212/247-4777, www.radiocity.com) often presents popular national and international music acts, and, of course, the annual Christmas spectacular. Historic **Beacon Theatre** (2124 Broadway, at 74th St., 212/465-6225, www.beacontheatre.com) is a charming smaller venue that also hosts national and international musicians and performers; the roster of events is especially well represented by favorite stand-up comics. Recent performers have included Wanda Sykes, Bill Maher, John Legend, and Van Morrison. **The Town Hall** (123 W. 43rd St., 212/840-2824, www.the-townhall-nyc.org) is a National Historic Site that presents a variety of jazz, world, and traditional music in an intimate setting.

The atmospheric **Apollo Theater** (253 W. 125th St., 212/531-5305, www.apollotheater.org) offers mostly R&B, soul, and rap. On Wednesdays, the famed amateur-night tradition continues. Don't hesitate to venture up here at night; 125th Street is always bustling.

LIVE MUSIC

Long, dark **Mercury Lounge** (217 E. Houston, 212/260-4700, www.mercuryloungenyc.com) features an antique wooden bar, exposed brick walls, heavy red drapes, and an excellent sound system. Hip rock and jazz acts play here. **The Bowery Ballroom** (6 Delancey St., 212/533-2111, www.boweryballroom.com) is one of the city's few midsize venues. Complete with a balcony, it presents a wide variety of music acts.

City Winery (155 Varick St., 212/608-0555, www.citywinery.com) is a posh, airy, blonde-wood-floored performance space and restaurant that often features big names in pop, rock, jazz, and folk.

The oldest and arguably best jazz club in the city is **Village Vanguard** (178 7th Ave. S., at 11th St., 212/255-4037, www.villagevanguard.com), a dark, wedge-shaped basement room filled with rickety tables and fading photographs. Established in 1934, Vanguard has booked all the greats, from Miles Davis and Dinah Washington to Wynton Marsalis and Terence Blanchard. Jazz lovers also trumpet **Blue Note** (131 W. 3rd St., 212/475-8592, www.bluenote.net). Though pricey, with overly commercial decor and mediocre food, the club has attracted jazz luminaries since 1981; nightly sets are at 8pm and 10:30pm. Less well-known but also good is **Fat Cat** (75 Christopher St., 212/675-6056, www.fatcatmusic.org), a spacious subterranean bar packed with locals playing pool, table tennis, shuffleboard, foosball, and board games. Three nightly sets of top-notch live jazz keep the party rocking until the 5am closing. Another basement jazz joint is **Smalls Jazz Club** (183 W. 10th St., 212/252-5091, www.smallsjazzclub.com), with an old-school Village vibe and stuffed to standing-room-only on weekends. Multiple sets

Blue Note jazz club

each evening (one cover admits you to them all) often focus on young talent.

After a Latin-inspired dinner, ditch your table for the nearby dance floor at **S.O.B.'s** (204 Varick St., 212/243-4940, www.sobs.com), New York's premier world music showcase, hosting everything from hip-hop and bhangra to the beats of Brazil, the Caribbean, Africa, and beyond.

Manhattan School of Music (120 Claremont Ave., 212/749-2802, www.msmnyc.edu), a competitive world-renowned music conservatory, offers degrees up to the doctoral level in the areas of classical and jazz performance and composition. The wealth of talent here is exhibited in free jazz and classical and orchestral concerts and performances throughout the year.

CLASSICAL MUSIC AND OPERA

Classical music thrives in New York City, especially at **Lincoln Center for the Performing Arts** (between 62nd and 65th Sts., and between Columbus and Amsterdam Aves.,

212/546-2656, www.lincolncenter.org). The center presents an astonishing 3,000 performances a year. On its north side is 2,700-seat **Avery Fisher Hall,** home to The New York Philharmonic (Sept.-May), Great Performers Series (Oct.-May), and Mostly Mozart Festival (July-Aug.).

Just north of Avery Fisher, above 66th Street, is 1,096-seat **Alice Tully Hall,** where The Chamber Music Society of Lincoln Center performs.

A dozen or so blocks from Lincoln Center is Manhattan's other major classical music venue, **Carnegie Hall** (7th Ave. and 57th St., 212/247-7800, www.carnegiehall.org). Saved from demolition by Isaac Stern and others in the early 1960s, this legendary hall remains a favorite spot among musicians of all genres.

On the west side of Lincoln Center is the grand **Metropolitan Opera House** (Lincoln Center, 212/362-6000, www.metoperafamily.org), home of the Metropolitan Opera Company. A good seat here costs over $100, but under-$20 seats and standing-room tickets

© FRANCISCO COLLAZO

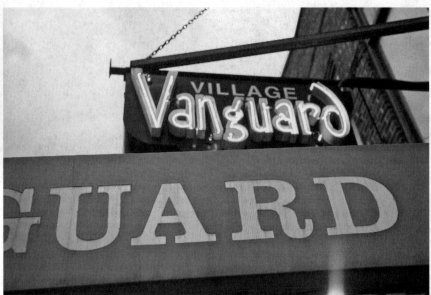

Village Vanguard jazz club

are often available in the upper balcony (bring binoculars).

THEATER

Attending a Broadway show is a quintessential New York experience. There's nothing quite like hurrying down the neon-splashed streets of Times Square along with thousands of other theatergoers, most of whom always seem to be running late. Among Broadway's many gorgeous, historic venues—most located just off Times Square—are the **Shubert** (225 W. 44th St., 212/239-6200, www.shubertorganization. com), **Booth** (222 W. 45th St., 212/239-6200, www.booth-theater.com), **Nederlander** (208 W. 41st St., 212/921-8000, www.nederland-ertheatre.com), **Majestic** (245 W. 44th St., 212/239-6215, www.majestic-theater.com), **Belasco** (111 W. 44th St., 212/239-6200, www.shubertorganization.com), and **Lyceum** (149 W. 45th St., 212/239-2949, www.shubertorganization.com).

Discount tickets to same-day performances are sold daily at three **TKTS** (www.

tdf.org) booths in the city, run by the Theater Development Fund. The **Times Square** location (under the red steps in Father Duffy Square on Broadway and 47th St., Mon. and Wed.-Sat. 3pm-8pm, Tues. 2pm-8pm, Sun. 3pm-7pm) sells tickets for evening performances. On days when matinee tickets are available, the booth opens at 10am. There is also a **South Street Seaport** location (corner of Front and John Sts., Mon.-Sat. 11am-6pm). The TKTS location in **downtown Brooklyn** (1 MetroTech Center, corner of Jay St. and Myrtle Ave. Promenade, Tues.-Sat. 11am-3pm and 3:30pm-6pm) sells same-day evening and next day matinee discount tickets.

DANCE

New York is home to two major ballet companies. **American Ballet Theater** (890 Broadway, 212/477-3030, www.abt.org), once directed by Mikhail Baryshnikov, and **New York City Ballet** (www.nycballet.com), founded by George Balanchine and Lincoln Kirstein, both

BEST OF BROADWAY AND BEYOND

There's nothing like seeing a Broadway show to really top off a full day in NYC. Times Square's garish lights beckon you to escape reality for a few hours through the work of the world's best actors and performers in some of the country's most beautiful, historic theaters.

Most visitors to New York City know they want to see a Broadway show, but many are intimidated by the process of choosing a show and buying tickets. And they may not know some of the most basic terms and tips for making the most of their Broadway experience. Here, then, is a Broadway primer:

"Broadway," "Off-Broadway," and "Off-Off-Broadway" are terms that refer to different types of theaters in Manhattan. Not determined solely by the theater's physical location on or off Broadway, the terms also take into account the number of seats a theater has and whether the actors are union or non-union. The general rule of thumb? **"Broadway"** shows occur in theaters between 40th and 54th Streets and 6th and 8th Avenues; these theaters have more than 499 seats. **"Off-Broadway"** shows play in theaters with 100-499 seats. **"Off-Off-Broadway"** shows play in theaters with fewer than 100 seats. Broadway productions lean toward the mainstream, and Off-Broadway productions almost equally so—despite having begun in the 1930s as a rebellion against Broad-

way values. Off-Off Broadway theater was a 1960s rebellion against the rebellion; its shows are often quirky and experimental.

"Stage door" refers to the door that actors and other employees use to enter and leave the theater. As such, it's the place you'll want to post yourself after the show if you hope to glimpse your favorite actor or try to get an autograph.

Broadway isn't just for adults. In addition to long-running kid-friendly shows like "The Lion King" and "Wicked," there are productions designed especially with kids in mind. If you're traveling with little ones, check the show schedule for **The New Victory Theater** (www.newvictory.org). This theater for kids features plays, puppetry performances, and much more, with shows for children as young as four months. Another kid-friendly tip? Once a year, **"Kids' Night Out"** (which actually takes place over several nights) (www.kidsnightonbroadway.com) offers free tickets to select Broadway shows for kids 6-18.

For discount tickets any time of the year, check Theatre Development Fund's **TKTS booths** (www.tdf.org) in the middle of Times Square, the South Street Seaport, or downtown Brooklyn. Here, you can score legit, day-of-show tickets for up to 50 percent off their regular price.

---

perform at **David H. Koch Theater** in Lincoln Center (212/496-0600).

NIGHTLIFE
Lower Manhattan

For a bar with a view, there's **Beekman Beer Garden Beach Club** (89 South St., 212/892-4600, www.beekmanbeergarden.com). Perched on the edge of the East River, this beer garden has fantastic views of the Brooklyn Bridge and Manhattan skyline, which you can enjoy from picnic tables or the umbrella-shaded, sand-floored "beach."

Jeremy's Ale House (228 Front St., 212/964-3537, www.jeremysalehouse.com) is

a jovial bar whose "Beer isn't the only thing for breakfast anymore" bumper stickers pretty much say all you need to know about this spot. Happy hour specials include 32-ounce Styrofoam cups of beer and half-price well drinks.

One of the city's most popular cocktail bars is **The Dead Rabbit Grocery and Grog** (30 Water St., 646/422-7906, www.deadrabbitnyc.com), whose unpleasant name belies its many charms, including craft cocktails that harken back to another era.

Macao Trading Company (311 Church St., 212/431-8750, www.macaonyc.com) is a sexy subterranean lounge with Eastern-influenced cocktails and a 1930s Macao theme. Food from the upstairs restaurant is served until 3:30am.

The appealing triumvirate of nightly jazz, gourmet bar snacks, and top-notch drinks makes **Silver Lining** (75 Murray St., 212/513-1234, www.silverliningbar.com), an old-fashioned cocktail lounge, a perfect place to start and end the evening.

Lower East Side

Ludlow, Stanton, and Clinton Streets are the hub of hip Lower East Side nightlife, where you'll find lots of laid-back bars and lounges; some are holes-in-the-wall, others are more upscale. If you're looking for a quick-n-easy bar crawl, a duo on Ludlow fit the bill: The domestic-sounding **Pianos** (158 Ludlow St., 212/505-3733) and **Cake Shop** (152 Ludlow St., 212/253-0036) sit conveniently near one other. Both are less precious than nearby hot spot, the popular **Stanton Social** (99 Stanton St., 212/995-0099).

BIG APPLE CIRCUS

Big Apple Circus (Damrosch Park at Lincoln Center, 800/922-3772, www.bigapplecircus.org) travels around the country, but releases the following year's new original show each winter right in the heart of the city. Performers come from America, Armenia, Brazil, Bulgaria, China, England, France, Germany, Italy, and Russia, exciting crowds with a more classic version of the all-too commercialized circus arts.

Trapeze acts, trampoline acrobatics, contortionists, jugglers, rousing music, and, of course, clowns all add to the fun, which is further enhanced by the intimate nature of the performance. With little resemblance to the massive arena filled with crying kids, whirring plastic light-up toys, and gimmicky overpriced treats that typically pop to mind with the term "circus," the not-for-profit Big Apple Circus offers an entertaining two hours where Big Top tent guests are never seated more than 50 feet from the action.

SoHo and TriBeCa

Stop by **Spring Lounge** (48 Spring St., 212/965-1774, www.thespringlounge.com), a.k.a the Shark Bar (so named for stuffed sharks mounted on walls), to enjoy a pint or two in a dive bar-chic spot where drinking starts at 8am.

Santos Party House (96 Lafayette St., 212/584-5492, www.santospartyhouse.com) is a black-walled bi-level dance club, where a diverse crowd of hipsters rocks to live acts and big-name DJs. Expect anything from electronica to hip-hop to reggae.

The classic bar in SoHo is **Fanelli's Cafe** (94 Prince St., 212/226-9412), an 1876 pub complete with beveled glass doors, tiled floors, and heavy, dark wood. Passable bar food is served on worn wooden tables. At **Pegu Club** (77 W. Houston St., 212/473-7348), colonial Asian decor characterizes this upscale cocktail bar where the mixologists produce beautiful drinks harking back to yesteryear.

Once an artists' hangout, **Puffy's Tavern** (81 Hudson St., 212/227-3912) now attracts everyone from bankers and bikers to police and firefighters. **Walker's** (16 N. Moore St., 212/941-0142) is an 1890s saloon that serves tasty pub grub and Guinness on tap. **Church Lounge** (2 Ave. of the Americas, 212/519-6600) in trendy TriBeCa Grand Hotel is an enormous bar-lobby always filled with downtown revelers.

East Village

McSorley's Old Ale House (15 E. 7th St., 212/473-9148) is one of New York's oldest bars, and was once a hangout of *New Yorker* writer Joseph Mitchell, who wrote of the place in his book *McSorley's Wonderful Saloon*. Inside, find a potbellied stove, old gas lamps, a carved mahogany bar, and pressed tin ceilings. Elegant **Temple Bar** (332 Lafayette St., 212/925-4242) is a lush hideaway with Oriental rugs and expensive drinks. Also in the neighborhood is **Angel's Share** (8 Stuyvesant St., 212/777-5415), a speakeasy-style bar tucked away in the restaurant Village Yokocho.

West Village

Sturdy old **White Horse Tavern** (567 Hudson St., 212/989-3956) was once a writer's hangout; Dylan Thomas drank himself to death here. Now the tavern caters mostly to a college crowd. Outdoor picnic tables are set up in summer.

Blind Tiger Ale House (281 Bleecker St., 212/462-4682) is considered one of New York's top craft beer bars with a prodigious selection of draft beers and an upscale bar menu.

They take libations seriously at **Little Branch** (20 7th Ave. S., 212/929-4360), a cozy nightspot where mixologists craft first-rate cocktails with ultra-fresh ingredients, hand-chipped ice, and chilled glasses. There's live jazz Sunday-Thursday.

Among gay bars, low-key **Stonewall Inn** (53 Christopher St., near 7th Ave. S, 212/488-2705) is named after the landmark riots. Across the street is **The Monster** (80 Grove St., 212/924-3558), featuring a drag cabaret. **Henrietta Hudson** (438 Hudson St., 212/924-3347) is a popular lesbian bar, drawing largely professional crowds.

Chelsea and Meatpacking District

In the Meatpacking District, find raucous, testosterone-filled **Hogs & Heifers** (859 Washington St., 212/929-0655). They put on quite a show here. Bartenders dance on the famed *Coyote Ugly* bar and purposefully give customers a hard time, while crowds spill out onto the street.

The Tippler (425 W. 15th St., basement level of Chelsea Market, 212/206-0000) is a complete contrast to Hogs & Heifers. Founded by two beverage consultants whose goal is to "help the world drink better," The Tippler is a trendy spot with classic architectural elements and artisanal cocktails.

Bar Americano (518 W. 27th St., 212/525-0000) is a popular option in Chelsea's gallery/High Line district. The downstairs bar is all sleek lines and low lights for the see-and-be-seen set.

Midtown

Midtown is *the* neighborhood to experience the city's best rooftop bars, among them **bar 54** (135 W. 45th St., 646/364-1234 www.timessquare.hyatt.com, 5pm-1am Sun.-Thurs., 5pm-2am, Fri.-Sat.). Its sweeping river-to-river views are thanks to its perch on the 54th story of the Hyatt Times Square. Indoor and outdoor fireplaces create a cozy ambience in colder weather, and creative cocktails and a full wine list are served year-round.

The newish **Refinery Rooftop** (63 W. 38th St., 646/664-0310), atop Refinery Hotel focuses on cocktails made of natural ingredients using biochemistry techniques. The bar has an indoor area with seats, an outdoor terrace, and an indoor-outdoor patio with retractable glass roof. For a drink in the city's only revolving bar, overlooking Times Square, take an elevator to the top of glitzy Marriott Marquis for the aptly named **The View** (1535 Broadway, 212/704-8900). Yes, it's an overpriced tourist attraction, but it's hard to beat the 360-degree view.

Back on ground level, elegant, wood-paneled **Algonquin Hotel** (59 W. 44th St., 212/840-6800), near the Theater District, offers several bars and lounges.

Another spot with overpriced drinks whose cost may be validated by the "only in New York" setting is **The Campbell Apartment** (15 Vanderbilt Ave., at 43rd St., 212/953-0409). Once the private office of railroad trustee John Campbell, the Grand Central Terminal spot is designed to resemble a 13th-century Florentine palazzo.

P.J. Clarke's (915 3rd Ave., 212/317-1616) is an out-of-time saloon sporting brass railings, worn wood, and sawdust on the floor. Featured in the 1945 movie *The Lost Weekend*, P.J.'s also serves pricey burgers and sandwiches.

In the post-modern Four Seasons Hotel is **The Bar** (57 E. 57th St., 212/758-5700), serving 15 different kinds of oversized martinis. Drinks at posh St. Regis Hotel's **King Cole Bar and Lounge** (2 E. 55th St., 212/753-4500) don't come cheap, but the room's stunning historic mural by Maxfield Parrish makes it worthwhile.

CRAFT COCKTAILS

Forget Cosmos, appletinis, and any drink tinged blue with curacao; now, New Yorkers want their cocktails artisanally titled and mixed, preferably with handcrafted, small-batch ingredients, the more locally sourced, the better. It's not enough, anymore, to stock trendy liquors, prepped in cocktail shakers, and strained into martini glasses or, worse, the grossly oversized, bowl-shaped margarita glass, rimmed with—gasp!—plain old salt. Now, New Yorkers out on the town for a drink expect bespoke glasses, special or vintage bar gear, and homemade garnishes (no shriveled orange peel or jarred Maraschino cherry, please) for specific, inspired drinks...all served by a bespectacled, mustachioed, vest-and-suspenders-wearing barkeep.

A growing number of the city's bartenders are happy to indulge these customers. After all, they're the ones who gave rise to the craft cocktail movement. Mixing bitters in their basements and cutting their own ice cubes, these drink artisans spawned the current craze for cocktails that can average $14 a pop. Here's a sampling of the best craft cocktails in NYC.

MANHATTAN

- Angel's Share
- The Dead Rabbit Grocery and Grog
- Little Branch
- Refinery Rooftop
- The Tippler

BROOKLYN

- Alameda
- The Clover Club
- Tooker Alley
- Weather Up

QUEENS

- The Astor Room
- Dutch Kills

Upper East Side

The Upper East Side is home to many singles bars that come and go with the seasons. One that's been around for a while is **Merchants NY** (1125 1st Ave., 212/832-4610), complete with a polished semicircular bar, small tables with flickering candles, and a good bar menu.

Upper West Side

Amsterdam Avenue between 79th and 85th Streets is teeming with bars. Mostly a younger twentysomething crowd prevails, but quieter choices include **Cava Wine Bar** (185 W. 80th St., 212/724-2282) and tiny **Dead Poet** (450 Amsterdam Ave., 212/595-5670).

Harlem

While many of Harlem's classic nightspots have closed, including famed Lenox Lounge, **Corner Social** (321 Lenox Ave., 212/510-8552) is one of several newer bar-restaurants that have both enjoyed and contributed to Harlem's gentrification. Crowds of young professionals venture uptown—some for the first time—to drink and eat at ample Corner Social, often spilling out onto the sidewalk, where a handful of tables are set up in warmer months.

Right across the street from Corner Social is **Red Rooster** (310 Lenox Ave., 212/792-9001), one of the many projects of ambitious chef-preneur Marcus Samuelsson. Upstairs, the restaurant serves Southern-U.S.-inspired dishes like fried chicken; downstairs, Ginny's Supper Club operates as "part raucous speakeasy, part debonair jazz lounge."

Shopping

If you can't find it—whatever the "it" is—in New York City, it either doesn't exist or you don't need it. Whether you're looking for vintage clothes, custom cookware, rare or specialized books, or notions of 900 sorts, you can probably find it in Manhattan...as long as you know where to look.

LOWER MANHATTAN

Lower Manhattan isn't the city's best shopping district; though a couple of big department and electronics stores draw shoppers down here, this area is mainly full of Wall Street types hurrying to and fro. Storefronts tend to close early. Two exceptions are **Century 21** (22 Cortlandt St., 212/227-9092), one of the city's largest and oldest discount clothing stores, and **J&R** (1 Park Row and adjoining buildings, near City Hall, 212/238-9000, www.jr.com). Once just a record store, J&R has branched out over the years to become a long row of shops selling every conceivable electronic device, including audio equipment, TVs, computers, cameras, and appliances. And, oh yes, they still sell recordings, too.

LOWER EAST SIDE

The Lower East Side is a destination for shoppers searching for vintage, handmade clothes, and accessories at chic, if small, boutiques. Don't expect lots of bargains, but you will find one-of-a-kind pieces, especially on Orchard and Rivington Streets. **Epaulet** (144 Orchard St., 212/228-3626) is a men's and women's boutique with clothes all designed and made in the United States with ethical standards. **Dressing Room Bar & Boutique** (75a Orchard St., 212/966-7330) is a totally unique shopping experience, part showroom for emerging designers, part clothing exchange, part cocktail bar, and part event space. If you're in need of undergarments, **Orchard Corset Center** (157 Orchard St., 212/674-0786) sells them, including, as its name indicates, corsets. And as long

as you're thinking about that part of the body, a visit to **Babeland** (94 Rivington St., 212/375-1701) might be in order; the sex shop is New York's cleanest and most professional.

SOHO AND TRIBECA

SoHo and TriBeCa are among the city's most popular neighborhoods for shopping, boasting a variety of clothing, novelty, design, and niche-interest shops. The area is especially known for trendy clothing stores, many very expensive, and gift and home furnishings shops. Chic designer stores include **Anna Sui** (113 Greene St., 212/941-8406), **Marc Jacobs** (163 Mercer St., 212/343-1490), **Prada** (575 Broadway, 212/334-8888), **French Connection** (435 W. Broadway, 212/219-1197), and **Stella McCartney** (112 Greene St., 212/255-1556).

If you're shopping on a more modest budget, stop in the stores along Broadway between Houston and Grand Streets, where you'll find chains like **Old Navy** (503 Broadway, 212/226-0838) and **H&M** (515 Broadway, 212/966-8975), as well stores like **Uniqlo** (546 Broadway, 877/486-4756), the Japanese casual-wear company with stacks of color, and **Yellow Rat Bastard** (483 Broadway, 212/334-2150) for street-wear. **What Comes Around Goes Around** (351 W. Broadway, 212/343-1225) houses over 60,000 vintage designer items, as well as denim and military threads. **Stella Dallas** (218 Thompson St., 212/674-0447) specializes in the 1940s look.

Once you're outfitted, complete your look with some accessories. You can find imaginative handmade women's hats at **The Hat Shop** (120 Thompson St., between Prince and Spring Sts., 212/219-1445), named one of the 10 best hat shops in the country by *USA Today*.

If you love chocolate, SoHo has a number of upscale chocolatiers where you can get your fix. **MarieBelle** (484 Broome St., 212/925-6999, www.mariebelle.com) has some of the fanciest chocolates in the city and a cute little café in the back to sit and sip hot chocolate. Try **Vosges Haut-Chocolat** (132 Spring St., 212/625-2929, www.vosgeschocolate.com) for truly original truffles, like the surprisingly delicious Indian curry truffle or their famous bacon and milk chocolate bars. **Kee's Chocolates** (80 Thompson St., 212/334-3284, www.keeschocolates.com) has some of the freshest truffles in town.

For decorative and design elements, stop by **The Evolution Store** (120 Spring St., 212/343-1114, www.theevolutionstore.com), an odd natural history store where you can pick up a giraffe skull or wild boar tusk, or bright and cheerful **Pylones** (69 Spring St., 212/431-3244, www.pylones-usa.com), filled with cute, colorful housewares and office gifts. For bigger pieces, there's **Wyeth** (315 Spring St., 212/243-3661, www.wyethome.com), which sells fine 20th-century vintage furniture, and **Urban Archaeology** (143 Franklin St., 212/431-4646, www.urbanarchaeology.com), which specializes in artifacts from demolished buildings.

SoHo and TriBeCa also have a number of children's bookstores. Among them are **Scholastic** (557 Broadway, 212/343-6166, www.scholastic.com/sohostore), which has a large play space that New York parents appreciate in cold months, and **Mysterious Book Shop** (58 Warren St., 212/587-1011, www.mysteriousbookshop.com), which sells hardcover, paperback, new, and used books. Another indie favorite is hip **McNally Jackson Books** (52 Prince St., 212/274-1160, www.mcnallyjackson.com), a two-level bookstore in SoHo, complete with café and a station where aspiring authors can print their own books.

If you're something of a writer yourself, then you'll want to at least peek at **Kate's Paperie** (435 Broome St., 212/941-9816, www.katespaperie.com), an upscale stationery shop filled with handmade paper products, or buy yourself a pen at **Fountain Pen Hospital** (10 Warren St., 212/964-0580, www.fountainpenhospital.com). This fix-it shop in TriBeCa also sells new, fine pens.

Finally, a unique SoHo shop is **Kid Robot** (118 Prince St., 212/966-6688, www.kidrobot.com), an anime and pop art store more for the kid in the adults than for kids who are towed along.

EAST VILLAGE

Shops in the East Village stay true to the neighborhood's punk and alt-everything roots, with vintage clothes and accessories and counter-culture books and goods all on offer here. **Screaming Mimi's** (382 Lafayette St., 212/677-6464) is known for 1950s-, 1960s-, and 1970s-era duds. **Stock Vintage** (143 E. 13th St., 212/505-2505) is one of the few vintage stores that specializes in menswear; it also has exceptional accessories, such as jewelry and cigarette cases. Complete the look with a Beat classic to stick in your back pocket. **St. Mark's Bookshop** (31 3rd Ave., 212/260-7853, www.stmarksbookshop.com) has an especially fine selection of fiction and alternative publications, and is open daily until midnight. **Sounds** (20 St. Mark's Pl., 212/677-3444) is stocked with a good selection of alternative music and used CDs, including some punk rock sounds that evoke the East Village's earlier days.

The East Village's ethnic roots are visible at long-time neighborhood favorite **Surma** (11 E. 7th St., 212/477-0729, www.surmastore.com). This one-of-a-kind shop sells Ukrainian crafts, books, and records. For offbeat souvenirs and postcards, step into **Alphabets** (64 Ave. A and 115 Ave. A., 212/475-7250). More stationery can be found for affordable prices at **Jam Paper and Envelope** (135 3rd Ave., 212/473-6666, www.jampaper.com).

If you're interested in something a little different, stop by the traditional **Tenth Street Russian and Turkish Baths** (268 E. 10th St., 212/674-9250, www.russianturkishbaths.com), a complex filled with saunas, steam rooms, and massage rooms. At one time, many such establishments existed in the East Village, but this is the last one left. Some days are co-ed, others for men or women only. If you need still more self-care, you'll love the 1851 flagship location of **Kiehl's** (109 3rd Ave., 212/677-3171, www.kiehls.com). You can buy a full line of natural, handmade beauty products at this store, which evokes an old-fashioned chemist's.

WEST VILLAGE

The West Village has loads of interesting shops of all sorts and has, so far, managed to stave off the big name brands that would colonize the neighborhood with boutique-size outlets. Supporting these smaller businesses helps ensure their survival.

For gently used clothes, visit **Star Struck** (47 Greenwich Ave., 212/691-5357), which carries a good selection of old coats, and **Beacon's Closet** (10 W. 13th St., 917/261-4863), which sells vintage and modern hand-me-downs.

The West Village is home to two popular apothecaries. One is the small but charming **Village Apothecary** (346 Bleecker St., 212/807-7566), which stocks colognes and perfumes, soaps, and a variety of toiletries. The much larger **C.O. Bigelow Apothecaries** (414 6th Ave., 212/533-2700) in the West Village is New York's oldest continuously operating pharmacy; the official historic landmark was established in 1838, and still sports its original oak fittings and gaslight fixtures.

Bond No. 9 (399 Bleecker St., 212/228-1732) features a collection of perfumes named after NYC neighborhoods, sold in cute NYC subway token-themed bottles. Also on Bleecker is **Murray's Cheese Shop** (254 Bleecker St., 212/243-3289, www.murrayscheese.com), a Village institution where you can buy cheeses from around the world. **McNulty's Tea & Coffee** (109 Christopher St., 212/242-5351, www.mcnultys.com) is an aromatic haven over 100 years old.

If you're looking for unique decorative items for your home, **Le Fanion** (299 W. 4th St., 212/463-8760, www.lefanion.com) sells beautiful pottery and chandeliers from the south of France, and **La Belle Époque** (115 Greenwich Ave., 212/362-1770) has French posters from the 1890s and 1900s.

For intellectual stimulation, visit **Three Lives & Co.** (154 W. 10th St., 212/741-2069, www.threelives.com), one of the city's top literary bookstores and host of frequent readings by well-known authors. **Bookbook** (266 Bleecker St., 212/807-8655, www.bookbooknyc.com) has an excellent selection of sale books and an extensive cookbook selection.

There are plenty more unique shops where you can browse and buy interesting goods. **Ink Pad** (37 7th Ave., 212/463-9876, www.theinkpadnyc.com) is a store that's stuffed to the gills with—what else?—rubber stamps and ink pads. Famed **Village Chess Shop** (82 W. 3rd St., 212/475-9580, www.chess-shop.com) moved out of its original location on Thompson St., and into a café, where baked goods and coffee are sold alongside chessboards and pieces. Chess games are always in session and players of all levels are welcome. The shop also offers one-hour lessons and runs Che$$ Ca$h Exchange, through which chess players can put their gently used games and pieces on consignment. If you're in the market for a guitar, **Matt Umanov Guitars** (273 Bleecker St., 212/675-2157, www.umanovguitars.com) sells (and repairs) new and rare guitars. Finally, you can find a full range of NYPD- and FDNY-themed items at **The Firestore** (17 Greenwich Ave., 212/226-3142, www.nyfirestore.com).

UNION SQUARE AND MADISON SQUARE PARK

Like the West Village, the neighborhoods in and around Union Square and Madison Square Park offer plenty of neat, independently-owned businesses; especially well represented are bookstores and foodstuffs and home decor shops. Mixed among them are recognizable brand name clothiers and megastores like the wildly popular Eataly and ABC Carpet and Home.

Lower 5th Avenue between 14th and 23rd Streets offer a large number of stylish clothing stores, with many upscale chains, including **Anthropologie** (85 5th Ave., 212/627-5885), offering an interesting mix of ethnic-influenced urban wear, and **Bebe** (100 5th Ave., 212/675-2323), with hip urban styles, some sleek, some frilly. **Emporio Armani** (110 5th Ave., 212/727-3240) is an expensive showroom for the designer brand. For outdoor wear and sports/recreation gear, stop by nearby **Paragon Sports**

(867 Broadway, 212/255-8889), the city's top sporting goods department store.

Many of the city's nonprofit, social service organizations and cultural organizations have thrift stores that funnel proceeds of sales back to their respective causes. One of the most popular is **Housing Works** (157 E. 23rd St., 212/529-5955, www.housingworks.org), which has a dozen thrift stores spread across Manhattan and Brooklyn. You can find one of them, along with thrift stores of several other non-profits, including City Opera, along E. 23rd Street between 2nd and Park Avenues.

A neighborhood novelty is New York's largest and oldest hat store, **J.J. Hat Center** (310 5th Ave., 212/239-4368). Established in 1911, J.J.'s stocks over 15,000 men's hats, including fedoras, Stetsons, homburgs, and caps.

Cooks and food lovers will enjoy the area, too. Venerable **Kalustyan's** (123 Lexington Ave., 212/685-3451) was the first store to import Indian foodstuffs into the city; the shop sells everything from homemade *labne* yogurt to naan bread to stuffed pita pockets to go. It also features spices, staples, and specialty items from many other countries around the world. And if you're hungry, there's a no-frills café upstairs. The neighborhood's other food institution is **Eataly** (200 5th Ave., 212/229-2560, www.eatalyny.com), an Italian-inspired market and food court where you can browse imported sweets and oils, buy handmade pasta and cheese, tip back a glass of wine, or sip a perfectly pulled espresso.

So you've got ingredients...now, in what vessels should you serve your inspired meals? **Fishs Eddy** (889 Broadway, 212/420-9020, www.fishseddy.com) can help; it's filled with retro and retro-inspired dinnerware. The shop features restaurant and diner overstocks as well as its own line of dishes and glassware. While you're in the neighborhood, you can browse the expensive but beautiful wares at **ABC Carpet and Home** (881 and 888 Broadway, 212/473-3000, www.abchome.com), which is hardly even a hop, skip, and jump across the street. While the store has an ample selection of rugs and carpets (very pricey ones, at that), it also stocks all manner of home goods and furniture, all sourced by buyers whose enviable jobs involve traveling around the world and purchasing beautiful objects that catch their eye. The clothes and jewelry are also worth a look.

Some of the city's best-loved bookstores are in the Union Square-Madison Square Park neighborhood. **Shakespeare & Co.** (716 Broadway, 212/529-1330, www.shakeandco.com) is a charming independent bookstore, nearly overshadowed by the granddaddy of New York City bookstores, **Strand Book Store** (828 Broadway, 212/473-1452, www.strandbooks.com, Mon.-Sat. 9:30am-10:30pm, Sun. 11am-10:30pm). The institution cherished by book-loving New Yorkers is the only one of 48 bookstores that used to line so-called "Book Row," which ran from Union Square to Astor Place. The Strand boasts 18 miles of shelves, which are loaded with more than 2.5 million new and used books. A rare books room is on the store's top floor. Just up the street from Strand is **Forbidden Planet** (832 Broadway, 212/473-1576, www.fpnyc.com), a gold mine for science fiction and comic book lovers, as well as gamers. The **Barnes & Noble flagship** (33 E. 17th St., 212/253-0810) borders the northern end of Union Square. About a half-dozen Barnes & Noble megastores, complete with cafés and reading series, are scattered throughout the city.

CHELSEA AND THE MEATPACKING DISTRICT

Shops in Chelsea and the Meatpacking District have undergone the same sort of transformation that has characterized the neighborhood itself over the past decade: trendy, expensive, and a little bit precious. Here, you'll find a clutch of high-end designers, including **Diane von Furstenberg** (874 Washington St., 646/486-4800) of 1970s wrap-dress fame, but once again a style icon, lately appearing on magazine covers and TV shows. If you're looking for more casual duds, popular denim label **Earnest Sewn** (821 Washington St., 212/242-3414) has a small shop where you can get your jeans custom-made.

The industrial ground floor of The National Biscuit Company's late-19th-century complex is now **Chelsea Market** (75 9th Ave., 212/243-6005, www.chelseamarket.com), a winding maze of gourmet butchers, cheesemongers, bakers, grocers, and vintners, as well as cute cafés and snack shops. The market also has a branch of **Posman Books,** featuring an excellent selection of New York City-themed books, and **Bowery Kitchen Supply,** where you're likely to spot a famous chef. Chelsea Market also hosts regular pop-up shops, selling everything from boutique and brand-name clothing to jewelry and fancy wine glasses.

Chelsea and the Meatpacking District have a fine selection of gift shops, stationery stores, bookstores, and novelty boutiques. **Abracadabra** (19 W. 21st St., 212/627-5194, www.abracadabranyc.com) features an enormous number of rubber Halloween masks and wacky gag gifts.

Books of Wonder (18 W. 18th St., 212/989-3270, www.booksofwonder.com) is a great children's bookstore. A bookstore dedicated to travel-related titles—mainly contemporary—is **Idlewild Books** (12 W. 19th St., 212/414-8888, www.idlewildbooks.com), which also hosts foreign language classes. **Revolution Books** (146 W. 26th St., 212/691-3345, www.revolutionbooksnyc.org), the country's largest radical bookstore, harks back to New York's inflammatory Sacco-and-Vanzetti days. For posters, **Chisholm Larsson Gallery** (145 8th Ave., 212/741-1703, www.chisholm-poster.com) specializes in European travel and product posters. Don't let the utterly boring name **Paper Presentation** (23 W. 18th St., 212/463-7035, www.paperpresentation.com) fool you: this is a paper-phile's paradise, peddling everything from fancy stationery and invitations to crafting supplies, gifts, and all sorts of paper-related novelties.

If you know where to go, you can score some collectibles in these neighborhoods, too. **Academy Records and CDs** (12 W. 18th St., 212/242-3000, www.academy-records.com) sells pretty much every American genre on CDs and LPs. If you're into rare jazz ephemera,

Jazz Record Center (236 W. 26th St., 8th Fl., 212/675-4480, www.jazzrecordcenter.com) is the place to go.

The Antiques Garage (112 W. 25th St., 212/243-5343, Sat.-Sun. 9am-5pm) is two floors of antiques sold out of a Chelsea parking garage. **West 25th Street Market** (W. 25th St. between Broadway and 6th Ave., 212/243-5343) features 125+ vendors selling mid-century modern and other vintage items.

MIDTOWN AND TIMES SQUARE

Midtown and Times Square represent a large swath of shopping pleasure in Manhattan. The neighborhoods are home to the city's most iconic department stores, including Saks Fifth Avenue, Bergdorf Goodman, and Tiffany & Co., all of which are located on Fifth Avenue. The king of department stores, of course, is **Macy's** (151 W. 34th St., 212/695-4400, www.macys.com). Ten stories high and a full block wide, the store was founded in 1858 by Rowland Hussey Macy, a Quaker from Nantucket. A few blocks farther northeast is **Lord & Taylor** (424 5th Ave., 212/391-3344), a comfortable midsize store that may not be as glamorous as some, but still carries a first-rate selection. **Saks Fifth Avenue** (611 5th Ave., 212/753-4000) is a wonderfully plush store with high-quality merchandise, and **Henri Bendel** (712 5th Ave., 212/247-1100) is frequented by the very rich and very thin. **Bergdorf Goodman** (754 5th Ave., 212/753-7300) is a favorite among wealthy socialites. Once a bargain basement, **Bloomingdale's** (1000 3rd Ave., 212/705-2000) is now one of New York's most glamorous department stores. It's well worth a browse, even if you're not planning to buy. **Barney's New York** (660 Madison Ave., 212/826-8900) carries fashionable and expensive clothing for men and women.

If your budget calls for more affordable clothes, cheap, cheerful, and trendy Swedish department store **H&M** (640 5th Ave., 212/489-0390) is perpetually busy at their multiple locations. You'll also find Gap, Desigual, Old

Navy, and the like ringing Herald Square, just steps away from Macy's.

More of a do-it-yourself kind of person? You can buy fabric and notions at **Margola** (48 W. 37th St., 212/695-1115), offering glass beads, rhinestones, and trinkets; **Manny's Millinery Supply** (28 W. 38th St., 212/840-2235), selling hats and notions; and **M&J Trimming** (1008 6th Ave., 212/391-6200), with a huge selection of beads, buttons, lace, and feathers.

Deep pocketed visitors looking to add to their jewelry boxes should head to 5th Avenue, home to two of the country's most famed jewelry stores, **Cartier** (653 5th Ave., 212/753-0111) and **Tiffany & Co.** (727 5th Ave., 212/755-8000). In Truman Capote's *Breakfast at Tiffany's,* character Holly Golightly opines, "Nothing bad can ever happen to you at Tiffany's," and she may be right. The store is as classy as Cartier, but much friendlier. Numerous other watch and jewelry shops line this part of 5th Avenue, too, including **Harry Winston** (718 5th Ave., 212/245-2000) and **Van Cleef and Arpels** (744 5th Ave., 212/896-9250). And at **Astro Gallery of Gems** (417 5th Ave., 212/889-9000) visitors can gawk at thousands of minerals and gems in a massive showroom.

Though neither as old nor as storied as some of the food shops in other neighborhoods, Midtown is nonetheless a sure-to-please destination for visitors with a sweet tooth. **Poseidon Bakery** (629 9th Ave., 212/757-6173) is a Greek shop that has been hand-rolling phyllo dough for nearly a century, and **Michel Cluizel** (584 5th Ave., 646/415-9126, www.chocolat-michelcluizel.com) has a lovely selection of truffles. The shop also sells delicious hot chocolate, which you can enjoy while strolling on 5th Avenue or seated at one of the shop's café tables.

In the technology and electronics realm, the flagship store of **Hammacher-Schlemmer** (147 E. 57th St., 212/421-9000) features imaginative and expensive high-tech gadgets. But it's **B&H** (420 9th Ave., 212/444-6615, www.bhphotovideo.com) that holds the undisputed title as *the* most popular electronics store in New York City—or *anywhere* for that matter. The scene is quintessential New York: The megastore, run by Hassidic Jews, is abuzz with customers from around the world, their purchases shuttling from storage to the ground-floor pay and pick-up area via an overhead trolley system. Free seminars on topics as wide-ranging as basic photographic techniques to advanced video editing are offered in the store's Event Space venue.

Museum shops are also good places to find unique gifts. **MoMA Design Store** (11 W. 53rd St., 212/708-9700, www.momastore.org) has interesting design-driven and art-inspired pieces. For gorgeous handmade jewelry, stop by the gift shop at **Museum of Arts and Design** (2 Columbus Circle, 212/299-7777, www.thestore.madmuseum.org). **Museum of the City of New York** (1220 5th Ave., 917/492-3330, www.shop.mcny.org), **The New York Public Library** (inside the main branch, the Schwarzman Building, at 42nd St. and 5th Ave., 212/930-0641, www.shop.nypl.org), and **The New York Transit Museum Store** in Grand Central Terminal (Shuttle Passage next to the Station Masters' office, 212/878-0106, www.transitmuseumstore.com) all feature a solid selection of New York City-themed items.

Book lovers have a number of options in Midtown, with many of the neighborhood's shops specializing in particular types of books. **Complete Traveller Antiquarian Bookstore** (199 Madison Ave., 212/685-9007, www.ctra-rebooks.com) features beautiful antique and rare travel books and literature. Classy, wood-paneled **Rizzoli** (31 W. 57th St., 212/759-2424, www.rizzolibookstore.com) stocks an especially fine collection of art and photography books, spread out over three floors. It also has a small but select offering of foreign newspapers and magazines. **Argosy** (116 E. 59th St., 212/753-4455, www.argosybooks.com) carries an excellent selection of old and rare books, as well as prints and maps.

If you're visiting with kids—or if you're a big kid yourself—you won't be able to leave New York without visiting **F.A.O. Schwarz** (767 5th Ave., 212/644-9400, www.fao.com), a vast, imaginative toy emporium that's as much fun for adults as it is for kids. Be sure to visit the BIG piano from the 1988 movie *Big* and the larger than life-sized LEGO sculptures. For a more exclusive experience, adults can arrange a private tour and breakfast with one of F.A.O.'s toy soldiers. No less crowded or popular is **Toys "R" Us** (1514 Broadway, 646/366-8800, www.toysrus.com) in Times Square, said to be the largest toy store in the world. Inside, find a 60-foot-tall Ferris wheel, along with three floors of toys and games. Many new "it" toys are launched here with events and concerts. If you're looking for toys on the go, **Kidding Around** (107 E. 42nd St., in Grand Central Terminal, 212/972-8697, www.kiddingaroundtoys.com), a small shop with ample selection in Grand Central Terminal, is a sure bet.

If you're looking for musical instruments—whether to spy or to buy—top-notch instrument stores in Midtown include **Sam Ash** (333 W. 34th St., 212/719-2299, www.samashmusic.com) and **New York Woodwind & Brass** (168 W. 48th St., 212/302-5893). **Steinway & Sons** (109 W. 57th St., 212/246-1100, www.steinwayshowrooms.com) is a lovely, old-fashioned piano showroom that opened in 1925. If you're lucky, you might be able to enjoy a free recital on the second floor.

Antique goods can be found at **Hell's Kitchen Flea Market** (W. 39th St., between 9th and 10th Aves., 212/243-5343, www.hellskitchenfleamarket.com, Sat.-Sun. 9am-5pm), which has over 100 vendors selling vintage and mid-century items.

UPPER EAST SIDE

Be prepared to spend a pretty penny in this tony neighborhood, where you'll find a number of exclusive clothiers and retailers on Madison, Park, and 5th Avenues.

Among the many upscale clothing stores you'll find on Madison Avenue is **Polo Ralph Lauren** (867 Madison Ave.-men's flagship, 888 Madison Ave.-women's/home flagship, 212/606-2100 and 212/434-8000, respectively), with its classic, upscale American fashion. **Second Chance Designer Resale** (1109 Lexington Ave., 2nd Fl., 212/744-6041) is the place to go for secondhand couture.

Food lovers will enjoy neighborhood institutions like **Schaller & Weber** (1654 2nd Ave., 212/879-3047, www.schallerweber.com), a 1937 German butcher shop that will mail sausages anywhere in the world. Younger and hipper, but just as popular, is cheery **Dylan's Candy Bar** (1011 3rd Ave., 646/735-0078, www.dylanscandybar.com), a Technicolor sweets store. More sophisticated spots for those with a sweet tooth are **Minamoto Kitchoan** (509 Madison Ave., 212/489-3747), selling Japanese delicacies, and **Ladurée** (864 Madison Ave., 646/558-3157), famous for its delicious *macarons*. If you want to don your own apron, **Kitchen Arts & Letters** (1435 Lexington Ave., 212/876-5550, www.kitchenartsandletters.com) stocks recent and hard-to-find cookbooks and literary titles related to food.

Other popular shopping spots in this neighborhood include **Star Magic** (1256 Lexington Ave., 212/988-0300), which sells a range of fun space-age gifts, including science kits, mobiles, prisms, kaleidoscopes, and books, and **The Manhattan Art & Antiques Center** (1050 2nd Ave., 212/355-4400, www.the-maac.com), a complex with about 100 small antique shops.

UPPER WEST SIDE

While it's not as interesting or as varied as the West Village, nor as expensive as the Upper East Side, the Upper West Side still has plenty to offer shoppers; this *is* still New York, after all.

Broadway, Amsterdam Avenue, and **Columbus Avenue** are the main thoroughfares here. On Columbus between 66th and 86th Streets, you'll find a large number of stylish clothing stores, with many upscale chains among them, including **Anthropologie, Banana Republic, Club Monaco, Eileen Fisher,** and **Free People. Columbus Avenue** is also home to boutiques like **Theory** (201 Columbus Ave. 212/362-3676) and **Malia Mills** (220 Columbus Ave., 212/874-7200), where attentive staff pick out beautiful designer bathing suits for you. **Off Broadway Boutique** (139 W. 72nd St., 212/724-6713) sells secondhand clothes once worn by stars.

Food lovers shouldn't skip **Zabar's** (2245 Broadway, 212/787-2000), one of the city's most beloved food stores. Dating back to the 1930s, Zabar's sells over 10,000 pounds of coffee, 10 tons of cheese, and 1,000 pounds of salmon a week, not to mention pots and pans, microwave ovens, vacuum cleaners, and the like. Some 10,000 customers are said to pass through its friendly portals on a Saturday afternoon. The best time to come is weekdays before 5pm. Not far away is **Citarella** (2135 Broadway, 212/874-0383, www.citarella.com), a gourmet market with elaborate window displays. **Jacques Torres** (285 Amsterdam Ave., 212/787-3256, www.mrchocolate.com) now has several Manhattan shops, including one on the Upper West Side; all Jacques Torres shops serve an amazing array of beautiful chocolate pieces, including over-the-top chocolate chip cookies.

For New York-themed gifts, stop by the gift shop at **The New-York Historical Society** (170 Central Park West, 212/485-9203, www.nyhistorystore.com), and for toys, visit **West Side Kids** (498 Amsterdam Ave., 212/496-7282, www.westsidekidsnyc.com), the neighborhood toy store every neighborhood wishes it had.

GreenFlea (Columbus Ave., between W. 76th and 77th Sts., 212/239-3027, www.greenfleamarkets.com, Sun. 10am-5:30pm) has a mix of new and used goods as well as a green market; it bills itself as the city's largest flea market.

HARLEM

125th Street cuts across Harlem, running from east to west, and is one long line of discount clothiers and chain retailers like **TJ Maxx** and **Old Navy.** To experience some of the neighborhood's best, most interesting shops, you'll need to explore beyond 125th.

One of the loveliest finds in Harlem is **La Casa Azul** (143 E. 103rd St., 212/426-2626, www.lacasaazulbookstore.com), a friendly, colorful space full of books in Spanish. It exists thanks to an ambitious crowdfunding campaign that raised $40,000 in 40 days. The store opened in El Barrio in 2012; in addition to selling an exceptional collection of books for children and adults, it also sells T-shirts, knickknacks, cards, and a small selection of music. The store also hosts a full schedule of readings and events.

At **Malcolm Shabazz Harlem Market** (52 W. 116th St., between Lenox and 5th Ave., 212/987-8131) dozens of vendors sell T-shirts, Kente cloth, African art, wool skullcaps, Gambian drums, African music, and even hair-braiding services.

For informative and interesting Harlem-themed books and gifts, visit the shops at **The Studio Museum in Harlem** (144 W. 125th St., 212/864-4500) and The New York Public Library's **Schomburg Center for Research in Black Culture** (103 W. 135th St., 212/491-2200).

Accommodations

With real estate values continually spiraling upward, cheap sleeps are not readily available in New York City. An "inexpensive" room costs $100-150 per night, while a moderately priced one with "nothing special" costs $150-250. The average hotel room now runs over $300 per night. It is likely to be small and cramped, with minimal amenities.

Some of the city's most affordable hotel rooms are found just outside Manhattan in the Queens neighborhood of Long Island City, one

stop from Midtown on the N and Q trains and just a few stops from Grand Central on the 7 train. Zoning changes intended to promote the neighborhood's growth have resulted in the recent construction of a cluster of hotels, many with lovely Manhattan views and affordable rates.

At the other end of the scale, New York is a glittering wonderland, home to some of the world's grandest hotels. The Plaza, Pierre, Four Seasons, Mandarin Oriental, and St. Regis are among the reigning monarchs. Even if you can't afford to stay in these elegant properties, they're well worth stepping into for afternoon tea, a cocktail, or just a look-see.

NYC & Company (800/NYC-VISIT or 212/484-1200, www.nycgo.com), the city's official convention and visitors' bureau, sponsors Hotel Week each January, a discount program intended to promote tourism in the slower winter months by making hotel rooms more affordable. Rooms that typically go for $300 and up may go as low as $100, with special amenities added as incentives to book.

Another option for saving money is booking online. Expedia.com, Orbitz.com, Hotels.com, and Hotwire.com are among the most popular, though many hotel managers say they will meet or beat these booking engines' rates if you call the hotel directly and inquire.

The hotels below are organized by neighborhood, with less expensive places listed first. Prices quoted are generally for high season. Keep in mind that in addition to the room rate, you'll also have to pay a hefty hotel tax of 14.75 percent.

LOWER MANHATTAN
$150-300
As far as location goes, it's pretty hard to beat **Conrad Hotel** (102 North End Ave., 212/945-0100, www.hilton.com, $250 and up), which is steps from both the Hudson River (some rooms overlook the waterway) and a massive complex of shops and restaurants.

$300 and Above
W New York Downtown (123 Washington St., 646/826-8600, www.wnewyorkdowntown.com, $485 and up) took a gamble with this location: Would people want to stay so close—practically atop–the site where the 9/11 terrorist attacks occurred? The answer has been a clear "Yes," and as the new World Trade Center nears completion, guests love the bird's-eye view of the gleaming tower's construction. The terrace bar is pretty spectacular, and the hotel is just a short walk from multiple subway lines.

LOWER EAST SIDE
Under $150
The **Chelsea Center** (83 Essex St., 646/669-8495, www.chelseacenterhostel.com, $35 pp bunk, $100 private room) is a small, friendly hostel with dorm-style accommodations, free luggage storage and a safe, and a light continental breakfast. All rooms share bathrooms.

$300 and Above
All of the 110 rooms at sleek and minimalist, 20-story **Hotel on Rivington** (107 Rivington St., between Essex and Ludlow Sts., 212/475-2600, www.hotelonrivington.com, $375-580) are wrapped in glass, offering stunning views of Manhattan. Velvet couches, heated-tile bathroom floors, private terraces, and in-room spa services are among the hotel's attractions, not to mention its hot location.

SOHO AND TRIBECA
Under $150
These neighborhoods are chock-a-block with pricey sleeps, but **Hotel Azure** (120 Lafayette St., 212/925-4378, www.hotelazure.com, $107-143) isn't one of them. It may lack charm and there are no special amenities to write home about, but the price is right and the location is convenient to major shopping and cultural attractions.

$300 and Above
When it opened in 1996, 370-room **☾ SoHo Grand** (310 W. Broadway, at Grand Ave., 212/965-3000 or 800/965-3000, www.sohogrand.com, $400-550) was SoHo's first hotel since the 1800s. Sleekly done up in industrial metals, oversized lamps, columns, and sofas in its lobby, the hotel has become a chic, minimalist haven for well-heeled fashionables and Europeans. Custom-designed guest rooms feature muted grays. Adjoining the lobby is a classy, high-ceilinged bar.

The Mercer (147 Mercer St., at Prince St., 212/966-6060 or 888/918-6060, www.mercerhotel.com, $550-760) is a stylish spot, located in the middle of SoHo. Each of its 75 understated rooms is done up in furniture made of exotic African woods and features a large bathroom with a tub made for two. Downstairs is Mercer Kitchen restaurant.

EAST VILLAGE
Under $150
"No frills" definitely describes **Bowery's Whitehouse Hotel of NY** (340 Bowery, www.whitehousehotelofny.com, $30-35 s, $60-70 d), which is a hostel-style budget accommodation geared toward students.

$300 and Above
From the moment you approach **The Bowery** (335 Bowery, 212/515-9100, www.theboweryhotel.com, $420-500) and the red-vested, black-bowler-hatted doorman welcomes you in, you feel as if you've slipped back into Old New York. Exceptional warm service and public areas are so inviting, you'll be tempted to tuck into a heavy leather chair before the crackling fire or greenery-filled courtyard or hide from the world, sipping a martini in the smokeless period bar. It really seems wasted on a city that has so much to offer outside the lobby doors. There are also floor-to-ceiling factory-style windows and generous tubs built for two.

"Haute minimalism" is how **Thompson LES** (190 Allen St., 212/460-5300, www.thompsonhotels.com, $299-499) describes its decor and vibe. Be sure to check out the rooftop pool, which features a filmstrip image of Andy Warhol on the bottom.

WEST VILLAGE
Under $150
The Jane (113 Jane St., 212/924-6700, www.thejanenyc.com, $105-135) is a lively, hip boutique hotel with an amazing bar housed in a century-old building, offering great amenities (free Wi-Fi, robes, flat-screen TV with DVD) and rooms reminiscent of a luxury train car. Larger "Captain's Cabins" offer private baths.

$150-300
Though small, the lobby of family-owned ◖**Washington Square Hotel** (103 Waverly Pl., 212/777-9515, www.washingtonsquarehotel.

com, $201-351) is stunning with all black and white tiles, lacy iron grillwork, gilded adornments, and Audubon prints. Recently renovated rooms feature Art Deco touches, and you can't beat the location, just off Washington Square.

UNION SQUARE AND MADISON SQUARE PARK
$150-300
High-spirited **Gershwin Hotel** (7 E. 27th St., 212/545-8000, www.gershwinhotel.com, $269 and up) looks dramatic from the outside, with elongated tear-drop lights protruding from the building's facade. A recent change in management also led to an updating of rooms, which are modern and comfortable. The hotel has a branch of the café Birch on the ground floor.

Nearby, **Ace Hotel** (20 W. 29th St., 212/679-2222, www.acehotel.com/newyork, $199 and up) has been wildly popular since it opened despite its small rooms. Design aficionados love the bold touches here, and the hotel's lobby is always buzzing with locals, who use the dark, café-like space as their personal office. An outlet of the popular Stumptown Coffee is located just off the lobby, and three popular restaurants—The Breslin, John Dory Oyster Bar, and No. 7 Sub—are on site.

$300 and Above
At the stylish **W Union Square** (201 Park Ave. S, at 17th St., 212/253-9119, $300-1,000), you'll find well-appointed rooms filled with ultra-comfortable furnishings and a lively lobby-bar filled with beautiful people. This is one of several W hotels in the city.

CHELSEA AND THE MEATPACKING DISTRICT
$150-300
Nautical-theme modernist **The Maritime Hotel** (363 W.16th St., 212/242-4300, www.themaritimehotel.com, $265-345) is a 126-room boutique hotel whose five-foot-diameter porthole windows add a decorative charm to the polished teak rooms, as well as views out onto Midtown and the Hudson River. The onsite

NYC'S DISCOUNT WEEKS

"Budget-friendly" isn't exactly the first adjective that comes to mind when you think of planning a trip to New York City. Budget travelers shouldn't be discouraged from visiting, however. Visitors can cut costs by taking advantage of one of the city's special discount weeks. Often running at least nine days and as long as nearly a month, these "weeks" offer deep markdowns or two-for-one specials on typically expensive services or experiences, ranging from meals and Broadway shows to hotel accommodations and spa services.

- **Hotel Week:** Each January, dozens of hotels—many of them trendy boutique properties where standard nightly rates can exceed $500—sign on to offer travelers rooms at $100, $200, or $300 per night.

- **Broadway Week:** Since launching in 2011, Broadway Week has been wildly successful, selling more than 300,000 tickets through its two-for-one pricing system. It typically runs for the first two weeks in September and again for two weeks in late January/early February.

- **Off-Broadway Week:** Like Broadway Week, Off-Broadway Week runs for nearly two weeks in winter, offering two-for-one priced tickets for popular and lesser-known shows at off-Broadway venues.

- **Comedy Week:** If you prefer stand-up, sketch, or improv comedy to dramas and musicals, time your visit to coincide with Comedy Week, which spans two weeks in late October-early November. Expect two-for-one tickets for well-known acts and emerging talent.

- **Spa Week:** Participating spas offer $50 treatments during this discount week, which is held each spring and fall.

- **Restaurant Week:** The original discount week and one of the city's favorites is Restaurant Week, which is held twice a year and typically runs as long as three weeks. Participating restaurants offer prix-fixe lunch and dinner menus at far more comfortable prices.

For information about all of these discount weeks, visit **NYC & Company's website** (www.gonyc.com). Get deeper discounts—or even freebies—by following the city's tourism organization, NYC & Company, on twitter (www.twitter.com/nycgo). During discount weeks, trivia questions spotlighting business participants are tweeted out; followers who respond correctly may win a free meal, tickets, or a service.

---

restaurant La Bottega, with its large indoor and outdoor spaces, has made this a popular place in the neighborhood for both guests and visitors alike.

$300 and Above

Hotelier André Balazs's modern brand **The Standard** (848 Washington St., 212/645-4646, www.standardhotels.com/new-york-city, $300-400) hits an architectural high note straddling the elevated High Line park. Floor-to-ceiling windows in the guest rooms, knockout views, and the outdoor Biergarten don't hurt.

Hotel Americano (518 W. 27th St., 212/216-0000, www.hotel-americano.com, $295 and up) was the first U.S. property opened by Mexican boutique hotelier Grupo Habita, and was one of the first hotels to pop up in the midst of this neighborhood's gallery district. The sleek, modern property attracts locals and visitors alike to its lobby bar-restaurant, where contemporary Mexican bites and trendy cocktails are served.

MIDTOWN AND TIMES SQUARE
$150-300

Charming **C Affinia Shelburne** (303 Lexington Ave., 212/689-5200, www.affinia. com, $230-299) in the Murray Hill neighborhood recently underwent a renovation that took it from baroque to boldly modern. Upstairs are

NEW YORK CITY

© FRANCISCO COLLAZO

Bikes are an amenity at the Maritime Hotel.

spacious suites with two double beds and well-equipped kitchens, making this a good value for the money.

Once the home of *LIFE* magazine, the friendly, Beaux-Arts **Herald Square Hotel** (19 W. 31st St., between 5th and 6th Aves., 212/279-4017 or 800/727-1888, www.heraldsquarehotel.com, $159-399) boasts a lovely facade complete with lacy iron fretwork and a plump, gilded cherub reading the magazine. Rooms are small, but adequate and very clean.

Built in 1901, the spiffy, neo-Art Deco **Metro** (45 W. 35th St., between 5th and 6th Aves., 212/947-2500 or 800/356-3870, www.hotelmetronyc.com, $250-380) offers 175 comfortable guest rooms and a large, comfortable lobby. An exercise room and lively rooftop terrace are on the top floor, where drinks are served in summer.

The New Yorker Hotel (481 8th Ave., 212/224-0719, www.newyorkerhotel.com, $220-380), a historic hotel in a central location, offers decent amenities and value. Rates vary as to category, with some view and tower rooms sporting a panoramic view of the city.

The Court NYC (120-130 E. 39th St., 212/685-1100, www.court.stgilesnewyork.com, $189-495) is one of two side-by-side hotels owned and operated by St. Giles, the other being The Tuscany NYC. The Court, built in 1927 as apartments, was converted to a hotel in the 1950s and features 199 guest rooms and suites, including some of the largest in the city, measuring as much as 1,000 square feet. Some of its suites feature terraces and patios that look out onto landmark sites, along with oversized living areas, and spacious baths.

The Tuscany NYC (120-130 E. 39th St., 212/686-1600, www.tuscany.stgilesnewyork.com, $289-595) received an extensive multi-million dollar renovation and reopened at the end of 2012 with 124 residential-style guest rooms (all with free Wi-Fi), suites, and a 17th-floor penthouse suite featuring a wrap-around terrace with stunning views of the Empire State and Chrysler Buildings.

The **Warwick Hotel** (65 W. 54th St.,

212/247-2700, www.warwickhotelny.com, $250-300), commissioned by William Randolph Hearst in 1926 for his silent movie actress paramour, celebrates its history through period photographic displays and entire recently-renovated floors of premium rooms with enhanced amenities. Murals on 54 offers elegant lunch dining, while Randolph's Bar serves fresh spins on bar classics along with more traditional entrées.

Filled with eclectic touches, the sleek **Paramount** (235 W. 46th St., near 8th Ave., 212/764-5500 or 800/225-7474, www.paramount-hotel.net, $159-500) is a fun place to stay. Created by Ian Schrager of Studio 54 fame, it features a darkened lobby filled with lollipop-colored chairs and a big-checked rug, and, in the rooms, beds slung close to the floor and stainless-steel sinks shaped like ice-cream cones. A second-story restaurant wraps around the lobby, and the hotel's Whiskey Bar is a popular late-night spot.

Still deliciously old-fashioned, with lots of wood paneling and brocaded chairs, is the 1902 **(Algonquin** (59 W. 44th St., between 5th and 6th Aves., 212/840-6800 or 800/555-8000, www.thealgonquin.net, $270-500). Each floor has a different color scheme, and the inviting rooms offer plump beds, comfy armchairs, and bathrooms equipped with plenty of amenities. Downstairs, where Dorothy Parker and friends once met, are several snug lounges perfect for afternoon tea, cocktails, or aperitifs.

$300-500

Hyatt Times Square New York (135 W. 45th St., 646/364-1234, www.timessquarehyatt.com, $399) is a brand new 487-room hotel in a mirror-like 54-story tower that literally reflects the city. Rooms are surprisingly large for a Midtown hotel (even bigger than some New Yorkers' apartments!), and are enlivened with New York City-themed pop, minimalist, and conceptual artwork. After you check in by iPad, you can explore onsite amenities, including a chic rooftop lounge, trendy diner, fitness center, and the only hotel spa in the neighborhood.

No two rooms are alike at the **Roger Smith** (501 Lexington Ave., at 47th St., 212/755-1400 or 800/445-0277, www.rogersmith.com, $299-499), a jazzy retreat complete with several art galleries, a gift shop selling arts and crafts, and a long, narrow restaurant painted with floor-to-ceiling murals. The rooms are quite spacious and tastefully furnished.

$500 and Above

The European-styled **(Hotel Elysée** (60 E. 54th St., between Madison and Park Aves., 212/753-1066 or 800/535-9733, $439-500) is furnished in dark woods, plush carpets, and Asian antiques. Most of the rooms have Italian marble bathrooms, and adjoining the lobby is the classy Monkey Bar, its walls covered with murals. Among the famous residents who once lived in the Elysée are Joe DiMaggio, Tallulah Bankhead, and Tennessee Williams.

Built in 1931, the famed **Waldorf-Astoria** (301 Park Ave., between 49th and 50th Sts., 212/355-3000 or 800/925-3673, www.waldorf.com, $500-1,000) continues to beckon with opulence and romance. Surrounding the Art Deco lobby are glittering stores selling jewelry, antiques, and rare books. Downstairs is Peacock Alley, an elegant café with a piano that once belonged to Cole Porter. Upstairs are 1,120 rooms in varying shapes and sizes.

One of the city's most opulent and atmospheric hostelries is the **St. Regis Hotel** (2 E. 55th St., at 5th Ave., 212/753-4500 or 800/759-7550, $750-1,200), built by John Jacob Astor in 1904. Filled with marble, crystal, and gold leaf, the St. Regis is home to the fabulous King Cole Bar, backed with a Maxfield Parrish mural. Guest rooms feature high ceilings, Louis XVI antiques, marble bathrooms with double sinks, and every conceivable amenity.

The **Plaza** (768 5th Ave., at 59th St., 212/759-3000 or 800/759-3000, www.fairmont.com, $700-1,400), one of New York's best-known hotels, was nicely restored by the Trumps in the late 1980s. The rooms come in all shapes and sizes and are furnished with both period antiques and reproductions. Some rooms offer grand four-poster beds, others marble fireplaces and crystal chandeliers.

UPPER EAST SIDE
$300-500
Downstairs at the small and stylish **Franklin** (164 E. 87th St., between Lexington and 3rd Aves., 212/369-1000, www.franklinhotel.com, $330-490) is a tiny streamlined lobby done up in black and burnished steel with mirrors and fresh flowers. Upstairs are 53 cozy guest rooms featuring beds with billowing canopies, cherrywood furnishings, and a fresh rose at each bedside.

$500 and Above
First-class service and unerring good taste have made **Carlyle Hotel** (35 E. 76th St., at Madison Ave., 212/744-1600 or 800/227-5737, www.thecarlyle.com, $650-1,300) one of the city's top hotels ever since it opened in 1930. The airy, spacious rooms are equipped with every conceivable amenity, while downstairs is the Cafe Carlyle, a superb cabaret.

A magnificent slice of the Old World can be found at the **(Pierre Hotel** (5th Ave. at 61st St., 212/838-8000 or 800/749-7734, www.fourseasons.com/pierre, $600-1,400). The stunning lobby is adorned with chandeliers, fresh flowers, silks, and damasks, while the guest rooms are lavishly furnished with antiques. A good way to sample the Pierre, even if you can't afford to stay, is to stop in at the baroque-styled Rotunda for an elegant afternoon tea.

UPPER WEST SIDE
Under $150
Hosteling International New York (891 Amsterdam Ave., between 103rd and 104th Sts., 212/932-2300, www.hinewyork.org, $29-40 pp dorm room, $150 private room with bath), occupying a block-long landmark building, is the nation's largest hostel, with 90 clean, dorm-style rooms, each sleeping 4-8 in bunk beds, as well as some family rooms. Also on the premises are kitchens, coin-operated laundry machines, and a garden. You must be a member of Hosteling International-American Youth Hostel (202/783-6161, www.hiayh.org, adults $29, seniors $18, youths under 18 free) to stay in the hostel, and reservations should be made 2-3 months in advance.

$150-300
The friendly **(Hotel Beacon** (2130 Broadway, at 75th St., 212/787-1100 or 800/572-4969, $245-295) offers good value for the money. Its rooms are large and attractive and equipped with two double beds and kitchenettes. The lobby gleams with black-and-white marble and brass.

HARLEM
Under $150
Efuru Guest House and Suites (106 W. 120th St., 212/961-9855, www.efuru-nyc.com, $85-129) is comprised of two brownstones in the heart of historic Harlem. Homey deluxe rooms and studio apartments have full kitchens, and each accommodation is equipped with cable TV and Wi-Fi, as well as access to the shared courtyard.

There's a laid-back vibe at **The Harlem Flophouse** (242 W. 123rd St., 347/632-1960, www.harlemflophouse.com, $125), an 1890s brownstone near Apollo Theater. Its four wood-floored rooms have no air-conditioning (just fans) and share two baths with claw-foot tubs.

Food

New Yorkers love to brag about the thousands of eating establishments in their city. Some come and go almost overnight; others have been around for decades. A few rules of thumb: the East Village is an excellent neighborhood for cheaper eats and ethnic restaurants; SoHo, TriBeCa, and Columbus Avenue boast lots of trendy spots; and Midtown and the Upper East Side are home to some of the city's most venerable, expensive restaurants.

LOWER MANHATTAN

A downtown branch of the acclaimed midtown bistro run by chef-turned-writer Anthony Bourdain (author of *Kitchen Confidential*), **Les Halles Downtown** (15 John St., 212/285-8585, www.leshalles.net, $26) is heralded for its "American beef, French style" and lively atmosphere. Don't keep your eyes open for Bourdain; the "chef at large" spends most of his time these days globetrotting for his popular TV show.

Feel like a Wall Street tycoon and have a drink on the balcony at **Cipriani Wall Street** (55 Wall St., 212/699-4096) and enjoy the private club atmosphere.

CHINATOWN

Chinatown is home to over 300 restaurants serving various cuisines, including Hunan, Szechuan, Shanghai, Cantonese, Vietnamese, and Thai. You can't go wrong with most of the restaurants here, especially those catering to a large Asian clientele. All are inexpensive to moderately priced, with the average entrée less than $12.

Bustling **C Joe's Shanghai** (9 Pell St., 212/233-8888, www.joeshanghairestaurants.com) features some of the freshest food in Chinatown (with other branches in Midtown Manhattan and Flushing, Queens) and is especially famous for its "soup dumplings"—a mouthful of soup *inside* dough.

A half-dozen or so cavernous, gaily decorated restaurants serve dim sum from mid-morning until late afternoon, and fixed-price banquets thereafter. One of the largest and best of these eateries is **Golden Unicorn** (18 E. Broadway, 212/941-0911, www.goldenunicornrestaurant.com), where waiters use walkie-talkies to communicate. Arrive early, as there's often a long wait.

Fresh and healthy Vietnamese food is the specialty at unassuming **Nha Trang** (87 Baxter St., 212/233-5948, www.nhatrangnyc.com). Some of the city's best Thai food can be found at **Pongsri** (106 Bayard St., 212/349-3132, www.pongsri.net).

Chinatown also has sweets. Try **Chinatown Ice Cream Factory** (65 Bayard St., 212/608-4170, www.chinatownicecreamfactory.com), where you can buy every flavor of ice cream from ginger to mango.

LITTLE ITALY

Though Little Italy is generally *not* the place to go for good Italian food, it does hold some bargain-priced eateries, cheery cafés, and a few noteworthy dinner restaurants.

Friendly, old-fashioned **Da Nico** (164 Mulberry St., 212/343-1212, www.danicoristorante.com), with a garden out back, specializes in excellent coal-oven pizza and savory roasted meats and fish. Homey **Benito One** (174 Mulberry St., 212/226-9171, www.benitoone.com) serves good, traditional Sicilian food.

One of Little Italy's best restaurants is **Il Cortile** (125 Mulberry St., 212/226-6060, www.ilcortile.com), a multi-roomed spot with brick walls and an indoor garden. Il Cortile specializes in Northern Italian cuisine. Also very good is **Taormina** (145 Mulberry St., 212/625-2332, www.taorminany.com), once former mobster John Gotti's favorite spot.

For an afternoon snack, try cozy, tile-floored **Caffe Roma** (385 Broome St., 212/226-8413), a wonderful espresso and pastry café that was once a hangout for opera singers. Another good choice is flashy **Ferrara Bakery & Cafe** (195 Grand St., 212/226-6150, www.ferraracafe. com).

LOWER EAST SIDE

The granddaddy of New York delicatessens is **Katz's** (205 E. Houston St., 212/254-2246, www.katzsdelicatessen.com), a huge, cafeteria-style place where you take a number at the door. Overhead hang WWII-era signs reading "Send a salami to your boy in the Army."

Also in the neighborhood, **'inoteca** (98 Rivington St., 212/614-0473, www.inotecanyc.com) offers small plate dining with a wide range of cheeses and a terrific wine list.

Schiller's (131 Rivington St., 212/260-4555, www.schillersny.com) is a hot spot, done up in casual bistro style. On the menu is everything from Cuban sandwiches to pasta.

Russ & Daughters (179 E. Houston St., between Allen and Orchard Sts., 212/475-4880, www.russanddaughters.com) is a bustling place filled with smoked fish and dried fruits, all arranged in neat rows. **Yonah Schimmel's** (137 E. Houston St., 212/477-2858, www.knishery. com) is a rickety old storefront selling some of the best knishes in New York.

SOHO AND TRIBECA

Once too hot for its own good, **Balthazar** (80 Spring St., 212/965-1414, www.balthazarny. com), a large and bustling brasserie, still draws a sleek, celebrity-studded crowd.

The Mercer Kitchen (99 Prince St., 212/966-5454, www.themercerkitchen.com), a cool subterranean restaurant in The Mercer Hotel, is a feast for the eyes. The eclectic menu is matched with a diverse wine list.

Dark and stylish ◖**Raoul's** (180 Prince St., 212/966-3518, www.raouls.com), a French bistro, is a downtown mecca and with good reason: The food and ambience are top-notch.

Kittichai (60 Thompson St., 212/219-2000, www.kittichairestaurant.com) serves high-end Thai food in a dramatically beautiful setting, frequented by beautiful people.

At the south end of SoHo is cozy **Cupping**

Room Cafe (359 W. Broadway, 212/925-2898, www.cuppingroomcafe.com), especially good for afternoon snacks. Another spot for a quick lunch is sandwich shop **Olive's** (120 Prince St., 212/941-0111, www.olivesnyc.com).

A long-time favorite among night-crawlers is the chic, Art Deco **Odeon** (145 W. Broadway, 212/233-0507, www.theodeonrestaurant. com), serving consistently good food in a lively, downtown setting.

The Harrison (355 Greenwich St., 212/274-9310, www.theharrison.com), a warm, New American cuisine eatery, has a succinct and spot-on seasonal menu. **Thalassa** (179 Franklin St., 212/941-7661, www.thalassanyc.com) is an upscale Greek restaurant that will take you far beyond taramasalata. The menu demonstrates the simple beauty of fish, charged by the pound.

Reserve months in advance to get a seat at **Nobu** (105 Hudson St., 212/219-0500, www. noburestaurants.com), arguably the most famous Japanese restaurant (with Peruvian touches) in America. Partly owned by Robert DeNiro, and a favorite among celebrities, the sleek eatery offers lots of innovative fare created by acclaimed chef Nobu Matsuhisa.

EAST VILLAGE

The East Village has traditionally been known for its cheap, Eastern European eateries, where the average main course costs $12. Two legendary 2nd Avenue spots are **Veselka** (144 2nd Ave., 212/228-9682, www.veselka.com), the place to go for borscht, pierogi, and scrumptious poppy-seed cake, and **Odessa** (119 Ave. A, 212/253-1482), serving heaping platters of Ukrainian food.

The East Village is also known for inexpensive Indian restaurants, most of which lie along 6th Street between 1st and 2nd Avenues. **Panna II** (93 1st Ave., 212/598-4610, www.panna2. com) is one fabulously festive BYOB spot covered in Christmas and chili pepper lights.

Still going strong after many years is **Angelica Kitchen** (300 E. 12th St., between 1st and 2nd Aves., 212/228-2909, www.angelicakitchen.com), serving the city's best vegan fare.

FOLLOW THAT FOOD TRUCK!

In New York City, the 21st century so far is indubitably the age of the food truck. Despite the constant threat of parking tickets and the stress of working in claustrophobic mobile kitchens, food trucks have allowed many entrepreneurial chefs who can't afford a brick-and-mortar restaurant the chance to build their own mini culinary empires. For the city's office workers, food trucks offer a welcome alternative to the uninspired sandwich. For travelers, they offer a chance to experience New York City's cultural and culinary diversity without securing coveted reservations or footing the bill for expensive sit-down meals.

Practically every cuisine imaginable is served from food trucks: Jamaican and Colombian, Mexican and Korean—even Mexican/Korean—and everything in between. You can wash your meal down with a lemonade from **Del's Frozen Lemonade Truck,** a juice from **Green Pirate Juice Truck,** or a coffee from **MUDtruck.** There's even a truck for happy hour: During summer, **Leblon Cachaca's** bright yellow-green "Caipi-Mobile" tools about

Manhattan selling caipirinhas, the national cocktail of Brazil. Got a sweet tooth? There are plenty of trucks to satisfy those cravings, too. Cupcakes, ice cream, doughnuts, cookies, brownies, and crepes are just some of the treats on wheels.

Many food trucks cluster around 48th and 49th Streets and Park Avenue during lunchtime. Simply walk up and down the street to see what strikes your fancy. You can also find a list of food trucks on the website of **The NYC Food Truck Association** (www.nycfoodtrucks.org). Most food trucks use the social media site twitter to broadcast their locations and daily specials; the tweat.it app (www.tweat.it) for smart phones gathers the food trucks' tweets and locations and constantly updates them on a single platform. And if you're in New York in September, consider attending **The Vendy Awards** (www.streetvendor.org/vendys). Started in 2004, Vendys are the Oscars of street food. Street cart and food truck vendors participate in a cook-off for attendees and judges as they vie for an award.

Two Boots (42 Ave. A, 212/254-1919, www.avenuea.twoboots.com) is known for its first-rate pizza and other spicy fare from the lands shaped like "Two Boots"—Italy and Louisiana. Creative American food with a Mediterranean flair is the specialty at ◖ **Five Points** (31 Great Jones St., between the Bowery and Lafayette St., 212/253-5700, www.fivepointsrestaurant.com), where the menu changes nightly.

One of the oldest pastry shops in the East Village is **Veniero's** (342 E. 11th St., 212/674-7070, www.venierospastry.com). Established in 1894, it features classic Italian treats. Across 1st Avenue is **De Robertis Caffe** (176 1st Ave., 212/674-7137, www.derobertiscaffe.com), a cheery Italian shop with a handful of tables and wonderful window displays.

KGB (85 E. 4th St., 212/505-3360, www.kgbbar.com) is a former speakeasy now filled with eclectic Soviet souvenirs. Especially popular among writers and editors, it hosts frequent readings and literary get-togethers.

WEST VILLAGE

One of the best places for a burger is **Corner Bistro** (331 W. 4th St., 212/242-9502, www.cornerbistrony.com), a dark pub with creaky wooden booths and an excellent jazz jukebox. For dessert, hit **Magnolia Bakery** (401 Bleecker St., 212/462-2572, www.magnoliabakery.com), still profiting from *Sex & the City* fame.

The city's best pizzeria is ◖ **John's** (278 Bleecker St., 212/243-1680, www.johnsbrickovenpizza.com), where the New York-style pies are thin, crispy, and low on grease. Pizza is sold by the whole pie only, no slices. Expect long lines unless you come during the off-hours. A large pizza costs $16.50.

Mexicana Mama (525 Hudson St., 212/924-4119) offers a simple Mexican menu in a diminutive space, warmed by its bright blue walls and proximity to the kitchen.

Pearl Oyster Bar (18 Cornelia St., 212/691-8211, www.pearloysterbar.com) is a New England clam shack in the heart of the Village. Try the sublime lobster roll.

Low-key, low-ceilinged **((Cafe Loup** (105 W. 13th St., near 6th Ave., 212/255-4746, www.cafeloupnyc.com) is a Village institution, serving a wide range of excellent French fare. A longtime favorite among connoisseurs of Italian food is comfortable, brick-walled **Il Mulino** (86 W. 3rd St., 212/673-3783, www.ilmulino.com), serving traditional Abruzzese fare.

Sleek and fashionable **Gotham Bar and Grill** (12 E. 12th St., near 5th Ave., 212/620-4020, www.gothambarandgrill.com) has won numerous top awards for both its design and food.

Bleecker and MacDougal Streets are known for their many Italian coffee and pastry shops. Among the best are **Cafe Dante** (79-81 MacDougal St., 866/681-0299, www.caffedante.com) and **Caffé Reggio** (119 MacDougal St., 212/475-9557, www.cafereggio.com). **Tea and Sympathy** (108 Greenwich Ave., 212/989-9735, www.teaandsympathynewyork.com) features a British-style afternoon tea.

Celebrity chef Mario Batali's rich, creative Italian food makes **Babbo Ristorante e Enoteca** (110 Waverly Pl., 212/777-0303 or 212/353-8064, www.babbonyc.com) one of the most sought-after reservations in Manhattan; happily, walk-ins can dine at the bar. It's in a classic Village carriage house, and the rock soundtrack, impeccable service, and constant crowds create a memorable experience. If you can't get in, try Batali's casual pizzeria, **Otto** (1 5th Ave., 212/995-9559, www.ottopizzeria.com).

CHELSEA AND MEATPACKING DISTRICT

Tiny **La Taza De Oro** (96 8th Ave., 212/243-9946) serves authentic and affordable Puerto Rican food, with a robust roster of daily specials. For hearty Cuban-Chinese fare, try hole-in-the-wall **La Chinita Linda** (166 8th Ave., 212/633-1791).

Numerous restaurants, many with outdoor tables in summer, line 7th and 8th Avenues between 14th and 23rd Streets. Among them is **Cafeteria** (119 7th Ave., 212/414-1717, www.cafeteriagroup.com), serving excellent brunches and a wide range of American fare. **Le Singe Vert** (160 7th Ave., 212/366-4100, www.lesingevert.com) is a popular French bistro.

Gourmet-style Mexican fare can be found at the bustling **Rocking Horse Cafe** (182 8th Ave., 212/463-9511, www.rockinghorsecafe.com).

Da Umberto (107 W. 17th St., 212/989-0303, www.daumbertonyc.com) is a classy, albeit noisy, spot acclaimed for its Northern Italian fare, wines, and well-dressed crowd.

Right next door is **Haven's Kitchen** (109 W. 19th St., 212/929-7900, www.havenskitchen.com), a popular café, cooking class center, and supper club.

For a taste of late-19th-century New York, visit **Keens Steakhouse** (72 W. 36th St., 212/947-3636, www.keens.com), an atmospheric multi-roomed pub with a crackling fireplace in winter.

Merchants (112 7th Ave., 212/366-7267, www.merchantsny.com) is a comfortable modern bar with a menu featuring gourmet sandwiches, salads, and desserts. The well-worn **Peter McManus** (152 7th Ave., 212/929-9691) attracts both long-time regulars and young professionals. Juicy burgers are served at the big, rickety booths in back. For a mellow gay bar that is less of a scene and more of just a relaxing place, try **Barracuda** (275 W. 22nd St., 212/645-8613).

In the Meatpacking District, **((Spice Market** (403 13th St., 212/675-2322, www.spicemarketnewyork.com) is a hot spot that's as acclaimed for its lush Eastern decor as it is for its Southeast Asian fare.

There's a happening scene at **The Standard Grill** (848 Washington St., 212/645-4100, www.thestandardgrill.com) in André Balazs's hip The Standard hotel, where showy dishes like saffron pappardelle with braised rabbit draw a trendy crowd. There's outdoor seating and a late-night menu served 1am-4am.

THE COFFEE THAT FUELS THE CITY THAT NEVER SLEEPS

There's a Starbucks on practically every corner in New York City, but many coffee-loving locals prefer to patronize hometown cafés and coffeehouses. Here are a few favorites:

- **Blue Bottle Coffee** (450 W. 15th St.) advertises "a six-stool counter where we feature a selection of single origin coffees prepared on Manhattan's first Lucky i. Cremas siphon bar, along with nel drip-style coffee." In other words, this is not a venti fat-free soy latté kind of place. It's for serious coffee intellectuals.

- **Café Grumpy** (224 W. 20th St.) has a silly name that belies its serious coffee. Selections are noted not only by the micro-region in which the single-origin beans were harvested, but also by who roasted them. Selections are then prepared in an $11,000 Clover machine, which brews each cup individually, not only adjusting to the ideal water temperature but tailoring the process to that particular bean. Starbucks has since bought the company that makes Clover machines and stopped sales to any other coffeehouse, so Café Grumpy remains one of only several hundred owners of this specialized brewmaster. They enforce a strict No Wi-Fi policy—better to enjoy your coffee without digital distractions.

- **Pennylane** (305 E. 45th St.) is a welcome addition to a neighborhood once blighted by bad coffee. Thanks to this minimalist café's location a stone's throw from the United Nations, it's popular among diplomats. You might feel out of place among all the well-tailored suits and multilingual conversations, but these regulars are a friendly bunch. If you can't find a seat, there's ample space at Dag Hammarskjold Plaza, just around the corner on 47th Street.

- **Stumptown Coffee Roasters at The Ace Hotel** (18 W. 29th St.) is good for an artisanal cup to go or, if you prefer, to be enjoyed in the trendy hotel's lobby, a de facto office for hip young entrepreneurial types.

UNION SQUARE AND MADISON SQUARE PARK

One of several restaurants from star chef Jean-Georges Vongerichten, busy **abc kitchen** (35 E. 18th St., 212/475-5829, www.abchome.com/abc-kitchen, noon-3pm Mon.-Fri., 5:30pm-10:30pm Mon.-Wed., 5:30pm-11:00pm Thurs., 5:30pm-11:30pm Fri.-Sat., 5:30pm-10:00pm Sun., 11:00am-3:30pm Sat.-Sun.) is farm-to-table inspired, with pastas, pizzas, fish-and poultry-focused entrees featuring local vegetables and cheeses. Its global designs are drawn from the on-site ABC Carpet & Home Store.

The refined, oak-lined **Gramercy Tavern** (42 E. 20th St., 212/477-0777, www.gramercytavern.com) serves award-winning, seasonal American fare, with an emphasis on local ingredients. Dinner is prix fixe in the dining room, but there are à la carte lunch options in the lowkey, no-reservations front room.

Equally pricey—and, most agree, worth every penny—is **Eleven Madison Park** (11 Madison Ave., 212/889-0905, www.elevenmadisonpark.com), whose multi-course tasting menu features New York State-sourced fare.

MIDTOWN AND TIMES SQUARE

If you're planning to eat in the Theater District before a show, make reservations or give yourself plenty of time. Many restaurants are packed 6:30pm-8pm. During warm weather, both Bryant Park (between 40th and 42nd Streets, 5th and 6th Avenues) and the steps of The New York Public Library are good spots for lunch. Nearby vendors sell everything from hot dogs to gourmet fare.

Top Chef fans can hit **'wichcraft** kiosk in Bryant Park, part of Tom Colicchio's empire. The kiosk serves sandwiches and soups right in Bryant Park. If you want to see what Colicchio is capable of with pricier plates (most of which are cooked with ingredients grown in a nearby garden), book a table at his exceptional— if oddly located—**Riverpark** (450 E. 29th St., 212/729-9790, www.riverparknyc.com), which, in warmer months, has a lovely terrace with views of the East River. **Hallo Berlin** (626 10th Ave., 212/977-1944, www.halloberlinrestaurant.com), "New York's Wurst Restaurant" as its menu proclaims, specializes in wurst (sausage) and provides great German food.

In the Theater District, popular **Virgil's Real BBQ** (152 W. 44th St., 212/921-9494, www.virgilsbbq.com) serves up enormous portions of spare ribs, smoked brisket, and the like in a lively, two-story setting. **Tony's DiNapoli** (147 W. 43rd St. in the Casablanca Hotel, 212/221-0100, www.tonysnyc.com) offers reasonably-priced, generous family-style platters of solid Southern Neopolitan Italian fare. There's a bustling atmosphere with warm service and salads made table-side under the gaze of Broadway's best in caricature.

West 46th Street between 8th and 9th Avenues is known as Restaurant Row. Here, you'll find **Joe Allen** (326 W. 46th St., 212/581-6464, www.joeallenrestaurant.com), a classic, well-known pub with a celebrity-studded clientele. Not far away is **Firebird** (365 W. 46th St., 212/586-0244, www.firebirdrestaurant.com). Housed in two posh brownstones, Firebird resembles a pre-revolutionary St. Petersburg mansion, complete with paintings, objets d'art, antiques, crystal, and authentic cuisine.

Overlooking Bryant Park behind The New York Public Library are **Bryant Park Grill** and the **Bryant Park Cafe** (25 W. 40th St., 212/840-6500, www.arkrestaurants.com). Both serve imaginative American fare in a handsome setting, but the grill is somewhat more formal. In summer, a rooftop terrace opens up. Just on the other side of the park is **LT Burger** (8 W. 40th St., 212/582-8200, www.ltburger.com/bryant-park). The inventive burgers don't come cheap, and neither do the adult milkshakes spiked with liquor, but they're both tasty and filling.

Farther north, **Rock Center Cafe** (20 W.

50th St., inside Rockefeller Center, 212/332-7620, www.patinagroup.com) serves American-style food in a superb setting overlooking the skating rink at Rockefeller Center. Be sure to make reservations.

Carnegie Deli (854 7th Ave., 212/757-2245, www.carnegiedeli.com) is a New York City landmark, famous for enormous overstuffed deli sandwiches. Similar in style is **Stage Deli** (834 7th Ave., 212/245-7850, www.stagedeli.com), Carnegie's major competitor.

Ninth Avenue between 42nd and 59th Streets is lined with one ethnic restaurant after another. Among them is the **Afghan Kebab House** (764 9th Ave., 212/307-1612), serving succulent kebabs in exotic surroundings, and airy, well-lit **Uncle Nick's** (747 9th Ave., 212/245-7992, www.unclenicksgreekrestaurant.com), one of Manhattan's few Greek restaurants.

Just north of Grand Central is **Num Pang** (148 W. 48th St., 212/421-0743, www.numpangnyc.com), a Cambodian sandwich shop with daily specials.

For a classic New York lunch, eat at Grand Central Terminal's **❰ Oyster Bar** (89 E. 42nd St., inside Grand Central, lower level, 212/490-6650, www.oysterbarny.com), complete with red-checked tablecloths and a vaulted ceiling. On the menu is a wide variety of fish dishes, priced at about $25. Adjoining the main restaurant is a cheaper counter area, where dishes average $12. If you've got a hankering for something sweet once you've slurped down your oysters, go across the hall and into the Grand Central food court for a slice of classic New York cheesecake at **Junior's** (45 Grand Central Terminal, 212/302-2000).

A top-tier Chinese restaurant is **Shun Lee Palace** (155 E. 55th St., 212/371-8844), featuring gourmet fare in an elegant black lacquer setting with a glowing cream satin dragon encircling the dining room. Sophisticated **Dawat** (210 E. 58th St., 212/355-7555) is considered to be one of the city's best Indian restaurants.

❰ Sushi Yasuda (204 E. 43rd St., 212/972-1001, www.sushiyasuda.com), frequently cited as New York's best Japanese restaurant, makes use of a Spartan aesthetic to focus all of the attention on the beautiful fish.

UPPER EAST SIDE

Barking Dog Luncheonette (1453 York Ave., 212/861-13600) is a cheery place with good soups, sandwiches, and simple entrées. The **Lexington Candy Shop** (1226 Lexington Ave., 212/288-0057, www.lexingtoncandyshop.net) is an old-fashioned luncheonette founded in 1925.

Good Persian food can be found at **Persepolis** (1407 2nd Ave., 212/535-1100, www.persepolisnewyork.com), offering succulent kabobs, unusual stews, and sour cherry rice.

At **Serafina** (1022 Madison Ave., 212/734-2676, www.serafinarestaurant.com), Northern Italian dishes are a pleasure to eat in the upstairs rooftop dining area. This is a great location for a bite after visiting 5th Avenue's museums.

Candle Cafe (1307 3rd Ave., 212/472-0970, www.candlecafe.com) offers scrumptious vegan food even a carnivore can enjoy.

Rosa Mexicano (1063 1st Ave., at 58th St., 212/753-7407, www.rosamexicano.com) is a haute-Mexican restaurant serving fresh, flavorful food that draws large crowds. At languorous, tropical **Le Colonial** (149 E. 57th St., 212/752-0808, www.lecolonialnyc.com), it's easy to imagine yourself in pre-war Saigon. Downstairs is a main dining room serving French-Vietnamese fare; upstairs is a sexy lounge.

Daniel (60 E. 65th St., 212/288-0033, www.danielnyc.com), named for chef Daniel Boulud, wins kudos from food critics all over Manhattan for its superb French cuisine, discerning wine list, and impeccable decor.

An institution in this part of town is **J.G. Melon** (1291 3rd Ave., 212/650-1310), a friendly saloon that also serves great burgers. For something classy, stop into the dark and gracious **Bemelmans Bar** (35 E. 76th St., 212/744-1600) in posh hotel The Carlyle.

UPPER WEST SIDE

For good people-watching during the summer, stake out an outdoor table in one of the many eateries located directly across from Lincoln Center.

Funky **Gray's Papaya** (2090 Broadway, 212/799-0243) sells some of the city's best cheap hot dogs—to be eaten standing up. Hole-in-the-wall **La Caridad 78** (2199 Broadway, 212/874-2780, www.lacaridad78.com) is the best of the Cuban-Chinese restaurants in this part of town—just look at the long line of cab drivers out front. The no-frills **Cafe con Leche** (424 Amsterdam Ave., 212/595-7000, www.cafeconlechenewyork.net) is a modern Latin diner with first-rate rice and beans.

The Upper West Side has become a bit of a brunch destination, due in no small part to restaurants like **Sarabeth's** (423 Amsterdam Ave., 212/496-6280, www.sarabethsrestaurants.com). Another neighborhood favorite is **Celeste** (502 Amsterdam Ave., 212/874-4559), which serves a solid selection of reasonable Italian dishes, though a no reservations policy could mean a wait. **Epicerie Boulud** (1900 Broadway, 212/595-9606, www.epicerieboulud.com) is also an option, with soups and sandwiches, cheese and charcuteries, an oyster bar, and lots of luscious pastries.

In Central Park, the sleek, upscale **Lakeside Restaurant** (East Dr., near 72nd St., 212/517-2233) serves grilled meats and fish, salads, and sandwiches on a veranda overlooking the lake.

Barney Greengrass (541 Amsterdam Ave., 212/724-4707, www.barneygreengrass.com) is best known for its traditional bagels and lox.

For Middle Eastern fare, along with live jazz and a circular bar, try **Cleopatra's Needle** (2485 Broadway, 212/769-6969, www.cleopatrasneedleny.com). Tiny **Awash** (947 Amsterdam Ave., 212/961-1416, www.awashny.com) is one of the best of the Ethiopian restaurants that dot the Upper West Side.

HARLEM

Miss Maude's Spoonbread Too (547 Malcolm X Blvd., 212/690-3100) serves up heaping portions of tasty Southern dishes, as does its sister restaurant, **Miss Mamie's Spoonbread Too** (366 W. 110th St., 212/865-6744, www.spoonbreadinc.com).

Legendary **Sylvia's** (328 Malcolm X Blvd., 212/996-0660, www.sylviasrestaurant.com) has been expanding over the years and attracts tourists by the busload. The food is still fine but the atmosphere is not what it once was.

On the part of 116th Street known as Little Senegal, **Africa Kine Restaurant** (256 W. 116th St., 212/666-9400, www.africakine.com) serves delectable Senegalese food. Share the grilled meats and stews, which come with bowls of rice.

Kitschy **Dinosaur Bar-B-Que** (700 W. 125th St., 212/694-1777, www.dinosaurbar-bque.com), a sister restaurant to the Syracuse hot spot, proves you can get decent bar-b-que in New York.

On Harlem's east side, **Patsy's Pizzeria** (2287 1st Ave., 212/534-9783, www.thepatsys-pizza.com) was the country's first coal-stoked brick-oven pizzeria. A Frank Sinatra favorite, it was established in 1932, and now has branches elsewhere in the city.

To get into tiny **Rao's** (455 E. 114th St., 212/722-6709), you have to book about three months in advance. The Rao family has been serving fine Neapolitan home-cooking in this former Dutch saloon since 1896.

The traditional **Hungarian Pastry Shop** (1030 Amsterdam Ave., 212/866-4230) sells mouthwatering strudel and other sweet treats.

Brooklyn

The largest borough in population (2.56 million) and the second largest in area (78.5 square miles), Brooklyn was a city in its own right, separate from New York, up until 1898. It had its own city hall, central park, downtown shops, museums, theaters, beaches, botanical garden, and zoo—all of which helps account for its fierce sense of identity and pride. Of all the boroughs, Brooklyn is the most individualistic, the most mythic, and the most complex.

Brooklyn is Walt Whitman, Coney Island, the Brooklyn Dodgers, the Brooklyn Bridge, Mae West, Nathan's Famous, Bazooka bubble gum, Lena Horne, John Travolta, Jackie Gleason, the Brooklyn Navy Yards, Mickey Rooney, Topps baseball cards, Pete Hamill, Barbra Streisand, Prospect Park, Chock Full o' Nuts, Junior's Cheesecake, and Spike Lee.

Brooklyn is also the borough of ethnic neighborhoods. In total, more than 90 ethnic groups call Brooklyn home, among them Hasidic Jews, West Indians, Latin Americans, Russians, Poles, Scandinavians, Asians, Italians, Middle Easterners, and Irish. Once quiet residential neighborhoods are now thriving. Brooklyn's housing stock of beautiful brownstones has attracted people looking for more space and charming digs. As artists and young people are priced out of Manhattan real estate, more and more have moved across the bridge, bringing along their support for creating a hip local arts and foodie haven.

BROOKLYN HEIGHTS

Quiet, tree-lined streets, dignified, perfectly preserved brownstones, well-dressed parents out playing with their apple-cheeked kids—such is the refined atmosphere of Brooklyn Heights, one of New York City's prettiest neighborhoods. Manhattanites even deign to visit, largely because of the **Promenade** that runs along the district's western edge, offering magnificent, bluff-high views of the skyline, the harbor, and the Brooklyn Bridge.

Used as a refuge by General Washington and his troops after an early defeat in the Revolutionary War, Brooklyn Heights became the country's first suburb when Robert Fulton started his ferry service in the early 1800s. Soon thereafter, wealthy Brooklyn Heights landowners, many of them bankers commuting to Wall Street, divided their property into standard building lots, and the neighborhood filled up with brownstones and churches.

Much of the pleasure of visiting Brooklyn

Heights lies in simply wandering its idyllic streets. Orange, Pineapple, Clark, Pierrepont, and Montague Streets all lead to the Promenade, which blooms profusely with flowers during warm weather. Montague Street is Brooklyn Heights' main commercial thoroughfare, where you'll find most of the neighborhood's restaurants, bars, and shops. During warm weather, many of these establishments set up tables on the street, giving it a vaguely European air.

From Manhattan, the best way to get to Brooklyn Heights is to walk over the Brooklyn Bridge, then cross through Cadman Plaza Park to the Heights. By subway, take the A train to High Street, or the No. 2 or 3 to Clark Street. You can also take the No. 4 to Borough Hall and walk west.

Brooklyn Historical Society

The pretty, terra-cotta building at Pierrepont and Clinton Streets is home to the **Brooklyn Historical Society** (128 Pierrepont St., 718/222-4111, www.brooklynhistory.org, Wed.-Sun. noon-5pm, adults $10, seniors and students $6), both a library and a museum. The museum showcases exhibits on such Brooklyn subjects as Brooklyn Navy Yard, the Dodgers, Coney Island, and the borough's many ethnic communities. The society also sponsors occasional walking tours.

New York Transit Museum

Two blocks southwest of Borough Hall is **The New York Transit Museum** (northwest corner of Schermerhorn St. and Boerum Pl., 718/694-1600, www.mta.info/mta/museum, Tues.-Fri. 10am-4pm, Sat.-Sun. 11am-5pm, adults $7, seniors and children 2-17 $5), run by The Metropolitan Transit Authority (MTA). Appropriately housed in a former subway station, the museum sports well-lit, tiled walls that seem to stretch out forever into the darkness. Some wonderful old restored subway cars are housed here, along with fascinating exhibits on the building of the subway, the history of the "Els" ("elevated" subways lines), trolleys, and buses.

DUMBO

Short for Down Under the Manhattan Bridge Overpass, happening DUMBO is a former warehouse district now gentrified by artists, galleries, boutiques, and restaurants. DUMBO has a gritty, industrialized feel, with its wide cobblestone streets and large converted factories. The neighborhood also has legitimate artistic chops with lots of good galleries, warehouse-size spaces, and huge rents to match.

Galapagos Art Space (16 Main St., 718/222-8500, www.galapagosartspace.com) is a cool performance space that hosts everything from burlesque to Quiz Night in a green building where you float on islands over the pool. **111 Front St.** houses more than a dozen galleries in one building, highlighting the work of local and international artists.

After you've had your fill of art spaces, find refuge in green spaces. Kick back in lovely **Brooklyn Bridge Park** (www.brooklynbridgepark.org), which has recently expanded and offers spectacular bridge and city views. Alternately, take a short walk to **Fulton Ferry Landing** (for summer water taxis to Manhattan go to www.nywatertaxi.com).

A clutch of historic buildings stands along Old Fulton Street leading down to the water. Among them is the medieval-looking **Eagle Warehouse** (28 Old Fulton St.), now a residential co-op. Near the entrance, a plaque honors Walt Whitman and *The Brooklyn Eagle,* which was published on this site from 1841 to 1892. Whitman served as the newspaper's editor until he was fired for his anti-slavery views.

COBBLE HILL AND BOERUM HILL

Atlantic Avenue runs alongside Brooklyn Heights, dividing it from the leafy brownstone neighborhoods of Cobble Hill and Boerum Hill (to the east). Once the center of New York's Middle Eastern community, Atlantic Avenue is now filled with antique shops and small boutiques. **Sahadi Specialty & Fine Foods** (187 Atlantic Ave., 718/624-4550, www.sahadis.com) is one of the few Middle Eastern stores left. This well-stocked supermarket has

a huge selection of olives and dried fruit, as well as some of the city's best prepared hummus and kibbeh. Also on Atlantic Avenue, **DARR** (369 Atlantic Ave., 718/797-9733) is another fun stop, with its eclectic collection of vintage furnishing.

Wander along Smith Street (in Boerum Hill) and walk back along Court Street (Cobble Hill). Both streets are representative of the fresh flavors of the neighborhoods, although Court Street has more of the older established stores that reflect the neighborhood's Italian-American heritage. If quirky kids' stuff is of interest, pop by charming Brooklyn mini empire **Area Kids** (196 Court St., 718/222-0869, www.areakids.com). Another borough-centric shop is **Brooklyn Industries** (100 Smith St., 718/596-3986, www.brooklynindustries. com) which sells clothes, bags, and accessories. Its Brooklyn-themed t-shirts are especially popular.

Food

Smith and Court Streets have exploded with great restaurants and bars over the past 10 years. Grab a pizza at old-style **Sam's Restaurant** (238 Court St., 718/596-3458) or great affordable Thai at **Joya** (215 Court St., 718/222-3484). Try **Zombie Hut** (261 Smith St., 718/875-3433) for your Tiki bar fix or **Floyd** (131 Atlantic Ave., 718/858-5810, www.floydny.com), where you can play a game of bocce while you drink. For top quality coffee, stop by **D'Amico Foods** (309 Court St., 718/875-5403, www.dami-cofoods.com).

For a higher-end meal, famed **River Cafe** (1 Water St., 718/522-5200, www.rivercafe.com) offers creative American cuisine and marvelous waterfront views of Manhattan. It's also possible to come just for a drink.

Nightlife

Speakeasy-style **Weather Up** (589 Vanderbilt Ave., www.weatherupnyc.com) is an always-busy, atmospheric, cash-only bar specializing in old-school cocktails. **Tooker Alley** (793 Washington Ave., 347/955-4743, www.

view of Manhattan from the Brooklyn Bridge Park

© INDI ERICKSEN

tookeralley.com) is a Chicago-inspired throwback to the Prohibition era, known for its "historical martinis."

The Clover Club (210 Smith St., 718/855-7939, www.cloverclubny.com) similarly evokes an earlier era with cocktails falling in the categories of fizzes, cobblers, and sours, among others.

FORT GREENE

Another up-and-coming Brooklyn neighborhood is Fort Greene. Come to Fort Greene for the amazing **Brooklyn Flea** (176 Lafayette Ave., www.brooklynflea.com, Sat. 10am-5pm) and you'll find it's well worth the trip. This flea market, full of local artisans and craftspeople and over 150 vendors, showcases what the new Brooklyn is all about: artisan food, local crafts, hip artists, vintage gear, and music.

If you prefer sitting down to strolling the stalls, **The General Greene** (229 DeKalb Ave., 718/222-1510, www.thegeneralgreene.com) offers fresh interpretations of seasonal American comfort foods.

Brooklyn Academy of Music (BAM)

BAM (30 Lafayette Ave. and other locations, 718/636-4100, www.bam.org) is a world-famous institution that's especially known for its avant-garde productions. BAM also holds several small movie theaters, presenting mostly foreign and art films, and the inviting BAMcafé, serving everything from gourmet sandwiches to simple entrées.

WILLIAMSBURG

For decades, Williamsburg was best known for its community of Satmarer Hasidim, a strict orthodox Jewish sect originally from Hungary. Since the mid-1990s, however, the area has been home to a steadily growing enclave of young artists and professionals, attracted to the area by its once low rents and abandoned industrial spaces. Most of the hipsterville newcomers live near **Bedford Avenue,** lined with a clutch of moderately priced restaurants, shops, bars, and clubs. As is the case with such cool new hot spots, things change quickly. A good website to access Williamsburg listings and happenings is www.freewilliamsburg.com. To reach the area from Manhattan, take the L train to Bedford Avenue.

Neighborhood galleries include **Momenta Art** (56 Bogart St., 718/218-8058, www.momentaart.org) and **Pierogi** (177 N. 9th St., 718/599-2144, www.pierogi2000.com). Tiny **Pete's Candy Store** (709 Lorimer St., 718/302-3770, www.petescandystore.com) presents lots of local singer-songwriters and the occasional jazz band. **Warsaw** (261 Driggs Ave., 718/387-0505), www.warsawconcerts.com), inside the Polish National Home, is "where pierogies meet punk" in an old dance hall that's now a premier music venue.

Food

Try **Fette Sau BBQ** (354 Metropolitan Ave., 718/963-3404, www.fettesaubbq.com, $25) with top barbecue in a converted auto-body repair shop, or appropriately named **egg** (135 N. 5th St., near Bedford Ave., 718/302-5151, www.eggrestaurant.com), open for breakfast and lunch and serving Southern-style breakfast foods.

Nightlife

Alameda (195 Franklin St., 347/227-7296, www.alamedabk.com), in Williamsburg's adjoining neighborhood, Greenpoint, is a restaurant whose bar turns out classic and seasonal cocktails, many of which include homemade vermouth and bitters.

PROSPECT PARK AND PARK SLOPE

Three of Brooklyn's finest attractions— Brooklyn Museum of Art, Brooklyn Botanic Garden, and Prospect Park—are all within a few minutes' walk of each other, and next door is one of the borough's most historic residential districts, Park Slope. West of Prospect Park and south of Grand Army Plaza, Park Slope was once known as the "Gold Coast"; the area is home to one of the country's largest concentration of Victorian brownstones. Park Slope fell on hard times after World War II, but has been on the upswing since the 1970s. Here, you'll find many young professionals strolling about with dogs and kids, along with a decreasing number of older families who've lived in the area for generations. From Manhattan, take the No. 2 or 3 train to Eastern Parkway.

The main commercial thoroughfares are **7th and 5th Avenues,** while most of the neighborhood's prettiest brownstones are on the side streets between Prospect Park and 6th Avenue. **Carroll Street** and **Montgomery Place** are especially worth a gander. **The Montauk Club** (25 8th Ave., at Lincoln), is one of Park Slope's finest buildings. It's an eclectic Venetian palace with a frieze depicting the history of Long Island's Montauk Indians.

Brooklyn Museum of Art

The lovely Beaux-Arts **Brooklyn Museum of Art** (200 Eastern Pkwy., 718/638-5000, www.brooklynmuseum.org, Wed. and Fri.-Sun. 11am-6pm, Thurs. 11am-10pm, adults $12, seniors and students $8, children under 12 free) was designed by McKim, Mead & White in 1897. Though one of the world's largest museums, it's always lived in the shadow of its mighty Manhattan cousin, The Metropolitan Museum of Art. But Brooklyn Museum is very different from The Met or any other Manhattan art museum. For one thing, it stages some of the more unusual shows in the city, among them are major retrospectives by African American artists such as Romare Bearden and Jacob Lawrence, and women artists such as Elizabeth Murray and Louise Bourgeois.

Like the Metropolitan, Brooklyn Museum's collections span virtually the entire history of art. Highlights include extensive Egyptian holdings, an excellent Native American collection, and a permanent collection of contemporary art. The museum also has one of the city's most eclectic gift shops, filled with handcrafts from around the world. On the first Saturday of every month, the museum is open until 11pm for an evening of special events, all free, thanks to corporate sponsorship.

Brooklyn Children's Museum

A hit with kids, **Brooklyn Children's Museum** (145 Brooklyn Ave., 718/735-4400, www.brooklynkids.org, Tues.-Sun. 10am-5pm, adults and children $9) is the first of its kind: a dedicated children's museum. Started in 1899, it underwent a complete renovation in 2008 and is now a green building. Hands-on activities explore Brooklyn's diversity through the World Brooklyn exhibit and let kids get physical in Totally Tots.

Brooklyn Botanic Garden

Next door to Brooklyn Museum is **Brooklyn Botanic Garden** (150 Eastern Pkwy./990 Washington Ave., 718/623-7200, www.bbg.org, Tues.-Fri. 8am-4:30pm, Sat.-Sun. 10am-4:30pm, adults $10, seniors and students $5, children under 12 free), another unusual and much beloved Brooklyn institution. Though considerably smaller than the world-famous botanical gardens in the Bronx, the Brooklyn gardens are in many ways more conducive to a visit, as they're more manageable in size. Spread out over 50 carefully designed acres are a rose garden, a children's garden, a Japanese scholar's garden, and a garden for the blind, complete with Braille signs. The Steinhardt Conservatory houses tropical and desert plants, along with the country's largest collection of bonsai. The best time to visit is May, when the cherry blossoms burst forth, all pink and white froth.

Prospect Park

Behind Brooklyn Museum and Brooklyn Botanic Garden is enormous **Prospect Park** (718/965-8999, www.prospectpark.org): 525 acres of forests and meadows, lakes and streams. Prospect Park was designed by Frederick Law Olmsted and Calvert Vaux, the two designers behind Central Park. The two men considered this park, which is considerably wilder than Central Park, to be their masterpiece.

The main entrance is at **Grand Army Plaza,** just up from Brooklyn Museum at the intersection of Eastern Parkway, Flatbush Avenue, and Prospect Park West. In the center of the plaza,

surrounded by an ever-present rush of traffic, is a towering triumphal arch honoring the Union soldiers of the Civil War.

Immediately inside the main entrance is the park's most glorious sight: Long Meadow. Stretching over a mile, this gently rolling lawn is lined with lush trees that completely hide the cityscape. During warm weather, the meadow attracts West Indian cricket players; in winter, cross-country skiers come out.

East of Long Meadow are an 18th-century **carousel;** the wooden Dutch farmhouse **Lefferts Homestead;** and **Prospect Park Zoo** (450 Flatbush Ave., 718/399-7339, www.prospectparkzoo.com, early Nov.-early Apr. daily 10am-4:30pm, early Apr.-early Nov. Mon.-Fri. 10am-5pm and Sat.-Sun. 10am-5:30pm, adults $8, seniors $6, children 3-12 $5). **Prospect Lake** shimmers at the park's south end.

Like Central Park, Prospect Park is generally safe, but it's not advisable to explore isolated areas alone or to enter the park after dark.

Food

Applewood (501 11th St., 718/788-1810, www.applewoodny.com, $25) brings sustainably-grown ingredients together in refined dishes that make this a Park Slope hit. Another local favorite, **Dram Shop** (339 9th St., 718/788-1444, www.dramshopbrooklyn.com) is a charming bar with better than average bar food.

On 5th Avenue, you'll find some of the neighborhood's best restaurants, including **al di la Trattoria** (248 5th Ave., at Carroll St., 718/783-4565, $17), which specializes in Northern Italian fare.

◖ CONEY ISLAND

If you've only got time to make one stop in Brooklyn, Coney Island should probably be it. Though no longer the amusement center it once was, there's something about this windy, run-down place—with its magnificent boardwalk, iconic rides, tawdry snack stands, buoyant Russian community, and hordes of summertime sunbathers—that's quintessential New York.

From Manhattan, take the D, F, or Q train to Coney Island/Stillwell Avenue. It's a long subway ride out, and you'll wind up on the elevated tracks above scrappy Surf Avenue. Go one block west to reach the beach and boardwalk. Coney Island is often crowded to the bursting point on hot summer days and pleasantly empty the rest of the year. The scene is classic: old Russian women sit gossiping beneath big black umbrellas; young boys run fishing lines off the piers; joggers kick up sand on the wide expanse of beach.

History

Coney Island was uninhabited until the early 1800s when several genteel resorts for the rich were built. After the Civil War, the railroad opened the area up to the masses, and the island's honky-tonk days and nights began. Saloons, gambling dens, boxing rings, and racetracks soon packed the place, followed by three enclosed parks, or "small cities of pleasure," called Steeplechase, Luna Park, and Dreamland.

But it was the building of the subway in 1920 that really transformed Coney Island: For just a five-cent fare, almost everyone could escape the oppression of the city for a day, and Coney Island grew and grew. New technologies led to the invention of the Ferris wheel and the roller coaster, and in 1923, the 80-foot-wide boardwalk was built.

Coney Island was magical. It seemed nothing could dull its shine. But Dreamland burned down in 1911, and Luna Park went up in flames in the 1940s. Next came the rise of the automobile, the flight to the suburbs, and the invention of a new kind of midway—a tamed, sanitized place known as Disneyland. Steeplechase Park closed in 1966, leaving only a remnant of itself behind.

Luna Park

Coney Island has always consisted of a group of privately run amusement parks. The largest, Astroland, closed in 2008, and New Yorkers were concerned that Coney Island—one of the city's very last holdouts against

gentrification—might lose its identity entirely. Fortunately, a second iteration of **Luna Park** (www.lunaparknyc.com), the amusement park that occupied the area from 1903 to 1944, opened in the summer of 2010. And **Deno's Wonder Wheel Amusement Park** (www.wonderwheel.com), damaged badly in the 2012 hurricane, is making a comeback. Though spiffed up considerably, the amusement park areas still have an edgy, authentically Coney Island feel, thanks, in part, to the parks' varied clientele.

The most famous rides, the Wonder Wheel, an iconic Ferris wheel, and the world-famous Cyclone are both still in operation.

Nathan's Famous

On the island side of the amusement park, find **Nathan's Famous** (Surf and Stillwell Aves., 718/946-2202). Nathan's was started in 1916 by Nathan Handwerker, a sometime employee of Charles Feltman. Feltman is said to have "invented" the hot dog by his simple act of putting a wiener inside a bun. Handwerker undersold his boss's fare by a nickel, and so secured his place in entrepreneurial history. Nowadays, on a busy summer weekend, the stand-up eatery sells as many as 50,000 hot dogs, 20,000 orders of French fries, and 500 gallons of lemonade. It also hosts the annual hot dog eating contest, attracting entrants from all over the world.

Sideshows by the Seashore

Heading east on the boardwalk from the amusement park, you'll soon come to the brightly painted storefront of the **Coney Island Circus Sideshow** (1208 Surf Ave., at W. 12th St., 718/372-5159, www.coneyisland. com, daily 1pm-8pm, adults $10, children $5). A fierce-looking tattooed man lounges by the door, while inside is a madcap scene crowded with Snake Ladies, the Fire Eater, Human Blockheads, the Elastic Lady, Escape Artists, and the Torture King. It's all a sort of shrine to the way Coney Island used to be, run by a group of actors and performance artists, many from the East Village.

Started in 1985 by Yale Drama School

graduate Dick Zigun, the nonprofit Sideshows also presents a whimsical, not-to-be-missed Mermaid Parade every June, a Tattoo Festival in late summer, and alternative rock-and-roll bands on summer nights. Next door to the theater you'll find a small museum of Coney Island memorabilia and a souvenir shop.

New York Aquarium for Wildlife Conservation

Between the boardwalk and Surf Avenue at West 8th Street is the delightful **New York Aquarium** (Surf Ave. at W. 8th St., 718/265-3474, www.nyaquarium.com, fall, winter, and spring daily 10am-4:30pm, summer daily 10am-6pm, call for current admission during rebuilding effort), which sustained heavy structural damage and loss of animal life during Hurricane Sandy in 2012. Previously, the beachside aquarium contained close to 4,000

residents, including walruses, beluga whales, sharks, stingrays, sea otters, and electric eels. The hurricane's effects have resulted in partial closure of some features; when complete, a massive rebuilding and renovation will introduce some entirely new features.

MCU Park and the Brooklyn Cyclones

New York Mets' minor league team, **Brooklyn Cyclones** (1904 Surf Ave., 718/449-8497, tickets 718/507-8499, www.brooklyncyclones.com), play in shiny, new MCU Park on the waterfront. This family-friendly entertainment has all the charm of other minor league teams, including goofy events and races during the game and seemingly unending giveaways. This is a very popular and affordable baseball option.

Queens

Until recently, Queens was widely regarded as a snore. This was where the complacent everyman lived in a row house exactly like his neighbor's. Queens was home to Archie Bunker and hundreds of thousands of others like him. Queens was mediocrity. Queens was suburbia. Queens was boring, boring, boring.

Whether or not this was ever really true, it certainly isn't so today. New York's largest borough now boasts some of the city's—nay, the *country's*—biggest and most vibrant ethnic neighborhoods, as well as some architectural and cultural gems that are just beginning to be appreciated. Queens is also where Louis Armstrong, Will Rogers, Jackie Robinson, and Jack Kerouac all once lived; where the early movie industry was headquartered; and where the wealthy once summered, on grand estates in Bayside or on the then-pristine beaches of the Rockaways.

Named for Queen Catherine of Braganza, the wife of England's Charles II, Queens was annexed to New York City in 1898. Western

Queens began developing in the mid-1800s, but it wasn't until the building of Long Island Rail Road in 1910 that the borough really boomed. Then, apartment houses and private homes sprang up all over, and thousands of New Yorkers moved out into the "country."

For information about what's happening while you're visiting, check the events calendar maintained by **Queens Council on the Arts** (www.queenscouncilarts.org).

Orientation

Theoretically, Queens is laid out according to a grid system. Streets run north-south, from 1st Street, paralleling the East River, to 250th Street, at the borough's eastern end. Similarly, the avenues run east-west, with the lowest numbered addresses to the north and highest numbered to the south. Addresses are supposedly coded with their nearest cross street or avenue: 28-13 23rd Avenue, for example, should mean that the building is at No. 13 on 23rd Avenue near 28th Street. Things don't always work out

© AVALON TRAVEL

that neatly, however, and addresses in Queens can be confusing because 23rd, for example, may refer to an avenue, street, place, or road. When in doubt, it's best to ask for clarification.

LONG ISLAND CITY

Directly east of the Queensboro Bridge (locals refuse to call it by its more recent official title, the Ed Koch Memorial Bridge) is Long Island City. Once a dreary industrial area filled with windowless factory buildings, Long Island City has in the last decade or so become home to a growing community of artists, young professionals with families, and others looking to escape Manhattan's astronomical rents. That fact went largely unnoticed by the general public until June 2002, when the Museum of Modern Art, undergoing extensive renovation, was temporarily located here. MoMA has since moved back to Manhattan, but, in the aftermath, Long Island City's other museums and galleries are flourishing.

Noguchi Museum and Socrates Sculpture Park

The austere **Isamu Noguchi Garden Museum** (9-01 33rd Rd. at Vernon Blvd., 718/204-7088, www.noguchi.org, Wed.-Fri. 10am-5pm, Sat.-Sun. 11am-6pm, adults $10, seniors and students $5) is housed in the late sculptor's former studio. Its many rooms are filled with stone, metal, and wood sculptures, along with models of many large-scale environments designed by Noguchi. A yard holds a peaceful sculpture garden. On Sundays a **shuttle bus** to the museum leaves from the Asia Society in Manhattan (70th St. and Park Ave., check the website for schedule, round-trip $10).

Across the street from Noguchi Museum is the delightful **Socrates Sculpture Park** (32-01 Vernon Blvd., 718/956-1819, www.socratessculpturepark.org, daily 10am-sunset, free). Dotted with huge outdoor sculptures, the park is the brainchild of artist Mark di Suvero. For 10 years, di Suvero and other area artists worked to turn the once-garbage-strewn lot into a bona fide park. The city officially recognized their efforts in 1994, and the site is now

part of New York's park system. The park offers great views of Manhattan. In summer months, it hosts a popular international movie series.

MoMA PS1

New York's premier center for art on the cutting edge, acquired by the Museum of Modern Art in 1999, **MoMA PS1** (22-25 Jackson Ave., 718/784-2084, www.ps1.org, Thurs.-Mon. noon-6pm, adults $10, seniors and students $5) specializes in the avant-garde, conceptual, and experimental art. Housed in a four-story building that was once a public school, it offers artwork in all sorts of nooks and crannies—stairwells, basements, holes in the floor—as well as in large galleries. Two or three shows are usually featured at once, and traveling international shows are showcased as well.

The museum is especially busy in summer, when its extremely popular "Warm-up" series runs, attracting young-ish hipsters for experimental live music and dancing. The recent addition of a well-regarded restaurant, the pricey bistro-like **M. Wells Dinette** (Thurs.-Mon. noon-6pm), has also attracted more visitors.

To reach MoMA PS1 from Manhattan, take the No. 7 train to 45th Road/Court House Square, or the E or F train to 23rd Street.

ASTORIA

Not far from Long Island City is Astoria, one of the oldest settlements in Queens. It was developed in 1839 by John Jacob Astor, who built it into a thriving shipping port. Later, in the 1920s and 1930s, the neighborhood was the center of the movie-making business on the East Coast; Astoria Movie Studios produced such legendary stars as Rudolf Valentino and Gloria Swanson.

Astoria today is a stable and well-kept working- and middle-class community with the largest concentration of Greeks outside of Greece. Greek shops can be found along 30th Avenue between 31st and Steinway Streets, while Broadway is home to numerous Greek bakeries and butcher shops, the latter advertising baby pigs, baby lambs, and baby goats for sale. In the past decade, the neighborhood has further diversified, as new immigrant groups settled in and began to call Astoria home.

Museum of the Moving Image

The **Museum of the Moving Image** (36-01 35th Ave., 718/777-6888, www.movingimage.us, Wed.-Thurs. 10:30am-5:30pm, Fri. 10:30am-8pm, Sat.-Sun. 11:30am-7pm, adults $12, seniors and students $9, children 3-12 $6) houses over 70,000 artifacts covering all aspects of the film industry, from make-up to fan magazines. The museum has hands-on exhibits where visitors can create their own animated films, design soundtracks, and the like. The museum also boasts an excellent screening program; call for the schedule.

In early 2011 the museum completed a $25 million expansion that doubled its exhibition space and introduced an outdoor theater and garden and a new virtual space, the VR room, where computer programs simulate three-dimensional alternative realities.

The museum is housed in a section of the old Astoria Movie Studios (34-12 36th St.), other parts of which were reopened as the **Kaufman-Astoria Studios** in the late 1970s. Among the many movies and television shows that have been completely or partially produced here are *The Wiz, The Verdict, The World According to Garp,* and *The Cosby Show.*

To reach the Museum of the Moving Image directly from Manhattan, take the R or G train to Steinway Street and walk south to 35th Avenue.

Food

Among Astoria's many Greek restaurants is informal **Telly's Taverna** (28-13 23rd Ave., 718/728-9056, www.tellystaverna.com, $16), which offers especially delicious grilled lamb dishes and an outdoor garden in summer. Another beloved spot that's busy in summer, **Bohemian Hall & Beer Garden** (29-19 24th Ave., 718/274-4925, www.bohemianhall.com), a huge Czech beer garden, serves amazing kielbasa and potato pancakes.

Increasingly, other immigrant groups are opening up restaurants in Astoria. For traditional Venezuelan fare, try **Arepas Cafe** (33-07 36th Ave., 718/937-3835, www.arepascafe.com), named for the country's signature food: the doughy, filled arepa. Nearby is the Brazilian food and variety store selling everything from Havaianas flip-flops to bikinis, **Rio Bonito** (32-15 36th Ave., 718/728-4300), which has a casual eatery inside. Contemporary Mexican fare is served up at popular **Pachanga Patterson** (33-17 31st Ave., 718/554-0525, www.pachangapatterson.com), and heaping platters of meat are the specialty at Colombian restaurant **Tierras Colombianas** (33-01 Broadway, 718/956-3012). The northern end of Steinway Street is home to a string of Egyptian cafés and hookah bars, serving everything from tea to kebabs. For dessert, locals favor **Omonia Cafe** (32-20 Broadway, 718/274-6650, www.omoniacafe.com), the bakery that made the cake for the popular 2002 movie *My Big Fat Greek Wedding,* and **Gulluoglu Baklava** (30-92 31st St., 718/406-9100, www.gulluoglubaklava.com). As long as you can say "baklava," don't worry about pronouncing the café's name.

To make your own meal, **Titan Foods** (25-56 31st St., 718/626-7771, www.titanfoods.net) is an especially popular stop for Greek groceries.

Nightlife

Nightlife in Queens may be tamer than in Manhattan, but that's just the way Queens residents like it. The drinks are cheaper and the bars less pretentious. If this sounds like your kind of scene, be sure to tipple at **The Astor Room** (34-12 36th St., Astoria, 718/255-1947), which calls up images of the Gilded Age. In Long Island City, **Dutch Kills** (27-24 Jackson Ave., Long Island City, 718/383-2724) evokes the Prohibition Era. Both are easily accessible by subway.

Shopping

Shopping in Astoria and Long Island City is reminiscent of what it must have been like to shop in Manhattan 20 years ago; the Queens neighborhoods have largely managed to stave off big box stores and chain restaurants, favoring local, independent businesses like **Astoria**

Bookshop (31-29 31st St., 718/278-2665, www.astoriabookshop.com), which opened in 2013. The neighborhood's **EuroMarket** (30-42 31st St., 718/545-5569, www.euromarketny.com) is a thrill for foodie shoppers who want to experience the best of Europe without crossing the pond.

JAMAICA BAY

At the far southern end of Queens is **Jamaica Bay Wildlife Refuge** (Broad Channel, 718/318-4340, www.nyharborparks.org, daily 8:30am-5pm), where 330 species of birds (half the total number of species in the Northeast), 80 types of fish, 60 species of butterflies, and dozens of kinds of reptiles and amphibians live. It seems amazing that wildlife can flourish here. JFK Airport is directly across the bay, and all around the refuge, traffic drones on incessantly. Still, the refuge is on the Atlantic flyway, and well worth a visit, especially during autumn and spring. You can also hike and kayak here.

FLUSHING MEADOWS CORONA PARK

Today, **Flushing Meadows Corona Park** (www.nycgovparks.org/parks/fmcp) is a peaceful green oasis attracting families, couples, and kids. But back in the early 1900s, it was a towering, reeking garbage dump that smoldered by day and glowed at night. More than a hundred railroad carloads of Brooklyn's refuse were dumped here daily, providing succulent meals for hordes of rats "big enough to wear saddles," as one observer put it.

Enter Robert Moses, city parks commissioner. Looking at the noxious heap, Moses saw not an irredeemable wasteland but a potential park. In 1934, he directed the removal of some 50 million cubic tons of garbage. Through sheer force of will, he won the site two World's Fairs, costing the city and its backers millions.

Remains of the fairs still dot the 1,225-acre park. Most conspicuous is the 1964 **Unisphere,** a shining 140-foot-high, 380-ton hollow globe

sitting in the middle of a pretty fountain. Other park attractions include a miniature golf course, playgrounds, a botanical garden, zoo, two lakes, and an old-fashioned carousel. Across the street is the huge, 55,000-seat **Citi Field,** home to The New York Mets.

From Manhattan, take the No. 7 train to Willets Point/Shea Stadium and follow the signs.

Queens Museum

Next to the Unisphere is the **Queens Museum** (Flushing Meadows Corona Park, 718/592-9700, www.queensmuseum.org), housed in what was the New York City pavilion at both the 1939 and the 1964 World's Fairs. Renovated in the late 1990s and again in 2013—the second renovation doubling its size—the museum presents first-rate temporary exhibitions and houses an unusual permanent exhibit: the New York Panorama. First showcased at the 1964 fair, the panorama is a scale model of the city, showing every single building and house in the five boroughs—some 895,000 of them, built of plastic and wood. The panorama was originally intended as a serious tool for urban planners but now feels more like a nostalgic work of art.

New York Hall of Science

Ranked as one of the country's top 10 science museums, the **New York Hall of Science** (47-01 111th St., 718/699-0005, www.nysci.org, Apr.1-Aug.31 Mon.-Fri. 9:30am-5pm and Sat.-Sun. 10am-6pm, Sept. 1-Mar. 31 Tues.-Fri. 9:30am-5pm and Sat.-Sun. 10am-6pm, adults $11, seniors, students, and children 2-17 $15) is housed in a dramatic, undulating building—another leftover from the 1964 World's Fair. Inside, you'll find 450 exhibits, many of them hands-on, including a distorted room that makes people appear to shrink or grow and an enlarged drop of water showing microscopic organisms going about their daily lives. Out back is a large Science Playground, where kids can learn about the laws of physics.

The Bronx

The Bronx is New York City's second smallest borough both in size and population, and it's the only one attached to the mainland. Purchased from the Algonquins by the Dutch West India Company in 1639, it was first settled in 1644 by a Scandinavian named Jonas Bronck. The area soon became known as "The Broncks," and remained a peaceful rural community up until the late 1800s, when the 3rd Avenue Elevated Railway arrived, bringing with it thousands of European immigrants. By 1900, the borough's population had soared to over 200,000.

Many consider the 1920s through the early 1950s to be the golden era of the Bronx. That's when the borough was filled with many tightly knit ethnic neighborhoods, each with its own vibrant community life. The arrival of the affordable automobile, however, soon allowed many of the Bronx's more affluent residents to move to Long Island or Westchester, and in 1950, Robert Moses' six-lane Cross-Bronx Expressway was constructed, destroying a number of the borough's most stable neighborhoods.

Today, the Bronx is best known as the home of such great New York institutions as the Bronx Zoo, the New York Botanical Garden, and Yankee Stadium. For more information on the borough, contact the **Bronx Tourism Council** (851 Grand Concourse, 718/590-3518, www.ilovethebronx.com).

◖ THE BRONX ZOO AND NEW YORK BOTANICAL GARDEN

Though the zoo and botanical garden are next door to each other, to visit both in one day would require much fortitude, as both are very large. It's smarter to opt for one, and combine it with a meal or coffee and dessert on Arthur Avenue.

One of the most beloved of New York institutions is the enormous **Bronx Zoo** (Fordham Rd. and Bronx River Pkwy., 718/367-1010, www.bronxzoo.org, Apr.-Nov. Mon.-Fri. 10am-5pm and Sat.-Sun. 10am-5:30pm, Nov.-Apr. daily 10am-4:30pm, adults $16.95,

seniors $14.95, children 3-12 $12.95), where New Yorkers have been spending weekends with their families for generations. It's among the world's largest and most important zoos, housing over 4,000 animals, many of which roam relatively freely in large landscaped habitats. The Bronx Zoo was one of the world's first wildlife centers to adopt this technique.

Among the 250-acre zoo's most popular attractions is its Wild Asia Monorail, a ride above a 38-acre savanna inhabited by elephants, Siberian tigers, rhinos, and many different kinds of deer. In World of Birds, centered on a towering waterfall, about 100 species flit from tree to tree.

To reach the zoo from Manhattan, take the No. 2 or 5 train to East Tremont Avenue-West Farms. Or, take the BMX11 Express Bus (718/652-8400, www.mta.info).

Just north of the zoo is 250-acre **New York Botanical Garden** (2900 Southern Blvd., 718/817-8700, www.nybg.org, spring-fall Tues.-Sun. 10am-6pm, winter Tues.-Sun. 10am-5pm, adults $13, seniors and students $6, children 2-12 $3). Made up of both the cultivated and the wild, the park contains dozens of constituent gardens, such as a rose garden and an herb garden, an arboretum, a hemlock forest, a children's garden, and—best of all—the enormous, shimmering, Victorian-style **Enid Haupt Conservatory** (separate admission, with price varying by season). Here, you'll find over 100 varieties of palms, tropical plants, desert flora, and ferns, and changing seasonal exhibits. The 1902 conservatory, with its 11 glass pavilions and many reflecting pools, was inspired by Kew Gardens in London and is the largest building of its type in America. The quirky Holiday Train Show features model trains rumbling past New York landmarks made entirely of plant parts.

To reach the botanical garden from Manhattan, take the No. 4 or D train to Bedford Park Boulevard and walk a half-dozen

or so long blocks east. Or, take a Metro North train (212/532-4900, www.mta.info).

BELMONT

Just west of Bronx Zoo is the Italian community of Belmont. A stable, middle-class haven of spic-and-span streets and small backyard shrines, Belmont is chock-a-block with Italian restaurants, pastry shops, butcher shops, and food markets. Most are located along **Arthur Avenue** or **187th Street**. Locals poo-poo Manhattan's Little Italy, calling their corner of The Bronx "The Real Little Italy of New York." To reach Belmont from the zoo, walk west seven long blocks, or catch the Bx22 bus on East Fordham Road. From the garden, walk south through the campus of Fordham University.

Food

At the heart of things is the indoor **Arthur Avenue Retail Market** (2344 Arthur Ave., at 187th St., www.arthuravenuebronx.com), where some of the city's freshest and cheapest fruits and vegetables can be found, along with fresh mozzarella, ravioli cutters, and espresso machines. Hand-rolled cigars and homemade sandwiches are also for sale here.

Just up the street are **Madonia Brothers Bakery** (2348 Arthur Ave., 718/295-5573), selling mouth-watering crusty bread, and **Biancardi Meats** (2350 Arthur Ave., 718/733-4058), selling whole baby lambs and goats (no place for the squeamish). Down the street is the **Calabria Pork Store** (2338 Arthur Ave., 718/367-5145), its ceiling densely hung with meats and sausages, and **Randazzo's Fish Market** (2327 Arthur Ave., 718/367-4139), piled high with crab, sole, scrod, and the like. In warm weather, Randazzo's operates a raw seafood bar out front.

A number of pastry shops and cafés are on 187th Street. **DeLillo's Pasticceria** (610 E. 187th St., 718/367-8198, www.delillopastryshop.com) serves both pastries and homemade gelato and spumoni. **Egidio Pastry Shop** (622 E. 187th St., 718/295-6077) is renowned for its miniature pastries.

Mario's Restaurant (2342 Arthur Ave., between 184th and 185th Sts., 718/584-1188, www.mariosrestarthurave.com, $16) serves huge portions of Southern Italian food. It may be Belmont's best-known restaurant; it was featured in the film *The Godfather*. **Dominick's** (2335 Arthur Ave., 718/733-2807, $12) has some of the neighborhood's best food, served family style at long tables covered with red tablecloths. Good pizza joints can also be found along Arthur Avenue.

CITY ISLAND

City Island is one of New York City's oddest communities, a sailors' haven that fancies itself part of New England. "Welcome to New York City's Nautical Community, 1645" reads the sign arching over the bridge leading from the mainland. And then you're here, on a narrow strip of land lined with boatyards, tiny clapboard houses, and bustling seafood restaurants.

Back in the 1700s, the inhabitants of City Island hoped to develop a port that would rival New York's. Their plan failed, but the community has been home to a number of thriving industries, including a shipbuilding industry that continues to this day. Several America's Cup yachts were built here.

City Island has only one real street: City Island Avenue. But some of its side roads, which are only a few blocks long, are pretty and worth a gander. To reach the island from Manhattan, take the No. 6 train to Pelham Bay Park, the last stop, and catch the Bx12 (summer only) or Bx29 bus to City Island. This area is perhaps best suited to visit by car to avoid desolate long stretches of waiting for the bus.

Food

City Island restaurants run the gamut from simple diners to elaborate (and expensive) old-fashioned affairs with nautical themes and plush booths. The rambling **Johnny's Reef Restaurant** (2 City Island Ave., 718/885-2086, $14) is a local favorite, offering huge portions of fried fish cafeteria-style, along with great views of the Sound. For a more sedate atmosphere and also very good food, head to the **Crab Shanty** (361 City Island Ave., 718/885-1810, www.originalcrabshanty.com, $24).

Staten Island

Sometimes dubbed "the forgotten borough," Staten Island is different from the rest of New York City. Significantly more rural and suburban than the other boroughs, it's also predominantly white, tends to be politically conservative, and is populated with working- and middle-class families.

These facts—and its geographic isolation—tend to leave Staten Island feeling estranged from the rest of the city, so much so that it periodically threatens to secede. The last time was in 1993 when the issue was put to a public vote; the referendum was enthusiastically passed, but more than 20 years later has never been implemented.

Fourteen miles long by seven miles wide, Staten Island is a hilly place made up largely of bedrock. A military camp for the British during the Revolutionary War, the borough remained predominantly agricultural until the early 1900s and was still largely undeveloped when the Verrazano-Narrows Bridge opened in 1964. The bridge connected the island to the rest of the city for the first time, bringing with it new industry, residents, and crime. Many Staten Islanders still blame the bridge for many of the island's current problems, and divide life into "Before the Bridge" and "After the Bridge."

Staten Island has its own minor league baseball team, the **Staten Island Yankees** (St. George Stadium, 75 Richmond Terr., 718/720-9265, www.siyanks.com). Their stadium is located next to the SI ferry terminal and makes for a fun day out when combined with a ferry trip to and from Manhattan.

To reach Staten Island from Manhattan, take the **Staten Island ferry** (718/727-2508, www.siferry.com) from Battery Park to St. George, where buses fan out to cover the island. For more information and help with travel directions, contact the **Staten Island Chamber of Commerce** (718/727-1900, www.sichamber. com).

STATEN ISLAND INSTITUTE OF ARTS & SCIENCES

Two blocks from the ferry terminal in St. George is **Staten Island Institute of Arts & Sciences** (75 Stuyvesant Pl., 718/727-1135, www.statenislandmuseum.org, Mon.-Fri. 11am-5pm, Sat. 10am-5pm, Sun. noon-5pm, suggested admission adults $5, seniors and students $3, children under 12 free), also known as the Staten Island Museum. Founded in 1881, the institute features small but well-done changing exhibits on the arts, natural sciences, and culture of the borough.

SNUG HARBOR CULTURAL CENTER AND BOTANICAL GARDEN

The 83-acre **Snug Harbor Cultural Center and Botanical Garden** (1000 Richmond Terr., 718/448-2500, www.snug-harbor.org, Wed.-Sun. noon-5pm, adults $8, seniors and students $7, children under 12 free) is set in a restored home for retired seamen. The 19th-century Greek Revival buildings now house all of the major Staten Island cultural institutions (varying fees for different museums), including The Nobel Maritime Collection, focusing on the art of John A. Nobel and featuring his houseboat studio; Art Lab, a school of fine and applied art; Newhouse Center for Contemporary Art; performing arts at the Veterans Memorial Hall Playhouse and the Music Hall; and Staten Island Children's Museum. The extensive grounds open to the public include the Chinese Scholar's Garden, Tuscan Garden, and the Connie Gretz Secret Garden (grounds-only admission $5).

Take the S40 bus at St. George Ferry Terminal to the Snug Harbor Road stop.

HISTORIC RICHMOND TOWN

Historic Richmond Town (441 Clarke Ave., 718/351-1611, www.historicrichmondtown. org, Wed.-Sun. 1pm-5pm, adults $8, seniors and students $6, children 4-11 $5) is a 30-acre

STATEN ISLAND

Newark Bay

Staten Island Ferry

THE BALLPARK AT ST. GEORGE

INSTITUTE OF ARTS AND SCIENCES ★ STATEN ISLAND FERRY TERMINAL

SNUG HARBOR CULTURAL CENTER ★ ST. GEORGE

CHILDREN'S MUSEUM ★

The Narrows

RICHMOND

TER

AVE

BLVD

FOREST

AUSTEN HOUSE

VERRAZANO-NARROWS BRIDGE

STATE

VICTORY

EXPY

ISLAND

RD

COLLEGE OF STATEN ISLAND

TODT HILL

HILL

Willowbrook Park

ROCKLAND

MANOR

AVE

RICHMOND

Railway

William Davis Wildlife Refuge

LaTourette Park

NEW JERSEY

RICHMOND

RD

RICHMOND TOWN RESTORATION

Island

Gateway National Recreation Area

KILL

WEST

PKY

AVE

WOODROW

Staten

SANDY GROUND

RICHMOND

BLVD

MTA

OUTERBRIDGE CROSSING

Arthur Kill

SHORE

VICTORY

Raritan Bay

TOTTENVILLE

HYLAN

ATLANTIC OCEAN

0   2 mi

0   2 km

© AVALON TRAVEL

NEW YORK CITY'S OTHER ISLANDS

Standing in Midtown, surrounded by skyscrapers and city buses, honking cars and hurried cyclists, it's easy to forget that New York City is bounded by water. Manhattan, Brooklyn, Queens, and Staten Island are the city's best-known islands, of course, but they're not the only ones. Three other islands accessible to the public are Governors, Randall's, and Roosevelt Islands, each with a unique history and distinct reasons to visit.

Governors Island (www.govisland.com) opened to the public as a multi-use recreational site in 2005 after serving as a military installation for more than 200 years. Even before artillery and infantry troops were stationed here during the War of 1812, the island served as a coastal defense for both the state and the nation. In the 20th century, it became the base for the Atlantic Area Command of the U.S. Coast Guard, and served a number of diplomatic and ceremonial functions, including a United Nations-sponsored talk intended to lead to the restoration of democratic rule in Haiti.

Now, the island is open to the public from early May to late September, and is the site of dozens of art exhibits, festivals, concerts, and events throughout the summer. Some are quirky, like the Unicycle Festival, and some are nostalgic, like the Jazz Age Lawn Party. Plenty of visitors to the island take the ferry over to just enjoy the grounds, which are perfect for a picnic or a snooze in the sun.

Neither as popular nor as easily reached as Governors Island, **Randall's Island** (www.randallsisland.org), open year-round, is still worth a visit if you want a respite from Manhattan's hustle and bustle. It's an underrated spot for taking stellar photos of Manhattan's East Side skyline or for running and cycling on eight miles of under-used, vehicle-free paths. The island is also home to a golf and tennis center, both of which are open to the public.

Roosevelt Island (www.rioc.ny.gov) has been an attraction for curious travelers since at least 1976, when a tramway connecting the island to Manhattan began operation, shuttling slowly over the East River at a peak height of 250 feet. Until recently, though, there wasn't much for visitors to see once they arrived on the island, and most just turned around and took the tram back to Manhattan.

That began to change in the mid 2000s, when new apartment buildings, marketed as a more affordable alternative to Manhattan real estate, were constructed. As these became occupied, more services and recreational installations popped up on the island. The newest of these is **Franklin D. Roosevelt Four Freedoms Park** (www.fdrfourfreedomspark.org), opened in 2012. The park, nearly four decades in the making, is a quiet beauty and offers lovely views of both Manhattan's East Side and Queens' Gantry Plaza State Park in the Long Island City neighborhood.

complex filled with 27 historic buildings, many of which are open to the public. Most have been moved here from elsewhere on the island, and they line up neatly along several streets that come alive in summer with craftspeople and guides in period dress.

Richmond Town sits on the site of an early Dutch settlement and interprets three centuries of daily life. The oldest building is 1695 Voorlezer's House (a *voorlezer* was a lay minister); one of the newest is New Dorp Railroad Station. Other interesting buildings include a two-story jail, tinsmith shop, general store, and carriage "manufactory."

Take the S74 bus from the ferry terminal; the ride takes 30-40 minutes.

Information and Services

TOURIST INFORMATION

New York City's Official Visitor Information Center (810 7th Ave., 212/484-1222, www. nycgo.com, Mon.-Fri. 8:30am-6pm, Sat.-Sun. 9am-5pm), run by NYC & Company, New York's tourism marketing organization, is open 365 days a year. Maps, brochures, and events calendars are available. The center also runs visitor information kiosks near key attractions. These are at **Macy's Herald Square** (151 W. 34th St., 212/484-1222); **City Hall** (southern tip of City Hall Park, 212/484-1222); and **Chinatown** (at triangle where Canal, Walker, and Baxter Sts. meet, 212/484-1222).

When out of town, written information can be ordered by calling **NYC & Company** (800/ NYC-VISIT or 212/484-1200).

Downtown Alliance (212/566-6700, www. downtownny.com) can provide you with information about Lower Manhattan. Various business partnerships operate carts stocked with tourist brochures near such visitor-heavy sites as Grand Central Terminal and the Empire State Building.

TOURS

No matter where your interests lie—in architecture, ethnic foods, or social history—chances are good that you'll find a tour tailor-made for you. Walking tours abound all over the city, especially in spring and fall, with each one more imaginative than the next (for example, "Famous Murder Sites" and "Edith Wharton's New York"). Most are reasonably priced.

City Tours

One of the best ways to get an overview of the city is to take a **Circle Line** cruise (Pier 83, W. 42nd St. and Hudson River, 212/563-3200, www.circleline42.com, prices vary by tour). Boats cruise daily year-round. Standard daytime cruises last three hours; "express" and evening cruises last two hours.

World Yacht (Pier 81, W. 41st St. and Hudson River, 212/630-8100, www.worldyacht.com, $50-125 per person) offers three-hour luxury dinner cruises with live entertainment and dancing, as well as brunch cruises.

Gray Line Sightseeing (777 8th Ave., 212/445-0848, www.graylinenewyork.com, prices vary by tour) offers over a dozen bus tours lasting anywhere from two hours to a full day. Tours are offered year-round. Gray Line also offers cruises and helicopter tours.

For a spectacular bird's-eye view of the city, try **Liberty Helicopter Tours** (212/967-6464, www.libertyhelicopter.com, $150 and up per person, reservations required).

Walking Tours

The Municipal Art Society (111 W. 57th St., 212/935-3960, www.mas.org) runs an extensive series of walking tours almost daily year-round. Most of the tours focus on architecture and history.

Context Travel (800/691-6036, www.contexttravel.com) offers walking tours on various topics, including architecture, art, and urban history; all are led by scholars. Groups are intimate, never booking more than six people.

Big Onion Walking Tours (888/606-9255, www.bigonion.com), founded by two Columbia University graduate students, offers some of the city's most fun and well-researched tours. Many of the tours concentrate on New York's immigrant history and on neighborhoods below 14th Street.

The 92nd Street Y (1395 Lexington Ave., 212/415-5500, www.92y.org), a leading cultural institution, offers many excellent walking and bus tours. They're very popular and must be reserved weeks in advance.

In Harlem, **Harlem Spirituals** (212/391-0900, www.harlemspirituals.com) specializes in visits to gospel services and soul food restaurants, as well as historic sites. **Harlem Heritage Tours** (212/280-7888, www.harlemheritage. com) offers about 30 different tours, ranging from "jazz nights in Harlem" to gospel walking tours.

Downtown, the **Lower East Side Tenement Museum** (103 Orchard St., 212/982-8420, www.tenement.org) sponsors walking tours of old immigrant neighborhoods. For a hip tour of the East Village and environs, check out **Rock Junket Tours** (212/209-3370, www.rockjunket.com). "Rocker guides" lead participants past legendary rock, punk, and glam sites from the 1960s to the present.

Other unique tours focus on niche interests, including food, and nature. **Foods of New York Tours** (212/913-9964, www.foodsofny.com, prices vary by tour, tastings included) explores some of the most famous restaurants and food shops in the West Village, Chelsea, and Chinatown. Worth watching out for are free nature walks offered in all five boroughs by the **Urban Park Rangers** (212/360-2774 or 866/692-4295, www.nyc.gov/parks).

The **Big Apple Greeter** (212/669-8159, www.bigapplegreeter.org) matches visitors with enthusiastic volunteers eager to introduce the city to out-of-towners. The service is completely free and especially helpful to the disabled and tourists interested in visiting off-the-beaten-track spots.

If you prefer to go on a **self-guided tour,** Downtown Alliance offers a comprehensive downtown walking tour guide on its website (www.downtownny.com/walkingtours).

TIPS FOR TRAVELERS
Tipping
A 15-20 percent tip is customary for waiters and taxi drivers. Hotel bellhops expect $1-2 a bag, porters $1-2 for hailing a cab, and room attendants $3-5 per person per night.

Restrooms
Finding a place to use the bathroom in Manhattan can be challenging when you're out and about; most restaurants and cafés post signs warning that bathrooms are for paying customers only. Some of the most accessible public restrooms in Manhattan are at Grand Central Terminal (42nd St. and Park Ave.), the main branch of The New York Public Library (5th Ave. and 42nd St.), on the southeastern edge of Madison Square Park (E. 23rd St. and Park Ave S.), and Barnes and Noble and Whole Foods (various locations).

Safety
As in most big cities, crime in New York can be a problem, and in the past, New York has had a bad reputation for all sorts of crime. In the past two decades, however, New York has consistently ranked as one of America's safest large cities. It doesn't even make the top-25 list of cities with the highest homicide rates. Statistically, your chances of being mugged are less than 30,000 to 1. To avoid being that one:

Act as if you know where you're going, especially when passing through empty neighborhoods. New Yorkers, forever blasé, keep up a brisk, disinterested pace at all times. If you spend too long ogling sites or looking nervously about, you'll be targeted as an easy mark. When unsure if you are headed the correct way, better to circle the block walking purposefully to head back in the correct direction than to flaunt your confusion.

Don't carry large quantities of cash or large bills, but do carry something; $20 is recommended.

Ignore hustlers and con artists, and don't be guilted into giving money to people who solicit money on the subway, which is illegal.

Avoid parks at night, and be extra careful around transportation centers such as Port Authority and Penn Station.

Don't carry valuables in lightweight backpacks that can easily be slashed open. Carry handbags close to your body.

When in rougher neighborhoods, stick to blocks where other people are in sight or at least where cars are passing by. At night, on empty streets, walk near the curb, away from dark overhangs.

If you're mugged, hand over your valuables immediately—they're not worth risking your well-being or your life.

Gay and Lesbian Travelers

Founded in 1983, **The Lesbian, Gay, Bisexual & Transgender Community Center** (208 W. 13th St., between 7th and 8th Aves., 212/620-7310, www.gaycenter.org) works with hundreds of organizations, including ActUP and GLAAD, and houses the National Museum and Archive of Lesbian and Gay History. Everything from dances to movies is presented here. Free information "Welcome Packets" about the city are available for travelers.

Travelers with Disabilities

New York is a difficult city for visitors with disabilities to navigate as so much of the city's core infrastructure is so old, but help is available. One source is the **Mayor's Office for People with Disabilities** (212/788-2830), which puts out a free Access Guide. Another is **Hospital Audiences, Inc.** (212/575-7676, www.hainyc.org), which publishes a guide to the city's cultural institutions that includes information on elevators, ramps, Braille signage, services for the hearing impaired, and accessible restroom facilities. The **Broadway Accessibility Initiative** (212/730-4750, www.inclusioninthearts.org) also helps theatergoers with different types of disabilities get the access or equipment they need to enjoy Broadway performances; the service and equipment are free.

For more general information, contact **Society for Accessible Travel and Hospitality** (212/447-7284, www.sath.org), a nationwide, nonprofit membership organization that collects data on travel facilities around the country.

The **Big Apple Greeter** program (212/669-8159), available free to all visitors, matches out-of-towners with New Yorkers eager to share their hometown. Of the 300 volunteer "Big Apple Greeters," many are specifically trained to help people with disabilities enjoy the city.

All of New York's buses are wheelchair accessible, but only a handful of subway stations are. **New York City Transit** (718/596-8585, www.mta.info) publishes the free brochures *Accessible Travel* and *Accessible Transfer Points within the NYC Subway*. The city also runs the Accessible Dispatch program for wheelchair users to call for **accessible taxis** (646/599-9999).

PUBLICATIONS

New York City has three major daily newspapers: *The New York Times, The Daily News,* and *The New York Post.* The *Times* is the country's unofficial paper of record, exhaustively covering national and international news. It also contains good information on happenings around town.

You'd be coming away with a skewed view of New York, however, if you didn't also pick up occasional copies of *The Daily News* and *The New York Post.* Both tabloids, with their in-your-face headlines, cover local news that *The New York Times* tends to ignore. *The Daily News* is also a good source for crisp, pithy features and reviews of local events. *The New York Post's Page Six* gossip column is must reading for many New Yorkers, and many of its reviews are excellent. Both papers also feature a daily movie schedule.

The Wall Street Journal and *The New York Observer* are other important daily papers. The former is focused on finance and world news, but has a strong local news and culture/entertainment section. The latter is focused almost exclusively on the cultural and artistic news of New York City, with some local politics sprinkled in.

When it comes to "alternative" papers, the weekly *Village Voice* is the granddaddy. Once known for its leftist politics and investigative features, *The Voice's* strongest suit these days is its events listings, which are among the city's most comprehensive. *The Voice* is free and can be found in red boxes on street corners, or in bookstores, music stores, clubs, and delis.

Among magazines, *New York, The New Yorker,* and *Time Out New York* cover the city extensively. *New York* is mostly lightweight, mainstream patter with occasional hard-hitting features. It has entertaining articles, good reviews, and solid events listings. *The New Yorker* is renowned for its acerbic, and usually deadly accurate, listings and reviews. *Time Out New York* features excellent round-up articles and a phenomenal listings section—the most comprehensive in the city.

EMERGENCIES

Dial 911 for emergency **police, ambulance,** or **fire department** response. For the location of the nearest police precinct, dial 646/610-5000.

Private hospitals with 24-hour emergency rooms include **Beth Israel Medical Center** (1st Ave. at 16th St., 212/420-2000), **New York University Medical Center** (1st Ave. at 34th St., 212/263-7300), **St. Luke's-Roosevelt Hospital** (9th Ave. at 58th St., 212/523-4000), **New York Hospital** (York Ave. at 68th St., 212/746-5454), and **Mount Sinai Hospital** (5th Ave. at 100th St., 212/241-6500).

POST OFFICES

Many post offices are open weekdays 9am-5pm and Saturdays 8am-1pm, but hours vary from branch to branch. The city's main post office on 8th Avenue at 33rd Street is open 24 hours a day, seven days a week.

TELEPHONES

The area code in Manhattan has historically been 212, while the other boroughs use 718. Since 1999, however, Manhattan now has a second area code—646—while the boroughs and upper Manhattan now also use 347. It is necessary to dial all 10 numbers when placing a call. 917 is the primary area code for New York City cell phones.

For **directory assistance** in Manhattan, call 411. For directory assistance in the other boroughs, call 718/555-1212.

For questions or complaints about any city agency, call the city government's catch-all hotline: 311.

Getting There

AIR

New York is serviced by three airports. **John F. Kennedy International Airport** (www.panynj.gov/airports/jfk.html) is about 15 miles from Manhattan in Queens. It's the largest of the three and handles primarily international flights. **La Guardia Airport** (www.panynj.gov/airports/laguardia.html), also in Queens, is about eight miles from Manhattan and handles primarily domestic flights. **Newark Liberty International Airport** (www.panynj.gov/airports/newark-liberty.html), across the Hudson River in New Jersey, handles domestic and some international flights. Kennedy is generally the most congested of the three airports, Newark the least.

Public transportation from the airports into Manhattan and the other boroughs is excellent; call 800/247-7433 for general information.

A **taxi ride** into Manhattan from La Guardia takes 20-30 minutes and costs about $40, including tolls and tip. The ride from Kennedy to Manhattan takes 30-45 minutes and costs a flat fare of $52, plus tolls and tip (when going the other way, from Manhattan to Kennedy, the trip is metered, but usually costs about the same). The 45-minute ride from Newark usually runs about $60. Cabs leave from well-marked stands staffed by dispatchers, just outside the flight arrival areas at all airports. Avoid the gypsy cabs and drivers asking "Taxi? Taxi?" near baggage-claim areas and just outside the terminal.

NYC Airporter (718/777-5111, www.nycairporter.com) offers frequent bus service to and from La Guardia ($13 one-way) and Kennedy ($16 one-way). Stops are made near Grand Central Terminal (Park Ave. between 41st and 42nd Sts.), inside the Port Authority Bus Terminal (42nd St. and 8th Ave.), and near Penn Station (33rd St. and 7th Ave.).

Olympia Trails of Coach USA (212/964-6233 or 877/894-9155, www.olympiabus.com) offers frequent bus service between Newark Airport and Manhattan ($16 one-way, $28 round-trip). Buses leave every 15 minutes, and make three stops in Manhattan: near Grand Central Terminal (41st St. and Park Ave.), next to Bryant Park (northwest corner of 42nd St. and 5th Ave.), and inside the Port Authority (42nd St. and 8th Ave.).

SuperShuttle (212/209-7000, www.supershuttle.com) offers door-to-door pick-up van service from homes and hotels to any of the three area airports. Fares start at $15.

TRAIN

Manhattan has two main railroad stations: **Pennsylvania Station** (33rd St. and 7th Ave.), commonly referred to as Penn Station, and **Grand Central Terminal** (42nd St. and Park Ave.). All **Amtrak** trains (800/872-7245) arrive and depart from Penn Station. **New Jersey Transit** (973/762-5100) and **Long Island Rail Road** (718/217-5477) also offer passenger-train service out of Penn Station. **Metro-North** (212/532-4900) runs commuter trains to suburban New York and Connecticut from Grand Central. Both stations are well serviced by buses, subways, and taxis.

BUS

Port Authority (8th Ave. between 40th and 42nd Sts., 212/564-8484) is the world's largest bus terminal, serving both commuter and long-distance travelers. Major bus lines departing from the terminal include **Greyhound** (800/231-2222, www.greyhound.com), **Peter Pan** (800/343-9999, www.peterpanbus.com), and **New Jersey Transit** (973/762-5100 or 800/772-2222, www.njtransit.com).

CAR

If you must drive into Manhattan, be prepared to pay a steep price for parking at a garage (often $20 or more an hour) or to spend 20 minutes or more looking for street parking. Street meters are disappearing in the city, but don't think that means they're free; each block has one or two machines where you make your payment via credit or debit card. Be sure to get the receipt, which must be displayed on the driver's side of your car's dashboard.

Getting Around

Most of Manhattan is laid out in a grid pattern, which makes it easy to find your way around. Avenues run north-south, streets east-west, and most are one-way. Fifth Avenue, which marks the city's center, separates the East and West Sides. Street addresses are labeled accordingly (1 E. 50th St., 1 W. 50th St.), with numbers increasing as you head away from 5th Avenue. Broadway, following an old Algonquin trail, cuts through the city on a diagonal.

Neighborhoods not laid out in a numbered grid pattern—essentially everything south of 14th Street—are more difficult to navigate; it helps to have a good map. The same applies in the other boroughs, where it's also a good idea to get exact directions to your destination before you set out.

If you don't know how to get where you're going, you can use mapping and directions services on the popular website, www.hopstop.

com, or on the MTA's own website (www.mta.info).

Walking is by far the best way to see New York City. In Manhattan, calculate about a minute to walk each north-south block and two minutes for each east-west block.

SUBWAY

Subways are the easiest and quickest way to get around town. Service is frequent, at least in Manhattan, and the trains run 24 hours a day, 7 days a week, year-round.

To ride the subways, you'll need a **MetroCard,** an electronic fare card, which can be purchased at kiosks in subway stations and can be bought in either value or time increments (7 day or 30 day; unfortunately, the popular day pass has been eliminated). Basic fare is $2.50. Fees change regularly; access www.mta.info for up-to-date information.

Subway maps are usually posted in each

© FRANCISCO COLLAZO

water taxi

station, and free copies are sometimes available at service booths. You can also see the map online at www.mta.info.

Three main subway lines service the city, each with multiple trains and routes. The IRT runs north-south on either side of Manhattan; the IND runs along 6th and 8th Avenues; and the BMT runs from lower Manhattan to Brooklyn and Queens. A new line, the Second Avenue subway, is under construction; the first phase is slated for completion in 2016.

Subway lines have numbers and colors, but New Yorkers typically refer to the trains they take by number, not color. They also don't typically use the terms IRT, IND, or BMT. Lines used most frequently by visitors are the No. 6 train, which makes local stops along the East Side of Manhattan, and the No. 1 train, which makes local stops along the West Side. There's also a Grand Central-Times Square Shuttle connecting the east and west sides on 42nd Street.

Over 3.5 million passengers travel the 700 miles of subway track every day without mishap. Still, crime is an occasional problem and you should take certain precautions. Keep a close eye on your belongings, especially during rush hours when the crush of the crowd makes pickpocketing easy. Don't wear expensive jewelry or have electronics, such as smartphones, visible. Avoid empty or near-empty cars, even during the day when the subways are theoretically the safest. When your train comes, sit in the center car, which has a conductor and is usually the most crowded car on the train. Finally, although many New Yorkers ride the subways at all hours, it's not especially advisable to take them after midnight.

BUS

Buses run 24 hours a day uptown along 10th, 8th, 6th, Madison, 3rd, and 1st Avenues, and downtown along 9th, 7th, 5th, and 2nd Avenues. East-west crosstown service can be found on Houston, 8th/9th, 14th, 23rd, 34th, 42nd, 49th/50th, 57th, 66th, 72nd, 79th, 86th, 96th, 116th, and 125th Streets. Bus stops are usually located every two blocks, and signs or shelters mark the spots.

The fare is $2.50, payable with either exact change (no bills) or the electronic MetroCard. Free transfers are available between uptown-downtown buses and crosstown buses, enabling you to make any one-way trip in Manhattan on a single fare. Good bus service is also available in the outer boroughs. Fees change regularly. Access the website for up-to-date information: www.mta.info. Also, note that the "Select Bus" service was introduced in 2010, turning some routes into "skip-stop" service. For these buses (indicated by "Select Bus" written on the front), fares are paid via machine at the bus shelter using your MetroCard (You'll need to grab the receipt as proof of payment; uniformed and undercover officers on board spot-check for fare evaders).

TAXI AND CAR SERVICE

Another mode of New York City transportation is the taxi cab, all painted yellow with lighted signs on their roofs. When the sign is lit, the cab is available and may be hailed anywhere. Fares begin at $2.50 for the first 0.25 miles, then jump $0.50 for each additional 0.2 miles and for every 60 seconds of waiting time. A $1 surcharge is added to rides begun between 4pm and 8pm; a $0.50 surcharge is added to rides begun between 8pm and 6am. A 15-20 percent tip is the norm and can be added automatically to the fare by the passenger when using a debit or credit card.

In late 2013, the city introduced a new series of taxis designed especially for the "outer" boroughs. The so-called "Boro Taxis" are "apple green," and can only be hailed in the boroughs *or* in Manhattan above E. 96th Street on the East Side and W. 110th Street on the West Side.

For decades, New Yorkers have often preferred to use a car service rather than taxi when making certain trips, especially trips to airports. Popular services include **Dial 7** (212/777-7777, www.dial7.com) and **Carmel** (866/666-6666, www.carmellimo.com). Many New Yorkers are also warming to **Uber** (www.uber.com), a relatively new car service that is hailed and paid for by smartphone app. Though convenient, the service is typically a bit more expensive than the other taxi or car service options listed here.

LONG ISLAND

Long, thin Long Island stretches east from New York City for about 120 miles. At the westernmost end of the island are the New York City boroughs of Brooklyn and Queens. So, in common parlance, Long Island begins at the Queens-Nassau County border. Remarkably though, given its proximity to New York City, much of Long Island is still farmland, dunes, and beach. The farther east you travel, the more the island resembles its Algonquin name, Paumanok, said to mean "the island with its breast long drawn out and laid against the sea."

Long Island's shape has often been compared to a whale. Its eastern bulk, never much more than 20 miles wide, splits at the 80-mile point into two curving spits of land, or "flukes," most commonly referred to as the North and South Forks. The island was once an extension of a barren plain that stretched east from the Alleghenies. About 15 million years ago, two glaciers moving southward dug out the deep valley that is now Long Island Sound and severed the island from the mainland. The glacier also cut hundreds of notches into the north shore, forming the coves, bays, and peninsulas seen here today. As the glacier melted, its waters ran south, flooding a huge meadow—now the Great South Bay and its neighboring waters—and creating low sand bars that became the foundation of today's miles-long barrier beach.

Although it's the largest island on the eastern seaboard, Long Island does not enjoy the idyllic, peaceful reputation of serenity that the term *island* usually brings to mind. Unfortunately, due to over-publicized reports of celebrities behaving badly and reality shows flaunting excess

HIGHLIGHTS

◖ **Old Westbury Gardens:** Resplendent as it is, the mansion isn't the main attraction at this estate. It's surrounded by the finest English gardens in the United States (page 135).

◖ **Sagamore Hill:** The former summer home of Theodore Roosevelt is packed with fascinating memorabilia (page 136).

◖ **Jones Beach:** Just 25 miles from midtown Manhattan is one of New York's most famous (and crowded) beaches, six miles of white sand lined with a wide, weathered boardwalk and Art Deco facilities (page 149).

◖ **Parrish Art Museum:** With the 2012 relocation of the Parrish to a new 34,000-square-foot building, the amount of exhibition space for this exceptional modern and contemporary art collection tripled (page 160).

◖ **Sag Harbor:** The lively old port holds a fascinating whaling museum, 19th-century sea captains' homes, and a wharf with great views of a busy harbor (page 164).

◖ **Montauk Lighthouse:** Commissioned by George Washington in 1792, this beacon stands sentinel on a lonely bluff at Long Island's easternmost tip (page 170).

LOOK FOR ◖ TO FIND RECOMMENDED SIGHTS, ACTIVITIES, DINING, AND LODGING.

over substance, the region's pristine nature preserves, charming fishing towns, and some of the finest white-sand beaches on the East Coast are all but forgotten.

The most spectacular shores are along the southern coast, where white sands and dunes stretch out for an incredible, all-but-unbroken 123 miles. Most beaches along the northern coast front the gentle waters of Long Island Sound, and are small and pebbly. Sailors satisfy their lust for wind, birders and anglers connect with the quiet, natural side of the island, and surfers ply the waves.

Beaches aside, both shores and forks have much to offer. The North Shore is home to many of Long Island's museums, as well as private mansions and nature preserves. South Fork, a magnet for the jetset, boasts the fashionable Hamptons, interesting historic sites, and a glittering social scene where people-watching abounds. More rural North Fork holds yet more historic sites, picturesque harbors and bays, orchards, organic farms, and a flourishing wine industry. Both the North and South Forks, with their historic villages and windswept shores, are astonishingly beautiful and remind visitors of a fact that's curiously easy to forget: This really is an island, with an idiosyncratic culture very different from that of the mainland.

PLANNING YOUR TIME

Each of Long Island's four sections—North Shore, North Fork, South Shore, and South Fork—can easily be explored in a day or two, depending on how many stops are made. Alternately, they can be combined into one long loop that begins and ends in New York City. If you do make the 120-mile trip from New York City to either busy **South Fork** or quieter **North Fork,** you'll want to spend at least two nights on the island. A five-day trip ensures enough time to explore both forks and make stops at the North Shore's **Oyster Bay** and **Cold Spring Harbor** on the way back. Oyster Bay and Cold Spring Harbor make for good day trips from New York City, as do **Jones Beach, Fire Island, Northport,** and **Port Jefferson.**

The North Shore

The farther east you travel along the North Shore, the more rural the landscape becomes. Traffic thins out considerably around Oyster Bay, and by the time you reach Centerport—located less than 20 miles from the Queens-Nassau border—you'll feel like you've left the city far behind.

Route 25A, also known as Northern Boulevard (and, in Nassau County, as North Hempstead Turnpike), is the northernmost major route that traverses Long Island. It's the best option for unhurried exploring. Long Island Expressway (LIE), or I-495, runs parallel to Route 25A to the south. It is the quicker route (except during rush hour) and therefore good to use when driving directly to a specific site.

GREAT NECK AND PORT WASHINGTON PENINSULAS

Heading into Long Island, you'll immediately cut across the bases of two large peninsulas: Great Neck and Port Washington. F. Scott

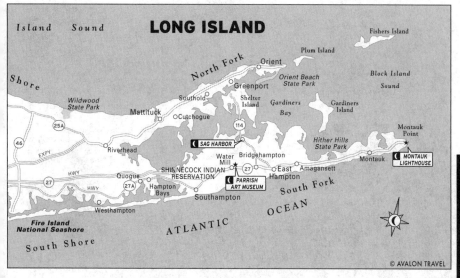

© AVALON TRAVEL

Fitzgerald and his wife Zelda once lived at 6 Gateway Drive, Great Neck, and it was on these two thick thumbs of land that he modeled his West and East Eggs of *The Great Gatsby.*

Many opulent estates such as the ones Fitzgerald describes are still scattered along the **Gold Coast,** which stretches 30 miles between Great Neck and Eatons Neck. Most were built in the early 20th century by captains of industry and commerce, including J. P. Morgan, F. W. Woolworth, and Louis Tiffany. At one time, there were some 600-700 mansions here, but only about 200 remain. About half are privately owned; most of the others have been converted into schools, religious retreats, and country clubs. Only a handful of the mansions are open to the public.

Mansions aren't the only attractions here, though; there are a number of historical, cultural, and natural sights worth slowing down for on the peninsulas. The towns of Port Washington and Roslyn are particularly dense with activities for visitors to enjoy.

American Merchant Marine Museum

American Merchant Marine Museum (300 Steamboat Rd., 516/726-6047, www.usmma. edu, Tues.-Fri. 10am-3pm, free), on the campus of the U.S. Merchant Marine Academy, showcases such odd treasures as models of well-known passenger liners and a life-size model of a cargo ship, used to train students during World War II. The academy's grounds offer good views of Throgs Neck Bridge, City Island, and the Bronx.

Sands Point Preserve

Just beyond Port Washington at the tip of the peninsula is 216-acre **Sands Point Preserve** (127 Middle Neck Rd., 516/571-7900, www. sandspointpreserve.org, daily 9am-4:30pm, $2 per person or $10 per car), filled with woods, shoreline, nature trails, ball fields, and several castle-like buildings. One of these, **Castlegould,** houses a visitors' center and natural history museum.

Sands Point was originally developed by railroad heir Howard Gould, and later purchased by the Guggenheims. Between the two families, they built three mansions: the immense Tudor-style **Hempstead House,** the much smaller **Mille Fleures,** and the Norman-style chateau, **Falaise** (guided

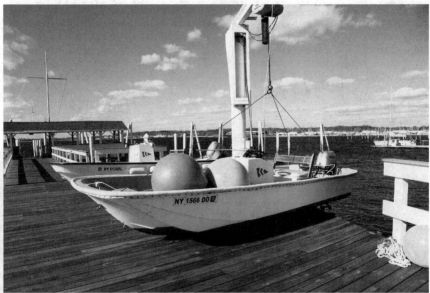

© FRANCISCO COLLAZO

dockside along Manhasset Bay

tours of Falaise offered on the hour, June-Oct. Thurs.-Sun. noon-3pm, adults $10, children under 10 not admitted). At Falaise, perched on a cliff overlooking the Sound, you'll find Guggenheim's purple Cadillac, parked next to the station wagon that once belonged to his good friend Charles Lindbergh.

Nassau County Museum of Art

Nassau County Museum of Art (Museum Dr., off Rte 25A/Northern Blvd., 516/484-9337, www.nassaumuseum.com, Tues.-Sun. 11am-5pm, adults $10, seniors $8, students and children over 4 $4; admission to grounds free) is at the northern end of the town of Roslyn. Occupying the 145-acre former Frick estate, the museum grounds boast about 30 outdoor sculptures by the likes of Roy Lichtenstein and Richard Serra, as well as formal gardens. Inside are first-rate temporary exhibits. An adjacent annex holds 100 miniature rooms depicting living environments from the 18th century to the present.

Accommodations and Food

Plush, elegant **⟨ Roslyn Hotel** (1221 Old Northern Blvd., 516/625-2700, www.theroslynhotel.com, $215-290) offers 77 well-appointed guest rooms decorated in deep roses and greens. Breakfast, Internet access, and parking are all complimentary.

There are a couple of notable places to eat in Roslyn. **Hendrick's Tavern** (1305 Old Northern Blvd., 516/621-1200, $30, Mon.-Thurs. 5pm-11pm, Fri.-Sat. 5pm-midnight, Sun. 5pm-10pm), located in a historic building where George Washington once ate breakfast, offers a menu heavy on steak and seafood dishes. On the other end of the cuisine and budget spectrum is plain and simple local favorite **Chicken Kebab** (92 Mineola Ave., 516/621-6828, www.chickenkebab.com, lunch and dinner, $9), serving Greek and Middle Eastern specialties.

For a town its size, Port Washington has a surprising number of restaurants. One popular spot is **Louie's Oyster Bar & Grill** (395 Main St., 516/883-4242, www.

louiesoysterbarandgrille.com, Mon.-Thurs. 11:30am-10pm, Fri.-Sat. 11:30am-11pm, Sun. 11:30am-3:30pm, $24), a local institution offering classic seafood dishes and great views of Manhasset Bay. **Chez Noelle** (34 Willowdale Ave., 516/883-3191, Tues.-Sun. 5pm-11:30pm, $26-30) is an upscale French restaurant serving both classic and modern dishes that draw raves from locals.

◖ OLD WESTBURY GARDENS

One of Long Island's most sumptuous mansions, now known as **Old Westbury** (71 Old Westbury Rd., 516/333-0048, www.old-westburygardens.org, May-Oct. Wed.-Mon. 10am-5pm, no admission after 4pm, adults $10, seniors $8, children 7-17 $5), is just a few miles beyond Roslyn, near the Long Island Expressway. Built in 1906 in a palatial Charles II style, this grand edifice was once home to John S. Phipps and his wife Margarita Grace, heirs to steel and shipping fortunes.

The mansion is magnificently furnished with 18th-century antiques, but it's the 88 acres of formal gardens out front and back that draw crowds. Considered to be the finest English gardens in the United States, Old Westbury's grounds are filled with tree-lined walks, grand allées, ponds, statuary, architectural "follies," and hundreds of species of plants, including historic varieties and new hybrids.

OYSTER BAY

In the mid-1700s, both the English and Dutch inhabited picturesque Oyster Bay, which accounts for the fact that the place has two main streets just a block apart. East Main Street was once controlled by the Dutch, West Main Street by the English. Named for Oyster Bay's most prominent resident, Theodore Roosevelt Memorial Park is a charming little downtown park along the water on Long Island Sound.

The towns of Oyster Bay, Cold Spring Harbor, and Old Bethpage can be combined into one nice day trip from New York City.

© AVALON TRAVEL

Start at Sagamore Hill in Oyster Bay, stop for lunch in Cold Spring Harbor, and move on to the Whaling Museum or Old Bethpage Village to round out the day. To reach Oyster Bay from Route 25A, head north on Route 106.

C Sagamore Hill

Sagamore Hill National Historic Site (20 Sagamore Rd., 516/922-4788, www.nps.gov/sahi, grounds daily dawn-dusk, staffed buildings Wed.-Sun. 9am-5pm, adults $5, children under 16 free) is the rambling hilltop estate that was once the summer home of Theodore Roosevelt. It sits on the outskirts of Oyster Bay. The former U.S. president, assistant secretary of the Navy, governor of New York State, police chief of New York City, and author of 30-odd books came here with his wife and six children to indulge in the "strenuous life": hiking, swimming, playing tennis, and horseback riding. Roosevelt never forgot his public duties while living here, however; out front is a wide porch with its railing removed so he could more easily address crowds who often assembled to hear him speak.

Sagamore is operated by the National Park Service, which has undertaken a massive restoration of the house that is expected to last into 2015. The grounds, visitors' center, and museum remain open to the public during this time.

Theodore Roosevelt Sanctuary and Audubon Center

Across the street from Sagamore Hill, 13-acre **Theodore Roosevelt Sanctuary and Audubon Center** (134 Cove Rd., 516/922-3200, www.ny.audubon.org, daily 9am-4pm, free) was established in 1923 as the first Audubon Songbird Sanctuary in the United States. The trees, shrubs, and vines planted on the grounds have been chosen to attract birds. A small **visitors' center** (Mon.-Fri. 9am-4pm, Sat. noon-4pm) features exhibits on the area's wildlife and Roosevelt's extensive involvement in the conservation movement. Visitors are also welcome to walk the sanctuary's trails.

Raynham Hall

Among Oyster Bay's notable historic homes-turned-museums is **Raynham Hall** (20 W. Main St., 516/922-6808, www.raynham-hallmuseum.org, Tues.-Sun. 1pm-5pm, adults $5, students and seniors $3, children under 6 free), once the home of prosperous Revolutionary War-era merchant Samuel Townsend. Townsend was a suspected Tory, but his son was George Washington's chief spy in New York City. When the war broke out, Raynham Hall was confiscated by the British, though Townsend's daughter Sally remained in the house. There, she overheard the British discussing Benedict Arnold's planned betrayal of West Point and conveyed that information to colonists.

Planting Fields Arboretum

Planting Fields Arboretum State Historic Park (1395 Planting Fields Rd., 516/922-9200, www.plantingfields.org, daily 9am-5pm, $8 per car), west of Oyster Bay, is a lush affair on the former estate of insurance executive William Robertson Coe. Some 160 acres of the property's 409 acres are planted with ornamental trees and shrubs, while about 200 other acres are preserved in their natural state.

At the heart of Planting Fields is **Coe Hall** (1395 Planting Fields Rd., 516/922-9200, www.plantingfields.org, Apr.-Sept. daily noon-3:30pm, adults $5, seniors $3.50, children 7-12 $1), a Tudor Revival stone mansion. The 1918 house is furnished with European antiques to give it the feel of an old English country manor.

Accommodations and Food

For overnight stays **East Norwich Inn** (6321 Northern Blvd., 516/922-1500, www.eastnor-wichinn.com, $125-150) is a pleasant, upscale motel offering comfortable rooms with double beds. Wi-Fi and continental breakfast are included in the room rate.

For dining in downtown Oyster Bay, there's **Wild Honey** (1 E. Main St., 516/922-4690, www.wildhoneyrestaurant.com, Tues.-Fri. 11:30am-2:45pm and 5pm-close, Sat.-Mon.

5pm-close, $24), which serves creative American food in a beautiful historic building that formerly served as Teddy Roosevelt's executive office.

Canterbury Ales Oyster Bar & Grill (46 Audrey Ave., 516/922-3614, www.canterburyalesrestaurant.com, $22) specializes in the Bay's namesake oysters. Various fish entrées, lobster, and pasta are also on the menu.

COLD SPRING HARBOR

During the mid-1800s, Cold Spring Harbor was a busy whaling port. Its main street, now Route 25A, was once called Bedlam Street for the cacophony of foreign languages heard there during whaling's heyday. The village's taverns were full of exotic objects sailors brought back from all ends of the earth. On the village's outskirts was Bungtown, a small settlement where barrels for whale oil were made.

Today, the boats bobbing in the harbor and the town's Whaling Museum recall the port's rich, adventurous past. The small, tourist-oriented village also offers shops, galleries, historic buildings, and a few other museums.

The Whaling Museum

The Whaling Museum (301 Main St., 631/367-3418, www.cshwhalingmuseum.org, Memorial Day-Labor Day daily 11am-5pm, winter Tues.-Sun. 11am-5pm, adults $6, seniors and children 4-18 $5) is a small, friendly institution founded in 1936. Exhibits in the trim, whitewashed building include a large collection of scrimshaw, a fully rigged whale boat from the 19th-century, huge iron cauldrons used to process whale blubber, thousands of journals and letters, and a great collection of historical photographs.

The museum also highlights the role that race played in whaling, explaining that whaling was the first racially integrated American industry. As early as the 1810s and 1820s, white and black seamen, captains, shipbuilders, and ship owners were working alongside each other. One boat, the *Industry,* out of Nantucket, Massachusetts, was captained and crewed entirely by African Americans.

SPLIA Gallery

The small but excellent **Society for the Preservation of Long Island Antiquities Gallery** (161 Main St., 631/692-4664, www.splia.org, hours vary seasonally) features changing exhibits tracing the island's social and cultural history. SPLIA was founded in 1948 in response to post-war changes in Long Island, namely suburbanization. The organization advocates historic preservation and strives to inform the public about Long Island's storied past through exhibits and events.

Cold Spring Harbor Fish Hatchery and Aquarium

Cold Spring Harbor Fish Hatchery and Aquarium (1660 Rte. 25A, 516/692-6768, www.cshfha.org, daily 10am-5pm, adults $6, seniors and children 3-12 $4), established in 1883, is just a few miles south of the village center. Until the early 1970s, this small plant produced about 100,000 brook trout a year, which were shipped upstate to stock the waters of the Adirondacks and the Catskills.

The hatchery suspended such mammoth operations in 1979, following the construction of larger facilities upstate, but it still operates as an educational institution. A half-dozen pools teem with hundreds of thousands of growing trout, all swimming together in one direction at one moment, switching to another the next. You'll also see a hatch house where eggs are incubated; a warm-water pond stocked with bass, bowfin, catfish, carp, bluegill, and the like; a turtle pond; and aquariums holding about 30 species of freshwater fish native to New York State.

Food

Grasso's (134 Main St., 631/367-6060, www.grassosrestaurant.com, Mon.-Sat. noon-3:30pm and 4pm-10pm, Sun. 11:30am-2:30pm and 3pm-9pm, $25-30) is a popular spot where live jazz accompanies upscale New American and Italian dishes. **Honu Kitchen and Cocktails** (363 New York Ave., 631/421-6900, www.honukitchen.com, Tues.-Thurs. 5pm-10pm, Fri.-Sat. 5pm-midnight, Sun. 4pm-9pm, $28)

LONG ISLAND

WALT WHITMAN: BIRTH OF AN AMERICAN POET

A few miles south of Huntington proper stands a farmhouse that's now preserved as the **Walt Whitman Birthplace State Historic Site** (246 Old Walt Whitman Rd., South Huntington, 631/427-5240, www.waltwhitman.org, June 15-Labor Day Mon.-Fri. 11am-4pm and Sat.-Sun. noon-5pm, winter Wed.-Fri. 1pm-4pm and Sat.-Sun. 11am-4pm, adults $6, seniors $5, students $4, children 6-12 $1). For all the congestion surrounding it, the Walt Whitman House sits in serene isolation behind a tall hedge.

Stepping into its snug, sunny hall is like stepping into a well-crafted poem. Whitman's father built this house, and everything in it is meticulously designed and constructed, from hand-hewn beams held together with wooden pegs to innovative storage closets built into the fireplace walls.

Whitman only lived here until he was five, when his family moved to Brooklyn. But he came back to Long Island as a young man to teach school, and the museum does a good job of chronicling his entire life. A short movie covers the highlights of his career, while upstairs and in an interpretive center next door are exhibit rooms filled with his papers, early editions of *Leaves of Grass*, and his schoolmaster's desk.

Other sites connected with Walt Whitman are located throughout the West Hills region. Some are buildings, while others are hills or hollows through which the poet liked to meander on his frequent trips back to the village of his birth. Ask at the Walt Whitman Birthplace for a copy of the booklet and trail map outlining these sites.

claims to have Long Island's longest bar. It also serves seasonal, contemporary American fare with plenty of surf and turf options.

OLD BETHPAGE VILLAGE RESTORATION

About 10 miles south of Cold Spring Harbor is **Old Bethpage Village** (1303 Round Swamp Rd., 516/572-8400, Wed.-Fri. 10am-4pm, Sat.-Sun. 10am-5pm, adults $10, seniors and children 5-12 $7), a restored 19th-century village filled with craftspeople and interpreters in period dress. A blacksmith shop, general store, hat shop, tavern, working farm, and about 45 other pre-Civil War buildings, most moved here from other locations on the island, are spread out over the village's 209 acres.

Thematic programming is offered throughout the year. In May, you'll spot Union soldiers training in the fields. Come in August for baseball games played according to 1860 rules. In December, you'll witness a 19th-century Christmas.

Camping is available nearby at 64-site **Battle Row Campground** (1 Claremont Rd., 516/572-8690), which also has a recreation center on site.

Accommodations and Food

Large, full-service **Melville Marriott** (1350 Walt Whitman Rd., Melville, 631/423-1600, www.marriott.com, $169-289) has 357 rooms and an indoor pool, fitness center, business center, and restaurant.

For Greek food or fresh fish, try bustling **Mediterranean Snack Bar** (360 New York Ave., Huntington, 631/423-8982, www.medsnackbar.com, Sun.-Thurs. 11am-10pm, Fri.-Sat. 11am-11pm, $17), where everything from souvlaki to soft-shell crab is served with Greek salad. If you're in the mood for Italian, **Jonathan's Ristorante** (15 Wall St., Huntington, 631/549-0055, www.jonathansristorante.com, Mon.-Thurs. noon-3pm and 5pm-10pm, Fri.-Sat. noon-3pm and 5pm-10:30pm, Sun. 4pm-9pm, $25) is a bistro serving eclectic Italian fare, including a wide range of pastas.

SUNKEN MEADOW STATE PARK

The main attraction at popular, 1,266-acre **Sunken Meadow State Park** (Rte. 25A and Sunken Meadow Pkwy., near Kings Park,

631/269-4333, www.nysparks.com/parks/37, daily dawn-dusk, $8-10 parking) is a mile-long beach, often packed in summer with thousands of sun worshippers tanning, swimming, napping, and playing. Three golf courses, lots of hiking trails, a salt marsh, and a small natural history museum are also within the park. Visitors can also enjoy the **Long Island Greenbelt Trail** (631/360-0753, www.li-greenbelt.org), which runs the 32-mile width of Long Island from Heckscher State Park to Sunken Meadow.

ST. JAMES

Continuing east on Route 25A, through large, traffic-clogged Smithtown, you'll soon come to tiny St. James. The town's biggest claim to fame is the **St. James General Store** (516 Moriches Rd., 631/854-3740, daily 10am-5pm), listed with the National Register of Historic Places. Used continuously since 1857, the creaky store is a hodgepodge affair stuffed to bursting with old-fashioned candy, scented soaps, historic postcards, and the like. A wooden cigar-store Indian presides out front.

STONY BROOK

Built on a hill sloping down to the water is the restored 18th-century village of Stony Brook. Just outside town is Stony Brook University, part of the State University of New York

(SUNY) system, which adds to the vitality of the village.

Although it's a popular tourist destination, complete with shopping malls and an ultra-clean feel, Stony Brook has managed to retain its rural character. Much of Stony Brook's charm is due to a man named Ward Melville, owner of the Thom McAn shoe company. Back in the 1940s, Melville—concerned about encroaching suburbia—had the village rebuilt along historical lines while successfully fighting for strict zoning codes. He paid for much of the rebuilding himself.

Along Main Street are the **harbor** and **village center** (www.stonybrookvillage.com), where well-marked signs point the way to shops and historic sites. To one side is an old **U.S. post office** (129 Main St.), equipped with a mechanical eagle that flaps its wings every hour on the hour. To the other side is **Three Village Inn** (150 Main St., 631/751-0555, www.lessings.com), built in 1751.

Beyond the post office is **All Souls' Episcopal Church,** designed by architect Stanford White and built in 1889. Pitched on the steep slope of a small hill, the tiny church, complete with zigzagging steps and a narrow steeple, has a fairy-tale quality, as if it were built for elves.

Continue walking a few blocks past the church to wide, dark Mill Pond and the

LONG ISLAND

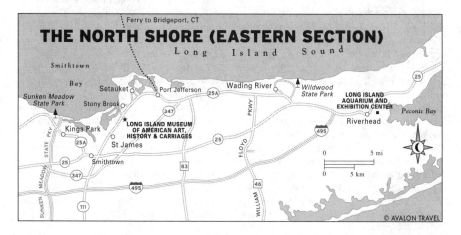

THE NORTH SHORE (EASTERN SECTION)

Ferry to Bridgeport, CT

Long Island Sound

Smithtown

Bay

Sunken Meadow State Park

Setauket   Port Jefferson   25A   Wading River   Wildwood State Park   25

Stony Brook   LONG ISLAND AQUARIUM AND EXHIBITION CENTER   Peconic Bay

347   Riverhead

Kings Park   ★ LONG ISLAND MUSEUM OF AMERICAN ART, HISTORY & CARRIAGES   495

25A   St James   25   495

25   Smithtown   83   FLOYD PKWY

347   46

495   0   5 mi

111   0   5 km

WILLIAM

SUNKEN MEADOW STATE PKWY

© AVALON TRAVEL

gray-shingled **Stony Brook Grist Mill** (100 Harbor Rd., 631/751-2244, Apr.-Nov. Sat.-Sun. noon-4pm, adults $2, children $1). Built in 1751, the restored mill still grinds corn.

Long Island Museum of American Art, History and Carriages

This nine-acre complex of the **Long Island Museum of American Art, History and Carriages** (1200 Rte. 25A, 631/751-0066, www.longislandmuseum.org, Thurs.-Sat. 10am-5pm, Sun. noon-5pm, adults $9, seniors $7, children 6-17 $4) on the outskirts of town focuses on American history and art. Foremost among its buildings is renowned Carriage House, which contains about 90 horse-drawn vehicles, ranging from hand-painted coaches and fire-fighting equipment to elaborate sleighs and a rare Roma wagon. Roma wagons seldom survive because of the culture's custom of burying all of a person's possessions—even wagons—after his or her death.

The art museum holds both changing exhibits and a large collection of works by William Sidney Mount, a 19th-century African American painter from Stony Brook who depicted rural Long Island life. The Bayman's Art Gallery features hand-carved antique decoys and 15 miniature period rooms. Also on site are a blacksmith's shop, barn, one-room schoolhouse, and other 19th-century buildings.

Accommodations and Food

Built in 1751 and once the home of Captain Jonas Smith, Long Island's first millionaire, **(Three Village Inn** (150 Main St., 631/751-0555, www.lessings.com, $129-399) is now a lovely inn with 21 rooms and a full-service restaurant. The rambling white house features period antiques, fireplaces, ceiling beams, and plenty of Colonial atmosphere in a setting overlooking the water. Some rooms are housed in the historic, white-clapboard main building; others are in an attractive modern wing. The adjoining **Restaurant Mirabelle** (150 Main St., 631/751-0555, $34) specializes in New American cuisine; in addition to à la carte options, a nine-course tasting menu is available.

Mirabelle Tavern is the other on-site restaurant; as its name suggests, tavern favorites, like fish and chips and burgers, are its menu staples.

A good choice for families is **Brook House** (123 Main St., 631/751-4617, Sun.-Thurs. 9am-8:30pm, Fri.-Sat. 9am-9pm, sandwiches $6-8, entrées $13-15), serving everything from burgers and sandwiches to dinner entrées such as steak and chicken. Kids will especially appreciate Brook House's ice cream parlor, which features 36 flavors.

PORT JEFFERSON

Located just beyond Stony Brook, Port Jefferson was once a thriving shipbuilding community and then home to several lace factories and gravel pits. Today, it's the main destination for visitors to the north shore, catering mostly to the tourist trade.

A number of historic homes are downtown. Most are privately owned, but **Mather House Museum** (115 Prospect St., 631/473-2665, www.portjeffhistorical.org, July-Aug. Tues.-Wed. and Sat.-Sun. 1pm-4pm, suggested donation $4), once owned by a shipbuilder, is open to the public. Inside, find an eclectic collection of 19th-century garments, Native American artifacts, and model boats. Out back are herb gardens, a marine barn, and a crafts house.

Downtown also offers several small tourist-oriented malls as well as some one-of-a-kind shops, including **Village Chairs & Wares** (402 Main St., 631/331-5791, Mon.-Sat. 11am-6pm, Sun. noon-6pm), which specializes in handmade chairs and tables inspired by Shaker and Farmhouse styles.

The **ferry** (631/473-0286) to Bridgeport, Connecticut, leaves from Port Jefferson's docks. For brochures and a map of the village, stop by **Port Jefferson Chamber of Commerce** (118 W. Broadway/Rte., 631/473-1414, www.portjeffchamber.com, year-round Mon.-Fri. 10am-4pm, June-Sept. Sat.-Sun. noon-4pm).

Accommodations and Food

Large and always bustling **(Danfords Hotel and Marina** (25 E. Broadway, 631/928-5200, www.danfords.com, $159-389) serves as a de

THE PINE BARRENS

Much of the eastern end of Long Island, from just east of Port Jefferson to Hampton Bays, is covered by a 100,000-acre pine-barren wilderness. Five times larger than Manhattan, the Pine Barrens sits over what is said to be the purest underground drinking-water supply on the island. In its scruffy wooded growth, dominated by pitch pine and scrub oak, are several rare plant and animal species, including unusual stands of dwarf pine.

For many years, the pine barrens were at the center of an intense environmental debate that pitted conservationists against builders and local government officials. In 1989, an environmental group, the Long Island Pine Barrens Society, sued Suffolk County for approving building projects in the wilderness area without studying the environmental impact. The New York State Court ruled no study was required but said the state needed to draw up a plan to protect the area. A Central Pine Barrens Joint Policy and Planning Commission was created, and, in 1994, they proposed establishing a 53,000-acre core area where building would be banned, surrounded by a 47,000-acre area open to controlled development.

The plan became law in July 1995 and is a major environmental victory. The Pine Barrens are now New York's third forest preserve, following the Adirondacks and the Catskills.

To access a five-mile trail that leads through the Pine Barrens, head south of the Riverhead Traffic Circle on Route 104 for about two miles and watch for signs. The trail should be avoided during hunting season, October-February. For more information, contact **The Long Island Pine Barrens Society** (547 E. Main St., Riverhead, 631/369-3300, www.pinebarrens.org), which has a downloadable trail guide on its website.

facto anchor for downtown Port Jefferson. Many rooms have balconies and views of the water; some have working fireplaces. The inn's upscale restaurant, **Wave Seafood Kitchen** (25 E. Broadway, 631/928-5200, www.danfords.com, $30), also overlooking the water, serves seafood and contemporary New American fare. During warm weather, guests can eat on the outside "Admiral's Deck."

Casual, laid-back **Village Way** (106 Main St., 631/928-3395, www.villagewayrestaurant.com, open daily, hours vary by season, $10-22) is a Port Jefferson institution. Seafood and pasta entrées, as well as sandwiches and burgers, are on the menu.

WILDWOOD STATE PARK

Continuing northeast from Fort Jefferson, past the small town of Wading River, you'll find **Wildwood State Park** (790 Hulse Landing Rd., 631/929-4314, www.nysparks.com/parks/68, daily dawn-dusk, $8-10 parking). Surrounded by farm country, Wildwood is blissfully empty during the off-season, but crowded during summer. Within its 600 acres are nearly 2 miles of beach, 12 miles of hiking trails, bathhouses, picnic areas, ball fields, refreshment stands, and a 314-site campground.

RIVERHEAD

Riverhead lies on the shore of Peconic Bay, right between the North and South Forks. The Suffolk County seat since 1727, Riverhead was once a thriving commercial center that benefited from the area's many farms. In more recent years, it suffered an economic downturn but is now experiencing something of a renaissance, thanks in part to popular Long Island Aquarium and Exhibition Center. Downtown Riverhead is also home to a number of lovely old brick buildings. Its revitalized waterfront is a good place for a summer stroll.

Long Island Aquarium and Exhibition Center

State-of-the-art **Long Island Aquarium** (431 E. Main St., 631/208-9200, www.longisland-aquarium.com, daily 10am-5pm, adults $22.50, seniors and children 3-12 $19.50) houses everything from native Long Island fishes to moray eels, Pacific octopuses, piranhas, stingrays, and seals. A large living coral reef is awhirl with colorful tropical fish, and an underwater cavern houses more than a dozen sharks. Visitors can also embark on a simulated submarine dive or take in a seal show.

Partner institution **Riverhead Foundation for Marine Research** (467 E. Main St., 631/369-9840, www.riverheadfoundation. org) maintains several exhibits on site. Among them are a rescue center for rehabilitating injured seals, sea turtles, and other marine life, and a touch-tank where children can handle starfish, crabs, snails, and small fish. Riverhead Foundation also offers seal-watching cruises

that depart from Point Lookout on the South Shore and naturalist cruises down the Peconic River.

Suffolk County Historical Society

At the other end of Riverhead's Main Street is **Suffolk County Historical Society** (300 W. Main St., 631/727-2881, www.suffolkcounty-historicalsociety.org, Wed.-Sat. 10am-4:30pm, adults $5, seniors $3, children 17 and under $1). This large, rambling museum filled with eclectic treasures is an excellent place in which to get a sense of Suffolk County's past. Browse the good-sized collections of Indian artifacts, Colonial furniture and ceramics, and other examples of early craftsmanship. There's also an excellent bookstore on-site.

The North Fork and Shelter Island

Like better-known South Fork across Great Peconic Bay, the North Fork was first settled in 1640 by colonists from New England. That heritage flavors everything from the look of its villages to the independent mindset of its people. Unlike the South Fork, the North Fork is still predominantly rural, with a correspondingly smaller number of "attractions." Expect fertile farms and rolling vineyards, as well as one-stoplight towns with white-steepled churches, colonial saltboxes, and village greens. For the moment, the North Fork still has the friendly, unpretentious feel of a small town.

The North Fork can be easily explored in a day, but the area is so achingly beautiful, especially near the windswept beaches of Orient Point, that it's worth lingering. Highlights include historic villages of Cutchogue, Southold, and Orient; the bustling harbor town of Greenport; and four-mile-long Orient Beach.

Accommodation options on the North Fork are limited to simple beachfront resort motels and B&Bs. Shelter Island has several historic inns. As in other shore areas, rates tend to be on the high side in season (Memorial Day-Labor Day) and reasonable the rest of the year.

Two- or three-night minimum stays are often required in summer, especially on weekends.

Two major roads traverse the North Fork. Route 25 to the south is the more popular route and can get congested on summer weekends. Sound Avenue/Route 48 to the north is a good alternative.

SOUND AVENUE

Heading east onto the North Fork via the northern route of Sound Avenue (which turns into Route 48), you'll soon come to **Briermere Farms** (4414 Sound Ave., 631/722-3931, www. briermere.com). Known for its homemade pies, Briermere features about 15 different varieties on any given day, ranging from standards like blueberry and peach to blends like blackberry-apple and strawberry-rhubarb.

Near the intersection of Sound Avenue and Herricks Lane is **Hallockville Museum Farm and Folklife Center** (6038 Sound Ave., 631/298-5292, www.hallockville.com, Mon.-Fri. 11am-4pm year-round; Sat.-Sun. 11am-4pm May-Dec. only, adults $7, seniors and children $5), a 102-acre farm that was owned by the Hallock family for over 200 years. Now

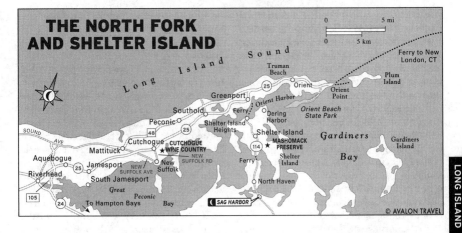

a museum listed on the National Register of Historic Places, Hallockville centers around a 1765 homestead, a large barn, a smokehouse, and a shoemaker's shop (where Capt. Zachariah Hallock made over 1,700 pairs of shoes between the years 1771 and 1820). The museum also stages frequent crafts demonstrations, festivals, and workshops.

CUTCHOGUE WINE COUNTRY

One of the prettiest North Fork hamlets, Cutchogue is filled with white churches, leafy trees, and weathered, shingled homes. The town is named after the Indian word for "principal place." **Historic wooden buildings** (Rte. 25, 631/734-7122, www.cutchoguenewsuffolkhistory.org, late June-early Sept. Sat.-Mon. 1pm-4pm, call for off-season hours, donations welcome), operated by Cutchogue-New Suffolk Historical Council, cluster around the village green.

The most interesting of the group is **Old House,** which dates to 1649. Dark and cozy inside, it's outfitted with all the luxuries of its day, including wood paneling, leaded glass windows, and a fluted chimney. The house was "lost" for close to 100 years, but was rediscovered in the 1930s by a WPA worker who noticed its unusual chimney.

Next to Old House are 1840 **Old Schoolhouse Museum** and **Wickham**

Farmhouse, equipped with furniture and farm implements from the early 1700s. Across the street is **Village Library,** housed in a lovely New England-style church. The church was built in 1862 because of a schism within its congregation. The Presbyterian minister was an ardent abolitionist who preached against slavery week after week until the church elders got tired and threw him out. The minister then gathered his followers and built the new church.

Wine-Tasting

Cutchogue—along with Peconic, just down the road—is the center of Long Island's wine-producing country. In general, wineries are open for tastings daily 11am-5pm; but during the off-season, it's best to call in advance. Tours can usually be arranged by appointment.

Before you even reach Cutchogue, you'll pass the sign "Entering Wine Country," and almost immediately you'll spy **Palmer Vineyards** (5120 Sound Ave., 631/722-9463, www.palmervineyards.com). One of Long Island's largest vineyards, it attracts hundreds of visitors on a summer's day. Palmer offers self-guided tours, a tasting room that looks like an English pub, and an outdoor deck overlooking its vineyards.

Off Route 25 east of Cutchogue are **Bedell Cellars** (36225 Main Rd., 631/734-7537, www.bedellcellars.com), a small but highly regarded winery that has won a number of awards, and **Pugliese Vineyards** (Main Rd., 631/734-4057, www.pugliesevineyards.com), which features a lovely collection of hand-painted bottles containing a chardonnay, blanc de blanc sparkling wine, cabernet sauvignon, and merlot, among other varietals.

Along Route 25 closer to Peconic is 500-acre **Pindar Vineyards** (37645 Main Rd., 631/734-6200, www.pindar.net), the largest vineyard on the island. Over 20 different wines are produced here annually, and tours run continuously throughout the day. Also popular is nearby **Lenz Winery** (Main Rd., 631/734-6010, www.lenzwine.com), a 70-acre vineyard with a striking modern main building.

To the north, along Route 48 in Cutchogue, are **Castello di Borghese-Hargrave Vineyard** (Sound Ave. and Alvah's Ln., 631/734-5111, www.castellodiborghese.com), the oldest vineyard on the island, founded in 1973, and **Vineyard 48** (18910 Middle Rd./Rte. 48, 631/734-5200, www.vineyard48winery.com).

Food

Not quite as old as the historic buildings in town, vintage, chrome-laden **Cutchogue Diner** (Main Rd./Rte. 25, 631/734-7016, www.cutchoguediner.com, $13) near the village green dates to the 1920s. The diner's pancakes and meatloaf are especially good. Also nearby is **Braun Seafood Co.** (Main Rd./Rte. 25, 631/734-6700, www.braunseafood.com), where you can purchase clam pies, an East End specialty (these can't be eaten on the spot; they must be cooked).

SOUTHOLD AND VICINITY

Settled in 1640, Southold is one of the oldest communities of European origin in New York State. The earliest white settlers to arrive here came from New Haven, Connecticut, starting up the industries of farming and whaling. Though the latter is no longer practiced, farming remains an important activity. You'll see plenty of roadside stands tempting you with fresh-from-the-garden fare. Some of the prettiest hamlets

on Long Island, including Greenport and Orient, are part of Southold.

Sights

Standing testimony to the town's long history is a **museum complex** (54325 Main Rd., 631/765-5500, www.southoldhistoricalsociety.org, July-Labor Day Wed. and Sat.-Sun. 1pm-4pm, suggested donation $2) conveniently located in the middle of low-key downtown. Among many historic buildings here are the weathered 1750 **Thomas Moore House**, lavishly furnished Victorian **Currie-Bell House**, and lovely, hand-hewn **Pine Neck Barn**. Also on the museum grounds are a working blacksmith shop, a buttery, and a millinery filled with an assortment of 19th- and early 20th-century hats. A map and more information about the museum complex can be picked up at 19th-century **Prince Building**, where Southold Historical Society is headquartered. Also in the building is the **Museum Shop** (Mon.-Fri. 9:30am-2:30pm), selling books and handcrafts.

Run by the Long Island chapter of the New York State Archaeological Association, the **Southold Indian Museum** (1080 Main Bayview Rd., 631/765-5577, www.southoldindianmuseum.org, Sun. 1:30pm-4:30pm year-round, Sat. 1:30pm-4:30pm June-Aug. only, adults $2, children $0.50) houses an extensive array of Algonquin artifacts. Here you'll find the country's largest collection of Algonquin pottery (from 3000 BC to colonial times).

Just north of downtown Southold is the striking **Horton Point Lighthouse** (off Lighthouse Rd., 631/765-5500 or 631/765-2101, June-Oct. Sat.-Sun. 11:30am-4pm, adults $3, children free), which stands high on a bluff at the end of Lighthouse Road. The first lighthouse on this site was commissioned by George Washington in 1790. The current lighthouse was built in 1857 and is still operational. Painted in stark white and surrounded by rhododendrons, the building overlooks a lonely stretch of beach. Lighthouse tours take visitors through the keeper's quarters and the working light tower. Downstairs is a small museum

THE ALGONQUINS

Thirteen Algonquin Indian tribes—including the Canarsees, Rockaways, Merricks, Massapeaques, Shinnecocks, Montauks, and Setaukets—occupied Long Island before the arrival of the Europeans. Today, many of the island's villages, harbors, and bays are named for these early peoples.

Algonquins fished in coastal waters, harvested quahog clams (producing much of the wampum used by Northeastern Indians from the shells), and grew corn, pumpkin, melon, and tobacco. According to one settler's journal, "[The Algonquins] were a tall, proud, and handsome people with grace of walk, active of body, carried straight as arrows."

Montauk chief Wyandanch, the grand sachem of Long Island tribes, befriended white settlers who began arriving in the 1640s. Ninicraft, chief of the Narragansetts who lived across the Sound, tried to enlist Wyandanch's help in killing off the whites in 1652. When Wyandanch refused, Narragansetts opened war on Montauks and nearly destroyed them.

Within a century after the arrival of the Dutch and English, only about 400 Indians remained on Long Island. Most had died of diseases introduced by Europeans; those who survived were subject to innumerable indignities. In 1759, for example, Indians had to beg for the right to cut firewood.

Today, a small Algonquin community of about 700 Shinnecocks still lives on Shinnecock Reservation near Southampton. Each Labor Day weekend, they celebrate their heritage with a three-day powwow that attracts Native Americans from across the country.

filled with artifacts, paintings, and "treasures" from sunken ships.

Accommodations and Food

North Fork Table and Inn (57225 Main Rd., 631/765-0177, www.northforktableandinn.com, $275-300) offers lovely accommodations. The Table (average entrées $34) at the inn prepares seasonally inspired dishes featuring locally grown biodynamic and organic produce, fresh local seafood from Peconic Bay and Long Island Sound, North Fork artisanal cheese, and a well-thought-out wine list. Prix fixe and tasting menus are available for lunch and dinner. Check the website for special events, such as beer pairing meals or harvest celebrations.

GREENPORT

North Fork's principal commercial center is bustling Greenport, laid out in neat squares that slope down to the harbor. Greenport has been a boating community since before the Revolutionary War. In the 1700s, cargo ships from the West Indies docked here to unload molasses and rum. Later, the port became a center for whaling and the oyster trade. Even today, an estimated two-thirds of Greenport's population earns its living from boats and related industries. The harbor is always full of fishing boats and pleasure craft and the streets are lined with restaurants and shops, some tourist-oriented, some not.

Sights

Waterfront **Mitchell Park** (115 Front St., 631/477-2200, www.greenportvillage.com) is a great place to watch all the maritime activity. Children will enjoy a ride on the 1920s **Mitchell Park Carousel** (June-Sept. daily 10am-9pm, off-season weekends and holidays 10am-9pm, ride $2) or a peek inside the public access **camera obscura** (summer daily daylight hours, off-season weekends and holidays daylight hours).

East End Seaport Museum and Maritime Foundation (end of 3rd St., 631/477-2100, www.eastendseaport.org, June 30-Labor Day daily 1pm-5pm, Memorial Day-June 30 and Labor Day-Columbus Day Sat.-Sun. 1pm-5pm, Nov.-Apr. by appointment only, suggested donation $5) is loaded with artifacts from the fishing and boatbuilding industries. Changing exhibits focus on such subjects as women and the sea and yacht racing.

Railroad buffs will want to visit the **Railroad Museum of Long Island** (440 4th St., 631/477-0439, www.rmli.us, Sat.-Sun. 11am-4pm, adults $7, children 5-12 $4). The museum, housed in what was once a freight station, traces the history of railroading on the island. A highlight is the 20-foot model of the Greenport freight yard as it looked in 1955.

Accommodations and Camping

The main building at [C] **Townsend Manor Inn** (714 Main St., 631/477-2000, www.townsend-inn.com, $150-375 in summer, $90-200 off-season) is a historic 1835 Greek Revival house complete with restaurant, old-fashioned cocktail lounge, and cozy living room. Guest rooms are located in several modern additions, and a pool is nearby as well.

Popular 1950s-era **Silver Sands Motel** (Rte. 25 at Silvermere Rd., 631/477-0011, www.silversands-motel.com, $150 standard room, $1,400/week apartments, $2,500/week cottages) is set on a quarter-mile of private beach. It offers a variety of accommodations, ranging from motel rooms to apartments and beach cottages. Also a good choice, with a variety of accommodation options, is smaller **Sunset Motel** (62005 Rte. 48, 631/477-1776, www.sunset-greenport.com, $175-365 summer, $110-145 off-season). At [C] **Sound View Inn** (58855 North Rd./Rte. 48, 631/477-1910, www.sound-viewinn.com, $195-255 summer, $130-155 off-season), also on the beach, all rooms have balconies, and some have kitchenettes. Tennis courts and a pool are on the grounds. All three motels are closed in winter.

Camping is available at the 150-site **Eastern Long Island Kampgrounds** (690 Queen St., 631/477-0022, www.easternlikampground.com). On site are a camp store, laundry facility, and playground.

Food

[C] **Claudio's** (111 Main St., 631/477-0627, www.claudios.com, hours vary seasonally, $28), a huge, rambling seafood restaurant, dominates the harbor area. Established by a Portuguese sailor in 1870, Claudio's bills itself as the "oldest same family owned restaurant in the United States." Design details include heavy carved wood, stained glass, and an enormous bar brought to the restaurant by barge from a New York City hotel in 1885. The less expensive **Claudio's Clam Bar on the Wharf** (111 Main St., 631/477-1889, www.claudios.com, hours vary seasonally, $20) features live music on summer weekends. Near Claudio's, **Aldo's** (103-105 Front St., 631/477-6300, www.aldos.com, hours vary seasonally, $15) is a café and bakery serving strong espresso.

ORIENT

At the far, far end of the North Fork is Orient, a tiny historical town located on one of the most glorious spots on the island. On this narrow windswept piece of land, you'll find gentle beaches, osprey nests, and only a few buildings, including houses that still fit the description in the 1930s WPA guide: "The little weathered shingle houses, few more than one-and-a-half stories high, sit primly behind picket fences. In sun or storm the Atlantic winds roll in...."

To reach Orient proper, cross a narrow isthmus. To the left are crescent-shaped Truman Beach and Long Island Sound, to the right, Orient Harbor and Gardiners Bay.

The town centers around an old-fashioned post office and **Orient Country Store.** The former is still equipped with turn-of-the-century stamp windows, while the latter sells groceries, sandwiches, home-baked treats, and arts and crafts made by locals.

Sights

Oysterponds Historical Society (1555 Village Ln., 631/323-2480, www.oysterpondshistoricalsociety.org, July-Sept. Thurs. and Sat.-Sun. 2pm-5pm, free), at the end of Village Lane, is a group of six well-preserved historic buildings. **Webb House** is a pre-Revolutionary War inn, while **Village House** is a 19th-century home containing memorabilia from the 1800s, when Orient was a popular resort with two big hotels. Temporary exhibits are showcased in **Schoolhouse Building,** the only building open year-round.

If you continue down Village Lane to King Street and turn onto Narrow River Road, you'll come to an early **slave burial ground,** in a pretty spot overlooking the sea. Twenty slaves are buried here, along with Dr. Seth Tuthill and his wife Maria. "It was [the Tuthills'] wish that they be buried with their former slaves," reads a plaque near the cemetery.

Orient Point and Beach

A few miles beyond Orient, at the very tip of North Fork, is Orient Point, where ferries dock on their way to and from New London, Connecticut. Abutting the point is **Orient Beach State Park** (N. County Rd., off Rte. 25, 631/323-2440, www.nysparks.com/parks/106, daily dawn-dusk, $8-10 parking), one of the finest beaches on Long Island. Stretching west over a long finger of land, the 357-acre park features miles of white, ocean-washed sands. It's especially popular among bird-watchers and nature-lovers, who appreciate the park's rare maritime forest. Facilities include a bathhouse, refreshment stand, horseshoe court, and hiking trails.

SHELTER ISLAND

In the middle of the bay between the North and South Forks is Shelter Island, a quiet retreat of wooded hills, uncrowded beaches, and expensive vacation homes, some dating back to the Victorian era. The island's first European resident was Nathaniel Sylvester, one of four businessmen who bought the island in 1651. Thanks to Sylvester, the island subsequently became a haven for Quakers fleeing persecution in Massachusetts. Sylvester gave the Quakers shelter—hence the island's name—and allowed them to practice their religion here.

Shelter Island has an exclusive air about it, due partly to its moneyed population and partly to the fact that it can be reached only by ferry. The high cost of the very short ferry ride ($10 one-way) keeps out the hoi polloi.

Sights

For day visitors, Shelter Island is the sort of place that's fun to explore without any particular destination in mind. Many roads wander past sun-splashed meadows and bays, dark woods, and historic homes. Near the North Ferry dock is **Shelter Island Heights,** filled with steep streets and Victorian-era gingerbread cottages. Across the bay from the Heights is **Dering Harbor,** the smallest incorporated village in the state, boasting a number of impressive mansions along Shore Road. At just 2.1 square miles, the year-round population hovers in the double digits.

History buffs might also want to stop at **Havens House** (16 South Ferry Rd./Rte. 114, 631/749-0025, www.shelterislandhistory.org, Apr.-Oct. Wed.-Fri. 11am-3pm, Sat. 9am-3pm, Sun. 11am-3pm, donation), a 1743 home on the National Register of Historic Places. The five-room house, run by the Shelter Island Historical Society, is outfitted with period furnishings and features a nice collection of antique dolls and toys.

Mashomack Preserve

Shelter Island's major treasure is **Mashomack Preserve** (79 S. Ferry Rd., 631/749-1001, www.nature.org/mashomack, Mar.-Sept. daily except Tues. 9am-5pm, Oct.-Feb. daily except Tues. 9am-4pm, adults $2, children $1), operated by The Nature Conservancy. Occupying nearly a third of the island, the preserve spreads out over 2,039 acres of oak woodlands, marshes, freshwater ponds, tidal creeks, and 12 miles of shoreline. One of the East Coast's largest concentrations of nesting osprey is within its confines, along with everything from ibis and hummingbirds to harbor seals and terrapins. Nature trails and hikes 1.5-11 miles in length meander through the preserve. The entrance to the preserve is located about a mile from South Ferry dock.

Accommodations and Food

Built on bluffs overlooking Coecles Inlet is the 1929 ◖ **Ram's Head Inn** (Ram Island Dr., 631/749-0811, www.shelterislandinns.com/ramshead, $105-375 in summer, with breakfast, closed Nov.-Apr.), boasting its own private beach, small boats, tennis courts, restaurant, and wide porch with wicker furniture. Most of the 17 rooms are filled with lots of light and simple antiques. Lunch and dinner (average entrée $32) consist of seasonal, local ingredients served in a high-ceilinged room hung with paintings.

Friendly, turn-of-the-century **House on Chase Creek** (3 Locust Ave., 631/749-4379, www.chasecreek.com, $130-245 summer, $85-175 off-season) offers three comfortable guest rooms and a suite year-round. **The Dory** (185 Bridge St., 631/749-4300, www.thedoryshelter-island.com, daily 11:30am-close, $23), also in town, serves simple seafood dishes on an outdoor deck during the summer.

Getting There and Around

To reach Shelter Island from the North Fork, take **North Ferry** (631/749-0139, www.northferry.com), which leaves from Route 114 at the foot of 3rd Street in Greenport. From the South Fork, take **South Ferry** (631/749-1200, www.southferry.com), which leaves from Route 114 in North Haven, about three miles north of Sag Harbor. Both ferries operate every 10-15 minutes from about 6am to 1:45am during summer, and cost $14 one-way for a car and driver, plus $1 for each passenger. Less expensive round-trip tickets to and from Greenport or to and from North Haven are available but cannot be applied to a trip that combines the two ferry services.

The South Shore

The South Shore is unbearably congested near New York City. However, just off its coast, the cityscape recedes into a long line of barrier islands and white sands. Beaches, beaches, and more beaches stretch out for miles and miles against the pounding surf of the Atlantic. Nearest to the city are Lido Beach, Long Beach, and famed Jones Beach, followed by Fire Island and South Fork.

FREEPORT

Heading into Nassau County on Sunrise Highway (Route 27), you'll soon come to Freeport, a busy fishing and boating community that's the largest town on the South Shore. Freeport's most famous native son is Canadian-American violinist and band leader Guy Lombardo. A long avenue named in his honor runs through downtown.

Freeport's main visitor attraction is its "Nautical Mile," located along **Woodcleft Canal,** bordered by a street of the same name. Much of Freeport was built on landfill, and Woodcleft is one of several canals in town. Along it, you'll find lots of shops, many selling arts and crafts, a plethora of seafood restaurants, and fishing boats sporting signs

advertising "Halfday Flounder." On summer evenings, music beckons from outdoor bars while party boats set sail for dinner and moonlight cruises.

For more information on Freeport, contact the **Freeport Chamber of Commerce** (46 N. Ocean Ave., 516/377-2200, www.freeportny.com). For more information on sport-fishing, call **Freeport Boatmen's Association** (540 Guy Lombardo Ave., 516/378-4838, www.freeportboatmens.com).

Cruises

In the fall, **Riverhead Foundation for Marine Research** (631/369-9840, www.riverheadfoundation.org), offers seal-watching cruises (adults $26, seniors and children 3-12 $22) that leave from Point Lookout, south of Freeport near Jones and Lido Beaches. Check the website for cruise schedules; reservations are required.

Accommodations and Food

The Freeport Inn and Marina (445 S. Main St., 516/623-9100, www.freeportinnandmarina.com, $125-325), just north of Jones Beach, is a recently renovated property popular with boaters and landlubbers alike.

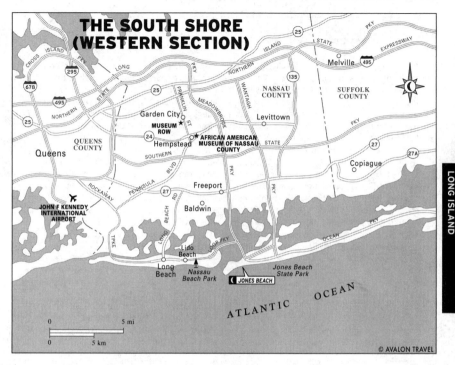

THE SOUTH SHORE
(WESTERN SECTION)

One of the best restaurants along Nautical Mile is **Hudsons on the Mile** (340 Woodcleft Ave., 516/442-5569, www.hudsonsonthemile. net, $27), serving seafood, sushi, and steak. Clientele here tend to be young and trendy. In summer, bands play on a crowded outdoor deck.

◖ JONES BEACH

Just 25 miles from midtown Manhattan, **Jones Beach** (1 Ocean Pkwy., Wantagh, 516/785-1600, www.nysparks.com/parks/10, daily dawn-dusk, free, parking $8-10) is Long Island's most famous and most accessible stretch of sand. Although its 6.5 miles are packed cheek-to-jowl on a hot summer's day, the beach is so magnificent that it still manages to impress. And talk about good people-watching!

City Parks Commissioner Robert Moses, who shaped much of the modern landscape of

New York, approached Jones Beach with the goal of transforming a sandbar off a windswept reef into the finest public beach in America. He largely succeeded, in an engineering feat that took two years to complete. Finished in 1929, the beach boasts an enormous number of well-worn but first-class facilities, including two lovely Art Deco bathhouses, wading and Olympic-size pools, ball fields, pitch-and-putt golf, shuffleboard courts, basketball courts, picnic areas, refreshment stands, a restaurant, a wide, weathered boardwalk, and a 200-foot-high water tower shaped like an obelisk. **Nikon at Jones Beach Theater** (Jones Beach, Wantagh, 516/221-1000, www.jonesbeach.com), which presents big-name acts in summer, is also here.

Jones Beach is open year-round, but lifeguards are only on duty Memorial Day-Labor Day. To reach Jones Beach, take the Wantagh State or Meadowbrook State Parkways south

BAY HOUSES

If you pay close attention while driving along the Wantagh, Meadowbrook, or Loop Parkways linking Jones Beach and Point Lookout to the mainland, you'll spot small cottages perched on platforms and surrounded by marshland and water. At one time, there were hundreds of such bay houses, as they are called, in the Town of Hempstead. Now there are only about 15; 20 were destroyed by Hurricane Sandy in 2012.

The building of the bay houses began in the early 1700s when the island's farmers, needing hay for their cattle, hired baymen to row out to remote marshlands and bring back hay for their animals. The journey often took several hours each way, so it wasn't long before baymen began building shacks in which to overnight. At first, these shacks were crude constructions. But as the years went by, baymen developed them into cozy cabins that they could also use for recreation and for the planting and harvesting of oysters and clams.

In the early 1900s, recreational fishermen discovered the South Shore, and the bay houses developed yet another purpose: bait

stations. Then, a decade or two later, Prohibition arrived. Some baymen, writes folklorist Nancy Solomon in her book *On the Bay*, "played an indispensable role in rum running, smuggling, via their bay houses, illegal booze from large cargo ships offshore to hotels.... "

All this history was almost lost in 1993, when the baymen's lease on their bay houses—last renewed by the Town of Hempstead in 1965—ran out. The town government had voted to have the houses destroyed, but Solomon's book, together with the efforts of the South Shore Bayhouse Owners' Association, convinced the town board of the homes' historic value. Their leases have since been extended virtually indefinitely.

Although the bay houses can be seen from the parkways, the best way to view them is by boat. Charter fishing boats that run out of Freeport pass close by.

Approximately 40 other bay houses are located in Suffolk County opposite Captree State Park near Captree Island, Sexton Island, and Havermeyer Island.

off the Sunrise Highway (Route 27), and watch for signs. Traffic is typically terrible in summer. If you're coming from New York City, consider taking Long Island Railroad (718/217-5477, www.mta.info/lirr). The train travels to Freeport, where shuttle buses operate to and from the beach.

West of Jones Beach are several smaller beaches, including **Long Beach** and **Lido Beach,** that are also fun to explore. To reach these often less-crowded locales, take Meadowbrook State Parkway to Loop Parkway.

Accommodations and Food

Allegria Hotel (80 West Broadway, 516/889-1300, www.allegriahotel.com, $225-500), a beachfront luxury hotel in Long Beach, has 143 guest rooms offering views of the Atlantic Ocean and New York City skyline. If that's not enough, there's also a 10,000-square-foot roof-top infinity pool. The hotel's restaurant,

Atlantica (80 West Broadway, 516/889-1300, www.allegriahotel.com, $30), specializes in seafood options and has an extensive wine list. The hotel also has two lounges: L'Onda Lounge and Jack's on the Rocks.

CENTRAL NASSAU COUNTY

Heading into Long Island on Southern State Parkway, you'll pass one of the state's only African American museums and two historic residential communities, Garden City and Levittown. Neither of the towns is a tourist attraction in the traditional sense, but both have played an interesting role in America's suburban development.

African American Museum of Nassau County

The **African American Museum of Nassau County** (110 N. Franklin St., Hempstead, 516/572-0730, www.theaamuseum.org,

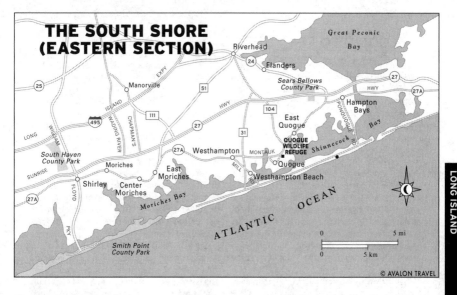

THE SOUTH SHORE
(EASTERN SECTION)

Tues.-Sat. 10am-5pm, free) is on a scruffy main drag in sprawling downtown Hempstead. It's a small but active institution where exhibits change every 8-10 weeks. Most exhibits are arts or history oriented, and range from locally produced shows to traveling Smithsonian productions. Past exhibits have included the role of African Americans in the Civil War, and contemporary Long Island artists.

Museum Row

The hangars of Mitchel Field, a former airfield just outside Garden City, have been transformed into **Museum Row.** At the heart of the project is the impressive **Cradle of Aviation Museum** (Charles Lindbergh Blvd., 516/572-4111, www.cradleofaviation.org, Tues.-Sun. 9:30am-5pm, adults $9, children 2-12 $8). Biplanes and fighter planes seem to soar up into the atrium, while all around are dozens of rare aircraft documenting the history of flight. Many major aviation events took place on Long Island; Charles Lindbergh's 1927 nonstop transatlantic flight, for instance, departed from nearby Roosevelt Field (now a shopping mall). An IMAX theater and Red Planet Cafe, designed to look like a 21st-century Mars space base, are other fixtures in the museum.

Long-established **Long Island Children's Museum** (11 Davis Ave., 516/224-5800, www.licm.org, summer daily 10am-5pm, Sept.-June Tues.-Sun. 10am-5pm, adults and children over age one $12, seniors $11) has hands-on exhibits for kids of all ages. Topics range from art to science, with plenty of activities, like bubble blowing, that are just plain fun.

The **Nassau County Firefighters' Museum and Education Center** (1 Davis Ave., 516/572-4177, www.ncfiremuseum.org, Tues.-Sun. 10am-5pm, adults $5, seniors and children $4) is also in Museum Row. This is a fun museum for families that features some antique fire engines, as well as interactive activities appropriate for kids.

FIRE ISLAND

A long skinny stick of land stretching 32 miles parallel to Long Island's south shore, Fire Island is a near-mythic place, known for its wildness—both in terms of its wilderness landscape and its party atmosphere.

Four distinct visitor areas and 17 resort communities make up the island, but it's all part of

WELCOME TO THE 'BURBS

Long Island is the archetypal American suburb. Early suburbs began springing up in western Nassau County in the 1920s. But the island's real transformation came with World War II, when factories producing aircraft and specialized weapons systems turned Long Island into an important manufacturing center. After the war, large housing tracts were built to accommodate returning soldiers. The most famous of these tracts was Levittown, the result of the transformation of potato fields into 17,447 inexpensive ranch homes by developer William Levitt in 1949. The largest housing development ever created by a single builder, Levittown was the American Dream come true for the working class, as well as the butt of countless jokes about "ticky-tacky houses" all looking just the same.

Levittown was originally built exclusively for GIs returning from World War II, but was later opened to the general public. Each preassembled house was built in five days using a 27-step process. Each had a living room, two bedrooms, a kitchen and bath, an attic, washing machine, barbecue grill, and television set. The cost to young families was $60 a month, no money down.

In the end, the individuality and imagination of Levittown's residents foiled many of the community's detractors. Drive down the streets here today and you'd be hard-pressed to find any house that closely resembles another. Some owners have added rooms and second floors, others have changed the facades or added driveways. To reach Levittown from Hempstead, head east on Hempstead Turnpike (Route 24).

Between 1950 and 1960, Long Island's population doubled from 670,000 to 1.3 million, and between 1960 and 1980 it doubled yet again. The island's population continues to swell; currently, more than 7.5 million people call Long Island home—and those are just year-round residents.

the National Seashore system. No cars are allowed on most of Fire Island, where park rangers administer a number of magnificent white sand beaches.

Take note of posters describing precautions to avoid poison ivy and deer ticks; both are abundant here and can quickly ruin a vacation. As long as you stick to beaches and boardwalks, or wear long pants when exploring grasses and woodlands, you shouldn't have a problem.

Free, excellent maps of Fire Island are available at various visitors' centers on the island, or from **Fire Island National Seashore Headquarters** (120 Laurel St., Patchogue, 631/687-4750, www.nps.gov/fiis, hours seasonal). Another helpful website is www.fireisland.com.

Resort Communities

Fire Island wasn't declared a National Seashore until 1964, by which time 17 resort communities had already been established. These

communities were allowed to remain, as long as they didn't grow beyond their designated boundaries. Today, they are popular vacation spots, especially among Manhattanites.

Each Fire Island community has its own distinct character. **Cherry Grove** and **Fire Island Pines** are the island's two gay retreats; **Kismet** and **Fair Harbor** attract a large singles crowd; **Saltaire** and **Seaview** cater primarily to families.

Most of these communities are not designed for the casual visitor. Their vacationers tend to rent or share houses—usually for the entire summer—and often arrive via hired water taxi. Most of these communities also do not offer bathhouses or other public facilities.

Two communities that *do* welcome day-trippers and overnight visitors are **Ocean Beach** and **Ocean Bay Park**. Ocean Beach attracts many families, Ocean Bay Park many singles. Both are friendly, middle-class communities equipped with public facilities and serviced by

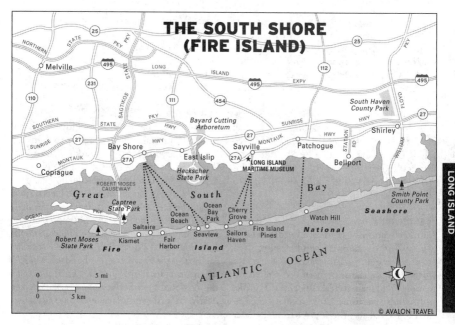

THE SOUTH SHORE
(FIRE ISLAND)

LONG ISLAND

© AVALON TRAVEL

Fire Island Ferries (Bay Shore, 631/665-3600, www.fireislandferries.com, adults round-trip $17, children round-trip $7.50).

Cherry Grove also welcomes casual visitors. Older, smaller, less expensive, and more exuberant than its sister community, the Pines, it centers around Grove Hotel, which always teems with a gay crowd, talking, drinking, and partying. Cherry Grove is serviced by **Sayville Ferry Service** (River Rd., Sayville, 631/589-8980, www.sayvilleferry.com, adults round-trip $16, children round-trip $7.50).

Robert Moses State Park

At Fire Island's westernmost end is 1,000-acre **Robert Moses State Park** (off Robert Moses Causeway, 631/669-0470, daily dawn-dusk, $8-10 parking), one of only two sections of the island that can be reached by car. A public beach since 1898, the park feels like a smaller, less crowded version of Jones Beach. The park, which is also a National Seashore, has bathhouses, shops, and snack bars.

At the park's western end is the black-and-white-striped **Fire Island Lighthouse** (4640 Captree Island, 631/661-4876, www.fireislandlighthouse.com, call for days and hours), built in 1827 to prevent shipwrecks. The current lighthouse dates to 1858. At its base is a **visitors' center** (631/661-4876, July-Sept. daily 9:30am-5pm). The lighthouse tower was restored in 2013 and **tower tours** (adults $7, seniors and children 12 and under $4) are available by advance reservation.

Sailors Haven

One of the island's most interesting beaches for day visitors is **Sailors Haven,** reached via ferry from Sayville. Sailors Haven is part wild beach and boardwalk, part dunes and grasses, and part **Sunken Forest**—a scrappy 300-year-old maritime forest located below sea level between two lines of sand dunes. A weathered gray boardwalk leads from the ferry dock through the 40-acre forest, lush with oak, maple, red cedar, and sour gum trees, as well as sassafras, bayberry, inkberry, and cattail. Due to the island's strong winds and salty air, none of the trees can grow taller than the dunes, even though fresh water extends as deep as 40 yards beneath their roots. Essential to the forest's existence, this fresh water exists because the island's annual rainfall exceeds its annual evaporation.

Sailors Haven, a National Seashore, has several facilities, including bathhouses, a snack bar, and a **visitors' center** (631/597-6183 seasonal). Ferries are operated by **Sayville Ferry Service** (River Rd., Sayville, 631/589-8980, www.sayvilleferry.com, adults round-trip $16, children round-trip $7.50).

Watch Hill

Another National Seashore **visitors' center** (631/597-6455, seasonal), similar to but larger than the one at Sailors Haven, is located at **Watch Hill,** on the eastern end of Fire Island. Remote and lonely in feel, Watch Hill is filled with windswept dunes and an often-unpopulated beach; adjacent to it is a national wilderness area that visitors are welcome to explore. Spring and fall are especially good times to come, as Fire Island is on the Atlantic flyway, a major avian migratory route. Watch Hill also has bathhouses, a snack bar, nature trails, and a visitors' center.

Ferries are operated by **Davis Park Ferry Co.** (West and Division Sts., Patchogue, 631/475-1665, www.davisparkferry.com, adults round-trip $16, children round-trip $10.50).

Smith Point County Park

East of Watch Hill and its adjacent National Wilderness Area is another beach park accessible by car. Like Robert Moses State Park, **Smith Point County Park** (William Floyd Pkwy., 631/852-1313, www.lirv.com/camps/Smith.htm) has plenty of bathhouses and concession stands, and attracts large crowds on summer weekends. Technically speaking, the park is not part of the National Seashore, but since it's located next to **Smith Point West**, which *is,* and both are lined with the same wide and wonderful beach, it all feels the same. Smith Point West also has a National Seashore

visitors' center (631/281-3010, seasonal) and a self-guided nature trail.

Smith Point County Park and Smith Point West are at the southern end of William Floyd Parkway, off Sunrise Highway (Route 27). In summer months, parking costs $10.

William Floyd Estate

As you drive down William Floyd Parkway to and from Smith Point, you'll pass signs for **William Floyd Estate** (245 Park Dr., 631/399-2030, seasonal, free), now part of the National Seashore. Floyd was a Revolutionary War general and one of the signers of the Declaration of Independence. After his death, his family's estate grew to include over 600 acres of forests and meadows, along with a grand 25-room mansion and 12 outbuildings. The estate remained in the Floyd family's hands until 1977 when Cornelia Floyd Nichols signed it over to the National Park Service one year before her death. Guided tours of the house are available.

Accommodations

One of the few hotels on Fire Island is simple but comfortable **(Fire Island Hotel and Resort** (25 Cayuga Walk, Ocean Bay Park, 631/583-8000, www.fireislandhotel.com, summer weeknight $230-345, weekend $285-543), housed in converted U.S. Life Saving Service buildings. The hotel caters primarily to families, but rooms go very fast. Reserve well in advance; weekend reservations require a three-night minimum stay. Another good choice for families is comfortable, air-conditioned, 1940s-era **Cleggs Hotel** (478 Bayberry Walk, Ocean Beach, 631/583-9292, www.cleggshotelfireisland.com, weeknight $165, weekend $395).

Grove Hotel (Ocean Walk, Cherry Grove, 631/597-6600, www.grovehotel.com, summer weeknight $75-160, weekend $500-750 for two-night minimum) caters to the gay community. Rates drop significantly during the off-season.

BAY SHORE AND VICINITY

Several Fire Island ferries leave from the town of Bay Shore. The ferry docks at the

STOP FOR A GANDER

Sitting all by itself by the side of the road on Route 24 in Flanders, the pure white bird—with its orange bill and bright red eyes made from Model-T taillights—makes the **Big Duck** look like a simple child's drawing come to life. The only giveaway that something else is afoot is the dark outline of a door just beneath the duck's throat.

The 20-foot-high, 30-foot-long Big Duck was built in 1931 by an ambitious duck-raising farmer who hoped to attract more customers and was inspired after a stop at a coffeepot-shaped coffee shop during a trip through California. Ducks were big business on Long Island

at that time; in 1939 there were 90 duck farms in Quogue alone. Ducks and eggs were sold from a shop within the building, seen as a model for large scale advertisement-building across the country. So influential was this particular Peking poultry that the term "duck" is still used in architecture whenever a building is made into a literal translation of an object.

Today, the Big Duck is listed on the National Register of Historic Places and it's open daily, year-round. The tourist stop is made complete by a shop with—what else?— duck books, duck T-shirts, duck coffee mugs, postcards, and books.

LONG ISLAND

foot of Maple Avenue, and on summer days, beachgoers stream down the thoroughfare, armed with coolers, beach chairs, and umbrellas. Few of them stop at **Gibson/Mack/Holt House** (22 Maple Ave., 631/665-1707, www.bayshorehistoricalsociety.org, Tues. and Sat. 1pm-4pm, free), but the very attractive historical home is well worth a look. Several rooms have been restored to their original 1820 condition, while others house memorabilia from the town's turn-of-the-century heyday. The house is run by the Bay Shore Historical Society and was restored almost entirely by volunteers.

Sightseeing cruises around Great South Bay are offered by **South Bay Cruises** (631/750-5359, www.laurenkristy.com, Apr.-Oct). The cruises leave from Bay Shore Manor Park at the foot of Clinton Avenue.

Heckscher State Park

Heckscher State Park (off Heckscher State Pkwy., East Islip, 631/581-2100, www.nysparks.com/parks/136, daily dawn-dusk, $8-10 parking) is a 1,500-acre spread east of Bay Shore. The park is an especially good place for families to go swimming because the water is calm, protected by the bay. Facilities include three beaches, a pool, bathhouses, nature trails, and a 69-site campground.

Long Island Greenbelt Trail, maintained by Long Island Greenbelt Trail Conference (631/360-0753, www.ligreenbelt.org), runs 32 miles, from Heckscher State Park on the South Shore to Sunken Meadow State Park on the North Shore. The trail follows the Connetquot and Nissequogue River valleys through wetlands, pine barrens, and forest.

Bayard Cutting Arboretum

One of the greatest estates along the South Shore is **Bayard Cutting Arboretum** (440 Montauk Hwy., Great River, 631/581-1002, www.bayardcuttingarboretum.com, Tues.-Sun. 10am-5pm, $8 parking), once owned by railroad magnate William Bayard Cutting. The 690-acre estate was designed by Frederick Law Olmsted, the famed landscape architect who also designed New York City's Central Park.

The arboretum centers on a dark baronial Tudor mansion. Inside are a few natural history exhibits and Hidden Oak Cafe, serving light lunch fare, but the place feels oddly empty. Perhaps that's because compared to the estate's glorious grounds, the mansion seems almost an afterthought.

Just outside the mansion is a verdant lawn, stretching 600 feet down to the Connetquot River. On either side stand huge old black oak trees, spreading out their leafy branches. All around are specialized gardens: azalea garden, rhododendron garden, lilac garden, and holly garden.

Parts of the arboretum were badly hit by Hurricane Gloria in 1985. An estimated 1,000 trees were lost during that storm, including about 20 of Long Island's oldest trees and 80 of the 120 species originally planted by Mr. Cutting. Younger trees were planted in their stead, but it will be many years before they reach their predecessors' 70-90-foot heights.

Long Island Maritime Museum

Laid-back **Long Island Maritime Museum** (86 West Ave., West Sayville, 631/854-4974, www.limaritime.org, Mon.-Sat. 10am-4pm, Sun. noon-4pm, adults $6, seniors and children $4) occupies an idyllic spot overlooking Great South Bay. Housed in shipshape buildings, the museum holds the largest collection of small craft in Long Island. On display is everything from oyster vessels and sailboats to ice scooters and clam boats.

A historic oyster house and an 1890s bayman's cottage, both of which were moved here from elsewhere on the island, are also on display. The oyster house holds an extensive exhibit on the harvesting of shellfish. Next door is a working boat shop where volunteers build new boats and restore old ones.

Food

Wine bar and bistro **fatfish** (28 Cottage Ave., Bay Shore, 631/666-2899, www.fatfish.info, seasonal, $28) has an extensive menu with plenty of fish, seafood, poultry, and meat options. Another excellent option is **The Lake House** (240 West Main St., Bay Shore, 631/666-0995, www.thelakehouserest.com, Tues.-Thurs. 5pm-9:30pm, Fri.-Sat. 5pm-10:30pm, Sun. 4pm-9:30pm, $30), which specializes in upscale New American dishes.

The Hamptons

The South Fork is perhaps best known for the Hamptons, New York City's playground. The rich and influential, the middle-class and obscure, all flock here during summer to rent weathered cottages, poke around in pictureperfect towns, indulge in fast-paced nightlife, and, most of all, explore some of the state's most magnificent beaches.

But the South Fork also has a culture all its own that has nothing to do with tourists. Farmers and, to a lesser extent, fisherfolk continue to practice their livelihoods here just as they have for hundreds of years. Humble potato fields adjoin multi-million-dollar second homes, and fishing boats share harbors with pleasure craft.

The English first arrived in Southampton from Lynn, Massachusetts, in 1640—the same year settlers from New Haven arrived on the North Fork. Much of their reason for coming was the fact that the Algonquin Indians made wampum on the island. Wampum could be exchanged for valuable beaver and other furs, and the English wanted to get access to the beads before the Dutch.

The Algonquins welcomed the English and in a matter of decades, English villages were flourishing. Most featured New England-style village greens, white-steepled churches, and colonial saltboxes. Many of these early buildings still stand today.

Tourists started arriving in the 1800s. Residents opened their homes to visitors, and by the 1850s, the local press was reporting that all rooms in East Hampton were fully booked, at $7 a night. Shortly thereafter, Southampton started building hotels, and in 1895, the railroad arrived, marking the beginning of the end of sleepy village life.

Note that several of the Hamptons (Westhampton Beach, Quogue, Hampton Bays) are actually west of the South Fork,

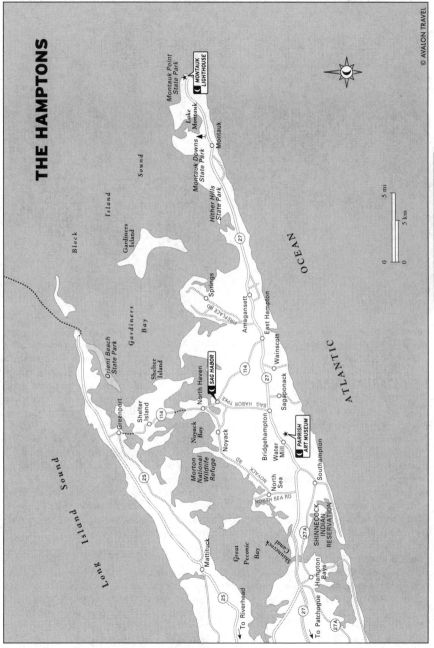

THE HAMPTONS

© AVALON TRAVEL

© FRANCISCO COLLAZO

general store in The Hamptons

but when people speak of the "Hamptons," they're generally referring to those towns east of Shinnecock Canal.

PRACTICALITIES
Accommodations

As in other resort areas, peak-season accommodations in the Hamptons don't come cheap. Peak season rates usually apply from mid-June through Labor Day, and minimum two- or three-night stays are often required, especially on weekends. Rates drop dramatically during the off-season.

Along the beach near Montauk, you'll find simple family-style resort motels that are more moderately priced. Rates listed for South Fork are for double rooms, but many places also offer family packages. Meanwhile, historic inns and B&Bs are plentiful throughout the region. Most resort motels are closed in winter; most inns and B&Bs are open year-round.

Beach Parking

Although all South Fork beaches are open to the public, parking can be a major problem. Many village and town beaches require parking permits (good for the entire summer), which usually cost non-residents over $100. However, some excellent public beaches have daily parking fees; the best of these are Atlantic Beach in Amagansett, Main Beach in East Hampton, and the beach at Hither Hills State Park in Montauk. Many hotels and motels also offer low-cost day-parking passes to their guests or include parking permits as an amenity; inquire when you book.

Parking illegally is not a good idea. Rules are strictly enforced, and violators will be ticketed with a heavy fine or towed. Most parking rules apply during summer only.

Nightlife

The South Fork is noted for its nightlife, which runs the gamut from casual bars to discos. In general, the nights get going as late in the Hamptons as they do in major urban centers—say 11pm—and don't shut down until 2am or even 4am on weekends. Here are a few favorite spots to see-and-be-seen. The French Riviera-themed **South Pointe** (125 Tuckahoe Rd., 631/377-3536, www.southpointenightclub.com) has 7,000 square feet of space to dance the night away to DJ-spun electronica. **SL East** (44 Three Mile Harbor Rd., 212/627-1235, www.emmgrp.com) offers pricey, exclusive bottle service. The wildly popular **Surf Lodge** (183 Edgemere St., 631/238-5190) has featured performers as diverse as Patti Smith and Willie Nelson.

QUOGUE

Turning south off Sunrise Highway onto Montauk Highway around Sayville or Patchogue will save you time and take you past a number of pretty villages. One of the prettiest is Quogue, a tiny place filled with big old shingled homes and wide empty streets.

Geographically part of the Hamptons, Quogue established itself as an autonomous village in 1928, allowing it, in the words of its village government, "to proudly stand apart from the 'Hamptons Scene'" to focus "on wholesome family oriented activities." True, it's not as popular as The Hamptons, but it *is* wholesome and family-friendly. Though the number of activities here is not boundless, two attractions are worth a stop.

Old Schoolhouse Museum

Quogue's **Old Schoolhouse Museum** (114 Jessup Ave., 631/996-2404, www.quoguehistory.org, hours vary seasonally, donations welcome) is a shingle-sided house built in 1822 and in use until 1893 as Quogue's first school. It is believed to be the oldest schoolhouse in Suffolk County and its longevity may be attributed to the fact that it has always been well cared for compared to other schools, which tended to be neglected within their communities. The schoolhouse has been operating as a museum since 1949.

Quogue Wildlife Refuge

Long Island has a number of beautiful, ecologically important wildlife refuges, one of which is in Quogue. **Quogue Wildlife Refuge** (3 Old Country Rd., 631/653-4771, www.quoguewildliferefuge.org, grounds open daily dawn-dusk, Nature Center open Tues., Thurs., and Sat.-Sun. 11am-4pm, free) was established in 1934. It is notable for its rare dwarf pines and, especially, for its Distressed Wildlife Complex, where wild animals with permanent injuries receive ongoing care. The refuge also offers over seven miles of trails spread out across its 305 acres.

Accommodations and Food

Dockers Waterside (94 Dune Rd., 631/653-0653, www.dockerswaterside.com, brunch, lunch, dinner, hours vary seasonally, $32) is a bustling restaurant on the waterfront, serving everything from steak to seafood. Live music is often featured on the weekends.

For accommodations right by the beach, **Hampton Ocean Resort** (30 Dune Rd., East Quogue, 631/653-3600, www.hamptonoceanresort.com, $225-600) is a hidden treasure. It offers warm and over-the-top service, including an excellent crew of polite, friendly staff who set up private cabanas and loungers for each room, hand pack personalized coolers filled with snacks and drinks, fire up the barbecue, and deliver everything from fresh beachside drinks and frozen treats to veggie burgers and hot dogs, all complimentary, so you never have to take your toes out of the sand or pull out your wallet. Two bedroom cottages ideal for families or couples traveling together feature a fully equipped kitchen and an outdoor covered patio with a large dining table. Resort highlights are the seemingly endless stretch of white sand with nary a hotel in sight and moonlight bonfires on the beach (s'mores included).

SOUTHAMPTON

The oldest of the Hamptons' villages is Southampton, a pristine and deceptively simple-looking town attracting a high quotient of socialites and the nouveau riche. Downtown is just a few blocks long, but it's lined with leafy trees, posh boutiques, and expensive cars. Its winding wooded lanes are dotted with splashy second homes, most of which are protected from prying eyes by tall privacy hedges.

Southampton, settled in 1640, was first called Conscience Point; its name was later changed to honor the Earl of Southampton. The town centers on the intersection of Main Street and Job's Lane. Walking maps and brochures can be picked up at the **Southampton Chamber of Commerce** (76 Main St., 631/283-0402, www.southamptonchamber.com, Mon.-Fri. 10am-4pm, Sat.-Sun. 11am-3pm).

◖ Parrish Art Museum

Founded in 1898 by a wealthy summer resident, **Parrish Art Museum** (279 Montauk Hwy., 631/283-2118, www.parrishart.org, hours vary seasonally, adults $10, seniors $8, children under 18 free) houses a notable collection of 19th- and 20th-century American art. William Merritt Chase and Fairfield Porter, both of whom spent much time in the area, are especially well represented. Out back, find an arboretum and a sculpture garden shaded by rare trees. In summer, the museum presents many lectures, concerts, films, and other special events.

Southampton Historical Museum

Southampton Historical Museum (17 Meeting House Ln., 631/283-2494, www.southamptonhistoricalmuseum.org, Tues.-Sat. 11am-4pm, adults $4, children under 17 free) administers a number of historic buildings. The museum is centered at **Rogers Mansion** (17 Meeting House Ln.), a Greek Revival home built by a whaling captain in 1843. Inside the home are period furnishings, a Shinnecock Indian exhibit, and Revolutionary War artifacts. Out back is a cluster of historical buildings, including a one-room schoolhouse, blacksmith's shop, carpenter's shop, and cobbler. The 1648 **Thomas Halsey Homestead** (249 South Main St.) is the oldest building in Southampton, a tiny gray cottage sitting primly behind a fence, oblivious to the modern world. Built by one of the town's original settlers, the house is still in excellent condition and is furnished with 17th- and 18th-century antiques. Nearby **Pelletreau**

Shop (78 Main St.) is the only 1600s-era trade shop in the United States that has been in continuous use; today, it is occupied by a jeweler who offers workshops to visitors.

Shinnecock Reservation

Just west of town, **Shinnecock Reservation** (631/283-6143, www.shinnecocknation.com) is home to about 700 Native Americans and the **Shinnecock Nation Cultural Center and Museum** (100 Montauk Hwy., 631/287-4923, www.shinnecockmuseum.com, Thurs.-Sun. 11am-5pm, adults $8, seniors $5.50, children 5-12 $4.75). Opened in 2001, the museum showcases historic birch-bark canoes and farm implements, beadwork, basketry, weavings, photographs, and an informative video.

Visitors are also welcome to attend the annual **Shinnecock Powwow,** held on Labor Day weekend. This major event attracts Native Americans from all over the country. Traditional dances, foods, and arts and crafts are featured.

Beaches

Southampton's main public beach is **Coopers Beach** (268 Meadow Ln., 631/283-0247, $40 a day parking fee), with full facilities including concession, bathhouse, and chair and umbrella rental. No parking permit is required at the often-uncrowded **Old Town Beach** (end of Old Town Rd.). There are only about 30 parking spaces, however, and no facilities.

Accommodations

Tudor-style ◖ **Southampton Inn** (91 Hill St., 631/283-6500, www.southamptoninn.com, summer $389-489, Sept.-June $129-489) offers 90 spacious rooms decorated with English country style accents. The inn has a heated outdoor swimming pool, a library with Steinway piano and fireplace, and tennis courts. The resort is especially popular with families and wedding parties.

Another excellent choice is historic, 70-room **Southampton Village Latch Inn** (101 Hill St., 631/283-2160, www.villagelatch.com, summer weekend $295-550, off-season $250-450). The inn was once an annex to the famous Irving Hotel, Long Island's oldest established lodging, which has since burned down. Tall hedges frame the mansion's green-shuttered front, while outside are a swimming pool and tennis courts. Exotic crafts such as Burmese puppets and African masks hang on the walls. Many rooms have refrigerators and some have private patios.

Food

The Golden Pear Cafe (99 Main St., 631/283-8900, www.goldenpearcafe.com, $12) offers homemade baked goods, sandwiches, and pasta. If you're looking to pick up food, try **The Village Gourmet Cheese Shoppe** (11 Main St., 631/283-6949, www.villagecheeseshoppe.com) for takeout.

More serious meals can be had at **C Le Chef Bistro** (75 Job's Ln., 631/283-8581, www.lechefbistro.com, hours vary seasonally), a French restaurant with a lively bar to one side, and dining to the other. Several prix fixe dinner menus are offered at $30, $35, and $40.

Red Bar Brasserie (210 Hampton Rd., 631/283-0704, www.redbarbrasserie.com, dinner nightly from 6pm, $30) serves creative American fare in a stylish, white-tablecloth setting. At night, the restaurant's bar is crowded with beautiful people. Guests can order à la carte or prix fixe.

WATER MILL AND BRIDGEHAMPTON

A few miles east of Southampton is the small village of Water Mill, named for the big gristmill near the town center. The village's first gristmill was built in 1644. The current one dates to 1800 and now operates as **Water Mill Museum** (41 Old Mill Rd., 631/726-4625, www.watermillmuseum.org, hours vary seasonally, adults $3, seniors $2.50). During the summer, the mill still grinds corn and wheat with its all-wooden gears, shafts, and wheel. A number of art exhibits and events are held here during the summer.

A few miles east of Water Mill is Bridgehampton, named for a small bridge that was built over Sagg Pond in 1686. During the 1800s, Bridgehampton was known for helping distressed ships at sea. The first headquarters of the Life Saving Service of Long Island was founded here in 1878; it merged with the Coast Guard in 1915. Today, Bridgehampton is another picture-perfect Long Island town. Big red-brick buildings line its Main Street, along with a number of antique shops.

Food

In Bridgehampton, sit indoors or outdoors at **Bobby Van's** (2393 Montauk Hwy., 631/537-0590, www.bobbyvans.com/bridgehampton.html, $35), a place to see and be seen. It was once frequented by the literati, and is now popular with celebrities. Classic steakhouse fare is what you can expect here. Another expensive-but-worth-it option is **Topping Rose House** (1 Bridgehampton-Sag Harbor Turnpike, 631/537-0870, www.toppingrosehouse.com), whose menu was designed by star chef Tom Colicchio. Most of the ingredients are sourced from the sea and nearby farms, including the hotel-restaurant's own plot, Topping Rose Farm.

EAST HAMPTON

At the center of the Hamptons lies East Hampton, an old money stronghold now better known for its famed artists and writers, actors and directors, publishers and media moguls. East Hampton has been a mecca for successful "creative types" since the 1870s, when artists William Merritt Chase, Childe Hassam, and others summered here.

In the late 1970s, the now-defunct *Saturday Evening Post* ran a contest asking readers to vote for the most beautiful town in America. East Hampton won, and it's not hard to see why. Even more than Southampton, East Hampton is an idyllic New England village that seems to have stepped out of time. Perfect colonial homes, emerald-green lawns, and white picket fences are everywhere. Nothing seems quite real, but who cares? What could possibly go wrong in a world such as this?

A pond, village green, and Old Burying

Ground split Main Street at the western end, while at the eastern end, in isolated splendor on a plush lawn, stands weathered Old Hook Mill. Between these two landmarks lie most of the town's shops, restaurants, and historic sites, all of which can be explored on foot. To catch a glimpse of the area's many posh summer homes, take a drive along Ocean Avenue or Lily Pond Lane.

East Hampton Chamber of Commerce (42 Gingerbread Ln., 631/324-0362, www. easthamptonchamber.com, June-Sept. Mon.-Sat. 10am-4pm, off-season hours vary) is well stocked with brochures and maps. **East Hampton Historical Society** (101 Main St., 631/324-6850, www.easthamptonhistory.org) sponsors walking tours of downtown and the cemetery in summer and fall. Many are led by guides dressed in colonial garb. Reservations are required.

Historic James Lane

At the western end of the village are Town Pond—once a watering hole for East

Old Hook Mill in East Hampton

© FRANCISCO COLLAZO

Hampton's cattle—and the snug **Home Sweet Home** (14 James Ln., 631/324-0713, May-Sept. Mon.-Sat. 10am-4pm, Sun. 2pm-4pm, adults $4, children $2), a nicely restored 1650 saltbox that was the boyhood home of John Howard Payne, composer of the song "Home Sweet Home." Inside the house is a good collection of English ceramics and early American furniture; out back are a windmill and garden.

Next door to Home Sweet Home is a complex of restored weathered buildings known as **Mulford Farm** (10 James Ln., 631/324-6850, Memorial Day weekend-Columbus Day weekend Sat. 10am-5pm, Sun. noon-5pm, or by appointment, adults $4, seniors $3, children $2). Owned by the same family from 1712 to 1944, the four-acre homestead includes a farmhouse, barn, garden, and various outbuildings. Costumed guides lead tours in summer.

Historic Main Street

Just east of James Lane stands **Clinton Academy** (151 Main St., 631/324-6850, www. easthamptonhistory.org, Memorial Day weekend-Columbus Day weekend Sat. 10am-5pm, Sun. noon-5pm, free), a large wood-and-brick building dating to the late 1700s. The building, which once housed the first prep school in the state and one of the first coed schools in the country, has also served as a theater and the office of the local newspaper. Today, it is a historical museum open to the public for tours.

Town House (149 Main St., 631/324-6850, www.easthamptonhistory.org, Memorial Day weekend-Columbus Day weekend Sat. 10am-5pm, Sun. noon-5pm, suggested donation adults $4, seniors $3, students $2), located next to Clinton Academy, is an elfin, one-room schoolhouse with a potbellied stove. The building also once served as the town hall and is the only remaining colonial-era town government meeting place still in existence.

Old Hook Mill (631/324-0713, July-Aug. Mon.-Sat. 10am-4pm, Sun. 2pm-4pm, adults $2, children under 12 $1), on the other end of Main Street, is the best surviving example of the many windmills that once dotted the South Fork. (Most of the few remaining windmills are not open to the public.) It was built by Nathaniel Dominy V, an innovative designer who included several then-unheard-of labor-saving devices, including a grain elevator, in his remarkably efficient mill.

Guild Hall

Across the street from Clinton Academy is **Guild Hall** (158 Main St., 631/324-0806, www.guildhall.org, July 1-Labor Day Mon. and Wed.-Sat. 11am-5pm, Sun. noon-5pm, Labor Day-June 30 Fri.-Sat. 11am-5pm, Sun. noon-5pm, suggested donation adults $7, seniors and students $5, children under 5 free), one of the premier art institutions on Long Island. Inside its three large galleries are temporary exhibits featuring top contemporary artists such as Chuck Close. Also part of Guild Hall is **John Drew Theater,** which presents dance, theater, and music performances, as well as literary readings by some of the famed authors who summer in the Hamptons. Every August, **The Clothesline Art Sale** presents work by both established and emerging artists.

Beaches

East Hampton has five beaches, all of which are owned and overseen by the village. From Memorial Day until the last Saturday in June and again from Labor Day until September 30, East Hampton's beaches are open only on weekends and holidays. From the last Saturday in June until Labor Day, beaches are open daily. Main Beach and Two Mile Hollow Beach are the only East Hampton beaches offering **day parking** ($25 per weekday, purchase at Main Beach's pavilion, Mon.-Fri. 9am-4pm). A useful, up-to-date resource for beachcombers seeking more information is the Village of East Hampton's website (www.easthamptonvillage.org).

Large crowds enjoy gorgeous **Main Beach** (101 Ocean Ave., 631/324-0074), which is staffed by lifeguards during the busy summer season. Facilities include bathhouses and concession stands. **Two Mile Hollow Beach** (Two Mile Hollow Rd.) is in the middle of a nature sanctuary and has no facilities. All the other beaches in East Hampton are usually less crowded, but require a resident parking permit.

Accommodations

Among the more moderately priced inns in this expensive town is **Bassett House Inn** (128 Montauk Hwy., 631/324-6127, www.bassetthouseinn.com, $145-375 July-Aug.), a large home built in 1830. It offers 12 guest rooms, all decorated with antiques. Some of the less expensive rooms share baths; some of the more expensive ones have fireplaces, and one has a whirlpool.

Boutique hotel **c/o The Maidstone** (207 Main St., 631/324-5006, www.themaidstone.com, $450-550 summer, $225-295 off-season) is housed in a 150-year-old Greek Revival home that was once a tannery. From the 1920s until the first decade of the 2000s, the house served as an inn. In 2008, it was bought by a Swedish hotelier who brought the property up to date and introduced his Scandinavian design sensibility and luxe amenities for a modern boutique hotel stay. In addition to organic linens and high-end toiletries, summer guests love the coveted beach parking permit that comes with each room. Pets are welcome ($25 fee) and are greeted with their own bowls and treats. Humans dine well at the hotel's Slow Food-certified restaurant, The Living Room (breakfast, lunch, dinner, $35), which focuses on fresh, local, organic ingredients.

Among the oldest accommodations on the South Fork is **Hedges Inn** (74 James Ln., 631/324-7101, www.thehedgesinn.com, $675-1,100 summer, $205-425 off-season). Built by one of the town's founding families, with sections dating back to more than three centuries, the inn features 12 nicely restored rooms, some overlooking Town Pond.

Another historic accommodation is **The Huntting Inn** (94 Main St., 631/324-0410, www.thepalm.com/Huntting-Inn, $250-750 summer, $195-450 off-season), with comfortable rooms and attentive staff. Its convenient location is noteworthy: The Hampton Jitney stops directly across the street and it's a three-minute walk to Main Street's shops and restaurants. Beach passes, towels, and chairs are included in the room rate in summer months.

Food

For a simple lunch or dinner, **Nichol's** (100 Montauk Hwy., 631/324-3939, daily 9am-10pm, $12) is an easygoing pub featuring seafood pie and 10 kinds of draft beer.

 Bostwick's Chowder House (277 Pantigo Rd., 631/324-1111, www.bostwickschowderhouse.com, Sun.-Thurs. 11:30am-10pm, Fri.-Sat. 11am-11pm, $22) is a casual, festive place specializing in fresh seafood.

East Hampton also has its share of posh eateries, where getting a reservation is no mean feat. **Nick & Toni's** (136 N. Main St., 631/324-3550, www.nickandtonis.com, daily 6pm-close, $36) offers Mediterranean and rustic Italian cuisine in a sophisticated yet relaxed setting, and **The Palm Restaurant** (94 Main St., 631/324-0411, www.thepalm.com, daily lunch and dinner, $42) serves pricy steaks from its location within the historic Huntting Inn.

As expected, some of the hotels and inns in town offer good dining options. The hotel at the Maidstone has **The Living Room** (207 Main St., 631/324-5494, www.themaidstone.com, daily breakfast, lunch, and dinner, $32), where the Slow Food philosophy informs the New American dishes on the menu, and **The 1770 House** (143 Main St., 631/324-3504, www.1770house.com, dinner, $40) has two on-site dining options: an upscale contemporary American restaurant featuring local ingredients and a tavern.

SAG HARBOR

Driving north from East Hampton along Route 114, through lush, fertile farm country, you'll soon come to the old whaling port of Sag Harbor. During its heyday, Sag Harbor was a bustling, bawdy commercial town, and some of that lively atmosphere—so different from the elegance of much of the Hamptons—lingers.

Sag Harbor is a good town to explore on foot. Lower Main Street is filled with shops and restaurants, while upper Main and side streets hold dozens of 19th-century homes and huge old trees. At the foot of Main Street is the weather-beaten 1,000-foot Long Wharf, which offers close-up views of the harbor.

Plentiful parking is available near the waterfront, especially between Main and Meadow Streets. Traffic usually doesn't get quite as congested here as it does in the Hamptons, but it can still be daunting.

In summer, **Sag Harbor Chamber of Commerce** (55 Main St., 631/725-0011, www.sagharborchamber.com) runs a **visitor information center** (July-Aug. daily 9am-4pm) in the old windmill at the entrance to Long Wharf.

Sag Harbor Whaling and Historical Museum

One of the most interesting buildings in town is **Sag Harbor Whaling and Historical Museum** (200 Main St., 631/725-0770, www.sagharborwhalingmuseum.org, May 15-Oct. 1 Mon.-Sat. 10am-5pm, Sun. 1pm-5pm, adults $6, seniors and students $5, children under 11 $2), its entrance marked with tall Corinthian columns and the impressive, large jawbones of a whale. The mansion was built in 1845 by architect Minard Lafever for whaling-ship owner Benjamin Huntting.

The hodgepodge of jumbled exhibits—some absolutely fascinating, others looking suspiciously like junk—makes exploring the museum a lot of fun. On display you'll find everything from wooden boats and tools used by whalers to ostrich eggs and a centuries old soda cracker.

Custom House

Around the corner from the whaling museum is the **Custom House** (Main St. and Garden St., 631/692-4664, www.splia.org/customhouse, Memorial Day weekend-Columbus Day Sat.-Sun. 10am-5pm, adults $6, seniors and students $5, children 6-11 $2), the former home of 18th-century customs inspector Henry Packer Dering. Dering's job was to record all the goods entering the harbor and collect entry taxes. He used his front room as an office; the

© FRANCISCO COLLAZO

Sag Harbor Whaling and Historical Museum

room is equipped with wooden window shields that Dering shut whenever he wanted to count money.

Other Historic Sites

All along Main Street near Custom House stand impressive **sea captains' houses,** and nearby is **Old Whaler's Church** (44 Union St., 631/725-0894, www.oldwhalerschurch. org, daily 9am-3pm). Designed in 1844 by Minard Lafever, the church is built in an unusual Egyptian Revival style, and has a soaring interior.

Wildlife Refuge

About four miles west of Sag Harbor is 187-acre **Elizabeth A. Morton National Wildlife Refuge** (2595 Noyack Rd., 631/725-7598, www.fws. gov, daily dawn-dusk, $4 parking). The refuge overlooks Peconic and Noyack Bays, and features sandy and rocky beaches, wooded bluffs, ponds, and nature trails. The refuge is open year-round, but much of the beach is closed April–mid-August to protect nesting birds, including the piping plover, which is a threatened species.

Shopping

Locals gripe about the gentrification of their town, epitomized by Main Street, where familiar urban retailers and restauranteurs are setting up South Fork outposts. For a town that has embraced its moniker "The Unhamptons," the quickening creep of non-local brands and stores is a nuisance.

A few locals hang on, though, attempting to stave off takeovers. **Sag Harbor Variety Store** (114 Main St., 631/725-9706, www.sagharborvariety.com) was established as an old-fashioned five-and-dime with lots of odds and ends. Today, its wares tend more toward dollar store-type items, but it's still fun to poke around the aisles and rifle through the bins here. **The Wharf Shop** (69A Main St., 631/725-0420, www.wharfshop.com) sells gifts and toys as well as Sag Harbor-themed souvenirs: postcards, magnets, ornaments, and fine chocolates inspired by the area. **Annyx** (150 Main

St., 631/725-9064, www.annyxsagharbor.com) is a home decor shop with unique recycled, vintage, and handmade accessories and gifts.

Accommodations

Sag Harbor Inn (45 W. Water St., 631/725-2949, www.sagharborinn.com, $230-499 summer, $110-295 off-season, includes breakfast), on the edge of downtown, is a modern, two-story hotel with 42 clean, spacious rooms, many with balconies overlooking the harbor. Similar in style is **❰ Baron's Cove Inn** (31 Water St., 631/725-2100, www.baronscove. com, $190-480 summer, $80-280 off-season), an upscale resort with 67 rooms that are all fresh from a 2013 renovation. Guests appreciate the hotel's complimentary beach shuttle, which eliminates the need for coveted beach parking permits.

Historic 1846 **❰ American Hotel** (49 Main St., 631/725-3535, www.theamericanhotel. com, $250-400 summer, $135-250 off-season) dates back to the town's whaling era. Built of red brick with a white porch out front, the hotel is a member of the Historic Hotels of America. Upstairs are eight guest rooms done up in Victorian antiques; downstairs is an acclaimed restaurant. The hotel's location is convenient to all the shops and restaurants on Main Street.

Food

Lively **La Superica** (2 Main St., 631/725-3388, daily 5:30pm-3am, $13) specializes in Mexican dishes made with healthy ingredients, accompanied by oversized margaritas. Not surprisingly, it's a favorite with twentysomethings.

A classic seafood shack, appropriately named **The Dockhouse** (1 Long Wharf, 631/725-7555, www.dockhouseny.com, daily 10:30am-9pm, $14), sits among bobbing yachts right on the pier. If you can't get a seat inside, take your lobster roll and wander to nearby park benches. The Dockhouse is also an excellent spot to pick up the freshest seafood for your own clambake as it doubles as a fish market. Check their chalkboard for prices.

For dinner and a view, check out **❰ Dockside Bar & Grill** (26 Bay St., 631/725-7100, www.

docksidesagharbor.com, hours vary seasonally, $16), serving lots of seafood, along with other American favorites, in a cavernous former American Legion Hall with an enormous patio.

The classic spot for dining in Sag Harbor is red-brick **American Hotel** (49 Main St., 631/725-3535, daily dinner, $38), which despite its name has a European feel and serves French-American cuisine. The restaurant has won numerous awards for its 85-page wine list.

AMAGANSETT

Small, picturesque Amagansett takes its name from the Algonquin word for "place of good waters." Indians traveling between East Hampton and Montauk often stopped here for fresh water. A monument and plaque on Bluff Road mark the spot.

Miss Amelia's Cottage

At the intersection of Montauk Highway and Windmill Lane stands a snug colonial home: **Miss Amelia's Cottage** (Montauk Hwy. and Windmill Ln., 631/267-3020, late June-Sept. Fri.-Sun. 10am-4pm, adults $3, children $1). Miss Mary Amelia Schellinger lived here between 1841 and 1930, and a look inside her house—still furnished with her belongings—gives visitors a good sense of what South Fork life was like back then. **Roy K. Lester Carriage Museum** (631/267-3020, late June-Sept. Fri.-Sun. 10am-4pm), just behind the cottage, contains about 30 restored carriages, including a surrey with a fringe on top.

East Hampton Town Marine Museum

Long, creaky **East Hampton Town Marine Museum** (301 Bluff Rd., 631/267-6544 or 631/324-6850, www.easthamptonhistory. org, early May-late Oct. Sat.-Sun. 10am-5pm, adults $4, seniors $3, children $2) is on the outskirts of town, filled with artifacts relating to whaling, fishing, and the sea. Boats and more boats, along with an exhibit on shipwrecks, are displayed on the first floor; upstairs are exhibits on shellfish harvesting, scalloping, ice-fishing, harpooning, and whaling. The museum also

JACKSON POLLOCK AND LEE KRASNER

In 1988, the unassuming 19th-century farmhouse where artists Jackson Pollock and Lee Krasner lived opened to the public as **The Pollock-Krasner House and Study Center** (830 Springs-Fireplace Rd., East Hampton, 631/324-4929, www.pkhouse.org, guided tour by appointment only May and Sept.-Oct. Thurs.-Sat. 11am-4pm, general admission July-Aug. Thurs.-Sat. 1pm-5pm, tours adults $10, children $5). Art workshops, changing exhibits, and lectures are held at **The Fireplace Project** (851 Springs Fireplace Rd., www.thefireplaceproject.com), just north of the Pollock-Krasner House.

The house, built in 1879 and since designated a National Historic Landmark, displays the artists' collection of Victorian furniture, books, and jazz records. Guests can also visit the barn where Pollock created many of his greatest works; the proof is on the floor, splattered in Pollock's signature style. In 1956, after a tragic car accident took Pollock's life less than a mile from their home, Krasner moved her own studio into the barn and continued her artistic career. She died in 1984.

On Accabonac Road, not far from Pollock's old residence, is **Green River Cemetery** (Accabonac Rd., just south of Old Stone Hwy.), which has recently become one of the Hamptons' odder tourist attractions. Pollock is buried in the cemetery beneath a boulder marked with an engraving of his signature. Since his death, numerous other creative luminaries—including visual artist Stuart Davis, poet Frank O'Hara, and art critic Harold Rosenberg—were also buried in Green River. Visitors often drop by to show their respects, sometimes leaving tributes such as paintbrushes behind.

inside the Pollock-Krasner House

offers great views of the dunes and the Atlantic Ocean.

Beaches

A wide and wonderful public beach is at the end of **Atlantic Avenue** (off Rte. 27, Amagansett, 631/324-2417). It was once known as "Asparagus Beach" because it attracted bunches of singles who stood together watching everyone else. Staffed by lifeguards and feeding hungry crowds from a large concession stand, the beach now attracts a more mixed crowd. Parking is fee-based on weekdays, but a permit is required on weekends.

Wildlife Refuge

Merrill Lake Sanctuary (off Springs Fireplace Rd., 631/329-7689, daily dawn-dusk, free), run by The Nature Conservancy, is an easily accessible salt marsh especially good for bird-watching. A trail leads through the refuge. Ospreys nest here in late June and early July.

Nightlife

The oldest and most beloved of nightspots on the South Fork is **Stephen Talkhouse** (161 Main St., 631/267-3117, www.stephentalkhouse.com), where first-rate musicians—everyone from Bob Dylan to Bo Diddley, and Patti Smith to Percy Sledge—have played for decades. The place has a nice, laid-back feel, with worn wooden tables and friendly waitstaff.

If you're wondering why parked cars line the road for a good quarter mile on an otherwise fairly desolate stretch of highway, you might have reached **Cyril's Fish House** (2167 Napeague Stretch., 631/267-7993, www.cyrilsfishhouse.webs.com, hours vary seasonally, $16-25). A happy, tan crowd is made slightly raucous with drinks like the house specialty, the BBC (Bailey's Banana Colada). The unpretentious, no-frills spot has a full menu that's heavy on fish and seafood.

Accommodations and Food

◖ **Mill-Garth Country Inn** (23 Windmill Ln., 631/267-5229, www.hamptonsweb.com/millgarth, $225-375, breakfast included) is a romantic and eclectic B&B comprised of cozy cottages and studios clustered around small patios. Part of the property dates to 1840. Lush vegetation and wicker furniture are everywhere. The beach is about a half mile away, so guests especially appreciate that room rates include a beach pass and parking permit.

Clam Bar at Napeague (2025 Montauk Hwy., 631/267-6348, $13) is the best spot to pull over and snag a picnic table for an unpretentious, satisfying meal of fried clams, lobster rolls, or clams on the half shell and a bucket of beer.

MONTAUK

I stand as on some mighty eagle's beak,
Eastward the sea absorbing, viewing, (nothing but sea and sky,)

The tossing waves, the foam,
the ships in the distance,

The wild unrest, the snowy, curling caps—
that inbound urge and urge of waves,

Seeking the shores forever.

Walt Whitman, "From Montauk Point"

The drive from Amagansett to Montauk is only about 10 miles, but the landscape changes dramatically along the way. Near Amagansett, the South Fork still feels like a well-tended region of small towns and farms; near Montauk, the terrain becomes windswept, barren, and wild. Despite all the tourists who flock here in summer, Montauk remains a somewhat isolated fishing village surrounded by dunes and a sandy beach. Commercial fishing is still big business here, though the introduction of new catch limits in recent years has forced some smaller commercial fishing operations to diversify their businesses by adding charter services to their roster of activities.

Montauk proper centers around a circular green with a weathered gazebo. On one side of the green, known as Village Plaza, is **White's**

Drug and Department Store (631/668-2994, daily, hours vary seasonally), a creaky old variety store where you can buy everything from postcards and sunglasses to small appliances and 14-carat-gold jewelry.

North of Montauk proper is **Montauk Harbor**, always teeming with fishing and pleasure craft and home to a number of restaurants. Every June, the harbor hosts the festive Blessing of the Fleet, in which hundreds of boats receive prayers for a safe season.

Montauk is a welcome respite after the heady, moneyed land of the Hamptons. Though it, too, now has its share of trendy hot spots, Montauk's main attraction remains the sea and shore.

Two-lane Montauk Highway is the only road that runs all the way from Southampton to Montauk. During the summer and on weekends, it often gets unbearably congested, but there is no alternate route.

Montauk Chamber of Commerce (742 Montauk Hwy., 631/668-2428, www.montaukchamber.com, Mon.-Fri. 10am-5pm, Sat.-Sun. 10am-2pm) is well stocked with brochures and maps. Parking is usually available in lots along Main Street or on side streets.

Second House Museum

The oldest building in Montauk is **Second House Museum** (Second House Rd., off Montauk Hwy., 631/668-5340, hours vary seasonally, adults $5, children $2), a dark and long-ceilinged affair, first built in 1746 and rebuilt in 1797. Inside, you'll find period furniture and small, casual exhibits on Montauk history.

One of the most interesting displays concerns Samson Occom, a Mohegan Indian born in Connecticut. Occom came to Montauk in 1744 after converting to Christianity. He married a Montauk woman and became a noted preacher, as well as the author of several hymns still sung today. Together with two white ministers, Occum went to England in the 1760s to raise money for indigent Indians. The earl of Dartmouth was so impressed with Occum's powerful preaching that he donated £10,000 to the cause. Back in America, however, the white ministers took over administration of the funds, which they used to found Dartmouth College in 1769. Occum withdrew from village life, a disillusioned, discouraged man.

Third House

Third House is a big, rambling property several times the size of Second House. Set in the middle of what is now **Montauk County Park** (off Rte. 27 east of the village center, 631/852-7878,

© DREAMSTIME.COM

Montauk Lighthouse

June-Sept. Wed.-Sun. 10am-5pm, free), it was used by Teddy Roosevelt and his Rough Riders in 1898, and currently functions as the park headquarters. A small exhibit on Roosevelt and his troops, along with early Montauk artifacts, are on display here.

Indian Field

At the end of Pocahontas Lane, off East Lake Drive, is Indian Field, a burial ground. The last piece of land owned by the Montauks on Long Island, Indian Field today sits surrounded by modern homes, but still retains a peaceful feel. According to ancient custom, Indians were buried here in a sitting position, in a circle relative to one another. Each grave is marked with a rough fieldstone.

The cemetery's largest and only engraved stone belongs to Stephen Pharaoh, better known as Stephen Talkhouse, who died in 1879. A whaler, Civil War soldier, and the last of the Montauk sachems, Talkhouse was also a famous walker who charged 25 cents to carry a letter from Montauk to East Hampton.

Legend has it that Talkhouse's long legs enabled him to make the 35-mile round-trip journey in a day.

Montauk Lighthouse

Within Montauk Point State Park, but not officially part of it, is the still-operating **Montauk Lighthouse** (2000 Montauk Hwy., 631/668-2544, www.montauklighthouse.com, hours vary seasonally, adults $9, seniors $8, children 12 and under $4, children under 41 inches tall not admitted to climb tower, parking $8), one of the most popular visitor attractions on Long Island. The lighthouse—the oldest in New York State and the fourth-oldest active lighthouse in the country—was commissioned by George Washington in 1792 and has been protecting vessels traveling the transatlantic trade route ever since. At one time, the lighthouse burned whale oil. Today it's automated and no longer requires a keeper. The Coast Guard still runs the technical end of the lighthouse but leases the building to the Montauk Historical Society.

FARMING AND FISHING

The Dutch were the first European settlers to arrive on Long Island and were quickly followed by the English, who began settling the North and South Forks in 1640. Unlike many colonial settlers elsewhere, those who established themselves on Long Island had it easy. The land was flat, rich, and easy to cultivate; the sea was brimming with seafood and shellfish. Soon, dozens of small communities were flourishing.

During the Revolutionary War, Long Island was occupied by the British, and many settlers chose to flee rather than remain under the king's rule. But post-war, the island prospered once again. Cattle ranching (in Montauk) and whaling (in Cold Spring Harbor, Sag Harbor, and Greenport) joined farming and fishing as important industries. In the mid-1800s, the Long Island Rail Road was built and agriculture became big business. To this day, Suffolk County remains one of New York's most productive farming regions.

While still an important player in commercial fishing in the United States, Long Island's fishing industry has not fared as well as the farming industry. Quotas introduced in the 2000s to protect waters from overfishing have impacted small commercial fishing operations on Long Island negatively, forcing them to establish side businesses, such as chartering themselves out as pleasure boats, to survive.

Long Islanders never go down without a fight, however, and the importance and influence of fishing are still visible across the island, especially in Montauk and other towns on the South Shore.

Beaches and Parks

About three miles west of Montauk is **Hither Hills State Park** (164 Old Montauk Hwy., 631/668-2554, www.nysparks.com/parks/122, daily dawn-dusk, parking $10). Home to the only official public beach in Montauk where you can park without a permit, Hither Hills has a bathhouse, general store, picnic area, and campground with 168 sites. The park is also laced with hiking trails leading into isolated dunes, which offer wonderful views of the ocean and bay.

An unofficial **public beach** borders Montauk's village center. Just park in Montauk, walk south down South Essex Street at the end of town, and you're here. Don't expect any facilities, however.

North of Montauk is **Montauk Downs State Park** (50 S. Fairview Ave., 631/668-3781, www.nysparks.com/parks/29, daily, hours vary by facility and season), which has tennis courts, a swimming pool, and a Robert Trent Jones-designed golf course, all of which are open to the public.

Six miles east of Montauk, at the tip of the South Fork, is **Montauk Point State Park** (2000 Montauk Hwy., 631/668-3781, www.nysparks.com/parks/61, $8 parking), a lonely, windy spot overlooking the sea. Hiking and biking trails are the main draws here, as are surfing and surf fishing.

Other Recreation

The nation's oldest cattle ranch, established in 1658, is **Deep Hollow Ranch** (Montauk Hwy. three miles east of village center, 631/668-2744, www.deephollowranch.com). Modern-day visitors can take guided trail rides through 3,000 acres of parklands, pastures, and beach.

Sportfishing (www.montauksportfishing. com) is one of Montauk's major attractions. "Party boats" take out large groups of anglers daily. To sign on, call **Lazybones in Montauk** (631/668-5671) or **Viking Fishing Fleet** (631/668-5700, www.vikingfleet.com). Viking Fishing Fleet also offers **whale-watching** cruises departing from Montauk Harbor in July and August.

Accommodations

◖**Hither Hills State Park** (164 Old Montauk Hwy., 631/668-2554, www.nysparks.com/

parks/122) has 168 popular campsites that must be reserved in advance. Sites can be reserved by the week only.

There are many resort motels in and near Montauk. One half mile west of the village is **The Breakers Motel** (769 Old Montauk Hwy., 631/668-2525, www.breakersmontauk.com, $150-210 summer, $105 off-season), which offers studios and one- and two-bedroom cottages, all of which face the beach and come with parking permits for the town beach. Another motel resort option is clean and friendly **Atlantic Terrace** (21 Oceanview Terr., 631/668-2050, www.atlanticterrace.com, $125-700), conveniently located right on the ocean and three blocks from downtown.

Royal Atlantic Beach Resort (126 S. Emerson Ave., 631/668-5103, www.royalatlantic.com, $105-1,240 summer, $70-105 off-season) offers a variety of accommodations, including studios, one-bedroom suites, and "two-story luxury beach houses." All units have kitchenettes and private terraces.

Modern, gray-shingled ⟨ **Surf Club Resort** (20 Surfside Ave., 631/668-3800, www.surfclub-montauk.com, $255-510 summer) is on the edge of Montauk village, by the beach. This condominium resort also rents one- and two-bedroom duplexes. The condos are built around an attractive pool.

Rooms at the hip **Surf Lodge** (183 Edgemere St., 631/483-5037, www.thesurflodge.com, $275-400) open onto a private sundeck, complete with hammocks for lazy afternoon siestas. Along with iPod docks, a complimentary bar of "sex wax" (which, of course, gives surfers a better grip on their boards) is provided in each room. Despite Wi-Fi throughout, this is a true getaway where phones are nonexistent. A stylish bar and restaurant are on-site. Each summer, the hotel plays host to an array of activities, including an impressive concert series, outdoor surf cinema, and live art installations.

Food

For brunch, **John's Pancake House** (721 Main St., 631/668-2383, daily 6am-3pm, $10) serves a solid breakfast at a good price. Their pancakes, waffles, and crepes bring in a crowd, so be prepared for a line. The **Naturally Good Foods & Cafe** (38 S. Etna Ave., 631/668-9030, www.naturallygoodfoodsandcafe.com, hours vary seasonally, $6 breakfast, $12 lunch) is a small natural-foods store that serves oatmeal, granola, and burritos for breakfast and salads, sandwiches, and wraps for lunch.

Shagwong (774 Main St., 631/668-3050, www.shagwong.com, daily noon-2am, $22), in business for over 40 years, offers quality seafood and steak. The place is equally well known for its lively nightlife scene.

Surfside Inn (685 Old Montauk Hwy., 631/668-5958, www.surfsideinnmontauk.com, lunch and dinner, $28) sits high above the ocean, offering great views from its porch and patio. The restaurant specializes in farm-to-table New American fare and its friendly bar is a favorite among locals.

Bustling ⟨ **Gosman's Dock** (500 West Lake Dr., 631/668-5330, www.gosmans.com, daily noon-10pm, $28) is now over 60 years old. A Montauk institution, this enormous dockside restaurant serves consistently fresh fare and has three dining rooms, all of which overlook the harbor and range in price from the cheap clam bar where you can grab a sandwich and a seat at the outside tables to the Topside restaurant.

⟨ **Dave's Grill** (468 West Lake Dr., 631/668-9190, www.davesgrill.com, May-Oct. daily from 5:30pm, $35) is a classy, intimate bistro specializing in grilled fish. During the summer, there's often a long wait, but it's worth it.

Byron at The Surf Lodge (183 Edgemere St., 631/483-5039, www.thesurflodge.com/byron, Mon.-Tues. and Thurs. 5pm-10pm, Wed. and Fri.-Sat. 5pm-11pm, $24) follows the local, seasonal Hamptons culinary trend, with an emphasis on seafood.

© FRANCISCO COLLAZO

The Hampton Jitney offers transport from New York City to The Hamptons.

Information and Services

For general information on Long Island, contact **Long Island Convention and Visitors Bureau and Sports Commission** (330 Motor Pkwy., Suite 203, Hauppauge, 631/951-3440 or 877/386-6654, www.discoverlongisland.com). For more information on attractions in Nassau County, contact **Nassau County Industrial Development Agency** (1550 Franklin Ave., Suite 235 Mineola, 516/571-1945 www.visitnassaucounty.com). For information on attractions in Suffolk County, visit the website of **Suffolk County Government** (www.suffolkcountyny.gov) and look for the visitors' section. **North Fork Promotion Council** (www.northfork.org) operates two seasonal visitor information centers, which are open May-October. One is located just before the village of **Greenport** (Main Rd./Rte. 25, 631/477-1383) and the other is located in **Laurel** (Main Rd./Rte. 25, 631/298-5757). For more information on any of the state parks or campgrounds, visit www.nysparks.com.

Getting There and Around

The major west-east thoroughfares traversing Long Island are Routes 25 and 25A to the north; Long Island Expressway (LIE), or I-495, mid-island; and Sunrise Highway/Route 27 and Montauk Highway (Routes 27A and 80) to the south. Southern State Parkway also traverses the South Shore but ends mid-island, at Heckscher State Park.

Keep in mind that traffic on Long Island is often slow and tangled, especially in summer. Avoid Long Island Expressway during rush hour and on summer Friday afternoons, when thousands of city dwellers head for the Hamptons.

A good alternative to driving is taking public transportation. Many Long Island communities, including those on the North and South Forks, can be reached from Manhattan via **Long Island Rail Road** (718/217-5477 or 516/822-5477, www.mta.info/lirr). Fares are reasonable

and taxis are usually available at stations. Several companies offer bus service to various points in Long Island. **BoltBus** (877/265-8287, www.boltbusli.com) leaves from Manhattan's Upper East Side and makes stops in the Long Island towns of Riverhead, Ronkonkoma, and Huntington. **Hampton Jitney** (631/283-4600, www.hamptonjitney.com) and **Hampton Luxury Liner** (631/537-5800, www.hamptonluxuryliner.com) service the Hamptons.

Ferries operate between Connecticut and Long Island. **Cross Sound Ferry** (631/323-2525 or 860/443-5281, www.longislandferry.com) travels between New London, Connecticut and Orient Point, New York. **Bridgeport/Point Jefferson Ferry** (631/473-0286, www.88844ferry.com) shuttles between Bridgeport, Connecticut and Port Jefferson, New York. From Port Jefferson, it's an easy one-hour drive to the west of the North Fork.

THE HUDSON VALLEY AND THE CATSKILLS

It's hard to believe, but to the immediate north of honking, teeming, steaming New York City lies some of the most splendid scenery in the Northeast. The beauty begins at the edge of the Bronx, where for a 21-mile stretch the blue-gray Palisade cliffs drop precipitously into the Hudson River. Farther north and to the west sprawl scrappy Ramapo Mountains, while to the east you'll glimpse the long, dark, silent reservoirs of New York City's water system. Midway up the Valley begin the Hudson Highlands, an extension of the Appalachian Mountains made up of steep cliffs, craggy bluffs, and brooding blue-black peaks. Lush, loamy farmland, heavy with fruits and vegetables, spreads across the regions to the east, west, and north of the Highlands.

Along with its seductive landscape, Hudson Valley lays claim to dozens of major historic sites, ranging from Revolutionary War battlefields to grand river estates. The region also offers first-rate cultural institutions, offbeat museums, gourmet restaurants, luxurious hotels and inns, and glorious state parks.

No less majestic are the Catskill Mountains, which lie to the west of Hudson Valley. One of the state's many natural playgrounds, the Catskills region is comprised by Ulster, Sullivan, Delaware, and Greene Counties, encompassing nearly 6,000 square miles. Many of those miles are covered by densely wooded mountains and threaded by rushing rivers and streams, making the area an ideal destination for visitors who enjoy being active outdoors. Hiking, fishing, and

HUDSON VALLEY

HIGHLIGHTS

◖ **Storm King Art Center:** This breathtaking hilltop park is filled with stunning sculptures by the likes of Louise Bourgeois, Alexander Calder, Mark di Suvero, and David Smith (page 201).

◖ **Walkway over the Hudson:** This rehabilitated railroad bridge spans the Hudson River, linking Poughkeepsie and Highland. It's the longest elevated pedestrian walkway in the world (page 204).

◖ **The Culinary Institute of America:** This lovely foodie haven features several award-winning, chef-student-staffed restaurants and a bakery open to the public. Tours, a culinary bookstore, and gift shop round out the offerings (page 211).

◖ **Rhinebeck:** This picturesque historic village is home to many antiques shops, pleasant lodgings, restaurants, and a lovely organic farmer's market (page 211).

◖ **Huguenot Street:** See "the oldest street in America with its original buildings," built by French Huguenot Protestants in the late 1600s (page 217).

◖ **Mohonk Mountain House and Preserve:** The Catskills were once dotted with lovely, sprawling mountain resorts, but none was ever lovelier than Mohonk. The storybook setting evokes bygone days (page 220).

◖ **Minnewaska State Park:** Located high in the Shawangunk Mountains, this park is filled with panoramic views, glacial lakes, and hiking trails for all expertise levels (page 221).

◖ **Downtown Woodstock:** Need more cowbell? Let your inner hippie loose and commune with the crowd on the village green in this famed arts colony (page 225).

◖ **Olana State Historic Site:** It's hard to pick a favorite among the Hudson Valley's epic estates, but Olana is particularly remarkable because of its unusual architecture and decor (page 240).

LOOK FOR ◖ TO FIND RECOMMENDED SIGHTS, ACTIVITIES, DINING, AND LODGING.

biking are all popular in summer months, while skiing and other snow sports are popular in winter. For more laid-back activities, visitors can explore the main streets of the Catskills' small towns, take one of several scenic train rides through the region, or enjoy fall's spectacular color show with an autumn leaf-peeping trip.

PLANNING YOUR TIME

To do the Hudson Valley or the Catskills justice would take two weeks, but you can see plenty over a long weekend or on day trips from New York City.

The gateways to both the Catskills and the Hudson Valley are about an hour's drive from

New York City. The Hudson Valley is particularly accessible, with many key sights within easy driving distance of each other, most on or just off Route 9.

The Hudson Valley is well serviced by trains arriving from New York City. But once in the region, it's easiest to explore all that's on offer with a car. Many travelers find that it's both easier and more affordable to take a train out of the city and into the Hudson Valley and then pick up a rental car in one of the smaller towns.

For a good one- or two-day trip from the Big Apple, stick to the lower Hudson Valley. **Tarrytown and Sleepy Hollow,** home to several major historic homes, including Sunnyside and Kykuit, make for an ideal day trip. Another option is **Beacon,** home to cutting-edge Dia:Beacon museum, and **Cold Spring,** an attractive village on the Hudson River. Outdoor lovers might want to take a day hike in **Harriman and Bear Mountain State Parks. West Point** and **Storm King Art Center** make up another good one- or two-day outing.

A three- or four-day trip could take in one of the lower Hudson Valley sights, plus two days in **Hyde Park,** home to the Roosevelt and Vanderbilt estates, with an overnight in or near **Rhinebeck** or **New Paltz.**

With six days, travel to two or three of the sights in lower and mid-Hudson Valley before heading to upper Hudson Valley. Here, visit the historic city of **Hudson,** home to Olana, a Persian-style castle.

Like the Hudson Valley, the Catskills are a quick getaway from New York City; they can be reached in about an hour, depending on traffic, which can be heavy on Friday afternoons as city-dwellers look to escape for the weekend. The Catskills are most easily reached by car, though bus service from New York City is available to some towns. Once here, however, visitors will find that a rental car is the best way to travel through the region.

If you intend to make the Catskills a day-trip destination, the most obvious choice is to go to **Woodstock,** which gained fame as the gateway to its namesake music-love-peace-and-happiness festival in 1969 (which was actually held on a farm over 50 miles away in Bethel). Spend the day browsing shops and galleries or see a concert at **Maverick** to get a sense of what the area is like today, and eat and shop your way along Tinker Street, the town's main thoroughfare.

For 2-4 days, start in Woodstock and then head north to **Boiceville,** where you can both see and stay at the impressive Onteora Mountain House, former home of mayonnaise magnate Hellman. From Boiceville, go west on Route 28 to **Mount Tremper,** where you can take a look at the Kaatskill Kaleidoscope, said to be the world's largest. Continue west on Route 28 and overnight in Phoenicia; the next day, you can either take a ride on the Catskill Mountain Railroad or go tubing on the river. After Phoenicia, you could choose to go southwest and explore the wilds of Catskill Park, or make the loop back to Woodstock by taking Route 212 east.

Lower Hudson Valley

First-time visitors will probably want to concentrate on Hudson River towns and villages, which are small, accessible, and charming. To explore them by car, follow Route 9, or Broadway, which is an extension of Manhattan's Broadway. To reach Route 9 from Manhattan, take the West Side Highway (Route 9A) north and watch for signs.

To head for destinations west, cross the George Washington Bridge on the upper level, taking the Palisade Parkway exit to your immediate right at the end of the bridge. Don't be alarmed by "Welcome to the Garden State" signs; this route takes you on a quick jog through New Jersey before you re-enter the Empire State.

HUDSON VALLEY

THE HUDSON VALLEY AND THE CATSKILLS

HUDSON VALLEY

BIKING THE BRIDGES

Rail trails and scenic biking abound in the Hudson Valley. The following bike-able bridges are just some of the options cyclists have for crossing the Hudson. All bridges offer lovely views and connections to scenic rides on both sides of the river. Bridges and walkways are listed from south to north.

GEORGE WASHINGTON BRIDGE

The south sidewalk is open to cyclists from 6am until midnight daily; the north sidewalk is usually closed. Access the sidewalk at Cabrini Boulevard and W. 177th Street on the New York side of the bridge. For information and alerts about construction and service changes that affect cyclists' access to the bridge visit the **Port Authority website** (www.panynj.gov).

NEWBURGH-BEACON BRIDGE

From dawn to dusk, cyclists are welcome to ride on the south sidewalk of the bridge, which offers views of Storm King Art Center. Take care, as the surface of the sidewalk is metal with a strong texture and can become slippery when wet.

MID-HUDSON BRIDGE

Bicycles may be taken across the north walkway from dawn to dusk. Ride down Church Street to approach from the east; from the west, look for the "Bicycle Route" signs to the walkway.

WALKWAY OVER THE HUDSON

This multi-use recreational path was created from an abandoned railroad bridge; it is now the longest elevated pedestrian bridge in the world (though cyclists are welcome, too). Visitors can approach from the Highland or Poughkeepsie end of the bridge; for specific directions visit the walkway's website (www.walkway.org/directions).

RIP VAN WINKLE BRIDGE

The roadway is open to cyclists, while the walkway on the south side is for pedestrians.

GREAT FREEDOM ADVENTURES HUDSON VALLEY BIKE TOURS

Longer cycling trips in the Hudson Valley are offered by **Great Freedom Adventures** (www.greatfreedomadventures.com). During its six-day Hudson Valley Bike Tour, guides lead cyclists on scenic routes, with stops at historic sites like Olana; award-winning restaurants, like those at the Culinary Institute of America; and shops and farms of artisanal producers.

YONKERS

Yonkers, on the Hudson just north of New York City, takes its name from *youncker* (young nobleman) Adriaen Van Der Donck, who first acquired it from the Dutch West India Company in the early 1600s. With a population of over 196,000, Yonkers is actually the fourth-largest city in New York State, but its identity is tied to New York City, and it serves as a sort of scruffy extension of its much larger neighbor to the south.

Originally a Lenape Indian village, Yonkers became an important manufacturing center in the second half of the 19th century. Among its chief products were textiles, carpets, patent medicines, insulated wire and cable, and elevators. Yonkers inventor Elisha G. Otis introduced the world's first "perpendicular stairway"—or elevator—in 1853.

Hudson River Museum

Yonkers' biggest visitor attraction is the **Hudson River Museum** (511 Warburton Ave., 914/963-4550, www.hrm.org, Wed.-Sun. noon-5pm, adults $5, seniors and children $3), partially housed in an impressive stone mansion overlooking the Hudson. Built by financier John Bond Trevor in 1876, Glenview Mansion is still outfitted with its original Victorian furnishings and art. Next door is a large, modern museum wing that presents first-rate exhibits on everything from regional flora and fauna to

LOWER HUDSON: WESTCHESTER COUNTY

PUTNAM COUNTY

9

684

North Salem

116

Somers

Muscoot Reservoir

Titicus Reservoir

121

Peekskill

202

35

Cross River

35

Yorktown Heights

Katonah

Cross River Reservoir

WARD POUND RIDGE RESERVATION

129

New Croton Reservoir

22

TACONIC STATE PKY

172

Croton-on-Hudson

100

Mount Kisco

Bedford

Hudson River

Croton Point Park

9A

9

117

Chappaqua

ROCKLAND COUNTY

Ossining

SAW MILL RIVER PKWY

Pleasantville

NEW YORK CONNECTICUT

684

137

Rockefeller State Park Preserve

★ BLUE HILL AT STONE BARNS
★ UNION CHURCH

Kensico Reservoir

22

North Tarrytown

Pocantico Hills

TAPPAN ZEE BRIDGE

Tarrytown

Valhalla

★ **LYNDHURST** ■

★ **SUNNYSIDE**

Elmsford

NEW YORK NEW JERSEY

Irvington

White Plains

287

★ **NEUBERGER MUSEUM OF ART**

Purchase

Greenwich

95

Dobbs Ferry

Scarsdale

Port Chester

87

100

Hastings-on-Hudson

9

Yonkers

Rye

CONNECTICUT NEW YORK

★ **HUDSON RIVER MUSEUM**

Eastchester

★ **RYE PLAYLAND**

■ **PHILIPSE MANOR** **YONKERS RACEWAY** ■

1

95

New Rochelle

Mount Vernon

NASSAU COUNTY

9A

87

Bronx

0   5 mi

0   5 km

© AVALON TRAVEL

HUDSON VALLEY

Hudson River history. Also at the museum are the exuberant *The Bookstore*—an "environmental sculpture" designed by Red Grooms—and the all digital, full-dome Andrus Planetarium, equipped with a Zeiss star machine (adults $2, seniors and children $1).

Philipse Manor Hall State Historic Site

A few miles south of Hudson River Museum is grand **Philipse Manor Hall** (29 Warburton Ave., 914/965-4027, www.nysparks.com/historic-sites/37, Apr.-Oct. Thurs.-Sat. 10am-4pm, Nov.-Mar. Thurs.-Sat. 10am-3pm, adults $5, seniors and students $3, children under 12 free), built in the 1680s for Frederick Philipse, who came to New York to work as a carpenter for Governor Peter Stuyvesant. Through his own skills and a strategic marriage, Philipse became one of the most powerful men in the Hudson Valley. By the end of his life, he owned an estate that covered virtually all of modern-day Westchester County.

A prominent Loyalist, Philipse was one of the 200-plus colonial New Yorkers who signed the Declaration of Dependence, swearing allegiance to King George III shortly after those 56 other Americans signed the Declaration of Independence. Documents and artifacts from that era are on display, along with an excellent collection of American portraits by Gilbert Stuart and other artists.

Empire City Casino at Yonkers Raceway

Nighttime harness racing can be seen year-round at **Yonkers Raceway** (810 Central Ave., 914/968-4200, www.empirecitycasino.com, post time Mon.-Tues. and Thurs.-Sat. 7:10pm). The current track dates back to 1958, but the first Yonkers track was built in 1898 and was long known as the "poor man's racecourse." In fact, one of its earliest owners, chain-store magnate James Butler, liked to pretend that he was poor. He once declined to play golf with John D. Rockefeller, Sr.—calling it a rich man's game—and rode around town in a rickety, out-of-date automobile. In addition to the raceway, **Empire City Casino** (810 Central Ave., 914/968-4200, www.empirecitycasino. com, daily 9am-4am) is here. It operates from the clubhouse, and features four restaurants, a food court, cocktail lounges, live entertainment, 5,300 slot machines, and electronic table games, including baccarat, craps, and roulette.

Food

If you want to eat in town, **La Belle Havana** (35 Main St., 914/920-9777, www.labellahavana.com, $16), in Yonkers, offers mojitos and *el sabor de Cuba* with fusion foodie flair via respected chef Alexandre Cheblal.

TARRYTOWN AND SLEEPY HOLLOW

Among the most popular visitor destinations in this area are Tarrytown and Sleepy Hollow. Washington Irving, one of the area's prominent residents from bygone times, quipped that the name Tarrytown came from the early Dutch farmers' tendency to linger too long at the village tavern. But most historians agree that "tarry" is a corruption of *tarwe,* the Dutch word for "wheat." Despite being busy commuter villages, the towns are home to several major historic sites and a handful of smaller ones.

Tarrytown is located at one of the Hudson River's widest points, the Tappan Zee. Tappan were an Algonquin tribe and *Zee* means "sea" in Dutch. Across the Tappan Zee runs the Tappan Zee Bridge, its graceful silver lines glinting in the sun.

Many of the historic sites in Tarrytown and Sleepy Hollow are operated by **Historic Hudson Valley** (914/631-8200, www.hudsonvalley.org), an educational institution founded by John D. Rockefeller in 1951 and originally called Sleepy Hollow Restorations. The philanthropist and preservationist Rockefeller, owner of the nearby Kykuit estate, acquired area properties of cultural, historical, and architectural significance and saved them from the wrecking ball. The organization changed its name to Historic Hudson Valley in 1987 and continues to operate several historic sites in the Hudson Valley.

Sunnyside

One of Tarrytown's earliest commuters was writer Washington Irving. In 1835 he moved into an old village farmhouse, now called **Sunnyside** (3 W. Sunnyside Ln., 914/591-8763 on weekends, 914/631-8200 on weekdays, www.hudsonvalley.org, hours vary seasonally, adults $12, seniors $10, children 3-17 $6), where he felt he could find the quiet he needed for his work, yet still be within easy reach of New York City. Almost immediately upon moving into his new abode, Irving began remodeling it, adding gables, dormers, and towers until the place was, as he described it, "as full of angles and corners as an old cocked hat."

Today, 17-room, wisteria-draped Sunnyside is open to the public. It's a charming, fairytale-like place, complete with costumed guides, a landscaped garden, and a pond with a bevy of swans. Much of Irving's furniture, including his desk and wood stove, is still in the house, along with many of his books. Just below Sunnyside runs the Hudson River Railroad, which Irving allowed to be built through his property on the condition that it stop to pick him up whenever he pleased.

Lyndhurst

Less than a mile north of Sunnyside is **Lyndhurst** (635 S. Broadway, 914/631-4481, www.lyndhurst.org, May-Oct. Mon. noon-5pm, Fri.-Sun. 10am-5pm, adults $14, seniors $13, children 6-16 $10), a magnificent Gothic Revival mansion designed by Alexander Jackson Davis in 1838. Originally built for William Paulding, a former New York City mayor, Lyndhurst was later owned by the unscrupulous financier Jay Gould. Among Gould's many questionable acts were his attempt to corner the gold market, which resulted in the disastrous panic of Black Friday, September 24, 1869, and his engineering of a deal that ruined his former business associate, Cyrus W. Field. Not surprisingly, none of this history is discussed at the site.

Covered with gables and chimneys, turrets, and towers, the exterior of Lyndhurst has a magical aspect. Inside, however, it feels dark.

Much of the Goulds' heavy furnishings and art collection are still in place.

Surrounding the mansion are 67 acres, complete with formal gardens, a children's playhouse, a bowling alley, nature paths, and spectacular views of the Hudson. Don't miss the romantic ruins of an enormous greenhouse, the 14 rooms of which once housed a renowned orchid collection.

Tarrytown Music Hall

Built in 1885, **Tarrytown Music Hall** (13 Main St., 914/631-3390, www.tarrytownmusichall. org) is the oldest live theater in Westchester County and a National Historic Landmark. Top-notch jazz, folk, and blues concerts are performed here; plays, musicals, operas, comedies, dance, and films are also on the schedule.

Old Dutch Church and Burying Ground

In Sleepy Hollow, the **Old Dutch Church** (540 N. Broadway, 914/631-1123, www.odcfriends. org, cemetery gates close at 4:30pm daily) dates back to 1685 and is believed to be the oldest church in continuous use in New York State. But except for its thick walls, little of the structure is original.

Surrounding the church is a Dutch cemetery that early settlers believed was haunted by a headless Hessian ghost. That local tale later became the inspiration for Washington Irving's *The Legend of Sleepy Hollow*. Irving took many of his characters' names from the cemetery's tombstones.

Adjacent to the Old Dutch cemetery is newer **Sleepy Hollow Cemetery** (540 N. Broadway, 914/631-0081, www.sleepyhollowcemetery.org, daily 8am-4:30pm), a scenic and peaceful place where Washington Irving, Andrew Carnegie, William Rockefeller, and other early movers and shakers are buried.

Philipsburg Manor

Across the street from the Old Dutch Church is **Philipsburg Manor** (381 N. Broadway, 914/631-3992, www.hudsonvalley.org, hours vary seasonally, adults $12, seniors $10,

GREAT RIVER ESTATES

- **Philipse Manor Hall,** Yonkers: This mansion, built for Frederick Philipse III, was confiscated by the state and sold at an auction after George Washington ordered Philipse arrested for his Loyalist beliefs. The state reacquired the house in 1908; today, it is a museum devoted to 18th-century history, art, and architecture.

- **Sunnyside,** Tarrytown: Writer Washington Irving's former abode, full of gables and towers, sits beside a pond with swans. Guides in period dress take you back to the mid-19th-century during a house and grounds tour.

- **Lyndhurst,** Tarrytown: The magnificent Gothic Revival estate, designed by the great Alexander Jackson Davis in 1838, was home to a mayor, a merchant, and a railroad magnate. It is now managed by the National Trust for Historic Preservation, whose staff offer guided tours of the house and grounds.

- **Philipsburg Manor,** Sleepy Hollow: This reconstructed 17th- and 18th-century manor house, which relied heavily upon slaves for its operation, is complete with a functional water-powered gristmill and guides in period dress.

- **Kykuit,** Sleepy Hollow: The former Rockefeller estate is famed for its magnificent grounds and collection of modern art, including Picasso and Calder. Staff offer guided tours.

- **Van Cortlandt Manor,** Croton-on-Hudson: This lovely 18th-century stone-and-clapboard house is not as well known as the Tarrytown mansions and is therefore a good place to visit on summer weekends. Guides show visitors one of the largest and best-equipped 18th-century kitchens in the United States, as well as colonial and federal period furniture.

- **Locust Grove,** Poughkeepsie: The romantic octagonal villa was once the summer home of artist-scientist-philosopher Samuel Morse, inventor of the telegraph. It is now a museum and 200-acre nature preserve.

- **Springwood,** Hyde Park: Perhaps the most interesting of the Hudson River estates, Springwood is FDR's former home, a deeply personal place. Adjoining it is a first-rate library-museum. Nearby is Eleanor Roosevelt's equally personal Val-Kill. Together, they comprise the Franklin D. Roosevelt National Historic Site, operated by the National Parks Service.

- **Vanderbilt Mansion,** Hyde Park: This was the most extravagant Hudson River estate, built in a posh Beaux-Arts style. Go here to drool over lavish furnishings, gold-leaf ceilings, Flemish tapestries, and the like.

- **Staatsburgh State Historic Site,** Staatsburg: The vast, 65-room mansion sits on a hill overlooking the Hudson River and Catskill Mountains. Edith Wharton based the Trenor estate in *The House of Mirth* on this place.

- **Wilderstein,** Rhinebeck: This whimsical, all-wooden Queen Anne mansion with interiors by Tiffany and grounds designed by Calvert Vaux is one of the smaller estates. Visitors can enjoy house tours and exploring the three miles of trails crisscrossing the estate.

- **Montgomery Place,** Annandale-on-Hudson: Though the classical revival style mansion is impressive, the grounds here are the main draw; 380 acres feature woodland trails with views of the Hudson River and Catskill Mountains, as well as carefully groomed gardens.

- **Clermont State Historic Site,** Germantown: This grand mansion has an especially fine front lawn lined with black locust trees. Historic house tours are offered or visitors can simply wander the 500 acres of grounds.

- **Olana State Historic Site,** Hudson: This eccentric Persian-style castle, perched high on a hill, was built by Hudson River School painter Frederic Church in 1870. The landscaped grounds are considered as impressive as Church's artwork.

© FRANCISCO COLLAZO

Philipsburg Manor

students 3-17 $6), a carefully reconstructed 17th- and 18th-century manor house, complete with a working gristmill and small farm. Once owned by Frederick Philipse of Yonkers, the estate is now often jammed with tour buses and groups of schoolkids; of all the Historic Hudson Valley properties, this one is best for families. Costumed guides describe life in colonial times as visitors pass through the main stone house, gristmill, Dutch barn, and other buildings.

Kykuit

Just northeast of Sleepy Hollow in the elite little village of Pocantico Hills, **Kykuit** (KYE-cut; visitor's center at Philipsburg Manor, 381 N. Broadway, 914/631-8200, www.hudsonvalley.org, hours vary seasonally, admission fees vary by type of tour and day of the week) served as the weekend home for three generations of the Rockefeller family. Compared to many of the estates along the Hudson, the Beaux-Arts Kykuit, built in 1908, is a relatively modest affair, decorated with 18th- and 19th-century antiques. The house tour doesn't become especially interesting until it descends to Nelson Rockefeller's astonishing subterranean art gallery, filled with more than 100 works by such modern masters as Picasso, Motherwell, Warhol, and Léger.

Even more wonderful are Kykuit's 87 acres of meticulously landscaped grounds, offering glorious views of the Hudson and Palisades. The gardens—complete with boxwood hedges, romantic arbors, and linden allées—are whimsically dotted with yet more modern-art masterpieces, including sculptures by Gaston Lachaise, Aristide Maillol, and Alexander Calder.

Kykuit **tours** leave from Philipsburg Manor (381 N. Broadway). Five different kinds of tours are offered and reservations for most are not required; same-day tickets are sold on a first-come, first-serve basis starting at 9am.

Union Church of Pocantico Hills
Union Church of Pocantico Hills (555 Bedford Rd. 914/631-8200, hours vary seasonally and

© FRANCISCO COLLAZO

the Kykuit estate

by church activities, $7) is a serene attraction. Inside are nine stunning stained glass windows by Marc Chagall and a luminous rose window by Henri Matisse. The Chagall windows depict biblical scenes. The Matisse window—a leafy swirl of green, yellow, and blue—was the final work completed by the artist before his death. Visitors can admire the windows on their own or request a guided tour.

Rockefeller State Park Preserve

Once part of the Rockefeller estate, the well-kept 750-acre **Rockefeller State Park Preserve** (off Rte. 117 near Rte. 9, Mount Pleasant, 914/631-1470, www.nysparks.com/parks/59, daily dawn-dusk, parking $6) is filled with meadows and woodlands, a small lake, a peony monument (a gift of Japan), and over 14 miles of mostly-level paths. The preserve is designated as an Important Bird Area by the National Audubon Society because more than 180 bird species have been documented here. Maps are available at the entrance.

Teatown Lake Reservation

Just a short drive from Tarrytown is peaceful 875-acre **Teatown Lake Reservation** (1600 Spring Valley Rd., 914/762-2912, www.teatown.org, trails daily dawn-dusk, visitors' center daily 9am-5pm), with a shimmering lake, hiking trails, an interpretive museum in two colonial buildings, and wildflowers galore in spring, summer, and fall. Most of the 230 species of native and endangered flowers grow on an isolated two-acre island in the middle of the park, accessible only by tour ($6 per person, reservations required, children under 12 not permitted on island).

Van Cortlandt Manor

In Croton-on-Hudson, 18th-century **Van Cortlandt Manor** (525 S. Riverside Ave., 914/631-8200, hours vary seasonally, adults $12, seniors $10, children 3-16 $6) is another splendid estate managed by Historic Hudson Valley. Oloff Van Cortlandt arrived in this county in 1638, and his son, Stephanus Van Cortlandt, became the first native-born mayor of New York City. The Van Cortlandt family once owned 87,000 acres of land stretching from Croton all the way east to Connecticut. They were staunch supporters of the Revolution, and among their many famous guests were Generals Washington and Lafayette.

The deed to the Van Cortlandts' property still hangs in the house, along with original family portraits. Also on display are period furnishings and a working kitchen where guides concoct colonial recipes. Outside, a long, brick-paved walk flanked with flower beds leads to a restored 18th-century inn.

Accommodations

Doral Arrowood (975 Anderson Hill Rd., Rye Brook, 914/939-5500, www.doralarrowwood.com, $199-249), a 114-acre resort and conference center, is situated on a Robert von Hagge–designed nine hole golf course and offers a Hot Stix facility, which uses a golfer's "swing DNA" for personalized club-fitting. Driving range, pool, tennis, squash, racquetball and sand volleyball courts are also available. Though largely used for meetings, the resort offers good deals and is a great location to use as a base for exploring the area.

Scoring high in the romance department is ◖ **Tarrytown House Estate & Conference Center** (49 E. Sunnyside Ln., 800/553-8118, www.tarrytownhouseestate.com, $209-399), housed in two pristine 19th-century estates: one a Greek Revival mansion once owned by B&O Railroad executive Thomas King, the other a sprawling "castle" that belonged to tobacco heiress Mary Duke Biddle. Together, the estates boast lavish gardens, a well-equipped health club, and a billiard room.

One of the most romantic hideaways in Westchester County is ◖ **Castle Hotel and Spa** (400 Benedict Ave., 914/631-1980, www.castlehotelandspa.com, $285-355). Perched on a hill overlooking the Hudson, this authentic castle, with its 75-foot-high main tower, was built near the turn of the 20th-century by the

© FRANCISCO COLLAZO

Castle Hotel and Spa

HUDSON VALLEY

son of a Civil War general. Now a luxury establishment that's a member of the Small Luxury Hotels of the World and National Trust Historic Hotels networks, it offers 31 luxurious accommodations, some with working fireplaces. On the premises is THANN Spa and the acclaimed Zagat 5-star Equus Restaurant.

Food

Mint Premium Foods (19 Main St., 914/703-6511, Tues.-Sun. 10am-10pm) is a must-stop for gourmands or anyone else really. The tiny shop stuffed with gorgeous international delicacies, hot and cold, makes this take-out a top option for foodies, especially considering the vast array of scenic picnicking spots in the area. **Horsefeathers** (94 N. Broadway, 914/631-6606, www.horsefeathersny.com, Sun.-Wed. 11:30am-9pm, Thurs.-Sat. 11:30am-10pm, $22) is a cozy local institution, known for home-style food, good burgers, sweet potato fries, and an extensive bar.

Ultra-romantic **Equus Restaurant** (400 Benedict Ave., 914/631-3646, www.castle-hotelandspa.com, daily breakfast, lunch, and dinner, $50 average dinner entrée) at Castle Hotel and Spa is spread out over several elegant rooms, including The Garden Room, The General's Bar, and Tapestry Lounge. It features unique and creative Auberge-style natural French cuisine based on locally-sourced ingredients.

(Blue Hill at Stone Barns (630 Bedford Rd., Pocantico Hills, 914/366-9600, www.bluehillfarm.com, tasting menu $148-208) is a branch of Manhattan's Blue Hill. Owner Dan Barber is a major figure in the locavore movement and a James Beard Outstanding Chef of the Year-award winner. His Hudson Valley outpost is in a beautifully restored barn located at **Stone Barns Center for Food and Agriculture** (914/366-6200, www.stonebarnscenter.org), a nonprofit education center and 80-acre farm. Known for being an experience where food is truly honored, the venue has no set menu; tasting menus are designed around the day's harvest, and range in price. Reservations are required.

If you're north of Tarrytown, Croton-on-Hudson has a good spot for lunch. **Justin Thyme** (171 Grand St., Croton, 914/271-0022, www.justinthymecafe.webs.com, Tues.-Thurs. 11:30am-9pm, Fri.-Sat. 11:30am-10pm, Sun. 11:30am-9pm, $16) offers everything from sandwiches to dinner entrées. To one side is a pub area with a copper-topped bar, to the other, the main dining room.

NORTHEASTERN WESTCHESTER
Katonah

The well-heeled, picturesque village of Katonah is about 10 miles east of the Hudson River, where Route 35 meets I-684. There are 55 historic homes on broad, tree-lined Bedford Street alone, all part of an area that's on the National Register of Historic Places. The homes were moved here between 1895 and 1897 when the original village of Katonah, located a half mile away, was flooded to create Cross River Reservoir. That event is known locally as "the Inundation."

Katonah Avenue, running parallel to Bedford Street, is also lined with Victorian-era buildings that were moved from the old village. Among them are the creaky, old-fashioned **Charles Department Store** (113 Katonah Ave., 914/232-5200, www.charlesdepartmentstore.com), still operated by descendants of the original owners.

Museum Mile

Route 22, just outside Katonah, is known as Museum Mile because of the three major cultural institutions found here. Most famous among them is the **Caramoor Center for Music and the Arts** (149 Girdle Ridge Rd., 914/232-5035, www.caramoor.org). An overgrown and romantic estate built in the 1930s by financier Walter Tower Rosen, Caramoor presents a highly acclaimed outdoor **music festival** (box office 914/232-1252, tickets $10-85) every summer, featuring many top names in classical music and opera and some top names in jazz.

Originally built by Rosen to house his outstanding art collection, **Caramoor Rosen**

House (149 Girdle Ridge Rd., 914/232-5035, www.caramoor.org, $10) is well worth visiting. The fascinating main house was created by combining entire rooms from historic European buildings and surrounding them with a Mediterranean-style shell. One of the bedrooms comes from a 1678 French chateau; the exquisite music room was originally part of a 16th-century Italian villa. Meanwhile, all around the house are sun-baked courtyards and deserted gardens strewn with weathering statuary.

Down the street from Caramoor is **John Jay Homestead** (400 Jay St., 914/232-5651, www.johnjayhomestead.org, Apr.-Oct. Wed.-Sat. 10am-4pm, Sun. 11am-4pm, Nov.-Mar. Wed.-Sat. 10am-3pm, Sun. 11am-3pm, free). Jay was president of the Continental Congress, first chief justice of the U.S. Supreme Court, and co-author of both the Federalist Papers and the Treaty of Paris (which ended the American Revolution). He retired here after leaving public office in 1801. The large wooden house with shutters and an inviting veranda is filled with period antiques and memorabilia. Surrounding the house are landscaped gardens and a farm.

Near John Jay's former home is the small but exceedingly lovely **Katonah Museum of Art** (134 Jay St., 914/232-9555, www.katonahmuseum.org, Tues.-Sat. 10am-5pm, Sun. noon-5pm, adults $10, seniors and students $5, children under 12 free). Designed by Edward Larrabee Barnes, the museum features unusual temporary exhibits by major contemporary artists such as Milton Avery and Mark Rothko.

North Salem

In the northeast corner of Westchester County lies North Salem, a rustic but moneyed one-stoplight burg surrounded by horse farms, wooded hills, and Titicus Reservoir. The village also boasts **Golden's Bridge Hounds** (www.goldensbridgehounds.org), the only hunt club left in Westchester. During the hunting season, the club's members ride to the hounds on nearby golf courses as often as three times a week.

The unusual **Hammond Museum and Japanese Stroll Garden** (28 Deveau Rd., 914/669-5033, www.hammondmuseum.org, Wed.-Sat. noon-4pm, adults $5, seniors $4, and children under 12 free) sits on a hill overlooking North Salem. Established by Natalie Hays Hammond in 1957, the place bills itself as a "cross-cultural center" for Eastern and Western arts. Inside the museum are changing exhibits on such subjects as antique Japanese fans and watercolors; outside are meticulously designed Japanese gardens.

Hammond was the daughter of John Hays Hammond, the mining engineer who discovered and developed the long-lost King Solomon Mines in South Africa. She traveled the world as a child, became engaged eight times but never married, and worked as a Broadway set and costume designer, author, miniaturist, and needlepoint artist.

Cross River

A few miles east of Katonah is 4,315-acre **Ward Pound Ridge Reservation** (Rtes. 35 and 121, 914/864-7317, daily 8am-dusk, parking $10), the largest park in Westchester County. Laced with 35 miles of good, fairly rugged hiking trails, the park also features two rivers for fishing and a small **Trailside Nature Museum** (Wed.-Sun. 10am-4pm). Year-round camping under lean-tos is available.

Shoppers might like to stop at nearby **Yellow Monkey Village** (792 Rte. 35, 914/763-5848, www.yellowmonkey.com, Tues.-Sat. 10am-5:30pm, Sun. noon-5pm), an attractive collection of shops housed in reproduction 18th-century buildings. The shops sell everything from Portuguese pottery to silk flowers.

Bedford

A few miles south of Katonah, where Route 22 meets Routes 121 and 172, is Bedford, another picture-perfect village. Here, pristine white 19th-century homes cluster around a village green, along with a carpenter-Gothic Presbyterian church and the nicely restored 1787 Court House, the oldest public building in Westchester County.

A walking tour of the village is printed on

a plaque in front of the Court House. Take the tour and you'll pass the 1681 Old Burying Ground, a general store, post office, and library that date back to the early 1800s. On Court Road just off the green is a row of shops selling antiques, clothing, and gifts.

Chappaqua

About eight miles south of Katonah is one of Westchester's more unusual lodgings, the 12-bedroom **C Crabtree's Kittle House Restaurant and Inn** (11 Kittle Rd., 914/666-8044, www.kittlehouse.com, $147 s, $167 d, with continental breakfast). Over 200 years old, the building has been a carriage house, roadhouse, girls' school, guesthouse for the Mount Kisco Little Theater, restaurant, and inn. Henry Fonda and Tallulah Bankhead were among the actors who overnighted here.

Attached to the inn is a restaurant (11 Kittle Rd., 914/666-8044, www.kittlehouse.com, Mon.-Fri. lunch and dinner, Sat. dinner, Sun. brunch and dinner, $32). The eclectic menu includes a mix of innovative Italian, French, Asian, and American dishes, with a tasting menu available. Live jazz is often played on the weekends. Reservations are recommended for this popular spot.

SOUTHEASTERN WESTCHESTER
Purchase

Despite its bland appearance, the wealthy community of Purchase is home to two remarkable cultural sites. **Neuberger Museum** (735 Anderson Hill Rd., 914/251-6100, www.neuberger.org, Tues.-Sat. noon-5pm, adults $5, seniors and students $3, children under 12 free), on the campus of Purchase College, State University of New York, is a first-rate art museum with an outstanding collection of modern works by such masters as Georgia O'Keeffe, Jackson Pollock, Henry Moore, Frank Stella, Mark Rothko, Edward Hopper, and—especially—Milton Avery. Avery was the favorite painter of the museum's founder, Roy Neuberger, and 20 of his canvases are on display.

Just down the street from Neuberger are **Donald M. Kendall Sculpture Gardens at PepsiCo** (700 Anderson Hill Rd., 914/253-2000, daily 9am-dusk, free). An impressive outdoor sculpture garden is filled with works by Alexander Calder, Jean Dubuffet, George Segal, Claes Oldenburg, and many others. More than 40 works are on display, installed on carefully landscaped grounds complete with dramatic fountains. A path winds through the area, and a map is available at the entrance.

To reach either the museum or the gardens from I-684, take the State University of New York exit and follow the signs. Note that the grounds are closed to the public during a renovation expected to last into mid-2015.

Rye Playland

Rye, a sprawling suburban town located on Long Island Sound, dates to the 1660s, when it was a notable stopping place on the Old Post Road between New York and Boston. Then, as now, the town centered around Purchase Street, which today is lined with trees and antiques shops.

At the southern end of Rye is the wonderful **Playland** (end of Playland Pkwy., 914/813-7000, www.ryeplayland.org). Opened in 1928 as the nation's first amusement park, this dreamy Art Deco refuge still boasts its original green-and-cream buildings and a number of original rides, including the Carousel, Derby Racer, Old Mill boat ride, and the wooden Dragon Coaster. Also in the park are about 40 other rides, a crescent-shaped beach with a weathered boardwalk, an Olympic-size pool, and a lake where rowboats can be rented.

Most of the rides at Playland are open May-Labor Day; hours vary. Admission for a non-rider is $10, for riders is $30, and kids under 48 inches ride for $20. To reach Playland from downtown Rye, head east on Playland Parkway. From I-95, take Exit 19.

Constitution Marsh

Constitution Marsh Audubon Center Sanctuary (127 Warren Landing Rd.,

Garrison, 845/265-2601, www.constitution-marsh.audubon.org, year-round Tues.-Sun. 9am-dusk), a 207-acre tidal marsh, is managed by the National Audubon Society. An interpretive nature trail and boardwalk run through the preserve, while at river's edge is a **visitors' center** (May-Oct. Tues.-Sun. 9am-5pm, free). The sanctuary is rich with birds—194 species have been spotted—and wildflowers.

The preserve also has canals created by farmers who hoped to use the marshlands to grow rice. Once a day at high tide, from May through early October, Audubon Society runs guided canoe trips through these canals. Trips are free and enormously popular; reservations must be made weeks in advance.

Manitoga

Heading North on Route 9D—watch closely for signs—you'll come to **Manitoga** (584 Rte. 9D, Garrison, 845/424-3812, www.russel-wrightcenter.org, trails: early May-late Oct. daily dawn-dusk, suggested donation $5; house tours: $15). Created by industrial designer Russel Wright over a period of about three decades beginning in 1947, Manitoga is designed, as the artist put it, to "bring to American culture an intimacy with nature." Throughout the center run three hiking trails that Wright carefully manipulated to their best natural effect. Some parts are reminiscent of a Japanese garden; others are considerably wilder.

At Manitoga's center is Wright's glass-walled home and studio, **Dragon Rock,** built on the edge of a small quarry. Wright rerouted a waterfall to turn the quarry into a pond.

Graymoor

A few miles due east of Manitoga is **Graymoor** (1350 Rte. 9, 845/424-3671, www.atonement-friars.org, grounds daily 9am-dusk), a monastery of the Franciscan Friars of the Atonement perched high on a hill with magnificent views of the Hudson Valley. Shrines, chapels, and Stations of the Cross are on the grounds, open for visitors to wander through and reflect upon.

Clarence Fahnestock Memorial State Park

Clarence Fahnestock Memorial State Park (1498 Rte. 301, Carmel, 845/225-7207, www.nysparks.com/parks/133, daily dawn-dusk, parking $7) spreads out over 14,000 acres of Putnam Valley. It's crisscrossed with a number of hiking trails, including the Appalachian Trail, and features lakes (boat rentals available), swimming beaches, fishing ponds, and an extensive performing arts program. A 77-site campground is open May-October.

Southeast Museum

This idiosyncratic **Southeast Museum** (67 Main St., Brewster, 845/279-7500, www.southeastmuseum.org, Apr.-Dec. Tues.-Sat. 10am-4pm, suggested donation $5) is full of oddities. Housed in the 1896 Old Town Hall, it contains a large collection of minerals from local mines, early artifacts from the Harlem Railroad Line, and an assortment of early memorabilia from the Borden condensed-milk factory. Gail Brewster began producing condensed milk here in the 1850s. He hit upon the idea while sailing home from England, when he longed for a glass of fresh milk. The town of Brewster has another famous resident: Rex Stout, creator of the orchid-loving detective Nero Wolfe and his sidekick Archie Goldwin.

Food

One of the few old-fashioned drive-ins left in the region is the ever-popular **Red Rooster Drive-in** (1566 Rte. 22, Brewster, 845/279-8046, Sun.-Wed. 10am-11:30pm, Thurs. 10am-midnight, Fri.-Sat. 10am-1am, $8), always crowded with families and enthused kids.

COLD SPRING

Legend has it that the quaint village of Cold Spring was first named by George Washington after he took a sip of the local waters. The village didn't flourish, however, until the 1800s when the federal government created an iron foundry here. Around the same time, tourists traveling by steamboat first discovered the glories of the Hudson Valley. Cold Spring, with

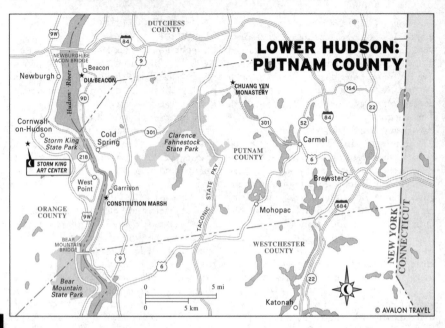

the granite dome of Storm King Mountain looming across the way, was a favorite overnight stop.

Today, much of Cold Spring still embodies the spirit and look of its Victorian heyday. Throughout the area are a number of old inns, and restored 19th-century buildings housing attractive antique and gift shops line Main Street. **Walking tours** (845/265-4010, www.putnamhistorymuseum.org) of the village are offered by Putnam History Museum.

At the foot of Main Street is the Hudson River, but you can't get there without first detouring south, under the Metro-North train tracks (a sign marks the way). Once at the shore, you'll find the **Riverfront Bandstand and Dock,** the latter jutting out into the river and offering outstanding views.

Putnam History Museum

Originally a school for children of the Irish immigrants employed by Cold Spring's foundry, this small 1820 building is now

Putnam History Museum (63 Chestnut St., 845/265-4010, www.putnamhistorymuseum. org, Wed.-Sun. 11am-5pm, adults $5, seniors and students $2). Run by the Putnam County Historical Society, the museum houses a recreated foundry room, school room, country store, and country kitchen, along with a dugout canoe, horse-drawn sleigh, and historic photographs.

Chuang Yen Monastery

Take a detour east from Cold Springs on Route 301 to view the largest indoor statue of the Buddha in the Western hemisphere at the largest monastery in the eastern United States, **Chuang Yen Monastery** (2020 Rte. 301, Carmel, 845/225-1445, Apr. 1-Jan. 1 daily 9am-5pm, free). Standing 37 feet tall, the Buddha sits surrounded by 10,000 small Buddha figurines in the Great Buddha Hall. Gravel walkways lead to several smaller halls, a lovely lake, and the Woo-Ju Library, a circulating library with titles in English and Chinese.

Accommodations

Right on the banks of the Hudson, with close-up views of Storm King Mountain, is boxy **Hudson House River Inn** (2 Main St., 845/265-9355, www.hudsonhouseinn.com, $170-250 with breakfast), the second-oldest continuously operating inn in New York. Built in 1832 to house steamboat passengers, the inn features 11 guest rooms and two suites, all nicely furnished with antiques. On site is an airy indoor-outdoor restaurant serving lunch and dinner.

Charming ◖ **Pig Hill Inn** (73 Main St., 914/265-9247, www.pighillinn.com, $150-230) is housed in a brick Georgian townhouse with antiques for sale. Six of the nine guest rooms have a fireplace or wood stove. Out back is a terraced garden.

Food

Friendly **Cold Spring Depot** (1 Depot Sq., 845/265-5000, www.coldspringdepot.com, $13) is a casual joint housed in an old railroad station. **Foundry Cafe** (55 Main St., 845/265-4504, $9) specializes in naturally healthy foods and regional American cooking, including soups, home-baked goods, and grain dishes.

On the shores of the Hudson River you'll find historic ◖ **Hudson House Restaurant** (2 Main St., 845/265-9355, www.hudsonhouse-inn.com, Mon.-Thurs. 11:30am-3:30pm and 5pm-9pm, Fri.-Sat. 11:30am-3:30pm and 5pm-10pm, Sun. 11am-8pm, $26) at Hudson House River Inn. The restaurant serves fresh seafood and regional American cuisine. An outdoor dining area opens in summer, and many tables have great views of the river.

One of the village's most upscale spots is **Plumbush Inn** (1656 Rte. 9D, 845/265-3904, www.plumbushinn.com, Mon.-Sat. dinner, Sun. brunch and dinner, $26), housed in an 1867 building. Here you'll dine by candlelight in a lush Victorian dining room complete with working fireplaces and dark wood paneling.

BEACON

Once a bustling manufacturing town best known for its brick and hat factories, Beacon, like many towns along the Hudson, fell on hard times in the 20th century. Many of its 19th-century buildings were boarded up. The town was used as the setting for the 1995 movie *Nobody's Fool*, starring a down-and-out Paul Newman. In the last few years, however, revitalizing change has come to town, thanks largely to Dia:Beacon, a major contemporary arts museum that opened here in 2003, bringing gentrification in its wake. During its first year of operation, Dia:Beacon attracted nearly 100,000 visitors, twice as many as projected. Main Street is now spiffy with artsy clothing boutiques, bistros, and antique shops, while second-home owners have contributed to the increase in real estate prices.

Mount Beacon towers over the city and has played an important role in its history. During the Revolutionary War, colonists set signal fires on the summit to warn compatriots of British troop movements. During the early 1900s, a casino serviced by a funicular sat atop the mountain; the tracks remain visible today.

Historic Houses

At **Mount Gulian Historic Site** (145 Sterling St., 845/831-8172, www.mountgulian.org, May-Oct. 31 Wed.-Fri. and Sun. 1pm-5pm, adults $8, seniors $6, children 6-18 $4), you'll learn about the Dutch, Native American, and African American cultures of the Revolutionary War-era Hudson Valley. Costumed guides conduct tours.

The 1709 **Madam Brett Homestead** (50 Van Nydeck Ave., 845/831-6533, Apr.-Dec. second Sat. of the month 1pm-4pm or by appointment), built by Catheryna and Robert Brett, has an interesting history. After the death of her husband by drowning, Madam Brett succeeded in establishing the region's first thriving business venture: the Frankfort Storehouse and Mill. The locals used to joke, "All roads lead to Mme. Brett's mill." During the Revolutionary War, Catheryna's granddaughter entertained Generals Washington and Lafayette here. The homestead is the oldest house in the county and is decorated with original furniture.

Dia:Beacon

Housed in a nearly 300,000-square-foot former printing plant, **Dia:Beacon** (3 Beekman St., 845/440-0100, www.diabeacon.org, Jan.-Mar. Fri.-Mon. 11am-4pm, Apr.-Oct. Thurs.-Mon. 11am-6pm, Nov.-Dec. Thurs.-Mon. 11am-4pm, adults $12, seniors $10, students $8, children under 12 free) displays the permanent collection of the Dia Art Foundation, an innovative arts institution based in New York City. Among the highlights are Andy Warhol's 1979 *Shadows,* composed of 102 paintings; Richard Serra's monumental Torqued Ellipses series; a large-scale sculpture by Walter De Maria; a series of fluorescent light works by Dan Flavin; and Agnes Martin's 1999 suite of paintings *Innocent Love,* created specifically for the institution.

Redesigned from a factory into a museum by artist Robert Irvin, Dia:Beacon sits on 34 landscaped acres with flowering fruit trees. The museum is within walking distance of Metro-North train station; on weekends, the Beacon Shuttle provides transportation to various stops in town. Fare is $2 per ride or $5 for an all-day pass.

Food

The name may be odd and somewhat cumbersome, but **SWIFT at The Roundhouse at Beacon Falls** (2 E. Main St., 845/440-3327, www.roundhousebeacon.com, Wed. 6pm-10pm, Thurs.-Sat. 11am-3pm and 6pm-10pm, Sun. 11am-3pm and 5pm-8pm, $30) is a top choice for upscale dining in Beacon, and is especially favored by art lovers who find themselves hungry after visiting Dia:Beacon. Dishes on the menu are seasonal, featuring local ingredients, and draw raves from guests, who also enjoy waterfall views from the restaurant's floor-to-ceiling windows.

PIERMONT

In its heyday, Piermont was a bustling commercial center at the terminus of the Erie Railroad. Today, it's a quieter, less touristy version of the nearby town of Nyack. Woody Allen filmed much of *The Purple Rose of Cairo* here in the early 1980s.

Most of the village's shops and art galleries are located on or just off Piermont Avenue. Among them are **Piermont Flywheel Gallery** (223 Ash St., 845/365-6411, www.piermontflywheel.com, Thurs. and Sun. 1pm-6pm, Fri.-Sat. 1pm-9pm, free), which features the work of its co-owners, all artists and sculptors. Another gallery featuring handmade objects by artisans is **The Outside In** (249 Ferdon Ave., 845/398-0706, www.outsideinpiermont.webs.com, Tues.-Sat. 11am-6pm, Sun. noon-5pm). Here, you can find larger pieces of handcrafted furniture and smaller objects suitable as gifts or souvenirs. A number of other vintage clothing boutiques and sundries shops line Piermont Avenue.

In the center of town is **Piermont Pier,** which extends into the river about a mile. Built by Chinese immigrants to allow the railroad easier access to Hudson River ships, the pier today is delightfully overgrown with cottonwoods, poplars, and goldenrod. From along its length you'll have unobstructed views of the Tappan Zee Bridge and Piermont Marsh, a 950-acre wetland and bird sanctuary.

If you're interested in visiting **Piermont Marsh,** enter **Tallman Mountain State Park** (off Rte. 9W, 845/359-0544, www.nysparks.com/parks/119, daily dawn-dusk, parking $6), just south of the pier and follow the bike path to the shore. The preserve, covered with wildflowers in the spring, is one of the most important fish-breeding areas along the Hudson and an excellent bird-watching spot.

Nightlife

One of the Hudson Valley's oldest and best-loved music clubs is **Turning Point** (468 Piermont Ave., 845/359-1089, www.turningpointcafe.com, tickets $15-35) in Piermont. The club presents mostly folk and folk-rock, along with some jazz and blues.

Food

A number of restaurants are located on Piermont Avenue. Classiest among them is **Xaviar's at Piermont** (506 Piermont Ave., 845/359-7007, www.xaviars.com, Wed.-Thurs.

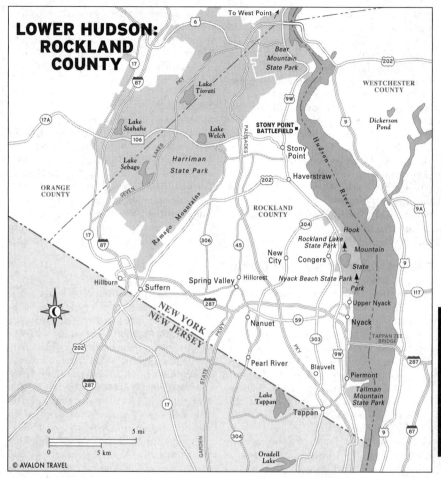

and Sat. 6pm-9pm, Fri. noon-2pm and 6pm-9pm, Sun. noon-2pm and 5pm-8pm, $36 à la carte, $90-100 tasting menu), a highly acclaimed fine dining restaurant serving contemporary American fare. Five- and ten-course tasting menus are available, though guests can also order à la carte if they prefer. Next door is a slightly less-expensive sister restaurant, the informal yet sophisticated C **Freelance Cafe and Wine Bar** (506 Piermont Ave., 845/365-3250, Tues.-Thurs. noon-3pm and 5:30pm-10pm, Fri. noon-3pm and 5:30pm-10:30pm,

Sat. noon-3pm and 5:30pm-11pm, Sun. noon-3pm and 5pm-10pm, $28), serving eclectic cuisine with Asian, French, and Italian influences.

Upstairs from the Turning Point club is **Tequila Sal y Limon** (468 Piermont Ave., 845/680-6741, www.tequilany.com, daily 3pm-close), a restaurant serving Mexican favorites like tacos and enchiladas.

NYACK

The town of Nyack was settled by Dutch farmers in the mid-1600s and became home to thriving shipping, boatbuilding, and shoe- and cigar-manufacturing industries in the 1800s. The village fell into decline after the Depression, but in the 1970s was reborn as an antiques and arts-and-crafts center. Today, most of Nyack's quaint Victorian downtown has been restored, and homes of the rich and famous perch on steep wooded hills surrounding the village. Famous Nyack residents have included Helen Hayes, Ben Hecht, Carson McCullers, Jonathan Demme, Ellen Burstyn, Harvey Keitel, and Toni Morrison.

In summer, when Nyack is flush with tourists, a Nyack Chamber of Commerce **information booth** (845/353-2221) operates daily at the corner of Main Street and Broadway. The booth is also open on weekends in spring and fall.

Edward Hopper House Art Center

The birthplace and home of painter Edward Hopper (1882-1967) is a two-story clapboard house in downtown Nyack now called the **Edward Hopper House Art Center** (82 N. Broadway, 845/358-0774, www.edwardhopperhouse.org, Thurs.-Sun. noon-5pm or by appointment, suggested donation $5). The son of a prosperous dry-goods merchant, Hopper grew up in Nyack and held title to the house until his death, even though he left the village in 1910 to live in New York City. Hopper is buried in Nyack's Oak Hill Cemetery.

The rooms of the Hopper House are wonderfully evocative, filled with a clean white light reminiscent of the artist's work. Only a small section of one room is devoted to Hopper's art. Most of the house is a gallery showcasing the work of local artists; out back is a picturesque garden where summer jazz concerts are presented.

Entertainment

Entertainment and nightlife options include lively, rollicking **O'Donoghue's Tavern** (66 Main St., 845/358-0180, www.odonoghuestavern.com), where you're bound to hear many a tale. Live Irish bands perform on Monday nights.

Nyack also hosts many street fairs and festivals. Three of the biggest, all featuring about 200 vendors, are **Art, Craft & Antiques Dealers' Fairs** (www.acadaofnyack.com), usually held on the third Sunday of May, July, and October.

Shopping

Most of the village's shops are found along Main Street and South Broadway. **Hickory Dickory Dock** (43 S. Broadway, 845/358-7474, www.hickorydock.com) sells clocks, handmade toys, and collectibles. **Saffron Trading Company** (14 S. Broadway, 845/353-3530, www.saffrontradingcompany.com) and **Maria Luisa Boutique** (77 S. Broadway, 845/353-4122, www.marialuisaboutique.com) are fun to browse for beautiful home accents and other lifestyle accessories.

Recreation

Riverfront **Memorial Park,** off Main Street in the village center, offers great views of the Hudson. Two miles farther north is **Nyack Beach State Park** (off N. Broadway, 845/268-3020, www.nysparks.com/parks/156, daily dawn-dusk, parking $6), a riverfront stretch offering hiking, fishing, and more great views.

Hook Mountain State Park (845/268-3020, www.palisadesparksconservancy.org/parks/10, daily dawn-dusk, parking $6), at the steep northern end of North Broadway, offers bird's-eye views of the Hudson, along with hiking and biking trails. Once a favorite campground among Native Americans, the park is said to be haunted by the Guardian of the Mountain, a medicine man who appears every September during the full moon to chant the ancient harvest festival. A hawk watch is held in the park in the spring and fall.

Food

Simple, casual **Strawberry Place** (72 S. Broadway, 845/358-9511, daily 7am-4pm, $10) is a local favorite that's especially good for breakfast. For after-meal treats, **Temptations Cafe** (80 Main St., 845/353-3355, www.temptationscafe.com, Mon.-Thurs. 11:30am-9pm,

Fri.-Sat. 11:30am-10:30pm, Sun. 11:30am-9pm, $5 average dessert) is the place to go for ice cream and desserts.

King & I (91-93 Main St., 845/358-8588, www.kingandinyack.com, Mon.-Thurs. and Sun. noon-10pm, Fri.-Sat. noon-11pm, $14) is known for its fresh, authentic Thai food. Asian-fusion cuisine is the order of the day at sleek, stylish 🄲**Wasabi** (110 Main St., 845/358-7977, www.wasabichi.com, $16).

For dinner in a historic setting, try 🄲 **Hudson House of Nyack** (134 Main St., 845/353-1355, www.hudsonhousenyack.com, Mon.-Fri. dinner, Sat.-Sun. brunch and dinner, $28), housed in an old town hall and former jailhouse with pressed tin walls and ceilings. On the menu is eclectic American cuisine and lots of homemade desserts. Patio dining is featured in summer.

TAPPAN

Tappan was the first town in New York State to establish an official historic district. Its Main Street is flanked with many nicely restored 18th- and 19th-century buildings, and in the town center is a village green that once held public stocks and a whipping post.

Revolutionary War Sites

Tappan is associated with both the beginning and the end of the planned betrayal of West Point by Benedict Arnold and British major John Andre during the Revolutionary War. It was in the DeWint House on Livingston Avenue that Washington entrusted West Point to Arnold, and it was in the Mabie House on Main Street that Andre—after his capture in Tarrytown—was imprisoned before being hanged.

Both buildings are still standing and open to the public. **DeWint House,** also known as **Washington's Headquarters** (20 Livingston Ave., 845/359-1359, www.dewinthouse.com, Tues.-Sun. 10am-4pm, free) is now a bona fide museum holding Washington memorabilia, artifacts regarding Masonic history, and information about the Andre trial. Washington was headquartered here in 1780 and 1783, and was

a Mason for 47 years. On the day of Andre's execution, Washington closed the shutters to his room.

Mabie House is now better known as **Old '76 House** (110 Main St., 845/359-5476, www.76house.com); it's a dark, low-ceilinged establishment that has functioned as a tavern and restaurant since 1800. Andre's former bedroom is now a dining room.

Also connected with Andre is **Andre Monument** (Old Tappan Rd. at Andre Hill Rd.). Here, a large crowd of spectators, held back by 500 infantrymen, watched Andre's execution on October 2, 1780. Only upon seeing the hangman's noose did Andre realize that his request to be shot as a soldier, rather than hung as a spy, was not to be granted. Impatient with his slow-moving hangman—a sympathetic fellow prisoner—Andre placed the noose around his own neck and the handkerchief around his own eyes. "All I request of you gentlemen," he said before the final signal was given, "is that you bear witness to the world that I die like a brave man."

Food

Old '76 House (110 Main St., 845/359-5476, www.76house.com, Mon.-Thurs. 11:30am-3pm and 5pm-9pm, Fri. 11:30am-3pm and 5pm-9:30pm, Sat. 11:30am-3pm and 5pm-10pm, Sun. 11:30am-3pm and 4pm-9pm, $24), complete with exposed beams, Dutch tiles, and fireplaces, specializes in traditional American fare for lunch and dinner. A jazz vocalist or pianist often performs on the weekend.

RAMAPO MOUNTAINS

Near the western edge of Rockland County rise the craggy foothills of the Ramapo Mountains. Nearly 600 million years old, the Precambrian Ramapos, which spill over into New Jersey, are one of the oldest land masses in North America. At one time, their slopes, now eroded and dotted with erratics left during the Ice Age, constituted a mountain system as grand as the Rockies.

In New York, most of the Ramapos fall within two very popular state parks: Harriman and Bear Mountain. The parks were created largely through the efforts of Mrs. E. H. Harriman, widow of railroad tycoon Edward Harriman and mother of the late statesman W. Averell Harriman. When the state proposed building a prison at Bear Mountain in 1908, Mrs. Harriman offered to give the Palisades Interstate Park Commission 10,000 acres in return for dropping the project. The proposal was accepted and since then the parks have been significantly enlarged through other gifts and purchases.

Harriman State Park

Straddling Rockland and Orange Counties is the second largest state park in New York: **Harriman State Park** (off Rte. 17 or Palisades Pkwy., Exits 17 or 18, 845/786-2701, www. nysparks.com/parks/145, open daily, hours vary by section of park), a 46,000-acre preserve that is considerably less developed than its better-known neighbor to the north, Bear Mountain State Park. **Seven Lakes Drive,** which hugs the shores of only a small portion of the many bodies of water to be found in this preserve, runs through the heart of the park. Two of the park's most spectacular lakes are crystal-clear **Lake Tiorati** and **Lake Sebago.** Ironically, their Native American names—bestowed upon them by white men eager to create a romantic atmosphere—are not local, but rather names that come from Western tribes. Both of the large, artificially constructed lakes have swimming beaches.

About 200 miles of **marked trails** loop through Harriman and its neighbor, Bear Mountain. Basic information on some of these trails can be picked up at the headquarters of the **Palisades Interstate Park Commission** (Bear Mt., Rte. 9W, 845/786-2701). For more detailed information and maps, stop at the superb **Park Visitor Information Center** (between Exits 16 and 17 on the Palisades Pkwy., 845/786-5003) or contact the **New York-New Jersey Trail Conference** (201/512-9348, www.nynjtc.com). The park also offers an excellent, 200-site **campground** (call 800/456-2267 for reservations).

Just south of the park, on a mountaintop near Hillburn, is ◖ **Mount Fuji** (296 Old Rte. 17, 845/357-4270, Mon.-Thurs. noon-2:30pm and 5pm-10pm, Fri. noon-2:30pm and 5pm-11pm, Sat. 5pm-11pm, Sun. 5pm-10pm, $34), a big, glitzy Japanese steakhouse offering stunning views of the valley below. On the western border of the park are Clove Furnace Historic Site, Tuxedo Park, and Sterling Forest.

Bear Mountain State Park

When New Yorkers think about getting out of the city for a day hike, they tend to think about **Bear Mountain State Park** (Palisades Pkwy., Exit 19, and Rte. 9W, 845/786-2701, www. nysparks.com/parks/13, daily 8am-dusk, parking $8), one of the most popular recreational areas in the region. Abutting Harriman to the north, the park offers dramatic views of the Hudson River and—on exceptionally clear days—New York City skyscrapers. Because Bear Mountain can get very crowded on weekends, it's best to come during the week. This is also no place for the outdoors purist; almost every inch of the 5,000-acre park has been trodden over many times.

To hike to the top of Bear Mountain and back takes 3-4 hours. For those who prefer to drive to the summit, **Perkins Memorial Drive** (open March-Oct.) offers stunning overlooks and historic markers that tell of Revolutionary War battles that took place here. Legend has it that Hessian Lake was named for the many dead Hessian soldiers whose bodies were weighted and dumped into the lake after the battle of Fort Clinton. The fort's ruins are nearby.

Though overrun with crowds on summer weekends, ◖ **Bear Mountain and Overlook Inn** (55 Hessian Dr., 845/786-2731, www.visitbearmountain.com, $95-145) is a charming spot, nearly 100 years old. The inn's rooms are divided among the Main Inn, four small stone cottages, and Overlook Lodge, a 24-room property near Hessian Lake. Come on a weekday in fall and you'll have the place to yourself! The Inn also has restaurants serving global cuisine made with locally-sourced ingredients:

Restaurant 1915, Blue Roof Tapas Bar, and Hiker's Cafe. Sunday brunch is also a popular dining event here.

Route 17 South

Route 17 runs along the western edge of Harriman State Park. In an earlier incarnation, Harriman was mining country, and its mountains are still pocked with mine shafts and foundries. A small museum documenting the area's mining history now stands at **Clove Furnace Historic Site** (21 Clove Furnace Dr., Arden, 845/351-4696, Mon.-Fri. 9am-11am and 1pm-4pm, free).

Just behind the museum is romantic, ivy-covered Arden House, which served as the residential estate of the Harriman family until 1972. Local lore has it that Edward Harriman built his mansion on this mountain site because he'd been shunned by the exclusive nearby community of Tuxedo Park and wanted his wife to be able to look down on it daily. Note that the privately owned house is not open to the public.

Continuing south on Route 17, you'll come to Route 17A. Travel west on the road about two miles to reach the dark, quiet woods of **Sterling Forest State Park** (845/351-5907, www.nysparks.com/parks/74, daily dawn-dusk). The spacious Visitors' Center has historical and nature exhibits, as well as a small gift shop. Special weekend hikes and events launch from here.

Nearby, popular **New York Renaissance Faire** (600 Rte. 17A, 845/351-5174, www.renfair.com, adults $22, children 5-12 $11) is presented on weekends in August-September. During the festival, which attracts about 175,000 visitors annually, knights in shining armor joust on horseback, minstrels strum love songs, a human chess game is played, and Shakespearean plays are staged. A special ShortLine bus leaves for the festival from Manhattan (212/736-4700).

Farther south on Route 17, you'll catch a glimpse of **Tuxedo Park.** Watch for a high stone wall and gatehouse on the right. The residential community was designed in the 1880s as a millionaires' refuge and is filled with turreted mansions. Etiquette maven Emily Post lived here for many years, and it was in Tuxedo Park that the formal dinner jacket of the same name was first introduced.

STONY POINT

South of Bear Mountain is **Stony Point Battlefield** (Park Rd., off Rte. 9W, 845/786-2521, www.nysparks.com/historic-sites/8, hours vary seasonally and by installation, parking $5), where the British army threatening West Point was based in the summer of 1779. Stony Point was captured by Americans in a daring midnight raid led by General "Mad" Anthony Wayne. A tour of the battlefield takes visitors through a small interpretive museum, past the ruins of the British fortifications, and past the oldest lighthouse on the Hudson River. Beautiful countryside surrounds the site.

WEST POINT

The section of the Hudson Valley between Dunderberg Mountain to the south and Storm King Mountain to the north is known as **Hudson Highlands.** Along this 15-mile stretch, the Hudson River, narrowing and deepening, cuts through the Appalachian Mountain Range, creating a spectacular rocky gorge.

About halfway up this stretch, where the river takes a sharp turn, is a rocky outcropping known as West Point. With its strategic views of both sides of the river, it's easy to see why it was such an important stronghold during the Revolutionary War. Today, West Point is best known as the home of the U.S. Military Academy, authorized by Congress in 1802.

U.S. Military Academy

About 4,400 cadets are enrolled at the **U.S. Military Academy** (www.usma.edu) each year. Graduates have included Generals Grant, Lee, Pershing, MacArthur, and Eisenhower; misfits have included James Whistler and Edgar Allan Poe.

Near the Thayer Gate entrance to the Gothic, fortress-like academy is a giant **visitors' center** (Rte. 218, 845/938-2638, daily

9am-4:45pm). The center stocks brochures and maps, holds a large gift shop, and screens a short movie about cadets' lives.

Next door to the visitors' center is **West Point Museum** (Rte. 218, 845/938-2203, daily 10:30am-4:15pm, free), filled with a wide and fascinating array of exhibits on military history. Here, you'll find everything from a Stone Age axe to weapons used in Vietnam and the Gulf War; dioramas of famous battles fought between the 16th and 20th centuries; the letter that Einstein wrote to President Roosevelt urging him to begin research on the uses of plutonium; and a pistol that once belonged to Adolf Hitler. One philosophical panel, simply entitled "Reflections," includes quotes by famous military leaders throughout history, from Thucydides to Eisenhower.

The academy can only be visited via escorted **tours** (adults $13, children 5-12 $10), which leave from the visitors' center throughout the day, except during special events such as football games. Tour highlights include **Cadet Chapel,** lined with lovely stained-glass windows donated by graduated classes; the **Plain,** where the cadets march out in formation at precisely 12:20pm every day; and **Trophy Point,** where you'll find unforgettable views of the blue-gray Hudson. Also at the point are links of the "Great Chain" that the patriots once stretched across the river here to prevent the passage of British ships.

Constitution Island

One of the more unusual spots at West Point is **Constitution Island** (845/446-8676, www. constitutionisland.org, hours vary seasonally, adults $10, seniors and students $9, children 3-6 $3, reservations required), accessible only by boat, which leaves from West Point's South dock. Strategically important during the Revolution, the island later became the home of Susan and Anna Warner, two 19th-century writers who taught Bible classes at West Point. Susan was the author of the popular 1850 novel *The Wide, Wide World;* Anna was best known for writing the words to the hymn "Jesus Loves Me." The sisters lived in **Warner House,** a 17-room Victorian mansion built on the island by their father in 1836. One wall of the mansion dates back to Revolutionary War days, and the whole house is furnished more or less as it was when the sisters lived here. At present, the house is under restoration and is not open to the public, but boat trips still leave you at the island to stroll the grounds and gardens.

Accommodations and Food

On the academy grounds just inside Thayer Gate off Route 218 stands the big, gray, castle-like ◖ **Thayer Hotel** (674 Thayer Rd., 845/446-4731 or 800/247-5047, www.thethayerhotel.com, $190-230), where the rooms are outfitted in the style of late-19th-century Americana. Some rooms overlook the Hudson, others the West Point campus. The lobby and restaurant are outfitted with marble floors and iron chandeliers. Outside is a pleasant terrace with more great views of the Hudson. The hotel's upscale **MacArthur's Restaurant** (674 Thayer Rd., 845/446-4731 or 800/247-5047, www.thethayerhotel.com, breakfast, lunch, and dinner, average dinner entrée $30) serves traditional American and Continental cuisine.

◖ STORM KING ART CENTER

Storm King Art Center (Old Pleasant Hill Rd., off Rte. 32 a few miles south of Vails Gate, 845/534-3115, www.stormking.org, early Apr.-late Nov. Wed.-Sun. 10am-5pm, adults $12, seniors $10, students $8, children under 5 free) is a breathtakingly beautiful sculpture park built on a hilltop. About 120 permanent works and many more temporary ones are scattered over green lawns and wheat-blond fields, while in the distance are the dusk blue Shawangunks. Nearly every major post-WWII sculptor is represented here, including Alexander Calder, Henry Moore, Louise Nevelson, Isamu Noguchi, and Richard Serra. A map of the 500-acre park and its sculptures is available at the gate. An imperial Norman-style building that was originally the home of lawyer Vermont Hatch stands in the center of the park; it houses temporary exhibits. An open air café sells light fare made from locally sourced ingredients. There's live music in the summer.

Accommodations

◖ **Storm King Lodge** (100 Pleasant Hill Rd., 845/534-9421, www.stormkinglodge.com, $175-195) offers excellent views of Storm King Mountain. Housed in a converted carriage house and centered around an expansive common room with a stone hearth, the lodge offers four cozy guest rooms, two of which have private fireplaces. There is also a cottage available for rent.

CORNWALL-ON-HUDSON

Storm King Highway (Route 218) runs from West Point north to the tidy village of Cornwall-on-Hudson; it's a twisting, narrow roadway that hugs the cliffs of the Hudson River gorge, offering stunning views of the landscape below. It's a particularly fine drive in fall, when the hills are ablaze with turning leaves.

Hudson Highlands Nature Museum

Hudson Highlands Nature Museum (25 Boulevard, Cornwall-on-Hudson, 845/534-7781, www.hhnaturemuseum.org, Fri.-Sun. noon-4pm, $3), founded in 1959, is one of the oldest environmental museums in the country, and is notable for its hands-on, down-to-earth feel. At its Wildlife Education Center, visitors can see living animals in recreated habitats. At the museum's second site, the **Outdoor Discovery Center** (100 Muser Dr., Cornwall, 845/534-5506, Sat.-Sun. 9am-4pm, $5 for all visitors over five), visitors can enjoy nature programs and trail walks on the grounds of this former 174-acre horse farm.

Accommodations and Food

Luxurious ◖ **Cromwell Manor Inn** (174 Angola Rd., 845/534-7136, www.cromwellmanor.com, $185-410) is an elegant 1820s B&B with nine guest rooms, some equipped with working fireplaces, whirlpool tubs, or steam rooms. Listed on the National Register of Historic Places, the manor is situated on a seven-acre estate surrounded by mountains and has its own formal gardens and croquet courts.

A Cornwall institution since 1985, ◖ **Painter's Restaurant** (266 Hudson St., 845/534-2109, www.painters-restaurant.com, $14) offers an eclectic array of sandwiches and burgers, salads and pasta, along with some Italian, Japanese, and Mexican specialties. Walls are hung with works by local artists. Upstairs are seven B&B guest rooms ($95-135).

NEWBURGH AND VICINITY

North of Cornwall-on-Hudson, Route 9W leads to the small city of Newburgh. Once a thriving whaling port and later an important factory town manufacturing everything from lawn mowers to handbags, Newburgh spent much of the late 20th century in a sorry state. Fortunately, Newburgh is coming out of its post-industrial slump, and now boasts a revitalized waterfront, Newburgh Landing, flush with restaurants, bars, and shops. Here, you can catch a narrated two-hour river cruise with **Hudson River Adventures** (845/220-2120, www.prideofthehudson.com, May-Oct.).

Washington's Headquarters State Historic Site

Washington's Headquarters State Historic Site (84 Liberty St. 845/562-1195, www.nysparks.com/historic-sites/17, Apr.-Oct. 31 Wed.-Sat. 10am-5pm, Sun. 1pm-5pm, adults $4, seniors $3, children under 12 free), the nation's first public historic site, sits at the far edge of downtown, on bluffs overlooking the Hudson. The general spent the last six months of the war here while his officers and troops waited farther south. It was from this headquarters—originally a farmhouse built by the Hasbrouck family—that Washington issued a victorious order for a "cessation of hostilities," bringing about an end to the Revolutionary War on April 19, 1783.

Now a state park, Washington's Headquarters has been restored to reflect his stay, and the place has a very personal feel. Its small, whitewashed rooms are simply furnished with cots, firearms, and facsimiles of Washington's account books, along with the desk he once used. The general remained in the house for about a year after the war ended, waiting for the British to leave New York. During much of that time, he was restless, bored, and resentful of public demands upon his time.

Surrounding the house are a wide lawn and high stone wall. An excellent visitors' center with new interactive displays is at the entrance, while the 53-foot Tower of Victory, built to commemorate the 100th anniversary of the war's end, sits near the bluffs.

Crawford House

History buffs might also want to visit the 1830 **Captain David Crawford House** (189 Montgomery St., 845/561-2585, www.newburghhistoricalsociety.com, Apr.-Oct. Sun. 1pm-4pm, also open by appointment, $5), just a few blocks away from Washington's Headquarters. The home of the Historical Society of Newburgh Bay and the Highlands, the house is filled with period antiques, Hudson Valley paintings, and an intriguing series of photo exhibits documenting Newburgh's more prosperous days.

Motorcyclepedia

Newburgh has added a modern twist to its cultural offerings with **Motorcyclepedia** (250 Lake St., 845/569-9065, www.motorcyclepediamuseum.org, Fri.-Sun. 10am-5pm, adults $11, children 3-12 $5, children under 3 free), the largest motorcycle museum in the United States. More than 450 motorcycles—some more than 100 years old—are displayed in the 85,000-square-foot space; collection highlights include rare vintage bikes, police and military bikes, sidecars, and more than 100 Indians, the first motorcyles produced in the United States, starting in 1901.

New Windsor Cantonment

Several other Revolutionary War sites are located within a few miles of Washington's Headquarters, in the town of New Windsor. Most interesting among them is **New Windsor Cantonment** (374 Temple Hill Rd., New Windsor, 845/561-1765, www.nysparks.com/historic-sites/22, Apr.-Oct. Wed.-Sat. 10am-5pm, Sun. 1pm-5pm, adults $4, seniors $3, children 5-11 $1), where the general's 7,000 troops, accompanied by some 500 women and children, waited out the last months of the war. Here they lived in log huts during a long, hard winter—a situation that almost led to rebellion. Today's cantonment re-creates the lives of the Continental

Army's soldiers and camp followers. Inside the visitors' center are two floors of exhibits and a slide show. Outside, a military drill including the firing of muskets and cannons is staged every afternoon.

National Purple Heart Hall of Honor

Right next to New Windsor Cantonment, the **National Purple Heart Hall of Honor** (374 Temple Hill Rd., New Windsor, 845/561-1765, www.thepurpleheart.com, hours vary seasonally, single admission free, $3 fee per person for groups of 10 or more) is a tribute to recipients of this prestigious military service award. Staff is devoted to collecting, preserving, and sharing stories of Purple Heart recipients, whose names are listed in a searchable electronic database that spans every war from the Civil War to present conflicts. Visitors can watch the film *For Military Merit,* as well as listen to interviews.

Gomez Mill House

Four miles north of Newburgh is the 1714 **Gomez Mill House** (Mill House Rd., off Rte. 9W, Marlboro, 914/236-3126, www.gomez. org, Apr.-Oct. Wed.-Sun. 10am-4pm, adults $8, seniors $6, and children 6-18 $3), the oldest extant house of a Jewish family in the nation. Continuously occupied for more than 275 years, the Mill House has been home to fur traders, merchants, Revolutionary War soldiers, farmers, artisans, and statesmen.

The house was originally built by Louis Moses Gomez, who bought 6,000 acres along the Hudson after fleeing the Spanish Inquisition. Several Indian paths converged on his property, and Native Americans once gathered near his home to hold ceremonial rites. In the early 20th century, Dard Hunter, a renowned craftsperson and papermaker, lived in the house.

Wineries

Seven wineries are in the area, including **Brotherhood** (100 Brotherhood Plaza Dr., Washingtonville, 845/496-3661, www.

brotherhood-winery.com), the oldest winery in the United States. Tours of the largest underground wine cellars in the country are given daily in April through December and on weekends the rest of the year. **Warwick Valley Winery and Distillery** (114 Little York Rd., Warwick, 845/258-4858, www.wvwinery.com) is open daily all year, making a variety of wines and Doc's Hard Apple Cider, which is distributed throughout the country.

Food

If your sweet tooth is aching, stop at **Commodore's** (482 Broadway, 845/561-3960), famous for its handmade chocolates.

Yobo (1297 Rte.300, 845/564-3848, www. yoborestaurant.com, Mon.-Thurs. 11:30am-10pm, Fri. 11:30am-11pm, Sat. 12:30pm-11pm, Sun. 12:30pm-10pm, $17) serves a wide variety of dishes from China, Korea, Indonesia, and other Asian countries in an artificially-constructed atmosphere of babbling brooks and waterfalls.

One of the area's most popular Italian restaurants is (**Il Cena'Colo** (228 S. Plank Rd., 845/564-4494, www.ilcenacolorestaurant.com, Mon. and Wed.-Thurs. noon-2:30pm and 5pm-9pm, Fri. noon-2:30pm and 5:30pm-11pm, Sat. 5:30pm-11pm, Sun. 4pm-9pm, $24), which serves Tuscan-style and Northern Italian fare. Among the tasty specials are oyster stew, fried baby artichokes, and gnocchi with venison sauce.

In downtown Marlboro, near the Gomez Mill House just north of the Orange-Ulster County border, is lively **Raccoon Saloon** (1330 Rte. 9W, 845/236-7872, www.raccoonsaloonny.com, $23). On the menu is an enormous selection of tasty burgers and beers, along with homemade ice cream.

The Wherehouse (119 Liberty St., 845/561-7240, www.thewherehouserestaurant.com, Tues.-Thurs. noon-11pm, Fri.-Sat. noon-midnight-, Sun. 11am-9pm, $11) is a casual, affordable spot close to Washington's Headquarters. Almost 50 different kinds of burgers are on the menu, alongside hot dogs, sandwiches, and chili.

A recent and welcome addition is **Newburgh Brewing Company** (888 S. Colden St., Newburgh, 845/569-2337, www.newburgh-brewing.com, Wed. 4pm-9pm, Fri. 4pm-midnight, Sat. 1pm-11am, Sun. noon-5pm), a craft brewery housed in a renovated box factory that dates to the 1850s. Its beautiful tasting room affords panoramic views of the Hudson River. Newburgh beer, local wine, and a menu of traditional beer-paired foods are served.

Mid-Hudson Valley

Many of the Hudson Valley's top attractions are clustered in the mid-Hudson region. Most of the grand riverfront estates for which the area is famous are located here, as are Vassar and Bard Colleges, the historic town of Rhinebeck, The Culinary Institute of America, and myriad country villages, pick-your-own farms, public gardens, and excellent restaurants and lodgings.

The historic museum-estates are all in a 20-mile riverfront stretch between Hyde Park and Clermont that in 1990 was declared a National Historic Landmark District, the second largest such district in the United States.

The district contains some 2,000 buildings, only a handful of which are open to the public. Of these, Franklin Delano Roosevelt's estate, Springwood, is by far the most personal and popular, and can be combined with a visit to Val-Kill, Eleanor Roosevelt's retreat. Between the two homes and nearby FDR Library and museum, you'll come away with a good sense of both the Roosevelts and the times in which they lived. Of the other museum-estates, Vanderbilt Mansion is the most lavish, Montgomery Place the most beautiful, Mills Mansion the most cavernous, Clermont the most elegant, and Wilderstein the smallest and least known.

South of Hyde Park is the river city of Poughkeepsie. While it has fallen on hard times, it has interesting historic and cultural sites to offer. A few miles east of Route 9, the expansive rural countryside is dotted with small villages, wineries, produce stands, and horse farms. The entire Hudson Valley is a major horse-breeding area, with about half of its horse farms located in Dutchess County.

POUGHKEEPSIE

Poughkeepsie (Wappinger Indian for "reed-covered lodge by the little water place"), the seat of Dutchess County, was founded in 1683 and designated the state capital in 1777. From the mid-1800s through the mid-1900s, the town was a major industrial center. It then served as home base for IBM following World War II. But the late 20th century was not kind to Poughkeepsie. Many of its factories closed down and urban renewal ravaged the city, destroying many of its historic 19th-century brick buildings. In the 1990s, IBM laid off thousands of employees.

Today, Poughkeepsie is poised for its comeback, as a revitalization project focuses on Main and Market Streets as a hub for commercial and cultural development. Near the river and railroad station, where Union and Academy Streets intersect Main and Mill, are two bustling, restored **historic districts** filled with shops, pubs, and restaurants.

(Walkway over the Hudson

This abandoned railroad bridge spanning the Hudson River, linking Poughkeepsie and Highland, was rehabilitated and reopened in 2009. The **Walkway over the Hudson** (www.walkway.org, daily 7am-dusk, free) has been a major draw for locals and visitors since. The multi-use pedestrian bridge is the longest elevated pedestrian walkway in the world, and, every day, runners, cyclists, and walkers enjoy the 1.28-mile path that sits 212 feet above the Hudson. The walkway can be approached from either the Poughkeepsie side or the Highland side; for directions, visit www.walkway.org. There is no fee to use the walkway; however, if

HUDSON VALLEY

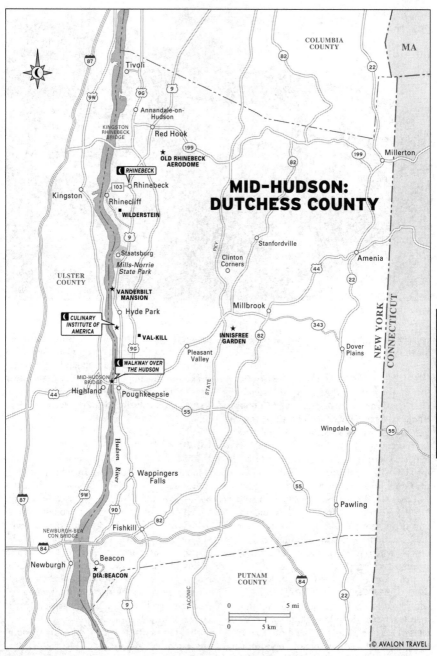

COLUMBIA COUNTY

MA

Tivoli

MID-HUDSON: DUTCHESS COUNTY

Annandale-on-Hudson

KINGSTON RHINEBECK BRIDGE

Red Hook

Millerton

OLD RHINEBECK AERODOME

RHINEBECK

Rhinebeck

Kingston

Rhinecliff

WILDERSTEIN

Stanfordville

Amenia

Clinton Corners

ULSTER COUNTY

Staatsburg

Mills-Norrie State Park

VANDERBILT MANSION

Millbrook

CULINARY INSTITUTE OF AMERICA

Hyde Park

VAL-KILL

INNISFREE GARDEN

Dover Plains

NEW YORK

CONNECTICUT

WALKWAY OVER THE HUDSON

Pleasant Valley

MID-HUDSON BRIDGE

Highland

Poughkeepsie

Wingdale

Hudson River

Wappingers Falls

Pawling

NEWBURGH-BEACON BRIDGE

Fishkill

Newburgh

Beacon

DIA:BEACON

PUTNAM COUNTY

TACONIC

0   5 mi

0   5 km

© AVALON TRAVEL

© FRANCISCO COLLAZO

Walkway over the Hudson

you're arriving by car, you'll pay a parking fee for the walkway's lot.

Cunneen-Hackett Arts Center

Just up the hill from the restored historic district near the railroad station is **Cunneen-Hackett Arts Center** (9 and 12 Vassar St., 845/486-4571, www.cunneen-hackett.org, Mon.-Fri. 9am-5pm, free). The center occupies two handsome 1880s Italianate buildings built by the nephews of Matthew Vassar, the Poughkeepsie brewer who founded Vassar College. No. 9 now houses a small art gallery; No. 12 is home to another gallery and an exquisite Victorian auditorium—complete with gold-cushioned seats and stained-glass windows—where plays, concerts, and films are presented.

The *Clearwater*

Built by a handful of river-loving volunteers, the *Clearwater* (845/265-8080, www.clearwater.org) has been sailing the Hudson since 1969, bringing with it a message of environmental urgency. The sloop often docks downtown at Main Street pier. It has been instrumental in helping clean up the Hudson, and is the impetus behind the popular, three-day **Clearwater Great Hudson River Revival** (www.clearwaterfestival.org), a festival held in the region every June.

Locust Grove, the Samuel Morse Historic Site

Immediately south of downtown Poughkeepsie is **Locust Grove** (370 South Rd./Rte. 9, 845/454-4500, www.morsehistoricsite.org, May 1-Nov. 30, hours vary seasonally, adults $10, children 6-10 $6), a romantic octagonal villa that was once the summer home of Samuel Morse, inventor of the telegraph. An artist and philosopher as well as a scientist, Morse bought his home in 1847 when he was already a widower in his fifties. With the help of renowned landscape architect Alexander Jackson Davis, he transformed it into a Tuscan-styled estate with a four-story tower, skylit billiard room, and extensive gardens.

A big visitors' center features an orientation video, a collection of telegraph equipment and other Morse inventions, and an art gallery showcasing paintings by Morse, John James Audubon, and other contemporaries of the inventor.

Vassar College and Frances Lehman Loeb Art Center

Vassar College (124 Raymond Ave., 845/437-7000, www.vassar.edu), at the southeastern edge of town, was founded as a women's college in 1861 by brewer Matthew Vassar, at the instigation of his friend Samuel Morse. Considered a risky experiment at the time, Vassar—now coeducational—is recognized as an exceptional college.

Surrounding much of the campus are towering stone walls with arched gates. Inside is the 1865 Main Building—reputedly designed in such a way that it could be converted into a brewery should the educational experiment fail—and a Norman-style chapel with five Tiffany windows. One of the windows depicts Elena Lucrezia Cornaro Piscopia, the first woman to receive a doctorate (from the University of Padua in 1678).

Near the main gate stands **Frances Lehman Loeb Art Center** (124 Raymond Ave., 845/437-5632, www.fllac.vassar.edu, Tues.-Wed. and Fri.-Sat. 10am-5pm, Thurs. 10am-9pm, Sun. 1pm-5pm, free), designed by Cesar Pelli. Vassar was the first college in the country to have its own art gallery, and today owns more than 12,500 works ranging in origin from ancient Egypt to modern-day New York. Especially strong are the collections of Hudson River landscape paintings, Old Master prints by Dürer and Rembrandt, and contemporary European and American art.

Entertainment

The local premier performing arts venue is **Bardavon 1869 Opera House** (35 Market St., 845/473-2072, www.bardavon.org). One of the oldest theaters in the country, it presents everything from top-caliber opera to serious drama. Two small but interesting professional theater groups connected with Vassar College are **New Day Repertory Co.** (29 N. Hamilton St., 845/485-7399) and **Powerhouse Theatre** (124 Raymond Ave., 845/437-5907, www.powerhouse.vassar.edu).

For live music, stop into **The Chance** (6 Crannel St., 845/471-1966, www.thechancetheater.com), where nationally known artists play everything from country to R&B. The weekend editions of *The Poughkeepsie Journal* contain good entertainment listings.

Accommodations

One of the nicest places to stay in Poughkeepsie is **❰ Inn and Suites at the Falls** (50 Red Oaks Mill Rd., 845/462-5770, www.innatthefalls.com, $145-230, with breakfast), which overlooks Wappingers Creek on the outskirts of town. Rooms are handsomely outfitted in contemporary European and country styles.

Downtown, you'll find the attractive, upscale **Poughkeepsie Grand Hotel and Conference Center** (40 Civic Center Plaza, 845/485-5300, www.pokgrand.com, $110-165, with full American breakfast). Popular among couples tying the knot, the hotel also has spacious suites for families and business travelers.

Food

For tasty baked goods in the historic district, try **Cafe Aurora** (145 Mill St., 845/454-1900, www.caffeaurora.com), which has been serving sweet treats since 1941.

Rosticceria Rossi and Sons (45 S. Clover St., 845/471-0654, www.rossideli.com, Mon.-Fri. 7:30am-6pm, Sat. 8am-5pm, $8) is a popular Italian deli selling panini, salads, and lunch standards like chicken, veal, and eggplant parmesan.

MILLBROOK AND VICINITY

About 12 miles northeast of Poughkeepsie on Route 44 is moneyed Millbrook, surrounded by large estates and horse farms. Though it seems hard to believe today, in this village of pricey antique stores and gift shops, Timothy Leary once ran his League for Spiritual Discovery out of the old Danheim estate on Franklin Avenue.

The estate, located about a mile from the village green, is recognizable by its large stone Bavarian-style gatehouse. Others who have made Millbrook their home in more recent years are Mary Tyler Moore, Daryl Hall, and Liam Neeson.

Innisfree Garden
The serene 200-acre **Innisfree Garden** (362 Tyrrel Rd., 845/677-8000, www.innisfreegarden.org, early May-mid-Oct. Wed.-Fri. 10am-4pm, Sat.-Sun. and holidays 11am-5pm, $5 weekdays, $6 weekends, children under 4 free) is landscaped around a small glacial lake just outside Millbrook. Founded by painter Walter Beck and his wife Marion, and designed according to Eastern principles, the so-called "cup garden" is actually a series of many little gardens, each arranged to draw attention to one especially beautiful object at its center. One of the small gardens focuses on a lotus pool, another on a group of "purple smoke trees," a third on a hillside cave. The Dragon, the Turtle, and the Owl—three large rocks standing sentinel over the preserve—sit on a spit of land jutting out into the lake.

Despite the garden's careful design, it has a wild and natural feel. Spreading out over a series of small hills and dales, dappled by sunlight, it features many isolated spots where visitors can linger.

Cary Institute of Ecosystem Studies
A few miles west of Millbrook is a 1,900-acre preserve that's home to both the **Mary Flagler Cary Arboretum** (Rte. 44A, just off Rte. 44, 845/677-5359, Mon.-Sat. 9am-4pm, Sun. 1pm-4pm, free) and the **Cary Institute of Ecosystem Studies** (Rte. 44A, just off Rte. 44, 845/677-5343, www.caryinstitute.org, trails: daily sunrise-sunset, internal roadways: Apr. 1-Oct. 31 daily 8:30am-7pm). The arboretum is open to the public, as is much of the institute's grounds, where ecological research is being conducted. Both are affiliated with the prestigious New York Botanical Garden in New York City.

Visitors to the arboretum must stop first at the Gifford House Visitor and Education Center to pick up a visitor permit, information, and maps. Directly behind the center are the perennial gardens, filled with over 1,000 species of plants. Among these gardens is a daffodil bed with 12 kinds of daffodils, a poisonous plants bed, and a garden specifically planted to attract butterflies. Surrounding the gardens are short hiking trails that lead past meadows, fern glens, and pine and hemlock forests.

Wing's Castle
One of the oddest sites in the Hudson Valley is whimsical **Wing's Castle** (717 Bangall Rd., 845/677-9085, www.wingscastle.com, Memorial Day weekend-Labor Day weekend Wed.-Sun. noon-4:30pm, adults $12, children 11 and under $8), set atop a rolling green hill with a panoramic view of the Hudson Valley. Built by Peter and Toni Wing and family, the castle has been a work-in-progress since 1970, lovingly put together out of everything from antique barn doors to toilet-bowl floats. Much of its stone came from abandoned railroad bridges.

It all began in the late 1960s when Peter, just back from Vietnam, and his wife Toni needed a place to live. They owned a piece of land, but had only $1,100 between them. The solution? They'd build the place themselves, out of salvaged materials; never mind the fact that they had no construction experience whatsoever.

Everyone told them it couldn't be done, but today the castle stands, quirky and proud. Each part is designed in a different style—Asian, Tibetan, Germanic, French—and it all works beautifully, with bits of colored fiberglass winking in the walls and a water-filled moat leading to an inviting hot tub. Inside is a hodgepodge collection of military artifacts, carousel animals, Native American arts, and the Wings' personal possessions.

The Wings turned part of their property into a two-room bed-and-breakfast in 2011. Children are not allowed at the bed-and-breakfast.

Wineries

Millbrook Vineyards and Winery (26 Wing Rd., at the Shunpike/Rte. 57, 845/677-8383, www.millbrookwine.com, Labor Day-Memorial Day daily noon-5pm, Memorial Day-Labor Day daily 11am-6pm) is spread out over 130 acres just below Wing's Castle. Known for its chardonnay, Millbook also produces a pinot noir, cabernet franc, and other wines.

About 10 miles northeast of Millbrook is award-winning **Cascade Mountain Winery** (835 Cascade Rd., Amenia, 845/373-9021, www.cascademt.com, Sat.-Sun. 11am-5pm). The family-owned winery produces whites, reds, and roses.

Accommodations

Camping is available at the 27-site **Wilcox Memorial Park** (Rte. 199, off Taconic Pkwy., Stanfordville, 845/758-6100), which has two lakes and a complex of farm buildings dating back to the 18th century.

Refreshingly down-to-earth, **A Cat in Your Lap** (Rtes. 82 and 343, 845/677-3051, www.acatinyourlap.com, $85 in the main house; $120 for studios in the barn) is a B&B housed in a gracious 1840s farmhouse and converted barn. Each room has a fireplace and private bath.

Food

Vintage, stainless-steel **Millbrook Diner** (3266 Franklin Ave., 845/677-5319) serves dependable diner fare and especially-good breakfasts. **Serevan Restaurant** (6 Autumn Lane, Amenia, 845/373-9800, www.serevan.com, Thurs.-Mon. 5pm-10pm, $28) earns raves from diners for Chef Serge Madikians' Mediteranean-Middle Eastern fusion flair, enhanced by local, organic, and free-range ingredients.

HYDE PARK AND VICINITY

Hyde Park's most popular destinations are the former homes of Franklin Delano Roosevelt, Eleanor Roosevelt, and a branch of the Vanderbilt family. Despite its blue-blood ancestry, the sprawling village is a downscale affair filled with aging shopping malls, tour buses, traffic jams, and motels named after the village's famous former residents.

Hugging the riverbank between the Vanderbilt Mansion and the Roosevelt homes is **Hyde Park Trail,** a 10-mile (and growing) system of easy hiking trails, well marked by white-and-green signs. Maps of the trails can be picked up at the **Wallace Center** (4079 Albany Post Rd./Rte. 9, 845/229-5320 or 800/FDR-Visit, www.nps.gov/hofr, daily 9am-5pm).

Henry A. Wallace Visitor and Education Center

Opened to the public in late 2003, the **Wallace Center** at the Franklin D. Roosevelt Presidential Library and Museum (4079 Albany Post Rd./Rte. 9, 845/229-5320 or 800/FDR-Visit, www.nps.gov/hofr, daily 9am-5pm) is now the best first stop for visitors to Hyde Park. The center provides a good, comprehensive orientation to the Roosevelt and Vanderbilt sites through exhibits and an introductory film. Visitors can buy tickets and get directions here; a large café and museum shop are also on site.

FDR's Home, Library, and Museum

Franklin Delano Roosevelt was born and raised at **Springwood** (4079 Albany Post Rd., 845/229-5320, www.nps.gov/hofr, daily 9am-5pm, adults $14, children under 15 free), a low-lying Georgian-style mansion along the Hudson. Later, he and his wife Eleanor raised their five children here, while Franklin rose through the political ranks. In 1928, he was elected governor of New York, and in 1932, president of the United States.

Now a National Historic Site, FDR's home has been restored to look much like it did during his presidential days. It has a very intimate feel. In the living room are the leash and blanket of his dog, Fala; in the "snuggery" are furnishings once belonging to his domineering mother, Sara Delano Roosevelt; in his office are books and magazines he was reading during his last visit here in March 1945. At the eastern end of the estate is **Top Cottage,** where Roosevelt entertained his closest friends.

Of at least equal interest is the adjacent **Franklin D. Roosevelt Presidential Library and Museum** (4079 Albany Post Rd./Rte. 9, 845/486-7770 or 800/FDR-Visit, www.fdrlibrary.marist.edu), which houses a superb series of exhibits on the family and their times. Here you'll find everything from FDR's christening dress and early political speeches to Eleanor's diary entries describing the enormous pain she felt upon learning of her husband's extramarital affairs.

Tickets to the FDR sites often sell out on fall weekends; to make a reservation, call 800/967-2283.

Val-Kill

By 1924, Eleanor Roosevelt had enough of both her husband's political cronies and her mother-in-law, so she built a weekend retreat for herself two miles east of the family estate. She moved there permanently after FDR's death in 1945.

Surrounded by fields and woodlands, the **Eleanor Roosevelt National Historic Site,** a.k.a. **Val-Kill** (54 Valkill Park Rd., 845/229-9115, www.nps.gov/elro, daily 9am-5pm, adults $10, children under 15 free) is a simple and rustic place that, compared to Springwood, attracts relatively few visitors. The former First Lady's tastes were delightfully unassuming; she used regular china, set up card tables for extra guests at Christmas, and hung family photographs helter-skelter over the cottage's rough-hewn walls. Nonetheless, it was in this simple setting that Mrs. Roosevelt drafted the U.N. Declaration of Human Rights and entertained important world leaders such as Nikita Khrushchev, Haile Selassie, Adlai Stevenson, and John F. Kennedy. A photograph of a 40-something JFK and a 70-something Eleanor is prominently displayed in the living room.

Vanderbilt Mansion

Two miles north of the Roosevelt homes is the extravagant **Vanderbilt Mansion National Historic Site** (119 Vanderbilt Park Rd., 845/229-9115, www.nps.gov/vama, daily 9am-5pm, adults $10, children under 15 free), built in a posh Beaux-Arts style complete with lavish furnishings, gold-leaf ceilings, Flemish tapestries, and hand-painted lampshades. Built between 1896 and 1898 by Frederick and Louise Vanderbilt, the mansion, designed by McKim, Mead & White, cost what was then a whopping $2.5 million. Nonetheless, it was the smallest of the Vanderbilt estates and was used only in spring and fall.

Next door to the mansion are extensive formal gardens and a coach house (not open to the public) in which the Vanderbilts housed six limousines that were always at their guests' disposal. The gardens have glorious views of the Hudson, with the smoky Shawangunk Mountains rising behind.

Staatsburgh State Historic Site

In Staatsburg, about five miles north of the Vanderbilt mansion, reigns the **Staatsburgh State Historic Site** (75 Mills Mansion Rd., 845/889-8851, Thurs.-Sun. 11am-5pm, adults $8, seniors and students $6, children under 12 free). Also known as **Mills Mansion,** the vast 65-room hilltop hideout is in a continual process of being restored. Guides take visitors through a series of cavernous rooms, some plush with Louis XIV, XV, and XVI furnishings, others filled with craftspeople busy at restoration work. The most beautiful room is the long dining room, flanked with Flemish tapestries and large windows overlooking the Hudson.

Parts of Mills Mansion date back to 1825, but most of the house was built in 1896 by McKim, Mead & White. Once owned by financier Ogden Mills, the mansion was frequented by Edith Wharton, who used it as the model for the Trenor estate, Bellomont, in *The House of Mirth.*

Surrounding Mills Mansion is **Mills-Norrie State Park** (9 Old Post Rd., 845/889-4646, www.nysparks.com/parks/171, daily dawn-dusk), a 1,000-acre preserve with a marina, campground, small environmental museum, and two nine-hole golf courses. Scenic hiking trails run along the west side of the park, overlooking the Hudson. The park also has a 46-site campground and 10 cabins for rent (reservations 800/456-2267, May-Oct.).

The Culinary Institute of America

A half-mile south of Hyde Park proper is **The Culinary Institute of America,** or **CIA** (1946 Campus Dr., 845/452-9600, www.ciachef.edu, daily, tour $6), the nation's most prestigious cooking school, founded in 1946. Housed in a former Jesuit seminary on 170 acres overlooking the Hudson River, the institute trains about 1,850 students at a time, in a 21-month program that includes courses in everything from pork butchering to provisions purchasing. Between classes, students hurry about campus dressed in traditional white chefs' tunics and white-and-gray checked pants.

The CIA is open daily and visitors are welcome to stroll the grounds, browse the well-stocked **Craig Claiborne Bookstore,** take a tour, or eat in one of several first-rate, student-staffed restaurants.

Entertainment

The Hyde Park Drive In (4114 Albany Post Rd., Hyde Park, 845/229-4738, www.hydepark-drivein.com, May-Sept. nightly, $9 adults, $6 children 5-11, show starts at dusk) features two screens. The drive-in is always bustling with friendly crowds. Bring blankets and lawn chairs or just recline the driver's seat to enjoy the classic 1950s atmosphere.

Accommodations

Directly across from Vanderbilt Mansion is attractive **Journey Inn Bed & Breakfast** (1 Sherwood Pl., 845/229-8972, www.journey-inn.com, $115-205), filled with antiques and memorabilia from the owners' international travels. The inn offers seven comfortable air-conditioned guest rooms, each done up to reflect a different destination, including Kyoto, Mombasa, and Tuscany.

Hyde Park has an abundance of decent budget motels, many of which cater to families and tour groups. Among them is the family-owned,

25-room **Roosevelt Inn** (4360 Albany Post Rd., 845/229-2443, www.rooseveltinnofhydepark.com, $95-120), where you can choose between "deluxe" or "rustic" style rooms.

Food

Hyde Park's best restaurants are at **The Culinary Institute of America** (1946 Campus Dr., 845/471-6608, www.ciarestaurants.com); reservations are essential. Each of the four restaurants has its own distinct style. The most casual is **Apple Pie Bakery Cafe** (Mon.-Fri. 7:30am-5pm, $6), which specializes in delicious desserts. The most elegant is **The Bocuse Restaurant** (Tues.-Sat. 11:30am-1pm and 6pm-8:30pm, $30-50), named for master Chef Paul Bocuse, whose "updated French" menu offers novel interpretations on classic bistro and provincial cuisine. Food can be ordered à la carte or from the tasting menu, and reservations are recommended. In between are **Ristorante Caterina de Medici** (Mon.-Fri. 11:30am-1pm and 6pm-8:30pm, $24), featuring contemporary and traditional Italian specialties, and **American Bounty Restaurant** (Tues.-Sat. 11:30am-1pm and 6pm-8:30pm, $26), dedicated to regional American dishes. Be aware that the restaurants are closed during school breaks; call ahead to avoid disappointment.

RHINEBECK

Continuing north along Route 9, you'll come to the picturesque village of Rhinebeck, the shady streets of which are lined with restored Victorian buildings. Rhinebeck was first settled in 1686 by Dutch immigrants and has been home to five illustrious Hudson Valley families: the Beekmans, Livingstons, Astors, Montgomerys, and Schuylers.

Rhinebeck Area Chamber of Commerce operates a **Visitor Information Booth** (Mill St., 845/876-5904, www.rhinebeckchamber.com, Mon.-Sat. 10am-4pm, Sun. noon-4pm), diagonally across from Beekman Arms.

Built in 1766, the famed **Beekman Arms** (6387 Mill St., 845/876-7077, www.beekmandelamaterinn.com, $140-250) is said to be the oldest inn in continuous operation in

America. Everyone from George Washington and Aaron Burr to William Jennings Bryan and FDR once ate or slept here. Even if you're not planning to do so yourself, the place is worth a look. Inside are low ceilings, heavy beams, wide floorboards, walk-in fireplaces, and benches dating to the Revolutionary War. The inn consists of a cluster of several small buildings. Rooms in the historic **main building** ($140-150) have plenty of atmosphere, but are small. Rooms in the handsome, American Gothic **◖ Delamater Inn** ($100-250), designed by Alexander Jackson Davis, are the most splendid.

Next door to Beekman Arms is a tiny **U.S. post office** (6383 Mill St.), a WPA project built in 1939 as a replica of the first home built in Rhinebeck. Inside are artifacts from the original building along with murals depicting the town's history.

Across the street from the post office stands **Rhinebeck Reformed Church** (6368 Mill St., 845/876-3727, www.rhinebeckreformedchurch.org, office open daily 9am-1pm), designed by Robert Upjohn in 1808. Next to the church is a picturesque graveyard with tombstones that date to the 1700s.

Old Rhinebeck Aerodrome

Most summer Sundays at the storybook **Old Rhinebeck Aerodrome** (9 Norton Rd., 845/752-3200, www.oldrhinebeck.org, May-Oct. daily 10am-5pm), Sir Percy Good Fellow climbs into his biplane to fight the Evil Black Baron for the heart of Trudy Truelove. Cheering the adversaries on as the rotary engines roar and the castor oil burns are excitable Madame Fifi, dashing Pierre Loop-da-Loop, and a crowd of early-21st-century citizens who have donned WWI-era hats, scarves, dresses, and coats at the gate.

Appearances to the contrary, this charming aerodrome—holding a hodgepodge of hand-painted signs and rickety hangars—is a serious place. On its grounds are about 75 historic airplanes dating back to the early 1900s. Among them are a 1911 Curtiss D, a 1929 Sopwith Camel, and a 1908 Voison whose double canvas

wings, light as gossamer, resemble those of a giant dragonfly. Summer weekends feature an air show reenacting historic flights.

At the aerodrome you can visit a **museum** (June-Oct. daily 10am-5pm, adults $10, seniors and children 13-17 $8, children 6-12 $3) or attend the **air shows** (June-Oct. Sat.-Sun, 2pm-4pm, adults $20, seniors and children 13-17 $15, children 6-12 $5; includes museum admission). **Flights** (summer Sun. from 10am, $75 for a 15-minute ride) over the Hudson River in a 1929 open-cockpit biplane are offered during the summer.

Wilderstein

Whimsical all-wooden Queen Anne mansion **Wilderstein** (330 Morton Rd., 845/876-4818, www.wilderstein.org, May-Oct. Thurs.-Sun. noon-4pm, adults $10, seniors and students $9, children under 12 free) sits in the middle of a 19th-century estate designed by Calvert Vaux, one of the two men who designed Central Park. *Wilderstein* means "wild man's stone" and was named after an Indian petroglyph found on the property. Inside the 1852 house—adorned with dormers, gables, and a magnificent, five-story tower—are lavish interiors by J. B. Tiffany. Outside are 40 acres of meadows and woods, including roads and trails offering great views of the Hudson.

Shopping

Rhinebeck is known for its antique stores and galleries, many of which are located along Route 9 or Market Street. One popular site is **Beekman Arms Antique Market** (Beekman Square at the Beekman Arms, 845/876-3477), which houses more than 30 vendors in an old red barn.

Tucked in between the newer stores are two creaky village institutions: **Rhinebeck Department Store** (1 E. Market St., 845/876-5500, www.rhinebeckdepartmentstore.com) and **A.L. Stickle Variety Store** (13 E. Market St., 845/876-3206). Both are veritable time capsules from the 1940s. **Oblong Books and Music** (Montgomery Row, 845/876-0500, www.oblongbooks.com) is a great indie bookshop. Stop by to catch an author reading or grab some tunes for the road.

Open air **Rhinebeck Farmers' Market** (summer location 61 E. Market St., winter location 80 E. Market St., www.rhinebeckfarmersmarket.com, Sun. 10am-2pm) is a meeting spot for local farmers, crafters, and the community, a pleasant mix of city weekenders and village residents. Live music provides a nice background against which vendors sell raw honey, local wines, sheep and goat cheese, cut flowers, free range farm-raised pheasant, venison and lamb, and organic potted herbs and greenery.

Entertainment and Events

Upstate Films (6415 Montgomery St., 845/876-2515, www.upstatefilms.org) is a revival movie theater screening foreign, independent, and documentary films, along with classics. The **Center for the Performing Arts at Rhinebeck** (661 Rte. 308, 845/876-3080, www.centerforperformingarts.org) offers theater, children's shows, concerts, jazz under the stars, and other events.

Rhinebeck's **Dutchess County Fairgrounds** (6550 Spring Brook Ave., 845/876-4000, www.dutchessfair.com) hosts a number of events throughout the year. Among them are an **Antiques Fair** in May, **crafts fairs** in October, and the six-day **Dutchess County Fair** in the summer. The latter is the largest county fair in the state, second in size only to the New York State Fair held in Syracuse.

Accommodations

Famed **Beekman Arms** (6387 Mill St., 845/876-7077, www.beekmandelamaterinn.com) is an inn that includes a cluster of several small buildings. Rooms in the historic main building ($140-150) have plenty of atmosphere, but are small; those in the handsome, American Gothic **C Delamater Inn** ($100-250), designed by Alexander Jackson Davis, are the most splendid and popular. Also at Delamater are six guesthouses perfect for families. Rooms in the other buildings cost $100-300.

The **Rhinecliff Hotel** (4 Grinnell St., 845/876-0590, www.therhinecliff.com,

$160-190), an 1854 renovated rooming house, offers all the modern luxury amenities you could need, including Wi-Fi, whirlpool tubs, and views of the Hudson from every room. This boutique country hotel has been touted for its authentic sense of place and features a restaurant and bar worthy of a pop in.

Delightful **C Whistle Wood Farm** (52 Pells Rd., 845/876-6838, www.whistlewood.com, $120-325) is on the outskirts of town, surrounded by fields and woodlands. Both a working horse farm and a friendly B&B, Whistle Wood boasts a whirlpool tub, decks overlooking the corral and fields of wildflowers, and plenty of in-room amenities. Stay in the main house or in the Carriage House, divided into two suites.

Motels in town include tiny, eight-room **Rhinebeck Motel** (6938 Rte. 9, 845/876-5900, www.therhinebeckmotel.com, $99-115) and family-owned **Rhinebeck Village Inn** (6260 Rte. 9, 845/876-7000, www.rhinebeckvillageinn.com, $80-98). Both are clean and friendly.

Food

A good place for burgers and fries, sandwiches, and salads is **Foster's Coach House Tavern** (6411 Montgomery St., 845/876-8052, www.fosterscoachhouse.com, Tues.-Thurs. and Sun.11am-11pm, Fri.-Sat. 11am-midnight, $9). Housed in an actual former coach house, Foster's is filled with wacky horse paraphernalia, including horseshoes, a horse carriage that's now a telephone booth, and mock horse stalls.

China Rose (1 Shatzell Ave., 845/876-7442, www.chinaroserestaurant.com, Wed.-Mon. 5pm-9:30pm, $17) is an upscale Chinese restaurant known for its use of fresh ingredients and its peaceful outdoor patio overlooking the Hudson.

If you're in the mood for Mediterranean or European cuisine, a couple of restaurants fit the bill. Lively, noisy **Gigi Trattoria** (6422 Montgomery St., 845/876-1007, www.gigihudsonvalley.com, Sun.-Thurs. 11:30am-9pm, Fri.-Sat. 11:30am-10pm, $28), housed in what was once an automobile showroom, bills itself as "Hudson Valley Mediterranean." On the menu are flatbread pizzas and lots of pasta dishes. **⟨ Le Petit Bistro** (8 E. Market St., 845/876-7400, www.lepetitbistro.com, Thurs.-Mon. 5pm-close, $18) is a classy yet casual bistro and bar with worn pine floors. The menu focuses on tasty French cuisine prepared with fresh local ingredients. **Tavern** (6387 Mill St., 845/876-1766, daily lunch and dinner, $25) at Beekman Arms is partially in the historic inn and partially housed in a greenhouse room filled with plants and flowers. The restaurant serves solid American fare with an emphasis on regional foods.

NORTH OF RHINEBECK
Red Hook

Five miles north of Rhinebeck is Red Hook, a small, low-key village filled with a surprising number of restaurants, inns and B&Bs, and historic buildings, such as **Octagonal House** (7444 S. Broadway), which now houses the **Red Hook Library** (www.redhooklibrary.org).

Anchoring the village is handsome, Federal-style **Red Hook Inn** (7460 S. Broadway, 845/758-8445, www.theredhookinn.com, $180-275), sporting a wide front porch. Inside are nine guest rooms and a restaurant (5-course prix fixe $69-79) serving fresh fare with international influences.

The striking, blue **Grand Dutchess Bed and Breakfast** (7571 Old Post Rd., 845/758-5818, www.granddutchess.com, $155-195), a Victorian Italianate mansion offering six light-filled guest rooms, is within walking distance of downtown. All rooms have private baths and air-conditioning, and antiques are everywhere.

A good spot for breakfast, lunch, or a simple dinner is the wonderful old **Village Diner** (7550 N. Broadway, 845/758-6232, www.historic-village-diner.com, daily 6am-9pm, $12). Built in 1927, the Art Deco-style eatery is still family owned and operated. Try the homemade doughnuts, soups, and egg creams.

The Hudson Valley region in general has been a supplier of cut flowers since Victorian times, and Dutchess County in particular was once the violet and anemone capital of the world. One of the oldest nurseries

still around is **F. W. Battenfeld & Sons** (856 Rte. 199, 845/758-8018, www.anemones. com), just outside Red Hook. The best time to visit is October-May, when the anemones are in bloom. Also of note near Red Hook is the large, family-owned **Greig Farm** (223 Pitcher Ln., 845/758-1234, www.greigfarm.com, July-Oct. daily), where you can pick your own apples, pumpkins, peaches, and berries.

Annandale-on-Hudson

Three miles west of Red Hook, in Annandale-on-Hudson, is **Montgomery Place** (River Rd., off Rte. 9G, 845/758-5461, www.hudsonvalley.org, grounds: year-round daily 9am-4pm, free; house tours: early May-late Oct., admission by timed tour, adults $10). One of the loveliest mansions along the Hudson, this quiet, 1802 Federal-style gem was remodeled in the 1860s by famed Alexander Jackson Davis. Every line of the classical structure and every inch of the romantic grounds seem perfectly in place. Stunning views of the Hudson and the Catskills beyond can be had from the mansion's circular, columned portico.

Montgomery Place was home to the prominent Livingston family for almost 200 years. Members of the family continued to live in the house until the 1980s, and it is still almost entirely furnished with their treasures.

Surrounding Montgomery Place are landscaped grounds laced with walking trails. Just outside the estate's gates are its still-thriving **Montgomery Place Orchards** (River Rd., off Rte. 9G, 845/758-6338, www.mporchards. com, June-Oct.), where you can pick your own fruits and berries.

Abutting Montgomery Place is **Bard College** (Rte. 9G at Annandale Rd., 845/758-6822, www.bard.edu), an idyllic 540-acre campus stippled with gardens and wooded groves. Once owned by Columbia University in New York City, Bard is now an independent institution known for its creative arts programs. Cutting-edge exhibits are showcased in its **Center for Curatorial Studies** (845/758-7598, www. bard.edu/ccs, Thurs.-Sun. 11am-6pm, free). Concerts and the critically acclaimed Bard

Music Festival (which focuses on a different composer each year) are presented in the dramatic, brushed-stainless-steel **Richard B. Fisher Center for Performing Arts** (845/758-7900, www.fishercenter.bard.edu, tours daily 2pm or by appointment, $5), designed by architect Frank Gehry and acoustical designer Yasuhisa Toyota. Daily tours show how the center's swooping lines reflect the surrounding landscape. The **SummerScape SpiegelTent** (845/758-7900, www.bard.edu/pac/summerscape) is a can't-miss burlesque show, modern dance, modified performing circus, and DJ-led event.

Tivoli

If you continue north of Annandale-on-Hudson on Route 9G to Route 78 and head west, you'll come to the hamlet of Tivoli. Henry Hudson is thought to have anchored offshore here in 1609, and nearby Cruger Island may once have been an important meeting ground for the local Wappinger and upstate Iroquois Indians.

Today, Tivoli is a popular hangout for Bard College students and professors, hence its many restaurants and bars. Among the most popular is boisterous **(Santa Fe** (52 Broadway, 845/757-4100, www.santafetivoli. com, Tues.-Thurs. and Sun. 5pm-9:30pm, Fri.-Sat. 5pm-10:30pm, $17), offering authentic Southwestern and Mexican food. In summer, a small outdoor dining area opens upstairs. Also a favorite, serving tasty, high-quality sushi, tempura, and noodles in a more relaxed setting is **Osaka** (74 Broadway, 845/757-5055, www. osakasushi.net, $18).

Clermont State Historic Site

Just north of the Dutchess County border is **Clermont State Historic Site** (Woods Rd., off Rte. 9G, Germantown, 518/537-6622, www. friendsofclermont.org, grounds: year-round daily dusk-dawn, free; house tours: early Apr.-Oct. 31 Wed.-Sun. 11am-4pm, adults $5, seniors and students $4, children under 12 free), a grand historic estate that was once home to seven generations of the Livingston family.

The Georgian manse sits on the edge of a wide lawn lined with enormous black locust trees. Views from the estate are superb; down below is the Hudson River, and in the distance are the high Catskill Mountains peaks that inspired the estate's name. *Clermont* is French for "clear mountain."

The 35-room mansion holds many of the Livingstons' heirlooms, including period furniture and family portraits by Gilbert Stuart and others. Robert R. Livingston (1746-1813) was arguably the most famous of the clan. He administered the first oath of office to George Washington, helped draft the Declaration of Independence, and served as minister to France under Thomas Jefferson.

Landscaped grounds include a Lilac Walk (in bloom in May), formal gardens, and many acres of fields, forests, and wetlands laced with carriage paths and hiking trails. On the front lawn near the river is a plaque honoring inventor Robert Fulton, whose steamboat, the *Clermont,* first traveled up the Hudson from New York City to Albany in August 1807.

Lake Taghkanic State Park and Vicinity

To the east of Clermont, amid rolling hills, is pristine **Lake Taghkanic State Park** (1528 Rte. 82, Ancram, 518/851-3631, www.nysparks. com/parks/38, daily dawn-dusk, parking $8), centering on cool, blue Lake Taghkanic, a 1,569-acre body of water ringed with bathing beaches and boat launches. Hiking trails climb small peaks to offer splendid views of the valley below. Also in the park are a top-rated **campground** (reservations 800/456-2267, May-Oct.) with 60 campsites, picnic areas, a boat-rental shop, ball field, and fitness trail.

Not far from Lake Taghkanic State Park is the classic **(West Taghkanic Diner** (1016 Rte. 82, 518/851-7117, Mon.-Thurs. 7am-9pm, Fri. 7am-11pm, Sat.-Sun. 7am-10pm, $10), where the red, neon-lit profile of a Native American chief greets motorists as they pull up.

Taconic State Park

Not to be confused with Lake Taghkanic

State Park, much larger **Taconic State Park** (253 Rte. 344, off Rte. 22, Copake Falls, 518/329-3993, www.nysparks.com/parks/83/details, daily 8am-sunset, parking $7) is another lovely preserve. It's on the New York-Massachusetts border, set against the Taconic Mountains, a small range that extends northward into Vermont. Two separate recreation areas—Rudd Pond and Copake Falls—are in the 5,000-acre park, which features hiking trails, beaches, campsites, boat rentals, picnic areas, and playgrounds.

The park's greatest attraction is Bash-Bish Glen, where Bash-Bish Brook cascades down a striking series of waterfalls. A craggy outcropping known as Eagle Cliff stands at the top of the cataract; local legend has it that several Indians once fell to their deaths over its edge. Among them was a woman named Bash Bish, after whom the brook was named. Her spirit is said to still inhabit the area. An ice-cold, 40-foot-deep quarry pool is also nearby.

The park also has **camping** facilities (reservations 800/456-2267, May-Oct.).

Copake Falls

On the edge of Taconic State Park is the serene village of Copake Falls, centered around a handful of historic wooden buildings and a small traffic circle with a historic four-faced clock. One of the county's most popular weekend events, attracting everyone from farmers to second-home owners, is the weekly **Copake Auction** (266 Rte. 7A, Copake, 518/329-1142, www.copakeauction.com).

Hillsdale

Winter brings skiers and snowboarders to Hillsdale's **Catamount Ski Area** (Breezy Hill Rd., off Rte. 23, 518/325-3200, www.catamountski.com). The small ski resort offers 32 slopes and trails, three terrain parks, and seven lifts, along with a laid-back atmosphere that makes it especially good for families.

Comfortable **Swiss Hutte** (Breezy Hill Rd., off Rte. 23, 518/325-3333, www.swisshutte.com, $150-220) sits in the middle of the Catamount ski area, overlooking the slopes. On

site is a cozy wood-paneled bar and separate dining room (bar dishes $5-18, restaurant entrées $32) that serve Swiss-American fare.

For good regional American cuisine or wood-fired pizza, try the circa-1811 **Hillsdale House** (Rte. 23 in the village center, 518/325-7111, $14).

The creaky, near-legendary **Rodgers Book Barn** (467 Rodman Rd., 518/325-3610, www.rodgersbookbarn.com, Apr. 1-Oct.31 Thurs.-Mon. 11am-5pm, Nov. 1-Mar. 31 Fri.-Sun. 11am-5pm) is filled with books, books, and more books—over 50,000 titles, all secondhand. They're housed in a two-story barn with lots of nooks and crannies.

Falcon Ridge Folk Festival (Dodds Farm, 44 Rte. 7D, 860/364-2138, www.falconridgefolk.com) comes to Hillsdale every late July-early August. On tap are top folk performers from around the country.

NEW PALTZ

Between the Hudson River and the Shawangunk Mountains lies the small town of New Paltz. New Paltz was founded in 1677 by a group of French Huguenot Protestants who came to the New World seeking religious freedom. The Huguenots first settled just north of New Paltz, in Kingston and Hurley. But in June 1663, the area's Esopus Indians raided the two small settlements, kidnapping 45 women and children. That September, a Huguenot search party found and freed the hostages. While embracing his family, one member of the party—Louis DuBois—noticed the fertile land around him. He returned in 1677 with 11 others to buy and patent a 33,000-acre tract of land, and the next year, the 12 families settled along what is now known as Huguenot Street.

The new town was governed by a kind of corporation called the Duzine, referring to the 12 partners. That arrangement continued until well after the Revolution, by special permission of the New York State legislature. The system apparently worked well; one later commentator wrote, "So fine and free from animosity and greed has been the life of the people of

MID-HUDSON AND
THE CATSKILLS:
ULSTER COUNTY

New Paltz that previous to 1873 no lawyer ever found a permanent residence here."

Today, the center of New Paltz lies just east of historic Huguenot Street, along Chestnut and Main Streets. Here, you'll find a clutch of attractive stores and restaurants. New Paltz is also home to a State University of New York (SUNY) branch that offers an especially strong arts department, which helps account for the town's strong cultural scene.

For more information on the area, visit **New Paltz Regional Chamber of Commerce** (257 Main St., 845/255-0243, www.

newpaltzchamber.org, Mon.-Fri. 9am-5pm, Sat.-Sun. 10am-3pm).

【 Huguenot Street

"The oldest street in America with its original buildings" is now a National Historic Landmark. Along its cool and shady time-ripened blocks stand six stone houses built in the early 1700s, as well as a reconstructed 1717 French church and cemetery, a 1799 house, a library, and museum.

All official walking tours of the street begin at the **1705 DuBois Fort Information Center** on Huguenot Street between Broadhead Avenue and North Front Street. A small museum here documents the street's history. Houses on the tours include the Abraham Hasbrouck House, once the village's social center, and the Bevier-Elting House. The most interesting house is **Jean Hasbrouck House,** which contains original woodwork and a beautiful "jambless" fireplace. Downstairs are rooms that once served as a tavern and general store, while upstairs are period furnishings, including a "senility cradle" used for the old and infirm.

Huguenot Street is run by the **Huguenot Historical Society** (88 Huguenot St., 845/255-1660, www.huguenotstreet.org, tours: adults $16, seniors $15, children 7-13 $10, families $40), which includes among its members many descendants of the original families. The society offers walking tours of the street; the standard tour lasts 90 minutes. During the **Colonial**

Street Festival (Huguenot St., second Sat. in Aug.) all the houses are open and various colonial-era skills, such as quilting and musket firing, are demonstrated.

Locust Lawn

Four miles south of New Paltz are yet more historic sites administered by the Huguenot Historical Society. Most important among them is **Locust Lawn** (436 S. Rte. 32, Gardiner), an elegant Federal-style mansion built by Revolutionary War hero Colonel Josiah Hasbrouck in 1814. After the war, the colonel became one of the wealthiest men in Ulster County. He filled his home with fine period furniture, magnificent china, and paintings by the likes of Ammi Phillips and John Vanderlyn.

Nearby is considerably more rustic **Terwilliger House,** built in 1738. A wonderful example of Huguenot and Dutch architecture combined, the stone-and-wood cottage features a wide central hallway, long sloping roof, and creaky front porch.

To arrange a tour of either site, call the **Huguenot Historical Society** (88 Huguenot St., 845/255-1660, www.huguenotstreet.org).

Wineries

Wine enthusiasts might want to visit **Adair Vineyards** (52 Allhusen Rd., 845/255-1377, www.adairwine.com, May-Oct. Sat.-Sun. 11am-6pm, Nov.-Apr. Sat.-Sun. 11am-5pm), which centers on a 200-year-old National Historic Landmark dairy barn. The tasting room is in the old hayloft.

Or, head east to **Route 9W**, which hugs the shores of the Hudson River. Many small wineries are located along the route between West Park and Marlboro. Most famous among them is **Benmarl Winery** (156 Highland Ave., Marlboro, 845/236-4265, www.benmarl.com, Apr.-Dec. daily noon-6pm, Jan.-Mar. Fri.-Sun. noon-5pm). First planted as a vineyard in the late 16th century, it sits on a hilltop with great views of the river. The winery produces award-winning varietals, including chardonnays and cabernets.

Entertainment and Events

Concerts and plays are often on tap at **The State University of New York at New Paltz** (Rte. 32, just south of New Paltz, one mile west of I-87, 845/257-2121), with many staged at the university's **Parker Theatre** (845/257-3880).

Though now primarily a casual restaurant, **P&G's** (91 Main St., 845/255-6161, www.pan-dgs.com, Mon.-Thurs. 11am-10:30pm, Fri. 11am-9pm, Sat.-Sun. 11am-10pm, $15) began as a dancehall in the 1900s and still presents live local bands on the weekends.

The **Ulster County Fair** (249 Libertyville Rd., 845/255-1380, www.ulstercountyfair. com, early Aug.) is held at the Ulster County Fairgrounds. The fairgrounds also host the **Woodstock-New Paltz Art & Crafts Fairs** (249 Libertyville Rd., 845/246-3414, www. quailhollow.com, Memorial Day and Labor Day weekends).

Accommodations

For the most popular resort in the New Paltz area, head to **Mohonk Mountain House** (1000 Mountain Rest Rd., 855/883-3798, www.mo-honk.com, $200-500), about five miles northwest of downtown, in the Shawangunks. The massive resort, which has been in operation since 1869, looks like a fairy castle; inside are many different room types, many with working fireplaces. Activities abound and the gorgeous landscape—pond, mountains, woods (particularly spectacular in fall)—ensure you'll never get bored. A restaurant and spa are on-site as well.

For lodging closer to town, family-oriented **Rocking Horse Ranch** (600 Rte. 44/55, 845/691-2927, www.rhranch.com, $99-255), a family-owned resort and dude ranch, is east of Highland proper. The Rocking Horse sits beside a lake and features indoor and outdoor pools, saunas, tennis courts, activities for kids, nighttime entertainment, and trail rides. In winter, the ranch offers cross-country skiing, ice-skating, snowshoeing, and sleigh rides.

In Wallkill, between Walden and New Paltz on Route 208, is the 1740 **Audrey's Farmhouse** (2188 Brunswick Rd., 845/895-3440, www.audreysfarmhouse.com, $115-195). The B&B offers comfortable guest rooms with feather beds, a swimming pool, library, and splendid views of the Shawangunks. Well-behaved dogs are welcome.

Food

With its outdoor café and homemade treats, **The Bakery** (13A N. Front St., 845/255-8840, www.ilovethebakery.com, daily 7am-7pm) is a good spot for breakfast or a simple lunch. Main Street also offers a number of dining options. Popular **A Tavola** (46 Main St., 845/255-1426, www.atavolany.com, Thurs.-Mon. 5:30pm-close, $25), complete with skylights, cooks up innovative Italian fare. **The Gilded Otter** (3 Main St., 845/256-1700, www.gild-edotter.com, Mon.-Thurs. 11:30am-10pm, Fri.-Sat. 11:30am-10:30pm, Sun. noon-9pm, $18) is the place to go for live music, local brews,

© FRANCISCO COLLAZO

Mohonk Mountain House

good pub grub, and views of the fabulous Shawangunks.

THE SHAWANGUNKS

Just west of New Paltz rise the Shawangunk Mountains, a tilted ridge of translucent quartz conglomerate cemented into sedimentary rock. One-tenth the age of the earth, the Shawangunks are often mistakenly assumed to be an extension of the Catskills, but are a distinct, separate range. The Shawangunks' steep escarpments make them a favorite spot for rock climbers. One local rock-climbing guide service and school is **HighXposure Adventures** (800/777-2546, www.high-xposure.com). Beginners are welcome.

Mohonk Mountain House and Preserve

High in the heart of the Shawangunks is **Mohonk Mountain House** (1000 Mountain Rest Rd., 855/883-3798, www.mohonk.com, $389-735, includes three meals and afternoon tea), an enormous castle-like structure

on the edge of a deep-blue glacial lake. Built by Quaker twins Albert and Alfred Smiley in 1870, Mohonk is the last of the magnificent resort hotels that once lined the Hudson.

In its heyday, Mohonk hosted a long line of distinguished guests, including Presidents Hayes, Taft, and Wilson. Albert Smiley was deeply concerned about the welfare of the American Indian, and, from 1883 to 1916, numerous important Friends of the Indian conferences were held here.

Mohonk is an ultra-romantic place, bursting with gables and chimneys, turrets and towers. The grounds offer lovely scenic hikes, natural cave spelunking, impressive gardens (with English maze), mountain biking, and crystal clear lake swimming. Trails, dotted with more than a hundred tiny gazebo-like sitting spots, provide resting spots to enjoy the view or a good book. Numerous activities are scheduled throughout the day, ensuring guests every possibility to tailor a visit to their interests. A sense of family and pride is pervasive among the excellent staff, who offer warm smiles and assurances that your needs will be met. Bonfires (where staff offer pre-loaded s'mores roasting sticks), square-dancing, movies under the stars, log rolling competitions, and other classic vacation activities make you feel as if you've stepped back in time.

To jump back into the present, hit the top-rated spa and outdoor mineral bath overlooking the mountains. Four-season fun means snow-tubing, Nordic skiing, snowshoeing, and ice-skating in the gorgeous stone pavilion or on Lake Mohonk.

The adjacent 5,600-acre **Mohonk Preserve** (845/255-0919, www.mohonkpreserve.org, daily dawn-dusk, hiking day pass: adults $12, children under 12 free) is ideal for hiking. Over 30 miles of trails and carriage roads crisscross the preserve. Hikers must purchase a day pass; passes do not permit access to the Mountain House or its facilities.

🅒 Minnewaska State Park

If the idea of spending $12 per person to hike the Mohonk Preserve sounds a bit steep, head farther west through fertile farmland to **Minnewaska State Park** (5281 Rte. 44/55, 845/255-0752, www.nysparks.com/parks/127, hours vary seasonally and by park facility, parking $8). Also located high in the Shawangunks, the park is filled with panoramic views, hiking trails, paved carriage roads, waterfalls, and lakes.

Near the center of the park is deep-blue **Lake Minnewaska**—Iroquois for "floating waters"—surrounded by white sandstone cliffs. The lake was created during the Ice Age when a glacier sliding by pulled out a hunk of soft sandstone. Lake Minnewaska has a sandy beach area where swimming is permitted, but if you like your bathing more secluded, hike the three-mile trail to **Lake Awosting.** This mile-long lake can only be reached on foot and is an idyllic spot surrounded by dark, piney woods.

Just minutes away from Minnewaska State Park is popular 🅒 **Minnewaska Lodge** (3116 Rte. 44/55, Gardiner, 845/255-1110, www. minnewaskalodge.com, $135-319). Catering to

outdoors enthusiasts, the 26-room lodge features rooms with cathedral ceilings and decks overlooking the 'Gunks, along with Mission-style furniture, oversized picture windows, and a wood-burning stove. Works by local artists hang on the walls.

After visiting the park, you might want to step into the old-fashioned, family-owned **Mountain Brauhaus** (junction of Rtes. 299 and 44/55, Gardiner, 845/255-9766, www. mountainbrauhaus.com, Wed.-Sat. 11:30am-9pm, Sun. 11:30am-8:30pm, $22) for a frothy mug of German beer and a plate of *rouladen* or *kassler rippchen*. The roadhouse sits at the base of the Shawangunks and offers spectacular views.

Ellenville

Southwest of Minnewaska State Park, where Route 209 meets Route 52, is the village of Ellenville. Located at the western base of the Shawangunks, Ellenville has traditionally been known for its Jewish boarding houses and mega-resorts. Most of these are gone now, but the town still has plenty of fine colonial and Greek Revival buildings, and a few remaining kosher shops and restaurants. Among them is **Cohen's Bakery** (89 Center St., 845/647-7620, www.cohensbakery.com), famed locally for its first-rate raisin-pumpernickel bread.

The Ellenville area also has a reputation for good hang-gliding. **Mountain Wings Hang Gliding Center** (77 Hang Glider Rd., 845/647-3377, www.mtnwings.com) rents equipment and offers introductory one-day hang-gliding courses.

NORTH ON ROUTE 209

Today's Route 209 closely parallels Old Route 209, reputedly the oldest highway in America. Originally known as the Old Mine Road, the old route ran between copper mines near Pahaquarry, New Jersey, and Kingston-on-the-Hudson, and was built sometime in the early 1600s. Many old homes and markers commemorating Indian raids are situated along Old Route 209, which runs concurrently with today's route in many places.

High Falls and Vicinity

Take Route 209 north to Route 213 east to High Falls, where the **D&H Canal Museum** (23 Mohonk Rd., 845/687-9311, www.canal-museum.org, June-Sept. Thurs.-Sat. and Mon. 11am-5pm, Sun. 1pm-5pm, off-season hours vary, adults $3, children $1) tells the story of the Delaware and Hudson Canal. Built in the 1820s, the canal was used to ship coal from the mines of Pennsylvania to the factories of New York. Later, it was used to ship cement made in the High Falls area to New York City. The museum has dioramas of the canal, working models of locks, and maps, photos, and artifacts.

❪ DePuy Canal House (1315 Rte. 213, 845/687-7700, www.depuycanalhouse.com, Fri. 5pm-10pm, Sat. 10am-10pm, Sun. 10am-4pm, $26 à la carte), built in 1797 by Simeon DePuy, overlooks Lock 16. Once an inn, the two-story building is now a renowned four-star restaurant serving innovative American cuisine in an intimate setting complete with fireplaces, steep staircases, and wide floorboards. Request the eagle-eye view of the kitchen to check out the chef in action via attic seating. Multi-course prix fixe meals are a popular choice here; there are five- and seven-course options.

For a simpler meal, try **The Egg's Nest** (Rte. 213, at Bruceville Rd., 845/687-7255, www.theeggsnest.com, daily 11:30am-11pm, $12), an eccentric spot offering tasty sandwiches and soups, or artsy **Northern Spy Cafe** (Rte. 213 at Old Rte. 213, 845/687-7298, www.northernspycafe.com, Tues.-Thurs. and Sun. 5pm-10pm, Fri.-Sat. 5pm-11pm, $20), which serves everything from burgers to Muscovy duck breast.

Stone Ridge

Stone Ridge Orchard (3012 Rte. 213, 845/687-2587, www.stoneridgeorchard.com), **Davenport Farms** (3411 Rte. 209, Stone Ridge, 845/687-0051, www.davenportfarms.com), and **Mr. Apples** (25 Orchard St., High Falls, 845/687-0005, www.mrapples.com) all offer country fresh prepared baked goods; you-pick apple, raspberry, and peach acreage; and farm activities like cider pressing or hay rides on busy summer weekends.

Bed-and-breakfast fans have an excellent choice in Stone Ridge. **The Inn at Stone Ridge/Hasbrouck House** (3805 Rte. 209, 845/687-0736, www.innatstoneridge.com, $195-425) is an elegant 18th-century colonial mansion. It offers nine guest rooms, an antique billiard room, 40 acres of gardens and woods, and a lake.

Hurley

Off Route 209 on the outskirts of Kingston lies this small village of 24 meticulously restored stone cottages. Almost all are private homes open to the public only once a year, during **Hurley Stone House Day** (www.stonehouseday.org), but they're also interesting to view from afar.

Hurley dates to 1651, when French Huguenots built wooden homes along Esopus Creek. The settlers didn't treat local Esopus Indians as well as they should have; in 1663, Indians retaliated by burning down the Huguenot settlement. Six years later, the settlers rebuilt, this time in stone.

Self-guided walking tour maps of Hurley can be picked up at the post office at the town's entrance, at the Hurley Library, or Elmendorf House, both on Main Street. A plaque with a town map also stands by the library.

Elmendorf House is believed to be the oldest house in Hurley. Known as the Half-Moon Tavern in Revolutionary days, it now houses a small museum run by the **Hurley Heritage Society** (52 Main St., 845/338-1661, www.hurleyheritagesociety.org, hours vary seasonally). The Heritage Society can also arrange tours of other historic buildings: **Polly Crispell Cottage,** also on Main Street, is equipped with a "witch catcher," or set of iron spikes set into the chimney; west of Main Street is the **Hardenberg House,** where abolitionist and suffragist Sojourner Truth, born a slave in Ulster County, spent her first 11 years.

KINGSTON

The small city of Kingston centers around a peaceful, tree-lined historic district known as the Stockade. A few miles away, down by the Hudson, is the city's equally pleasant harbor, Rondout Landing. There you'll find more nicely restored buildings, along with historic vessels and tour boats.

Kingston was settled by the Dutch in 1652, making it the third oldest settlement in the state after Albany and New York City. In 1777, the town served as state capital; in the early 1800s, it was known for its boat-building and cement industries. Remnants of these can still be seen at Rondout Landing. The landing is also the endpoint of the Delaware & Hudson Canal. Built in 1828 to help transport coal from Pennsylvania to the Hudson River, the canal turned Kingston from a humble port into a major commercial center.

Historic Stockade Area

In 1658, hostilities broke out between the new Dutch settlers and the Esopus Indians, prompting Governor Peter Stuyvesant to come from Manhattan to oversee the building of a stockade. The settlers moved their homes inside the 13-foot-high stockade walls, and no Esopus were allowed in after dark. By 1700, the stockade itself was gone, but the site continued to function as the village center. Over the next 200 years, many of Kingston's most important buildings were erected here. Today, the eight-block district is lined with shady trees, inviting shops and restaurants, and historic sites.

The district centers around the **Old Dutch Church** (272 Wall St., 845/338-6759, www.olddutchchurch.org), designed in 1852 by Minard Lafever. Renaissance Revival in style, the church features a vaulted ceiling reminiscent of Christopher Wren.

Nearby stands the 1818 **Ulster County Courthouse** (285 Wall St.). A plaque out front honors Sojourner Truth, who was born a slave in Ulster County in 1797. It was in this courthouse on November 26, 1883, where Truth won a lawsuit that saved her son from slavery

in Alabama. It was the first such case ever won by a black parent.

Senate House State Historic Site (296 Fair St., 845/338-2786, www.nysparks.com/historic-sites/18, Apr.15-Oct.31 Wed.-Sat. 10am-5pm, Sun. 1pm-5pm, other times of year by appointment, adults $4, seniors $3, children 12 and under free) was the meeting place of the first New York State Senate. Inside the former Dutch home, viewable only by guided tour, is the parlor where the 24-member Senate met in 1777 to ratify the first New York State Constitution. A museum with exhibits on Kingston's history and a collection of paintings by John Vanderlyn, one of America's first landscape painters, is connected to the house. Vanderlyn painted the enormous *Landing of Columbus* that hangs in the Capitol rotunda in Washington, D.C. Nonetheless, he lived most of his life in penury and died of starvation in his Kingston apartment.

A printed **walking tour** (845/339-0720) of the stockade area can be picked up from the City of Kingston. Many of the area's shops and restaurants are located along Wall, John, and North Front Streets.

SAUGERTIES

About 15 miles north of Kingston, where Route 212 meets Route 9W, is Saugerties, filled with turn-of-the-century brick buildings. Saugerties was once a river port known for its packet-trade and racing steamers. Most famous among them was the *Mary Powell,* the fastest ship on the Hudson between 1861 and 1885.

Opus 40

Between Saugerties and Woodstock is one of the most unusual spots in Ulster County, an environmental sculpture known as **Opus 40** (50 Fite Rd., 845/246-3400, www.opus40.org, June-Oct. Thurs.-Sun. 11am-5:30pm, adults $10, seniors and students $7, children 6-12 $3). Created by artist Harvey Fite over a period of 37 years, Opus 40 covers more than six acres of an abandoned bluestone quarry. Its pools and fountains, sculptures and walkways, all center on a towering blue-gray monolith reminiscent

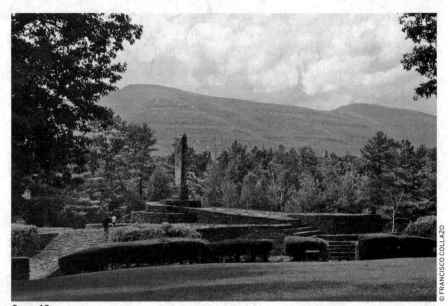

© FRANCISCO COLLAZO

Opus 40

of Stonehenge. The dark crest of Overlook Mountain rises behind Opus 40.

Fite, a professor at Bard College, created his monumental work using traditional quarrier's tools. Adjacent to the site is **Quarryman's Museum,** itself a work of art. The museum is filled with hammers and screws, chains and wagon wheels, with everything arranged according to size and shape. A seven-minute video on the site is featured.

Shopping

Downtown Saugerties is full of antique shops, most of which are located along Main and Partition Streets. Some are serious affairs, others sell what looks suspiciously like junk. One of the largest emporiums is **Saugerties Antique Center & Auction House** (220 Main St., 845/246-8234), which houses about 25 dealers. A guide to the town's antique stores can be picked up in many shops.

Camping and Accommodations

The largest campground in Saugerties is **Rip Van Winkle** (149 Blue Mountain Rd., 888/720-1232, www.ripvanwinklecampgrounds.com, $10 pp), offering 170 sites. The **Saugerties-Woodstock KOA** (882 Rte. 212, 845/246-4089, www.koa.com/campgrounds/Saugerties, $35.95 per night) offers 100 sites and camping cabins.

At C **Saugerties Lighthouse B&B** (168 Lighthouse Dr., 845/247-0656, www.saugertieslighthouse.com, $135-160), adventurous guests can watch boats pass by on the Hudson from their basic second-story rooms. From the parking lot, it's a 10-minute walk to the lighthouse, though this can be a wet experience.

Food

C **New World Home Cooking Co.** (1411 Rte. 212, 845/246-0900, www.ricorlando.com/nwhc, daily dinner, $21) is a "funky world cuisine café" offering a variety of dishes with Asian, Creole, Cajun, and Caribbean influences, including a broad selection of vegetarian options. Wild art-filled walls and live music reigns, from Celtic to Zydeco, and provides a fitting backdrop to what comes out of the wall-less kitchen. The inventive menu revolves around the best of seasonal local organic and sustainable delicacies. Former punk rocker turned slow food chef, Ric Orlando, makes sure the vibe is never dull.

Chic yet casual (**Cafe Tamayo** (91 Partition St., 845/246-9371, www.cafetamayo. com, $18) is housed in an attractive 1864 brick building complete with ceiling fans, an old-style bar, and patio. The menu features contemporary American fare.

The Catskills

WOODSTOCK AND VICINITY

The famed arts colony of Woodstock is still a picturesque and unusual spot, inhabited by an idiosyncratic bunch of artists and craftspeople, individualists and ne'er-do-wells. But the place is often so overrun with tourists that it's hard to tell.

Woodstock the town dates to the 1700s. But Woodstock the arts colony dates to 1902, when a wealthy Englishman, freethinker, and lover of the arts named Ralph Radcliffe Whitehead came here to set up an arts-and-crafts community. A student of John Ruskin who railed against the evils of the Industrial Revolution, Whitehead envisioned his colony as living apart from the modern world, surrounded by scenic splendor, and supporting itself with its arts and crafts.

Whitehead went in with two partners, bought 1,300 acres, and built a small village, Byrdcliffe, just above Woodstock. A few years later one of his followers, poet Hervey White, became fed up with Whitehead's authoritarian demands and started a second arts community, Maverick, on the south side of town. Then, in 1906, the Art Students League of New York City arrived, opening a summer school in Woodstock's downtown. The village was thronged with ever-increasing numbers of painters, potters, weavers, poets, dancers, musicians, novelists, hangers-on, and tourists eager to "see the artists."

By mid-century, folk singers Pete Seeger, Joan Baez, and Peter, Paul, and Mary discovered Woodstock, and in the 1960s, Bob Dylan moved in, buying a farm on an isolated mountaintop. The town's first recording studio was built, and a series of small concerts, the Woodstock Soundoffs, was staged. The Soundoffs were the immediate forerunner of the legendary 1969 Woodstock Music Festival that took place in Bethel, 60 miles away. The concert organizers wanted to hold the event closer to home, but Woodstock had no open space large enough, and last-minute ordinances imposed by nervous officials prevented the concert from taking place in Saugerties as originally planned.

(Downtown Woodstock

For all its renown, Woodstock remains a small village, with a population of about 6,000. Its main thoroughfare is **Tinker Street,** which according to legend is named after a tinker's wagon that sank into the mud here one fine spring day.

Where Tinker Street meets Rock City and Mill House Roads is the **village green,** often filled with teenagers wearing the tie-dyed T-shirts and long dresses of their parents' or grandparents' generations. Nearby is the Millstream, immortalized in Tell Taylor's classic song, "Down By the Old Millstream."

Dozens of small shops, restaurants, galleries, and museums crowd the streets of Woodstock. Among the oldest is **Woodstock Artists Association and Museum** (28 Tinker St., 845/679-2940, www.woodstockart.org, Sun.-Mon. and Thurs. noon-5pm, Fri.-Sat. noon-6pm, closed for the month of Jan.), which has exhibited the works of area artists since 1920. Among the newest is first-rate **Center for Photography at Woodstock** (59 Tinker St., 845/679-9957, www.cpw.org, Wed.-Sun.

BY THE TIME THEY GOT TO WOODSTOCK...

By the time they got to Woodstock... they had to keep going for over 50 miles. The famed 1969 Woodstock Music Festival actually took place on Max Yasgur's farm in Bethel, as opposed to the Catskill mountain town that provided its name.

To get to Bethel from Route 52, head east on Route 17B, through mile after mile of scenic farm country. The former Yasgur farm is off Hurd Road. Signs off Route 17B point the way to an enormous lime-green field sloping down to borders of dark green trees. A horizontal stone marker near the road reads: "This is the original site of the Woodstock Music and Arts Fair held on Aug. 15, 16, 17, 1969." It also lists the festival's many performers: Richie Havens, Arlo Guthrie, Joan Baez, Joe Cocker, Ravi Shankar, Santana, and Janis Joplin, to name a few.

Bethel Woods Center for the Arts (200 Hurd Rd., 866/781-2922, www.bethelwoodscenter.org), opened in 2006 with a performance by The New York Philharmonic. The $65-million center was built on the site of the 1969 Woodstock Festival and features the pavilion amphitheater, outdoor stage area, theater, interpretive center with impressive multimedia interactive exhibits about the 1969 festival, and a seasonal craft and farmers' market.

The venue attracts an ambitious line-up of performers ranging from The New York Philharmonic to ballet troupes, jazz greats, and pop-music stars, as well as arts workshops and film festivals. During big concerts, area campgrounds are the first to fill, though the Bethel Woods Center for the Arts website offers a comprehensive directory of additional accommodations. Those visiting the museum on concert days should buy advance tickets to avoid disappointment.

Not far from Bethel Woods Center for the Arts is exquisite **Lake Superior State Park** (Dr. Duggan Rd., off Rte. 17B, 845/794-3000, ext. 5002, nysparks.com/parks/87, daily 9am-dusk, parking $7 in summer), an all-but-untouched recreation area open for swimming, picnicking, boating, and fishing. Boats are available for rent.

noon-5pm), housed in what was once the Espresso Café, where Bob Dylan, Janis Joplin, and other 1960s-era icons performed. Tinker Street is also home to **The Golden Notebook** (29 Tinker St., 845/679-8000, www.golden-notebook.com), a good bookstore.

Overlook Mountain

Looming behind Woodstock is Overlook Mountain, the summit of which offers splendid views of the valley and river below. To reach the mountain from town, take Rock City Road to Meads Mountain Road; the trailhead is opposite **Karma Triyana Dharmachakra** (335 Meads Mountain Rd., 845/679-5906, www.kagyu.org, shrine room Mon.-Fri. 2pm-6pm, Sat.-Sun. 10am-noon and 1pm-6pm, hours may differ if a teaching is in session), a Tibetan Buddhist monastery. In its shrine room is a 13-foot-high statue of the Buddha, which was used by Martin Scorsese in his film *Kundun,* about the life of the Dalai Lama.

The two-mile walk to the top of the mountain follows an old roadbed, is of easy-to-moderate difficulty, and takes about an hour. Along the way you'll pass the ruins of the Overlook Mountain House, once a popular resort that was anchored to the mountain by strong cables to keep it from being blown away. Plaques tell the resort's fascinating history.

Entertainment

Founded by poet Hervey White, the **Maverick Concerts** (120 Maverick Rd., Woodstock, 845/679-8217, www.maverickconcerts.org, mid-July-late Sept.) are the oldest chamber-music series in the country, featuring top musicians in a relaxed woodsy setting. The remarkable "music chapel," hand-hewn in 1916, boasts perfect acoustics and seats only 400. It's changed little since its creation. The concerts attract an eclectic crowd, drawing from NYC's metro-music lovers as well as those who remember Woodstock because they were there. Following a nearly century-old tradition, very little reserved seating is available (26 online ticketed seats, $40). Join excited concert-goers for first-come seating ($25) under the rustic chapel's dome or on handmade wooden benches decorated with woven branches under the canopy of leafy trees. Some take advantage of Maverick's "Rock Bottom, pay-what-you-can" seating and bring their own chair or blanket to lounge and soak in the venue's unique atmosphere and artistry of world-class musicians.

The **Colony Café** (22 Rock City Rd., 845/679-8639, www.colonycafewoodstock.com) presents local, regional, and national performers most nights of the week. The café serves beer, wine, coffee, and dessert.

Now housed in the 1902 Byrdcliffe art colony is **Woodstock Byrdcliffe Guild** (34 Tinker St., 845/679-2079, www.woodstockguild.org), an arts center featuring performance art, theater, and film. Since 2000, Woodstock has been home to the **Woodstock Film Festival** (www.woodstockfilmfestival.com), held each fall.

Bearsville Theater (291 Tinker St., 845/679-4406, www.bearsvilletheater.com), in Bearsville, includes two restaurants, several off-site studios secluded in the woods, and a 250-seat theater that presents original drama throughout the summer. The complex was originally planned and financed by the late Albert Grossman, former manager of Bob Dylan and Janis Joplin.

To find out what's going on in the area, check the **Woodstock Times** (www.woodstockx.com) or listen to Woodstock's independent radio station, WDST, FM 100.1.

Accommodations

The mustard yellow **Twin Gables** (73 Tinker St., 845/679-9479, www.twingableswoodstockny.com, $89-160) has functioned as a homey, affordable guesthouse since the 1920s and claims to be the oldest house in Woodstock. Some rooms share baths.

Also downtown, you'll find the attractive

Woodstock Inn on the Millstream (48 Tannery Brook Rd., 845/679-8211, www.woodstock-inn-ny.com, $129-245), an upscale property with a variety of room types. The inn is in walking distance of Millstream, a natural brook and swimming hole and a favorite cool-down spot in the summer.

Elegance and convenience mingle at **The Wild Rose Inn** (66 Rock City Rd., 845/679-8783, www.thewildroseinn.com, $150-250), just a block from the village green. This B&B offers cushy furnishings, private whirlpool bathtubs, and private entrances to all rooms. The friendly owner is well versed in all things local.

Built as the home of Woodstock artist Jo Cantine, the elegant hideaway **Woodstock Country Inn** (185 Cooper Lake Rd., 845/679-9380, www.woodstockcountryinn.com, $185-300) offers four guest rooms filled with light and antiques. There is also an outdoor pool and great mountain views.

Food

One of Woodstock's oldest restaurants is the hole-in-the-wall **Joshua's** (51 Tinker St., 845/679-5533, www.joshuascafe.com, Mon.-Tues. and Thurs.-Fri. 11am-close, Sat.-Sun. 10am-close, $23), serving simple but tasty Middle Eastern food. **The Garden Café** (6 Old Forge Rd., 845/679-3600, www.gardencafe-woodstock.com, Mon. and Wed.-Fri. 11:30am-9pm, Sat. 10am-9:30pm, Sun. 10am-9pm, $14) on the village green serves up vegetarian and vegan fare even carnivores can appreciate.

Another local favorite is **The Red Onion** (1654 Rte. 212, 845/679-1223, www.redonionrestaurant.com, Sun.-Thurs. 5pm-9pm, Fri.-Sat. 5pm-10pm, $25). Housed in an 1830s farmhouse on the outskirts of town, the restaurant serves an eclectic international menu.

Streamside **C Bear Cafe** (295 Tinker St., 845/679-5555, www.bearcafe.com, Mon. and Wed.-Thurs. 5pm-9:30pm, Fri.-Sat. 5pm-10:30pm, Sun. 5pm-9pm, $28) is in the Bearsville Theater Complex in Bearsville and is housed in a modern barn-like building with a big, comfortable bar. Expect imaginative

THE ROXBURY EXPERIENCE

For those who didn't get enough of the wonderfully weird Woodstock experience, the village of **Roxbury,** which lies right up Route 28W, has plenty to offer. Between the **Roxbury Arts Group**'s (venues vary, 607/326-7908, www. roxburyartsgroup.org) gallery and single-day workshops in felting and clay-work, **walking tours** (Town of Roxbury Department of Community Resources, 607/326-3722) of town led by costumed historical figures, and **Roxbury Nine Vintage** (www.roxburyny.com) baseball games played by 19th-century rules, you will quickly understand why the entire town was placed on the National and State Registers of Historic Places.

Perhaps the best reason to visit is **The**

Roxbury Motel (2258 County Hwy. 41, Roxbury, 607/326-7200, www.theroxburymotel. com, $90-645), the grooviest boutique hotel in the Catskills. A stay in "Genie's Bottle," "George's Spacepad," or "The Shagadelic" will offer suite dreams. Themed studios like "Fred's Lair" or "Samantha's Cloud" feature chunky rock walls or illuminated chromatherapy bathtubs. Fortunately, the owners' incredible attention to detail pulls off this trip back to the 1960s and '70s with style and class. Stop at the local bakery to buy your own to-die-for coffee cake, part of the motel's impressive continental breakfast spread, as you head back out on the road to reality.

American dishes. Next door to the Bear Cafe is **Little Bear** (Bearsville Theater Complex, 845/679-8899, www.thelittlebearchinesrestaurant.com, $16), offering tasty Chinese food with lovely streamside outdoor seating.

WEST ON ROUTE 28

Route 28 runs right through the heart of **Catskill Park** and **Catskill Forest Preserve** (no entrance fee). Just past Boiceville, the land turns wooded, wild, and wonderful, with mountains rising to the left and right. Five of the Catskills' highest peaks are located in Ulster County.

Twelve-mile-long **Ashokan Reservoir** begins near the park's entrance. Built between 1909 and 1919, despite fierce local opposition, the reservoir displaced eight communities, 2,600 graves, 64 miles of road, and 11 miles of railroad. Around the reservoir runs Route 28A, a marvelous **scenic drive** that skirts Ashokan Dam, fountains, and a picnic area. Peaks rising to 3,000 feet surround the western end.

To either side of Route 28 are small, wistful villages that were once major resort destinations but now aren't much more than clutches of well-worn buildings, huddled together against the modern world. The original Route

28 once ran through their centers; the modern route bypasses them completely.

Boiceville

On the outskirts of Boiceville is **(Onteora Mountain House** (96 Piney Point Rd., 845/657-6233, www.onteora.com, $185-265), a noteworthy B&B. Onteora sits high on a mountaintop overlooking Catskill Park. Once the posh retreat of mayonnaise mogul Richard Hellman, the home features huge picture windows, cathedral ceilings, and a massive stone fireplace. The B&B offers seven guest rooms, all with private baths and most with magnificent views.

The very popular **Bread Alone Bakery & Cafe** (3962 Rte. 28, 845/657-3328, www. breadalone.com/boiceville, Mon.-Thurs. 7am-5pm, Fri.-Sat. 7am-6pm, $8) offers much more than just great fresh bread baked in a wood-fired oven. Also on the menu are homemade soups, sandwiches, pastries, and coffees.

Mount Tremper

One of the odder attractions in the Catskills is **Emerson** (5340 Rte. 28, 877/688-2828, Mon.-Thurs. 10am-5pm, Fri.-Sun. 10am-6pm, adults $5, children under 11 free), where you'll find the world's largest kaleidoscope, housed in a former grain silo painted with blue sky, white clouds, and a pair of honey-colored eyes. Inside the nearly 60-foot-tall tower, visitors stare straight up into myriad images multiplied by 254 facets covering about 45 feet. Three different shows are presented in the kaleidoscope: America, The House We Live In; Metamorphosis; and Hexagram Holiday. Also in the complex are shops selling kaleidoscopes, furniture, clothing, books, and gifts.

C Four Corners Country Inn (1564 Wittenberg Rd., 845/688-3054, www.fourcornerscountryinn.com, $80-150), built in 1850 as a guesthouse, is both an inviting B&B and a popular French restaurant run by a French-born owner. Perched on a small hill surrounded by woodlands, the inn offers about eight guest rooms, many of which share bathrooms, and a wide, lovely veranda. The romantic dining room (average entrées $21) serves classic French favorites such as assorted pâtés, escargot, and scallops Provençal, and offers a French and American wine list.

Another classic French restaurant in the area is luminous **Catskill Rose** (5355 Rte. 212, 845/688-7100, www.catskillrose.com, $24), its front door framed with pink neon. To one side is an Art Deco bar glowing blue, to another a clutch of dining tables. Dishes are prepared by a husband-and-wife team.

The Emerson resort includes the **Catamount Restaurant** (5340 Rte. 28, 77/688-2828, www.emersonresort.com, Mon.-Thurs. 5pm-9pm, Fri.-Sat. 5pm-10pm, Sun. 4pm-9pm, $22), which serves classic American fare in a setting overlooking Esopus Creek and Mt. Tremper; the family-friendly **Lodge at Emerson** (5340 Rte. 28, 877/688-2828, www.emersonresort.com, $190-300), furnished in upscale log-cabin-style decor, and adults-only **Inn at Emerson** (5340 Rte. 28, 877/688-2828, www.emersonresort.com, $299-399). There is also a spa on the premises.

A good area campground is **Kenneth L. Wilson Campground** (859 Wittenberg Rd., one mile off Rte. 28, 845/679-7020, reservations 800/456-2267), which has 71 sites, picnic areas, showers, boat rentals, and mountain bike trails for advanced riders. Reservations should be made well in advance.

Phoenicia

One of the most prosperous villages along Route 28 is Phoenicia, known for its trout fishing, kayaking, and tubing, all done on Esopus Creek, which runs through the town. From May to September, floating down the creek on huge black inner tubes is one of the county's most popular activities. Several tube rental shops are located at the entrance to Phoenicia, among them is **Town Tinker** (10 Bridge St., 845/688-5553, www.towntinker.com).

Less than a mile away, housed in the old railroad station at the town's east end is the **Empire State Railway Museum** (70 High St., 845/688-7501, www.esrm.com, Memorial Day-Oct.31 weekends and holidays 11am-4pm, $3), which documents the history of the five different railroads that serviced the Catskills between the late 1860s and the 1940s.

Between the railroad museum and nearby Mt. Pleasant runs **Catskill Mountain Railroad** (845/688-7400, www.catskillmtrailroad.com, hours vary seasonally). Though damaged by a 2011 hurricane and currently under threat by local governments, which want to shut the railroad down, scenic train rides along Esopus Creek are still chugging along and are particularly popular during fall foliage in September-October.

Phoenicia's Main Street is short, which makes it easily walkable. On it, you'll find a handful of shops like **The Tender Land Home** (64 Main St., 845/688-7213, www.tenderlandhome.com), selling handcrafts and home accessories, and the self-described "antique emporium and odditorium," **Homer & Langley's Mystery Spot** (72 Main St., 845/688-7868, www.lauralevine.com/mystery-spot), a "shrine to clutter" that is "packed to the rafters" with "knick-knacks and doo-dads" curated by artist Laura Levine.

C Sweet Sue's (49 Main St., 845/688-7852, Thurs.-Mon. 8am-3pm) is Phoenicia's obligatory spot for breakfast and brunch. Over a dozen types of pancakes are on the menu.

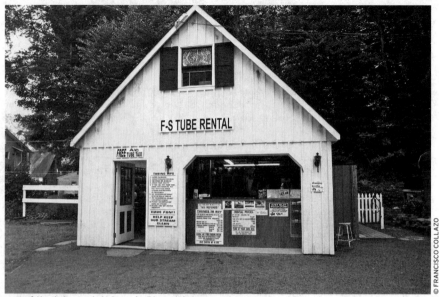

© FRANCISCO COLLAZO

one of the tube rental shops in Phoenicia

Brio's (68 Main St., 845/688-5370, www. brios.net, summer 7am-11pm daily; off-season hours vary, $12) is a dependable pizzeria that also serves pasta and salads.

"Catskills vs. Hamptons" read buttons sitting in a bowl on the check-in desk at **The Graham & Co.** (80 Rte. 214, 845/688-7871, www.thegrahamandco.com), Phoenicia's newest—and so far only—boutique hotel. You'll be forgiven if you feel confused about your coordinates when you glance at the cool kids lounging around the pool here: Might Phoenicia be the next East Hampton? Twenty rooms are spare on design but perfectly comfortable; some even have kitchenettes. A bunkhouse is intended for snowboarders and skiers. A pool, bikes, and a fire pit round out the on-the-grounds amenities at this hip hotel.

Woodland Valley Recreation

Off Route 28 one mile west of Phoenicia, Woodland Valley Road turns off to the left and leads through Woodland Valley, one of the deepest and most romantic valleys in the Catskills. Four miles in, the road comes to a parking lot at **Woodland Valley State Campground** (1319 Woodland Valley Rd., 845/688-7647, reservations 800/456-2267), where reservations should be made well in advance.

There is also a well-marked trail that takes hikers to the top of Wittenberg Mountain. The 3.4-mile, 2,800-foot ascent takes about three hours. It's steep near the beginning and again near the top, but only of moderate difficulty most of the way. The spectacular view from the summit—one of the best in the Catskills—encompasses almost all of Ashokan Reservoir.

From Wittenberg Mountain, a short, narrow trail leads via a connecting ridge to Cornell Mountain, which offers good views of Slide Mountain, the highest peak in the Catskills. The hike from Wittenberg to Cornell takes about 30 minutes.

Pine Hill and Highmount

Good downhill skiing can be found in Highmount at New York State-owned

© FRANCISCO COLLAZO

the Catskill Mountain Railroad

Belleayre (Belleayre Rd., off Rte. 28, Highmount, 845/254-5608, www.belleayre. com). There are more than 45 trails for skiers of all skill levels. The vertical drop is 1,404 feet. The longest run is over 12,000 feet. During off-season, you can hike or take a chairlift to the summit.

Anchoring the small village nearby is old-fashioned **Pine Hill Arms Hotel** (288 Main St., 845/254-4012, www.pinehillarms.com, $75-85), which features a beautiful old bar, a restaurant serving an especially good breakfast, and live music on some weekends. One of the most economical places to stay in all of the Catskills is the friendly **Belleayre Lodge and Cabins** (15 Hostel Dr., Pine Hill, 845/254-4200, www.belleayrelodge.com, $95-270), which offers cabin-style accommodations.

WEST ON ROUTE 23A

Some of the most dramatic scenery in the Catskills lies west of Route 32 on Route 23A. For about four miles, between Palenville and Haines Falls, the road winds steeply up nearly 1,500 feet, past craggy cliffs and rocky streams, forested walls and outstanding views. The incline continues at a gentler angle between Haines Falls and Hunter, then levels out to run along Schoharie Creek.

Kaaterskill Falls

Off Route 23A about three miles west of Palenville are **Kaaterskill Falls,** marked with a sign and roadside parking lot. At 260 feet (compared to Niagara's 167 feet), these are the highest waterfalls in the state. During the Romantic Age, everyone from Thomas Cole and Asher Durand to James Fenimore Cooper and William Cullen Bryant were inspired by this long glittering torrent. The falls were portrayed in countless paintings, illustrations, and poems until they became an icon for the American wilderness. Near the top of the falls once stood Catskill Mountain House, the nation's first mountain resort.

To reach the lower basin of Kaaterskill Falls, follow the trail on the north side of Route 23A. The hike, which begins at Bastion Falls, takes

© FRANCISCO COLLAZO

The Graham & Co. hotel in Phoenicia

less than an hour round-trip, and although there are steep spots, the trail is mostly level.

Escarpment Trail

The **Escarpment Trail** stretches 24 miles between Route 23A in Haines Falls and Route 23 in East Windham without crossing a single highway. Parts of the trail have been used for more than 150 years, as initials and dates carved along its ledges attest.

To access the popular section of the Escarpment Trail that leads past the former site of the Catskill Mountain House, continue about two miles past the Kaaterskill Falls parking area and take the first right onto County Road 18, following signs to North-South Lakes Campground. At the end of this four-mile road, just before the campground, turn right onto Scutt Road, where you'll find a parking area and a blue-marked trail.

Follow the trail through a forested area, past Spruce Creek and a four-way intersection, toward Layman Monument and Sunset Rock. Soon after the intersection, the trail skirts along

the top of the Great Wall of Manitou. The terrain here is fairly level and all along the way are overlooks offering magnificent views. Near the Layman Monument you can see Kaaterskill Clove ("clove" comes from the Dutch word for "gorge"), with Hunter Mountain behind.

About 1.5 miles past Inspiration Point is a red-marked cutoff trail leading to the site of the former Catskill Mountain House. Take this shorter trail, or continue on the more scenic blue trail past Split and Boulder Rocks. Either way, in 20-30 minutes you'll reach the large open ledge upon which the famed resort once stood. An informative plaque marks the spot.

To hike from the parking lot to the Catskill Mountain House site takes about an hour and a half. From there, you can return the way you came or take the service road back to the parking lot.

Catskill Mountain House Site

Don't miss the view from the **Catskill Mountain House site,** just east of Haines Falls. The whole world seems to lie at your feet. Straight ahead, in the distance, are the gray-blue Taconic and Berkshire Mountains; below is the Hudson, shrunk to a slim silver line. The view is perhaps best described in James Fenimore Cooper's *The Pioneers,* one of his Natty Bumppo tales: "'What see you when you get there?' asked Edwards. 'Creation!' said Natty,...'all creation, lad.'"

The site can be reached by hiking the Escarpment Trail or by driving into **North-South Lakes Campground** (County Rd. 18, Haines Falls, 518/589-5058, closed late Oct.-mid-May). Drive to the end of the service road. The short trail that leads to the site is located at the far end of the parking lot. For those with more time and more stamina, the site can also be reached by hiking the 24-mile Escarpment Trail.

North-South Lakes

According to legend, North and South Lakes are the two eyes of a great reclining giant, Onteora; nearby Lake Creek was made from his tears. South Lake, formerly known as Sylvan Lake, was one of Thomas Cole's favorite subjects. He painted his well-known *Lake With Dead Trees* and *Catskill Lake* here.

The 219-site **North-South Lakes Campground** (County Rd. 18, Haines Falls, 518/589-5058, reservations 800/456-2267, closed late Oct.-mid-May) is part of a state park by the same name, where you'll find two long, pristine lakes ringed by deciduous trees that erupt with fiery color in fall, a sandy beach, bathhouses, and hiking trails. Rowboats can be rented, and fishing is good.

Tannersville

Part scruffy mountain village, part cheery tourist town, Tannersville—named for its once-extensive tanning industry—is now home to a few shops and cafés, several inns and B&Bs, and more than its fair share of tattoo parlors. In the village center, you'll find **Maggie's Krooked Cafe** (6000 Main St., 518/589-6101, www.krookedcafe.com, daily 7am-7pm, $13), offering home-cooked specialties such as pancakes and beer battered shrimp. Another café

on Main Street, **Last Chance Antiques and Cheese Cafe** (6009 Main St., 518/589-6424, www.lastchanceonline.com, daily 11am-close, $16), is a combination store/café featuring overstuffed sandwiches, homemade soups, cheeses, and chocolates.

Hunter Mountain

In winter, New York City residents by the thousands flock to the slopes of Hunter Mountain Ski Area, the Catskills' best-known ski center. In summer and fall, Hunter Mountain Festivals are staged here. Annual events include the German Alps Festival, the International Celtic Festival, and Oktoberfest, among others.

Before becoming a ski town, Hunter was known first for its tannery and then for its chair factory. Today you'll find lodges and restaurants along its Main Street, many done up in ersatz Swiss motifs. Many shut down during the off-season.

SKIING

Hunter Mountain Ski Area (off Rte. 23A, 518/263-4223, www.huntermtn.com) actually covers three mountains, with 58 trails, 10 lifts, and 100 percent snowmaking capability. On summer weekends, **Summer Sky Ride** (early July-early Sept. Wed.-Fri. 11am-4pm, Sat.-Sun. 10am-5pm, hours vary in the off-season, adults $10, seniors $8, children 7-12 $6) travels to the mountain's summit.

HIKING

A number of good, well-marked hiking trails crisscross the area around Hunter Mountain. Many start at the back of the mountain on Old Spruceton Road. To get here, continue west on Route 23A past the Ukrainian church and turn left onto Route 42 south. Continue to the hamlet of Westkill, turn east onto County Road 6, and follow it six miles through pastoral Spruceton Valley. You'll find two parking lots and the trailheads at the end, after the road has become dirt.

The main trail leading to Hunter's summit is of moderate difficulty, covers 7.2 miles round-trip, and takes about 6-7 hours. Along the way is a mile-long spur leading to **Colonel's Chair,** a northern protuberance of the mountain supposedly resembling a giant armchair. The chair was named after Colonel William Edwards, an early tanner who made his fortune decimating the area's hemlock forest. It was Edwards who first put Hunter, then known as Edwardsville, on the map.

One of the easiest hikes in the Catskills, leading to Diamond Notch Falls, also begins at the parking lots. The gently inclining trail is about a mile long and runs alongside West Kill Creek. Wildflowers and birds are abundant.

For more information on hiking Hunter Mountain, stop in at the main **Hunter Mountain Ski Area** (off Rte. 23A in the heart of the village, 518/263-4223, www.huntermtn. com).

FISHING
In summer, anglers can be found **trout fishing** in Schoharie Creek along Route 23A, while hikers take to the slopes of Hunter Mountain. Four miles south of town is the 24-site **Devil's Tombstone Campground** (Rte. 214, 845/688-7160, reservations 800/456-2267), one of the oldest campgrounds in the Catskills and an ideal base camp for skilled hikers.

ACCOMMODATIONS
Charming (**Fairlawn Inn** (7872 Main St., 518/263-5025, www.fairlawninn.com, $129-250) is a three-story Victorian inn with nine attractive guest rooms, many with brass or four-poster beds. Stained-glass windows, parquet floors, 19th-century antiques, wraparound porches, and a stunning central staircase add to the ambiance.

The modern (**Scribner Hollow Lodge** (13 Scribner Hollow Rd., 518/263-4211, www. scribnerhollow.com, $115-260 pp, with breakfast and dinner) is a full-service lodge with an outdoor pool, an unusual indoor grotto, saunas, and fireplaces. Each of the rooms is furnished differently, and artwork is everywhere.

Near the base of Hunter Mountain is chalet-style **Hunter Mountain Inn** (7433 Main St., 518/263-3777, www.hunterinn.com,

$100-180), whose bar is a favorite haunt of the après-ski crowd; live music is often featured on weekends. The inn holds 42 rooms, which feature cathedral ceilings and whirlpool tubs.

Lexington
Continuing west on Route 23A, you'll pass through the nondescript hamlets of South Jewett and Jewett Center before coming to the startlingly beautiful **St. John the Baptist Ukrainian Catholic Church** (Rte. 23A just east of Lexington, 518/263-3862, www.brama.com/stjohn). The church was built in 1962 in memory of Ukrainians killed by Communists in World War II. The entire edifice, with its rich brown cedar shingles, onion domes, and steeply pitched roofs, was constructed without nails in the traditional Ukrainian manner. The interior features a stunning hand-carved altar, along with woodcarvings and icons. On Saturday evenings in July and August, classical chamber-music concerts are presented in the adjacent *Grazhda,* or community center.

EAST ON ROUTE 23
Route 23A cuts east to west across the northern part of the Catskill Mountains. If you want to loop back to Palenville, passing through some spectacular scenery along the way, take Route 23 east from Lexington.

Ashland
Heading east along Route 23, you'll pass a wide and wonderful waterfall on the right known as **Red Falls.** At its base is a deep, dark swimming hole. From the waterfall, Route 23 winds through the hamlet of Ashland, an excellent place to stop to take photographs of the iconic Catskills scenery.

One lodging option in the area is **The McElroy House Bed & Breakfast** (11376 Rte. 23, 518/734-3643, www.mcelroyhouse.com, $79-119). Each of the rooms has a private bath and all guests can take advantage of shuttle service to and from Ski Windham.

Windham
Route 23 continues past Ashland to the busy

FLY FISHING

At a roadside park deep in the Catskills, a plaque quoting the Fisherman's Prayer says it all: "God grant that I may live to fish until my dying day, and when it comes to my last cast I then most humbly pray, when in the Lord's safe landing net I'm peacefully asleep, then in His mercy I be judged good enough to keep."

Livingston Manor, on the banks of the Willowemoc, is primarily known for its superb trout fishing. The Willowemoc offers nearly 7 miles of public water from Livingston Manor downstream to Roscoe, and the Beaverkill's 15 miles below Roscoe are all public and easily wadable. Covered bridges dating to the mid-1800s span the trout streams.

Appropriately situated about midway between Livingston Manor and Roscoe is state-of-the-art **Catskill Fly Fishing Center and Museum** (1031 Old Rte. 17, 845/439-4810, www.catskillflyfishing.org). Started by a group of local fisherfolk in 1981, the center does an excellent job of documenting the history of fly fishing in the United States.

Hundreds of meticulously crafted flies, along with rods, reels (some dating back to 1850), historic photos, and other artifacts are on display. To the uninitiated, that might sound ho-hum, but don't pass judgment until you've seen the bumble puppy, midge, quill gordon, wet spider, cow dung, or red ant. Fly-tying is a bona fide folk art, and each fly is an intricate affair, individually designed and named. At one time, flies were made out of feathers and furs; today, the material is usually synthetic.

The center also hosts fly-tying demonstrations, lectures, and fly-tying classes for beginners. The Willowemoc, usually lined with fisherfolk in waders casting their lines, runs out front.

Roscoe, a.k.a. **Trout Town U.S.A.,** is considerably larger and more sophisticated than Livingston Manor, but its raison d'être is the same. American fly-fishing was developed at **Junction Pool,** just west of Roscoe, where the Willowemoc and Beaverkill meet. The town boasts five of the country's best trout streams and plenty of other fishable waterways.

A number of expert fly-tiers still live and work in Roscoe. **Dette Trout Flies** (68 Cottage St., 607/498-4991, www.dettetroutflies.com) is a family-owned fly-tying business started in 1928. Among anglers, the Dette name is known around the world. The shop gives straight intel on what to expect throughout the area in their Daily Report (online and by phone), including river flows, temperatures, turbidity, insect hatches, and local weather.

Continuing farther up Lewbeach Road, you'll enter Catskill Park and soon come to the hamlets of Beaverkill and Lewbeach. State-run **Beaverkill Campground** (792 Berrybrook Road Spur, 845/439-4281) is situated on the banks of Beaverkill River, another world-famous trout-fishing stream. The 52-site campground has a picnic area with grills and hot shower facilities. Keep an eye out for the covered bridge on the property, which dates to 1865.

Wulff School of Fly Fishing (845/439-5020, www.wulffschool.com), in Lewbeach, offers weekend trout-fishing and fly-casting workshops May-June. Run by Joan Wulff, a champion fisherwoman and author, the school is set on 100 acres and includes a private stretch of the Beaverkill River.

ski-resort village of Windham. More upscale than Hunter, Windham is filled with Greek Revival buildings, ski lodges, and restaurants.

Ski Windham (33 Clarence D. Lane Rd., 518/734-4300, www.skiwindham.com) is considerably smaller than Hunter Mountain, but it's also less hectic. The resort offers 52 trails, a 3,100-foot summit, and 97 percent snowmaking capability.

There are a number of dining options in Windham. For a hearty breakfast or lunch, or a glass of Guinness, try **Jimmy O'Connors Windham Mountain Inn** (South St., 518/734-4270, www.windhaminn.com), a lively Irish pub. The homey **Michael's Diner** (5339 Main

St., 518/734-4831, daily 7am-9pm, $10) serves breakfast all day, along with sandwiches, homemade soups, and Greek specialties. German-Swiss cuisine is served at cozy **Chalet Fondue Restaurant** (55 Rte. 296, 518/734-4650, chaletfondue.com, Mon. and Wed.-Sat. 5pm-10pm, Sun. 1pm-8pm, $18), decorated in traditional German style with fireplaces, giant wine casks, and carved woodwork.

🄲 **Albergo Allegria B&B** (43 Rte. 296, off Rte. 23, a half mile east of Windham, 518/734-5560, www.AlbergoUSA.com, $93-249), a charming Victorian manor house that feels more like an inn than a B&B, is in a rural setting on the outskirts of town. Twenty-one guest rooms are nicely done up in period antiques. Downstairs is a comfortable lounge with overstuffed couches and a fireplace.

Cairo

Between Windham and Cairo (KAY-ro), Route 23 turns from scenic to spectacular as it traverses the big wide slopes of Windham High Peak, Burnt Knob, and Acra Point. Expansive Helderberg Valley opens up below, while the Green Mountains of Vermont and the White Mountains of New Hampshire make themselves visible on the horizon. A scenic overlook is located midway.

At Acra, you can continue east directly into Cairo, or loop south through the community of Round Top, once known for its German resorts, one or two of which are still in operation. The hamlet's foremost accommodation, however, is the wonderful 🄲 **Winter Clove Inn** (2965 Winter Clove Rd., Round Top, 518/622-3267, www.winterclove.com, $95-140 pp including all meals; weekly rates available), a big white colonial sitting on a hillside. Owned by the same family since 1830, Winter Clove has swimming pools, tennis courts, a nine-hole golf course, hiking trails, and an antique bowling alley.

Buddhist Temple

Just beyond the town of Cairo, off Route 23B, is Ira Vail Road and signs that will lead you to the **Mahayana Temple at South Cairo** (700 Ira Vail Rd., 518/622-3619, daily 7am-7pm), the retreat of the Eastern States Buddhist Temple of America, based in New York City. The red-and-gold enclave sits in a peaceful woodsy area at the end of a dirt road. Not far from the red-gated entrance are the serene Lake of Fortune and Longevity and the Pagoda of Jade Buddha. To one side are the Grand Buddha Hall and several smaller temples.

A plaque at the Grand Hall tells the story of the Yings who immigrated to the United States from China in 1955, only to find no organized Buddhist temple in New York. Seven years later they founded the first, at 64 Mott Street in New York City's Chinatown, and soon thereafter built the Mahayana retreat.

Inside the Grand Hall is an altar laden with three golden Buddhas, fruit, and flowers. Two monks in orange robes sit against one wall. The retreat actively welcomes visitors, as the many unobtrusive donation boxes attest.

Don't leave the Mahayana retreat without visiting the fascinating Five Hundred Arhats Hall. Here, 500 golden Buddhas, each one different from the next, sit in a darkened room lit only with small spotlights.

EAST DURHAM

On Route 145, about five miles northwest of Cairo, is the village of East Durham. At first, nothing seems too out of the ordinary in this scenic spot surrounding by rolling hills, but then you start to notice one shamrock after another, one green building after another, one Irish name after another: O'Sullivan, Kelly, McGrath, McGuire, O'Connor, McLaughlin, Ryan, O'Shea. Ethnic resorts may be dying out in the Catskills, but someone forgot to tell East Durham.

Variously nicknamed Ireland's 33rd County, the Irish Catskills, or the Irish Alps, East Durham and environs have been an Irish resort since the late 1800s, when immigrants living in New York City escaped the summer heat by coming up here to the hills that reminded them of home. Much of this tourist trade died down in the 1970s with the advent of affordable flights to Ireland, but it's recently begun to enjoy a resurgence, thanks to a new wave of Irish immigrants to New York.

Guaranteed Irish

One unique stop in the village center is **Guaranteed Irish** (2220 Rte. 145, 518/634-2392, Apr.-Dec. daily, Jan.-Mar. weekends only), which bills itself as "the largest Irish import store in the United States." Inside this sprawling building you'll find everything from Irish sweaters and china leprechauns to an excellent selection of Irish music and literature. Most everyone who shops here seems to have at least a touch of Irish brogue, so even if you don't intend to buy, it's great fun just to listen.

Entertainment and Events

The **MJQ Irish Cultural & Sports Centre** (2267 Rte. 145, 518/634-2286, www.mjqirishculturalcenter.com) presents theater, music, dance, and sporting events.

Irish music can also be heard at many of the casual pubs along Route 145, or the more formal lounges situated in the village's resorts. Popular **East Durham Irish Festival** (518/634-2286, www.eastdurhamirishfestival.com), featuring Irish bands, bagpipes, and dancers, takes place over Memorial Day weekend.

Accommodations and Food

Gavin's Irish Country Inn (118 Golden Hill Rd., off Rte. 145, 518/634-2582, www.gavins.com) offers lodging as well as live music several nights a week. **Shamrock House** (2388 Rte. 145, 518/634-2897, www.shamrockhouse.com, $110-140 with breakfast and dinner), owned by the Kellegher family since 1938, is a well-kept motel with a restaurant, pub, and live Irish music on weekends.

Upper Hudson Valley

CATSKILL

The town of Catskill, the Greene County seat, sits on the sloping banks of the Hudson River at the mouth of Catskill Creek. The natural harbor here helped the town grow steadily after its founding in the late 1600s. By the early 1900s, Catskill was the prosperous home of small knitting factories, brickyards, and distilleries.

During Prohibition, the town was known for its "retailers of liquid damnation." Catskill applejack was brewed in the hills surrounding town and buried in jugs whenever the law came around. The lucrative moonshine trade coupled with the inaccessible hills made Catskill a favorite haunt of New York City gangsters Legs Diamond and Vincent Coll. Diamond was once tried in the **Greene County Courthouse,** an imposing neoclassical building that still stands at the corner of Main and Bridge Streets.

Today, the town feels worn around the edges, but it retains a distinct charm. Besides the courthouse, **Main Street** showcases one big wooden building after another, many housing

friendly, old-fashioned businesses. **Catskill Gallery** (398 Main St., 518/943-3400, www.greenearts.org, Mon.-Sat. 10am-5pm, free), run by the Greene County Council on the Arts, presents exhibits, concerts, readings, and plays throughout the year. Running parallel to Main Street is **Spring Street,** a treasure trove of Victorian homes. In the summer, check out the **HI-Way Drive-In Theater** (10699 Rte. 9W Coxsackie, 518/731-8672, www.driveinmovie.com/NY/Hi-way/schedule, May-Oct. nightly, $9 adults, $4 children 3-11, show starts at dusk), which offers three screens and FM radio-generated audio for the double features shown nightly, complete with dancing popcorn and games of chance during intermission.

Cedar Grove

The father of the Hudson River School, Thomas Cole, lived in Catskill much of his adult life. Born in England in 1801, Cole came to New York City in 1818. He taught himself to paint landscapes, and in 1825 took his first sketching trip up the Hudson. The works he produced on that trip won him instant recognition.

Cole's former home, **Cedar Grove** (218 Spring St., 518/943-7465, www.thomascole. org, May-early Nov. Wed.-Sun. 10am-4pm, adults $10, seniors $9, children under 12 free) is a big yellow-and-white house with a wide veranda overlooking the Hudson. The house features exhibits on Cole and his family, other Hudson River artists such as Frederic Church, and the Catskills. Also on display are a few small works by Cole, and memorabilia such as his paint box and Bible.

Out back is Cole's old studio, housed in what were once slave quarters.

ATHENS

About four miles north of Catskill on Route 385 is the attractive village of Athens, first settled by the Dutch in 1686. At one time or another, the town has been a center for brick making, shipbuilding, ice-harvesting, and mushroom-growing (grown in icehouses, after the advent of refrigeration).

Today, Athens feels like a smaller, sleepier version of Catskill. Its streets, too, are lined

Guaranteed Irish

One unique stop in the village center is **Guaranteed Irish** (2220 Rte. 145, 518/634-2392, Apr.-Dec. daily, Jan.-Mar. weekends only), which bills itself as "the largest Irish import store in the United States." Inside this sprawling building you'll find everything from Irish sweaters and china leprechauns to an excellent selection of Irish music and literature. Most everyone who shops here seems to have at least a touch of Irish brogue, so even if you don't intend to buy, it's great fun just to listen.

Entertainment and Events

The **MJQ Irish Cultural & Sports Centre** (2267 Rte. 145, 518/634-2286, www.mjqirishculturalcenter.com) presents theater, music, dance, and sporting events.

Irish music can also be heard at many of the casual pubs along Route 145, or the more formal lounges situated in the village's resorts. Popular **East Durham Irish Festival** (518/634-2286, www.eastdurhamirishfestival.com), featuring Irish bands, bagpipes, and dancers, takes place over Memorial Day weekend.

Accommodations and Food

Gavin's Irish Country Inn (118 Golden Hill Rd., off Rte. 145, 518/634-2582, www.gavins.com) offers lodging as well as live music several nights a week. **Shamrock House** (2388 Rte. 145, 518/634-2897, www.shamrockhouse.com, $110-140 with breakfast and dinner), owned by the Kellegher family since 1938, is a well-kept motel with a restaurant, pub, and live Irish music on weekends.

Upper Hudson Valley

CATSKILL

The town of Catskill, the Greene County seat, sits on the sloping banks of the Hudson River at the mouth of Catskill Creek. The natural harbor here helped the town grow steadily after its founding in the late 1600s. By the early 1900s, Catskill was the prosperous home of small knitting factories, brickyards, and distilleries.

During Prohibition, the town was known for its "retailers of liquid damnation." Catskill applejack was brewed in the hills surrounding town and buried in jugs whenever the law came around. The lucrative moonshine trade coupled with the inaccessible hills made Catskill a favorite haunt of New York City gangsters Legs Diamond and Vincent Coll. Diamond was once tried in the **Greene County Courthouse,** an imposing neoclassical building that still stands at the corner of Main and Bridge Streets.

Today, the town feels worn around the edges, but it retains a distinct charm. Besides the courthouse, **Main Street** showcases one big wooden building after another, many housing friendly, old-fashioned businesses. **Catskill Gallery** (398 Main St., 518/943-3400, www.greenearts.org, Mon.-Sat. 10am-5pm, free), run by the Greene County Council on the Arts, presents exhibits, concerts, readings, and plays throughout the year. Running parallel to Main Street is **Spring Street,** a treasure trove of Victorian homes. In the summer, check out the **Hi-Way Drive-In Theater** (10699 Rte. 9W Coxsackie, 518/731-8672, www.driveinmovie.com/NY/Hi-way/schedule, May-Oct. nightly, $9 adults, $4 children 3-11, show starts at dusk), which offers three screens and FM radio-generated audio for the double features shown nightly, complete with dancing popcorn and games of chance during intermission.

Cedar Grove

The father of the Hudson River School, Thomas Cole, lived in Catskill much of his adult life. Born in England in 1801, Cole came to New York City in 1818. He taught himself to paint landscapes, and in 1825 took his first sketching trip up the Hudson. The works he produced on that trip won him instant recognition.

Cole's former home, **Cedar Grove** (218 Spring St., 518/943-7465, www.thomascole. org, May-early Nov. Wed.-Sun. 10am-4pm, adults $10, seniors $9, children under 12 free) is a big yellow-and-white house with a wide veranda overlooking the Hudson. The house features exhibits on Cole and his family, other Hudson River artists such as Frederic Church, and the Catskills. Also on display are a few small works by Cole, and memorabilia such as his paint box and Bible.

Out back is Cole's old studio, housed in what were once slave quarters.

ATHENS

About four miles north of Catskill on Route 385 is the attractive village of Athens, first settled by the Dutch in 1686. At one time or another, the town has been a center for brick making, shipbuilding, ice-harvesting, and mushroom-growing (grown in icehouses, after the advent of refrigeration).

Today, Athens feels like a smaller, sleepier version of Catskill. Its streets, too, are lined with big old wooden buildings, many of them from the Victorian age. Route 385 south of Athens parallels the Hudson at water level, offering splendid views of the river and the 1874 **Hudson-Athens Lighthouse** (located in the Hudson River, 518/828-5294, www.hudson-athenslighthouse.org, tours offered in summer, adults $25, children $10).

Downtown, right on the Hudson's shore, is the Victorian **Stewart House** (2 N. Water St., 518/567-1642, www.stewarthouse.com, lunch $13, dinner $22). Downstairs is a formal dining room and a more casual bar/bistro area where contemporary American and French fare is served. There is also a small **hotel** ($100-125 d) on the property that is fresh from a total renovation following 2011 Hurricane Irene. Its nine rooms each feature views of the Hudson River and have queen beds.

HUDSON

Hudson is one of the most interesting towns along its namesake river. Once a whaling port and 19th-century boomtown, the town has been gentrified by New Yorkers seeking second homes. Today, amid handsome antique stores and weathered Victorian buildings, proud descendants of whalers and Manhattan weekenders live side by side.

The Dutch began arriving in Hudson in the 17th century, but the town wasn't really settled until the 1780s, when a group of seafaring New Englanders seeking a harbor safe from British attack discovered the area's deep waters and steep bluffs. They purchased the land in 1783; by the following spring, several families had arrived and built homes.

Many of the new settlers were Quakers who carefully designed their new city to be a shipping center, complete with straight main streets, a shipyard, wharves, and warehouses. In 1785, Hudson received the third city charter granted in New York State, and by 1790, 25 schooners—most in the whaling business—were registered in the city. In 1797, Hudson missed becoming the capital of New York State by one vote.

By the mid 1800s, the whaling industry

HUDSON VALLEY

© AVALON TRAVEL

THE HUDSON RIVER

Most of the Hudson River isn't a river at all but an estuary, or arm of the sea; ocean tides run as far north as Albany. Algonquin Indians, recognizing this natural phenomenon, called the Hudson "Muhheakantuck," or "the river that flows both ways."

Navigable as far north as Albany, the Hudson begins at Lake Tear in the Clouds atop Mt. Marcy in the Adirondacks. Only 315 miles long from its source to New York Harbor, it varies in width from 2 feet to about 2 miles, and in depth from a few inches to 216 feet. The Hudson's widest point is at Haverstraw Bay; its deepest is between Newburgh and West Point.

When European settlers first arrived in New York, they found the banks of the Hudson–like all the Northeast–lined with primeval forest. The trees were of gargantuan size, with foliage so dense there was virtually no undergrowth.

By the mid-1800s, most of those trees were gone, cleared away for agriculture. Then came the Industrial Revolution, and cities, towns, and factories sprang up all along the river, bringing with them increasingly toxic levels of pollution. By the early 1970s, the Hudson had become, in the words of one local newspaper, a "flowing cesspool that was the shame of the Empire State."

Today, thanks largely to the Clean Water Act of 1972 and the work of the nonprofit organization Riverkeeper, the Hudson is a much cleaner place. Towns no longer spew untreated sewage into its waters, and factories have significantly reduced their chemical discharge. Much work remains to be done, but the Hudson is now regarded as a "recovering" river with an "improving" environmental condition.

had all but disappeared, but the coming of the railroads enabled an industrial transformation. Business boomed until the early 1900s, when industrial demands changed and Hudson began a slow decline. In the 1980s, the city was rediscovered by New Yorkers seeking refuge and began its rebirth.

Warren Street

The heart of downtown Hudson and the gentrification process is Warren Street, lined with one historic building after another. On the block closest to the river, there's a Greek Revival mansion with a "widow's walk" that once belonged to a whaling captain (No. 32). Along the 100 block alone are a Federal-style brick house with "eyebrow" windows (No. 102), a Queen Anne clapboard house with attractive trim (No. 114), and a rare Adam-style house with an ornamental marble frieze (No. 116).

The 1811 **Robert Jenkins House** (113 Warren St., 518/828-9764, July-Aug. Sun.-Mon. 1pm-3pm, or by appointment, adults $3, seniors $2, children under 12 free) houses a small local history museum. Exhibits include

paintings by several lesser-known Hudson River School artists, the jawbone of a whale, General Grant's "personal table," and other curious odds and ends.

◖ Olana State Historic Site

Perched high on a hill just south of Hudson is **Olana State Historic Site** (5720 Rte. 9G, 518/828-0135, www.olana.org, grounds: year-round daily 8am-sunset, parking fee may apply in summer and fall; house: mid-May-early Nov. Tues.-Sun. 10am-5pm, hours vary off-season, adults $9, seniors and students $8, children under 12 free; $5 vehicle fee May-Oct. Sat.-Sun.), an eccentric, Persian-style castle built in 1870 by landscape artist Frederic Church, with the help of architect Calvert Vaux. Church was then at the height of his career and had just returned from a trip to the Middle East, a land with which he had fallen in love.

A tour of Olana begins in the formal greeting room, which is hung with a dozen paintings, including one by Church's teacher and the founder of the Hudson River School, Thomas Cole. Here, a guide explains that one of the largest contributions the Hudson River School made to America was its portrayal of the wilderness as something approachable and worth preserving; before, it had been regarded as hostile and dangerous. One of Church's most famous paintings, of Niagara Falls, was used to spearhead a movement to save the falls from destruction.

Throughout the castle, painted in deep blues, reds, and yellows, are romantic arched doorways, wide-open windows, stenciled Persian lettering, and plush Persian rugs. Every room is filled with unique objects carefully picked out by the artist, who one critic said had the "best taste of his time." Each room also houses a number of Church's majestic, luminous canvases. The dining room is an amazing picture gallery, hung floor to ceiling with hundreds of canvases from the 16th to 18th centuries.

FASNY Museum of Firefighting

The delightful, spit-and-polish **FASNY Museum of Firefighting** (117 Harry Howard Ave., 518/822-1875, daily 10am-5pm, adults $5, children 5 and older $2, children under 5 free) boasts the nation's largest collection of firefighting equipment and related paraphernalia, including dozens of exquisite old horse-drawn fire carriages, many equipped with fairy-tale finery. Several carriages sport engraved lanterns and velvet-covered seats. One even has silver- and gold-plated hubcaps.

Part of the museum's charm is its location on the grounds of New York's retirement home for volunteer firefighters. You'll see the retirees hanging out on the porch as you drive up, and you'll meet them as you tour the museum. From them you'll learn that 80 percent of New York State's firefighters are still volunteers, a fact that poses a serious problem as the demands of firefighting are not compatible with busy modern-day lives.

Shopping

In recent years, Warren Street has become a destination for antiques lovers; dozens of stores of varying quality are located here, most between 5th and 7th Streets. Among them are **Theron Ware Gallery** (548 Warren St., 518/828-9744, www.theronwarehudson.com), specializing in classic Americana and ornate European antiques, and **Ornamentum** (506-½ Warren St., 518/671-6770, www.ornamentumgallery.com), part jewelry store and part art gallery. The two-story **Carrie Haddad Gallery** (622 Warren St., 518/828-1915, www.carriehaddadgallery.com) exhibits paintings, photographs, and sculpture by both established and up-and-coming artists.

Accommodations

The Victorian **◖Hudson City B&B** (326 Allen St., 518/822-8044, www.hudsoncitybnb.com, $129-209) was built by Joshua Waterman, a former Hudson mayor, in the 1860s. Outside, find a wide veranda lined with wicker chairs. Inside, find a parlor with a fireplace and guest rooms filled with antiques.

Built in the late 1800s, the red-brick **St. Charles Hotel** (16-18 Park Pl., 518/822-9900, www.stcharleshotel.com, $105-139, with continental breakfast) offers simple, adequate rooms.

Food

As the commercial hub of the community, it's not surprising that the area's best restaurants are along Warren Street. A good place for breakfast is **Nolita Bakery Cafe** (454 Warren St., 518/828-4905, Thurs.-Tues. 8am-4pm, $9).

At the sleek and trendy **◖ Red Dot** (321 Warren St., 518/828-3657, www.reddotrestaurant.com, Wed.-Mon. 5pm-10pm, $20), you can order everything from calamari to Thai curried vegetables. Sister restaurant to a Manhattan eatery of the same name, **Mexican Radio** (537 Warren St., 518/828-7770, www.hudson.mexrad.com, daily 11:30am-11pm, $18) offers high-end Mexican fare in a room filled with Mexican art.

KINDERHOOK

The charming village of Kinderhook, or "children's corner," was first settled by the Dutch, a fact reflected in the town's neat tree-lined streets, historic wooden buildings, and laid-back atmosphere. The village's most famous native son was Martin Van Buren, and signs directing visitors to the former president's birth site, home, and gravesite are everywhere. It is to Van Buren, nicknamed "Old Kinderhook," that we owe the expression "O.K."

To reach Kinderhook from Hudson, take Route 9 north about 10 miles.

Martin Van Buren National Historic Site

Martin Van Buren, a tavern owner's son who rose to hold the highest office in the land, spent the last 21 years of his life in this large yellow house surrounded by linden trees, now called the **Martin Van Buren National Historic Site** (1013 Old Post Rd., 518/758-9689, www.nps.gov/mava, grounds: year-round daily 7am-dusk, free; house: mid-May-Oct. 31 9am-4pm daily, $5 per person or $12 per family). Before Van Buren bought the property in 1839, Washington Irving had often visited here, sometimes even tutoring the former residents' children.

A visit to Lindenwald, as the house is known, begins with a short film on the "Little

Magician" (Van Buren was only five feet six inches), who avidly supported Jeffersonian democracy, served as vice-president under Andrew Jackson, and established the country's independent treasury. In his day, Van Buren was regarded as a cool and competent diplomat who operated most effectively behind the scenes, "row[ing] to his object with muffled oars."

A fine collection of musical instruments is in the sitting room, all done up in elegant gold and light blue. A magnificent French wallpaper mural depicting a hunting landscape is in the banquet room, which is kept dark at all times to preserve the mural, which can only be viewed by flashlight.

Luykas Van Alen House

Also off Route 9H, just north of Lindenwald, is the **Luykas Van Alen House** (Rte. 9H, 518/758-9265, www.cchsny.org, early July-Columbus Day Sat.-Sun. noon-4pm, adults $7, seniors $2, children under 12 free), a 1737 Dutch farmhouse complete with a steeply pitched roof, wide chimneys, delft tile, and sturdy furnishings. If the place looks familiar, it's because it was used in Martin Scorsese's film *The Age of Innocence,* based on the Edith Wharton novel.

In front of the farmhouse is a dark and peaceful pond that's home to several swans; to one side is the one-roomed **Ichabod Crane School House.** Washington Irving apparently based his famous character on a schoolteacher from Kinderhook; the building has been restored to look as it did in the 1920s.

Downtown Historic Sites

1820 **James Vanderpoel House** (16 Broad St., 518/758-9265, by appointment, adults $7, seniors $2, children under 12 free) is by the village green. Vanderpoel, a contemporary of Martin Van Buren, was a prominent attorney, state assemblyman, and judge. The house is an excellent example of Federal-style architecture and contains an interesting collection of period furnishings and paintings by early area artists.

Nearby is **Columbia County Historical**

Society Museum and Library (5 Albany Ave., 518/758-9265, Mon.-Wed. and Sat.-Sun. 10am-4pm and by appointment, free), housed in what was once a Masonic temple. Changing exhibits focus on the county's history and culture.

Accommodations and Food

Housed in an 1852 colonial farmhouse is **Mile Hill B&B** (2461 Mile Hill Rd., 917/691-8757, www.milehillbandb.com, $100-185), offering two guest rooms and a pool on the grounds.

The log cabin **Carolina House** (59 Broad St., 518/758-1669, www.carolinahouserestaurant.com, Sun.-Thurs. 5pm-9:30pm, Fri.-Sat. 5pm-10pm, $22) is a family-owned local favorite that attracts diners from miles around. Contemporary American fare is featured on the menu.

THE CHATHAMS

To the east of Kinderhook, in a countryside of rolling hills and horse farms, are the Chathams: the Village of Chatham, Chatham Center, East Chatham, North Chatham, and Old Chatham. Old Chatham, settled in 1758, is little more than a crossroads; the Village of Chatham is the Chathams' commercial hub. During the late 1800s, over 100 trains a day passed through here on their way to Albany or Boston. The streets are still lined with Italianate brick storefronts dating back to that era.

Near East Chatham is **Librarium** (126 Black Bridge Rd., 518/392-5209, www.thelibrarium. com, hours vary seasonally), a homey book barn with over 35,000 used titles. There are also picnic tables on site where you can enjoy your lunch should you so choose.

Columbia County Fair (junction of Rtes. 66 and 203, 518/392-2121, www.columbia-fair.com) comes to the Chatham fairgrounds over Labor Day weekend. It's the nation's oldest continuously running county fair.

Accommodations and Food

In the village center you'll find **Chatham Bakery and Coffee Shoppe** (1 Church St., 518/392-3411), a family-run institution known for its baked goods and burgers served on homemade bread.

The **Inn at Silver Maple Farm** (1871 Rte. 295, East Chatham, 518/781-3600, www.silvermaplefarm.com, $90-230) is an 1830s dairy farm turned lovely B&B. Complete with pine floors, exposed beams, and hand-painted murals, the inn is surrounded by fields and woods. The rooms are airy and comfortable, while a deck offers scenic views of the Berkshire Mountains.

Camping is available in nearby Austerlitz at the 200-site **Woodland Hills Campground** (386 Fog Hill Rd., 518/392-3557, www.whcg.net). Between Chatham and Chatham Center, budget travelers will find **Chatham Travel Lodge** (Rte. 295 and Taconic State Pkwy., 518/392-4066, www.chathamtravellodge.com, $65-95).

Information and Services

For general information on the region, contact **Hudson Valley Tourism** (845/615-3860, www.travelhudsonvalley.com).

Hudson Valley (www.hvmag.com) is a glossy monthly magazine about the region, available at area newsstands. Its restaurant and shop listings are especially useful.

Each county has its own tourist information office. Most are open Monday-Friday 9am-5pm.

- **Westchester County Tourism** (148 Martine Ave., Suite 104, White Plains, 914/995-8500 or 800/833-9282, www.visitwestchesterny.com)

- **Rockland County Tourism** (18 New Hempstead Rd., New City, 845/708-7300, www.rockland.org)

- **Orange County Tourism** (124 Main St., Goshen, 845/615-3860 or 800/762-8687, www.orangetourism.org)

- **Putnam County Visitors Bureau** (110 Old Rte. 6, Carmel, 845/225-0381, www.visitputnam.org)

- **Dutchess County Tourism** (3 Neptune Rd., Poughkeepsie, 845/463-4000, www.dutchesstourism.com)

- **Columbia County Tourism** (401 State St., Hudson, 518/828-3375, www.columbiacountytourism.org)

Getting There and Around

The easiest way to explore the Hudson Valley is by car. However, many towns along the east bank of the Hudson River and some in Westchester's Harlem Valley are reached by trains that depart from Grand Central in Manhattan. On the west banks of the Hudson, communities in Rockland and Orange Counties (Tuxedo, Harriman, Salisbury Mills, Campbell Hall, Middletown, Otisville, and Port Jervis) are serviced by **Metro-North Railroad** (212/532-4900 or 800/638-7646), which leaves from Manhattan's Penn Station. Taxis are usually available at the villages' railroad stations. **Amtrak** (800/872-7245) provides rail service between New York City and more than 40 stations in the Hudson Valley.

If traveling up Metro-North's Hudson Line, sit on the left-hand side of the train car. The railroad hugs the eastern shoreline and offers spectacular views.

Adirondack-Pine Hill-New York Trailways

THE CAPITAL-SARATOGA REGION

(800/225-6815, www.trailwaysny.com) and **ShortLine Bus** (800/631-8405, www.coachusa.com/shortline) offer daily bus service between Manhattan's Port Authority Bus Terminal and many Hudson Valley communities.

Travelers can opt to fly into either New York City's JFK or LaGuardia airports or Stewart International or Albany International Airport. Among the major airlines flying into Stewart are **Delta** (800/221-1212), **JetBlue** (800/538-2583), and **USAir** (800/428-4322); those flying into Albany are Delta (800/221-1212), **Southwest** (800/435-9792), **United** (800/241-6522), and USAir (800/428-4322).

HUDSON VALLEY

THE CAPITAL-SARATOGA REGION

There's no lack of reasons to visit central New York. The Capital-Saratoga region benefits from both the glory days of Hudson River and Erie Canal commerce, as well as the beauty of its riparian landscapes. Plus, there's Albany's political intrigue and Saratoga's social strutting during summer horse-racing season. And it's close enough to New York City for a quick getaway.

Still, residents tend to feel slighted by travelers, who aren't quite sure where the region begins and ends, much less what single characteristic defines the area and sets it apart. Hudson Valley draws visitors with charming villages and farm-to-table food. The Adirondacks and Catskills sell themselves with postcard-perfect mountains. And the western end of the state has Niagara Falls. The Capital-Saratoga region doesn't have a singular, cohesive identity. Not knowing what, exactly, the area is famous for, it's easy to make the decision to skip the region altogether.

That would be a mistake. This area is worth visiting because so much history happened here, and it's documented and shared so passionately. This is where the United States claimed the first major victory of the Revolutionary War. Nearly 60 years later, this is where New York's abolitionist movement was fostered. It's the part of the state where Ulysses Grant raced against time and the ravages of throat cancer to finish his best-selling memoirs. It's where both state and national political careers have been born (and died). It's where passionate people in tiny towns build museums and shrines to the people and creeds they believe in, from

© FRANCISCO COLLAZO

HIGHLIGHTS

☾ Empire State Plaza: Love it or hate it, you've got to appreciate the sheer, Rockefellerian ambition that made the modern art and architecture of this plaza possible, especially when viewed from Corning Tower's observation deck (page 250).

☾ New York State Capitol Building: The centerpiece of the stunning castle-like edifice is its stone staircase, hand-carved with 300 tiny faces, each different from the next (page 251).

☾ Saratoga Race Track: There's a reason this course has endured 150 years, turning an entire town into a summer destination. Even visitors who know little about horse-racing will find themselves swept up in Saratoga's equine traditions (page 263).

☾ New Skete Monastery: This region of New York gave rise to many religious, spiritual, and utopian communities. This one is alive and well and worth a visit, not the least for its buy-it-on-the-honor-system cheesecake (page 273).

☾ National Baseball Hall of Fame and Museum: This massive, enthusiastic tribute to America's national sport wins over even those who don't root, root, root for a home team (page 282).

© AVALON TRAVEL

LOOK FOR ☾ TO FIND RECOMMENDED SIGHTS, ACTIVITIES, DINING, AND LODGING.

the most secular (baseball and boxing) to the most sacred (the Eastern Orthodox religion). To travel the region is to be treated to the full throes of these passions, which can't help but rub off on you.

PLANNING YOUR TIME

The Capital-Saratoga region isn't quite as road-trip friendly as some of the state's other regions, mainly because the key attractions look like random scatter plots on a map. Visitors shouldn't be discouraged by this information, however; well-maintained interstates (including I-87 and I-90) and secondary roadways connect noteworthy cities and towns, making for fast travel. Most of the top spots to visit are clustered in and just around downtown zones. Comfortable accommodations are often right alongside them, making it easy for travelers to maximize their time and get the most out of a visit.

Albany is the ideal stopover, an urban home base for exploring the region. Though not exactly equidistant to the other main points of interest, it's just off the interstate, allowing quick access to other towns and cities recommended here. Plus, the capital's hotels, restaurants, and services offer lots of options for a range of budgets.

The Capital-Saratoga region is increasingly promoting itself as a four-season destination and, in fact, there *is* plenty to see and do, year-round. Keep in mind, though, that summer months are when the region really shines. It's this season when most attractions are open daily, with longer hours, and when the area's most famous sights and experiences—especially Saratoga's horse racing—are polished up for an influx of visitors. Plan on three full days to see the highlights of Capital-Saratoga, which could be an extension of a Hudson Valley visit or your gateway to the Adirondacks or Catskills.

Albany

From a distance, Albany looks like just another average, midsize city clustered around a handful of high-rise office buildings, but beneath its apparently calm surface you'll find a surprisingly complex soul. Albany, as William Kennedy writes in *O Albany!*, is "as various as the American psyche itself, of which it was truly a crucible."

The oldest city in New York and one of the oldest in the nation, Albany is located at the head of the navigable portion of the Hudson River, and this strategic position has shaped much of its history, both colonial and industrial. Explorer Henry Hudson arrived in 1609 (he thought the river might lead to Asia's lucrative silks and spices), and by the mid-1600s, the Dutch settlement of Fort Orange had become a flourishing trading post. The Erie Canal and the railroad cemented Albany's role as a hub of early American industry. Large groups of Irish immigrants settled in Albany while building the Canal, and thousands more Irish and Germans arrived with the coming of the Industrial Revolution. Factories manufacturing everything from checkers and dominoes to textiles and woolens lined the Hudson during this manufacturing boom. The number of full-time residents soared: The authors of the WPA's *A Guide to the Empire State* reported that Albany's population doubled between 1820 and 1830.

It's not surprising, then, how many famous figures in 19th and 20th century industry, arts, and politics got their start in Albany. The city was an early home to writers Herman Melville, Bret Harte, and Henry James. Presidents Martin Van Buren, Millard Fillmore, Grover Cleveland, Theodore Roosevelt, and Franklin Roosevelt all got their starts here, and President Chester A. Arthur is buried here.

Today, Albany is home to a large branch of the State University of New York (SUNY), and as part of New York's "Tech Valley," it's diversifying its traditional economic base. As the state capital, though, Albany's main business is government. Come here at lunchtime when legislature is in session and you'll see thousands of workers hurrying out for a sandwich and a few moments of sun. Alliances are made and deals are forged over meals and drinks; this is a city notorious for political wheeling and dealing.

Orientation

Albany is an easy city to navigate, thanks to generally light traffic and its accessibility via several major interstates, including 87, 88, and 90. Most visitor sights are located in or near downtown, where the most dramatic architectural sights are Empire State Plaza and the Capitol, which sit side by side on a hill. From here, downtown slopes eastward to the river, whose banks are being reclaimed for recreation. Hudson River Way is a pedestrian bridge connecting downtown Albany to Albany Riverfront Park and Corning Preserve, and the Mohawk Hudson Bikeway runs along the river as well.

Tours

Albany Heritage Area Visitor Center (25 Quackenbush Sq., 518/434-0405, www.albany.org) offers free walking-tour maps of downtown. More than 20 of the city's architectural, historical, and cultural highlights are included on the self-guided itinerary.

One of Albany's foremost attractions is its

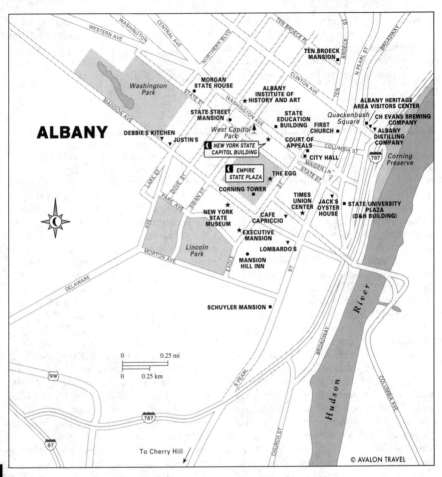

architecture. A few highlights are mentioned here; for a thorough, self-guided architectural tour, pick up a copy of *Albany Architecture* (Mount Ida Press, 518/426-5935), edited by Diana S. Waite. Though it has not been updated since its publication in 1993, the main attractions outlined in the book's eight architectural walking and driving tours remain relevant and accessible to visitors.

To experience Albany by water and learn why the Hudson River and Erie Canal were so central to the city's early growth, take a tour with **Dutch Apple Cruises** (boarding at Broadway and Madison Ave., 518/463-0220, www.dutchapplecruises.com).

SIGHTS
◖ Empire State Plaza

Dominating downtown Albany is **Empire State Plaza** (between Eagle and Swan Sts., Madison Ave. and State St.), the extravagant brainchild of Governor Nelson Rockefeller. An enormous marble platform sitting atop a hill, the plaza covers 98.5 acres and includes 10 buildings, among them the Legislative Building, Justice Building, and The Egg—a round, whimsical performing arts center. A long reflecting pool cuts a ribbon through the main part of the plaza, which is also a destination for art lovers. More than 90 abstract expressionist works, including sculptures by Calder and Noguchi, can be found on the Plaza and in its buildings.

Legend has it Rockefeller conceived of the plaza during a 1959 visit from Princess Beatrix of the Netherlands: It humiliated him to drive royalty through the moldering capital. The plaza cost at least $1 billion—an extraordinary sum for the time—and displaced 3,600 households, many of them poor. The ambitious project generated great controversy, but the plaza has been largely responsible for the rejuvenation of Albany's downtown.

Visitors can relax by the **reflecting pool** (which becomes a public skating rink in winter) or ascend to the 42nd-floor **observation deck** (daily 9am-2:30pm, free) in **Corning Tower,** which offers an exceptional view of Albany, the Hudson River, and beyond (on a clear day, Massachusetts, Vermont, and Connecticut can also be seen). Maps are available at the **Visitors Assistance Office** (concourse level, north end of the Plaza, 518/474-2418), which also offers tours of the Plaza during the work week on a seasonal basis.

New York State Museum

America's oldest and largest state museum, **New York State Museum** (222 Madison Ave., 518/474-5877, www.nysm.nysed.gov, Tues.-Sun. 9:30am-5pm, free), is located on Madison Avenue at the southern end of Empire State Plaza. Spread out over a maze of high-ceilinged rooms, it's packed with life-size dioramas, multimedia shows, historical artifacts, and scientific specimens of all types.

As might be expected, a large part of the museum's collection is comprised of artifacts and ephemera from "New York's natural and human heritage." Permanent exhibits are dedicated to topics as diverse as Native Americans, birds of New York, the Harlem Renaissance, and the 2001 terrorist attacks on the World Trade Center; the museum also hosts about a

dozen temporary exhibits annually. One popular stop for visitors with kids is The Carousel, which features 40 animals, two chariots, and a round tub. It's free and runs every 15 minutes during museum hours.

New York State Capitol Building

The stunning **State Capitol Building** (tours 518/474-2418, Mon.-Fri. 10am, noon, 2pm, and 3pm, free, reservations recommended) sits on State Street at the northern end of Empire State Plaza. Begun in 1867, the castle-like edifice required 32 years and $25 million to complete; it is one of only a handful of capitols in the United States that does not have a dome. A clutch of architects, including Thomas Fuller, Henry Hobson Richardson, and Frederick Law Olmsted, participated in the design, which explains its diverse—but ultimately cohesive—collage of architectural styles.

Capitol tours lead visitors past gold-leaf walls of the Senate Chamber and granite columns of the Assembly Chamber before culminating at the "Million Dollar Staircase." Here, 300 tiny, hand-carved faces smile, glare, or stare at passersby. Seventy-seven of the faces are of famous figures, including Susan B. Anthony, Frederick Douglass, Abraham Lincoln, and Walt Whitman, but most are anonymous, and each is different from the next.

Free tours and free self-guided audio tours are available. Be prepared to pass security clearance and present an ID.

Albany Institute of History & Art

One of the oldest museums in the United States, founded in 1791, **Albany Institute of History & Art** (125 Washington Ave., 518/463-4478, www.albanyinstitute.org, Wed.-Sat. 10am-5pm, Sun. noon-5pm, adults $10, seniors and students $8, children 6-12 $6, children under 6 free) is housed in an elegant Beaux-Arts building and contains some wonderful gems, including many paintings by artists of the Hudson River School. Early works of American portraiture are in the museum's collection, along with Dutch ceramics,

© FRANCISCO COLLAZO

The USS *Slater* is America's only restored World War II destroyer escort.

Albany-made silver, and New York-made furniture. Changing exhibits on the Hudson Valley and Capital District are also featured.

Albany Heritage Area Visitor Center

The **Albany Heritage Area Visitor Center** (25 Quackenbush Sq., at Broadway and Clinton Ave., 518/434-0405, Mon.-Fri. 9am-4pm, Sat. 10am-3pm, Sun. 11am-3pm, free) is a good place to learn about Albany's history and culture. This large, refurbished water pumping station contains informative exhibits on everything from the city's ethnic heritage to its industrial past, as well as cultural curiosities, such as the tale of the modern billiard ball, invented in Albany in 1868.

Albany Distilling Company

The city's first licensed distillery since Prohibition, **Albany Distilling Company** (78 Montgomery St., 518/621-7191, www.albanydistlling.com, Tues. 4pm-8pm, Sat. noon-8pm, other days by appointment) is a small but passionate two-person operation where craft spirits are made. Local New York State ingredients go into ADC's bourbon and whiskey, while their rum is made from Caribbean molasses. The founders and distillers give tours and offer tastings twice a week and by appointment; their facility is adjacent to the wildly popular C.H. Evans Brewing Company at Albany Pump Station.

USS *Slater*

Albany's waterfront is home to America's only restored World War II destroyer escort, the **USS *Slater*** (Broadway and Quay St., 518/431-1943, www.usslater.org, Apr.-Nov. Wed.-Sun. 10am-4pm, adults $8, seniors $7, children 6-14 $6, children under 6 free), which is open to the public for guided tours. The galley and mess hall, officers' and sailors' quarters, and watch and battle stations all have objects from the destroyer's active period.

Albany Riverfront Park and Corning Preserve

From downtown Albany, walk across the

CAPITAL-SARATOGA

Hudson River Way, a pedestrian bridge, to reach these two Hudson River parks. In them you'll find walking/biking trails, picnic tables, exercise stations, and panoramic views of the Hudson, often busy with fishing boats, college crew teams, private yachts heading to and from the Erie Canal, and, at times, the *Half Moon,* an exact replica of the ship Henry Hudson used to reach Albany in 1609. Free concerts are presented during summer at the 1,000-seat riverfront amphitheater. A restaurant on a barge is at Corning Preserve's north end.

The entrance to Hudson River Way is off Broadway, not far from the visitors' center; note the lampposts, each of which tells about a different episode in Albany history.

New York State Executive Mansion

One block south of Empire State Plaza is the governor's mansion, **New York State Executive Mansion** (138 Eagle St., tours: 518/473-7521, Sept.-June Thurs. only 10am, 11am, noon, 1pm, and 2pm, free), open to the public by reserved tour only. An impressive Italianate building with a wraparound porch, the mansion dates to 1856, when it was constructed as a private residence. The state purchased the property in 1877, and each successive governor has put his stamp on it: Theodore Roosevelt built a gym; FDR sunk a pool; and animal-lover Al Smith installed a zoo.

Free **tours** of the mansion are arranged through Empire State Plaza's visitor services center. Reservations must be made two weeks in advance of the tour.

Schuyler Mansion

The gracious 1761 Georgian **Schuyler Mansion** (32 Catherine St., 518/434-0834, May-Oct. Wed.-Sun. 10am-5pm, adults $5, seniors $4, children 5-12 free) is perched on a hill that once offered a great view of the Hudson. The home, now a State Historic Site, was built by Philip Schuyler, a leading Albany citizen and general during the Revolutionary War. Daniel Webster once honored Schuyler as "second only to Washington in the services he performed for his country," but Schuyler was relieved of his duties and court-martialed for ordering the evacuation of Fort Ticonderoga. A probable victim of political infighting, Schuyler was eventually acquitted, though he resigned his post.

Schuyler Mansion hosted major political players of the day—Benjamin Franklin, Benedict Arnold, George Washington, Aaron Burr—and served as a prison for General Burgoyne following the British surrender at Saratoga. Schuyler's daughter, Elizabeth, married Alexander Hamilton here.

Historic Cherry Hill

To the south of downtown Albany stands homey, colonial-era **Historic Cherry Hill** (523 S. Pearl St., 518/434-4791, www.historiccherryhill.org, tours on Wed. and Sat. afternoons, adults $5, seniors $4, students $2, children 6-17 $1), which is undergoing an extensive renovation, but remains open to the public for special restoration tours. Built in 1787 by Philip and Mary van Rensselaer, the house was home to five generations of the van Rensselaer and Rankin families; the last member died in 1963.

The frugal van Rensselaers had a hard time throwing anything away. Inside, you'll find an odd assortment of furnishings from all five generations. Highlights include early Dutch tiles, a striking sleigh bed, turn-of-the-20th-century swimming trunks, 1920s postcards, and an early Castro convertible. The kitchen is equipped with both a colonial-era wall oven and a freestanding gas stove.

Lark Street

Two blocks west of Empire State Plaza is Lark Street, Albany's bohemian hub, lined with an eclectic array of small shops, ethnic restaurants, and nightclubs. Most are located in the eight blocks between Madison and Washington Avenues.

Lark Street sits on the edge of Center Square, a prosperous residential neighborhood notable for its fine architecture. Some of the best examples stand along State Street between Lark Street and Empire State Plaza. In these two short blocks you'll find one opulent 19th-century home after another, many designed by Albany architects Charles Nichols, Albert Fuller, and Ernest Hoffman.

Washington Park and State Street

Continue another block west of Lark Street to **Washington Park,** a lush green oasis considered an "Olmstedian" style park, given the influence of famed landscape architect Frederick Law Olmsted on its design. Curved roads, wooded glades, open meadows, ornate gardens, and Washington Lake can all be found on its 90 acres. Though not original to the park's 1870s beginnings, **Lake House,** an extravagant terra-cotta affair with pink terrazzo floors and wrought-iron chandeliers, is also found here.

State Street's opulence continues along the north side of the park. Highlights include **Grange Sard, Jr. House** at No. 397, designed by Henry Hobson Richardson, and No. 441, the work of William Ross Proctor.

Ten Broeck Mansion

The imperial, Federal-style **Ten Broeck Mansion** (9 Ten Broeck Pl. between Ten Broeck and N. Swan Sts., 518/436-9826, www.tenbroeckmansion.org, May-Oct. Thurs.-Fri. 10am-4pm, Sat.-Sun. 1pm-4pm, Nov.-Apr. by appointment, adults $5, seniors and students $4, children 5-12 $3) stands on the north side of Albany, in the city's Arbor Hill neighborhood. It was built for Abraham Ten Broeck and his wife Elizabeth van Rensselaer in 1797-98. Ten Broeck served as a general in the Continental Army and later as state senator, judge, and mayor of Albany.

Now owned by Albany County Historical Association, the mansion contains a fine collection of period furniture and showcases changing historic exhibits. Tours, free with admission, are given on the hour. Curiosities include a snug wine cellar that wasn't rediscovered until the 1970s. Its rare contents were sold for $42,000; proceeds were used to restore the house.

"Nipper"

All along Broadway in northern Albany hulk old factory buildings dating back to the city's era of industrial activity. A highlight is the former **RTA Building** (991 Broadway, at Loudonville Rd.). RTA was a distributor of RCA electrical appliances, and on the building's roof sits a 25-foot-high, four-ton statue of Nipper, the canine symbol of the RCA-owned Victor Company. Nipper's head is cocked to the side and he wears a quizzical expression, as if to ask, What am I still doing here? The statue was built in Chicago around 1858 and shipped in five sections on railroad flat cars.

ENTERTAINMENT

The city's best sources for information about entertainment are the Thursday and Sunday editions of *The Times-Union* (518/454-5694, www.timesunion.com) and *Metroland* (518/463-2500, www.metroland.net), a free alternative weekly published each Thursday.

Performing Arts and Film

The Egg (Empire State Plaza, Madison Ave. and Swan St., 518/473-1845, www.theegg.org), named for its shape, is the capital's premier arts venue. It houses two theaters; one has 982 seats and the other is more intimate with 450 seats. Both present a wide range of music, theater, and dance.

The **Capital Repertory Theatre** (111 N. Pearl St., 518/445-7469, www.capitalrep.org) presents classical, contemporary, and world-premier works October-June. The company performs in the 286-seat Market Theater, formerly a grocery store.

The 1931 **Palace Theatre** (19 Clinton Ave., 518/465-3334, www.palacealbany.com), which seats 2,800, was once an opulent movie palace. Today, it's home to the Albany Symphony Orchestra and host to touring concert acts, Broadway shows, and movies.

Tiny **Albany Civic Theater** (235 2nd Ave., 518/462-1297, www.albanycivictheater.org), occupying a converted turn-of-the-century firehouse, presents four theater productions

THE SHAKERS

Brought "across the pond" from England, 19 official Shaker communities sprang to existence in the United States in the 18th century, with most in Ohio, Kentucky, and parts of the Northeast, including the communities of New Lebanon and Albany. American Shakers lived a pacifist communal life and believed in equality of the sexes, common ownership of property and goods, innovation in agriculture and manufacturing, confession of sins, simplicity in their own mannerisms and dress, and celibacy. Living in rural colonies consisting of several "families" of non-blood related members, who occupied separate quarters based on sex, Shakers sought to avoid corruption in the outside world.

New Lebanon, in the Capital region's Columbia County, is just a few miles from the New York-Massachusetts border. Established in 1785, New Lebanon was one of the earliest Shaker communities, and was an organizational, architectural, and spiritual model for those that followed. Though no Shakers live at **Mt. Lebanon Shaker Village** today (the last Mt. Lebanon Shaker died in 1947), the site is a National Historic Landmark with a museum open to the public. Visitors can learn more about the community through guided tours that lead visitors through the North, Center, and Church Family buildings, as well as the Meetinghouse, which has a unique arched roof.

Watervliet Shaker National Historic District (25 Meeting House Rd., 518/456-7890, www.shakerheritage.org, Tues.-Sat. 9:30am-4pm, free), just outside Albany in the town of Colonie, is the Capital region's other significant Shaker community and America's first Shaker settlement, established in 1776. It too is a national historic site open to the public. During its height, this Shaker settlement was active not only in the women's rights movement, but in abolition, and recent research confirmed that Watervliet was a safe haven for fugitive slaves.

In Watervliet, eight sturdy, clean-lined Shaker buildings still stand, grouped around a crossroads. The splendid 1848 Meeting House has been converted into a visitor center, where you'll find a small exhibit area, a gift shop offering Shaker crafts, and a large hall where Shakers once held their meetings. Bleacher-style rising seats in back were set aside for "World's People"—nonbelievers—who often came to meetings to watch and listen to the Shakers' music. Today, the hall is used for Shaker concerts, workshops, and crafts shows. One of the most important features of this site is its cemetery, where spiritual leader Mother Ann Lee is buried. Visitors can also take self-guided tours, picnic on the grounds, and browse or pick up a free walking-tour map in the gift shop.

every year. Each runs just three weeks; tickets sell out quickly.

Times Union Center (51 South Pearl St., 518/487-2000, www.timesunioncenter-albany. com) is a multipurpose facility with adaptable seating arrangements that can accommodate crowds ranging in size from 6,000 to 17,500. Concerts, family shows, sporting events, and trade shows are presented.

Comedy Works (500 Northern Blvd., 518/275-6897, www.thecomedyworks.com) features nationally recognized comedy acts several nights a week; dinner is available before the show.

Nightlife

Pearl Street is home to **The Merry Monk** (90 N. Pearl St., 518/463-6665, www.merry-monkalbany.com, daily 11:30am-11pm), a Belgian beer bar with more than 100 selections. On Lark Street, long Albany's center for nightlife, you'll find a wide variety of restaurants and bars, including **Lionheart Blues Cafe** (258 Lark St., 518/436-9530, daily from 3pm). **Bomber's Burrito Bar** (258 Lark St., 518/463-9636, www.bombersburritobar.com, daily 11am until at least 12:30am), featuring a tequila and beer bar in addition to burritos, is in the same building. **DeJohn's Restaurant and Pub** (288 Lark St., 518/465-5275, www.

dejohns.com, daily 4pm-11pm) and the jazz joint **Justin's** (301 Lark St., 518/436-7008, www.justinsalbany.com, Mon.-Fri. 11:30am-1am, Sat.-Sun. 10:30am-1am) round out some of the options on Lark. LGBT-friendly **Oh Bar** (304 Lark St., 518/463-9004, www.ohonlark.com, Mon.-Wed. 2pm-3am, Thurs.-Sat. 2pm-4am, Sun. 2pm-3am) features an outdoor patio and garden.

Other LGBT-friendly bars in Albany are found on Central Avenue, including the city's oldest gay bar, **Waterworks** (76 Central Ave., 518/465-9079, www.waterworkspub.com, daily 1pm-4am), and **Rocks** (77 Central Ave., 518/472-3588, www.rocks77.com, daily 2pm-4am).

Intimate **Valentine's** (17 New Scotland Ave., 518/432-6572, www.valentinesalbany.com) is a top club for local rock. **Lark Tavern** (453 Madison Ave., 518/694-8490, www.albanylarktavern.com, Mon.-Sat. 11am-4am, Sun. noon-4am) hosts local rock, reggae, and "psycho-country" bands; it also has a full-service dining room where lunch and dinner are served.

Albany's recently created **Warehouse District** is an increasingly popular place to spend the evening. All of the following watering holes are located on Broadway between Clinton and Pleasant Streets: **The Olde English Pub and Pantry** (683 Broadway, 518/434-6533, www.theoldeenglish.com, Mon.-Sat. 11am-2am, Sun. 11am-11pm); German-style **Wolff's Biergarten** (895 Broadway, 518/427-2461, www.wolffsbiergarten.com, Mon.-Fri. 11am-2am, Sat. 9am-2am, Sun. 9am-midnight); Irish pub **Graney's Stout** (904 Broadway, 518/427-8688, www.graneysbarandgrill.com, Mon.-Fri. 11am, Sat. 11:30am, Sun. noon, close times vary based on number of customers); and self-described rock-n-roll country bar **Barrel Saloon** (942 Broadway, 518/694-0670, www.barrelsaloon.com, Tues.-Sat. 2pm-4am, Sun. 12:30pm-8pm).

EVENTS

Albany celebrates its Dutch heritage with the impressive **Tulip Festival** (518/434-1217), held on the second weekend of May.

Throughout the summer, **free concerts** (518/474-2418) and other special events are staged at Empire State Plaza. **Park Playhouse** (518/434-2035) presents free musicals and plays at Lake House in Washington Park in July and August.

Fairgrounds in the nearby village of **Altamont** (fairs 518/861-6671, www.altamontfair.com) host some of the region's top special events. Among them are the **Old Songs Festival of Traditional Music and Dance** in June, **Altamont Fair** in August, and **Capital Region Scottish Games** in early September. The fairgrounds also host local craft beer and wine fests in the fall.

ACCOMMODATIONS

There's much to recommend about **Hilton Albany** (40 Lodge St., 518/462-6611, www.hiltonalbany.com, $169-285), fresh off a multimillion rebrand and renovation completed in 2013. First is the hotel's unbeatable location,

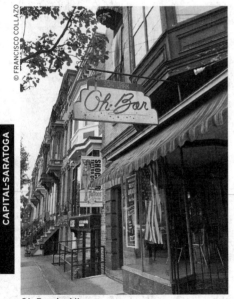

© FRANCISCO COLLAZO

CAPITAL-SARATOGA

Oh Bar, in Albany

within comfortable walking distance to Empire State Plaza, the Capitol, and numerous downtown restaurants and attractions. Size (385 rooms and suites), service (extensive breakfast buffet), and amenities, including free Wi-Fi, are also notable. Some higher floor rooms and suites have exceptional views of the Hudson River, Capitol, or other architectural stunners, like the Albany Home Savings Bank building.

Elegant, 19th-century **Morgan State House** (393 State St., 518/427-6063, www.statehouse.com, $160-260 d) on Washington Park has both rooms and full suites. If traveling with children, this inn is not a good option, as kids under 16 are not allowed.

Neoclassical **State Street Mansion** (281 State St., 518/462-6780, www.statestreetmansion.com, $105-175 d) dates to 1881. It offers 12 guest rooms; several are "European plan," which means they share a bathroom with another room. All guests receive free continental breakfast each morning.

Historic **Century House** (997 New Loudon Rd./Rte. 9, Latham, 518/785-0931, www.thecenturyhouse.com, $129-149), a third-generation family-run property with a pool and tennis court, is just outside Albany in the town of Latham. The mansion makes use of an 1800s public house as the base for its handsome restaurant and Federal-style Tavern, serving hearty, tasty meals with a gourmet flair and great attention to detail. The hotel features a complimentary hot country breakfast buffet with chef on hand for special requests. A 1.5-mile nature trail is also on-site.

Desmond Hotel and Conference Center (660 Albany-Shaker Rd., 518/869-8100, www.desmondhotels.com, $145-185 d), a lovely hotel-inn filled with period furnishings, artwork, rich dark-wood paneling and warm, top quality service, is convenient to Albany's airport. Faux Colonial Williamsburg villages form charming interior courtyards around airy fountains, garden seating, and poolside lounging. Many rooms feature balconies or private patios. The large property has two heated indoor pools, a health club, The Tavern, and several good restaurants, including Simpson's Grille (casual)

and Scrimshaw (fine dining), offering the same high level of service and the talents of five chefs. Wi-Fi, parking, and an airport shuttle are all free for guests.

About 15 minutes east of Albany is **Gregory House Country Inn** (3016 Rte. 43, Averill Park, 518/674-3774, www.gregoryhouse.com, $115-125 d), a gracious homestead and modern inn with 12 nicely appointed guest rooms. On site are a popular Italian restaurant called La Perla and pub room serving coffee, dessert, appetizers, and drinks. Wi-Fi and continental breakfast are included in the room rate.

FOOD

Jack's Oyster House (42 State St., 518/465-8854, www.jacksoysterhouse.com, $22, daily 11:30am-10pm) is a classic downtown seafood restaurant frequented by legislators. Run by the same family for more than 100 years, the restaurant serves up lunch and dinner against a backdrop of white tablecloths, tiled floors, and big pane-glass windows. Reservations are recommended.

Many small restaurants along lively Lark Street serve both lunch and dinner. For imaginative, contemporary American fare, try **Justin's** (301 Lark St., 518/436-7008, www.justinsalbany.com, Mon.-Fri. 11:30am-1am, Sat.-Sun. 10:30am-1am, $16), an inviting basement spot partially housed in a historic building. Jazz is often featured on the weekends. **Debbie's Kitchen** (456 Madison Ave., near Lark St., 518/463-3829, www.debbieskitchenllc.com, Mon.-Fri. 10am-7pm, Sat. 11am-6pm, $8) specializes in overstuffed sandwiches.

New World Bistro Bar (300 Delaware Ave., 518/694-0520, www.newworldbistrobar.com, Mon.-Thurs. 5pm-9:30pm, Fri.-Sat. 5pm-11pm, Sun. 11am-3pm and 5pm-9:30pm, $19), near Lark Street, offers "global soul food" using seasonal and sustainable products, many from regional farms. There's an extensive small plate menu, as well as a number of gluten-free and vegan options.

Mingle (544 Delaware Ave., 518/915-1468, www.minglealbany.com, Mon. 5pm-9pm, Tues.-Thurs. 11:30am-9pm, Fri.

11:30am-10pm, Sat. 5pm-10pm, $22) is billed as a "Korean-fusion" restaurant, but its lunch and dinner menus are heavily inflected with other global influences. Alongside Korean classics like bibimbap, you'll find Portuguese clams and jambalaya.

C.H. Evans Brewing Company at the Albany Pump Station (19 Quackenbush Sq., 518/447-9000, www.evansale.com, Mon.-Thurs. 11:30am-11pm, Fri.-Sat. 11:30am-midnight, Sun. noon-8pm, $16) is a popular microbrewery and full-service restaurant (think pasta, beef, and burgers) with a 120-year family heritage. It's located in the building that once housed the original pumping station for Albany Water Works.

Modern, upscale **Cafe Capriccio** (49 Grand St., 518/465-0439, www.cafecapriccio.com, Sun.-Thurs. 5pm-9pm, Fri.-Sat. 5pm-10pm, $22) is a local favorite specializing in Northern Italian fare. For a more old-fashioned Italian dining experience, try classic **Lombardo's** (121 Madison Ave., 518/462-9180, www.lombardosofalbany.com, Mon.-Fri. 11am-11pm, Sat. 3pm-11pm, $16), frequented by politicians. In operation since 1919, the historic building once housed an Italian consulate and ice cream parlor.

Angelo's 677 Prime (677 Broadway., 518/427-7463, www.677prime.com, Mon.-Fri. 11:30am-2pm and 5:30pm-10pm, Sat. 5:30pm-10pm, $35) is Albany's go-to upscale restaurant for steak and seafood. Its wine list features more than 400 varieties.

Yono's (25 Chapel St., 518/436-7747, www.yonos.com, Mon.-Sat. 5:30pm-11pm, $30) is headed up by a husband-wife team whose menu features Indonesian specialties alongside French and continental dishes inspired by Chef Yono's travels. Diners can order à la carte or enjoy the chef's tasting menu accompanied by a vintage from the 600-bottle strong wine list.

VICINITY OF ALBANY
Troy

Seven miles northeast of Albany, Troy is said to be the home of Uncle Sam, both the man and the patriotic icon. Though born in Massachusetts, meatpacker Samuel Wilson inspired the Uncle Sam figure when he stamped "U.S." on barrels of meat he sent to U.S. troops during the War of 1812. Soldiers receiving the shipment began referring to Wilson as "Uncle Sam"; the name stuck and a folkloric tale was born. Today, statues and images of Uncle Sam abound in Troy, and an annual **"Uncle Sam Parade"** rivals July 4 for its display of patriotism.

Troy is also home to the **New York State BBQ Championship,** and the city is increasingly attracting foodies of all tastes to its restaurants. One excellent downtown option is the always-busy **Brown's Brewing Company** (417 River St., 518/273-2337, www.brownsbrewing.com, Mon.-Thurs. 11:30am-11pm, Fri.-Sat. 11:30am-midnight, Sun. 11:30am-10pm, $18), which was the region's first brewery-restaurant. Better-than-usual pub food from an extensive menu is served alongside one of more than a dozen beers on tap. Customers who can't decide which beer to drink can order a "paddle"—a sampler flight of six or eight brews.

Another favorite is **The Charles F. Lucas Confectionery and Wine Bar** ("Confectionery" to locals; 12 Second St., 518/326-3450, lucasconfectionery.wordpress.com, Mon.-Wed. 4pm-11pm, Thurs.-Fri. 4pm-midnight, Sat. noon-midnight, Sun. noon-9pm, $16), which specializes in cheese, charcuterie, confections, and wine. All are served in a warm, charming setting. The former confectionery shop, dating to the 1860s, features reclaimed wood, tile, and other materials salvaged from old buildings in Troy.

Crailo State Historic Site

Directly across the Hudson from Albany in Rensselaer is the 1704 **Crailo State Historic Site** (9 Riverside Ave., 518/463-8738, May-Oct. Wed.-Sun. 11am-4pm, adults $5, seniors $4, children 5-12 free). Home to the van Rensselaer family until the mid-1800s, the mansion is now a museum focusing on the history of Dutch culture in the Hudson River Valley. Exhibits range from archaeological artifacts to a restored cellar kitchen. Surrounding

The Charles F. Lucas Confectionery and Wine Bar in Troy

the house is a riverside park where summertime concerts are held.

John Boyd Thacher State Park

For terrific views of the Hudson and Mohawk Valleys and Adirondacks, head 18 miles west of Albany to **Thacher State Park** (1 Hailes Cave Rd., 518/872-1237, www.nysparks.com/parks/128, daily 8am-dusk, parking $6-8). Here you'll also find the unusual **Indian Ladder Geologic Trail,** (May-Nov. daily, weather permitting) a half-mile-long ledge that is one of the richest fossil-bearing formations in the world.

Rensselaerville

About 25 miles southwest of Albany is the charming one-street village of **Rensselaerville,** originally settled in the late 1700s by Connecticut families who arrived via Long Island. On the National Register of Historic Places, the village is filled with restored post-colonial and Greek Empire homes, many built by Ephraim Russ (1784-1853), a talented carpenter-architect who once lived in the village.

On Main Street, you'll find lots of shops selling the handiwork of Valley craftspeople, including jewelers, fiber artists, glass-blowers, and ceramists. Rensselaerville is also home to the **Rensselaerville Institute** (Rte. 85, 518/797-3783, www.rinstitute.org, gallery: Mon.-Fri. 9am-5pm), which houses a small gallery and presents concerts during the summer.

CAPITAL-SARATOGA

Saratoga Springs and Vicinity

For most of the year, Saratoga Springs is a charming Victorian town known for its first-rate arts scene, grand romantic architecture, sophisticated shops and restaurants, and therapeutic mineral springs. Come summer, though, the town turns itself upside down with buyers and sellers of dreams. From dawn until dusk, and then from dusk until dawn, gossiping socialites, shrewd businesspeople, and innocent tourists mix with breeders, trainers, and grooms...all for the love of horses.

The Saratoga Race Course, built in 1864, is America's oldest racetrack, and it has long represented the very best of what racing has to offer. Louisville may have its Kentucky Derby, Baltimore its Preakness, but serious horse fans come to Saratoga for six weeks of exclusive racing. Attendance at the sprawling, Victorian-era grandstand—complete with striped awnings, clapboard siding, and gilded cupolas—averages about 25,000 a day, which just about matches Saratoga's year-round population.

Saratoga is slower but no less interesting once the horses are back in their stables. Arts thrive at the Saratoga Performing Arts Center, Skidmore College, and Yaddo, a renowned artists' retreat. The town also supports several fine museums, Saratoga Spa State Park, and a number of good hotels and B&Bs, as well as a robust local food culture. Surrounding Saratoga is lush, rolling countryside offering more cultural, historical, and scenic attractions. Best known among them is the Saratoga National Historic Park, where the 1777 battles that turned the course of the Revolutionary War were fought.

Orientation

Saratoga Springs is a small, compact city (population 26,000), with many attractions sitting squarely on Broadway, one of two main avenues. The track lies to the east of downtown, off Union Avenue, while Saratoga Spa State Park is to the south, off South Broadway (Route 9). The Thruway (I-87) passes within a few miles of the city.

Points of interest along Broadway lie within easy walking distance of each other. The track and state park are each about a mile from downtown. Park downtown in large, free lots between Broadway and Circular Street.

The **Saratoga County Chamber** (28 Clinton St., 518/584-3255, www.saratoga.org) operates an **information booth** (Broadway near the entrance to Congress St., June-Sept. daily 9am-5pm, extended hours during racing season).

SIGHTS
Heritage Area Visitor Center

A good place to start a tour of Saratoga is at the **Heritage Area Visitor Center** (297 Broadway, 518/587-3241, www.saratogaspringsvisitorcenter.com, May-Nov. Mon.-Sat. 9am-5pm, Sun. 10am-3pm, free), housed in Drink Hall, where mineral waters were once sold. Back then, different waters were recommended for different times of the day: Hathorn in the morning, Coesa before dinner, and Geyser in the evening.

Today, the Beaux-Arts hall with its barrel-vaulted ceiling is filled with history exhibits and racks bursting with tourism brochures. Free walking-tour maps pinpointing the area's springs and other points of interest can be picked up here.

Congress Park

Congress Park (Broadway and Congress St., 518/587-3241), directly across from the Visitor Center, is a small jewel of a retreat filled with lawns, graveled walkways, and flowering plants. In the center of it all reigns the Italianate red-brick Canfield Casino, now home to Saratoga Springs History Museum.

One of the oldest parks in the country, Congress Park dates back to 1792 when Nicholas Gilman, a member of the first U.S. Congress, "discovered" and named Congress Spring. Then along came Gideon Putnam, who in 1806 bought swampland next to the spring, siphoned off some of its waters, and built Saratoga's first mineral-water bathhouse. In 1876, Frederick Law Olmsted completely redesigned the park, replacing old structures with high Victorian Gothic buildings. Tours of the park are offered in summer.

Canfield Casino

Lavish **Canfield Casino** in Congress Park was built by John Morrissey in 1870 as an adjunct to his new racetrack. One writer of the day described the place as having "gorgeously furnished toilet rooms, faro parlors, and drawing rooms."

In 1883, Richard Canfield purchased the building and embellished it with more ostentatious touches, including stained-glass windows. Fabulous sums were won and lost in the casino's gaming rooms, and many "Monte Carlo suicides" were said to have been committed. Before the casino was shut down in 1907, Canfield purportedly netted the then-enormous profit of $2.5 million.

Today, the casino houses **Saratoga Springs History Museum** (1 E. Congress St., Congress Park, 518/584-6920, www.saratogahistory.org, Feb.-Mar. Sat.-Sun. 10am-4pm, Apr.-May Wed.-Sun. 10am-4pm, Memorial Day-Labor Day daily 10am-4pm, adults $5, seniors

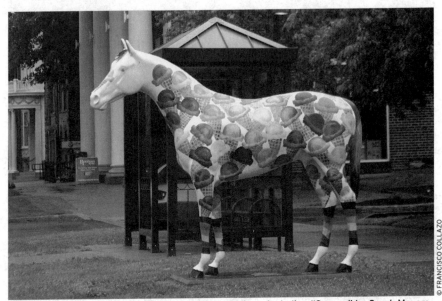

© FRANCISCO COLLAZO

Painted horses decorate the streets of Saratoga Springs, including "Scoops" by Sarah Maxam.

$4, students $4, children under 12 free). Downstairs, temporary exhibits focus on the history and culture of Saratoga. Upstairs are period rooms and an oddball collection of artifacts, including Egyptian spears, bullets from Battles of Saratoga, and old gaming tables.

Broadway

Lined with shops and restaurants, the bustling blocks of downtown Broadway begin north of Congress Park. Leafy trees spread their boughs, and inviting park benches beckon here and there.

At one time, Broadway was flanked with one grand hotel after another, some sporting balconies stretching hundreds of feet. Today, only the 1877 **Adelphi** (365 Broadway) remains and its future is uncertain; it closed in late 2012 for a renovation, no specific date has been set for its reopening. The exterior remains intact, though, and gives visitors a good sense of what Saratoga's Victorian era hotels looked like.

Other buildings worth noting along Broadway include the 1916 Classic Revival

Adirondack Trust, No. 473, adorned with Adirondack symbols and bronze Tiffany doors, and the 1910 Beaux-Arts **post office,** No. 475. At Lake Avenue, across from the post office, is the 1871 Italian palazzo **city hall,** birthplace of The American Banking Association and The American Bar Association.

Tang Teaching Museum and Art Gallery

The dynamic **Tang Teaching Museum and Art Gallery at Skidmore College** (815 N. Broadway, 518/580-8080, www.skidmore.edu/tang, Tues.-Sun. noon-5pm, suggested donation adults $5, children over 12 $3, seniors $2, children under 12 and students free) hosts contemporary art exhibits and cultural events, all of which are open to the public. Donated to Skidmore College in 2000 by Chinese-born American businessman Oscar Tang, whose wife and daughter are both Skidmore alumni, the museum is dedicated to "fostering interdisciplinary thinking." The permanent collection includes works in a wide range of media, while

THE WICKEDEST SUMMER RESORT

Saratoga Springs didn't really take off until the 1860s, when prizefighter, gambler, and general roustabout John Morrissey built Saratoga Race Course. The track was a near-instant success and was soon joined by elaborate gambling casinos and posh, block-long hotels where fluttering socialites danced with hard-nosed gamblers beneath crystal chandeliers.

Saratoga regulars included prominent horsemen such as William R. Travers, financiers such as J. Pierpont Morgan, actresses such as Lillian Russell, and high rollers such as Diamond Jim Brady, who sometimes wore as many as 2,548 diamonds with his evening outfits. New York City reporters, including intrepid Nellie Bly of *The New York World*, were dispatched to Saratoga to file stories about the country's "Wickedest Summer Resort."

By the early 1900s, vice-fueled fun seemed to be over. A reform movement closed down casinos, some springs dried up due to excessive commercial pumping, and the fashionable crowd moved on.

New York State intervened, establishing a state reservation to preserve the largest cluster of springs in 1909. Over the next 25 years, the state transformed the reservation into Saratoga Spa State Park, complete with a hotel and two magnificent bathhouses. Saratoga's golden era of the spa began, with people coming from all over to take "the cure": drinking mineral waters, soaking in baths, and exercising. Casinos were also in full swing again, this time under control of gangsters like Lucky Luciano and Dutch Schultz.

Saratoga suffered another decline after World War II as interest in spa therapy declined and casinos were shut down again, this time for good. Only the race course mustered on, with races held every August without fail.

Saratoga's many charms were discovered by a new generation in the 1960s, when old Victorian buildings were snatched up and renovated, and a new wave of socialites and vacationers moved in.

---

temporary exhibits focus on everything from pop art to site-specific installations.

Union Avenue

Union Avenue, Saratoga's other main drag, is a wide boulevard leading east to Saratoga Race Course. The avenue features some of the town's grandest Victorian architecture. Several buildings now operate as upscale B&Bs charging exorbitant prices during racing season; others hold offices, apartments, and condominiums. During the summer, Union Avenue, like the race course itself, is planted with thousands of white, purple, and pink impatiens.

National Museum of Racing and Hall of Fame

Even non-racing fans will want to step into the one-of-a-kind **National Museum of Racing and Hall of Fame** (191 Union Ave., 518/584-0400, www.racingmuseum.org, hours vary seasonally, adults $7, seniors and students $5,

children under 5 free), filled with intriguing exhibitions on the history and mechanics of thoroughbred racing. Learn why all thoroughbreds trace their origins to one of three Arabian progenitors and how, at a full gallop, a horse takes in five gallons of air a second. Exhibits on racing champs tell stories of Man o' War and Secretariat, Seattle Slew and Affirmed, while exhibits on Saratoga tell of the resort town's gambling heyday.

In summer, the museum offers **tours** (summer Wed.-Sun. 8:30am, $10 pp) of the training track.

◖ Saratoga Race Track

The nation's oldest thoroughbred track, **Saratoga Race Track** (267 Union Ave., 518/584-6200, www.nyra.com/saratoga), comes to life every mid-July through early September. Most U.S. tracks present one weekly stakes race, featuring top-of-the-line horses; Saratoga has one every day. The meet's

© FRANCISCO COLLAZO

Grand Victorian architecture is a highlight of Union Avenue.

highlight is the Travers Stakes, held on the fifth Saturday; other big events are the Whitney, the Alabama, and the prestigious Fasig-Tipton yearling sales.

Saratoga, filled with striped tents and bright flowers, remains one of the world's best tracks for a close-up view of the horse-racing world. Thoroughbreds are walked through the crowd before being saddled in the paddock, and jockeys stop to talk and sign autographs between races.

Breakfast at the track is a race-day tradition. Early access and the long-standing honor system policy of reserving a shaded picnic table with a personal item ensure visitors a comfortable spot to enjoy the day. A buffet breakfast is served 7am-9:30am on The Porch of The Clubhouse. Thoroughbreds prepare for races in sight, with workout commentary offered during the meal. A much-anticipated bonus of the breakfast is the free 45-minute tram and walking tour of the historic stable area posttoast. The first tour leaves the main Clubhouse entrance at 8am; five additional trams leave approximately every 15 minutes. Trams run on a first-come, first-served basis and often fill to capacity early.

Yaddo

Just east of the racetrack lies the artists' retreat **Yaddo** (312 Union Ave., 518/584-0746, www.yaddo.org, gardens and grounds daily 8am-dusk, free), housed in a Victorian Gothic mansion that was once home to Spencer and Katrina Trask. Spencer was a New York financier and philanthropist, Katrina a poet.

Artists come to Yaddo to get away from the noisy outside world and work in uninterrupted peace. About 4,000 writers, composers, and visual artists have enjoyed residencies here since the program began in 1926, including Flannery O'Connor, Saul Bellow, Leonard Bernstein, Langston Hughes, John Cheever, and Aaron Copland.

The house is off-limits to the public, but visitors are welcome to stroll through an Italian garden featuring over 100 varieties of roses, and a rock garden planted with flowering

RACING SEASON

Saratoga Race Course, the country's oldest race track, is a cultural and historical gem enjoyed by thoroughbred horse racing aficionados and betting novices alike. With attendance capacity of 50,000, this hot spot was named one of the top 10 sporting venues in the world by *Sports Illustrated* , and it retains its Old World charm. Here are some tips to make the most of your day at the races.

Track Basics: The 40-day season starts in mid- or late July and runs through early September. Races are held daily, except Tuesdays. The venue opens at 11am weekdays, 10:30am weekends, and post time is 1pm. General admission is $3; clubhouse admission is $5. A dress code is enforced for box seat and clubhouse ticket holders; details are available on the course's website (www.nyra.com).

For general information during the meet, call Saratoga Race Course at 518/584-6200. For advance ticket sales, contact **New York Racing Association** (718/641-4700, www.nyra.com).

Parking and Traffic: New York Racing Association maintains large parking lots across from the track; prices vary according to proximity. Parking is also available in many private lots surrounding the track. You can park for free at Saratoga Casino and Raceway, which has ample lots, and take the free shuttle to the racecourse. If you're *not* planning to go to the track, avoid traffic-clogged Union Avenue between noon and 1pm, and again around 5:30pm.

Seating: Most of the nearly 7,000 reserved seats in the grandstand and clubhouse are sold by mail in January. However, about 1,000 grandstand seats go on sale every race day at the track's Union Avenue entrance. On weekdays, tickets are often available until post time; on weekends, they're typically gone by 10 or 11am.

Many fans bring lawn chairs, blankets, and coolers to the shady grounds behind the track, which are equipped with large, flat-screen TVs. Others watch the races on their feet, then retreat to benches near the betting windows.

How to Bet: Easy-to-follow instructions are printed inside *Post Parade*, the daily program, available at the gate. Minimum bets are $1.

After the Races: The most popular racetrack hangout is **Siro's** (168 Lincoln Ave., 518/584-4030), adjacent to the south side of the track. A long bar is set up beneath a striped canvas tent, and live bands play until about 8:30pm, when the party then moves inside.

Polo Matches: Coinciding with racing season, world-class polo matches (518/584-8108, www.saratogapolo.com) take place on Fridays and Sundays at Saratoga Polo Field (Bloomfield and Denton Rd.). Most games begin at 5:30pm; gates open at 4pm.

Accommodations: Most hotels and B&Bs double their prices during racing season, and many of the most popular places are booked solid months in advance. Even if you arrive at the last minute, however, you will find something. Saratoga County Chamber (www.saratoga.org) maintains an updated list of available rooms.

perennials. Wistful marble statues and a picturesque fountain provide other photo ops.

Saratoga Casino and Raceway

South of the main track stretches the half-mile-long **Saratoga Casino and Raceway,** a foremost trotting track. Opened in 1941, the track features evening racing January-November with a short break in April. Some of the track's top races take place during the thoroughbred meet.

In the old horseman's building is **Saratoga Harness Hall of Fame** (352 Jefferson St., 518/587-4210, July-Sept. Tues.-Sat. 11am-3pm, hours vary off-season, free). On display are antique horseshoes, racing silks, high-wheel sulkies, and other memorabilia. One exhibit honors Lady Suffolk, the "Old Grey Mare" of folk-song fame, who raced in Saratoga in 1847.

CAPITAL-SARATOGA

© FRANCISCO COLLAZO

the artists' residence at Yaddo

National Museum of Dance and Hall of Fame

South Broadway leads out of downtown and past the **National Museum of Dance and Hall of Fame** (99 S. Broadway, 518/584-2225, www.dancemuseum.org, June-Oct. Tues.-Sun. 10am-4:30pm, adults $6.50, seniors and students $5, children under 12 $3), the only museum in the country devoted exclusively to professional American dance, including ballet, modern dance, vaudeville, and tap. Housed in Saratoga Spa State Park's former Washington Bathhouse, the museum spreads out over four spacious halls filled with blown-up photographs and plaques. Temporary exhibits hang near the entrance, while TV monitors screening famous performances are featured throughout. The museum also has an interactive kids' wing.

Saratoga Spa State Park

More European than American in feel, **Saratoga Spa State Park** (off S. Broadway, just south of downtown, 518/584-2535, www. saratogaspastatepark.org, hours vary by facility and season, parking $8) spreads out over 2,200 pristine acres, every one of which was meticulously planned. At one end is Avenue of the Pines, flanked with towering green-black trees. At the other, Loop Road leads past a half-dozen mineral springs, each with a different taste, depending on its mineral content. In between are multiuse recreation trails, tennis courts, swimming pools, mineral baths, golf courses, Spa Little Theater, Saratoga Performing Arts Center, and Gideon Putnam Hotel, a grand Georgian affair built in the 1930s.

Though no longer the drawing card they once were, the mineral baths remain the heart of the park. **Roosevelt Baths** (518/584-3000 or 800/452-7275, www.gideonputnam.com, daily 9am-7pm, treatments $30-300), within walking distance of Gideon Putnam Hotel, includes a fitness center and private rooms and tubs, where clients relax in bubbling golden-brown waters, indulge in algae body wraps, and enjoy muscle-relief treatments.

Victoria Pool (late June-early Sept. daily 10am-6pm, adults $8, children $4),

© FRANCISCO COLLAZO

the Gideon Putnam hotel

embellished with colored tiles, romantic archways, and a small café, is near the park's center. Even on the hottest days, the pool often remains uncrowded, partly because the park also boasts a second, larger pool—**Peerless Pool** (late June-early Sept. Wed.-Mon. 10am-6pm, adults $2, children 5-12 $1), adjoined with diving and wading pools. **Catherine's in the Park** (58 Roosevelt Dr., 518/583-4657) is a convenient lunch spot near the pools, offering soups and sandwiches.

ENTERTAINMENT
Performing Arts

Saratoga Performing Arts Center (108 Ave. of the Pines, 518/584-9330, www.spac.org) is an outdoor amphitheater with a capacity of 25,000 spectators. As the preeminent performing arts center of the Capital-Saratoga Region, SPAC presents The New York City Opera, The New York City Ballet, The Philadelphia Orchestra, and well-known rock, pop, and jazz stars throughout the summer. Picnicking before performances is a Saratoga tradition.

Nightlife

Saratoga has a lively nighttime scene, thanks largely to the presence of Skidmore College and the racetrack. **Caroline Street** is especially known for its many clubs and bars, most catering to twentysomethings. **Desperate Annie's** (12-14 Caroline St., 518/587-2455, www.desperateannies.com, daily 4pm-4am), a.k.a. DA's, is a popular college and local hangout, complete with pool table. Around the corner, **9 Maple Ave.** (9 Maple Ave., 518/583-2582, www.9mapleave.com, daily 4pm-3am) is the place to go for serious jazz.

Caffe Lena (45-47 Phila St., 518/583-0022, www.caffelena.com, Wed. 7pm-9:30pm, Thurs. 7pm-11pm, Fri.-Sat. 8pm-10:30pm, Sun. 7pm-9:30pm) is the oldest continuously run coffeehouse in America, founded in 1960 by Lena Spencer. Little wonder that it was named Best Small Venue in North America by the International Folk Alliance: Bob Dylan played here on his first tour of the East and Don McLean first played "American Pie" on the café's small

CAPITAL-SARATOGA

SARATOGA'S MINERAL SPRINGS

Saratoga's springs gurgle up from ancient seas trapped in limestone layers sealed by a solid layer of shale. A geological fault line runs through the layers, cracking the shale and allowing water to escape to the surface. The limestone enriches the water with minerals, and carbon dioxide adds natural carbonation.

Most of the springs bubble up in Congress Park, High Rock Park, and Saratoga Spa State Park. Some are marked by pavilions, others by fountains, and each has its own distinct taste. A complete guide to the springs and their reputed therapeutic values can be picked up at Saratoga Springs' **Heritage Area Visitor Center** (297 Broadway, Saratoga Springs, 518/587-3241, www.saratogaspringsvisitorcenter.com).

One bottling company continues to operate in the city: world-famous **Saratoga Spring Water Company** (www.saratogaspringwater.com). The Saratoga Spring Water Company has been located on Geyser Road at the Route 50 entrance to Saratoga Spa State Park since 1872. Take time to see its lovely Victorian gazebo, built in the late 1800s.

Saratoga Spa State Park still offers mineral baths and other treatments at **Roosevelt Baths** (518/584-3000 or 800/452-7275, www.gideonputnam.com). **Crystal Spa** (120 S. Broadway, 518/584-2556, www.thecrystalspa.net) offers mineral baths as well.

one of Saratoga's many mineral springs

© FRANCISCO COLLAZO

---

stage. Lena is gone now, but her legacy continues with a lineup of top acoustic acts—Odetta, Jimmie Dale Gilmore, Tom Paxton, and others. Small plates, coffees, and desserts are served up alongside music at weekend concerts; self-serve refreshments are offered during "emerging artist" shows.

Big, boisterous **Parting Glass** (40-42 Lake Ave., 518/583-1916, www.partingglasspub.com, daily 10am-3am) has 170 beers and Guinness on tap, along with a wide selection of pub grub. Live music and poker nights keep regulars and visitors entertained.

Lively bar scenes can also be found at many restaurants, including **Siro's** (168 Lincoln Ave., 518/584-4030, www.sirosny.com, Mon.-Thurs. 11:30am-10:30pm, Fri. 11:30am-11pm,

Sat. 5pm-11pm, Sun. 5pm-10:30pm), **Sperry's** (30-1/2 Caroline St., 518/584-9618, www.sperrysrestaurant.com, Mon.-Thurs. 4:30pm-10pm, Fri.-Sat. 5pm-11pm, Sun. 11am-2:30pm and 4:30pm-10pm), **Cantina** (430 Broadway, 518/587-5577, www.cantinasaratoga.com, Mon., Wed., and Sun. 11:30am-9pm, Tues. and Thurs.-Sat. 11:30am-10pm), and **Olde Bryan Inn** (123 Maple Ave., 518/587-2990, www.oldebryaninn.com, Sun.-Thurs. 11am-10pm, Fri.-Sat. 11am-3pm).

SHOPPING

Broadway is Saratoga's main shopping street, though its side streets hold treasures, too. **Lyrical Ballad Bookstore** (7 Phila St., 518/584-8779, www.lyricalballadbooks.com), housed in the old Saratoga National Bank building, is a packed-to-the-rafters antiquarian shop that stocks about 30,000 books. Rare volumes are stored in the bank's old safe-deposit vault. Back on Broadway, **G. Willikers** (461 Broadway, 518/587-2143, www.gwillikerstoys.com) upholds its nearly 30-year tradition of selling toys (plenty of horse-themed games, figurines, and books, of course!), alongside newer specialty shops like **Saratoga Salsa & Spice Company** (398 Broadway, 518/580-0792, www.saratogasalsaandspice.com) and **Saratoga Olive Oil Co.** (484 Broadway, 518/450-1308, www.saratogaoliveoil.com).

ACCOMMODATIONS
Hotels
Well-maintained grounds and friendly staff make **Roosevelt Inn and Suites** (2961 S. Broadway/Rte. 9, 800/524-9147, www.rooseveltsuites.com, $79-99 off-season, $195-255 racing season) a solid choice for reasonably priced lodging. Located a few miles out of town, the hotel has two tennis courts, a pool,

health club, and day spa, all of which make this a popular spot for an off-season getaway.

Longfellows (500 Union Ave., 518/587-0108, www.longfellows.com, $145-165 off-season, $225-265 racing season), with its airy loft rooms built inside a renovated 1915 dairy barn, offers modern amenities. On-site casual dining choices include a tavern, courtyard, and fireside seating.

It's hard to beat **Gideon Putnam** (24 Gideon Putnam Rd., 866/890-1171, www.gideonputnam.com, racing season $325-479, off-season $99-269) for location; the hotel enjoys pride of place in a particularly peaceful part of Saratoga Spa State Park, but is still close to downtown (a five-minute drive when there's no traffic). Rooms are large and comfortable, and a restaurant is on-site for guests who don't feel like venturing out for a meal. The hotel also manages the Roosevelt Baths; spa treatments can be booked directly through the concierge.

Bed-and-Breakfasts
Downtown Saratoga has a plethora of Victorian-era B&Bs. One of the most spectacular is the High Victorian Gothic **Batcheller Mansion Inn** (20 Circular St., 518/584-7012, www.batchellermansioninn.com, $160-245 off-season, $335-425 racing season), which offers nine spacious guest rooms, including one that features a pool table. Equally unique is the 1901 Queen Anne **Union Gables** (55 Union Ave., 518/584-1558, www.uniongables.com, $165-190 off-season, $335 racing season), notable for its wonderful wide porch, rose garden, and pool. Each guest room has a private bath and small refrigerator; seven of the rooms are pet-friendly.

Westchester House B&B (102 Lincoln Ave., 518/587-7613, www.westchesterhousebandb.com, $145-255 off-season, $285-490 racing season) dates back to 1885, when master carpenter Almeron King built this Queen Anne style home for his family. Look for original design details, such as hand-carved chestnut moulding. **Brunswick Bed & Breakfast** (143 Union Ave., 518/584-6751, www.brunswickbb.com, $109-149 off-season, $229-335 racing season) is a Gothic Victorian home built in 1886; it is particularly popular with horse lovers, as the B&B is directly across the street from the racetrack.

Inviting **❰ Harren Brook Inn** (738 Rte. 9P, 518/583-4009, www.harrenbrookinn.com, $125-195 off-season, $195-295 racing season) sits on the shores of Saratoga Lake and is run by two former schoolteachers with a good knowledge of the area. Nine rooms—all named after champion horses—are nicely appointed, each with queen beds and private baths. All guests can enjoy a cozy sitting room, breezy porch, and small private beach.

FOOD
Bakeries, Breakfast, and Diners
Mrs. London's (464 Broadway, 518/581-1652, www.mrslondons.com, Mon.-Thurs. 7am-6pm, Fri.-Sat. 7am-9pm, Sun. 7am-6pm) offers a mouth-watering selection of desserts, baked goods, and gourmet coffees.

Shirley's Restaurant (74 West Ave., 518/584-4532, Mon.-Sat. 6:30am-8pm, Sun. 7am-1:30pm), open since the 1960s, is a good spot for breakfast, lunch, and homemade pies.

Gideon Putnam Hotel (24 Gideon Putnam Rd., 518/584-3000, Sun. 10:30am-1:30pm, $28) is well known for its Sunday brunch buffet. Cheese and pastry options are offered while egg and carvery stations serve up brunch favorites. Expect an enormous array of options.

Restaurants
❰ Hattie's (45 Phila St., 518/584-4790, www. hattiesrestaurant.com, daily 5pm-10pm, $16) has been a Saratoga institution since 1938. This is the place to go for tasty fried chicken, barbecued ribs, catfish, and sweet potato pie.

Another institution is casual **Olde Bryan Inn** (123 Maple Ave., 518/587-2990, www.oldebryaninn.com, Sun.-Thurs. 11am-10pm, Fri.-Sat. 11am-3pm, $20), housed in a rustic 1825 stone house with dark, thick-beamed ceilings and a big, comfortable bar. The extensive menu features American pub fare and comfort food favorites.

Lillian's (408 Broadway, 518/587-7766,

www.lilliansrestaurant.com, Mon.-Thurs. 11am-10pm, Fri.-Sat. 11am-11pm, Sun. 11am-9pm, $24) is outfitted with woodwork, brass, Tiffany-style lamps, and stained glass. The dependable menu includes lots of standard steak, chicken, and fish dishes, along with lighter fare.

❰ Sperry's (30-1/2 Caroline St., 518/584-9618, www.sperrysrestaurant.com, Mon.-Thurs. 4:30pm-10pm, Fri.-Sat. 5pm-11pm, Sun. 11am-2:30pm and 4:30pm-10pm, $26), a favorite haunt of horsemen and -women during racing season, is an upscale bistro filled with memorabilia dating back to Saratoga's days as a fashionable spa. Specialties include fresh fish, jambalaya, and homemade pasta.

Only open during racing season, **❰ Siro's** (168 Lincoln Ave., 518/584-4030, www. sirosny.com, Mon.-Thurs. 11:30am-10:30pm, Fri. 11:30am-11pm, Sat. 5pm-11pm, Sun. 5pm-10:30pm, $30-48) boasts the best after-track bar scene, as well as the most exclusive restaurant in town. Featured are both innovative and traditional continental dishes. Reservations are essential.

Max London's Restaurant and Bar (466 Broadway, 518/587-3535, www.maxlondons. com, Mon.-Thurs. 5pm-close, Fri.-Sun. 11am-3pm and 5pm-close, $19) serves consistently tasty pizzas and pastas in a hip atmosphere, as well as a popular weekend brunch.

Cantina (430 Broadway, 518/587-5577, www.cantinasaratoga.com, Mon., Wed., and Sun. 11:30am-9pm, Tues. and Thurs.-Sat. 11:30am-10pm, $14) is a Victorian barroom with patio seating serving good Mexican cuisine and occasional live music. Ask about Burrito Palooza and Taco Tuesday specials.

The Wine Bar (417 Broadway, 518/584-8777, www.thewinebarofsaratoga.com, Mon.-Sat. 4pm-last call) offers nearly 50 wines by the glass, live music, a smoking lounge, patio dining in season, and a broad menu of small plates and half entrées. An impressive suite with oversized bedroom and full amenities is also available.

A little pricier than the others, candlelit **Chianti II Ristorante** (18 Division St., 518/580-0025, www.chiantiristorante.com,

Mon.-Thurs. 5pm-9:30pm, Fri.-Sat. 5pm-10:30pm, Sun. 5pm-9pm, $21) is known for authentic Northern Italian cuisine and an award-winning wine list.

Dessert

For a small town, Saratoga sure has a lot of sweet spots, each specializing in its own sugary confections.

"Have Fun and Make People Happy" is the motto at **Bettie's Cakes** (371 Broadway, 518/894-1179, www.bettiescakes.com, Mon.-Thurs. 11am-9pm, Fri.-Sat. 11am-10:30pm, Sun. 11am-9pm), a pink- and mint-colored, retro-themed "cupcakery" that also sells cakes and homemade ice cream. Music is loud, employees are on a permanent sugar high, and the frosting just might make you lick your fingers. Keep an eye out for Bettie's mobile location, a cotton candy-pink double decker bus, during summer months.

The Chocolate Mill (382 Broadway, 518/871-1210, www.chocolatemillcafe.com, Mon.-Thurs. 7am-9pm, Fri.-Sat. 7am-11pm, Sun. 7am-6pm) is a small café and bakery. With its dark wood and sculptural pastries, it looks like it was lifted straight out of Paris (pretension, thankfully, was left behind). There are cakes and truffles, as well as other brilliant, uncommon creations like Chef Vollkommer's delicious s'mores on a stick. Though desserts and coffee are the main draw, there are also breakfast and lunch menus.

Eugenio's Cafe Gelato (458 Broadway, 518/691-6000,www.eugenioscafegelato.com, Mon.-Thurs. 1pm-9pm, Fri. 1pm-11pm, Sat. 10:30am-11pm, Sun. 10:30am-9pm) is a small café where owner Eugenio Bizarro makes and serves Italian-style gelato fresh each day.

EXCURSIONS FROM SARATOGA

Stillwater

Battles that turned the course of the American Revolution were fought about 12 miles southeast of Saratoga. The former battlefield is now part of **Saratoga National Historical Park** (648 Rte. 32, 518/664-9821, www.nps.gov/sara, May-Oct. daily 9am-dusk, weather permitting, $5 per car, $3 per hiker or biker).

In October 1777, British general Burgoyne and his forces marched south from Canada to take control of the Hudson River. They planned to meet Colonel Leger and his forces in Albany, and continue to New York City to join General Howe. Instead, just outside Saratoga, General Burgoyne came upon the American forces, 9,000 strong. Led by General Horatio Gates and General Benedict Arnold, the Americans defeated the British in two fierce battles.

A tour of the park begins at the **visitors' center** (May-Oct. daily 9am-5pm), where you can watch an informative film. Beyond the center is a nine-mile, self-guided driving tour past strategic points equipped with audio recordings, plaques, and maps. Only a few bunkers remain, but the countryside is exceptionally lovely, especially in late afternoon, when mists roll in from nearby Hudson River.

Schuylerville

Continue north of the battlefield on Route 4 for about eight miles to reach Schuylerville, lined with worn white buildings and empty storefronts. Just south of the Route 32 intersection stands **Schuyler House** (Rte. 4, 518/664-9821, June-Sept. Thurs.-Sun. 9:30am-4:30pm, free). Also part of the Saratoga National Historical Park, the house once belonged to the Schuyler family, who ran a self-sufficient estate here that employed about 200 people. The house was burnt by Burgoyne during the Battles of Saratoga but was rebuilt that same year.

Take Route 32 west of Schuyler House about a half mile to reach **Saratoga Monument** (Rte. 32, June-Sept. Thurs.-Sun. 9:30am-4:30pm, fall weekends only, free), a beautifully restored gray obelisk on a hill. The third part of Saratoga National Historical Park, the monument features four niches honoring the battles' American leaders—General Philip Schuyler, General Horatio Gates, Colonel Daniel Morgan, and General Benedict Arnold. Statues stand in the first three niches; the fourth stands deliberately empty.

CAPITAL-SARATOGA

Ballston Spa

Before the Civil War, Ballston Spa outranked Saratoga as a fashionable resort and watering hole. After the war, however, the racetrack and casinos drew the crowds away, and Ballston Spa turned to knitting mills and tanneries. Today little evidence of any of these industries remains except at Saratoga County Historical Society's **Brookside Museum** (6 Charlton St., 518/885-4000, www.brooksidemuseum.org, Tues.-Fri. 10am-4pm, Sat. 10am-2pm, adults $2, seniors $1.50, children over 5 $1, children under 5 free). Housed in what was once a resort hotel, Brookside showcases exhibits on the town's 19th-century spas, 20th-century amusement parks, early African American settlers, and dairy farming.

Also in Ballston Spa is the eclectic **National Bottle Museum** (76 Milton Ave., 518/885-7589, www.nationalbottlemuseum. org, June-Sept. daily 10am-4pm, Oct.-May Mon.-Fri. 10am-4pm, donation). Thousands of antique and handmade bottles are displayed, most without signage; a video on antique bottles is featured. The museum hosts the annual Saratoga Antique Bottle Show and Sale, an impressive event where aficionados have their goods appraised or trade and sell bottles. It has also opened a small glassworks studio in a nearby facility, where visitors can take classes.

Wilton

One of the oddest and most moving house museums in New York State is **Grant Cottage** (off Ballard Rd., 518/584-4353, www.grantcottage.org, Memorial Day-Labor Day Wed.-Sun. 10am-4pm, Labor Day-Columbus Day Sat.-Sun. 10am-4pm, adults $5, seniors and children 6-18 $4), a state historic site.

President Ulysses S. Grant came to Mt. McGregor in June 1885. Afflicted with throat cancer, he spent the last six weeks of his life here, completing his memoirs. Grant had become bankrupt paying back the money he had urged friends to invest in his son's company; the company went belly-up after his son's partner absconded with the funds. As a result, Grant

was working frantically to finish his book so his family would have something to live on after he was gone. At the time, Mt. McGregor was home to popular Hotel Balmoral, owned by W.J. Arkell. Arkell, an admirer of Grant, lent the general his cottage when he learned that New York City's summer heat was preventing Grant from finishing his memoirs. Grant—often sleeping as few as two hours a night—did succeed in finishing his memoirs just four days before his death on July 23, 1885. They are considered to be among the finest ever written by an American general and earned the family half a million dollars in royalties.

The house remains as it was when Grant and his family left it. In one room are Grant's toothbrush, his nightshirts, and a half-empty bottle of medicinal cocaine. In another are wreaths sent by mourners, preserved in beeswax more than a century ago, and the bed where Grant died, the bedspread stained with flowers brought by mourners.

The cottage currently shares land with Mt. McGregor Correctional Facility; to access the cottage, guests must stop at a guard booth and enter a walled minimum-security complex topped with barbed wire. The New York State's governor's office has announced that the prison is likely to be closed, which may result in even easier access to the historic site.

Bed-and-Breakfasts

In Schuylerville, the wood-frame, Federal-style **Dovegate Inn** (184 Broad St., 518/695-3699, www.dovegateinn.com, $95-130 off-season, $185-195 racing season) is a welcoming B&B offering three spacious guest rooms with private baths. A small restaurant and gift shop are also on-site.

About five miles south of Ballston Spa is the **Olde Stone House Inn** (Round Lake, 518/899-5048, www.oldestonehouseinn.com, $90-150 off-season, higher in racing season), an elegant 1820 cobblestone home with four guest rooms (two with shared bath) and extensive grounds. In the United States, cobblestone houses are all but unique to New York.

The Mansion Inn (801 Rte. 29, Rock City

Falls, 518/885-1607, www.themansionsaratoga.com, $140-225 off-season, $250-499 racing season) lies seven miles west of downtown Saratoga. This 1866 Victorian mansion sits on four acres, built by 19th-century industrialist George West, known as The Paper Bag King, and is listed on the National Register of Historic Places. Modern conveniences and luxury amenities make this a good out-of-town lodging for racing season.

Washington County

This sliver of a county sits between Saratoga and Vermont, the Adirondack Mountains and the Green Mountains, reaching north as far as Lake Champlain. Though often overlooked by travelers, Washington County is exceptionally lovely, its small towns filled with little-known history and charm. Hills are smaller, greener, and closer together; villages are more genteel and picturesque. If it looks familiar, it might be: This is Grandma Moses country. The self-taught folk artist grew up near Eagle Bridge in southern Washington County and painted scenes she saw around her. Her legacy is acknowledged by the many artists who live in the area.

CAMBRIDGE

About 25 miles east of Saratoga Springs, Cambridge is the official birthplace of pie à la mode. The historic moment occurred one evening in the mid-1890s when Professor Charles Watson Townsend, dining at Hotel Cambridge, ordered ice cream with apple pie; a neighbor eating at the next table dubbed the concoction "pie à la mode." The professor ordered it by its new name during a subsequent visit to Delmonico's in New York City. The waiter had never heard of it and called for the manager, who declared in consternation, "Delmonico's never intends that any other restaurant shall get ahead of it.... Forthwith, pie à la mode will be featured on the menu every day." A *New York Sun* newspaperman, overhearing the conversation, reported it the next day; before long, pie à la mode was a fixture on menus across the country.

Today, Hotel Cambridge sits empty on Main Street, waiting hopefully for a new owner to restore it to its former glory. The hotel's neighbors, however, are evidence of vibrant small-town life and the trend of Main Street restoration movements around the state and country. A prime example is indie bookstore **Battenkill Books** (15 E. Main St., 518/677-2515, www.battenkillbooks.com), which features new titles on a range of topics, as well as magazines, gifts, toys, and a remarkably full schedule of readings, book club meetings, and other events. The bookstore's neighbors include **Cambridge Food Co-Op** (1 W. Main St., 518/677-5731), featuring local, natural, and organic food, and **The Village General Store** (25 E. Main St., 518/677-2495), an old-fashioned general store with a 100-year history. Profits from the general store support **Hubbard Hall** (25 E. Main St., 518/677-2495, www.hubbardhall.org), a rural opera house dating to 1878. Today, the restored hall is host to a wide range of music, dance, and theater events throughout the year, including the popular **Music from Salem** classical series held during the summer, which has featured renowned international chamber music performers.

◖ New Skete Monastery

If you wonder whether you've driven into a cultural and geographical warp hole when you happen upon gold, onion-domed structures on a thickly wooded hilltop between Cambridge and Vermont, don't worry: You've just stumbled upon the Eastern Orthodox **New Skete Monastery** (273 New Skete Ln., 518/677-3928, www.newskete.org, grounds Tues.-Sun. dawn-dusk). Home to a handful of brothers, the monastery centers around a rough-hewn wooden renewing public interest in the monastic community.

Though kennels are off-limits to the public, guests can visit the chapel and gift shop. The nuns of New Skete, famous for their cheesecake, run a similar **gift shop** (343 Ash Grove Rd., 518/677-3810). When no staff is present, the gift shops run on an honor system. New Skete also offers accommodations and meals for visitors who want a quiet retreat of two or more days; reservations must be made in advance and the suggested donation is $60 per night. The main church is open during Sunday morning services only.

SALEM

The town of Salem is about 15 miles north of Cambridge. Blink and you might miss downtown and surrounding spots like **Fort Salem Theater** (11 E. Broadway, 518/854-9200, www.fortsalemtheater.com), housed in a building that was a church (twice) and a fort before being transformed into a performance space known locally for music, musicals, and cabaret. Just down the street is **Courthouse Community Center** (58 E. Broadway, 518/854-7053, www.salemcourthouse.org), another repurposed building, this one a former courthouse turned performing and visual arts venue. Still more art can be enjoyed at **Salem Art Works** (19 Cary Ln., 518/854-7674, www.salemartworks.org, hours vary seasonally), where resident artists work in a variety of media, including ceramics, glass, and iron. Visitors can view sculptures, installations, and other pieces in a massive barn gallery, the farmhouse gallery, and on the grounds of the property.

chapel filled with icons painted by the monks. A more elaborate church presides nearby.

Apart from its religious mandate, New Skete's secular claim to fame is dogs. Monks began breeding and training German shepherds shortly after moving here in 1966, when it became apparent they could not support themselves by farming. The business took off, especially after 1978, when one of the brothers wrote a best-selling, award-winning book, *How to Be Your Dog's Best Friend* (Little, Brown). The 2007 TV series *Divine Canine* introduced the New Skete monks to a new generation,

Rural Washington County is known for farming and for having the largest dairy cow population in the state. Visitors can get a literal taste of the land's bounty at spots like **Battenkill Valley Creamery** (691 Rte. 30, 518/854-9400, www.battenkillcreamery.com), which has an on-site ice cream parlor. Just a couple minutes up the road is **Gardenworks** (1055 Rte. 30, 518/854-3250, www.gardenworksfarm.com, hours vary seasonally), a third-generation family farm where you can pick

GRANDMA MOSES

Her legal name was Anna Mary Robertson Moses, but most people knew her during her lifetime and know her now as "Grandma Moses." In the three decades between the time the self-taught folk artist started painting in her 70s and her death at age 101 in 1961, she produced more than 1,600 paintings. She became the most recognized (and recognizable) American folk artist. Her appeal endures: One painting fetched more than a million dollars in 2006.

Born in the quiet rural town of Eagle Bridge, New York, she rocketed out of the relative obscurity of rural life and into the international art scene after being discovered by New York City art collector Louis Caldor in 1938. He purchased multiple works, which he then exhibited in Manhattan. Many critics and curators were ambivalent about Moses's work; they were busily trying to convince the world that the United States had art movements as vital and viable as those in Europe. But the public loved Moses's simple depictions of quintessential American scenes.

Visiting the Grandma Moses homestead today, it's not hard to see the sources of her inspiration. It's surrounded by fields. The bucolic, country life depicted in her paintings has changed little. In fact, it's also the subject of the artwork painted by her grandson, artist Will Moses, who exhibits and sells his pieces at Mt. Nebo Gallery, located on the homestead and open to the public.

Moses preferred to stay close to home, surrounded by those scenes, but her work traveled far and wide. Biographer Jane Killar, the foremost expert on Grandma Moses, has written that Moses was considered "democracy's ideal cultural ambassador" because of both her all-American personal story (ancestors from both sides of her family arrived in America on the *Mayflower*) and her subject matter. Her accessible rendering of Americana stimulated patriotism at a crucial post-war moment and served as a welcome, concrete antidote to the abstractions of Modernist art.

Though visitors passing through Eagle Bridge can't enter the home itself, they can stop to take photos of the house and a historical plaque marking the site where Grandma Moses produced her iconic works. They can also observe how her folk art legacy has been carried on in her own family by visiting grandson Will's gallery. In addition to original work and prints, **Mt. Nebo Gallery** (60 Grandma Moses Rd., 518/686-4334, www.willmoses.com, hours vary seasonally, free) sells cards, puzzles, and books featuring Will's work.

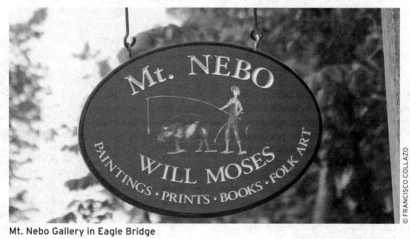

Mt. Nebo Gallery in Eagle Bridge

© FRANCISCO COLLAZO

CAPITAL-SARATOGA

© FRANCISCO COLLAZO

Battenkill Valley Creamery

your own blueberries and raspberries in season. Earlier in the year, visitors can experience the sugaring tradition at **Mapleland Farms** (647 Bunker Hill Rd., 518/854-7669, www.maplelandfarms.com, hours vary seasonally), where the fifth generation of the Campbell family gives sugarbush and sap lineage tours and offers pancake breakfasts (with maple syrup, of course) to guests who want to learn how maple syrup is produced.

Sightseeing and outdoor activities are big draws in Salem, too. Popular photo opportunities include the area's **covered bridges,** among them, **Rexleigh** (Rexleigh Rd., off Rte. 22 South) and **Eagleville** (Eagleville Rd., off Rte 313). Both bridges are still operational; each spans the Battenkill River and is listed on the National Register of Historic Places.

The river is popular for fly-fishing, canoeing, kayaking, and floating, and Salem and its neighboring villages are bike-friendly; detailed cycling itineraries can be found on the county's tourism website (www.washingtonnycounty.com/cycling.html).

Accommodations and Food

Bunker Hill Inn (412 Bunker Hill Rd., 518/854-9339, www.bunkerhillinn.com, $53-105), a 19th-century farmhouse, is one of the best options for a home base while exploring Washington County. The comfortable, welcoming B&B may seem remote, but it's a 10-15 minute drive to most of Salem's attractions.

In summer months, farm-to-table dinners at **Gardenworks** (1055 Rte. 30, 518/854-3250, www.gardenworksfarm.com) aren't to be missed. But if you're looking for lunch or you're in Salem in another season, **Jacko's Corner** (190 Main St., 518/854-7449, www.jackoscorner.com, Mon.-Thurs. noon-7pm, Fri.-Sat. noon-8pm, Sun. 10am-5pm) is a reliable spot for a café-style meal. In addition to its soda fountain and old-fashioned candy selection, Jacko's has a light lunch menu of quiche and soup.

GRANVILLE

This sturdy town of red-brick buildings was originally settled by Vermont Quakers in 1780. Later, in the mid-1800s, it was famed for its colored slate quarries—producing maroon, green, and blue slate—worked primarily by people of Welsh descent. Today, Granville still sports slate roofs, chimneys, patios, sidewalks, and even slate business signs.

Pember Museum of Natural History

Housed in a striking Victorian mansion, **Pember Museum of Natural History** (33 W. Main St., 518/642-1515, www.pembermuseum.com, Tues.-Fri 1pm-5pm, Sat. 10am-3pm, free) is a surprisingly Old World place filled with elegant glass and wood exhibit cases displaying hundreds of preserved birds, insects, reptiles, and mammals collected by amateur naturalist Franklin Pember in the late 1800s.

Some species, such as the passenger pigeon and Carolina parakeet, are now extinct. Others, such as the South American possum and red kangaroo are exhibited with their offspring. Larger specimens, such as the Alaskan

©FRANCISCO COLLAZO

Rexleigh's covered bridge

brown bear and brown pelican, almost burst out of their cases. Walk down the aisles here and you'll feel as if you're surrounded by a magical, about-to-awaken menagerie.

Slate Valley Museum

Step into this renovated 19th-century Dutch barn to learn more about Granville's slate history at the **Slate Valley Museum** (17 Water St., 518/642-1417, www.slatevalleymuseum. org, Tues.-Fri., 1pm-5pm, Sat. 10am-4pm, adults $5, children under 12 free). Inside, memorabilia, tools, machinery, photography, and artwork date back to the days when Granville was known as the "Colored Slate Capital of the World." During the town's heyday around the turn of the 20th century, 64 slate companies employing 3,000 men were located here.

At the heart of the collection is a powerful 25-foot mural depicting 13 men at work in a slate quarry. The mural was painted in 1939 by Woodstock artist Martha Levy for the federal Works Progress Administration.

WHITEHALL

Whitehall, birthplace of the U.S. Navy, is at the head of Lake Champlain and near the end of the Erie Canal. The first American fleet was built here in 1776 under the supervision of Benedict Arnold.

A trim historic Main Street, listed on the National Register of Historic Places, runs along the eastern edge of Whitehall. Nearby are pleasant waterfront parks and **Skenesborough Museum** (off Rte. 4, 518/499-1155, June-Sept. Mon.-Sat. 10am-4pm, Sun. noon-4pm, $2), housing models of the first U.S. Navy ships, along with canal and railroad exhibits. The museum also runs the **Heritage Area Visitors Center,** which is stocked with free walking-tour maps. Another interesting attraction is **Skene Manor** (8 Potters Terrace, 518/499-1906, www.skenemanor.org, mid-Apr.-Dec. Fri.-Sun. noon-4pm, donations welcomed), a Victorian Gothic mansion staffed by volunteers offering free tours. Sandwiches and soups are available for purchase at the manor's Tea Room and there's an on-site gift shop as well.

CAPITAL-SARATOGA

© FRANCISCO COLLAZO

Bunker Hill Inn, Salem

Central New York

SCHENECTADY

Schenectady is best visited for its history. The oldest European settlement in the Mohawk Valley, the city boasts one of the largest and best collections of 18th-century buildings in New York—**the Stockade,** the state's first historic district. Visitors walking along this district's quiet, crooked streets, heavy with trees, will be transported back to a gentler age.

Museum of Innovation and Science and Suits-Bueche Planetarium

Formerly called Schenectady Museum, the **Museum of Innovation and Science** (15 Nott Terrace Heights, off Nott Terrace, 518/382-7890, www.schenectadymuseum.org, June-Sept. Mon.-Sat. 10am-5pm, Sun. noon-5pm, off-season hours vary, adults $9.50, seniors $8, children 3-12 $6.50) recently underwent a name change to better reflect its focus: the city's industrial and technological history. The transformation wasn't just nominal; exhibits became more modern, interactive, and kid-friendly, all with the intention of fostering an understanding of how technology and science affect modern-day visitors in their own daily lives. The museum is also known for its 30-foot-high planetarium; an additional fee is charged at admission for guests who want to see a planetarium show.

Stockade District

Along the banks of Mohawk River, in the triangle formed by State and North College Streets, lies the **Stockade** (www.historicstockade.com), one of the nation's oldest continuously occupied neighborhoods. Settled in 1661 by Dutch merchants and fur traders, the outpost flourished until 1690, when a party of French-Canadians

HAPPY GOATS, GREAT CHEESE

At **Nettle Meadow Goat Farm and Cheese Factory** (484 S. Johnsburg Rd., Warrensburg, 518/623-3372, www.nettlemeadow.com), you'll see a sign with these words: "Happy Goats. Great Cheese!"

A tour of the picturesque farm affirms that both statements are true. It would be hard to find a better place to be a goat...or a cheese lover. The farm is a goat's utopia, with a designated retirement home for old milk-goats no longer able to produce, as well as a bachelor pad housing the male goats born on the farm. The pampered goats—all of which are called by their own name—munch on organic feed made of wild herbs, nettles, garlic, kelp, and wild raspberry branches.

Determined to keep from the slaughterhouse the young males they bottle-fed by hand as babies, owners Lorraine Lambiase and Sheila Flanagan allow the goats to roam the land until they can find a good home as a pet or 4H project. Nettle Meadow's no-kill policy even extends

to the wolves and coyotes that threaten the herd. Finding the idea of shooting the intruders repugnant, they hired a top-of-the-line security force of no nonsense llamas.

To outsiders, it probably seemed unlikely that a business that spoils its goats so and ladles (as opposed to drains, which is less time-consuming) the product to protect the architecture of the curds could survive. But, its cheeses have won lots of awards, and Nettle Meadow's unique organic Kunik cheese, a goat milk-cow's cream blend, has even been listed by the celebrated Murray's Cheese as one of the World's Best 300 Cheeses. It is also featured in many top New York City restaurants, and respected New York City cheesemonger Anne Saxelby has declared "It may well be the sexiest cheese in the U.S.A."

Farm and rescue sanctuary tours are available at noon on Saturdays. The farm is open for cheese sales Thursday-Monday 11:00am-3:00pm.

and their Indian allies burnt it to the ground, massacring most of the inhabitants and marching the rest off to Québec.

Native Mohawks encouraged the Dutch to rebuild, and two years later the Stockade was flourishing once again. During the next two centuries all of Schenectady's most important families settled here. Today the residential district is a wonderful spot, filled with architectural landmarks of all styles and periods. The oldest are churches and graveyards dating back to the 1690s; the newest are homes built in the 1930s.

Plaques pinpointing some of the Stockade's more interesting sites are located throughout the district. Maps are available in the Schenectady County Historical Society Museum, located on the southern edge of the Stockade.

Schenectady County Historical Society Museum

On display in the friendly, three-story

Schenectady County Historical Society Museum (32 Washington Ave., 518/374-0263, www.schist.org, Mon.-Fri. 9am-5pm, Sat. 10am-2pm, adults $2, children under 12 $1) is everything from antique dolls and guns to period costumes and furniture. Highlights include an elaborate dollhouse that once belonged to the family of Governor Yates, and the notebooks and letters of GE's electrical genius, Dr. Charles Steinmetz.

Union College

The first planned college campus in America, **Union College** (807 Union St., 518/388-6000, www.union.edu) was designed in 1814 by classical landscape architect Joseph Jacques Ramee. Filled with broad lawns and giant elms, Union admitted only men until 1970.

At the center of the campus is high-Gothic **Nott Memorial,** the only 16-sided building in the northern hemisphere. Nearby are **Jackson's Gardens,** beautifully landscaped formal gardens first planted in the early 1800s by math professor Isaac Jackson.

Union College is located between Lenox Road, Seward Place, Union Avenue, and Nott and Union Streets. Parking is available in the lots at Nott Street and Seward Place.

Entertainment

Try to catch a show at historic **Proctor's Theatre** (432 State St., 518/346-6204, www. proctors.org), an architectural gem built in 1926. Once a vaudeville palace, it also hosted the first public demonstration of the television and has seen the likes of Cab Calloway and Duke Ellington performing in the ornate, 2,700-seat auditorium, which features a 1931 Golub Mighty Wurlitzer Organ. The events calendar is packed with Broadway musicals, concerts, operas, dance troupes, and classic movies.

Accommodations and Food

In the Stockade find **Café 1795** (35 N. Ferry St., 518/372-4141), selling gourmet sandwiches

and salads, as well as simple entrées. Located on the site of the 17th-century Old Public Market, Café 1795 sits on an attractive patio with a handful of picnic tables. For heaping platters of diner fare, try **Blue Ribbon Restaurant and Bakery** (1801 State St., 518/393-2600, www.blueribbonrestaurant.com, Mon.-Thurs. 6am-11pm, Fri.-Sat. 6am-midnight, Sun. 6am-10pm, $13), especially known for its cheesecake.

Overlooking the Mohawk River across from Schenectady is ◖ **Glen Sanders Mansion** (1 Glen Ave., Scotia, 518/374-7262, www.glen-sandersmansion.com, $154-350), an upscale inn housed in a historic stone home with original Dutch floors and doors. The inn's on-site restaurant, **Angelo's Tavolo** (1 Glen Ave., Scotia, 518/374-7262, www.glensandersmansion.com, $24), serves modern Italian cuisine in a formal setting, while a downstairs pub has a more casual take on the same. Ten standard guest rooms offer double queen-size beds; 10 suites offer king-size beds and sitting areas, some with fireplaces.

FULTON COUNTY

It's hardly surprising that this county's primary attraction is its outdoor splendor since its nickname is "Land of 44 Lakes" and its geographic junction is Adirondack Park and the Mohawk Valley. In fact, 59 percent of the county sits in the park itself.

There are plenty of opportunities to explore by land and by water regardless of the season. Winter is an increasingly popular time to visit Fulton County, as ice fishing draws hearty souls to cast a line, especially during the annual **Walleye Challenge** in January. More than 1,500 contestants descend upon Great Sacandaga Lake and compete to catch the heaviest fish for cash prizes.

In warmer weather, cyclists might want to take to **Powley-Piseco Road,** considered one of the best seasonal roads in the Adirondacks and one of the only remaining dirt roads in the region. Eight miles of the 17-mile trail wind through Fulton County.

Hiking is also a popular activity in Fulton County, which has nearly 75,000 acres of forest. Trails vary in level of difficulty as well as type of terrain; **Willie Wildlife Marsh Trail,** for example, takes hikers through a wetland habitat.

SCHOHARIE COUNTY

Schoharie County, like much of central New York, is defined by its picturesque farmland. It's beautiful enough, but if you're driving through without knowing the county's less visible attractions, you'll miss out. Many of the best sights in Schoharie County can't even be seen at eye-level; you'll have to go underground to discover them. Schoharie's prehistoric caves and 100-foot underground waterfall are two of the county's subterranean wonders.

Howe Caverns (255 Discovery Dr., Howes Cave, 518/296-8900, www.howecaverns.com, May 1-Oct. 31 daily 9am-6pm, Nov. 1-Apr. 30 Fri.-Mon. 10am-3pm) is a living, limestone cave carved out by an underground river over the course of six million years. Today, it's a veritable amusement park. Passing through the somewhat touristy offerings at the surface

(geode cracking and gemstone, arrowhead, or fossil panning) brings you to a lobby where groups wait for their timed tour. Hopping in an elevator drops you down 15 stories to explore the cavern, which includes an underground boat ride and a particularly lovely passage called the "winding way." Visitors looking for something out of the ordinary can take a two-hour adventure spelunking tour through areas not accessible to the general public or explore the old-fashioned way—by lantern, the way Lester Howe might have done it when the caverns were discovered in 1842...by his cow, Millicent. In addition to cave tours, visitors can also zip-line, rock climb, or test out a ropes course.

Secret Caverns (671 Caverns Rd., Howes Cave, 518/296-8558, hours and admission fees vary seasonally) may not actually be a secret but they are less commercialized and crowded than Howe. Secret Caverns are also smaller than Howe, with formations that may not seem as impressive until you see the 100-foot waterfall that helped form the caverns in the first place.

Once underground but now housed safely in **Gilboa Museum** (122 Stryker Rd., Gilboa, 607/588-9413, www.gilboafossils.org, early June-early Sept. Sat.-Sun. 12:30pm-4:30pm) are nine of the world's oldest tree fossils and the first fossil tree stumps that were documented in North America. An amateur naturalist made the initial discovery of these Devonian Period fossils, which were found in a tree trunk in Schoharie Creek after a flood. Seventy years later, an expedition from New York State Museum found almost 50 more; some were retained for the museum's collection, and others were shipped near and far to other collectors and institutions. Though the nine fossils at this museum represent just a portion of the museum's interests and collection, they comprise its most compelling exhibit.

The caverns and the Gilboa Museum are about halfway between Albany and Cooperstown, and can be taken as day trips from either city or as interesting stops when traveling between the two. For an excellent lodging and dining option in Schoharie

County, there's **American Hotel** (192 Main St., Sharon Springs, 518/284-2105, www.americanhotelny.com, $150-175 Nov.-May, $215-235, June-Oct.). Built in 1847, it sat vacant for nearly a third of the 20th century until it was bought and restored by its current owners in 1996. Nine comfortable rooms feature Frette linens, free Wi-Fi, and breakfast; the on-site restaurant sources most of its produce from nearby farms.

COOPERSTOWN

With its friendly, old-fashioned Main Street, population of about 2,000 residents, and, of course, the National Baseball Hall of Fame and Museum, Cooperstown likes to think of itself as the most famous small town in America. To the north are the still waters of Otsego Lake; to the south, east, and west are the rolling, forested hills of Leatherstocking Country.

Cooperstown was first settled in 1790 by William Cooper, father of James Fenimore, America's first internationally recognized author. Fiercely ambitious Cooper Sr. obtained the land through unscrupulous means during the chaos following the Revolutionary War, then immediately set about establishing himself as a grand gentleman. Within a decade he'd built the largest private home west of Albany, won widespread respect for his skill as a land developer, and established Cooperstown as the Otsego County seat. Later, he became a county judge and representative to Congress.

James Fenimore Cooper wrote about Cooperstown in his novel *The Pioneers,* and set many of his Natty Bumppo tales on the shores of "The Glimmerglass"—Otsego Lake. After travels at sea and abroad, he settled down in his hometown and took over where his father had left off, playing lord of the manor. Cooper was buried in the town's Christ Church Cemetery in 1851.

In the late 1800s Cooperstown became home to the Clark family, who'd made a fortune with Singer Sewing Machines. Edward Clark, the family patriarch, built a miniature castle called Kingfisher Tower on Otsego Lake in 1876. In the late 1930s and 1940s one of his descendants, Stephen C. Clark, established the town's three famous museums—the National Baseball Hall of Fame, Farmers' Museum, and Fenimore Art Museum.

On summer days, Cooperstown's population swells by the thousands. Tourists wearing baseball caps and T-shirts are everywhere, and parking can be a problem. The best approach is to park in one of the park-and-ride lots on Routes 80 and 28 and ride the free trolley into town. During the off-season, street parking is generally available.

◖ National Baseball Hall of Fame and Museum

The National Baseball Hall of Fame and Museum (25 Main St., 607/547-7200, www. baseballhall.org, June-Sept. daily 9am-9pm, Oct.-May daily 9am-5pm, adults $19.50, seniors $12, children 7-12 $7) was established in 1939 as an homage to America's favorite pastime. It's loaded with state-of-the-art displays covering every aspect of the sport, from famous ballparks and women's baseball, to the World Series, Negro League, and baseball in the Caribbean. Aficionados and collectors crowd displays to see such memorabilia as Jackie Robinson's warm-up jacket, Hank Aaron's locker, Willie Mays's glove, Yogi Berra's catcher's mitt, and that rarest of all baseball cards, the Honus Wagner 1909 T-206 tobacco card, recalled at the request of the nonsmoking ballplayer.

Occupying three floors and 60,000 square feet, the museum begins with a cavernous Hall of Fame honoring the greats. A ramp to one side leads to exhibits on such subjects as "Scribes and Mikemen" and "Baseball at the Movies," while stairs lead to the 2nd and 3rd floors, where the heart of the collection is housed. One room honors Babe Ruth; another, baseball in the 19th century; a third, "Today's Game." Separate exhibit cases are devoted to such major players as Hank Aaron, Jackie Robinson, and Ty Cobb. A 13-minute multimedia show, "The Baseball Experience," is presented throughout the day, while film and audio clips supplement exhibits' visuals.

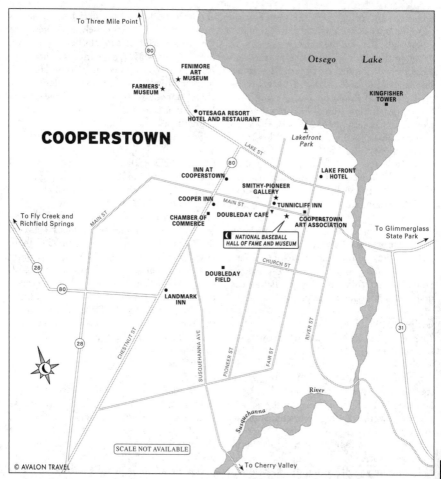

To Three Mile Point

FENIMORE ART MUSEUM

FARMERS' MUSEUM

Otsego Lake

KINGFISHER TOWER

OTESAGA RESORT HOTEL AND RESTAURANT

COOPERSTOWN

LAKE ST

Lakefront Park

INN AT COOPERSTOWN

LAKE FRONT HOTEL

SMITHY-PIONEER GALLERY

COOPER INN

MAIN ST

TUNNICLIFF INN

CHAMBER OF COMMERCE

DOUBLEDAY CAFE

COOPERSTOWN ART ASSOCIATION

To Fly Creek and Richfield Springs

MAIN ST

NATIONAL BASEBALL HALL OF FAME AND MUSEUM

To Glimmerglass State Park

CHURCH ST

DOUBLEDAY FIELD

LANDMARK INN

CHESTNUT ST

SUSQUEHANNA AVE

PIONEER ST

FAIR ST

RIVER ST

River

Susquehanna

SCALE NOT AVAILABLE

© AVALON TRAVEL

To Cherry Valley

Daily trivia games and educational programs are also featured. Combination tickets with the Farmers' Museum and Fenimore Art Museum are available.

Doubleday Field

Just down Main Street from the Hall of Fame is **Doubleday Field** (1 Doubleday Court, 607/547-2270, year-round daily), the oldest baseball diamond in the world and the site of the first official game in 1839. Originally built for 8,000 spectators and later expanded

to accommodate 10,000, the field is now available for rent and is very popular among local groups, meaning that a game is often in progress. The field is also the site where Hall of Fame inductees are presented awards during the annual Induction Weekend.

Lakefront Park

Two blocks north of the Baseball Hall of Fame lies Otsego Lake, created during the last great Ice Age. Like many glacial lakes, Otsego is cool and deep, with steep banks and overhanging trees. Fed by springs, it is the source of the Susquehanna River, which flows south to Chesapeake Bay and the Atlantic Ocean.

Along the lake's edge is **Lakefront Park,** a pleasant spot frequented by families. To one side is a statue called *Indian Hunter;* to the other, **Council Rock,** once a meeting place for various Indian tribes. The rock was employed by Cooper in *The Deerslayer* as a rendezvous point for Deerslayer and his friend Chingachgook. "The rock was not large . . .," wrote Cooper, "The incessant washing of the water for centuries had so rounded its summit, that it resembled a large beehive." Today, a flight of stone steps leads down to a terrace overlooking the rock.

From the park you can see 60-foot-high, 1907 **Kingfisher Tower,** designed in the style of a European castle by architect Henry Hardenbergh, who also designed The Plaza Hotel in New York City. The miniature castle/tower is not open to the public.

Galleries

The galleries of the **Cooperstown Art Association** (22 Main St., 607/547-9777, www.cooperstownart.com, Mon. and Wed-Sat. 11am-4pm, Sun. 1pm-4pm, free) are diagonally across from the Baseball Hall of Fame. Founded in 1928, the association showcases a variety of works ranging from contemporary to traditional.

Flanking **Pioneer Street,** which intersects Main Street by the flagpole, are some of Cooperstown's oldest buildings. Foremost among them is the dark, low-ceilinged **Smithy-Pioneer Gallery** (55 Pioneer St., 607/547-8671, www.smithyarts.org, May-Oct. Tues.-Sat. 10am-5pm, Sun. noon-5pm, free), part of which was built around 1786 by William Cooper. Originally a storehouse, the building was later converted into a blacksmith's shop and now contains both historic artifacts and an art gallery.

Cooper's Town

Although the old Cooper family mansion was torn down long ago, Cooperstown still contains about 20 buildings that date back to James Fenimore's time. Most closely associated with Cooper is **Christ Episcopal Church** (46 River St., 607/547-9555, www.christchurchcooperstown.org), consecrated in 1810 on land donated by his father. In Cooper's fiction, the church appears as "New St. Paul's"; the Cooper family plot is located in the cemetery behind the church.

For more Cooper-related sites, pick up a copy of *Cooper's Otsego County* by Hugh Cooke MacDougall (New York State Historical Society, 607/547-1400, www.nysha.org).

Farmers' Museum

Just outside downtown Cooperstown is the second of its famous museums, **Farmers' Museum** (5775 State Hwy. 80/Lake Rd., 607/547-1450, www.farmersmuseum.org, May-Oct. daily 10am-5pm, hours vary off-season, adults $12, seniors $10.50, children 7-12 $6), composed of meticulously restored pre-Civil War buildings. Run by New York State Historical Association, this is not just another living history museum; rather, it's the granddaddy of them all. Founded in 1944, it was the first open-air museum in New York State and one of the first in the country.

The museum is spread along one looping street, lined with a general store, blacksmith's shop, printing office, doctor's office, and druggist's shop. In the Main Barn near the entrance hang imaginative exhibits on early rural life; skillful guides roam about in period dress, some demonstrating such arts as broom-making and open-hearth cooking. Sheep graze in the village common. Fat cows wander a nearby hill.

One of the museum's odder exhibits is the 2,900-pound Cardiff Giant. Supposedly unearthed in nearby Cardiff in 1869 by the hitherto unassuming William Newell, the sleeping stone man with the mysterious smile soon drew visitors from all over the country. A Harvard professor claimed the Giant dated back to Phoenician times; Oliver Wendell Holmes drilled a hole behind his left ear to see if the brain was petrified. Only after Newell had raked in tens of thousands of dollars was the statue proven to be a hoax.

Combination tickets with the Baseball Hall of Fame and Fenimore Art Museum are available.

Fenimore Art Museum

Directly across the street from Farmers' Museum is the third of Cooperstown's museum triumvirate. **Fenimore Art Museum** (5798 State Hwy. 80/Lake Rd., 607/547-1400, www.fenimoreartmuseum.org, mid-May-mid-Oct. daily 10am-5pm, hours vary off-season, adults $12, seniors $10.50, children 12 and under free), also run by New York State Historical Association, holds the state's premier collection of folk art, fine art, and Native American art. Highlights include Thomas Cole's *Last of the Mohicans,* Gilbert Stuart's *Joseph Brandt,* a version of Edward Hicks' *Peaceable Kingdom,* and an eclectic collection of weathervanes, trade signs, cigar-store Indians, and decoys.

One wing of the museum houses The Eugene and Clare Thaw Collection of American Indian Art. Perhaps the most important privately owned collection of its kind, the collection includes about 700 works spanning 2,500 years of native North American culture. Among the many stunning items on display are a flowing Blackfoot headdress, a Lakota-painted horsehide, and a brilliant blue Heiltsuk moon mask.

A first-rate book store is also on-site, as is a café serving light lunch with a view of Otsego Lake. Combination tickets with the National Baseball Hall of Fame and Farmers' Museum are available.

Breweries

Cooperstown has two breweries offering tastings and tours. **Brewery Ommegang** (656 County Rd. 33, 607/544-1800, www.ommegang.com, daily noon-5pm, adults $3) was built on an old hops farm in 1997 and has been brewing Belgian-style beer ever since. Belgian-inspired food is served in an on-site café. **Cooperstown Brewing Company** (110 River St., Milford, 607/286-9330, Mon.-Sat. 10am-6pm, Sun. noon-5:30pm, adults $3, children free) is a small, independently-owned brewery making beer from homegrown hops. Tasting pours are generous and label names reflect Cooperstown's baseball history: Nine Man Ale, Old Slugger, and Strike-Out Stout.

Entertainment

Glimmerglass Festival is an acclaimed musical event taking place every July-August at **Glimmerglass Opera** (7300 State Hwy. 80), a partially open-air theater by Otsego Lake. Three operas and a musical typically comprise the festival's musical menu, rounded out with backstage tours and symposia. The **box office** (18 Chestnut St., 607/547-2255, www.glimmerglass.org) is downtown. Apart from the festival, chamber-music concerts, lectures, and plays take place regularly in **Hyde Hall** (Glimmerglass State Park, 607/547-5098, www.hydehall.org).

For an elegant evening out, step into Templeton Lounge of **Otesaga Resort Hotel** (60 Lake St., 607/547-9931, www.otesaga.com). Live music and dancing are offered Thursday-Saturday evenings (8:30pm-11:30pm).

Shopping

Numerous shops occupy Cooperstown and the surrounding area. A few miles south of Cooperstown is **Fly Creek Cider Mill** (288 Goose St., 607/547-9692, www.flycreekcider.com, daily 9am-6pm), where apples are pressed in a 19th-century wooden cider mill. The mill is water-powered and all original equipment is used. Also on site is an extensive gift shop and a snack bar selling lots of tasty homemade treats, including cider donuts and cider floats and slushes. A duck pond and play area will delight kids.

Among the region's more unusual stores is **Wood Bull Antiques** (3920 Rte. 28, 607/286-9021, www.woodbullantiques.com), in a large barn eight miles south of Cooperstown. According to the owners, the merchandise has been gathered from over 35 years of attic rummaging and close to 3,000 auctions.

Sports and Recreation

You'll find good swimming at public beaches on Otsego Lake at **Glimmerglass State Park** (off County Rd. 31, 607/547-8662, www.nysparks.com/parks/28, $7 vehicle entrance fee); **Three Mile Point** (East Lake Rd., 607/547-2777), off Route 80; and **Fairy Springs** (East Lake Rd., 607/547-2150), off County Road 31.

On summer Saturday nights, the bleachers are always filled with families and fans of stock car racing at **Lebanon Valley Speedway** (1746 Rte. 20, 518/794-9606, www.lebanonvalley.com). Racing season runs April-October.

Accommodations

The 1902 **◖ Otesaga Resort Hotel** (60 Lake St., 607/547-9931, www.otesaga.com, $465-550 d with full breakfast, dinner, and afternoon tea) is a delicious grande dame of a hotel affiliated with Historic Hotels of America. Stately white columns tower out front. Out back, a long, circular porch with rocking chairs overlooks the lake. Facilities include a romantic ballroom with a 20-foot-high coffered ceiling, a main dining room, the appealing Hawkeye Bar & Grill, tennis courts, and first-rate Leatherstocking Golf Course. All rooms are outfitted with period furnishings.

The Otesaga also operates **The Cooper Inn** (Main and Chestnut Sts., 607/547-2567, www.cooperinn.com, $265 d summer, $110-160 off-season, breakfast included), built between 1813 and 1816. Reigning over its own little park in the heart of the downtown, the luxurious inn offers 15 handsomely decorated rooms and the use of all Otesaga facilities.

◖ Inn at Cooperstown (16 Chestnut St., 607/547-5756, www.innatcooperstown.com, $187 d summer, $115-375 off-season, breakfast included) is all that an inn should be—big, creaky, lined with a wide porch, and shaded with magnificent trees. All 18 guest rooms have private baths and queen or double beds. The two-story luxury suite features a king bed, hydro spa tub, and wet bar.

Cooperstown's oldest inn, now somewhat worn but still atmospheric, is 1802 **Tunnicliff Inn** (34-34 Pioneer St., 607/547-9611, www.

tunnifcliffinn.net, $155-375 d summer, $89-200 d off-season). Here, you'll find 17 guest rooms, a restaurant, and a historic bar. A hot breakfast buffet is included in the room rate.

Among the many inviting B&Bs in Cooperstown is stately **◖ Landmark Inn** (64 Chestnut St., 607/547-7225, www.landmarkinncooperstown.com, $200-295 d July-Aug., $115-210 d off-season), in an 1856 Italianate mansion. Beautifully restored, the inn offers a plush parlor complete with fireplace, hardwood floors polished to a high gleam, a game room, various cozy sitting areas, and 10 spacious guest rooms, each with feather duvet bed, refrigerator, air-conditioning, cable TV, Wi-Fi, and antiques.

Cooperstown also has a number of good, clean motels. Forty-five room **Lake Front Hotel** (10 Fair St., 607/547-9511, www.lakefrontmotelandrestaurant.com, $169-259 d summer, $85-189 d off-season) is in the heart of the village, overlooking Otsego Lake. An onsite restaurant serves breakfast, lunch, and dinner; a deck overlooks the lake.

Seven miles north of Cooperstown is **◖ Lake 'N Pines Motel** (7102 Rte. 80, 607/547-2790, www.lakenpinesmotel.com, $130-165 d summer, $55-95 off-season). As its name suggests, it is also on the lake. Here, guests can choose between motel rooms and cottages. On site are indoor and outdoor pools and a small beach with paddleboats. Breakfast is included in the room rate.

In addition to **Glimmerglass State Park's** campground (1527 Hwy. 31, 607/547-8662), camping options include **Cooperstown Beaver Valley Campground** (138 Towers Rd., Milford, 607/293-7324, www.beavervalleycampground.com), which offers cabin and tent camping, three beaver ponds (one with catch and release fishing), a pool, baseball field, and playground. **Cooperstown Shadow Brook Campground** (2149 Hwy. 31, 607/264-8431, www.cooperstowncamping.com) offers tent and RV sites as well as cabin lodging. There's also a heated pool. The commercial campgrounds have Wi-Fi and all the campgrounds are open May-October.

Food

High-ceilinged 🍷 **Doubleday Cafe** (93 Main St., 607/547-5468, Mon.-Thurs. 7am-9pm, Fri.-Sat. 7am-10pm, Sun. 7am-9pm, under $12) has a friendly small-town feel, with a counter bar to one side and lots of tables and chairs in back. The menu has a nice variety of sandwiches, salads, and simple entrées.

Otesaga Resort Hotel's **Hawkeye Bar & Grill** (60 Lake St., 607/544-2524, breakfast, lunch, and dinner, hours vary seasonally) is especially good for lunch in summer, when lakeside patio seating opens up. Sandwiches and soups are staple lunch fare; the dinner menu is more elaborate.

🍷 **Nicoletta's Italian Cafe** (96 Main St., 607/547-7499, www.nicolettasitaliancafe.com, daily 4pm-9:30pm, $16), housed in an airy, high-ceilinged, former storefront, is a local favorite. Specialties include tasty pasta dishes made from fresh, local ingredients and classics like veal piccata.

A variety of international dishes are offered at the lovely lakeside 🍷 **Blue Mingo Grill** (Sam Smith's Boatyard, 6098 Hwy. 80, 607/547-7496, www.bluemingogrill.com, daily 11am-10pm, hours vary seasonally, $19). Lunch dishes include salads, grilled fish, and pizzas, while the dinner menu changes weekly and can include anything from Thai dishes to fresh lobster.

GLIMMERGLASS STATE PARK

Glimmerglass State Park (1527 Hwy. 31, 607/547-8662, www.nysparks.com/parks/28, daily 8am-dusk, parking $6-8) occupies the northern end of Otsego Lake. Features of this peaceful green oasis include a swimming beach, plenty of hiking and biking trails, a playground, and a 43-site campground.

Grand neoclassical **Hyde Hall** (607/547-5098, www.hydehall.org, June-Oct. daily 10am-5pm, adults $10, seniors $8, children 6-17 $8) stands in the heart of the park. Once home to the Clarke family, the mansion had fallen into serious disrepair but has been undergoing restoration for several years. Admission includes a guided tour, offered on the hour beginning at 10am and ending at 4pm.

UTICA

If ever a city deserved its nickname, it's Utica. The "Second Chance City" is a smaller burg flecked with gems most travelers miss. Utica, though, is accustomed to having its potential overlooked. Located halfway along the Erie Canal corridor, it seems the city should have been—and should be—more important than it ever has been. Because it's also on the shallowest part of the Mohawk River, however, it's never been able to benefit from the robust commerce other canalside towns enjoyed. Still, Utica has been a stopover point for plenty of travelers, including Mark Twain, and an attractive home for many refugees arriving in the United States, a demographic trend that has made the city remarkably diverse. That diversity is reflected most of all in the city's culinary scene, which boasts everything from Bosnian to Cuban cuisine. In addition to fantastic food from far-flung lands, you'll also find a surprising amount of impressive art in Utica, primarily at Munson Williams Proctor Arts Institute.

Sights

Munson Williams Proctor Arts Institute (310 Genesee St., 315/797-0000, www.mwpai.org, Tues.-Sat. 10am-5pm, free) houses 20 galleries exhibiting American and European paintings and decorative objects from its 25,000-item collection, which spans genres and generations. Notable pieces include work by Dali, Picasso, and Pollock.

Stanley Center for the Arts (261 Genesee St., 315/724-1113, www.thestanley.org) was designed by Thomas Lamb, a 20th-century architect renowned for theaters and cinemas. The Stanley opened as a movie house in 1928 and is one of just three remaining "Lamb theaters" in the country (all three are in New York). Today, it hosts year-round performances of Broadway shows, Utica Symphony Orchestra concerts, and visiting musical and comedic acts.

FX Matt Brewing Company, also known as **Saranac Brewery** (830 Varick St.,

CAPITAL-SARATOGA

800/765-6288, www.saranac.com, tours daily, adults $5, must make reservation by phone), is a family-owned brewery offering tours and a tasting tavern; it also hosts numerous community events throughout the summer, including a concert series. Tour guides get rave reviews for being friendly and knowledgeable.

Accommodations and Food

The Pratt-Smith House (10497 Cosby Manor Rd., 315/732-8483, $75-90) is a Federal-era colonial brick home that was once a working farm. Today, it's a welcoming B&B whose owners are consistently commended by guests for their friendly warmth. Affordability and a generous breakfast make up for areas that are crowded with knickknacks and the mattresses that could use an update.

Rosemont Inn Bed and Breakfast (1423 Genesee St., 866/353-4907, www.rosemontinnbb.com, $109-189) is an Italianate Victorian home in a central downtown location, just a few minutes from both Stanley Center for the Arts and Munson Williams Proctor Arts Institute. All seven guest rooms have private baths and one has a working fireplace.

The Tailor and the Cook (94 Genesee St., 315/793-7444, www.thetailorandthecook.com, Wed.-Sat. 4pm-11pm, $25) is Utica's most celebrated farm-to-table restaurant. Two executive chefs share responsibility for the kitchen and seasonal menu changes. Many plates have hints of global influences, such as Jamaican Blue Crab and Scallion Dumpling and North African Chickpea Stew.

MADISON COUNTY

Madison County's small towns are sandwiched between larger cities, namely Utica and Cooperstown to the east and Syracuse to the west, which make them perfect stop-off points if you're in the area. The county, which is the geographical center of the state, isn't necessarily stocked with superlatives; its attractions tend to be more modest, asking only for quiet appreciation. The highlights included here form a near perfect triangle on the map, and together they make an interesting day trip.

Though the town that is home to **The National Abolition Hall of Fame and Museum** (5255 Pleasant Valley Rd., Peterboro, 315/684-3262, www.nationalabolitionhalloffameandmuseum.org, mid-May-mid-Sept. Sat.-Sun. 1pm-5pm, adults $3, children free) may seem sleepy today, that was hardly the case in the 1830s, when Peterboro was a hotbed of antislavery activism. The New York State Anti-Slavery Society held its inaugural meeting here in 1835 and the town had at least one safe home, that of Gerrit Smith, participating in the Underground Railroad network. The museum interprets this history and is the first such institution in the country to serve as a single place of honor for abolitionists.

The International Boxing Hall of Fame (1 Hall of Fame Dr., 315/697-7095, www.ibhof.com, Mon.-Fri. 9am-5pm, Sat.-Sun. 10am-4pm, adults $9.50, children $6.50) opened in 1989 with the goal of honoring the sport's heroes and showcasing prized memorabilia. Expect lots of photos, champion belts, and autographed mementos.

Named one of America's top 10 sculpture parks by National Geographic, **Stone Quarry Hill Art Park** (3883 Stone Quarry Rd., Cazenovia, 315/655-3196, www.stonequarryhillartpark.org, daily dawn-dusk, suggested donation $5 per car) is a 104-acre outdoor sculpture gallery featuring work by established and emerging artists. The park also offers hikers four miles of trails; maps are available at the hilltop kiosk.

ONEIDA

If the name of this small New York town between Utica and Syracuse sounds familiar, it probably is. Like the famous china and silver manufacturer, it took its name from the Native American Oneida tribe. The town's history is a curious one. Like many villages along the Erie Canal, Oneida owes its founding and initial flourishing to both the waterway and the railroad. By the late 19th century, the town had become the home of a utopian socialist commune called the Oneida Community, whose own manufacturing activities preceded those of the Oneida china and flatware empire. Today, the stories of these varied chapters in the town's history are told at historic parks, museums, and other sites of interest.

Sights

Old Erie Canal State Historic Park (315/637-6111, www.nysparks.com/parks/17) is a 36-mile section of the 363-mile long Old Erie Canal, straddling Oneida and Madison Counties. You can dip into the park at various points. To get there, take NYS Thruway exit 34 (Canastota); turn left on N.Peterboro St., then left on E. North Canal St. The **Erie Canalway Trail** (www.ptny.org/canalway), a multiuse national recreation trail paralleling the canal, also runs through the park. Several small, canal-themed museums can be found in the park, including **Chittenango Landing Canal Boat Museum** (7010 Lakeport Rd., Chittenango, 315/687-3801, www.clcbm.org, May-June and Sept.-Oct. Sat.-Sun. 11am-3pm, July-Aug. daily 11am-3pm, adults $6, seniors $5, children $3) and **Canastota Canal Town Museum** (122 Canal St., Canastota, 315/697-5002, www.canastota.com, May-June and Sept.-Oct. Tues.-Sat. noon-3pm, July-Aug. Tues.-Sat. 11am-3pm, adults $3, children 12 and under free). The former is dedicated to the watercraft that plied the canal, while the latter emphasizes just how profoundly the canal shaped the small towns along its banks through trade.

Cross Island Chapel (Pond off Sconondoa Rd.) is reputed to be the smallest church in the United States and was once the smallest church in the world before being ousted by a slightly smaller house of worship in Switzerland.

Though it's open to the public by appointment, it may be better appreciated as a photo op, since just two people can fit inside it at the same time. The church, which dates back only to 1989, is just shy of 29 square feet in size and can only be reached by boat, as it's in the middle of a pond.

Shako:wi Cultural Center (5 Territory Rd., 315/829-8801, Apr. 2-Nov. 30 Mon.-Sat. 9am-5pm, Dec.1-Apr. 1 Mon.-Fri. 9am-5pm, free) offers visitors the opportunity to learn about Oneida tribal history and culture through exhibits that were established and are managed by the Oneida nation. A shop with authentic, handmade crafts is also on site.

Accommodations and Food

It's amazing that the oddly-named, 93,000-square-foot, 19th-century **Oneida Community Mansion** (170 Kenwood Ave., 315/363-0745, www.oneidacommunity.org, $115-200) even functions as a B&B, given its national historic landmark status and its dual existence as a museum. The former home of the utopian experiment, the Oneida Community, this property sits on 33 acres of old-growth trees and gardens. Room rates include a tour of the mansion, as well as modern amenities like free Wi-Fi.

Turning Stone Resort (5218 Patrick Rd., Verona, 800/771-7711, www.turningstone.com, rates vary by accommodation type) is a massive complex with a variety of accommodation types (hotel rooms and suites and RV sites, among others), a dozen bars and restaurants, a casino, spa, and five golf courses, three of which are championship courses. It's like Vegas...but in central New York.

Information and Services

For information on the state parks mentioned in this chapter, visit the website of the **New York State Office of Parks, Recreation, and Historic Preservation** (www.nysparks.com). The major cities and counties also have their own tourist information offices and websites.

- **Albany Heritage Area Visitor Center** (25 Quackenbush Sq., Albany, 518/434-0405, www.albany.org)

- **The Saratoga County Chamber** (28 Clinton St., Saratoga Springs, 518/584-3255, www.saratoga.org)

- **Washington County Tourism** (383 Broadway, Fort Edward, www.washingtonnycounty.com)

- **Oneida County Tourism** (www.oneidacountytourism.com)

- **Madison County Tourism** (www.madisontourism.com)

- **Schenectady County Visitors Agency** (www.visitschenectady.com)

- **Fulton County** (www.44lakes.com)

- **Schoharie County** (www.upstatevacation.com)

Getting There and Around

If you want to reach the area by air, **Albany International Airport** (junction of I-87 and I-90, 518/242-2200, www.albanyairport.com) is the region's biggest and most central airport; however, the region is also easily reached by **trains** (Amtrak, 800/872-7245, www.amtrak.com) or **buses** (Trailways, 800/776-7548, www.trailwaysny.com) departing New York City. Once here, however, travelers will find that a car is the best way to get around and see the area's highlights. Major national car rental chains have rental outposts at the airport.

If arriving by car, visitors will find it's easy to reach the region's main cities and secondary towns, as major interstates, including I-87 and I-90, facilitate accessibility.

THE ADIRONDACKS

Nearly one-third of New York State is a big, blank space on the map. Most of it is contained within Adirondack Park, a six-million-acre refuge that includes vast, silent forests, thousands of gleaming lakes and ponds, hundreds of rugged smoke-blue peaks, and miles of rushing rivers and streams. During the region's short summers, vacationers flock here by the thousands to canoe, fish, camp, and hike.

Once the hunting grounds of the Iroquois and Algonquin, the Adirondacks were largely overlooked by early settlers. Military outposts went up along the shores of Lakes George and Champlain in the mid-1700s, but the rest of the region remained the haunt of hunters and trappers until well into the 1800s. In 1837, New York State commissioned a natural-history survey of the wilderness, led by geologist and botanist Ebenezer Emmons. Accompanying Emmons was artist Charles Cromwell Ingham, whose paintings of the Adirondacks astonished the general public. Few realized that so great a wilderness remained in the Northeast. Soon outdoor enthusiasts discovered the region. Most famous among them were the members of the Philosophers' Camp. Organized by William Stillman of Cambridge, Massachusetts, the camp included such eminent men as Ralph Waldo Emerson and Louis Agassiz, who came to hike, fish, canoe, botanize, talk, and write.

In 1879, William West Durant created an architectural camp style that combined the features of a log cabin with those of a Swiss chalet. Wealthy families such as the Vanderbilts and Rockefellers embraced the style and built luxurious "great camps" that resembled

© DREAMSTIME.COM

HIGHLIGHTS

◖ **Hyde Collection:** An important collection of Old Masters, including works by Rembrandt, El Greco, and Degas, is housed in this 1912 mansion styled as a Renaissance villa (page 297).

◖ **Fort Ticonderoga:** The French, British, and Americans all once held control of this now-meticulously restored fort, which counts a lock of Washington's hair among its objects on display (page 305).

◖ **Olympic Ski Jump Complex:** The Olympic ski jumps offer a gasp-worthy view of the 90- and 120-meter high jumps from an elevator-accessible sky deck, while the nearby freestyle aerial training center boasts a year-round training and competition site for free-

stylers who perfect their incredible feats using a 750,000-gallon landing pool in the summer (though winter showoffs must hit the 37-degree slope just right) (page 314).

◖ **Lake Placid Sliding Center:** Passenger rides are given on bobsleds year-round on the 1980 Olympic bobsled track in charming Lake Placid. Don't worry, professional drivers are included (page 314).

◖ **Hiking:** The **Adirondak Loj** is the trailhead for many stunning trails that ascend up the region's incomparable peaks. Its helpful information center will advise you in selecting the right trail before sending you on your way (page 314).

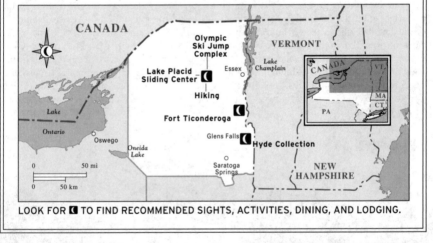

LOOK FOR ◖ TO FIND RECOMMENDED SIGHTS, ACTIVITIES, DINING, AND LODGING.

self-contained villages. Nearly a dozen of these great camps still stand, saved, in part, by recognition conferred upon them through National Historic Landmark status.

Today, the Adirondacks are an unusual mixture of public and private land. Forty-three percent of the park is Forest Preserve that belongs to the people of New York. Fifty-seven percent is privately owned by industries and individuals, and devoted primarily to forestry, agriculture, and recreation. Within Adirondack Park

live about 130,000 people in 103 towns and villages, many of which have populations of less than 1,000.

Contrary to popular belief, the Adirondacks are not an extension of the Appalachian Mountains, but rather are part of the vast Canadian Shield. Nearly twice as old as the Appalachians, the Adirondacks are composed of Precambrian igneous and metamorphic rock thrust upward about 10 million years ago. Atop the summits is a bluish, erosion-resistant

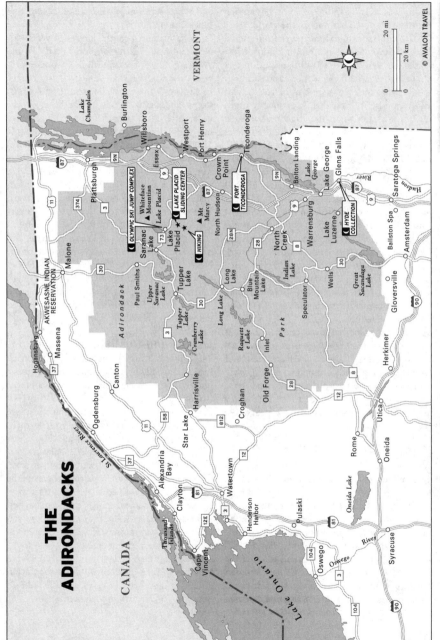

THE
ADIRONDACKS

© AVALON TRAVEL

bedrock that, at 1.2 million years old, is among the oldest exposed bedrock in the world.

Also contrary to popular perception, much of the Adirondacks is not mountainous. Most of the area lies between 1,000 and 2,000 feet above sea level, with the western and southern sections composed of gentle hills strewn with lakes, ponds, and streams. Most of the highest summits, known as the High Peaks, are in the northeastern section, around Lake Placid. Forty-two of the 46 High Peaks are over 4,000 feet; Mount Marcy, at 5,344 feet, is the highest.

Throughout the Adirondacks run 1,200 miles of rivers fed by an estimated 30,000 miles of brooks and streams. Most significant among them are the Hudson—whose highest source is Lake Tear of the Clouds on Mount Marcy—Raquette, Ausable, Sacandaga, Beaver, Oswegatchie, St. Regis, and Moose. The park also contains about 3,000 lakes and ponds, including the large and well-known Lake George and Lake Champlain. Between Lake Champlain and the mountains runs the long and fertile Champlain Valley.

Tourism, which has always been important here, is an increasingly vital part of the year-round economy. In the wake of the decline of factory, logging, and commercial fishing work that were the traditional economic mainstays here, more businesses in the tourism industry are looking for ways to extend the appeal of the region to all four seasons.

PLANNING YOUR TIME

A minimum of four or five days is necessary to explore the highlights of the Adirondacks. One to two weeks allow for more leisure and flexibility, especially if you want to do some hiking or canoeing. **Lake Placid** and **Saranac Lake** make good bases of operations. From these two scenic villages, located amidst the **High Peaks,** it's an easy drive to attractions and good hiking trails. Alternatively, to tack the Adirondacks onto the Capital-Saratoga region, you could base yourself in charming **Saratoga Springs**

and take overnight trips to **Lake George** and **Lake Champlain.**

I-87 runs north-south along the eastern side of the Adirondack region; local roads 28 and 28N cut across the mountains from east to west, offering access to some key attractions, including **Adirondack Museum** and **Great Camp Sagamore.** Roads 73 and 86 are in the northeastern Adirondacks, providing access to top sights, like **Lake Placid** and the **Olympic Training Center,** as well as **John Brown Farm** and **Adirondak Loj.** But travelers who stick only to roads and villages will get a one-sided sense of the place. While offering superb views, roads make it easy to underestimate the park's vast, haunting wildness. The only way to truly experience the Adirondacks is by canoe or on foot.

With the exception of ski resort areas and major towns such as Lake Placid, much of the North Country closes during the off-season, which begins in mid-fall and runs through mid-to-late spring. If traveling during that period, call ahead to make sure attractions, restaurants, and hotels are open.

Guides and Outfitters

The guide is a firmly entrenched Adirondack institution. Traditionally thought of as a crusty, plaid-jacketed man wise in the ways of the woods, he's been around since the mid-19th century, when naive visitors coming to explore the wilderness needed someone to help them find their way around and stay alive.

The Adirondack Guides' Association was formed in 1891 to establish a uniform pay scale. Today, hundreds of guides operate throughout the region. They're not as necessary as they once were, thanks to well-marked trails, detailed maps, and regional guidebooks, but they can still lead you to out-of-the-way spots. Many guides offer group trips, too; some also rent or sell outdoor gear.

For a complete list of guides, contact the **New York State Outdoor Guides Association** (1936 Saranac Ave., Lake Placid, NY 12946, 866/469-7642, www.nysoga.com).

© VISITADIRONDACKS.COM

the scenic Adirondacks

Lake George and Southeastern Adirondacks

Christened Lac du St. Sacrement in 1609 by Father Jogues, the first European to discover it, Lake George lies in a deep fault valley, the ends of which are blocked by glacial debris. Thirty-two magnificent miles long, the dark, spring-fed lake surrounds hundreds of islands. The busy tourist village of Lake George sprawls at the lake's southern end, but otherwise the shoreline is crowded with dense pine.

As part of a strategic water route connecting Canada with New York City, Lake George played an important role in both the French and Indian War and the American Revolution. Between 1690 and 1760, the French and British fought four major battles along the shores of Lake George and nearby Lake Champlain. Fort Ticonderoga, at the foot of Lake George overlooking Lake Champlain, and Fort William Henry, at the head of Lake George, date to that period. The taking of Fort Ticonderoga from the British in 1775 marked the Americans' first major military victory in the Revolutionary War.

Surrounding Lake George are the forested foothills of the Adirondacks. Their summits offer glorious views of the lake below and the higher peaks farther north. To the west gleam a smattering of smaller lakes, including Lake Luzerne, Schroon Lake, and Brandt Lake.

GLENS FALLS

Between Saratoga Springs and Lake George lies Glens Falls, a town of wide, empty downtown streets, dotted with handsome brick buildings. Nearby flows the Hudson River and a

ADIRONDACKS

LAKE GEORGE AND SOUTHEASTERN ADIRONDACKS

28N

87

22

BLUE RIDGE RD

North Hudson

9

9N

Schroon Lake

74

Ticonderoga

🌙 **FORT TICONDEROGA** ★

Lake Champlain

Schroon Lake

ROGERS ROCK

28

28N

Pottersville

Brant Lake

8

Hague

Silver Bay

Brant Lake

VERMONT

Chestertown

9

8

Tongue Mountain ▲

The Glen

28

Bolton Landing

Lake George

22

Warrensburg

87

9

Whitehall

4

9N

Prospect Mountain ▲

Lake George

9N

9L

Lake Luzerne

9

4

Hadley

Glens Falls

🌙 **HYDE COLLECTION**

Great Sacandaga Lake

Hudson River

87

9

9N

Saratoga Springs

0	10 mi
0	10 km

© AVALON TRAVEL

60-foot-high waterfall that was responsible for turning the town into an early industrial center. An Adirondacks **information booth** (between Exits 17 and 18 off northbound I-87, 518/792-2730) is located in Glens Falls.

◖ Hyde Collection

The main reason to stop in Glens Falls is to tour the first-class **Hyde Collection** (161 Warren St., 518/792-1761, www.hydecollection.org, Tues.-Sat. 10am-5pm, Sun. noon-5pm, adults $8, seniors and students $6, children under 12 free), housed in a 1912 American Renaissance mansion. Step inside and you'll find yourself surrounded by palm trees, balconies, tile floors, fine antiques, and an important collection of Old Masters, among them, Rembrandt, Rubens, El Greco, Botticelli, Tintoretto, Degas, Cézanne, van Gogh, and Picasso. American artists are also well represented, including Eakins, Homer, and Whistler.

The Hyde Collection was amassed by Louis Fiske Hyde and Charlotte Pruyn Hyde in the first half of the 20th century. Mrs. Hyde turned the family mansion into a museum in 1952, following her husband's death.

Chapman Historical Museum

Also worth a stop, especially for photography buffs, is **Chapman Historical Museum** (348 Glen St. 518/793-2826, www.chapmanmuseum.org, Tues.-Sat. 10am-4pm, Sun. noon-4pm, adults $5, seniors and students $4, children under 12 free). Housed in an a mid-19th century Victorian mansion, complete with several period rooms, the museum showcases an outstanding collection of photographs by Seneca Ray Stoddard. An artist, writer, cartographer, and surveyor, Stoddard wrote numerous early guidebooks to the Adirondacks and captured the region's majesty through his photographs.

LAKE GEORGE VILLAGE

Everything at Lake George, from the House of Frankenstein Wax Museum to Million Dollar Beach, seems to date to the 1950s.

Mom-and-pop motels, mini golf courses, and the Magic Forest with its giant Uncle Sam statue looming out front all cajole visitors back in time.

Lake George is basically a one-street town, with the majority of its souvenir shops and restaurants laid out along Canada Street (Route 9). Intersecting Canada Street at the lakefront, Beach Road leads to Fort William Henry and **Million Dollar Beach** (Beach Rd., vehicle fee: car $10, motorcycle $4), which is *much* smaller and tamer than its name implies. Along the way are docks where boats and water-sports equipment can be rented.

During summer, Lake George village is packed with tourists, most of them families. After Labor Day, the place shuts down abruptly and remains shuttered until Memorial Day of the following year.

Lake Excursions

Brave the hordes of tourists and take a cruise on Lake George. Though the boats are highly commercialized, they do take you out into deep, dark blue waters framed with moody forests and peaks.

Affiliated with Shoreline Restaurant, **Lake George Shoreline Cruises** (2 Kurosaka Ln., 518/668-4644, www.lakegeorgeshoreline.com, May-Oct.) offers day and evening cruises onboard two different boats. **Lake George Steamboat Cruises** (Steel Pier, 57 Beach Rd., 518/668-5777, www.lakegeorgesteamboat.com, May-Oct.) offers sightseeing, dinner, and entertainment cruises onboard three large boats, including a paddle wheeler.

Fort William Henry

In a small, hilly park, you'll find the largely unexcavated ruins of the original Fort William Henry, along with plaques explaining various aspects of the 1757 battle. The original fort was built in 1756 by British general William Johnson, the man responsible for naming the lake for King George III. The fort was attacked in 1757 by 1,600 French soldiers and 3,000 Native Americans under the command of General Montcalm. James Fenimore Cooper

To Schroon Lake

To Warrensburg, Schroon
Lake, and Bolton Landing

9N
9

**LAKE GEORGE
HISTORICAL MUSEUM**

87

AMHERST STREET

MONTCALM STREET

Prospect Mountain Hiking Trail

Shepard
Park

L a k e

G e o r g e

CANADA STREET

▼ **SHORELINE
RESTAURANT**

SMITH STREET

9L

BEACH ROAD

Million Dollar
Beach

MOHICAN STREET

FORT ★
WILLIAM
HENRY

LAKE GEORGE
BATTLEFIELD
PARK

**LAKE GEORGE
VILLAGE**

9N

Prospect
▲ Mountain

9L

STATE PARKWAY

SCALE NOT AVAILABLE

87

9N

To Lake
Luzerne

9

■ **ADIRONDACK
MOUNTAIN CLUB**

To Amusement Parks

© AVALON TRAVEL

based *The Last of the Mohicans* on the incident. Picnic tables throughout the park offer good lake views.

Nearby is **Fort William Henry Museum** (48 Canada St., 518/668-5471, www.fwhmuseum. com, May-Oct. daily 9am-6pm, adults $16.95, senior $13.95, children 5-12 $7.95, children under 5 free), a facsimile reconstruction of the fort. Featured are some French and Indian War artifacts and life-size dioramas and demonstrations of cannon and musket firings.

The fort museum does not present much that's original (and tours offer sensationalized accounts of the history); it's better to save your money for the considerably more authentic

Fort Ticonderoga, located at the northern end of Lake George.

Lake George Historical Association and Museum

Housed in the Old Court House, the **Lake George Historical Association and Museum** (290 Canada St., 518/668-5044, www.lakegeorgehistorical.org, hours vary seasonally, free) has three floors of exhibits on the history of Lake George. Of particular interest are the jail cells in the basement (circa 1845), an exhibit on lake shipwrecks, photos from the steamboat era, and an elaborate, doll-size wooden church carved by convicted murderer George Ouellet in 1881. After finishing his church, Ouellet sold it for a sizable sum, hired a new lawyer to appeal his conviction, and was acquitted.

Prospect Mountain

For a terrific view of Lake George and the southeastern Adirondacks, drive up **Prospect Mountain Veterans Memorial Highway** (formerly Prospect Mountain State Parkway), which intersects with Route 9 just south of the village. The 5.5-mile drive leading up the 2,030-foot mountain offers 100-mile views of five states. Park your car near the top and board one of the "viewmobiles" to travel to the mountain's crest.

An easy 1.6-mile hiking trail, marked with red blazes, also leads to the summit. To reach the trailhead from Lake George village, take Montcalm Street to Smith Street and turn south. The trail begins midway down the block, and follows the roadbed of an old cable railroad.

Amusement Parks

Lake George wouldn't be Lake George without its amusement parks. Five miles south of the village is the largest of them, **Great Escape & Splashwater Kingdom** (1172 Rte. 9, 518/792-3500, www.sixflags.com/greatEscape, late June-Labor Day daily, hours vary, adults $54.99, children under 48 inches $44.99, children under age 2 free), offering over 135 rides, shows, and attractions, including Steamin' Demon Loop Rollercoaster and the Sasquatch drop ride.

Three miles south of the village, **Magic Forest** (1912 Rte. 9, 518/668-2448, www.magicforestpark.com, late June-Labor Day daily 9:30am-5pm, adults $19.99, children under 12 and seniors $17.99) offers 20 rides for children and a handful for adults.

One mile south of the village, **Water Slide World** (2136 Rte. 9, at Rte. 91, 518/668-4407, www.waterslideworld.info, late June-Labor Day daily 10am-5pm, adults $31.95, children under 11 $28.95, seniors $15, toddlers 35-39" tall $12) includes a wave pool, water slides, bumper boats, and a lazy river.

Adirondack Mountain Club (ADK)

Also to the south of Lake George village, near the intersection of Route 9 and Route 9N, is an **information center** run by **Adirondack Mountain Club** (ADK, 814 Goggins Rd., off Rte. 9N west of I-87, 518/668-4447 or 800/395-8080, www.adk.org, Mon.-Sat. 8:30am-5pm), a nonprofit organization dedicated to broadening the public's appreciation of the Adirondack wilderness. Stop here for information on hiking trails and camping areas. The center also has a bookstore where you can buy maps and guidebooks or make a purchase from a limited but carefully chosen selection of gear. Experts are on hand to answer questions. Take Exit 21 to reach the center directly from I-87.

Hiking

Buck Mountain is on the southeastern shore of Lake George. A well-marked, 3.3-mile hiking trail leads to the summit and great views of Lake George, Lake Champlain, the Adirondacks, and Vermont's Green Mountains. To reach the trailhead, head east from the village to Route 9L. Turn left and continue for about seven miles until you see a turn for Pilot Knob and Kaatskill Bay. Follow this road about 3.5 miles to the trailhead, marked with a large sign and parking lot. The easy-to-moderate round-trip hike takes about four hours.

Accommodations and Camping

This area is best appreciated for the natural beauty of the lake and surroundings, so consider camping or look further up the lake for accommodations. If you prefer being in the heart of a town with tourist services, consider a chain, as the franchises are most likely to provide the expected level of quality. Dozens of small motels are located along Routes 9 and 9N, many of them classic Adirondack 1950s-style properties. Ask to see the room before committing; many are outdated or well worn from waterlogged families making themselves at home over the years. Value is questionable and the level of service and amenities often does not match the rates.

Six Flags Great Escape Lodge (89 Six

THE BIRTH OF THE PARK

In 1872, years after explorers had discovered the sources of the Nile and various rivers out West, a young surveyor named Verplanck Colvin finally traced the Hudson River to its mysterious source. Starting in the Champlain Valley, he and his party hiked from peak to peak until reaching Mount Marcy and what is now known as Lake Tear of the Clouds. "Far above the chilly water of Lake Avalanche," Colvin later reported to the state legislature, "at an elevation of 4,293 feet, is *Summit Water,* a minute unpretending tear of the clouds as it were–a lonely pool, shivering in the breezes of the mountains, and sending its limpid surplus through Feldspar Brook to the Opalescent River, the well-spring of the Hudson."

From that expedition on until 1900, Colvin surveyed the entire Adirondack region. Often financing his own expeditions, he sent back frequent reports to the state legislature, passionately arguing for the creation of a park to preserve the forest and its watershed.

Few listened at first, but as the century wore on, downstate New Yorkers began to worry about their water supply, and businesses worried about the buildup of silt in New York Harbor. Protecting the forests would help solve both problems and create a giant "pleasuring-grounds for the people." Largely because of the businessmen's influence, the idea took hold, and in 1885, the state passed an unprecedented bill establishing a 681,374-acre Adirondack Forest Preserve. This law, strengthened in 1892 and again in 1894, even went so far as to dictate that the preserve remain "forever wild," a phrase that has created considerable controversy ever since.

Flags Dr., 518/824-6060, www.sixflagsgreatescapelodge.com, $149-239) boasts the kid-friendly amenity of an indoor water park. The hotel's 200 reasonably priced rooms are clean and comfortable and offer a microwave and fridge. The attractive Adirondack-style lobby with its massive stone fireplace is a nice contrast to the area's largely motel-style offerings. The 1950s diner chain, Johnny Rockets, with dancing servers, cheese fries, and malteds, as well as several other restaurants, is on the property. This resort is one of a few that are open year-round. They offer Holiday in the Lodge packages, which include entrance to the theme park's ice-skating, sledding, live music, and holiday light festival.

For camping, visit the 68-site **Lake George Battleground State Campground** (2224 Rte. 9, 518/668-3348, reservations 800/456-2267) or the 251-site **Hearthstone Point** (3298 Lake Shore Dr., 518/668-5193, reservations 800/456-2267).

Food

A number of fast food and sandwich shops are located along Canada Street and Beach Road. Among them is **Garrison Koom Café** (220 Beach Rd., 518/668-5281, www.menumart.com/garrison, $6), serving burgers, sandwiches, and simple entrées. The café also claims to have more than 100 brands of beer, 16 of which are on tap.

For finer dining, try the airy ☾ **Shoreline Restaurant** (2 Kurosaka Ln., 518/668-4644, www.lakegeorgeshoreline.com/restaurant, Fri. 4pm-10pm, Sat.-Sun. 11am-10pm, $19), which looks out on a small marina. Menu selections range from fresh fish to chicken teriyaki. Sit on the deck and enjoy live entertainment in summer. Also overlooking the water is the big, boisterous **Boardwalk** (2 Lower Amherst St., 518/668-5324, www.lakegeorgeboardwalk.com, $22), offering burgers and sandwiches at lunch, and considerably more elaborate entrées at dinner.

LAKE LUZERNE

Take Route 9N out of Lake George village to reach Lake Luzerne, a quieter resort community about 10 miles away. The village, bounded by two rivers, consists of a few small streets crowded with Victorian homes. Lake Luzerne traditionally has been known for its dude ranches, which is why you'll notice signs pointing to Big Hat Country along the way. Though the dude-ranch business is not what it once was, the country's oldest weekly rodeo still takes place weekend nights in summer at **Painted Pony Ranch** (703 Howe Rd., 518/696-2421, www.paintedponyrodeo.com).

The free **Lake Luzerne Chamber Music Festival** (203 Lake Tour Rd., 518/696-2771), featuring members of the Philadelphia Orchestra, takes place on Monday nights during the summer at the Luzerne Music Center.

Water Sports

The Hudson River flows along the east side of town, where bubbling Rockwell Falls rushes downstream through a small park. At the western end, the Sacandaga River attracts white-water rafters and canoeists. Rental equipment and guided white-water raft trips down Sacandaga's Class II and III waters are offered by **Wild Waters Outdoor Center** (518/494-4984, www.wildwaters.net) in nearby Warrensburg.

Hiking

Although **Hadley Mountain** is just under 2,700 feet high, it affords magnificent views from its summit. To the north loom the High Peaks, to the south are the Catskills and Great Sacandaga Lake, and to the east are Lake George and the Green Mountains. The Adirondack Mountain Club considers the four-mile round-trip hike to the summit easy-to-moderate in difficulty. The hike should take about three hours.

To reach the trailhead, take Route 9N north of Lake Luzerne to Hadley and head north on Stony Creek Road. Continue three miles to Hadley Hill Road and turn left. Proceed slightly over 4 miles to Tower Road, turn right, and continue another 1.5 miles to the trailhead on the left, marked with a sign.

Accommodations and Camping

For camping, visit the 174-site **Luzerne State Campground at Fourth Lake** (Rte. 9N south

of the village, 518/696-2031, reservations 800/456-2267).

The gracious **Lamplight Inn B&B** (231 Lake Ave., 518/696-5294, www.lamplightinn.com, $175-250 summer, about a third less other seasons) is an award-winning 1890 inn featuring eight bedrooms, most with fireplaces. A carriage house and cottage on the property are also available for rental.

Roaring Brook Ranch and Tennis Resort (Luzerne Rd./Rte. 9, 518/668-5767, www.roaringbrookranch.com; inclusive rates $85-122 per person, including riding, use of all facilities, breakfast, and dinner; family rates available), located between Lake George and Lake Luzerne, has been operating one of the oldest and best dude ranches in the area since 1945. Spread out over 500 acres, the well-kept resort includes simple but comfortable rooms, nearly 30 horses, three lighted tennis courts, and swimming pools, saunas, and fitness rooms.

BOLTON LANDING

Back along the shores of Lake George, about 10 miles north of Lake George village, is Bolton Landing, another congested tourist town. Traffic here is bumper to bumper during summer.

For many visitors, Bolton Landing's main attractions are its gift shops, most along Main Street, which are a step up in class from Lake George village offerings. **Bolton Historical Museum** (4924 Main St., 518/644-9960, July 4-Labor Day daily 9am-4pm and 7pm-9pm, spring and fall Sat.-Sun. 9am-4pm, free), housed in a former Catholic church, includes a collection of photographs by Seneca Ray Stoddard and an exhibit on sculptor David Smith, who once lived in the area.

Sagamore Resort (110 Sagamore Rd., 518/644-9400, www.thesagamore.com), isolated on its own private island at one end of the village, opened in 1883 and is now listed on the National Register of Historic Places. The columned, gabled hotel remains a luxurious year-round resort. Features include six excellent restaurants, a full-service spa, tennis courts, playground, nearby golf course, and a sandy beach with great views of Lake George. **Cruises** on the lake are offered by *The Morgan,* a replica of a 19th-century touring boat (sightseeing cruise free for guests, $30 for non-guests).

The Sembrich

Marcella Sembrich, a soprano who sang with the Metropolitan Opera, summered in Bolton Landing from 1921 to 1935. In those days, the village was a favorite resort of opera stars, and Sembrich brought several students with her each year. Today, the diva's former studio **The Sembrich** (4800 Lake Shore Dr., 518/644-2431, www.thesembrich.org, June 15-Sept. 15 daily 10am-12:30pm and 2pm-5pm, free, donations accepted) houses her sizable collection of music, along with her costumes, furniture, and other memorabilia.

Accommodations and Food

Across the street from the Sembrich estate is **Ballymore Guest Cabin at Hilltop Cottage** (4825 Lake Shore Dr., 518/644-2492, www. hilltopcottage.com, $100/night, May 1-Oct. 31 only). Marcella Sembrich's opera students stayed in the cottage back in the days when she was teaching here.

The **Ⓒ Sagamore Resort** (110 Sagamore Rd., 518/644-9400, www.thesagamore.com, $229-335 off-season, $389-659 summer) offers 100 luxurious rooms and suites in the historic main hotel and 240 private lodge rooms. The Sagamore Resort has a variety of **restaurants** (110 Sagamore Rd., 518/644-9400, www.thesagamore.com, hours vary). **Mr. Brown's Pub** ($9-18) serves sandwiches and salads; the **Pavilion** has a similarly casual menu, with meals served lakeside. **Club Grill Steakhouse** ($18-36) serves hamburgers and basic fare at lunch and steaks at dinner. **La Bella Vita** specializes in innovative Italian cuisine.

The casual **Algonquin Restaurant** (Lake Shore Dr., 518/644-9442, www.thealgonquin. com, daily, $22), built over the water, is a local favorite for lunch and dinner. On the menu is everything from burgers to fresh fish.

NORTHERN LAKE GEORGE

Route 9N continues north of Bolton Landing into much wilder countryside. Tourist centers are left behind as you veer away from the lakeshore, past the Tongue Mountain Range, and then return to it once again, passing the isolated resort communities of Sabbath Day Point, Silver Bay, and Hague.

Scenic Route 8 heads west out of Hague to Brant Lake, about 10 miles away. En route, lookouts offer great views of the High Peaks. In the fall, the surrounding Dixon Forest turns vivid hues of red, yellow, and orange. Mohawk legend describes this as the land of Broken Wing, a crippled brave who saved his village and is remembered every autumn by the turning of the leaves.

About two miles north of Hague on Route 9N are **Indian Kettles,** shallow glacial potholes 1-3 feet in diameter said to have been used for cooking by Native Americans.

Rogers Rock State Park

Just north of Indian Kettles, **Rogers Rock State Park** (Rte. 9N, 518/585-6746, camping reservations 800/465-2267, $6-8 parking) offers a 332-site campground, beach, and bathhouse, along with a 2.5-mile hiking trail that leads up 500 feet to Rogers Slide. At first, the trail winds mostly uphill and northerly, but then it flattens out to run along a ledge and open expanse. Keeping to the right at a fork just past the ledge will bring you to cliffs overlooking Lake George.

Accommodations and Camping

Forty-eight of the islands dotting Lake George are available for camping, though you'll need a boat to pack in and out. The gorgeous setting, absolute privacy, and crystal clear swimming make these an obvious draw. For more information, contact the **Department of Environmental Conservation** (518/623-1200, www.dec.ny.gov/outdoor/camping.html). Alternately, you can be spontaneous and take a quick sightseeing cruise on the **Sagamore boat** (110 Sagamore Rd., 518/644-9400, www. thesagamore.com, $30 for non-guests, daily)

THE SUNKEN TREASURE OF LAKE GEORGE

Beneath the waters of Lake George lie approximately 300 shipwrecked vessels in three "submerged heritage preserves" that are open to the public. Two of the three sites date to the mid-18th century French and Indian War. The third submerged heritage preserve is an underwater classroom for SCUBA divers who want to learn more about the lake's ecology and these sunken treasures.

Among the wrecks are bateaux, flat-bottom boats that were part of a large fleet deliberately scuttled by the British and the American colonists in 1758 to protect the craft from the French and Native Americans. The British returned to the lake in 1759 and raised close to 200 of the ships. No one suspected the remaining bateaux still existed until two teenage div-

ers discovered them in 1960. That same year, three of the boats were raised from the lake; one was put on exhibit at the Adirondack Museum, which has the second largest watercraft collection in the country.

Yet another ship was discovered in 1990, a 52-foot radeau (seven-sided battleship) named the *Land Tortoise*. Also part of the scuttled fleet, this fragile vessel is North America's oldest intact warship. It is also one of the country's few shipwrecks designated as a National Historic Landmark. Divers can only approach this wreck with advance registration.

To learn more about Lake George's Shipwreck Preserves, contact the **Department of Environmental Conservation** (518/897-1276, www.dec.ny.gov/outdoor/7830.html).

to handpick which island from the multitude best suits your needs.

One of the last of the old lakeside hotels that once flourished in this region is **Northern Lake George Resort** (Rte. 9N, Silver Bay, 518/543-6528, www.northernlakegeorge.com, $99-145). It was built in 1896 and originally called Hotel Uncas. The resort has been altered over the years but still features an old-fashioned rustic lobby complete with stone fireplace and high ceilings. Accommodation options include lakeside villas and motel rooms.

SCHROON LAKE AND VICINITY

Schroon Lake, a quiet resort community with a laid-back Main Street and good-size public beach, is situated west of Lake George. During the summer, one-hour narrated cruises of the lake are offered by **Schroon Lake Boat Tours** (518/532-7675). The area is also home to the **Seagle Music Colony** (999 Charley Hill Rd., 518/532-7875, www.seaglecolony.com), a music retreat founded by concert baritone Oscar Seagle in 1915. The colony stages opera concerts and musical theater July-early August.

Natural Stone Bridge and Caves

At the lake's southern end, near Pottersville, lies **Natural Stone Bridge and Caves** (535 Stone Bridge Rd., off Rte. 9, 518/494-2283, www.stonebridgeandcaves.com, hours vary seasonally, adults $12.98, children 5-12 $8.50). Formed by the Ausable River, this geological park features odd-shaped rock formations, waterfalls, and potholes large enough to park a truck in.

Hiking Pharaoh Mountain

To the east of Schroon Lake rises Pharaoh Mountain, surrounded by the Pharaoh Lake Wilderness Area. The splendid views from the mountaintop, covered with open rock, take in nearby ponds and craggy hills, as well as the more distant High Peaks. The nine-mile round-trip hike is of moderate difficulty and takes 4-5 hours.

To reach the trailhead, head north of Schroon Lake on Route 9 about two miles. Turn right onto Alder Meadow Road and continue 2.2 miles to a fork. Bear left on Crane Pond Road and travel 1.4 miles to a parking lot. Continue on the road on foot 1.9 miles to Crane Pond, where the trailhead begins at the end of another parking lot (parking is not permitted here).

Detour to North Hudson

On the edge of the High Peaks region about seven miles north of Schroon Lake village is North Hudson, a tiny mountain hamlet surrounded by ponds and wilderness; its year-round population is about 240. The place is well worth a detour for the magnificent views along the way.

Blue Ridge Road (Route 2) heads west out of North Hudson to skirt the southern edge of the High Peaks. The route runs alongside the Branch, which flows between Elk Lake and Schroon River; about three miles from the village cascade the lovely **Blue Ridge waterfalls.**

Accommodations and Food

Schroon Lake Bed and Breakfast (Rte. 9, 518/532-7042, www.schroonbb.com, $135-160) offers five comfortable guest rooms furnished with antiques. A breezy front porch provides good views of the lake and Adirondacks.

Tucked into the mountains north of North

Hudson is ultra-secluded ◖ **Elk Lake Lodge** (1106 Elk Lake Rd., 518/532-7616, www. elklakelodge.com, $130-210 per person, includes all meals). One of the finest rustic lodges in the Adirondacks, Elk Lake Lodge is situated on its own private lake surrounded by a 12,000-acre preserve. The main lodge, built in 1904, offers six rooms with private baths, as does the more modern Emerson Lodge. Eight cottages sit on the lakefront.

One of the finest restaurants in the area, specializing in innovative American dishes, is the rambling Civil War-era ◖ **Friend's Lake Inn** (Friends Lake Rd., 518/494-4751, www.friendslake.com, $28), about seven miles south of Schroon Lake in historic Chestertown. The wine list alone runs about 25 pages long. A full menu of New American fare is offered at dinner only, though in summer, a bar and light lunch menu are also available. Upstairs and out back are 17 lovely guest rooms ($359-550, including breakfast and dinner; $319-510 breakfast only), all with queen-size beds and private baths. Many rooms also have whirlpool tubs, and two have fireplaces.

Champlain Valley

In 1609, 11 years before the Pilgrims landed in Massachusetts, French explorer Samuel de Champlain "discovered" the long, thin, sparkling blue lake that now bears his name. Shortly after his arrival, he encountered and killed two Iroquois, establishing the tenor of European-Native American relations for centuries to come.

One hundred and ten miles long and 400 feet deep in spots, Lake Champlain is the largest freshwater lake in the United States after the Great Lakes. Encompassing 490 square miles, it stretches from New York north into Canada and east into Vermont. Even bigger than the lake itself is the basin in which it sits. On the New York side, that basin extends as far west as the Adirondack Mountains and as

far south as Hudson Falls. About 25 percent of Adirondack Park lies within the Champlain Valley.

Compared to Lake George, the shores of Lake Champlain appear sparsely forested and surprisingly undeveloped. The countryside becomes especially magnificent north of Port Henry, where the raw, jagged High Peaks of the Adirondacks rise to one side and the moody, rounder peaks of Vermont's Green Mountains to the other.

Throughout the 19th and much of the 20th centuries, Lake Champlain supported numerous iron-ore and manufacturing plants, most of them along the shore. Many of these have closed in recent years, which helps account for the region's current high unemployment rate.

CHAMPLAIN VALLEY

To Canada↗
Plattsburgh
Ausable Chasm
Lake Champlain
Hurricane Mountain
Elizabethtown
ADIRONDACK HISTORY CENTER MUSEUM
Willsboro
Essex
Westport
VERMONT
Port Henry
CROWN POINT HISTORIC SITE
North Hudson
Crown Point
CORDUROY RD
Ironville
FORT TICONDEROGA
Schroon Lake
Ticonderoga
Lake George
© AVALON TRAVEL
0   10 mi
0   10 km

TICONDEROGA

Ticonderoga, the town and the fort, is sandwiched in the two miles between Lake George and Lake Champlain. The town sits at the foot of Lake George; the fort overlooks Lake Champlain.

The Town

Sprawling, scruffy Ticonderoga centers around a historic downtown containing several interesting buildings. Among them is **Ticonderoga Heritage Museum** (Montcalm St. at Bicentennial Park, 518/585-2696, www.ticonderogaheritagemuseum.org, Memorial Day-Columbus Day, hours vary seasonally), which houses displays on the area's industrial history. Traditionally, Ticonderoga has been known for its pencil- and paper-making plants. The first commercial pencils, which bore the name "Ticonderoga," were produced in the area in 1840. The industry has not entirely disappeared; International Paper still operates in town.

◖ Fort Ticonderoga

One of the Adirondacks' most popular visitor attractions, **Fort Ticonderoga** (100 Fort Ti Rd., 518/585-2821, www.fortticonderoga. org, mid-May-mid-Oct. daily 9:30am-5pm, hours vary off-season, adults $17.50, seniors $14, children 5-12 $8, children under 4 free), sits within a shade-filled park. Originally built by the French in 1755, the fort bore the nickname "Key to a Continent." Strategically located along the Canada-New York waterway, Ticonderoga was attacked six times during the French and Indian and Revolutionary Wars. Three times it held successfully, and three times it fell. Control changed hands among the French, British, and Americans.

Inside the fort are meticulously restored barracks, kitchens, stables, cannons, and artifacts from both wars. Among the more unusual items on display are a lock of George Washington's hair, a pocket watch once owned by Ethan Allen, and a rum horn given to General Schuyler by Paul Revere. Numerous special events are staged daily throughout the

Away from the shore, the valley opens into rich farmland. Red barns, silver silos, and a patchwork of green fields spread out over one gentle slope after another. Dairy farming is especially big business.

Pick up brochures and maps at **Lake Champlain Visitors Center** (814 Bridge Rd., 518/597-4649, www.lakechamplainregion. com, Mon.-Fri. 9am-4pm), which is near the Lake Champlain Bridge, which connects New York with Vermont.

summer, including parades, cannon firings, and fife-and-drum musters.

America's Fort Cafe (518/585-2821, $10), on-site in the Log House Visitors' Center, serves reasonably priced soups, salads, and sandwiches and has great views of Lake Champlain and Vermont's Green Mountains.

Fort Ticonderoga Ferry

Continue east past the fort on Route 74 to reach a public boat ramp and dock for the **Fort Ticonderoga Ferry** (4831 Rte. 74, 802/897-7999, www.forttiferry.com, $9 per car with up to four passengers one-way, $16 round-trip; $2 per bicycle and rider; $1 per pedestrian), in operation in one form or another since the mid-1700s. From May to October, the flatbed ferry crosses whenever there's traffic to Shoreham, Vermont. The low-key journey only takes a few minutes.

CROWN POINT

About eight miles north of Ticonderoga is the village of Crown Point, not to be confused with the Crown Point Historic Site a few miles farther north. The village of Crown Point was once known for its iron industry. The remains of two forts are at the historic site.

Ironville

Hard as it is to believe today, the quiet, near-deserted area just west of Crown Point was once a major industrial center filled with dirty, clanking machinery. A rich bed of iron ore was discovered here in the early 1800s, and throughout that century, the region teemed with mines, forges, and railroads. The high-quality ore attracted the U.S. Navy, intent on securing iron to build its first iron-clad warship, the Civil War-era *Monitor.*

Crown Point's industrial activity centered around the company town of Ironville, now a village so small it's all but disappeared. In its heyday, Ironville boasted a company store, company housing, and company script. Today, it's an exceptionally lovely hamlet with a strong New England feel.

Penfield Homestead Museum (703 Creek Rd., 518/597-3804, www.penfieldmuseum.org, June-Oct. Sat.-Sun. 11am-4pm, suggested donation $5), an 1828 Federal-style building, was once home to industrialist Allen Penfield, the first man to use electricity for industrial purposes (in 1831). Exhibits tell the story of Penfield's inventions and the area's industrial past. A collection of ancient machinery slumbers out back.

To reach Ironville from Ticonderoga, take Route 74 to Corduroy Road. From Crown Point, take Route 47 west, which becomes Ironville Road and then Corduroy Road.

Crown Point State Historic Site

A pudgy spit of land juts into Lake Champlain north of Crown Point. Flat and windswept, with sweeping views of the north, the point once provided an ideal lookout spot. The French built Fort St. Frederic here in 1734, only to be conquered by the British in 1759, who in turn built Fort Crown Point.

The remains of both forts still stand near a **visitors' center** (21 Grandview Dr., 518/597-4666, mid-May-Columbus Day Thurs.-Mon. 9:30am-5pm, adults $4, seniors and students $3, children under 12 free) that provides historical background. Much of the area has not been fully excavated, but it has a lonely and haunting appeal.

PORT HENRY

Port Henry, a large town of red-brick buildings spread over several steep hills, is on the mainland just north of Crown Point Historic Site. Like Crown Point, Port Henry was once known for its iron industry, which peaked here during World War II. A giant 18-million-ton mountain of ore tailings that's visible for miles around is just west of town.

"Welcome to the Home of the Champ" reads the sign at the town's entrance. A cheerful green serpent with a zigzagging tail stands nearby. **The Champ** is a legendary monster who is purported to live in the depths of Lake Champlain. Stories about him have circulated for hundreds of years, first among the Iroquois and later among explorers and settlers. In

THE ADIRONDACK ECOSYSTEM

The Adirondack forest supports over 70 different species of trees, most of which are in the spruce and fir, or beech, birch, and maple families. White pines grow at the park's lowest elevations in the Champlain Valley, while spruce grows above 2,500 feet. In between thrive spruce swamps and hardwood forests.

Woodland wildflowers such as dewdrops and lily-of-the-valley flourish in the lower Adirondacks, while bright specks of alpine flora, mosses, lichens, and other hardy plants grow on the peaks. Several good guides to the park's flora and fauna are published by the Adirondack Mountain Club.

As for mammals, the Adirondacks are home to 53 species, including raccoon, porcupine, weasel, mink, otter, bobcat, fox, coyote, white-tailed deer, and black bear, as well as the elusive moose and lynx, which were reintroduced into the forest in the 1990s.

Birdlife in the park ranges from the very small (chickadees and nuthatches) to the very large (grouse and osprey). More than 200 species have been spotted, including hawks, kingbirds, peregrine falcons, and bald eagles. One of the most characteristic sounds of the Adirondacks is the haunting call of the loon.

Eighty-six species of fish swim in Adirondack waters, including trout, salmon, northern pike, and small- and large-mouth bass. The region also supports 35 species of reptiles and amphibians. Pesky blackflies thrive in the mountains in late May-June, and mosquitoes are plentiful throughout the summer.

1609, Samuel de Champlain reported seeing the 20-foot-long creature in the lake. Since then, there have been over 300 reported sightings of the Champ, many near Port Henry. Although there is no concrete proof that the Champ exists, the legislatures of both New York and Vermont have passed resolutions encouraging scientific inquiry into the depths of the lake.

WESTPORT

Lying on a natural terrace above a deep bay, the tidy Victorian village of Westport has been a favorite stopping-off place since steamship days, when families traveling north on Lake Champlain debarked here to catch stagecoaches for points farther west. Later, Westport became a destination in its own right, as evidenced by the elegant homes along Route 22. Today, Westport remains one of the few villages in the Adirondacks that's accessible by rail; Amtrak travels through here on its way between New York and Montréal.

Westport is known for its historic inns and **Depot Theater** (6705 Main St., 518/962-4449, www.depottheatre.org), which presents professional summer stock in a restored 19th-century railway station. A busy marina, where boats can be rented, and a public beach are on the lakeshore. A variety of shops border Main Street, including **Westport Trading Company** (6521 Main St., 518/962-4801), which sells the work of more than 100 area artists and artisans.

Accommodations

The clapboard **Westport Hotel** (6691 Main St., 518/962-4501, www.thewestporthotel.com, $45-130) dates to 1876, the same year that the railroad came to town. Inside are 10 guest rooms nicely outfitted in early Americana; outside is an inviting wraparound porch.

The stately 1855 **Inn in Westport** (1234 Stevenson Rd., 518/335-1966, www.innwestport.com, $89-176, with breakfast), situated across the street from the town library, features 11 spacious guest rooms with period furnishings, each named after a famous writer. A sitting room with a fireplace, a bookstore styled like a personal library, and an outdoor deck are common areas enjoyed by guests.

The fine Dutch colonial **All Tucked Inn** (53 S. Main St., 518/962-4400, www.alltuckedinn.com, $80-160), set back on a lawn behind a white picket fence, offers nine guest rooms and a glass-enclosed porch that overlooks the lake. Three of the rooms have fireplaces.

Food

For casual dining at the marina, try **The Galley** (20 Washington St., 518/962-4899, www.westportmarina.com/galley, $18), which offers pasta, fish, and burgers. Live bands play on weekend nights in the summer. The **Westport Hotel** (6691 Main St., 518/962-4501, www.thewestporthotel.com, Mon.-Fri. lunch and dinner, Sat.-Sun. breakfast, lunch, and dinner, $24) runs a tavern whose walls were made from wooden siding reclaimed from an area barn. The stone bar and cozy fireplace also contribute to the authentic Adirondack ambience.

ESSEX

The loveliest village along the Lake Champlain shore is Essex. Filled with trim, white pre-Civil War buildings, the entire village is on the National Register of Historic Places. The Adirondacks' dramatic High Peaks rise to the west; to the east sparkle the blue waters of the lake, offset by the dusk-blue mountains of Vermont.

Essex, founded in 1765, was one of the earliest European settlements on Lake Champlain. The community was completely destroyed during the American Revolution but soon rose again to become a prosperous shipbuilding center and lake port. By 1850, Essex was one of the largest and busiest towns on the lake, with a population of 2,351.

Then came the Civil War, the opening of the West, and the building of the railroads, all of which drew commerce away from Lake Champlain. Essex's economy suffered and its population dwindled. There was little money for building; standing structures had to suffice. And so it remains today.

Essex centers around two parallel streets, Main and Elm, both just two blocks long. Excellent examples of Federal, Greek Revival, and Victorian architecture abound, while a park and small marina stretch along the waterfront.

Lake Champlain Ferries (802/864-9804, www.ferries.com, car and driver $9.50, cyclists $4.75, adult pedestrians $3.75, seniors $3.20, and children $1.50; all prices quoted are one-way) dock at the northern end of the village, crossing between Essex and Charlotte, Vermont. The ride takes 20 minutes one-way.

Accommodations and Food

At the heart of Essex sits the 200+-year-old **Essex Inn** (2297 Main St., 518/963-4400, www.essexinnessex.com, $195-395, with full breakfast), which was fully renovated in 2010 and has nine guest rooms. Breakfast and dinner (average dinner entrée $14) are served outside in warm weather.

ELIZABETHTOWN

Elizabethtown, the Essex County seat, is about 10 miles west of Westport and Lake Champlain. Settled in 1791 by pioneers from Vermont, Elizabethtown was at first known for its lumber mills and later for its resort hotels.

Essex County Court House

Essex County Court House (Court. St./Rte. 9N), where the body of abolitionist John Brown lay in state on the way to burial in nearby North Elba, is in the town's center. Brown's wife and other members of the funeral entourage spent the night at the town's Deer's Head Inn while four young men from the village stood guard over the body. Today, the courthouse features a mural of Brown speaking in his own defense at his 1859 trial in West Virginia. Another mural depicts Samuel de Champlain firing his arquebus at the Iroquois.

Adirondack History Center Museum

Housed in a big old schoolhouse on the edge of town, the laid-back **Adirondack History Center Museum** (7590 Court St., 518/873-6466, www.adkhistorycenter.org, late-May-mid-Oct. daily 10am-5pm, adults $5, seniors $4, children 6-16 $2, children under 6 free) corrals an enormous hodgepodge of exhibits. A recreated log-cabin kitchen and artifacts from an iron mine take up one floor; on another is an exhibit on the Iroquois and displays about the lumbering industry. A light-and-sound show offers some perspective on the French and Indian War, while Adirondack guide boats, early farm implements, antique bobsleds, and a roomful of dolls tell stories of everyday Adirondack life.

Hiking

On the north side of Route 9N, 6.8 miles west of Elizabethtown and 1.6 miles past Hurricane Road, a small parking area and sign point the way to **Hurricane Mountain.** The red-marked trail passes through a pretty coniferous forest before heading up a ridge to the rocky summit pass. Superb views of Jay Range, the Green Mountains, Mount Marcy, and Whiteface Mountain await at the top. The Adirondack Mountain Club lists the moderate-to-difficult hike as 5.3 miles round-trip, averaging about 4.5 hours.

KEENE

Route 9N leads northwest from Elizabethtown to Keene, the "Town of High Peaks." Completely surrounded by jagged mountaintops, Keene's main street is lined with white frame houses, white picket fences, and tourist-oriented shops. Most noticeable among them is **North Country Taxidermy and Trading Post** (Main St./Rte. 73, 518/576-4318), with stuffed bears and wolves out front. The shop stocks a wide array of North Country souvenirs, including antlers, stuffed birds, mounted heads, leather goods, and bearskin rugs. **Adirondack Alpine Adventures** (518/576-9881, www.alpineadven.com) offers rock- and ice-climbing guide service and instruction in the area, as well as backcountry ski trips.

Route 73 climbs west out of Keene to Lake Placid. For much of the way, the route follows the riverbed of the wide Cascade Brook. En route you'll pass two sparkling lakes ringed with trees.

Accommodations

Keene Valley Lodge (Rte. 73, Keene Valley, 518/576-2003, www.keenevalleylodge.com, $80-225), housed in a lovely Italianate building, is a B&B offering a variety of rooms, some of which share baths; others are suites. Guest rooms are furnished with antiques. Common areas include a den with fireplace and the inn's wraparound porch. Another excellent option is **The Snow Goose Bed & Breakfast** (1433 Rte. 73, 518/576-9460, www.thesnowgoose.com, $115-140), a comfortable B&B with three rooms. The property is set on 13 acres, and hiking trails begin practically just outside the front door.

Food

A Keene Valley landmark, **Noon Mark Diner** (Main St./Rte. 73, 518/576-4499) is the place to go for homemade fruit pies, as well as homemade donuts, soups, and bread. Chili, burgers, and simple dinners are also on the menu. Another popular spot is **Lisa G's** (6125 Sentinel Rd., 518/523-2093, www.lisags.com, daily lunch and dinner, $17), a friendly place serving "comfort food with a twist."

NORTH TO AUSABLE CHASM

Continuing north of Essex on Route 22, you'll hug the lakeshore for a few glorious miles before heading inland to **Willsboro,** which is on the Bouquet River. Willsboro is a favorite spot among anglers thanks to its fish ladder at the Willsboro Dam. The ladder, off Route 22, allows landlocked salmon to ascend the river to spawning grounds farther upstream; you can watch the action from a viewing window.

Continue another 13 miles north and you'll bump into **Ausable Chasm** (2144 Rte. 9, 518/834-7454, www.ausablechasm.com, spring, fall, and winter daily 9am-4pm, summer daily 9am-5pm, adults $16.95, children 5-12 $9.95, children under 5 free). Carved out by the Ausable River over the past 500 million years, this massive stone gorge stretches out over 1.5 miles. It is 20-50 feet wide, 100-200 feet deep, and is filled with odd rock formations, caves, rapids, and waterfalls. After the serene back roads and

FOREVER WILD

During the past 100 years, numerous land purchases by the state have increased the Adirondack Forest Preserve from its original 681,374 acres to its present size. The park's Blue Line—a term derived from the color ink used in 1884 to delineate the park's boundaries on a map—now encompasses nearly six million acres.

With this growth has come conflict, exacerbated by increased tourism and a boom in second homes. The conflict has pitted conservationists concerned about the park's ecological future against those advocating varying forms of economic development.

The conflict reached one early crisis point in the late 1960s, when the building of I-87 opened up the region to yet more visitors. As a result, Governor Nelson Rockefeller appointed a state commission to study the future of the park in 1968. Among the commission's proposals was the establishment of an Adirondack Park Agency (APA) to encourage wise land-use planning.

Duly established in 1971, the APA has since instituted zoning laws for both the park's state *and* private lands. This has infuriated many residents who feel that the state has no right to tell them what they can or cannot do with private property. Many also feel that zoning laws, along with the original "forever wild" clause, are inhibiting economic growth in an area already suffering from out-migration and severe unemployment.

For conservationists, of course, there is no real debate. In a world of ever-decreasing blank spots on the map, the park must be preserved.

---

peaceful vistas of Lake Champlain, this place comes as a shock.

Ausable Chasm is one of the oldest tourist attractions in the United States, opened in 1870. Count on dozens of tour buses crowding its parking lot. A 0.75-mile trail leads through the gorge to Table Rock, where visitors can opt to take **rafts** (adults $12, children 5-12 $10, children under 5 $5) the rest of the way.

NORTH ON 9N

Heading into the High Peaks region from Ausable Chasm on Route 9N, you'll pass through **Au Sable Forks,** once home to illustrator Rockwell Kent, and tiny **Jay,** beautifully situated on the East Branch of the Ausable River. Several old-fashioned country stores and **Jay Craft Center** (Rte. 9N, 518/946-7824, www.jaycraftcenter.com), housing a pottery studio and a gift shop, are located in Jay. A few miles south in **Upper Jay** are **antique shops** just waiting to be browsed.

From Jay, take Route 86 west to reach **Wilmington,** a small ski town huddled at the base of towering Whiteface Mountain, or keep heading north for Plattsburgh.

PLATTSBURGH

The small industrial city of Plattsburgh played an important role in both the American Revolution and the War of 1812. In 1776, the British won the Battle of Lake Champlain off Plattsburgh's shores. In 1814, American Commodore Thomas MacDonough defeated a British fleet from Canada here by using an intricate system of anchors and winches that enabled him to swivel his vessels completely around.

Plattsburgh-North Country Chamber of Commerce runs a **visitor information center** (off I-87 heading south between Exits 41 and 40, 800/487-6867).

Riverwalk Park

Historic Plattsburgh centers around **Riverwalk Park,** which runs along the banks of the Saranac River downtown. The park begins at Bridge Street and extends to the Champlain Monument at Cumberland Avenue. Addresses worth noting along the way include the 1830 **Trinity Episcopal Church** (Trinity Pl.); the 1917 **City Hall** (City Hall Pl.), designed by John Russell Pope; and the **Champlain Monument**

PLATTSBURGH

COURT ST

ST

TRINITY
EPISCOPAL
■ CHURCH

CITY
HALL
■

PL

Park

CUMBERLAND AVE

KENT-DELORD
HOUSE MUSEUM
P
★

TRINITY PL

HALL

OAK ST

CITY

Riverwalk

CHAMPLAIN
MONUMENT
■

BRIDGE ST

Lake

MARGARET

ST

River

Champlain

DURKEE

Saranac

SCALE NOT AVAILABLE

To Clinton County
Historical Museum

© AVALON TRAVEL

(Cumberland Ave.), a gift to the city from France in 1909, commemorating the tercentenary of Samuel de Champlain's voyage.

Kent-Delord House Museum

The city's foremost visitor attraction, **Kent-Delord House Museum** (17 Cumberland Ave., 518/561-1035, www.kentdelordhouse.org, May-Oct., hours vary seasonally, adults $5, children under 12 $3), stands across from Champlain Monument. Built in 1797 and enlarged in 1811, the gracious house was commandeered by the British during the War of 1812. Home to three generations of the Delord family, the house contains nine period rooms and an interesting collection of portraits. Of special interest is an exhibit on Fanny Delord Hall, a self-taught healer who in the late 1800s patented and marketed her own home remedy, Fanoline, "a healing, antiseptic and curative ointment, in cases of Eczema, Fever-sores, Catarrh, Saltrheum, Piles, Sore Nipples, Burns, Blisters, Scratches, Corns, Sore Eyes, Chapped Hands, and Lips."

Clinton County Historical Museum

To learn about Plattsburgh's history, visit the **Clinton County Historical Museum** (98 Ohio Ave., 518/561-0340, www.clintoncountyhistorical.org, Wed.-Sat. 10am-3pm and by appointment, adults $5, seniors $3, children under 12 $2), which presents exhibits on North Country themes, including mining and other local industry.

Lake Placid and High Peaks

Though it was known to avid hikers and skiers and to those who'd been around long enough to have attended the 1932 Winter Olympics, it wasn't until the 1980 Winter Olympics that Lake Placid transformed from a sleepy town to a destination on the state map.

Today, almost everyone who visits the Adirondacks visits Lake Placid, which centers on one long and sometimes very congested Main Street running alongside the lake. The village draws almost as many visitors because of its upscale shops and restaurants as it does for its lonely, mountainous countryside. Even the former Olympic sites, managed by the Olympic Regional Development Authority, have become popular tourist attractions.

© DREAMSTIME.COM

view of Mirror Lake, located in Lake Placid

Keep in mind that Lake Placid is not actually on Lake Placid, but on Mirror Lake. Lake Placid, a much larger body of water, lies to the immediate north of the village.

The term "High Peaks" generally refers to the heart of the Adirondacks, where 46 of the region's highest peaks can be found. Just west of the Champlain Valley, the High Peaks are loosely bounded by Elizabethtown to the east, Wilmington to the north, the Franklin County line to the west, and Newcomb to the south. Lake Placid lies at the center.

Many hikers come to the High Peaks region intent on climbing all 46 of its highest summits and thereby becoming "46ers." The tradition dates back to the early 1920s, when two young brothers, George and Robert Marshall, climbed to the top of Whiteface Mountain with their guide, Herb Clark. Upon reaching the summit, they made a pact to climb all the peaks in the park measuring 4,000 feet or more in height. Later, it turned out that some of the peaks on their list were under 4,000 feet, but no matter, a pattern had been set. Today, hikers come from all over the country to carry on the tradition. If you intend to join them, Adirondack Mountain Club has a special website devoted to the 46 Peaks (www.adk46er.org), which is rich with information, including a list of the peaks, their elevations, and hiking tips.

SIGHTS AND RECREATION
Olympic Center

Olympic Center (2634 Main St., 518/523-1655, www.whiteface.com/facilities/olympic-center), built for the 1932 Winter Olympics and renovated for the 1980 Games, stands at the entrance to the village. The center still houses four Olympic **ice-skating arenas** (three indoor, one outdoor), which are open for public skating. In Olympic Center, **Lake Placid Olympic Museum** (daily 10am-5pm, adults $7, seniors and children 7-12 $5, children 6 & under free) has an extensive collection of Olympic memorabilia.

Lake Placid-North Elba Historical Society Museum

Now occupying the old Lake Placid railroad station, the eclectic **Lake Placid-North Elba Historical Society Museum** (242 Station St.,

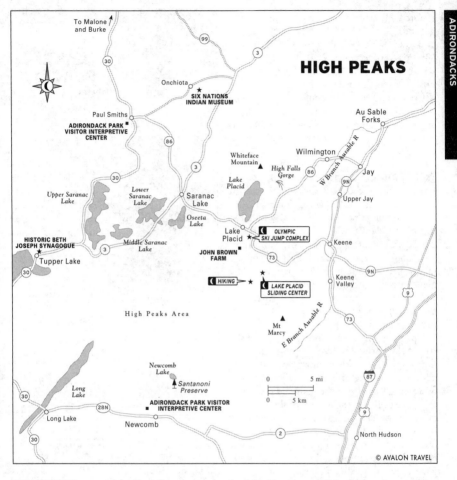

HIGH PEAKS

518/523-1608, www.lakeplacidhistory.com, Memorial Day-mid-June Sat.-Sun. 10am-4pm, mid-June-Columbus Day Wed.-Sun. 10am-4pm, free) houses everything from antique sporting equipment to mementos of conductor Victor Herbert, who once summered on the lake. Exhibits on the experimental colony for former slaves founded in 1849 by abolitionist John Brown are especially interesting.

John Brown Farm State Historic Site

In 1849, abolitionist Gerrit Smith, later joined by John Brown, established a farming community for free blacks and escaped slaves in the Adirondacks. Each new farmer was given 40 acres to till, but since few came prepared to cope with the region's harsh climate, most left within a few years. The area is now designated the **John Brown Farm State Historic Site** (115 John Brown Rd., 518/523-3900, www.nysparks.com/historic-sites/29/details.aspx, May-Oct. Wed.-Mon. 10am-5pm, adults $2, seniors and students $1, children under 12 free). Brown himself lived on the farm for several more years, in a cabin that has been nicely restored. He erected his own gravestone on the grounds.

Brown was executed in Charlestown, Virginia, on December 2, 1859, following his seizure of the U.S. Arsenal at Harper's Ferry. His body was shipped north to New York City, where his coffin was exchanged for a new one so he would not be buried in Southern property. At each stop along the way upstate, his entourage was greeted with sympathetic crowds and tolling bells.

◖ Olympic Ski Jump Complex

If you approached Lake Placid from the east on Route 73, the first thing you undoubtedly noticed were the stark towers of the **Olympic Ski Jump Complex** (5486 Cascade Rd., 518/523-2202, www.whiteface.com, daily 9am-4pm, $8-16 depending on whether special events are taking place), looming out of the landscape like giant misshapen thumbs. The site still serves as a training center and is open year-round, thanks to plastic mats, water ramps, and snowmaking machines.

Upon entering the complex, stop first at the **freestyle aerial facility,** where—with any luck—you'll see athletes practicing their maneuvers by sailing off water-filled ramps and over pools. Next, visit the main lodge to view a photo exhibit on the history of ski jumping, and catch the chairlift to the 90-meter jump. If training is taking place, you can watch from an observation deck. If not, take the glass-enclosed elevator to the top of the 120-meter jump for great views of the High Peaks.

◖ Lake Placid Sliding Center

South of the ski-jumping complex rises Mount Van Hoevenberg, site of Olympic bobsled, luge, and skeleton runs at **Lake Placid Sliding Center** (518/523-4436, www.whiteface.com, daily 9am-4pm, bobsled rides $60-70 per person). The track measures almost a mile long. Passenger rides on bobsleds are offered year-round.

Excellent **Olympic Cross-Country Biathlon Center,** also on Mount Van Hoevenberg, offers a 31-mile system of trails. In winter, trails

are groomed frequently and are open to cross-country skiers of all levels. In summer, trails are used by mountain bikers and horseback riders. Skis and bikes can be rented on-site, and guided horseback rides are available.

◖ Hiking

Mount Marcy, elevation 5,344 feet, is the highest mountain in the Adirondacks, and the one that draws the most hikers each year. In 1872, Verplanck Colvin first hiked the mountain and discovered **Lake Tear of the Clouds,** the source of the Hudson River. "But how wild and desolate this spot!" he wrote. "It is possible that not even an Indian ever stood upon these shores. There is no mark of ax, no barked tree, nor blackened remnants of fire; not a severed twig or a human footprint?"

Since that day, many have followed in Verplanck's foorsteps; an estimated 45,000 people make the seven-mile trek annually. Anticipating the problems that come with over-use, park personnel urge hikers to shy away from famed Mount Marcy and tackle lesser-known peaks instead. The information center at **Adirondak Loj** (1002 Adirondak Loj Rd., 518/523-3441, www.adk.org), eight miles south of Lake Placid, is the starting point of many trails that ascend into the park. It's also the site of a first-rate information center, staffed by the nonprofit **Adirondack Mountain Club,** which can help you choose the hike that's right for you.

Also on Averyville Road, 1.2 miles past the intersection with Old Military Road, is a blue-marked trail that leads to **Wanika Falls.** The 13.4-mile hike takes about seven hours, but the terrain is easy, and the waterfalls make the trip worthwhile. According to Adirondack Mountain Club, the route leads through some of the finest forest in the region before ascending an old road leading to Chubb River and cascading falls, several hundred feet high. The trail is part of the much longer Northville-Placid Trail laid out by the Adirondack Mountain Club in 1922 and 1923.

Boating

A small **public beach** (Parkside Dr., off Main St., 518/523-2445, daily dawn-dusk) is situated south of Olympic Center. Just beyond the northern end of Mirror Lake lies Lake Placid and **Lake Placid Marina** (Mirror Lake Dr., 518/523-9704, www.lakeplacidmarina. com), where one-hour lake cruises depart May-October.

Canoes and other boats can be rented at **Jones Outfitters** (2419 Main St., 518/523-3468, www.jonesoutfitters.com) and **Captain Marney's** (35 Victor Herbert Dr., 518/523-9746).

Guides and Tours

Bear Cub Adventure Tours (30 Bear Cub Rd., 518/523-4339) offers guided canoeing, fishing, backpacking, and hiking trips.

For a scenic flight over the High Peaks, contact **Adirondack Flying Service** (Airport Rd., off Cascade Rd., 518/523-2473, www.flyanywhere.com).

ENTERTAINMENT AND EVENTS

Lake Placid Center for the Arts (17 Algonquin Dr., 518/523-2512, www.lakeplacidarts.org) presents music, dance, theater, film, and special events throughout the year. The 18-piece **Lake Placid Sinfonietta** (Mid's Park, 518/523-2051, www.lakeplacidsinfonietta.org, July-Aug. Wed. evenings) performs free concerts.

Figure-skating, hockey games, and speed-skating events take place in the **Olympic Center Ice Arena** (2634 Main St., 518/523-1655) throughout the year.

SHOPPING

Main Street heads north of the Olympic Arena past about 100 shops, some of them one-of-a-kind, others ubiquitous chains. One must-see is **The Adirondack Store** (2024 Saranac Ave., 518/523-2646, www.theadirondackstore.com), which sells everything from hand-knit sweaters to Winslow Homer prints.

ACCOMMODATIONS
Luxury Inns and Lodges

High Peaks Resort (2384 Saranac Ave., 518/523-4411, www.highpeaksresort.com, $149-269) features a choice of private dock or three pools for swimming, as well as a health club and full service spa. The resort also offers two on-site restaurants.

Entering the large, heavy-beamed lobby of the all-suite **Whiteface Lodge** (7 Whiteface Inn Ln., 800/582-0505, www.thewhitefacelodge.com, $400-488), guests are greeted with that quintessential Adirondack scent of woody goodness. Resort offerings are extensive, including top-rated restaurant Kanu, generous and luxurious suites, romantic surroundings, a movie theater, full service spa, indoor/outdoor pool, lake swimming, and canoeing. Guests can also enjoy cigars and cognac in outdoor lean-tos.

Posh (**Mirror Lake Inn Resort and Spa** (77 Mirror Lake Dr., 518/523-2544, www.mirrorlakeinn.com, $240-350 for rooms, $420-660 for suites in summer, about a third less off-season) is a grand colonial-style structure that was rebuilt after a 1988 fire. Also on-site at this AAA Four Diamond resort are The View Restaurant, Taste Bistro, a bar, cozy lounges, a spa, tennis courts, indoor and outdoor pools, and a private beach.

On the shores of Lake Placid lies secluded **Lake Placid Lodge** (144 Lodge Way, 518/523-2700, www.lakeplacidlodge.com, $440-900), an authentic great camp complete with a stone fireplace and moose head. Now a member of exclusive Relais & Chateaux, the lodge boasts 30 guest accommodations, ranging from lodge rooms and suites to private cabins and cottages. Two restaurants are on-site.

The retreat of the Adirondack Mountain Club (ADK), **Adirondak Loj** (1002 Adirondak Loj Rd., 518/523-3441, www.adk.org, from $169 private rooms, from $69 bunk beds, from $59 lofts per person) is eight miles south of Lake Placid, high in the mountains on the shores of Heart Lake. Meals can be arranged for an additional fee ($9 for breakfast and lunch, $19 for dinner). You don't have to be an ADK member to stay here, but you must make reservations well in advance. The Loj is also the starting point of the Van Hoevenberg Trail, which leads to the summit of Mount Marcy.

Motels and Hotels

Wildwood on the Lake (2135 Saranac Ave., 518/523-2624, www.wildwoodmotel.com, $78-285) offers a cozy fireplace lobby, indoor heated pool, lakeside barbecues, and free boat rentals for guests. The picturesque locale is a 10-minute walk from the village.

Art Devlin's Olympic Motor Inn (2764 Main St., 518/523-3700, www.artdevlins.com, $78-200) offers friendly service and an easy location for wandering around town.

In the upscale motel category there is **Golden Arrow Lakeside Resort** (2559 Main St., 518/523-3353, www.golden-arrow.com, $129-220), offering excellent value accommodations. The resort, located on the lake as its name suggests, has its own small beach, which is equipped with boats (free for guests). Golden Arrow also has a heated indoor pool, sauna, restaurant, lounge, and nightclub.

FOOD

For tasty scones and other baked goods, step into **Bluesberry Bakery** (2436 Main St., 518/523-4539, www.bluesberrybakery.com, Thurs.-Mon. 7:15am-3pm). For a more extensive breakfast, **Chair 6** (5993 Sentinel Rd., 518/523-3630, www.chair6.com, $10) fits the bill; the restaurant also serves lunch and dinner. For mouthwatering barbecue stop at **Tail o' the Pup** (Rte. 86, 518/891-0777, www.tailofthepupbbq.com, $10), a classic roadside eatery located halfway between Lake Placid and Saranac Lake. Local favorite **The Cowboy** (2226 Saranac Ave., 518/837-5069, www.placidcowboy.com, hours vary seasonally, $28) is also good, serving tasty starters like shrimp and black bean fritters in an unassuming hole-in-the-wall location.

Lake Placid Pub and Brewery (813 Mirror Lake Dr., 518/523-3813, www.ubuale.com, daily lunch and dinner, $13) is a popular spot, offering pub food upstairs and a boisterous bar below. At **Nicola's on Main and Grill 211** (211 Main St., 518/523-5853, www.nicolasandgrill211.com, $24), you'll find two restaurants in one. Nicola's is an upscale Italian restaurant serving pasta, fresh fish, veal, and pizza baked in a wood-fired oven. Grill 211 is a New York City-style steakhouse that also serves seafood.

High Peaks Resort is home to the casual restaurant, **The Dancing Bears** (2384 Saranac Ave., 518/523-4411, www.highpeaksresort.com), which claims to serve the coldest beer in Lake Placid. The evidence? Draught beers are encased in ice blocks.

WHITEFACE MOUNTAIN

From Lake Placid, take Route 86 northeast to reach Wilmington, a small ski town huddled at the base of towering Whiteface Mountain. The largest ski resort in New York, state-owned **Whiteface Mountain** (5021 Rte. 86, 518/946-2223, www.whiteface.com) boasts 86 trails, 11 chairlifts, and the highest vertical drop in the Northeast at 3,216 feet. The mountain attracts expert skiers, but intermediate and novice trails are also plentiful.

During the summer, the mountain's peaks are accessible via the **Whiteface Mountain Cloudsplitter Gondola Ride** (late June-early Oct. daily 9am-4pm, adults $20, seniors and children 7-12 $14, children 6 and under free) and **Whiteface Veterans' Memorial Highway** ($10 per car and driver, $7 each additional passenger). The chairlift leads to Little Whiteface Peak (3,676 ft.), while the highway leads to Whiteface Summit (4,867 ft.). Both afford superb views of the High Peaks to the south, Lake Champlain and the Green Mountains to the east, the St. Lawrence River and Canada to the north, and Saranac Lake Valley to the west. Of the Adirondacks' 46 High Peaks, only Whiteface is accessible by car.

Santa's Workshop

Near the entrance of Whiteface Mountain Memorial Highway stands **Santa's Workshop** (324 Whiteface Veterans' Memorial Highway, 518/946-2211, www.northpoleny.com, hours vary seasonally, theme park: adults $21.50, seniors and children 2-16 $19.35), a cheery red-and-white cottage surrounded by flowers. Inside is a post office/gift shop where visitors can send letters postmarked "North Pole" or buy "I believe in Santa Claus" T-shirts. Out back, a cozy, kid-oriented theme park includes amusement park rides, Santa's reindeer, and Santa's elves. Special events such as a Santa Claus Parade are presented daily.

Accommodations and Food

C **Hungry Trout Motor Inn** (5239 Rte. 86, Wilmington, 518/946-2217, www.hungrytrout.com, $119-199) offers 22 upscale motel rooms, all with picture windows, along with a pool and playground. The inn's restaurant (average entrée $22), overlooking the churning white waters of the Ausable River, specializes in its namesake trout, prepared a myriad of tasty ways, along with continental fare.

Stop at **Country Bear** (5830 Rte. 86, Wilmington, 518/946-2691, www.country-beardiner.com, daily, $9) for a satisfying breakfast or lunch.

SARANAC LAKE

After the heavy tourist traffic of Lake Placid, Saranac Lake village comes as a relief. Although classified as a village, Saranac Lake is a sizeable town (pop. 5,400), with a busy, unpretentious Main Street where stores, banks, churches, and supermarkets cater to residents, not tourists. It is not located on the shores of its namesake, but on smaller Lake Flower. A pleasant public beach (daily dawn-dusk) is located on Lake Colby, just north of downtown. The Saranac

---

THE LEGEND OF WHITEFACE

There once was a young brave who wanted to win the hand of a beautiful Iroquois princess. The princess asked him to prove his love by bringing her the skin of the Great White Stag who roamed the region's highest peak.

Armed with two magic arrows an old chief had given him, the brave went to the mountain. For weeks, he hunted for the stag in vain. At last, late one evening, he found him standing in the mist at the top of the mountain. The brave deftly shot his two arrows. One pierced the stag's neck, the second his haunch; but when the brave rushed forward to claim his trophy, he couldn't reach him—the mountainside was too steep. The stag remained pinned to a ledge by the magic arrows, just out of reach.

When the brave awoke the next morning, the stag had disappeared, but the rock where he had hung had turned white. From then on, the Iroquois called the mountain Whiteface.

© DREAMSTIME.COM

half-way to the top of Whiteface Mountain

Lakes—Lower, Middle, and Upper—are farther west. Upper Saranac Lake is famous for its rustic Adirondack architecture, best glimpsed by boat.

Settled in 1819 by Jacob Smith Moody, Saranac Lake soon established itself as a center for Adirondack guides. All of Moody's sons became guides, and their Uncle Martin once guided everyone from President Grover Cleveland to Ralph Waldo Emerson.

In 1876, Dr. Livingston Trudeau, suffering from tuberculosis, came to Saranac Lake to die. Instead, the fresh mountain air restored him, and in 1884 he opened the first outdoor sanatorium for the treatment of tuberculosis. By the early 1900s, Trudeau Sanatorium was famed worldwide, with thousands flocking to "The City of the Sick" to take "the cure."

Trudeau Sanatorium closed in 1954, after antibiotics were developed, but its legacy lives on in the Trudeau Institute, a scientific research institute. *Doonesbury* cartoonist Garry Trudeau is the great-grandson of Dr. Livingston Trudeau.

Robert Louis Stevenson Memorial Cottage and Museum

Among the pioneer "lungers" who came to Saranac Lake to take the cure was Robert Louis Stevenson. In 1887, fresh from the success of his just-published *Dr. Jekyll and Mr. Hyde,* the author rented a cozy cottage on a hill within easy reach of Dr. Trudeau. While living here, Stevenson wrote some of his best essays and started his long tale, *The Master of Ballantrae.* "I was walking on the veranda of a small house outside the hamlet of Saranac. It was winter, the night was very dark, the air clean and cold and sweet with the purity of forests. For the making of a story, here were fine conditions," reads the quote by the door.

Today, the **Robert Louis Stevenson Memorial Cottage and Museum** (11 Stevenson Ln., 518/891-1462, July-Oct. Tues.-Sun. 9:30am-noon and 1pm-4:30pm, adults $5, children under 12 free) houses a large collection of Stevenson memorabilia, including his ice skates, playing cards, letters to Henry James, autographed first editions, and the velvet jacket that he always wore while writing. On the mantelpiece are Stevenson's cigarette burns, which he left everywhere he went.

Entertainment and Nightlife

Pendragon Theatre (15 Brandy Brook Ave., 518/891-1854, www.pendragontheatre.org) presents professional regional theater, performing both classic and contemporary works.

A number of popular bars, many hosting local bands on the weekends, hug Main Street near Hotel Saranac and along Broadway north of Main. Among them is the popular, teeming, indoor-outdoor **Water Hole** (48 Main St., 518/891-9502, www.saranaclakewaterhole. com), which offers live music several nights each week.

Outfitters, Guides, and Recreation

Saranac Lake is ideally situated between the High Peaks and the Northwest Lakes, which offer some of the best canoeing in the Northeast.

Large and friendly **St. Regis Canoe Outfitters** (73 Dorsey St., 518/891-1838, www. canoeoutfitters.com) is both a sprawling retail shop and the place to go to set up a canoeing or kayaking trip. St. Regis rents boats and camping gear, provides instruction and trip-planning advice, and offers guided trips and shuttle services. Trips can be arranged for as short as one morning or as long as two weeks or more.

Adirondack Foothills (518/359-8194, www.adkfoothills.com) offers customized hiking, camping, canoeing, and fishing trips. **McDonnell's Adirondack Challenges** (518/891-1176, www.macscanoe.com) rents canoes by the day or longer; staff can provide information about recommend canoe routes.

Accommodations and Food

A regional landmark run by students from Paul Smith's College, ◖ **Hotel Saranac** (100 Main St., 800/937-0211, www.hotelsaranac.com, $68-120) provides a good base from which to explore the area. Built in 1927, the snug, full-service brick hotel has 82 small but comfortable rooms. The lobby is a replica of the foyer in the Danvanzati Palace in Florence, Italy.

Blue Moon Cafe (55 Main St., 518/891-1310, www.bluemooncafe-adk.com, daily breakfast, lunch, and dinner, $18) serves an eclectic range of dishes—from Amelia Island Gumbo to Kung Pao Chicken—inspired by a variety of international cuisines. **The Downhill Grill** (74 Main St., 518/891-3663, daily lunch and dinner, $14) serves reliably tasty grill fare, including burgers and steak.

PAUL SMITHS

About 10 miles northwest of Saranac Lake lies the hamlet of Paul Smiths, named after Appollos (Paul) Smith, a famed Adirondack guide who established one of the Adirondacks' first hotels here in 1859. Charles Dickens once said of Smith, "He has no bad habits, and is, withal, the best rifle shot, paddler, and compounder of forest stews in the whole region." When Smith died in 1912, his funeral was the largest ever held in northern New York, drawing more than 700 people.

The original Paul Smiths hotel has closed, but its spirit lives on through **Paul Smith's College** (Rtes. 86 and 30, 800/421-2605, www.

ALMANZO WILDER, FARMER BOY

Fans of Laura Ingalls Wilder might want to head north of Paul Smiths about 35 miles to the **Almanzo Wilder Homestead** (177 Stacy Rd., 518/483-1207, www.almanzo-wilderfarm.com, late May or early June-Sept. Mon.-Sat. 11am-4pm, Sun. 1pm-4pm, adults $7.50, seniors $7, children 6-16 $4), located in farm country east of Malone. Wilder's husband, Almanzo Wilder, grew up here, and the author based her book *Farmer Boy* on his childhood.

The trim, airy house has been carefully restored to reflect the book. Downstairs is the parlor where "Almanzo didn't mean to throw the blacking brush," and upstairs is his "soft, cold feather bed." In the kitchen are kerosene lamps, tallow candles, and a butter churn—all similar to the ones used by Almanzo—while out back is the red barn where he did his chores. In 2013, a replica schoolhouse opened on the grounds.

Ingalls Wilder, who met her husband in South Dakota, never visited the Wilder homestead, but according to family members, the house was "as described in the book." Photocopies of the sketches Almanzo drew for Wilder, along with several of her letters, are on display in the entrance hall.

---

paulsmiths.edu), founded by the hotelier's son in the 1930s. The school is known for its degrees in hotel management and culinary arts.

The college's 3,000-acre **Visitor Interpretive Center** (VIC, www.adirondackvic.org) offers free and fee-based sports, arts, children's, and nature-oriented activities throughout the year. Its expanse is spacious enough for 25 miles of trails, many of which have comfortable walking surfaces and signage that explains the ecology of the area.

White Pine Camp

White Pine Camp (White Pine Rd., a half mile east of the Rtes. 86/30 intersection, 518/327-3030, www.whitepinecamp.com, cabins $155-375 daily) served as President Calvin Coolidge's summer White House in 1926. Built in 1907, the camp overlooks Osgood Pond and contains about 20 asymmetrical buildings, complete with soaring rooflines, unusual angles, and skylights. In the main cabin, exhibits explain the site's history and architecture, while among the surrounding outbuildings are a tennis house, indoor bowling alley, and a Japanese teahouse. There are also cabins and cottages available for rent by the week.

Tours (July-Labor Day Wed. and Sat. 10am and 1:30pm, adults $10, children $5) of the camp are offered and reservations are not required.

ONCHIOTA

"Leaving 67 of the friendliest people in the Adirondacks (plus a couple of soreheads)" reads the sign at the northern end of Onchiota. No one seems quite sure exactly who those soreheads are, but to meet the first variety, stop into the one-of-a-kind **Six Nations Indian Museum** (1462 Rte. 60, 518/891-2299, www.sixnationsindianmuseum.com, July-Aug. Tues.-Sun. 10am-5pm, adults $4, children $2). From the outside, the museum looks much like an ordinary house. Inside, though, you'll find yourself surrounded by a kaleidoscopic array of pictographs, paintings, basketwork, beadwork, quillwork, pottery, canoes, masks, drums, and lacrosse sticks, all very neatly arranged to cover virtually every square inch of wall and peaked wooden ceiling. The museum is the creation of one man, Ray Fadden, a Mohawk who drew most of the elaborate pictographs himself. The works tell traditional Iroquois tales.

Fadden, who spent much of his life as a teacher, began fighting for the preservation of Iroquois culture as early as the 1940s. Back then hardly anyone listened, but Fadden never faltered and eventually was instrumental in the founding of numerous Iroquois heritage programs. Many of his former students are now major leaders in the Mohawk Nation.

The museum is run by Fadden's son and daughter-in-law. Visitors are warmly greeted at the door and taken on personalized tours. To reach Onchiota from Paul Smiths, take Route 86 east to County Roads 31 or 30 north (not to be confused with state Route 30, which leads to Malone). The museum is in the hamlet's center and is easy to find.

Northwest Lakes

The northwestern section of the Adirondacks is a sparsely populated area often overlooked by vacationers. Much of the land here is quite flat and covered with hundreds of lakes and ponds, along with seemingly endless unbroken forest. Though the region is primarily a canoer's paradise, it also has much to offer in the way of easy-to-moderate hikes.

ST. REGIS CANOE AREA

To the immediate west of Paul Smiths begins the St. Regis Canoe Area, a 20,000-acre region encompassing 58 lakes and ponds. St. Regis Mountain stands alone at the area's northern edge, offering wide-angled views of the watery terrain.

St. Regis Canoe Outfitters (Floodwood Rd. at Long Pond Portage, 518/891-8040, www.canoeoutfitters.com), one of the area's largest outfitters, based in Saranac Lake, maintains an outpost in the canoe area at Lake Clear. To reach the outpost and several good boat-launch sites, take Route 86 north from Saranac Lake to Route 186. Turn left and follow Route 186 west to its end and junction with Route 30. Continue straight, past the junction, for 5.5 miles, crossing the Saranac Inn Golf Club. Just beyond the course, at a paved four-way intersection, turn right on Floodwood Road. Continue straight ahead 4.1 miles to the base.

Accommodations, Camping, and Food

Secluded **Fish Creek Pond Campground** (518/891-4560, reservations 800/465-2236, www.fishcreekpond.com), with more than 300 sites, and 287-site **Rollins Pond Campground** (518/891-3239, reservations 800/465-2236) sit off Route 30 between the St. Regis Canoe Area and Tupper Lake village.

Sunday Pond B&B (5544 Rte. 30, Saranac Inn, 518/891-1531, www.sundaypond.com, $99) is tucked into the woods near a fish hatchery. It's a simple, Adirondack-style lodge with three guest rooms, a sleeping loft that's good for families, and a lean-to. All rooms have private baths. The proprietors also offer lunch and dinner for an additional fee.

Just west of St. Regis Canoe Area is the classic **Lake Clear Lodge & Retreat** (6319 Rte. 30, 518/891-1489, www.lodgeonlakeclear.com, $169-289), where you can choose among guest rooms filled with Adirondackiana, chalets, or suites with whirlpool tubs. The snug lodge is renowned locally for its restaurant, **Hohmeyer's,** which serves German and Adirondack specialties. The menu changes nightly, but entrées such as Wiener schnitzel or sauerbraten are always available. A German **Bierkeller** is downstairs in the main lodge.

The region's most exclusive accommodations can be found at **The Point** (Upper Saranac Lake, 518/891-5674, www.thepointsaranac. com, $1,250-2,500), an ultra-luxurious great camp once owned by the Rockefellers. Now open to the public, The Point features the absolute utmost in hedonistic delights, with the Relais & Chateaux stamp of approval.

TUPPER LAKE

Once a major industrial center known for its lumber and paper mills, as well as its woodworking factories, Tupper Lake still harbors its share of smokestacks, especially along the lakefront. Made up of early-20th-century brick buildings, downtown remains small, tightly

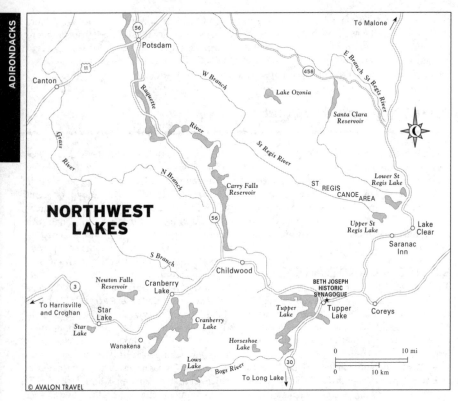

NORTHWEST LAKES

knit, and compact. Many of the street names bear evidence of the town's French-American heritage.

Raquette River Outfitters (1754 Rte. 30, 518/359-3228, www.raquetteriveroutfitters. com) rents canoes, provides car shuttles, and offers guided canoe trips.

Historic Beth Joseph Synagogue

The oldest synagogue in the Adirondacks, **Historic Beth Joseph Synagogue** (2026 Rte. 30, 518/359-7229, July-Aug. Tues.-Fri. 11am-3pm, July-Aug. Fri. services 7pm, free), is an architectural gem built in 1905 by Russian Jewish immigrants who came to the region as peddlers. At its peak in the mid-1920s, the synagogue served about 35 families but was closed in 1959 due to a dwindling congregation. Now on the State Registry of Historic Buildings, the

synagogue functions as a small museum. All fixtures and furnishings are original, and the vestibule houses an exhibit on the town's early Jewish community. A small art gallery is downstairs.

Accommodations and Food

The motels and hotels in town are extremely spare and somewhat outdated. It's best to spend the night elsewhere. Similarly, the options for eating well in Tupper Lake are limited. At local favorite **Larkin's Deli and Bakery** (58 Main St., 518/359-9000, www.larkinsdeliandbakery.com, breakfast, lunch, and dinner), you can buy fresh homemade donuts, among other delights.

CRANBERRY LAKE

Mostly state-owned, Cranberry Lake has been virtually bypassed by civilization. Its 11 square miles include 55 miles of shoreline. A village of the same name sits on Route 3 at the eastern end of the lake. To the west of the village is a boat launch, and to the east, the public Cranberry Lake Campground.

One of the area's most popular canoe trips begins at Inlet, off Route 3 southwest of the lake, and continues 16 miles along **Oswegatchie River** to the lake itself. An easy hiking trail up **Bear Mountain** on the east side of the lake begins at Cranberry Lake Campground. The hike is 3.6 miles round-trip, takes about two hours, and offers good views of the lake.

Accommodations and Food
There are 173 sites at **Cranberry Lake Campground** (Long Pine Rd., off Rte. 3, 315/848-2315, reservations 800/465-2267). Campers who prefer to rough it can row out to one of 46 primitive tent sites designated with yellow markers along the lake's shoreline. If you'd prefer a motel, try the simple but comfortable **Cranberry Lake Lodge** (7209 Rte. 3, 315/848-3301, www.cranberrylakelodge.com, $68-195), which also has a family-style restaurant (average entrée $8) and lounge.

WEST ON ROUTE 3
From Cranberry Lake, Route 3 heads west through flat, woodsy, isolated countryside. Harrisville, built on the banks of the Oswegatchie River, is just over the St. Lawrence-Lewis County border, about 35 miles from Cranberry Lake.

If you head north of Harrisville on Route 812 about 50 miles, you'll arrive in the Thousand Islands region. If you continue south about 14 miles along Route 812 toward Croghan, you'll come to the hamlet of Indian River and an astonishing outdoor **Concrete Sculpture Garden.** Created by the late Veronica Terrillion, a folk artist, the park is alive with over 400 brightly painted statues of animals, people, and religious figures. Zebras, leopards, and a giraffe are poised near the driveway; a boat transporting the figures representing Terrillion's family floats in a small lily-filled pond.

Visitors are welcome to stop and take pictures of the park from the road, but please keep in mind that this is private property.

Central Adirondacks

Nestled into the center of Adirondack Park are more still blue lakes, encircled by densely packed forests and small to moderate peaks. The climate here is not as harsh as it is farther north, and the landscape has a more human-size feel. Some sections of the Central Adirondacks, such as Indian Lake, attract only a handful of visitors; others, such as Old Forge, are overrun with vacationers.

LONG LAKE
Heading south from Tupper Lake on Route 30, you'll come to Long Lake, a 14-mile stretch of water that is really just an engorged section of Raquette River. At the intersection of Routes 30 and 28N is the village of Long Lake, dominated by the rectangular Adirondack Hotel, an 1870s lodging with wide verandas. Just across Long Lake bridge from the hotel is a **public beach** (Rte. 30, just south of the bridge, daily dawn-dusk, with year-round heated bathrooms) and boat launch.

One of the region's most popular **canoe trips** begins at Long Lake launch and heads north along Raquette River through the High Peaks region. Past the High Peaks, paddlers can choose to continue on Raquette River to Tupper Lake or portage to Upper Saranac Lake. Either way, the trip covers about 40 miles and takes about four days. Boats and canoes can be rented at **Long Lake Marina** (Rte. 30, 518/624-2266, www.longlakemarina.com), in the village center. To take a scenic seaplane flight, contact

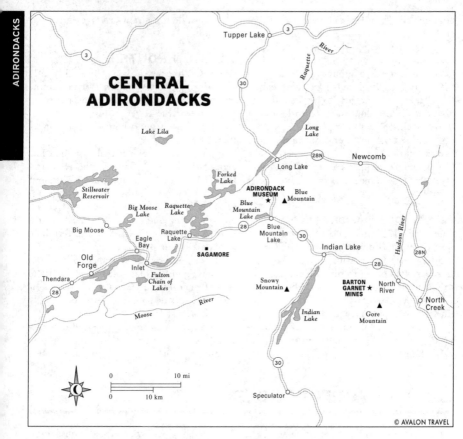

Tupper Lake

CENTRAL
ADIRONDACKS

Lake Lila

Stillwater
Reservoir

Big Moose
Lake

Raquette
Lake

Big Moose

Eagle
Bay

Old
Forge

Inlet

Thendara

Fulton
Chain of
Lakes

Moose

River

Forked
Lake

Long
Lake

Long Lake

Newcomb

ADIRONDACK
MUSEUM

Blue
Mountain

Blue
Mountain
Lake

Blue
Mountain
Lake

SAGAMORE

Indian Lake

Snowy
Mountain

BARTON
GARNET
MINES

North
River

North
Creek

Indian
Lake

Gore
Mountain

Raquette River

Hudson River

Speculator

0   10 mi

0   10 km

© AVALON TRAVEL

Helms Aero Service (Rte. 30, 518/624-3931, www.helmsaeroservice.com, May-Oct. daily).

Hiking

At the southern end of Long Lake ascends the double-peaked **Owls Head Mountain.** The well-marked, 3.5-mile trail leading to the top is of moderate difficulty and takes about four hours to hike round-trip. Along the way you'll pass streams, valleys, a fire tower, Lake Eaton—a good place for a swim—and good views of the High Peaks. To reach the trailhead, take Route 30 one mile north of Long Lake village to Endion Road and watch for signs.

Shopping

You can't miss **Hoss's Country Corner** (1142 Main St., 518/624-2481, www.hossscountry-corner.com), a big, square emporium built in the classic Adirondack style. Inside, you'll find everything from groceries and clothing to handicrafts and a good selection of regional books.

Accommodations and Camping

Two miles north of the village is 135-site **Lake Eaton Campground** (Rte. 30, 518/624-2641, reservations 800/456-2267). Five miles west of Long Lake is 80-site **Forked Lake Campground** (381 Forked Lake Campground Ln., 518/624-6646, reservations 800/456-2267).

© VISITADIRONDACKS.COM

one of the Adirondacks' many fire towers

On the shores of the lake is **(Quackenbush's Long View Wilderness Lodge** (681 Deerland Rd., 518/624-2862, www.quackenbushlongviewwildernesslodge. com, $100-160, with breakfast), a comfortable, low-key place with guest rooms, cottages, and a private beach equipped with canoes and other boats.

Though now better known for its restaurants than for its guest rooms, **Adirondack Hotel** (1245 Main St., Rte. 30, 518/624-4700, www. adirondackhotel.com, $90-120 summer, $68-85 off-season, some rooms share baths) still accommodates overnight visitors. Rooms are spartan but clean.

Food

Long Lake Diner (Rte. 30, 518/624-3941) serves breakfast and lunch. **(Adirondack Hotel** (1245 Main St., Rte. 30, 518/624-4700, www.adirondackhotel.com, $16) holds a popular café open for breakfast, lunch, and a light dinner; the hotel's more formal dining room, The Victorian Room, serves full-course dinners.

BLUE MOUNTAIN LAKE

One of the loveliest lakes in all the Adirondacks is dark, spring-fed Blue Mountain Lake. Situated 1,800 feet above sea level, the isolated lake is dotted with small islands and flanked by towering Blue Mountain, a moody peak that the Iroquois once called "Hill of Storms." The lake, one of a chain of three, is stocked with bass, whitefish, and trout.

The village of Blue Mountain Lake sits at the water's southern edge, along Routes 28 and 30. Though home to only about 100 permanent residents, the village is a major cultural center, thanks to the presence of the renowned Adirondack Museum and the much smaller Adirondack Lakes Center for the Arts. A postage-stamp-size **public beach** (off Route 28, July-Sept.) is situated in the heart of the village, and several crafts galleries are located along Route 30.

A popular **canoe trip** starts at Blue Mountain Lake and heads west through Eagle and Utowana Lakes to the 0.4-mile Bassett Carry. At the end of the portage flows the Marion River, which leads to Raquette Lake, which in turn leads to the Fulton Chain of Lakes. Depending on how far you paddle, the trip can take anywhere from 1-5 days. A lean-to is situated on the north shore of Utowana Lake about a half mile above the dam.

Adirondack Museum

High on a slope overlooking Blue Mountain Lake presides the **Adirondack Museum** (9097 Rte. 30, 518/352-7311, www.adkmuseum.org, late May-mid-Oct. daily 10am-5pm, adults $18, seniors $16, students 13-17 $12, children 6-12 $6, children under 6 free), a compact complex of 22 buildings that covers virtually every aspect of Adirondack life. By far the most important museum in the region, the complex has been described by *The New York Times* as "the best of its kind in the world."

Featured in the museum's two main buildings are first-rate exhibits on Adirondack history, natural science, culture, and art. Dioramas simulate scenes such as a logging camp, an early Adirondack hotel, and a hermit's cabin, while nearby are displays on fishing, trapping, and surveying. In one room is a Victorian hearse equipped with wheels for summer and runners for winter; in another, over 800 wooden miniatures carved by one man.

Smaller buildings focus on specific themes. The Boat Building is packed with dozens of sleek wooden vessels; the Transportation Building has 50 horse-drawn vehicles and a private railroad car. At the Photo Belt, visitors watch historic photographs slide by on a moving belt.

Adirondack Lakes Center for the Arts

The inviting **Adirondack Lakes Center for the Arts** (3446 Rte. 28, 518/352-7715, www. adirondackarts.org, Thurs.-Sat. 10am-4pm, gallery admission free, evening events prices vary) presents both visual and performing arts. Past exhibits have covered everything from traditional quilts to contemporary pottery, while concerts have ranged from the Tokyo String Quartet to Aztec Two-Step. A gift shop selling regional arts and crafts is also at the center.

Hiking

One of the best ways to get a good view of Blue Mountain Lake is to hike up brooding **Blue Mountain,** elevation 3,750 feet. Though quite steep in parts, the four-mile round-trip hike is of moderate difficulty overall and takes about three hours. At the summit gleams the restored 1917 Blue Mountain Fire Tower, staffed with a ranger/guide on summer weekends. The trailhead and a well-marked hiking trail begin off Route 30, a half mile north of the Adirondack Museum.

Outfitters

Boats and canoes can be rented at the friendly, family-run **Blue Mountain Lake Boat Livery** (3429 Rte. 30 at Rte. 28, 518/352-7351, www. boatlivery.com). Docked outside are two classic wooden launches that take visitors to isolated parts of Blue Mountain Lake and two smaller neighboring lakes. Low-key **sightseeing tours**

(July-Sept. daily, adults $20, seniors $18, students and children over three $15, reservations recommended) are filled with interesting historical information.

Blue Mountain Outfitters (Rte. 30, 518/352-7306) rents canoes and kayaks, sells outdoor gear, and offers guided canoe trips.

INDIAN LAKE

Southeast of Blue Mountain Lake lounges long, skinny Indian Lake, named after Sabael Benedict, an Abenaki and the area's first settler. A hamlet of the same name clusters around the intersection of Routes 28 and 30 at the lake's northern end, while to the east stretches Siamese Ponds Wilderness Area.

Siamese Ponds Wilderness Area

Covering an area of 112,000 acres, the Siamese Ponds region is roughly bounded by Route 28 to the north, Route 30 to the west and south, and Route 8 to the east. Often overlooked by vacationers, the area encompasses gentle mountains, dense forests, crystal-clear ponds, and rushing streams. In certain sections, you can hike all day without encountering another person.

Thirty-three miles of marked hiking trails and many more unmarked ones run through the wilderness. Major trailheads are located at the end of Big Brook Road (off Rte. 30 a half mile south of Indian Lake village); at Thirteenth Lake and the end of Old Farm Clearing Road (take Rte. 28 east to Thirteenth Lake Rd.); and on Route 8 about four miles west of Bakers Mills.

Hiking

One of the trails at the end of Big Brook Road leads up **Chimney Mountain,** named after its unusual central bulwark of layered gneiss, granite, and marble. The mountain is also known for its many crevices and caves. These should be explored by expert spelunkers only. Most visitors shouldn't proceed further than shining a flashlight down into the depths. The round-trip hike up and down Chimney Mountain covers three miles, takes 2.5 hours, and is quite rugged in spots. From up top are good views of Kings Flow, Round Pond, and the High Peaks.

The tallest of the southern Adirondacks, **Snowy Mountain** (3,899 ft.) offers a long, challenging climb best suited for hikers in good condition. The hike to the summit, which offers excellent views of the surrounding lakes, is about seven miles round-trip and takes about five hours. Steep sections are located near the trailhead and again near the top, while in between are rolling terrain and a sparkling brook that follows the trail for close to a mile. To reach the trailhead, take Route 30 south of the hamlet of Indian Lake 6.5 miles. Watch for a sign marking the trail on the right and a paved parking area on the left.

Rafting Trips

White-water rafting trips down nearby Hudson River Gorge and Moose River are offered by **Adventure Sports Rafting Co.** (Main St., 518/648-5812, www.adventuresportsrafting. com) and **Adirondac Rafting Company** (Rtes. 27 and 30, 518/523-1635, www.lakeplacidrafting.com).

NORTH CREEK

Off Route 28 midway between Indian Lake and Warrensburg in the southeastern Adirondacks lies North Creek, a small town wedged between mountains and the **Hudson River Gorge.** Towering over North Creek to the south is Gore Mountain; to the north flows the Hudson River and a 16-mile stretch of white water that's considered the finest rafting run in the east.

The Hudson River Gorge begins east of Indian Lake, just beyond the confluence of the Indian and Hudson Rivers. During the spring, the water runs high, with near continuous Class III and IV rapids. The river should be tackled by experts only; a number of deaths have occurred here over the years.

Gore Mountain

One of New York's largest ski resorts, **Gore Mountain** (793 Peaceful Valley Rd., 518/251-2411, www.goremountain.com) particularly attracts intermediate skiers. Featured are 94 trails, a vertical drop of more than 2,500 feet, and 14 ski lifts. The **gondola ride** (July 4-Columbus Day, adults $9, seniors and kids under 12 $7) operates to the summit, offering bird's-eye views of the countryside.

Barton Garnet Mines

On the back side of Gore Mountain lies **Barton Garnet Mines** (Barton Mines Rd., North River, just north of North Creek, off Rte. 28, 518/251-2706, www.garnetminetours.com, July-Aug. Mon.-Sat. 9:30am-5pm and Sun. 11am-5pm, Sept.-Oct. Sat. 9:30am-5pm and Sun. 11am-5pm, adults $10, seniors $9, children $7), a sprawling operation that produces 90 percent of the world's industrial garnet. Garnets are also New York State's stone. During the summer, visitors can tour the open-pit mines with guides who explain the area's geology and history.

Outfitters and Guides

One of the oldest rafting outfitters in the state, **Hudson River Rafting Company** (1 Main St., 518/251-3215, www.hudsonriverrafting. com) offers guided trips down the Hudson River Gorge and along the Moose, Black, and Sacandaga Rivers.

Accommodations and Food

At the C **Copperfield Inn** (307 Main St., 877/235-1466, www.copperfieldinn.com, $159-285) you'll find 31 spacious rooms with plenty of amenities, a heated pool, health club, hot tub, and tennis courts. Also on the premises is **Trappers Tavern,** serving casual meals like pizza and chili.

NORTHWEST ON ROUTE 28N

Scenic Route 28N heads out of North Creek in the southeastern Adirondacks to skirt the southern edge of the High Peaks region. Along the way you'll pass one splendid lake and mountain vista after another. The ride is especially magnificent in autumn.

ADIRONDACKS

Adirondack Park Visitor Interpretive Center

In Newcomb, the Adirondack Park Agency maintains the **Adirondack Park Visitor Interpretive Center** (5922 Rte. 28N, 518/582-2000, www.esf.edu/aic, Tues.-Sat. 10am-4pm, free), which offers an excellent introduction to the park. Exhibits range from the region's logging history to local flora and fauna. Print out free information about trailhead locations and canoe routes at one of the touch-screen stations, or follow one of the interpretive trails outside. Trails lead onto a peninsula in Rich Lake, past beaver ponds and old-growth hemlocks.

Camp Santanoni

Deserted **Camp Santanoni,** one of the old great camps, stands on the shores of Newcomb Lake. Built in 1892 by Albany industrialist Robert Pruyn and surrounded by 12,900-acre Santanoni Preserve, the eerily empty camp built of massive logs includes a central lodge, boathouse, studio, and guest cottages. None of the deteriorating buildings is open to the public, and the only way in is **hiking** five miles along Santanoni Road.

The road is located on the north side of Route 28N, about a mile east of Adirondack Park Visitor Center. A parking area is near the camp's gatehouse; beyond, stretch fields crisscrossed with stone fences. About 1.5 miles in is a deserted farmstead that once provided the great camp with its provisions.

A yellow-marked trail runs north of the great camp along Newcomb Lake. Here you'll find several remote campsites with their own private beaches.

For more information, inquire at the Park Visitor Interpretive Center.

RAQUETTE LAKE

Heading west of Blue Mountain Lake on Route 28 instead of east, you'll come to Raquette Lake. It was here that W. W. Durant built Camp Pine Knot, the first Adirondack great camp, in 1877. Durant combined elements of the Adirondack log cabin and the Swiss chalet, a style that continues to predominate in the

Adirondacks. Camp Pine Knot still stands near the lake, along with four other great camps: Camp Echo, Bluff Point, North Point, and Sagamore. Only Sagamore is open to the public, but you can glimpse the other four by touring Raquette Lake by boat.

At the southwestern edge of Raquette Lake lies a hamlet of the same name, equipped with three marinas and little else. At the lake's southeastern edge stretches **Golden Beach State Park** (Rte. 28, 315/354-4230), offering a swimming beach, hiking trails, boat rentals, 205-site campground, and good fishing spots.

Great Camp Sagamore

A self-contained rustic village hidden deep in the woods, **Great Camp Sagamore** (Sagamore Rd., off Rte. 28, 315/354-5311, www.sagamore.org, tours given late May-mid Oct., hours vary seasonally, adults $16, children $8) was built by W. W. Durant in 1897 and sold to Alfred G. Vanderbilt, Sr. in 1901. Considered the prototypical great camp, Sagamore centers on a seemingly indestructible main lodge built of huge dark logs, while outbuildings house a dining hall, guest cottages, boathouse, horse barn, icehouse, and bowling alley.

One of Sagamore's most interesting buildings is the casino playhouse, the walls of which are covered with animal "trophies" killed by generations of Vanderbilts. The camp was once known as the "headquarters of the gaming crowd," and the Vanderbilts entertained lavishly, inviting everyone from Gary Cooper and Gene Tierney to Lord Mountbatten and Madame Chiang Kai-Shek.

Now a National Historic Landmark owned by the Sagamore Institute, Sagamore hosts weekend and week-long learning vacations focusing on such subjects as woodcarving, storytelling, and folk music. You can also book a simple "Outdoor Weekend" with no classes. Summer weekend packages start at $299 per person.

Shopping

Inside the sprawling **Raquette Lake Supply**

© VISITADIRONDACKS.COM

Great Camp Sagamore

Co. (1 Main St., 315/354-4301), owned by the same family since the late 1800s, you'll find everything from a post office and launderette to groceries and fishing supplies.

Outfitters

Boats, canoes, and water-sports equipment can be rented at **Bird's Marine** (179 Rte. 28, 315/354-4441, www.birdsmarine.com).

Raquette Lake Navigation Co. (254 Antlers Rd., 315/354-5532, www.raquettelakenavigation.com, June-Oct.) offers lunch, dinner, sightseeing, and moonlight cruises. Brunch cruises are also offered on Sundays.

OLD FORGE AND THE FULTON CHAIN

Nestled in the western foothills of the Adirondacks, the Fulton Chain is a series of eight lakes, flanked by long ridges. None of the ridges reaches higher than 600 feet, but they feature steep, glaciated cliffs that drop dramatically down into the lakes. Excellent bird's-eye views can be had by hiking up Bald Mountain

or by taking a ride up the McCauley Mountain chairlift.

Heading west from Raquette Lake on Route 28, you'll come first to Eighth and Seventh Lakes—the most pristine of the Fulton Chain—and to the attractive hamlet of Inlet. About two miles beyond Inlet is Big Moose Public Road (County Road 1), a wooded back lane that leads north four miles to Big Moose Lake. So far, so good. But then, about 10 miles beyond Inlet lies Old Forge. After the relative solitude of Blue Mountain Lake, Indian Lake, and even Raquette Lake, built-up Old Forge and much of the Fulton Chain may come as a surprise. The towns here have a number of souvenir shops, motels, and attractions, including the theme park **Enchanted Forest/Water Safari** (3183 Rte. 28, 315/369-6145, www.watersafari.com, early June-early Sept., $26.95 kids, $29.95 adults), a total kid-pleaser.

If you're keen to get back into the wilderness, take heart: One of the Adirondacks' most famed and popular **canoe trips** begins in Old Forge and proceeds north through the Fulton

THE TRAGEDY THAT BECAME AN AMERICAN TRAGEDY

On July 11, 1906, a young man named Chester Gillette overturned a rowboat in the middle of Big Moose Lake, drowning—accidentally or deliberately?—his pregnant girlfriend, Grace Brown. The case riveted the nation and became the basis for Theodore Dreiser's novel *An American Tragedy*. Dreiser stuck surprisingly close to the facts of the case. Like Gillette, Dreiser's protagonist, Clyde Griffiths, grew up in a religious family that roamed the West; he traveled east to work in his uncle's skirt factory and was desperate to achieve the American Dream no matter what it took.

Gillette was arrested the day after the drowning and incarcerated in the Herkimer County jail. Visitors lined up around the block to walk past his cell, and reporters flocked there from all over the country. Among those cover-

ing the case was ex-lawman Bat Masterson, who had become a sportswriter for *The New York Morning Telegraph*. Masterson was one of the few to question whether Gillette could receive a fair trial in Herkimer County, a charge that infuriated local officials.

Several buildings connected with the Gillette case still stand. In Cortland, south of Syracuse, is the rooming house where Gillette lived while working at his uncle's factory. In Herkimer, in the Mohawk River Valley, stand the courthouse and jail in which he was tried and incarcerated. And the railroad station through which the couple passed just hours before the fateful event remains in Big Moose Lake.

Chester Gillette was found guilty of first-degree murder and was electrocuted at Auburn State Prison on March 30, 1907.

Chain to Raquette Lake, Long Lake, and the Raquette River. Canoeists can then head to either Saranac or Tupper Lakes. The entire route is about 100 miles long, involves about 9 miles of portage, and takes about six days. To canoe just the 18-mile-long Fulton Chain, from Old Forge to the Eighth Lake Campground, takes a full day and involves 1.7 miles of portage.

Detour to Big Moose Lake

Located off the beaten tourist track, Big Moose Lake is worth a detour, especially for fans of Theodore Dreiser's novel *An American Tragedy* or its 1951 film adaptation, *A Place in the Sun*. Dreiser based his classic on an actual tragedy; it was in the lake's South Bay that Chester Gillette drowned Grace Brown. Bear left on Big Moose Road upon reaching the lake and you'll come to the old railroad station (now Big Moose Station Restaurant) where Gillette and Brown disembarked. Bear right and you'll reach the former site of the Hotel Glennmore, where the couple registered and rented their boat. The hotel is gone now, but several outbuildings remain.

Dreiser wrote: "The quiet, glassy, iridescent surface of this lake...seemed, not so much like water as oil—like molten glass that, of enormous bulk and weight, resting upon the substantial earth so very far below...Everywhere pines—tall and spearlike. And above them the humped backs of the dark and distant Adirondacks beyond."

View

The oldest multi-arts center in the Adirondacks, **View** (3273 Rte. 28, Old Forge, 315/369-6411, www.viewarts.org, Mon.-Sat. 10am-4:30pm, Sun. noon-4pm, $10) began its life in the early 1950s as the Old Forge Arts Center. It occupies a 28,000-square-foot facility with performance, gallery, and studio spaces. The galleries feature work inspired by the Adirondacks. Film, concert, and lecture series are presented throughout the summer, along with crafts workshops, children's programs, and nature hikes.

Hiking

Bald Mountain, which offers superb views of the Fulton Chain for surprisingly little effort, is 4.5 miles east of Old Forge. From the well-marked parking lot at the foot of the mountain, the trail climbs only 400 feet in less than a mile: "If the climb were not too short to call a hike, or if you were not apt to meet hordes of other hikers, it could be one of the most satisfying treks in the Adirondacks," writes hiking guru Barbara McMartin in *50 Hikes in the Adirondacks.* To access the trailhead, turn left on Rondaxe Road, just north of Old Forge off Route 28, and follow signs for the trail.

Shopping

Old Forge Hardware (104 Fulton St., Old Forge, 315/369-6100, www.oldforgehardware. com) bills itself as the "Adirondacks' Most General Store." Inside, you'll find everything you could possibly need, from snowshoes and camp stoves, to plenty of things you don't, like paperweights. Also on Route 28, **Moose River Trading Company** (Rte. 28, Thendara, 315/369-6091) stocks classic Adirondack gear.

Outfitters and Guides

In Old Forge, boats and canoes can be rented at **Rivett's Marine** (102 Lakeview Ave., 315/369-3123, www.rivettsmarine.com). **Adirondack River Outfitters** (800/525-7238, www. aroadventures.com) conducts guided rafting trips down the Hudson, Moose, Black, and Salmon Rivers. **Tickner's Moose River Outfitter** (113 Riverside Ln., 315/369-6286,

www.ticknerscanoe.com) offers guided canoe and kayak trips, along with instruction, rentals, and sales.

Accommodations

Van Auken's Inne (108 Forge St., Thendara, 315/369-3033, www.vanaukensinne.com, $90-130), with its long, two-tiered porch, contains 12 renovated guest rooms with private baths. Some open out onto a breezy second-story balcony. On the ground floor are a comfortable lobby, tavern, and restaurant, all filled with antiques.

Food

Big Moose Station (2138 Big Moose Rd., Eagle Bay, 315/357-3525, www.bigmoosestation.com, daily breakfast, lunch, and dinner, $17), in the old Adirondack Railroad station, serves American diner-style food.

Housed in its namesake, complete with soaring ceilings, exposed beams, and a waterwheel, is the historic **Old Mill Restaurant** (Rte. 28, 315/369-3662, www.oldmilloldforge.com, daily dinner, $24) in Old Forge. Traditional American favorites, including steak, pork chops, and shrimp and chicken dishes, are on the menu.

In Thendara, the 1893 **Van Auken's Tavern and Inne** (108 Forge St., 315/369-3033, www. vanaukensinne.com, Tues.-Sun. dinner, $20) serves contemporary American and continental fare. The menu includes everything from grilled veal chops to fresh fish.

Information and Services

The **New York State Outdoor Guides Association** (1936 Saranac Ave., Lake Placid, NY 12946, 866/469-7642, www.nysoga.com) provides a complete list of guides and outfitters operating in the Adirondacks.

For general information on the Adirondacks, contact **Adirondack Regional Tourism Council** (Box 911, Lake Placid, 518/846-8016, www.visitadirondacks.com).

For more information on Lake George and the southeastern Adirondacks, contact the **Lake George Regional Chamber of Commerce** (Box 272, Lake George, 518/668-5755, www.lakegeorgechamber.com).

For more information on the Lake Champlain Valley and High Peaks region, contact the **Lake Placid/Essex County Visitors Bureau** (2608 Main St., Lake Placid, 518/523-2445, www.lakeplacid.com).

Other useful area information centers include:

- **Franklin County Tourism** (355 W. Main St., Malone, 518/481-1573, www.adirondacklakes.com)

- **Hamilton County Tourism** (White Birch Lake, Indian Lake, 518/648-5239, www.hamiltoncounty.com)

- **Oswego County Division of Promotion and Tourism** (46 E. Bridge St., Oswego, 315/349-8322, www.visitoswegocounty.com)

- **Plattsburgh-North Country Chamber of Commerce** (7061 Rte. 9, Plattsburgh, 518/563-1000, www.northcountrychamber.com)

- **Town of Webb/Old Forge Tourism Department** (3140 Rte. 28, Old Forge, 315/369-6983, www.oldforgeny.com)

- **Warren County Department of Tourism**

(Municipal Center, 1340 Rte. 9, Lake George, 800/958-4748, ext. 143, www.visitlakegeorge.com)

HIKING AND CANOEING

With 2,000 miles of hiking trails, and canoe routes stretching 100 miles or more, the Adirondacks is an outdoor lover's paradise. Free, basic information on hiking trails, canoe routes, and tips for using the state's lands can be obtained from the **Department of Environmental Conservation** (DEC, 518/402-8013, www.dec.ny.gov).

Some of the DEC's brochures include enough information to actually embark on a hike or canoe trip, but many do not. The best source for more detailed information and maps—essential in many areas—is **Adirondack Mountain Club** (ADK, 814 Goggins Rd., Lake George, NY 12845, 518/668-4447, www.adk.org). ADK maintains visitor information centers at Lake George and Lake Placid and runs Adirondak Loj, a rustic lodge and campground at Lake Placid.

The Adirondack Mountain Club publishes a number of hiking and paddling guidebooks that are updated regularly. These guidebooks, along with detailed topographic maps of the region, are sold online through the Club's store (www.adk.org).

FISHING

Among the many fish swimming Adirondack waters are landlocked salmon, brook trout, lake trout, northern pike, pickerel, and small- and large-mouth bass.

Fishing licenses are mandatory for everyone over age 16 and can be obtained in sporting-goods stores, bait shops, and town offices. Prices differ based on the length of time for which the permit is requested (one-day, seven-day, or year) and whether the person in need of the permit is a New York State resident or visitor. Once you've got your permit in hand,

canoeing in the Adirondacks

check with the Department of Environmental Conservation (www.dec.ny.gov), which maintains fishing hotlines dispensing information about good fishing spots. Call 518/402-8924 for current regional hotline numbers for the Adirondacks and High Peaks and northwestern lakes. The same information is also updated regularly on the DEC's website.

Getting There and Around

No major airports service the North Country, though there are regional airports in Lake Clear and Plattsburgh. The latter has limited commercial flights on Allegiant, PenAir, and Spirit. Most visitors, however, fly to New York City, Albany, Syracuse, Boston, or Montréal, and then drive.

Amtrak (800/872-7245, www.amtrak. com) operates daily between New York and Montréal, with stops in Glens Falls, Fort Ticonderoga, Port Henry, Westport, and Plattsburgh. The scenery along the way is spectacular. In fact, the ride has been called one of the 10 most scenic in the world.

Adirondack-Pine Hill Trailways (800/776-7548, www.trailwaysny.com) is the only bus company that provides service throughout the Adirondacks. **Greyhound** (800/231-2222, www.greyhound.com) travels to Glens Falls and Plattsburgh.

By far the best ways to explore the North Country are by car, canoe, and foot. **The Adirondack North Country Association** (ANCA, 67 Main St. Saranac Lake, 518/891-6200, www.adirondack.org) publishes a good map that outlines scenic and historic driving and cycling routes; copies can be picked up for free in most tourism offices.

THE FINGER LAKES AND THOUSAND ISLANDS-SEAWAY

This massive region, equal to New Hampshire or New Jersey in size, really seems to have it all: fascinating history, picture-perfect landscapes, farm-fresh food, and some of the country's best wines.

And that's just for starters.

According to Iroquois legend, the Finger Lakes were created when the Great Spirit reached out to bless the land, leaving imprints of his hands. Six of his fingers became the major Finger Lakes—Skaneateles, Owasco, Cayuga, Seneca, Keuka, and Canandaigua. The other four became the Little Finger Lakes—Honeoye, Canadice, Hemlock, and Conesus. He must have had an extra finger, too; that one became Otisco.

Geologists have a different creation story. They say the long, skinny parallel lakes formed from steady progressive grinding of at least two Ice Age glaciers. As the glaciers receded, lake-valleys filled with rivers that were backed by dams of glacial debris.

Depending on the weather, the water varies in hue from a deep sapphire blue to a moody gray. Along the lakes' southern edges, deep craggy gorges are sliced through the middle by silvery waterfalls. To the north are hundreds of drumlins, gentle glacier-created hills. All around lie fertile farmlands with fruit trees, buckwheat, and, especially, grapevines.

Scenic beauty is only part of the Finger Lakes story. The region's small towns abound with markers of important moments in American history. There are the homes of abolitionists Harriet Tubman and William Seward in Auburn; the National Park site

© FRANCISCO COLLAZO

HIGHLIGHTS

◖ **Skaneateles Village:** One of the prettiest of the Finger Lakes is anchored by this picturesque village, filled with cute shops and cafés (page 345).

◖ **Women's Rights National Historical Park:** The site of the first women's rights convention, organized by Elizabeth Cady Stanton and friends, met in Seneca Falls in 1848. The park has an informative visitors' center and historic sites (page 353).

◖ **Wine Routes:** Routes 414 and 14 are chock-a-block with wineries, with one tasting room after another tempting you inside to savor the flavor (pages 366).

◖ **Watkins Glen State Park:** It's hard to believe that such incredible natural beauty is so accessible to the main drag. A single turn and you're in the parking lot; two minutes later, you're at the trailhead, where you'll feel drops from the first impressive waterfall stippling your face (page 369).

◖ **Mark Twain's Study:** Modeled after a Mississippi steamboat pilot house, the stand-alone octagonal study holds the iconic writer's typewriter, hat, pipe, and other belongings (page 373).

◖ **Soaring over Harris Hill:** Climb into a tiny engineless glider and soar over the Seneca Lake Valley. The pilot tailors the flight to your tastes—from serene to exhilarating (page 374).

◖ **Corning Museum of Glass:** This remarkable collection of glass art spans over 3,000 years. Dozens of daily interactive shows and a studio where you can try your hand as a gaffer make for a fun, informative museum experience (page 376).

◖ **Rockwell Museum of Western Art:** This fantastic museum features an exceptional collection of painting, sculptures, photos, and multimedia work from the American West. Special children's activities make it a must-visit for families (page 377).

◖ **National Museum of Play:** Kids won't want to miss this sprawling children's museum, where interactive exhibits and hands-on exploration are encouraged (page 393).

◖ **Boldt Castle:** If you can't live in a castle that was built in tribute to you, visiting Boldt Castle—built at the bidding of George Boldt in honor of his wife—is probably the next best thing (page 409).

LOOK FOR ◖ TO FIND RECOMMENDED SIGHTS, ACTIVITIES, DINING, AND LODGING.

FINGER LAKES

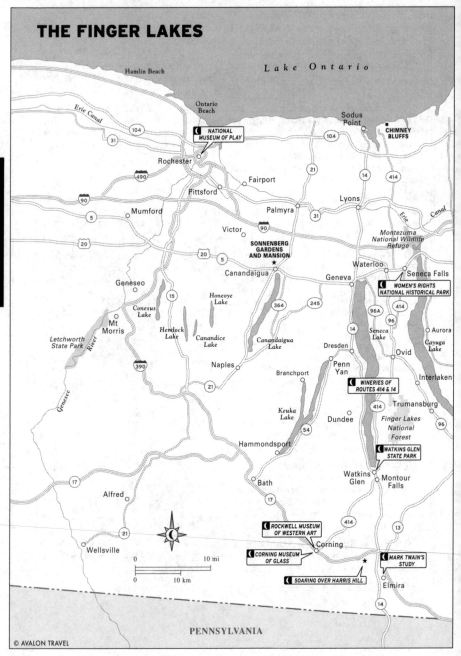

THE FINGER LAKES

Lake Ontario

Hamlin Beach

Erie Canal

Ontario Beach

Sodus Point

CHIMNEY BLUFFS

NATIONAL MUSEUM OF PLAY

Rochester

Fairport

Pittsford

Lyons

Mumford

Palmyra

Montezuma National Wildlife Refuge

Victor

SONNENBERG GARDENS AND MANSION

Waterloo

Seneca Falls

WOMEN'S RIGHTS NATIONAL HISTORICAL PARK

Canandaigua

Geneva

Geneseo

Honeoye Lake

Aurora

Conesus Lake

Mt Morris

Hemlock Lake

Canandice Lake

Canandaigua Lake

Dresden

Seneca Lake

Ovid

Cayuga Lake

Letchworth State Park

Naples

Penn Yan

Interlaken

Branchport

WINERIES OF ROUTES 414 & 14

Keuka Lake

Dundee

Trumansburg

Finger Lakes National Forest

Hammondsport

WATKINS GLEN STATE PARK

Bath

Watkins Glen

Montour Falls

Alfred

ROCKWELL MUSEUM OF WESTERN ART

Corning

MARK TWAIN'S STUDY

CORNING MUSEUM OF GLASS

SOARING OVER HARRIS HILL

Elmira

Wellsville

0   10 mi

0   10 km

PENNSYLVANIA

© AVALON TRAVEL

commemorating the first women's rights convention in Seneca Falls; and the Book of Mormon Historic Publication Site in tiny Palmyra, where Joseph Smith, Jr. experienced his "First Vision," leading to the establishment of the Mormon religion. The region also holds a number of interesting small cities. Syracuse was once an Erie Canal boomtown. Ithaca, home to Cornell University, is surrounded by awesome steep gorges and waterfalls.

More watery landscapes await in the Thousand Islands, an archipelago in the St. Lawrence River that separates New York and Canada. There are actually far more than 1,000—nearly 1,900 in all. Some are inhabited and can be visited, while others offer barely enough room to stand. To be counted among them, an island must be at least one square foot in size, support at least one tree, and remain above water year-round. Many scions of industry built lavish vacation homes here, including Boldt Castle, now one of the region's top tourist attractions. In the early 20th century, wealthy families from northeastern and midwestern cities would decamp to the Thousand Islands to escape the pressures of urban life and revel in the calm, unhurried pace of the islands. Despite over a century of tourism, that slower pace thankfully remains today.

PLANNING YOUR TIME

The Finger Lakes and Thousand Islands-Seaway is one of the largest regions in New York State and the distance between the two areas is considerable. Fortunately, I-90 east to I-81 north makes for a speedier connection between the Finger Lakes and the Thousand Islands-Seaway.

Given the region's size, the number of historical and natural points of interest, and the variety of wineries in the area, one could easily spend a week or two exploring the Finger Lakes and Thousand Islands. If you don't have the luxury of time, you can still experience the best of either area by training your focus on a micro-region. The Finger Lakes particularly lend themselves to settling in a single town as a home base and exploring the wineries and natural features of the lake on which that town sits.

Most travelers will probably want to start their tour in **Skaneateles,** the prettiest of the Finger Lakes, which can easily be explored in an afternoon. Just down the road is **Auburn,** home to the fascinating house-museums of abolitionists William Seward and Harriet Tubman. Beyond that is the town of **Seneca Falls,** a must stop for anyone interested in women's history.

Outdoor lovers might want to focus on the southern side of the Finger Lakes region. Here, you'll find **Ithaca,** a university town surrounded by dramatic gorges and great hiking trails; **Finger Lakes National Forest;** and, at the far western edge of the region, **Letchworth State Park,** home to the "Grand Canyon of the East." There's also the little-known Finger Lakes Trail. More than 950 miles long, it runs from the Pennsylvania-New York border in Allegany State Park to the Long Path in the Catskill Forest Preserve. Branch trails lead to Niagara Falls, the Genesee River Valley, the Great Eastern Trail south of Corning, the central Finger Lakes, and Syracuse.

Wine lovers should focus on **Hammondsport** and **Keuka and Seneca Lakes,** which have an especially large number of vineyards, as well as lovely scenic vistas.

Culture buffs will want to spend one or two days in **Rochester,** which has an impressive children's museum and The George Eastman House, one of the finest collections of photography and film in the country. In Corning, the world-famous glass museum and Rockwell Museum of Western Art are must-sees. A visit to Corning can be paired with a stop in Watkins Glen, whose popular state park by the same name offers easy hikes with rewarding views of dramatic waterfalls and glacier-carved gorges.

The Thousand Islands are best visited in the summer months, when attractions are all open and activities are in full swing. From the Finger Lakes, you'll take I-90 east and then I-81 north to reach the region.

Syracuse

The main streets of Syracuse are oddly wide and flat, like fat rubber bands stretched out to their sides. They beg the question: who would lay out a city with so much empty space? The answer is simple. One street—Erie Boulevard—was once the Erie Canal, another, Genesee Street, was the Genesee Valley Turnpike.

Like many towns in central New York, Syracuse boomed with the opening of the Erie Canal. But long before the canal, settlers were attracted to the area for its many valuable salt springs. As early as 1797, the state took over the springs to obtain tax revenues on salt, worth so much it was referred to as "white gold."

With the opening of the Erie Canal, the salt industry developed rapidly, reaching a high point of eight million bushels a year during the Civil War. Other Syracuse industries flourished as well, including foundries and machine shops. The Irish, who had arrived to dig the canal, remained to work the factories and were soon joined by large numbers of German immigrants. Little surprise, then, that breweries were another booming industry in Syracuse.

After the Civil War, other industries took over, among them, typewriters, ceramics, and Franklin cars, equipped with air-cooled engines. The Irish and Germans were joined by Italians, Poles, Russians, and Ukrainians.

Today, the fifth-largest city in the state (pop. 145,000) still supports a wide variety of people and industries, including National Grid, Lockheed Martin, and Syracuse University.

Orientation

The heart of Syracuse is Clinton Square, where Erie Boulevard and Genesee Street meet. The main business district lies just south of the square and is dominated by Salina and Montgomery Streets. From Clinton Square, head south on Franklin Street three blocks, and you'll find yourself in the red-brick Armory Square District, Syracuse's answer to Greenwich Village. At one end hulks the old Syracuse Armory; all around are shops, cafés, and restaurants. The district centers on the junction of Franklin and Walton Streets.

Syracuse University sits on a hill to the southeast; to the northwest is Onondaga Lake. South of the city, the sovereign 7,300-acre Onondaga Nation is home to about 750 Haudenosaunee. The Iroquois Confederacy's Grand Council of Chiefs still meets here every year, as it has for centuries.

The New York State Thruway runs east-west north of downtown. I-81 runs north-south through the center of the city. Street parking is generally available. Sights downtown are within easy walking distance of each other.

SIGHTS
Heritage Area Visitor Center and Erie Canal Museum
The long, 1850s building of the **Heritage Area Visitor Center and Erie Canal Museum** (318 Erie Blvd. E., 315/471-0593, www.erie-canalmuseum.org, Mon.-Sat. 10am-5pm, Sun. 10am-3pm, free) was once an Erie Canal weigh station for boats. Today, it's the only remaining weighlock building in the country,

and it is home to a visitors center, historical exhibits, a theater where a good introductory film on the city is screened, and a 65-foot-long reconstructed canal boat. In the boat remain the original personal effects of some early passengers, including one heart-breaking letter from an Irishwoman who buried her husband at sea.

Clinton Square

Heading west two blocks from the visitors center, you'll reach **Clinton Square,** the heart of the city. The former intersection of the Erie Canal and Genesee Valley Turnpike teemed with farmers' wagons, peddlers' carts, canal boats, hawkers, musicians, and organ grinders in the old days. Today, many free outdoor events are held here.

In the mid-1800s, Clinton Square evolved from a marketplace into a financial center. Four bank buildings along Salina Street—all listed on the National Register of Historic Places—hark back to those days. Another noteworthy historic item is the four-sided, 100-foot clock tower on the 1867 Gridley Building, which was originally lit by gas jets.

At the western end of Clinton Square, near Clinton Street, stands **Jerry Rescue Monument.** The monument commemorates William "Jerry" McHenry, born into slavery in North Carolina around 1812. Jerry successfully escaped to Syracuse, where he got a job in a cooper's shop making salt barrels. He was discovered and arrested by federal marshals in 1851. A vigilante abolitionist group headed by Gerrit Smith and Dr. Samuel J. May attacked the police station and rescued Jerry, who fled to Canada a few days later. That rescue, which challenged the Fugitive Slave Act of 1850, was one of the early events precipitating the Civil War.

One block farther west on Erie Boulevard at Franklin Street is the stunning **Niagara Mohawk Power Corporation** building. Completed in 1932, the steel-and-black structure is a superb example of Art Deco architecture. The edifice is especially worth seeing at night, when it's lit by colored lights.

Rubenstein Museum of Science and Technology

The MOST, a.k.a. **Rubenstein Museum of Science and Technology** (500 S. Franklin St., 315/425-9068, www.most.org, Wed.-Sun. 10am-5pm, adults $8, seniors and children 2-11 $7), is an interactive, hands-on center that's family-friendly. Exhibit subjects include the earth, the human body, the environment, and space. Kids especially love Science Playhouse, a climbing maze, and Discovery Cave, a life-size replica of a cave, where they can learn more about cavern and fossil formation. The MOST also has a planetarium and an IMAX theater; entry to each requires a separate ticket from that presented for museum admission.

Landmark Theatre

The 2,922-seat **Landmark Theatre** (362 S. Salina St., 315/475-7980, www.landmarktheatre.org, Mon.-Fri. 10am-5pm, tours by appointment) is less than two blocks from the MOST. Designed in 1928 by Thomas Lamb, a preeminent movie-palace architect, the building's relatively sedate exterior does little to prepare you for its riotous interior—an ornate Indo-Persian fantasy rich with gold carvings. Nearly destroyed by a wrecking ball in the 1970s, the Landmark Theatre is now a beloved local institution that features traveling Broadway performances and other cultural events.

Onondaga Historical Association Museum

One of the best county museums in the state, **Onondaga Historical Association Museum** (321 Montgomery St., 315/428-1864, www.cnyhistory.org, Wed.-Fri. 10am-4pm, Sat.-Sun. 11am-4pm, free, donations welcome) covers virtually every aspect of Central New York history, from the Onondaga Nation and early African American settlers to the Erie Canal and the salt industry. Permanent exhibits include Freedom Bound: Syracuse and the Underground Railroad, Syracuse's Brewing History, and Syracuse China, which features almost 200 pieces of china made by Syracuse

China over a 130-year period. A variety of historic maps, photographs, paintings, and artifacts are also displayed.

Everson Museum of Art

Housed in a sleek, modern building designed by I. M. Pei in 1968 and widely credited for launching his career, **Everson Museum of Art** (401 Harrison St., 315/474-6064, www.everson.org, Tues.-Fri. and Sun. noon-5pm, Sat. 10am-5pm, $5 suggested donation) contains one of the world's largest collections of ceramics. The museum also displays fine collections of 19th-century American portraits, post-World War II-era photographs, and art videos from the 1960s and 1970s. Temporary exhibits often focus on contemporary American artists working in a variety of media.

Rosamond Gifford Zoo at Burnet Park

The 36-acre **Rosamond Gifford Zoo** (1 Conservation Pl., 315/435-8511, www.rosamondgiffordzoo.org, daily 10am-4:30pm, adults $8, seniors $5, students $4, children 2 and under free) on the west side of town houses about 700 animals living in recreated natural habitats, including an arctic tundra, a tropical rain forest, and an arid desert. Public overnights and meet-the-elephant opportunities are a couple of the zoo's highlights.

Tipperary Hill

West of downtown, at the juncture of West Fayette and West Genesee Streets, is the "Gateway to Tipperary Hill." Syracuse's oldest Irish neighborhood, Tipperary Hill is known for its **upside-down traffic light,** the only one in the country, at the intersection of Tompkins and Lowell Streets. When the stoplight was installed in 1925, right-side-up, members of the predominantly Irish neighborhood were irate: "British" red was placed above "Irish" green. Local boys protested by hurling stones at the light, breaking the lenses. City officials, realizing this was one battle they could never win, reversed the lenses in conciliation. Today, the green-over-red light remains and

a monument to the stone throwers sits at the same intersection.

Cashel House (224 Tompkins St., 315/472-4438, www.cashelhousegifts.com), packed with goods imported from Ireland, stands in the heart of today's Tipperary Hill. Across the street, **Coleman's Authentic Irish Pub** (100 S. Lowell Ave., 315/476-1933, www.colemansirishpub.com) has been serving Irish pub grub since 1933. Look for its "leprechaun doors" as you enter and leave the restaurant.

Salt Museum

To the north, in the suburb of Liverpool, lies lozenge-shaped Onondaga Lake, whose rich salt deposits first attracted settlers to the area. The lake is currently undergoing a major clean-up to remediate pollution. To one side stands **Salt Museum** (106 Lake Dr., Liverpool, 315/453-6715, www.onondagacountyparks.com/salt-museum, early May-mid Oct. Sat.-Sun. 1pm-6pm, free), equipped with an original "boiling block." Brine was once turned into salt here through boiling and solar evaporation. Battered antique iron kettles, wooden barrels, and other equipment, along with a fascinating collection of historic photographs, are on display.

The museum and lake comprise **Onondaga Lake Park** (www.onondagacountyparks.com/onondaga-lake-park), which also offers bicycle rentals, a tram ride, a playground, and **Skä•noñh–Great Law of Peace Center** (6680 Onondaga Lake Pkwy., 315/428-1864, www.skanonhcenter.org), a second museum and heritage center on the other side of the parkway. At present, the museum itself is closed while it is repurposed from its former identity as the Ste. Marie among the Iroquois Museum. Visitors can walk the grounds during renovation, which is expected to last well into 2014.

Matilda Joslyn Gage House

History has all but forgotten Matilda Joslyn Gage, who doesn't enjoy nearly as much renown and recognition as fellow suffragettes Elizabeth Cady Stanton and Susan B. Anthony. The staff of the **Matilda Joslyn**

THE PEOPLE OF THE LONGHOUSE

When French explorers first arrived in the Finger Lakes area in the early 1600s, they found it occupied by a confederacy of five Indian nations. The French called the Indians "Iroquois"; the Indians called themselves "Haudenosaunee," or "People of the Longhouse."

The Mohawk Nation (Keepers of the Eastern Door) lived to the east of what is considered the Finger Lakes region, along Schoharie Creek and the Mohawk River Valley. The Seneca (Keepers of the Western Door) lived to the west, along the Genesee River. In the middle were the Onondaga (Keepers of the Council Fire), and it was on their territory the chiefs of the Five Nations met to establish policy and settle disputes. The two other "little brother" nations were the Cayuga, who resided between the Onondaga and the Seneca, and the Oneida, who lived between the Onondaga and the Mohawk. A sixth nation, the Tuscarora, joined the Iroquois confederacy in 1722.

During the Revolutionary War, all of the Iroquois except the Oneida sided with the British, as they had during the French and Indian War. Together with the Tories, they terrorized the pioneer villages and threatened the food supply of the Continental Army. In 1779, an angered General Washington sent Major General John Sullivan into the region, ordering him to "lay waste all the settlements around so that the country may not only be overrun but destroyed." Sullivan carried out his orders, annihilating 41 Iroquois settlements and burning many fields and orchards. By the time he was done, the Iroquois nation was in ruins. Thousands fled to Canada; others were resettled onto reservations in 1784.

Gage House (210 E. Genesee St., 315/637-9511, www.matildajoslyngage.org, hours vary seasonally), Gage's former home turned museum, is committed to doing their small part to restore Gage to history. Gage, a historian and scholar, was instrumental in drafting seminal documents of the suffrage movement; she was also an ardent abolitionist. Interestingly, she had another influence on American society as well: She was the mother-in-law of writer L. Frank Baum, famous as the author of *The Wizard of Oz*. Her life and work inspired Baum to explore the themes of courage and compassion that formed the crux of his most famous book.

At the Gage House visitors can learn a great deal about 19-century history in rooms that are devoted to the suffrage and abolition movements, as well as Iroquois influence on democracy and women's rights. There is also a room that interprets some of Baum's and Oz's history. Baum married Gage's daughter in this house and he lived here for a short time. The house is part of the National Underground Railroad Network to Freedom.

ENTERTAINMENT AND EVENTS
Performing Arts

One of the more unusual arts organizations in town is **Open Hand Theater** (518 Prospect Ave., 315/476-0466, www.openhandtheater.org), featuring giant puppets from around the world. Connected to the theater is a **Museum of International Masks and Puppets** (518 Prospect Ave., 315/476-0466, www.openhandtheater.org, by appointment), complete with hands-on activities.

Landmark Theatre (362 S. Salina St., 315/475-7980, www.landmarktheatre.org) hosts concerts, plays, dance troupes, and classic movies throughout the year.

Syracuse Stage (820 E. Genesee St., 315/443-4008, www.syracusestage.org) is the region's premier professional theater and puts on up to seven plays and musicals annually.

Red House Art Center (201 S. West St., 315/362-2785, www.theredhouse.org) is a cultural center that presents many types of work, including theater, music, and visual art, year-round.

Nightlife

The best source for what's going on where is **Syracuse New Times** (www.syracusenewtimes. com), a free alternative newsweekly published on Wednesdays, available throughout the city.

Many bars and clubs are located in the **Armory Square District** (www.armorysquare. com).

One of the liveliest music clubs in town is **Dinosaur Bar-B-Que** (246 W. Willow St., 315/476-4937, www.dinosaurbarbque.com), a friendly spot filled with dinosaurs and blues paraphernalia. Guests run the gamut from bikers to businesspeople. Live blues is performed most nights.

A good club in which to hear local bands is **Shifty's** (1401 Burnet Ave., 315/474-0048, www.shiftysbar.com), which has live music Wednesday-Sunday. On weekends, traditional Irish music can be heard at **Coleman's Authentic Irish Pub** (100 S. Lowell Ave., 315/476-1933, www.colemansirishpub.com).

Events

Syracuse Jazz Fest (www.syracusejazzfest. com) is the largest free jazz festival in the Northeast. The celebration usually runs for three days in early July, and features a wide variety of jazz events, artists, and styles. The city also hosts a smaller but growing **Blues Festival** (www.nysbluesfest.com) each summer.

One of the state's grandest parties is the **New York State Fair** (New York State Fairgrounds, 581 State Fair Blvd., Exit 7 off I-690, 315/487-7711, www.nysfair.org), featuring agricultural and livestock competitions, music and entertainment, amusement rides and games of chance, business and industrial exhibits, and talent competitions. The fair runs for 12 days, ending on Labor Day, and has attracted as many as one million visitors in past years.

SHOPPING

If there's something you forgot to pack, it would be nearly impossible not to find a replacement at **Destiny USA** (9090 Destiny USA Dr., 315/466-6000, www.destinyusa.com), a six-story shopping mall with more than 200 stores. It's the largest mall in the state and the sixth largest in the country.

SPORTS AND RECREATION

Mid-Lakes Navigation (315/685-8500, www. midlakesnav.com) offers sightseeing and dinner cruises on the Erie Canal and Skaneateles Lake. The company also offers two- and three-day cruises and has boats available for weekly rental.

Take in a Syracuse University football, basketball, or lacrosse game at the 50,000-seat **Carrier Dome** (900 Irving Ave., 315/443-4634, www.carrierdome.com).

ACCOMMODATIONS

◖ **Barrington Manor B&B** (1504 James St., 315/472-7925, www.barringtonmanor.org, $99-350 d) is in a lovely residential neighborhood just east of downtown. This stately English Tudor B&B offers five attractive guest rooms filled with antiques. There's a small garden out back, and a guest kitchen is generously stocked with snacks, beer, and wine.

Comfortable **Craftsman Inn** (7300 E. Genesee St., 315/637-8000, www.craftsmaninn.com, $99-180) is in Fayetteville, 10 miles southeast of Syracuse. All 90 rooms and suites are furnished in Arts and Crafts style.

Downtown **Parkview Hotel** (713 E. Genesee St., 315/476-4212, www.theparkviewhotel. com, $129-675) is a charming boutique hotel with large, Art Deco-styled rooms. A good coffee bar, Stefon's Marketplace, also serves light meals on the first floor. The complimentary airport shuttle and free Wi-Fi add to the good value of this convenient downtown option.

◖ **Jefferson Clinton Hotel** (416 S. Clinton St, 315/425-0500, www.jeffersonclintonhotel. com, $215-350), with warm, genuine service, impresses guests with little touches, from the rubber ducky atop the generous stack of bath towels to an omelet station at the complimentary breakfast buffet. Free Wii, X-Box 360, DVD and GPS rentals, Wi-Fi, and parking are added perks. What might be most winning, though, is the hotel's habit of scooting guests to their room on early arrivals whenever possible and offering free upgrades to available junior suites. The Armory Square location offers easy access to pubs, museums, and the large ice-skating pavilion during winter.

Hotel Skyler (601 S. Crouse Ave., 800/365-4663, www.hotelskyler.com, $189-399) is one of Syracuse's most interesting accommodations, built in a former temple and theater in the middle of the Syracuse University campus. The hotel's 58 rooms are decorated in a bohemian chic style, and all have free Wi-Fi. All guests enjoy complimentary access to the hotel's gym and business center, and parking is free.

Courtyard Syracuse Downtown at Armory Square (300 W. Fayette St., 315/422-4854, www.marriott.com, $199-249) opened in July 2013 in a location that is incredibly convenient to restaurants, shops, and other Syracuse attractions. The seven-story Marriott property has 96 rooms and six suites, all of which have free Wi-Fi.

FOOD

In the Armory Square District, try **Pastabilities** (311 S. Franklin St., 315/474-1153, www.pastabilities.com, Mon.-Sat. lunch and dinner, Sun. dinner, $14) for Italian fare. Also in the neighborhood, **Lemon Grass** (238 W. Jefferson St., 315/475-1111, www.lemongrasscny.com, Mon.-Sat. lunch and dinner, Sun. dinner, $20) and **Bistro Elephant Steakhouse** (238 W. Jefferson St., 315/475-1111, www.bistroelephant.com, Mon.-Sat. 5pm-close, $21) are owned by the same duo and share the same address and phone number. Lemon Grass is a Thai restaurant; Bistro Elephant is a steakhouse with some international influences.

◖ Dinosaur Bar-B-Que (246 W. Willow St., 315/476-4937, daily lunch and dinner, www.dinosaurbarbque.com, $14), known statewide for its winning sauces, is awhirl with murals of frolicking dinosaurs. Business folks on lunch breaks slip past the row of Harleys parked out front to get their 'cue on. It was ranked best BBQ in North America by *Good Morning America*. The fun, bustling hot spot

serves straightforward barbecue dishes and home-style comfort foods for lunch and dinner; fried green tomatoes and pulled pork sandwiches are two favorites.

In its past life, **◖ The Mission Restaurant** (304 E. Onondaga St., 315/475-7344, www.themissionrestaurant.com, Tues.-Sun. lunch and dinner, Mon. lunch, $18) was a Methodist church, and today it still has a steeple and stained-glass windows. The church was also a stop on the Underground Railroad. Today, the repurposed building is a restaurant where Pan-American fare, with a heavy emphasis on Mexican cuisine, is served.

The Clam Bar (3914 Brewerton Rd., 315/458-1662, www.theclambarrestaurant.com, daily lunch and dinner, $18), with a deceptively 1950s kitsch, dive-ish look, complete with knotty pine walls and motorcycle parking, fronts a family-owned place touted for the best seafood in town. This claim is backed up by the crowd, which you'll want to get here early to avoid.

In Tipperary Hill, **Coleman's Authentic Irish Pub** (100 S. Lowell Ave., 315/476-1933, www.colemansirishpub.com, daily lunch and dinner, $16) is a neighborhood institution. Its menu, written in both Gaelic and English, features lots of hearty Irish fare. For Old World German food in a simple setting, try **Danzer's** (153 Ainsley Dr., 315/422-0089, $16), also a Syracuse institution, located south of downtown.

EXCURSIONS FROM SYRACUSE
Beaver Lake Nature Center

The serene, 560-acre **Beaver Lake Nature Center** (8477 East Mud Lake Rd., Baldwinsville, 315/638-2519, www.onondagacountyparks.com/beaver-lake-nature-center, daily 7:30am-dusk, $3 per car), 18 miles northwest of Syracuse, offers 9 miles of well-marked trails and boardwalks, along with a 200-acre lake that's a favorite resting spot for migrating ducks and geese. A visitors' center displays exhibits on local flora and fauna.

Highland Forest

Onondaga County's largest and oldest park is the 2,700-acre **Highland Forest** (1254 Highland Forest Rd., 315/683-5550, www.onondagacountyparks.com/highland-forest, daily dawn-dusk, $1 per person), in Fabius, about a 30-minute drive southeast of Syracuse. Spread out atop Arab Hill, the park offers great views of the surrounding countryside.

Adirondack-like in appearance, the forest is laced with four hiking trails ranging in length from less than a mile to eight miles. One-hour guided trail rides on horseback are offered May 1-October 31; hay and sleigh rides are offered on fall and winter weekends.

Green Lakes State Park

About 10 miles due east of Syracuse, 2,000-acre **Green Lakes State Park** (7900 Green Lakes Rd., Fayetteville, 315/637-6111, camping reservations 800/456-2267, www.nysparks.com/parks/172, daily dawn-dusk, $8 parking) has two aquamarine glacial lakes. Facilities include a swimming beach, hiking and biking trails, playground, campground, and 18-hole golf course. Boats can also be rented.

Camillus Erie Canal Park

Part of the much larger Erie Canalway National Heritage Corridor, **Camillus Erie Canal Park** (5750 Devoe Rd., Camillus, 315/488-3409, www.eriecanalcamillus.com) is a great place to get a sense of the significant role of the canal in the history of New York. While the **Sims Store Museum** (noon-4pm Sat. year-round, noon-4pm Wed.-Thurs. May-Oct.), modeled after an old-fashioned general store, is certainly interesting, a guided **boat tour** (1pm-5pm May-Oct.) on the canal is even more informative and engaging.

Skaneateles Lake

The farthest east of the Finger Lakes, deep blue Skaneateles is also the highest (867 feet above sea level) and most beautiful. Fifteen miles long and 1-2 miles wide, the lake is surrounded by gentle rolling hills to the south and more majestic, near-mountainous ones to the north. Iroquois for "long lake," Skaneateles is spring fed, crystal clean, and clear. In the summer, its waters are specked with sailboats; in the winter, ice fishers build igloos.

The only real village on the lake is Skaneateles. Handsome summer homes placed judicious distances apart preside elsewhere along the shoreline.

◖ SKANEATELES VILLAGE

The charming village of Skaneateles spreads out along one long main street (Route 20) at the north end of the lake. Graceful 19th-century homes, white-columned public buildings, and trim brick storefronts are everywhere and make for excellent strolling. Skaneateles has been a favorite retreat among wealthy Syracusans for generations.

The first Europeans in Skaneateles were Moravian missionaries who visited an Onondaga village here in 1750. From 1843 to 1845, the village was the short-lived site of a Utopian community that advertised in the newspapers for followers and advocated communal property, nonviolence, easy divorce, and vegetarianism. The area also served as a stopping place on the Underground Railroad, with English-born Quaker James Fuller spearheading the local abolition movement.

Clift Park, in the center of the village, is a waterfront refuge with a gazebo and wide-angled views of the lake. Docked at the end of a small pier are the two classic wooden boats of **Mid-Lakes Navigation Co.** (315/685-8500, www.midlakesnav.com, mid-May-Oct.). During warmer months, the family-owned spit-and-polish vessels offer enjoyable sightseeing, and lunch and dinner cruises. These same craft also deliver the mail on Skaneateles Lake—a 100+-year-old tradition. The knowledgeable captain offers insight into passing sights and properties, some of which her family settled generations before.

The Creamery

To learn about the lake's history, step into **The Creamery** (28 Hannum St., 315/685-1360, www.skaneateleshistoricalsociety.org, Nov.-Apr. Fri. 1pm-4pm, May-Oct. Fri.-Sat. 1pm-4pm, donations welcome), a small, local museum housed in the former Skaneateles Creamery building. From 1899 to 1949, area farmers brought their milk here to be turned into buttermilk, cream, and butter. Displays include scale models of the boats that once sailed the lake, exhibits on dairy farming, and information about the teasel, a thistle-like plant once used in woolen mills to raise a cloth's nap. For 120 years, Skaneateles was the teasel-growing capital of the United States. The Creamery is run by the **Skaneateles Historical Society** (28 Hannum St., 315/685-1360, www.skaneateleshistoricalsociety.org), which also offers walking tours of the village.

New Hope Mills

For spectacular views of the lake, drive down either Route 41 to the east or Route 41A to the west. Route 41A veers away from the shoreline at the southern end and leads to **New Hope Mills** (181 York St., Auburn, 315/252-2676, www.newhopemills.com, Mon.-Fri. 8am-4pm, Sat. 10am-2pm), an 1823 flour mill that is currently being converted into a museum. Unbleached flours and grains are for sale in the mill's store, and coffee and baked goods are served in the café.

Events

Weekly **sailboat races** (2745 East Lake Rd., www.skansailclub.com, June-Aug. Wed. 5:30pm, Sat.-Sun. 2pm) take place throughout the summer, while free **band concerts** (W. Genesee St., across from the Sherwood Inn, www.skaneateles.com, July Fri. 7:30pm, Aug. Fri. 7pm) are held on Friday evenings in Clift Park. **Polo games** are played on Sunday afternoons in July and August at **Skaneateles Polo**

Club (783 Andrews Rd., 315/685-8545). Since 1980, the **Skaneateles Festival** (www.skanfest.org) has been bringing top chamber-music artists to town in August. The town's largest event is the **antique and classic boat show** (north end of Lake Skaneateles, 315/685-0552, www.skaneateles.com) in early July.

But not all of the fun happens in the summer. The cold weather brings what Skaneateles calls "the world's smallest Christmas parade": Scrooge, Bob Cratchit, Tiny Tim, and a handful of other characters from Charles Dickens' *A Christmas Carol* kick off holiday festivities with a march around town. **Dickens Christmas** (www.skaneateles.com) celebrated its 20th anniversary in 2013. Beloved by locals and visitors alike, the festival features free horse and carriage rides, free roasted chestnuts, and free hot cider and donuts (or hot chocolate served by village Girl Scouts). There's also caroling on most every street corner, a sing-along in the village gazebo, Mother Goose story-time, and Father Christmas giving out free treats for the best little visitors. Live Dickens characters interact with townsfolk and visitors in the shops and along the streets and perform scenes from the Dickens classic. It's enough to warm the cockles of the Scrooge-iest visitor's heart.

Accommodations

Across from the park is the hospitable 【**Sherwood Inn** (26 W. Genesee St., 315/685-3405, www.thesherwoodinn.com, $185-295), a rambling, colonial blue building that was once a stagecoach stop. The inn was established in 1807 by Isaac Sherwood, a man who began his career by delivering the mail on foot between Utica and Canandaigua and ended it as the "stagecoach king." Upscale yet casual, the inn includes a very popular restaurant, a tavern with frequent live entertainment, and 25 attractive guest rooms, all decorated with antiques. Contributing to the inn's relaxed atmosphere are a big screened-in porch with wonderful views of the lake, an outdoor patio for summer dining, lots of fresh flowers, and a snug lounge. **The Gray House** (47 Jordan St., 315/685-0131, www.gray-house.com, $99-185), near the heart of downtown, is a welcoming B&B housed in a spacious Victorian home. It has five guest rooms, a large parlor, two breezy porches, and gardens.

Hobbit Hollow Farm (3061 West Lake Rd., 315/685-2791, www.hobbithollow.com, $100-170), a century-old colonial Revival farmhouse, overlooks Skaneateles Lake from its picturesque 400-acre perch. This four-season property offers a full country breakfast, afternoon wine and cheese tasting, Wi-Fi, spa robes, snowshoes, and private baths.

Ultra-luxurious **Mirbeau Inn and Spa** (851 W. Genesee St., 315/685-5006 or 877/647-2328, www.mirbeau.com, $185-385) is on the outskirts of Skaneateles. The elegant, European-style inn, complete with wall frescoes, waterfalls, soft lighting, and 18 spacious guest rooms, also has an on-site spa. The inn is also known for its serene restaurant.

Food

The laid-back ◖ **Doug's Fish Fry** (8 Jordan St., 315/685-3288, www.dougsfishfry.com, daily lunch and dinner, $12) is a local favorite, renowned for its chowder, fried scallops, gumbo, and fish sandwiches.

Rosalie's Cucina (841 W. Genesee St., 315/685-2200, www.rosaliescucina.com, $27) offers first-rate Italian fare, ranging from pizza and pasta to grilled lobster tails, in an adobe tavern.

In addition to great accommodations, Sherwood Inn and Mirbeau Inn both have excellent restaurants. The restaurant at **Mirbeau** (851 W. Genesee St., 315/685-5006 or 877/647-2328, www.mirbeau.com, daily breakfast, lunch, and dinner, $32) serves creative American cuisine made with fresh local ingredients. Mirbeau also hosts special dinners with visiting chefs and special guests as well as cooking classes. The restaurant at **Sherwood Inn** (26 W. Genesee St., 315/685-3405, www.thesherwoodinn.com, $26) features traditional American fare. Check out **Patisserie** (4 Hannum St., 315/685-2433), which provides all the breads for the Sherwood Inn, a perfect stop for a great morning coffee and pastry.

Independent bookshop and café **Creekside Books and Coffee** (35 Fennell St., 315/685-0379, www.creeksidecoffeehouse.com) is a great place to stop for an espresso or glass of wine while leisurely browsing books. The café hosts wine tastings, author readings, cooking demos, and live music in a cozy, bookish atmosphere.

CORTLAND

About 12 miles from the southern tip of Skaneateles Lake sprawls the city of Cortland (pop. 19,292). Set in the midst of fertile farm country, Cortland was once a small industrial center, best known for its wire cloth, lingerie, and corset factories. A **National Historic District** of handsome homes and commercial buildings is found on Main Street between Tompkins Street and Clinton Avenue.

Cortland also has a claim to literary fame. It was here that Chester Gillette, the real-life counterpart to the character Clyde Griffiths in Theodore Dreiser's *An American Tragedy*, met Grace Brown. Writes Dreiser of Griffiths's arrival in his new hometown: "He found himself ambling on and on until suddenly he was...in touch with a wide and tree-shaded thoroughfare of residences, the houses of which, each and every one, appeared to possess more room space, lawn space, general ease and repose and dignity even than any with which he had ever been in contact...." Gillette once worked in his uncle's Gillette Skirt Factory on the north side of town, and lived in the double house at No. 17 East Main Street, which stands today.

1890 House Museum

Perhaps one of the houses spotted by Gillette/Griffiths in his ramble was the castle-like **1890 House Museum** (37 Tompkins St., 607/756-7551, www.the1890house.org, year-round Thurs.-Sat. noon-4pm, adults $8, seniors and students $5, children under 10 free), built by wire manufacturer Chester F. Wickwire. Now an informal museum, the house holds 30 rooms notable for their parquet floors, stained-glass windows, ornate stenciling, and hand-carved woodwork. A tower provides excellent views of the town. Walking-tour maps of Cortland's Historic District can be picked up here.

Cortland Country Music Park

Part RV camp, part country-music mecca, the 18-acre **Cortland Country Music Park** (1824 Rte. 13, 607/753-0377, www.cortlandmusicpark.com) bills itself as the "great Nashville of the Northeast." During summer, four or five concerts by top performers are staged, along with two-steppin' dance classes, square dances, and jamborees. The park offers live music by regional bands on weekends year-round and special events including horseshoe tournaments, the Old Timers Show, and the Festival of Bands.

The music park, which was built by volunteer country music fans, started in 1975. Centered around an Opry barn, it is equipped with one of the largest dance floors in the Northeast, an outdoor stage, and a Hall of Fame Museum (open only during events). In the museum, you'll find everything from a black-sequined dress formerly owned by Tammy Wynette to white boots once worn by Roy Acuff.

Shopping

It's worth traveling about eight miles south of Cortland to visit the **Book Barn of the Finger Lakes** (198 North Rd., Dryden, 607/844-9365, Mon.-Sat. 10am-5:30 pm, Sun. noon-5pm). The complex, which actually consists of three barns, houses 2.5 miles of shelves laden with nearly 100,000 books in 254 categories. It is run by Vladimer Dragan, who buys and sells all his books in person, even making house calls to estates and libraries.

Accommodations

Greek Peak Mountain Resort and Hope Lake Lodge and Indoor Waterpark (2000 Rte. 392, 800/955-2754, www.greekpeak.net, $340 fireplace suite for 2-4 people) is a four-season resort catering to skiers, families, and spa lovers. There are waterpark-inclusive packages and accommodations tailored to guests' individual interests. The resort offers several cafés and restaurants, 32 ski trails, a tubing center, and Nordic skiing and snowshoeing. Full service Waterfalls Spa gives non-snowbunnies plenty of treatments to enjoy.

Owasco Lake

The smallest of the major Finger Lakes, Owasco is 12 miles long and 1.5 miles wide at its widest point. Iroquois for "the crossing," Owasco lies 720 feet above sea level. For great views of the lake, take Route 38 south, hugging the western shore, or Route 38A south, which travels high above the lake to the east. A few miles down, Route 38A bumps into Rockefeller Road, a shoreline route lined with 150-year-old camps and houses.

The city of Auburn, population 27,365, sits at the northern end of Owasco. At the southern end are the village of Moravia, birthplace of President Millard Fillmore, the Fillmore Glen State Park, and miles of farm country.

AUBURN

For a small city, Auburn has been home to an unusually high number of remarkable men and women: Logan, or Tahgahjute, Iroquois orator; Harriet Tubman, African American leader; William H. Seward, visionary statesman; Thomas Mott Osborne, pioneer of prison reform; and Theodore W. Case, the inventor of sound film. Tributes to all can be found in the city.

Auburn was originally a Cayuga Indian village established at the junction of two trails. Revolutionary War veteran Colonel John Hardenbergh arrived in 1793 and built the area's first gristmill. By 1810, the village boasted 90 dwellings, 17 mills, and an incorporated library containing 200 books.

The opening of the Auburn State Prison in 1817 and the Auburn Theological Seminary in 1821 greatly stimulated growth. By the mid-1800s, Auburn was thriving. It even

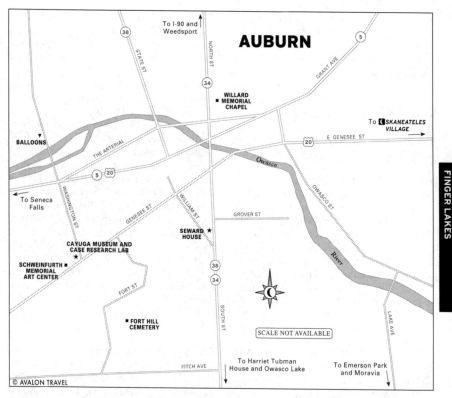

entertained hopes of becoming the state capital. The impressive public buildings on Genesee Street and lavish private homes on South Street date back to those heady days.

Seward House

One of the most interesting house museums in New York is **Seward House** (33 South St., 315/252-1283, www.sewardhouse.org, June-Labor Day Tues.-Sat. 10am-5pm and Sun. 1pm-5pm, hours vary off-season, closed Jan.-Feb., adults $8, seniors $7, students $5, children under 6 free), a stately 1816 Federal-style home shaded by leafy trees. The house belonged to William H. Seward, ardent abolitionist, New York governor, and U.S. senator, best remembered for purchasing Alaska from the Russians in 1857. Seward also served as Lincoln's secretary of state and was almost assassinated by a co-conspirator of John Wilkes Booth at the same time as the president.

Amazingly, almost everything in the Seward house is original. Inside, you'll find not only Seward's furniture, but his grocery bills, top hats, pipe collection, snuff-box collection, 10,000 books, political campaign buttons, tea from the Boston Tea Party, personal letters from Abraham Lincoln, and calling cards of former visitors Horace Greeley, Frederick Douglass, Millard Fillmore, and Daniel Webster.

Seward first moved to Auburn for the love of Miss Frances Miller, whose father, Judge Elijah Miller, built the house. As a newly minted lawyer, Seward got a job in the judge's law firm and proposed to his daughter. The ornery judge allowed the liaison on one condition: Seward could never take his daughter away from him.

Seward agreed and, despite his enormous worldly success, lived under his father-in-law's thumb for the next 27 years.

Excellent guides bring the past alive and a fascinating collection of visiting leaders makes for a fun "Guess Who" game. Perhaps the most interesting aspect of the museum is the revelation and proof, in the form of photographs, news clippings, an eyewitness account, and a bloodied, rent garment, that Lincoln was not a solo target that fateful night in the theater.

Harriet Tubman Home

On the outskirts of Auburn, next door to the AME Zion Church, stands the **Harriet Tubman Home** (180 South St., 315/252-2081, www.harriethouse.org, Tues.-Fri. 10am-4pm, Sat. 10am-3pm, adults $4.50, seniors $3, children $1.50), comprised of a brick house and adjacent white clapboard house wrapped with a long front porch. Known as the "Moses of her people," Harriet Tubman settled here after the Civil War, largely because her close friend and fellow abolitionist William Seward lived nearby.

Born a slave in Maryland in 1820 or 1821, Tubman escaped in 1849, fleeing first to Philadelphia and then to Canada. Yet as long as others remained in captivity, her freedom meant little to her. During the next dozen years, she risked 19 trips south, rescuing more than 300 slaves. She mostly traveled alone and at night. Her motto was "Keep going; children, if you are tired, keep going; if you are scared, keep going; if you are hungry, keep going; if you want to taste freedom, keep going."

A visit to the Tubman property begins in the Visitor Center with interpretive panels that follow the timeline of Tubman's life and pertinent events. Afterward, a member of the AME Zion Church takes visitors on a tour of the clapboard house where Tubman tended to the elderly and where a few of her belongings, including her bed and Bible, are on display. Tubman herself lived in the brick house. Though not open at present, there are future plans to make the house accessible to the public.

Fort Hill Cemetery

Harriet Tubman, William Seward, and numerous other Auburn notables are buried in **Fort Hill Cemetery** (19 Fort St., 315/253-8132, www.cayuganet.org/forthill, Mon.-Fri. 9am-4pm), on a hill to the west side of South Street. Native Americans used the site as burial grounds as early as AD 1100.

A large stone fortress-gate marks the cemetery entrance; inside towers the 56-foot-high **Logan Monument.** Erected upon a mound believed to be an ancient Native American altar, the monument pays homage to Logan, or Tahgahjute, the famed Cayuga orator born near Auburn in 1727. Logan befriended European settlers until 1774, when a group of marauding Englishmen massacred his entire family in the Ohio Valley. In retaliation, he scalped more than 30 white men. Later that same year in Virginia, at a conference with the British, he gave one of the most moving speeches in early American history. "Logan never felt fear," he said. "He will not turn his heel to save his life. Who is there to mourn for Logan? Not one."

Cayuga Museum and Case Research Lab

Housed in a Greek Revival mansion, **Cayuga Museum** (203 Genesee St., 315/253-8051, www.cayugamuseum.org, Feb.-Dec. Tues.-Sun. noon-5pm, suggested donation $3) is devoted to local history. Exhibits cover early Native American culture, the Civil War, the Auburn Correctional Facility, Millard Fillmore, and women's rights.

Behind the museum mansion stands a simple, low-slung building known as the **Case Research Lab** (203 Genesee St., 315/253-8051, www.cayugamuseum.org, Feb.-Dec. Tues.-Sun. noon-5pm, suggested donation $3). Here, in 1923, Theodore W. Case and E. I. Sponable invented the first commercially successful sound film, ushering in the talking movie era. Displays include the first sound camera and projector, original lab equipment, and Case's correspondence with Thomas Edison and Lee De Forest, a self-promoter who claimed *he* was the inventor of sound film.

Schweinfurth Memorial Art Center

Next to the Cayuga Museum, **Schweinfurth Memorial Art Center** (205 Genesee St., 315/255-1553, www.schweinfurthartcenter.org, Tues.-Sat. 10am-5pm, Sun. 1pm-5pm, closed between exhibits, adults $6, children 12 and under free) features temporary exhibits by contemporary and classic artists. Shows feature everything from fine art and photography to folk art and architecture. Each winter the museum hosts a popular juried quilt show.

Willard Memorial Chapel

The only complete and unaltered Tiffany chapel known to exist, **Willard Memorial Chapel** (17 Nelson St., 315/252-0339, www.willard-chapel.org, Feb.-Dec. Tues.-Fri. 10am-4pm, Jan. Thurs.-Fri. 10am-4pm, $5) glows with the muted, bejeweled light of 15 windows handcrafted by Tiffany Glass and Decorating Company. Louis C. Tiffany also designed the chapel's handsome oak furniture, inlaid with mosaics, leaded-glass chandeliers, and gold-stenciled pulpit.

A visit to the chapel begins with a video on the chapel's history and the now-defunct Auburn Theological Seminary of which it was once a part. In July and August, free organ recitals and concerts are played in the chapel.

Accommodations and Food

One mile south of Auburn you'll find **Springside Inn** (6141 W. Lake Rd., 315/252-7247, www.springsideinn.com, $100-250, with continental breakfast), a striking red Victorian with big white porches. Upstairs are seven guest rooms furnished with antiques and nice touches like canopy beds and claw-foot or whirlpool tubs.

The Springside Inn is well known for its modern gastropub, **Oak & Vine** (6141 W. Lake Rd., 315/252-7247, www.oakandvine.com, Mon.-Sat. dinner, Sun. brunch, $22), a local favorite for special occasions. The menu features American cuisine, including organic pasta and locally sourced organic produce.

Balloons (67 Washington St., across from the state prison, 315/252-9761, www.balloonsrestaurant.net, Tues.-Sat. dinner, $14) is a friendly spot with Art Deco decor, serving heaping platters of Italian-American food since 1934.

The Restaurant at Elderberry Pond (3712 Center Street Rd., 315/252-6025, www.elderberrypond.com, mid-Mar.-Dec. Wed.-Sun. lunch and dinner, $30) is surrounded by 100 acres of organic ingredients, from herbs to free range meats, grown right on Elderberry Pond Farm. The menu changes daily; a sampling includes items like organic whole wheat pasta served with an assortment of daily garden pickings. The adjacent farm store, located in an 1800s smokehouse, is a good spot to pick up some favorites for the road.

MORAVIA

At the southern end of Owasco Lake is Moravia, birthplace of President Millard Fillmore. Well off the beaten track, this small village boasts a number of handsome 19th-century buildings and the 1820s **St. Matthew's Episcopal Church** (14 Church St., 315/497-1171, Mon.-Fri. 8am-5pm, tours by appointment). The sanctuary's interior is covered with elaborate oak carvings designed and executed in Oberammergau, Germany.

FILLMORE GLEN STATE PARK

Just south of Moravia lies the 857-acre **Fillmore Glen State Park** (1686 Rte. 38, 315/497-0130, camping reservations 800/456-2267, www.nysparks.com/parks/157, daily dawn-dusk, $7 parking), centered on a deep, rugged ravine with five spectacular waterfalls. At the foot of the main falls is a geometric rock formation known as the Cowpens, and a popular swimming hole. Nearby are hiking trails, a campground, and a playground.

The park also contains a replica of the tiny log cabin in which President Millard Fillmore was born. His actual birthplace lies about five miles east of the park. Fillmore grew up dirt poor and went to work at an early age; he later described his upbringing as "completely shut out from the enterprises of civilization and advancement."

Cayuga Lake

The longest of the Finger Lakes, Cayuga stretches out for just under 40 moody miles, 382 feet above sea level. It varies in depth from a few feet to 435 feet, and supports a wide variety of marine life, with carp and large-mouth bass swimming in shallow waters and northern pike and lake trout inhabiting deeper ones.

Cayuga was named after the Iroquois nation that originally lived along its shores (the literal translation of Cayuga is "boat landing"). The Cayugas were called Gue-u-gweh-o-no, or people of the muckland, exemplified by the once-enormous Montezuma Marsh at the northern end of the lake.

Seneca Falls, the small industrial town where the first Women's Rights Convention met in 1848, sits just south of the marsh. Anchoring the southern end of the lake is Ithaca, a friendly cultural center that's home to Cornell University, Ithaca College, and craggy gorges

with waterfalls higher than Niagara. Along the lake's eastern and western shores are approximately 20 wineries; on the eastern shore is the historic village of Aurora.

SENECA FALLS

Seneca Falls owes its early development to a series of waterfalls dropping over 50 feet. The first gristmill was built here in 1795, and by the 1840s, the town supported dozens of water-powered factories. Many employed women worked 14-hour days for wages they had to turn over to their husbands. In 19th-century America, women were not allowed to own money or property or to even serve as legal guardians of their own children. This was the environment in which Elizabeth Cady Stanton gathered the historic 1848 convention that issued a Declaration of Sentiments calling for greater rights for women.

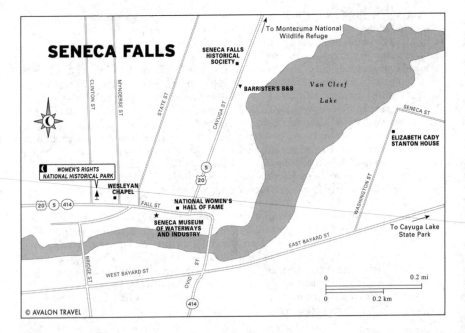

© AVALON TRAVEL

Today, Seneca Falls centers around Fall Street (Rtes. 5 and 20). Running parallel to Fall Street is the Seneca River and the Cayuga-Seneca Canal, which links Cayuga and Seneca Lakes. At the eastern end of town is the artificially constructed Van Cleef Lake.

Heritage Area Visitors Center

For a good general introduction to Seneca Falls, stop into the **Heritage Area Visitors Center** (115 Fall St., 315/568-1510, Mon.-Sat. 10am-4pm, Sun. noon-4pm, free). The exhibits cover virtually every aspect of the town's history, from its Iroquois beginnings and early factory days to its women's history and ethnic heritage, as well as the area's industrial past. Seneca Falls once held world fame for its knitting mills and pump factories.

Don't leave the center without learning about the destruction of the city's once invaluable waterfalls. The falls were eliminated in 1915 to create the Cayuga-Seneca Canal and, by extension, Van Cleef Lake. The flooding destroyed more than 150 buildings; today, many foundations are still visible beneath the lake's clear waters.

◖ Women's Rights National Historical Park

Elizabeth Cady Stanton and her abolitionist husband Henry Stanton moved to Seneca Falls from Boston in 1847, a time when the town was both a major transportation hub and a center for the abolitionist movement. Often home alone, caring for her children, Stanton felt isolated and overwhelmed by housework. She also noticed the plight of her poorer neighbors: "Alas! alas!," she wrote in her autobiography *Eighty Years and More*, "Who can measure the mountains of sorrow and suffering endured in unwelcome motherhood in the abodes of ignorance, poverty, and vice...."

On July 13, 1848, Stanton shared her discontent with four friends. Then and there, the group decided to convene a discussion on the status of women. They set a date for six days thence and published announcements in the local papers. About 300 people—men

and women—showed up. During the meeting, the group's Declaration of Sentiments was issued, calling for greater rights for women. Stanton and her friends deemed the convention a success. They were little prepared for the nationwide storm of outrage and ridicule that followed. Their lives, the town of Seneca Falls, and the nation would never be the same.

Wesleyan Chapel (126 Fall St.), where the historic 1848 convention took place, still stands. However, the structure is not entirely original. After suffering decades of weathering and vandalism, most of the chapel was in ruins. A restoration project improved the exterior, providing protection for some of the original elements of the architecture; National Park Service rangers now lead guests on tours of the chapel.

Nearby is a 140-foot-long wall and fountain inscribed with the Declaration of Sentiments: "We hold these truths to be self-evident; that all men and women are created equal...."

Next to the wall is the spacious, two-story **Visitor Center** (136 Fall St., 315/568-2991, www.nps.gov/wori, daily 9am-5pm, free), managed by the National Park Service. Here, you'll find exhibits on the convention, its leaders, and the times in which they lived. Other sections focus on employment, marriage, fashion, and sports. There's a lot of interesting information, along with free handouts and a good bookstore.

Elizabeth Cady Stanton House

Elizabeth Cady Stanton House (32 Washington St., tours June-Sept. daily, $1 pp) is about a mile from the visitors center on the other side of Van Cleef Lake. Stanton lived here with her husband and seven children from 1846 to 1862. During much of that time, she wrote extensively about women's rights.

Among the many reformers who frequented the Stanton home was Amelia Bloomer, the woman who popularized the clothing that bears her name. Though a resident of Seneca Falls, Bloomer did not sign the Declaration of Sentiments, believing it to be too radical.

The meticulously restored Stanton House is full of authentic, original ephemera from

Stanton's life and era, including the bronze cast of Stanton's hand clasping that of Susan B. Anthony. Stanton met Anthony soon after the 1848 convention, and the women worked closely together throughout their lives.

In summer months, **house tours** are offered daily; visitors must sign up for the tours at the Women's Rights Visitor Center (136 Fall St., 315/568-2991).

Seneca Museum of Waterways and Industry

Housed in a historic building, the **Seneca Museum of Waterways and Industry** (89 Fall St., 315/568-1510, www.senecamuseum.com, Sept.-mid-June Tues.-Sat. 10am-4pm, mid-June-Aug. Tues.-Sat. 10am-4pm and Sun. noon-4pm, adults $2, families $5) is filled with exhibits on the history of the village and its surrounding waterways. A colorful 35-foot mural lines one wall. The museum has antique fire engines, pumps, looms, and printing presses. One exhibit shows how the Erie Canal was built, another is a working lock model.

National Women's Hall of Fame

The **National Women's Hall of Fame** (76 Fall St., 315/568-8060, www.greatwomen.org, Sept.-May Wed.-Sat. 10am-4pm, June-Aug. Wed.-Sat. 10am-4pm and Sun. noon-4pm, adults $3, seniors and students $1.50, children under 5 free) bills itself as "the only national membership organization devoted exclusively to the accomplishments of American women." Enlarged photos and plaques pay homage to everyone from painter Mary Cassatt to anthropologist Margaret Mead.

Seneca Falls Historical Society

Seneca Falls Historical Society (55 Cayuga St., 315/568-8412, www.sfhistoricalsociety. org, Mon.-Fri. 9am-4pm, adults $7, students $5, families $20) is housed in a notable Queen Anne home, set back from the street behind an iron fence. Inside, 23 elegant rooms feature period furnishings, elaborate woodwork, and an extensive costume collection. A rare collection of 19th-century circus toys is strewn through the children's playroom.

Montezuma Audubon Center

Five miles east of Seneca Falls is the **Montezuma Audubon Center** (2295 Rte. 89, Savannah, 315/365-3580, www.ny.audubon. org/montezuma, Apr.-Nov. daily dawn-dusk, free), a haven for migrating and nesting birds. Spread out over 6,300 acres of swamplands, marshlands, and fields, the refuge includes a visitors' center, nature trail, driving trail, and two observation towers. Nearly 315 species of birds have been spotted in the refuge since it was established in 1937. Migrating waterfowl arrive by the tens of thousands in mid-April and early October. Late May to early June is a good time to spot warblers; in mid-September, the refuge fills with shorebirds and wading birds.

Before the turn of the century, Montezuma Marsh was many times its current size, stretching about 12 miles long and up to 8 miles wide. The Erie Canal and Cayuga Lake dam projects greatly reduced its size.

Cayuga Lake State Park

Three miles east of Seneca Falls lies the 190-acre **Cayuga Lake State Park** (2678 Lower Lake Rd., 315/568-5163, camping reservations 800/456-2267, www.nysparks.com/parks/123, daily dawn-dusk, parking $6-8), offering a swimming beach, a bathhouse, hiking trails, a playground, and a 287-site campground. In the late 1700s, the park was part of a Cayuga Indian reservation, and in the late 1800s it was a resort area serviced by a train from Seneca Falls. The state park was established here in 1928.

Finger Lakes National Forest

The 16,212-acre **Finger Lakes National Forest** (National Forest Headquarters, 5218 Rte. 414 Hector, 607/546-4470, www.fs.usda.gov/fingerlakes) lies between Seneca and Cayuga Lakes and is the state's sole National Forest. Gorges, woods, pastures, shrub lands, and many wildlife ponds are intermingled to provide excellent opportunities for wildlife viewing and fishing. Over 30 miles of trails, including the 12-mile Interloken Trail, part of the **Finger Lakes Trail,** allow for hiking and horseback riding in the warm months and snowmobiling and skiing in the winter. Apples, raspberries, and other fruits are abundant throughout the forest, with five acres managed specifically for blueberry bushes. Free camping is available on three developed campgrounds on a first-come, first-served basis.

Events

Convention Days Celebration (315/568-8060, www.conventiondays.com), commemorating the first Women's Rights Convention, takes place each year on the weekend closest to July 19-20. Concerts, dances, speeches, historical tours, food, kids' events, and a reenactment of the signing of the Declaration of Sentiments form the schedule of activities.

Accommodations and Food

Several lovely B&Bs are in the heart of Seneca Falls. The 1855 **Hubbell House** (42 Cayuga St., 315/568-9690, www.hubbellhousebb.com, $155-300), built in Gothic cottage style, overlooks Van Cleef Lake. Downstairs are a large double parlor, library, and dining room; upstairs are four guest rooms furnished with antiques.

The large, historic **◖ Barristers Bed and Breakfast** (56 Cayuga St., 800/914-0145, www.sleepbarristers.com, $159-179), built by master craftsmen in the 1800s, features five spacious guest rooms furnished with antiques, a large front porch, cozy common room, and stone patio with a fire pit, perfect for sitting around on cool evenings. Guest amenities include a refreshment center.

The fresh, modern **Gould Hotel** (108 Fall St., 315/712-4000, www.thegouldhotel.com, $99-189) offers 48 rooms and suites with clean contemporary lines and extensive amenities (robes, Keurig coffee machines, iPod docking stations). The excellent **Restaurant at the Gould Hotel** (average entrée $22) and a hipster-ish bar experience await downstairs.

Don't call it "just" a grocery store: **Wegmans** (1 Loop Rd., Auburn, 315/255-2231, www.wegmans.com, open 24 hours daily) is a local institution. Visitors come to love it too because of sprawling hot and cold buffet bars, with a wide array of options for a quick, delicious, and healthy lunch.

WATERLOO

A few miles west of Seneca Falls on Routes 5 and 20 is Waterloo, a surprisingly busy village filled with aging red-brick buildings and shady trees. As a plaque along Main Street attests, Waterloo claims to be the birthplace of Memorial Day. Originally known as Declaration Day, the event apparently first took place here on May 5, 1866, in honor of the Civil War dead. Flags flew at half-mast, businesses closed, and a solemn parade marched down Main Street. In 1966, Congress and President Johnson officially recognized Waterloo as the birthplace of Memorial Day.

In the middle of town you'll find **Terwilliger Museum** (31 E. Williams St., 315/539-0533, Tues.-Fri. 1pm-4pm), which has a reconstructed Native American longhouse and village store, along with antique pianos, carriages, fire equipment, and a 1914 Waterloo mural.

You can also rent kayaks, canoes, and campsites from **Canal Side Experiences** (706 Waterloo-Geneva Rd., 315/651-4443, www.canalside.net). If you prefer that someone else take the helm, you can hire them to take you on a canal excursion on one of their pontoon boats. The quirky one-stop-shop also offers shopping, snacks, and entertainment. The owners operate a paint-your-own-pottery studio and rent time on their radio-controlled "theme park" with cars, trucks, and tanks you can drive around a homemade obstacle course.

Also on the canal, **Fuzzy Guppies** (1278 Waterloo-Geneva Rd., Waterloo, 315/539-8848, www.fuzzyguppies.com), rents canoes, kayaks, and paddleboats by the hour or the day, and welcomes campers who want to pitch a tent. You can also rent time in the "human waterball," a huge, inflatable ball bobbing on the water. Climb inside, try to walk on water—and see if you can keep your balance.

After you've worked up an appetite paddling on the canal, nab a table at **RiverPark Grille** (1314 Waterloo-Geneva Rd., Waterloo, 315/539-0509, www. riverparkgrille.com, 11am-9pm Mon.-Sat.), conveniently located next door to Fuzzy Guppies. Expect loaded nachos, chicken wings, and burgers.

AURORA

Halfway down Cayuga's expansive eastern shore is picture-perfect Aurora, with its houses laid out like beads on a string. Most date back to the mid-1800s; the village is on the National Register of Historic Places.

Called Deawendote, or Village of Constant Dawn, by the Cayuga, Aurora attracted its first European settlers in the late 1780s. Henry Wells founded Wells College here in 1868, and the school—a premier liberal arts college for women, which only went coed in 2005—remains a focal point of Main Street.

Also in Aurora is **MacKenzie-Childs** (3260 Rte. 90, 315/364-7123, www.mackenzie-childs. com, daily 10am-5pm), a classy home furnishings-design studio best known for its whimsical terra-cotta pottery. The studio employs about 100 craftspeople, who design everything from glassware to lamps, and is housed on a 19th-century estate with great views of the lake. Though the studio itself is no longer open for tours, MacKenzie-Childs hosts a visitors' center, where a video about the studio's craftsmanship is shown, and guests can take a free tour of the **Farmhouse,** a charming 15-room Victorian built in the 1800s. The tour features many MacKenzie-Childs products.

In the Tudor-style Aurora Free Library building, the charming, turn-of-the-century **Morgan Opera House** (Rte. 90 at Cherry Ave., 315/364-5437, www.morganoperahouse.org, May-Sept.) offers musical and dramatic events.

Accommodations and Food

One of the best options in the area is the lovely 1833 **Aurora Inn** (391 Main St., 315/364-8888, www.innsofaurora.com, $175-465). Inside, find 10 luxurious guest rooms furnished with antiques and Oriental rugs, a waterside restaurant (entrées $18-27) with views of the lake, and a cozy tavern with a fireplace and mahogany bar. On the menu of the highly-thought-of restaurant is refined American cuisine inspired by the seasons and fresh regional products paired perfectly with Finger Lakes wines.

E.B. Morgan House (431 Main St., 315/364-8888, $165-390) rents rooms individually or all seven for larger groups. When the entire house is rented, a private epicurean dinner option for up to 14 is available via Aurora Inn's Executive Chef Patrick Higgins.

For more casual dining, **Pumpkin Hill Bistro** (2051 Rte. 90, 315/364-7091, www.pumpkinhillbistro.com, lunch and dinner, hours vary seasonally, $9-14), housed in an 1820s hand-built dwelling, was transported to its current location in 2001. Burgers, panini sandwiches, and country favorites are enhanced by regional farm goods. Nightly specials and harvest brunches bring in a steady flow of locals.

ROMULUS

Midway down the west side of the lake lies Romulus, known for its vineyards and wineries. Two of the best wineries are only five miles apart. A very large operation, **Swedish Hill Winery** (4565 Rte. 414, 607/403-0029, www. swedishhill.com, tasting room year-round daily 9am-6pm) produces about 30,000 cases of 25 different kinds of wines a year. **Knapp Winery** (2770 County Rd. 128, 800/869-9271, www. knappwine.com, Apr.-Nov. daily 10am-5:30pm, Dec.-Mar. Mon.-Sat. 10:30am-5pm and Sun. 11:30am-5pm) is much smaller, but its wines are among the region's finest. Knapp's breezy **Vineyard Restaurant** (2770 County Rd. 128, 800/869-9271, Apr.-Nov. daily 11am-5pm, hours vary off-season, $13) emphasizes local produce.

OVID

Heading south of Romulus on Route 96, you'll come to the hamlet of Ovid, astride a small ridge surrounded by farmland. In the heart of the village stand three red-brick Greek Revival buildings known as the **Three Bears** because of the way they diminish progressively in size. "Papa Bear" was once the county courthouse; "Mama Bear," the village library; and "Baby Bear," the county jail. Today, the buildings house county offices.

Accommodations and Camping

Off Route 89 overlooking Cayuga Lake is **Sned-Acres Campground** (6590 S. Cayuga Lake Rd., 607/869-9787, www.sned-acres. com), a good place for families as it's equipped with a playground and miniature golf course.

Nearby is **Driftwood Inn B&B** (7401 Wyers Point Rd., Ovid, 607/532-4324, www.driftwoodny.com, $125-180), offering six guest rooms in the main house, and four cottages, which are available by the week. Out front is a 260-foot-long waterfront equipped with small boats and views of the lake.

TAUGHANNOCK FALLS

About 10 miles north of Ithaca thunder **Taughannock Falls,** a skinny but dazzling 215-foot-long stream of water flanked on either side by towering stone walls. Just 10,000

© JACK AIELLO/123RF

Taughannock Falls

years ago, the falls cascaded straight down into Cayuga Lake, but erosion has moved them almost a mile inland. Thirty feet higher than Niagara, Taughannock Falls are the highest straight falls east of the Rockies.

The falls are situated within the 783-acre **Taughannock Falls State Park** (2221 Taughannock Rd., 607/387-6739, camping reservations 800/456-2267, www.nysparks. com/parks/62, daily dawn-dusk, parking $7), which also offers lake swimming, fishing, boating, hiking, cabins, and a 76-site campground. Children will enjoy the park's imaginative playground, equipped with wooden towers and platforms. An overlook before the park gate offers a nice chance to see the falls without a commitment for those short on time. In July and August, free jazz, Latin, folk, and rock concerts take place weekly in the park.

Accommodations

Two lovely options in Trumansburg, close to Taughannock Falls, are the best bet for this area. The proximity to Ithaca (10 minutes) makes this peaceful alternate locale worthy of consideration for a base to explore that city.

The Halsey House (2057 Trumansburg Rd., 607/387-5428, www.halseyhouse.com, $209-289) sits at the entrance to the Taughannock Falls road and offers the perfect mix of romantic elegance and modern convenience (Wi-Fi, flatscreen TVs and a DVD collection, robes, complimentary snacks and drinks) in sumptuous bedded rooms with gorgeous upscale whirlpool bathrooms. Lovely innkeepers, a common area made cozier by a fireplace, and the included gourmet breakfast add to the experience.

Inn at Gothic Eves (112 E. Main, 607/387-6033, www.gothiceves.com, $189-259) is an 1855 inn nestled in the heart of the tiny village. This unique property offers a selection of rooms, most of which are named after wines, and a true farm-to-table breakfast using eggs, berries, and local cheeses, often harvested that very morning. A can't miss at this spot is a session in the outdoor wood-fired hot tub, which is included in the stay and is stoked by the innkeeper by appointment.

FINGER LAKES

Ithaca

Idyllically situated at the southern edge of Cayuga Lake, Ithaca is all but surrounded by steep hills and gorges. Three powerful waterfalls plunge right through the heart of the city and give Ithaca the tagline that it's used for years: "Ithaca is gorges." The small, progressive university town has a population of just over 30,000—which nearly doubles in size whenever its two colleges, Cornell University and Ithaca College, are in session.

Ithaca was originally a Cayuga settlement that was destroyed during General Sullivan's ruthless 1779 campaign. The first white settlers arrived in 1788, but the town didn't really begin to grow until the opening of Cornell University in 1868.

For several years beginning in 1914, Ithaca was a center for the motion picture business. The Wharton Studios based itself here; *Exploits of Elaine,* starring Lionel Barrymore and Pearl White, and *Patria,* starring Irene Castle, were both filmed in Ithaca. The region's unpredictable weather proved less than ideal for moviemaking, however, and in 1920 the industry moved west.

Ithaca also claims to be the birthplace of the sundae, supposedly first concocted here in 1891. "As the story goes," writes Arch Merrill in *Slim Fingers Beckon,* "an Ithaca preacher came into C. C. Platt's drugstore, weary and sweating after the Sunday morning service. He asked the druggist to fix a dish of ice cream and pour some syrup on it...and thus another American institution was born."

Orientation

Downtown is small and compact. In its flat center lies **Ithaca Commons,** a pedestrian mall spread out along State Street. Perched on a steep hill to the east is Cornell University. The roller-coaster streets surrounding Cornell are known as **Collegetown.** On another hill to the south sits Ithaca College.

The best way to explore Ithaca and environs is by foot and car. Street parking is generally available, but there are also several municipal garages downtown.

SIGHTS
Ithaca Commons

The pedestrian-only Commons runs along State Street between Aurora and Cayuga Streets and along Tioga Street between Seneca and State Streets. Somewhat European in feel, it's filled with fountains, trees, flowers, and benches, and is flanked by shops and restaurants.

Most of the buildings along the Commons were constructed between the 1860s and the 1930s. Note the handsome Italianate building at **No. 158 E. State Street,** and the Art Deco storefront at **No. 152 E. State Street.** Just beyond the Commons, at **No. 101 W. State Street,** glows a 1947 neon sign of a cocky chanticleer.

The **Sagan Planet Walk** was built in memory of astronomer Carl Sagan, who was a resident of Ithaca. It starts at the "sun" on the Commons and continues on to visit nine "planets" along a 0.75-mile route leading to the ScienCenter Museum (www.sciencenter.org). Visitors who get their "Passport to the Solar System" stamped along the way earn a free visit to the museum.

Historic DeWitt Park

The oldest buildings in the city are located on or near DeWitt Park, a peaceful retreat at East Buffalo and North Cayuga Streets, one block north of DeWitt Mall. Many buildings in this National Historic District date to the early 1800s.

On the park's north side stands the 1817 **Old Courthouse** (121 E. Court St., 607/273-8284), thought to be the oldest Gothic Revival building in the state, and **First Presbyterian Church,** designed by James Renwick, the architect of St. Patrick's Cathedral in New York

City. On the east side is the Romanesque **First Baptist Church,** built in 1890.

History Center in Tompkins County

Inside this large, renovated building you'll find the **History Center in Tompkins County** (401 E. State St., 607/273-8284, www.thehistory-center.net, Tues., Thurs., and Sat. 11am-5pm, free), run by the DeWitt Historical Society. The society owns an impressive collection of over 20,000 objects, 3,000 books, and 100,000 photographs.

Permanent displays show the city's beginnings, its industries, and its surprising film history. Temporary exhibits have focused on such subjects as folk arts, alternative medicine, Italian immigrants, and Finnish-American saunas.

The ScienCenter

The hands-on **ScienCenter** (601 1st St.,

607/272-0600, www.sciencenter.org, Tues.-Sat. 10am-5pm, Sun. noon-5pm, adults $8, seniors $7, children 3-17 $6) primarily appeals to young ones, but adults can learn something here as well. Pre-schoolers can play in the Curiosity Corner, which has a water table and craft area, while older kids will probably head to the Animal Room or space exhibits. The museum has an extensive set of activities outside, too. In addition to mini-golf, there's a "create your own waterfall" activity, a geometry climber, the world's only Kevlar cable suspension bridge, a giant lever, whisper dishes, and a "bubble-ology" section in outdoor Emerson Science Park.

Ithaca Falls

At the corner of Falls and Lake Streets thunder Ithaca Falls, the last and greatest of the six waterfalls along the mile-long Fall Creek gorge. These "pulpit falls" are closely-spaced rapids created by layers of resistant rock. To reach the site from Ithaca Commons—about a 20-minute walk—head north along Cayuga Street to Falls Street and turn right. To one side is a small grassy park and a wooded path that leads to a popular fishing hole.

Cornell University

Cornell University, built around a long, lush green lined with ivy-covered buildings, sits high on a hill overlooking downtown Ithaca. The views from here are especially fine at twilight, when Cayuga's waters glow with the setting sun and the gorges begin a slow fade into black.

Cornell was founded in 1865 by Ezra Cornell and Andrew D. White, who vowed to establish an "institution where any person can find instruction in any study." In so doing, they challenged a number of long-standing mores. Their university was one of the first to be non-sectarian; to offer instruction to all qualified applicants, regardless of sex, race, or class; and to feature courses in everything from agriculture to the classics.

Traffic and information booths are located at each entrance to the central campus. Except in

a few metered areas, parking is by permit only; purchase a permit at the traffic booths. Visitors to the Herbert F. Johnson Museum can park in metered spaces out front. To tour the campus, contact the **Information and Referral Center** (Day Hall, Tower Rd. and East Ave., 607/254-4636, www.cornell.edu).

HERBERT F. JOHNSON MUSEUM OF ART

At the northern end of the Cornell campus is the **Herbert F. Johnson Museum of Art** (114 Central Ave., 607/255-6464, www.museum.cornell.edu, Tues.-Sun. 10am-5pm, free), housed in a striking modern building designed by I. M. Pei. The museum features especially strong collections of Asian and contemporary art but is also a teaching museum, containing a little bit of almost everything.

The Asian collection is situated on the 5th floor, where big picture windows open out onto 360-degree views of Cayuga Lake and the surrounding countryside. Among the many exquisite objects on display are funerary urns from the T'ang dynasty, silk paintings from 19th-century Japan, and bronze Buddhas from 15th-century Thailand.

WILDER BRAIN COLLECTION

Those interested in the odd and macabre will want to step into Cornell's Uris Hall (East Ave. and Tower Rd.) and ride an elevator up to the second floor. In a small case to the rear of the building are eight of the surviving stars of the Burt Green Wilder brain collection, which once numbered about 600 floating specimens.

Wilder, a former Civil War surgeon, was Cornell's first zoologist. He began assembling his collection in the late 1800s in the hopes of proving the size and shape of a person's brain were related to his or her race, sex, intelligence, and personality. Alas, his studies only disproved his theories, and in 1911 he rocked the scientific world by declaring that there was no difference between the brains of black and white men.

The pickled collection includes the extraordinarily large brain of criminal Edward Howard Ruloff, who was hanged in Binghamton on

FINGER LAKES

May 18, 1871. Ruloff allegedly killed his wife and daughter and was convicted of killing three men. He was also highly intelligent, and had published several scholarly papers despite his lack of formal education.

Burt Green Wilder's brain is also in the collection. Considerably smaller than Ruloff's, it sits yellowing in viscous formaldehyde. The creator has joined his creation.

Cornell Plantations

Just north of the Cornell campus, 2,800-acre **Cornell Plantations** (124 Comstock Knoll Dr., 607/255-2400, www.cornellplantations. org, daily dawn-dusk, free) is an oasis of green. It encompasses a botanical garden, nature preserve, and arboretum, with specialty gardens devoted to everything from wildflowers to poisonous plants. Walkable nature trails wind through the Fall Creek gorge. Pick up maps in the **visitors' center** (Tues.-Sat. 10am-4pm).

Sapsucker Woods Bird Sanctuary

At the eastern edge of the city lies a world-class center for the study, appreciation, and conservation of birds. Not everything is open to the public, but key attractions include 4.2 miles of trails through the Sapsucker Woods Sanctuary and Stuart Observatory, which overlooks a waterfowl pond and bird-feeding garden.

The 230-acre Sapsucker Woods were named by bird artist Louis Agassiz Fuertes in 1901 after he spotted a pair of yellow-bellied sapsuckers—unusual for the region—nesting in the area. Sapsuckers continue to breed here each year. Near the woods you'll find a **visitors' center** (159 Sapsucker Woods Rd., 800/843-2473, www.birds.cornell.edu, Mon.-Thurs. 8am-5pm, Fri. 8am-4pm, Sat. 9:30am-4pm, Sun. 11am-4pm, free), where you can pick up maps and view paintings by Agassiz Fuertes.

Buttermilk Falls State Park

Just south of downtown is **Buttermilk Falls State Park** (Rte. 13, 607/273-5761, camping reservations 800/456-2267, www.nysparks. com/parks/151, May-Nov. daily dawn-dusk, parking $7), plummeting more than 500 feet past 10 waterfalls, churning rapids, sculptured pools, and raggedy cliffs. Alongside the falls runs a trail leading up to spire-like Pinnacle Rock and Treman Lake. At the base of the falls are a natural swimming hole, ball fields, and a campground.

Robert H. Treman State Park

Robert H. Treman State Park (105 Enfield Falls Rd., 607/273-3440, camping reservations 800/456-2267, Apr.-Nov. daily dawn-dusk, parking $7), five miles south of Ithaca, is 1,025 acres of wild and rugged beauty. Near the entrance is Enfield Glen, a forested gorge traversed by a stone pathway and steps. The steps lead to 115-foot-high Lucifer Falls and a vista stretching 1.5 miles down into a deep glen threaded by the Gorge Trail. A three-story 1839 gristmill, a natural swimming pool, and a campground are also on the grounds.

ENTERTAINMENT AND EVENTS

Cornell's **Schwartz Center for the Performing Arts** (430 College Ave., 607/254-2787) stages 6-12 plays September-May, along with the Cornell Dance Series and numerous guest performances. Professional regional theater is staged by acclaimed **Hangar Theatre** (801 Taughannock Blvd., 607/273-8588, www. hangartheatre.org, June-Aug.). The **Kitchen Theatre** (417 W. State St., 607/272-0403 or 607/272-0570, www.kitchentheatre.org) presents contemporary theater year-round in an intimate space.

Among the groups performing regularly in the city is **Cayuga Chamber Orchestra** (171 E. State St., 607/273-8981, www.ccoithaca.org), the official orchestra of Ithaca. **Ithaca Ballet** (607/277-1967, www.ithacaballet.org) performs both classical and contemporary works.

Good club listings can be found in *Ithaca Times* (www.ithaca.com), a free alternative news weekly.

Many of the local galleries participate in the monthly **First Friday Gallery Night** (www. gallerynightithaca.wordpress.com), a free event that takes place from 5pm-8pm. Galleries and shops stay open late, inviting visitors to browse art and enjoy special exhibits and live performances.

SHOPPING

One block north of the Commons, at the corner of Seneca and Cayuga Streets, is **DeWitt Mall** (215 N. Cayuga St.). This former school building now contains about 20 shops, galleries, and restaurants. Among the galleries is **Sola Art Gallery** (607/272-6552, www.solagallery.com, Mon.-Sat. 10:30am-5:30pm), which specializes in Japanese woodblock prints.

Handwork (102 W. State St., 607/273-9400, www.handwork.coop, Mon.-Wed. and Sat. 10am-6pm, Thurs.-Fri. 10am-8pm, Sun. noon-5pm) is a craft co-op showcasing the work of over 30 local craftspeople. Here, you can find jewelry, clocks, glass, ceramic, fiber, and leatherwork, and home accessories, such as handmade wooden cutting boards.

As its name suggests, **Ithacamade** (430 W. State St., 607/272-1396, www.ithacamade.com) is a gallery specializing in arts and crafts made by Ithacans. In addition to jewelry, pottery, and decorative arts, Ithacamade also has soap and snacks like macarons and biscotti for sale.

SPORTS AND RECREATION

Circle Greenway is a 10-mile self-guided walk or bike ride that leads to many of Ithaca's foremost natural and urban attractions, including gorges, the waterfront, Cornell, and the Commons. A free map can be picked up at **Ithaca/Tompkins County Convention and Visitors Bureau** (904 E. Shore Dr., 607/272-1313, www.visitithaca.com).

Cayuga Lake Cruises (708 W. Buffalo St., 607/256-0898, www.cayugalakecruises.com) offers dinner, lunch, brunch, and cocktail cruises aboard the M/V *Columbia*. **Ithaca Boat Tours** (607/697-0166, www.ithacaboattours.com, $12 adults, $10 seniors and students, $8 children 5-12) offers narrated one-hour tours of the lake that depart from the Farmers Market pier at 11am and 12:30pm Saturdays

and Sundays, May 1 to October 31. Two-hour tours (adults $18, seniors and students $16, children 5-12 $12) are offered on Tuesdays, Wednesdays, and Fridays, and ecotours (adults $18, seniors and students $16, children 5-12 $12) are scheduled for Thursdays and Sundays.

ACCOMMODATIONS

As the teaching hotel of Cornell's School of Hotel Administration, the **Statler Hotel** (130 Statler Dr., 607/257-2500, www.statlerhotel.cornell.edu, $165-680) is Ithaca's hotel of choice for visiting parents, academics, and travelers. The hotel features 153 guest rooms, two restaurants, and a café and lounge; guests have access to most of Cornell's facilities, including the gym, pool, tennis courts, and golf course.

The very unique **Log Country Inn B&B** (4 Larue Rd., 607/589-4771, www.logtv.com/inn, $70-150) may sound rustic but it features soaring cathedral ceilings, fireplaces, a sauna, and 11 guest rooms, some with whirlpool tubs. Each room is named for a particular country or region of the world. A trip to the website is suggested to handpick a vibe of choice. Next door is a 7,000-acre forest, perfect for hiking and cross-country skiing. Some rooms share baths.

City Lights Inn (1319 Mecklenburg Rd., 607/227-3003, www.theinnatcitylights.com, $135-155) offers warm service, roomy suites (some with full kitchen and wood stove), and cozy bedrooms, all with private bath and modern amenities. The garden is a nice place to relax or to enjoy Ithaca's fireworks displays on holidays.

The picturesque **William Henry Miller Inn** (303 N. Aurora St., 607/256-4553, www.millerinn.com, $155-185) is an 1880 home and carriage house filled with stained glass and carved wood details. It has high-ceilinged rooms with private baths (some with whirlpool tubs) and modern amenities, warm service, evening dessert with coffee, and gourmet breakfast with offerings such as poached eggs with sun dried tomato hollandaise or crème brulee French toast.

For more bed-and-breakfast suggestions, contact the **Ithaca/Tompkins County**

Convention and Visitors Bureau (904 E. Shore Dr., 607/272-1313, www.visitithaca.com) or **Bed & Breakfast of Greater Ithaca** (800/806-4406, www.bbithaca.com). You can also check room availability by visiting the visitors bureau's website www.visitithaca.com.

FOOD

A number of casual eateries are located along Ithaca Commons. The 100 block of Aurora Street just off the Commons has one restaurant after another.

The cooperatively owned █ **Moosewood Restaurant** (215 N. Cayuga St., DeWitt Mall, 607/273-9610, www.moosewoodcooks.com, Sun. 5:30pm-8:30pm, Mon.-Thurs. 11:30am-3pm and 5:30pm-8:30pm, Fri.-Sat. 11:30am-3pm and 5:30pm-9pm, $18) opened in 1973 and has been serving creative vegetarian cuisine ever since. It has made a name for itself worldwide for its best-selling cookbooks and natural foods. An outdoor dining area is open in summer.

Also serving contemporary American cuisine, as well as seafood, **BoatYard Grill** (525 Taughannock Blvd., 607/256-2628, www.boatyardgrill.com, daily lunch and dinner, $17) overlooks the waterfront.

Just a Taste (116 N. Aurora St., 607/277-9463, www.just-a-taste.com, Sun.-Thurs. 5:30pm-10pm, Fri.-Sat. 5:30pm-11pm, average tapa $8-10), Ithaca's wine and tapas bar, serves 50 wines by the glass and a menu inspired by Spain's small, sharable dishes, called tapas. Outside is a lovely garden. A couple blocks north, **Madeline's** (215 E. State St., 607/277-2253, www.madelines-restaurant.com, Sun.-Wed. 5pm-10pm, Thurs.-Sat. 5pm-11pm, $20) offers excellent "Euro-Asian fusion."

Hot spot **Maxie's Supper Club and Oyster Bar** (635 W. State St., 607/272-4136, www.maxies.com, daily 4pm-11pm, $14), evokes New Orleans with its decor, attitude, and, of course, spicy Cajun cuisine and stick-to-your-ribs Southern soul food. Everything is homemade at this family-run affair.

Seneca Lake

At just over 36 miles long and 618 feet deep, Seneca Lake is the deepest lake in New York State. It seldom freezes over and is renowned for its superb lake-trout fishing. Given to sudden, capricious gusts of wind, it's the most mysterious of the Finger Lakes.

Ever since the days of the Native Americans, area residents have reported strange, dull rumblings coming from Seneca's depths. The sounds are usually heard at dusk in the late summer or early fall and are most distinct midway down the lake. Native Americans believed the rumblings were the voice of an angry god. Early settlers considered them omens of disaster. Science attributes them to the popping of natural gas released from rock rifts at the bottom of the lake.

Whatever the cause, the dull rumbles—a sound much like gunfire—may have had some portent, for during World War II, a

huge munitions depot was built along Seneca's eastern shore. The 10,500+-acre Seneca Army Depot remains, though it ceased operations in the 1990s and was shuttered in 2000. A herd of snow-white deer roam the grounds and can best be seen from Route 96A at dawn and dusk.

At the northern end of Seneca Lake lies Geneva, a historic town whose South Main Street has been called "the most beautiful street in America." At the southern end is Watkins Glen, a village known for the birth of American road racing. It's also home to a rugged, 700-foot-deep gorge that's been turned into a natural theme park.

GENEVA

One of the larger towns in the region, Geneva is home to about 13,200 residents. Though overall a nondescript place, elegant South Main

Street, lined with leafy trees, stately homes, and Hobart and William Smith Colleges, runs through its center.

Geneva was once a major Seneca settlement known as Kanadesaga. During the French and Indian War, the British erected a fort here from which they and the Seneca conducted murderous raids, only to be massacred themselves during the 1779 Sullivan campaign.

Soon after the Revolution, European settlers began to arrive. A visionary land agent laid out the town along a broad Main Street and a public green. This gave the place an air of dignity, which, during the 1800s, attracted an unusually large number of retired ministers and spinsters. Geneva soon earned the nickname "The Saints' Retreat and Old Maids' Paradise."

In 1847, the Medical College of Geneva College (now Hobart) received an application of admission from Elizabeth Blackwell of Philadelphia. The students and deans, assuming it to be a joke, laughingly voted to admit her. A few weeks later, to everyone's amazement, Ms. Blackwell arrived, and in 1849, she graduated—the first woman ever granted a medical diploma in America.

Rose Hill Mansion

Three miles east of downtown lies Geneva's foremost visitor attraction, the 1839 **Rose Hill Mansion** (3373 Rte. 96A, 315/789-3848, May 1-June and Sept.-Oct. 31 Mon.-Fri. 9:30am-4:30pm and Sat. 1:30pm-4:30pm, Nov. 1-Apr. 30 Tues.-Fri. 9:30am-4:30pm and Sat. 1:30pm-4:30pm, July-Aug. Mon.-Fri. 9:30am-4:30pm and Sat.-Sun. 1:30pm-4:30pm, adults $7, seniors $6, children 10-18 $4, children under 10 free), built in the Greek Revival style with six Ionic columns out front. The mansion was once home to Robert Swan, an innovative farmer who installed the country's first large-scale drainage system. Tours of the house take visitors past a fine collection of Empire-style furnishings. Next door is the former carriage house; out front, the green lawn slopes down to Seneca Lake.

Prouty-Chew House

Built in the Federal style in 1829 by a Geneva attorney, the **Prouty-Chew House** (543 S. Main St., 315/789-5151, www.genevahistoricalsociety.com, hours vary seasonally, free) was enlarged several times in the 1850s and 1870s, which accounts for its eclectic look. It's now home to the Geneva Historical Society, which showcases changing exhibits on local history and art.

Wine Tasting

The regional wine passport program offers the best deal for tastings at wineries throughout the area.

Three Brothers Wineries & Estates (623 Lerch Rd., Geneva, 315/585-4432, www.3brotherswinery.com, open 10am-5pm) offers three distinct wineries and one microbrewery. The tasting room of each has its own unique vibe. Stony Lonesome Estates is all hard wood and class, while Passion Feet is sexy with velvet accents, and Bagg Dare is down-home, kick-back casual.

Five bucks gets you five tastings at **Zugibe Vineyards** (4248 East Lake Rd., Geneva, 315/585-6402, www.zugibevineyards.com, 11am-5pm daily). Take a seat on the porch and enjoy the unobstructed views of Seneca Lake as you sip your way through Cab Sauvs, Gruner Veltliners, and the lesser-known Lembergers.

The tasting room at **Ventosa Vineyards** (3440 Rte. 96A, Geneva, 315/719-0000, www.ventosavineyards.com, 11am-5pm Mon.-Thurs. and Sat., 10am-9pm Fri., noon-5pm Sun.) opens up to beautiful lake views, but it's popular among oenophiles in part because it's open late on Friday, when it also hosts live music. The Italian cafe just off the tasting room serves light bites (11am-5pm daily).

Accommodations and Food

For dockside dining, try **The Crow's Nest** (415 Boody's Hill Rd., 315/781-0600, www.thecrowsnestrestaurant.com, daily lunch and dinner, $14). Sandwiches, salads, seafood, and beef are on the menu here.

Red Dove Tavern (30 Castle St., 315/781-2020, www.reddovetavern.com, hours vary seasonally, $25) features American fare comprised of local ingredients. Entrées change weekly based on what's in season.

The extravagant, Romanesque **Belhurst Castle** (4069 West Lake Rd., 315/781-0201, www.belhurst.com, $110-395 d, with breakfast) took 50 workers toiling six days a week for four years to complete. Finished in 1889, it features everything from turrets to stained-glass windows. Inside is **Edgar's** (average lunch entrée $9, average dinner entrée $24), an upscale restaurant serving continental fare for both lunch and dinner, and **Stonecutters** (daily lunch and dinner, $12), which offers a tavern-style menu. Fourteen modern guest rooms vary greatly in size and price. An on-site spa-salon pampers guests and a winery offers tours and tastings. Out front are formal gardens and a lakefront beach. Also operated by Belhurst Castle are the lovely Georgian **White Springs Manor** (315/781-0201, www.belhurst.com, $110-395 d) and **Vinifera Inn** (315/781-0201, www.belhurst.com, $110-395 d).

The luxurious, all-suite **Geneva-on-the-Lake** (1001 Lochland Rd., 315/789-7190, www.genevaonthelake.com, $210-550, with continental breakfast) is especially popular among honeymooners. The property centers around a 1911 mansion built in the style of a 16th-century Italian villa. Each suite differs from the next. Outside are 10 acres of formal gardens. The **dining room** (average dinner entrée $36), open to the public for lunch and dinner, serves continental fare using fresh local produce.

Stivers Seneca Marina (401 Boody's Hill Rd., Waterloo, 315/789-0377, www.stiverssenecamarine.com) offers a unique lodging alternative. You can remain docked at Stivers' own marina, which has a very good on-site restaurant, or choose to motor slowly along the canal on a multi-day itinerary in the houseboat, which has four bedrooms, a full kitchen, two full baths, a living room, a hot tub, and a slide. Weekly rentals are $4,550.

DETOUR TO SODUS POINT

Sodus Point, which overlooks Lake Ontario, is worth a 30-mile detour north of Geneva on Route 14. The village boasts gorgeous views and an inviting public beach.

Sodus Bay Lighthouse Museum

The handsome 1870 **Sodus Bay Lighthouse Museum** (7606 N. Ontario St., 315/483-4936, www.soduspointlighthouse.org, May 1-Oct. 31 Tues.-Sun. 10am-5pm, $4 adults, children 8-17 $2) in a three-story stone block structure is dedicated to maritime and regional history. The lighthouse tower, about 50 feet high, is open to visitors who can climb the 52 circular steps into the lens room. From there, it's a gorgeous view of the Lake Ontario shoreline.

Chimney Bluffs State Park

Located on the eastern side of Sodus Bay, the **Chimney Bluffs** rise 150 feet above the lake like some giant confectionery delight. All pinnacles, spires, and peaks, they're part of a glacier-created drumlin that has been eroded, carved, and shaped by water, wind, and snow. Atop some of the pinnacles sit lone trees; below them extends a stony beach. Scuba divers exiting Lake Ontario are another unexpected sight on the beach.

Dozens of other drumlins (minus the pinnacles and peaks) can be found throughout this part of the Lake Ontario region. The only other places to view drumlins in North America are the areas bordering Lake Superior in Minnesota.

Chimney Bluffs and its beach form part of the undeveloped **Chimney Bluffs State Park** (7700 Garner Rd., Wolcott, www.nysparks.com/parks/43, daily dawn-dusk, free).

Alasa Farms and Crackerbox Palace

On your way to and from Sodus Point, you'll pass through farm country, heavy with rich black soil. Apples, cherries, and peaches thrive in this climate, as do corn, wheat, potatoes, onions, and lettuce.

Off Route 14 just south of Sodus Point lies

Alasa Farms. Once a 1,400-acre Shaker religious community, the site passed into private hands in the 1800s. Throughout the 1920s and 1930s, the farm raised everything from shorthorn cattle and hackney ponies to timberland and orchards. Today, it's home to **Crackerbox Palace** (6450 Shaker Rd., Alton, 315/483-2493, www.crackerboxpalace.org, Sat. 10am-3pm and by appt., $5 per person), a nonprofit farm haven that rescues and cares for abused and abandoned animals. Tours are available on Saturdays and by appointment.

Events

One of the region's foremost events is **Sterling Renaissance Festival** (800/879-4446, www.sterlingfestival.com), held in Sterling, near Fair Haven, about 25 miles west of Sodus Point. For seven weekends in July and August, the fest celebrates the Middle Ages with music, jousting, outdoor theater, crafts, and food.

Accommodations

Several lovely B&Bs are in the heart of Sodus Point.

Carriage House Inn (8375 Wickham Blvd., 315/483-2100, www.Carriage-House-Inn.com), an 1870s Victorian B&B, offers four guest rooms, all with king beds and private baths. Guests can walk along the beach for about a half mile to reach the Sodus Bay Lighthouse Museum.

Maxwell Creek Inn B&B (7563 Lake Rd., 315/483-2222, www.maxwellcreekinn-bnb.com, $135-159) is an historic 1846 cobblestone house located on the Seaway Trail. It has five guest rooms in the main building, as well as a private cobblestone cottage that has two efficiency suites, each with a kitchenette and private bath.

Silver Waters B&B (8420 Bay St., 315/483-8098, www.silver-waters.com, $85-139) is an historic inn in the center of Sodus Point Village, featuring four guest rooms, each with a private bath. From here, it's a quick walk to the Sodus Bay Lighthouse Museum.

Situated on 5.4 acres with a combination of woods and 340 feet of lakeshore, **The Cliffs at Sodus Point** (7961 Lake Rd., 315/483-4309. www.thecliffsatsoduspoint.com, $135-155) features five guest rooms with private baths. The B&B also has a gift shop on-site, where you can buy hand-painted wine glasses and handmade wine stoppers and jewelry.

◖ WINE ROUTES

Heading south from Geneva on either side of Seneca Lake, you'll find a series of vineyards worth a visit. Route 14 runs south along the western shore of the lake, while Routes 96A and 414 run along the eastern shore. Both routes offer excellent wineries and scenic views, both from the vineyards and tasting rooms, as well as the roads you take to reach them. If you don't have time for both routes, choose the Route 14 wineries, which will allow the opportunity to pass through Watkins Glen and catch a view of its spectacular falls and gorges.

South on Route 14

From Geneva, Route 14 heads south along the western shore of Seneca Lake past two excellent wineries. **Fox Run Vineyards** (670 Rte. 14, Penn Yan, 315/536-4616, www.foxrunvineyards.com, Mon.-Sat. 10am-6pm, Sun. 11am-6pm) is housed in an 1860s dairy barn with sweeping views of the lake. Fox Run produces more than 90 wines, including ports. **Anthony Road Wine Company** (1020 Anthony Rd., Penn Yan, 800/559-2182, www.anthonyroadwine.com, Mon.-Sat. 10am-5pm, Sun. noon-5pm) produces a variety of reds, whites, and dessert wines.

More good wineries are clustered near the lake's southern end. Among them is **Hermann J. Wiemer Vineyard** (3962 Rte. 14, Dundee, 607/243-7971, www.wiemer.com, Mon.-Sat. 10am-5pm, Sun. 11am-5pm), founded by a foremost viticulturist who came from a family that made wine in Germany for more than 300 years. The winery is best known for its Rieslings.

About five miles farther south is **Glenora Wine Cellars** (5435 Rte. 14, Dundee, 607/243-9500, www.glenora.com, hours vary seasonally). Established in 1977, Glenora is best

THE VINEYARDS OF THE FINGER LAKES

The hills of the Finger Lakes, covered with vineyards, glow pale green in spring, brilliant green in summer, and red-brown-purple in fall. The conditions for ideal grape-growing were set into motion tens of thousands of years ago when retreating glaciers deposited a layer of topsoil on shale beds above the lakes, which create a microclimate that moderates the region's temperatures.

It wasn't until the 19th century, though, that winemaking began to take root in the Finger Lakes. A minister whose intent was to make sacramental wine planted some vines near Hammondsport in 1829. The yield was successful; soon, neighbors planted their own vines, and vineyards ringed the village. In 1860, 13 Hammondsport businesspeople banded together to form the country's first commercial winery: Pleasant Valley Wine Company. Dozens of other entrepreneurs soon followed suit.

For many years, the Finger Lakes vineyards produced only native American Concord, Delaware, and Niagara grapes, used in the production of ho-hum sweet and table wines. About 25 years ago, however, several viticulturists began experimenting with the more complex European Vinifera grape. Today, a staggering number and variety of wines are produced here, including cabernet franc, cabernet sauvignon, Cayuga white, chardonnay, gewurztraminer, lemberger, merlot, pinot gris, pinot noir, Riesling, seyval blanc, vidal blanc, traminette, and both ice and iced wines.

Called "Napa Valley of the East," the Finger Lakes region currently boasts more than 100 wineries, most of which overlook Canandaigua, Cayuga, Keuka, or Seneca Lakes. Each lake has its own wine trail program, which publishes free maps and brochures and manages a "passport" program offering tasting discounts. Information about the wine trails can be found on the official Finger Lakes Wine Country website (www.fingerlakeswinecountry.com).

Most wineries are open daily 10am-5pm, year-round. Smaller wineries may close their tasting rooms in winter or reduce days or hours; call first. Tastings typically cost $2-5, an amount that's usually applied against your bill if you buy any bottles.

For a complete list of wineries, contact **Finger Lakes Wine Country** (607/936-0706, www.fingerlakeswinecountry.com).

---

known for sparkling wines. Its tasting room offers views of vineyards and of Seneca Lake. The winery also runs **Inn at Glenora Wine Cellars** (5435 Rte. 14, 607/243-9500, www.glenora. com, $160-255), whose spacious rooms feature picture windows overlooking vineyards, as well as private balconies or patios. Whether you're a guest at the inn or just passing through, you can dine at the winery's restaurant, **Veraisons** (5435 Rte. 14, 607/243-9500, www.glenora. com, average entrées $28), where the specialty is "regional fusion" fare. In summer months, enjoy your meal on the restaurant's outdoor dining patio.

Fulkerson Winery (5576 Rte. 14, Dundee, 607/243-7883, www.fulkersonwinery.com, daily 10am-5pm) has a large, light-filled tasting room, where staff will happily pour sips for you while sharing the Fulkerson family's fascinating history. Now in their seventh generation of farming, the Fulkersons trace their ancestry all the way back to the family's original farm...on New York City's Wall Street. Today, operations are firmly rooted in the Finger Lakes, where visitors can tour vineyards on foot or horseback or take a free winemaking class on weekends. An adjacent house owned by the family, and built in 1856, can be rented out by families or small groups. With four bedrooms, an enormous and fully-equipped kitchen, large dining room and living room, and 2.5 bathrooms (plus a washer and dryer), the house is a fantastic home base for exploring the region.

South on Routes 96A and 414

From Geneva, Route 96A heads south along the eastern shore of Seneca Lake. About 10 miles down is the 1,852-acre **Sampson**

© FRANCISCO COLLAZO

grounds of the Glenora Wine Cellars

State Park (6096 Rte. 96A, 315/585-6392, camping reservations 800/456-2267, www. nysparks.com/parks/154, parking $7), once a naval station where thousands of service members trained during World War II. Today, the park is equipped with a marina, swimming beach, bathhouses, picnic area, playground, and 245-site campground. South of Willard, Route 96A veers inland to Ovid, in the Cayuga Lake area, where it meets Route 414. Continue south on Route 414 to more small villages and a cluster of vineyards and wineries.

You'll find several wineries around the village of Lodi. Among them is **Lamoreaux Landing Wine Cellars** (9224 Rte. 414, 607/582-6011, www.lamoreauxwine.com, Mon.-Sat. 10am-5pm, Sun. noon-5pm), housed in a Greek Revival building with great views of the lake. Lamoreaux produces everything from chardonnay to pinot noir.

A few more miles down the road sprawls **Wagner Vineyards** (9322 Rte. 414, 607/582-6450, www.wagnervineyards.com, daily 10am-5pm). Its hub is a weathered octagonal building overlooking the lake. Established in 1979, Wagner produces over 30 different wines. On the premises is a microbrewery (www. wagnerbrewing.com) and **Ginny Lee Cafe** (607/582-6574, www.theginnylee.com), open for lunch and Sunday brunch only. On summer Friday nights, Wagner hosts "Fridays on the Deck," a hugely popular live music series. Locals crowd the deck and the generous-size lawn to eat, drink, and dance.

WATKINS GLEN AND VICINITY

Watkins Glen, named for the astonishing gorge that cuts through its center, sits at the southern tip of Seneca Lake. The glen, which is a popular state park, is easily accessible from the main roadway, where you'll find many family-friendly restaurants and lots of shops.

From 1948-1952, the main street of Watkins Glen and the steep roads surrounding it were the speedway of the American Grand Prix.

© FRANCISCO COLLAZO

FINGER LAKES

the distinctive octagonal building at Wagner Vineyards

During the races, as many as 75,000 spectators descended on the village, whose year-round population was under 3,000. Today, world-class auto races take place at the **Watkins Glen International** (2790 Rte. 16, 607/535-2486, www.theglen.com), a racetrack four miles south of Watkins Glen. The **Grand Prix Festival** (www.grandprixfestival.com) in early September commemorates the town's legacy, re-enacting the 1948 American Grand Prix, complete with vintage vehicles.

Watkins Glen State Park

Created some 12,000 years ago during the last Ice Age, **Watkins Glen State Park** (off Rte. 14, 607/535-4511, www.nysparks.com/parks/142, daily 8am-dusk, parking $8) is a wild and raggedy gorge flanked by high cliffs and strange, sculpted rock formations. Glen Creek—which drops some 700 feet in two miles over rapids, cascades, and 19 waterfalls—rushes through its center.

Alongside the gorge runs the 1.5-mile Gorge Trail, made up of 832 stone steps, stone paths, and numerous bridges. The trail leads past tunnels, caves, and a natural stone bridge, all carved out of the sedimentary rock by Glen Creek. If you hike the trail on a fine summer's day, you'll have lots of company, but the gorge inspires awe nonetheless.

The park also offers **campgrounds** (reservations 800/456-2267).

Montour Falls

Route 14 leads south of Watkins Glen through narrow, winding Pine Valley to Montour Falls, a small industrial community surrounded by seven glens. In the middle of town is **Shequaga Falls,** plunging downward 165 feet into a deep pool. The falls are illuminated at night; near the top is a pedestrian bridge.

Along Genesee and Main Streets you'll find a handsome **National Historic District,** known as the Glorious "T" District, composed of 24 brick buildings dating back to the 1850s. Among them is Memorial Library with its Tiffany windows and the Greek Revival Village Hall.

FINGER LAKES

© FRANCISCO COLLAZO

a marina on Seneca Lake, in Watkins Glen

Sports and Recreation

World-class auto racing takes place April-October at **Watkins Glen International** (2790 Rte. 16, 607/535-2486, www.theglen.com). Ticket prices vary by event.

From early May until late October, 50-minute cruises of Seneca Lake are offered every hour on the hour by **Captain Bill's Seneca Lake Cruises** (1 N. Franklin St., 607/535-4541, www.senecaharborstation.com). Captain Bill also runs dinner cruises.

Another way to experience the lake by boat is to go on an excursion on the *True Love* (Dock at Village Pier, 607/535-5253, www.schoonerexcursions.com, $29-49 per person), a restored 1926 schooner made famous by its role in the movie *High Society,* which featured Louis Armstrong, Bing Crosby, Grace Kelly, and Frank Sinatra. Morning, mid-day, afternoon, and sunset sails are offered early May-late October. Charter sails are also available.

If you're looking for a more active way to experience Watkins Glen, **Summit to Stream Adventures** (3192 Abrams Rd., 607/535-2701, www.summittostream.com) offers chartered fly-fishing and steelhead/salmon fishing excursions, as well as guided kayak and canoe trips and gear rentals.

Accommodations

One of the more idiosyncratic lodging options in the area is **Seneca Lodge** (3600 Rte. 419, 607/535-2014, www.senecalodge.com, $75-99). A favorite haunt of bow hunters and race mechanics, the lodge centers around a restaurant and tavern whose back wall, bristled with arrows, looks like the hide of a porcupine and from whose ceiling hang NASCAR champs' tires and Formula One laurel wreaths. Accommodations consist of basic camp-style A-frames, cabins, and motel rooms.

Magnolia Place Bed and Breakfast (5240 Rte. 414, Hector, 607/546-5338, www.magnoliawelcome.com, $140-190), an 1830 farmhouse located about seven miles outside of Watkins Glen, offers eight suites overlooking Seneca Lake. Innkeepers talented in the culinary arts host wine tastings and create hot

© FRANCISCO COLLAZO

Watkins Glen State Park

breakfasts of "Dutch babies" with cinnamon biscuits, or corn fritters with house-smoked salmon, crème fraiche, and a poached egg. They also provide homemade evening sweets and dinner or hors d'oeuvres on request. **Watkins Glen Harbor Hotel** (16 N. Franklin St., 607/535-6116, www.watkinsglenharborhotel.com, $159-339), situated on Seneca Lake's waterfront, is a newer hotel that's a favorite of NASCAR drivers and their entourages during race weekends. Large, airy rooms feature lush bedding and spa-style baths. Lake-facing rooms, which have balconies, are particularly coveted. The hotel's dining options include alfresco in season, a classic country club sports bar, and Blue Pointe Grille restaurant.

Food

Classic Chef's (2250 Rte. 14, Montour Falls, 607/535-9975, Sun.-Thurs. 6:30am-8:30pm, Fri.-Sat. 6:30am-9:30pm) is a classic American eatery, now in its sixth decade. Come here for tasty pancakes or grilled cheese sandwiches.

Wildflower Café & the Crooked Rooster Brewpub (223-301 N. Franklin St., 607/535-9797, www.roosterfishbrewing.com, $14) offers tasty organic fare, from creative sandwiches to hearty meals and fresh, house-made pizzas. Roosterfish ales are another big draw.

Chef-owned **Dano's Heuriger on Seneca** (9564 Rte. 414, Lodi, 607/582-7555, www.danosonseneca.com, $12), with glass-walled lakeside dining, combines the tastes of a traditional Viennese wine restaurant with the Finger Lake's best vintages. Charcuterie and schnitzel, authentic Viennese casual ordering style and Austrian traditions, like a festival celebrating the harvest with newly fermented wine, add to the charm. A chef's table is available on request for parties of six or more.

Just west of the village, you'll find **Castel Grisch Estate** (3380 County Rd. 28, 607/535-9614, www.castelgrisch.com, hours vary seasonally, $16), a winery with a Swiss-style restaurant. Outside is a deck with lake views.

Blue Pointe Grille (16 N. Franklin St., 607/535-6116, www.watkinsglenharborhotel.com, $26) at Watkins Glen Harbor Hotel, is a casual fine dining restaurant where the talents of Chef Chris Hascall are expressed through signature dishes such as Rack of Lamb, Eggplant Strato, and Wild Mushroom Ravioli. The restaurant participates in Finger Lakes Culinary Bounty, a program where properties sign on to use freshly delivered locally grown products in their menus.

Nickel's Pit BBQ (205-207 N. Franklin St., 607/210-4227, www.nickelspitbbq.com, Wed.-Fri. 5pm-close, Sat.-Sun. noon-close, $11), located in the old Watkins Glen Fire Department building, serves authentic BBQ and craft beers. Its outdoor beer garden makes it an especially popular spot on weekends.

Village Marina Bar & Grill (Seneca Harbor Park, 607/535-7910, www.village-marina.com, hours vary seasonally, $9) is a hometown favorite located on the shore of Seneca Lake. Burgers and other bar food can be paired with local beer and wine. Summer weekends see plenty of live entertainment here.

FINGER LAKES

Elmira

Elmira sits on both sides of the Chemung River, a few miles north of the Pennsylvania border. Some parts of the city are quite historic, with handsome stone and red-brick buildings.

Once the site of a Seneca village, Elmira was settled by Europeans in the 1780s. By the 1840s, the town was known for its lumbering and woolen mills, and by the 1860s, for its metal industries and iron furnaces. Elmira also served as a major transportation center, sitting at the crossroads of the Erie Railroad, the Chemung River, and the Chemung and Junction Canals.

Elmira has played an important role in the country's military and literary history. During the Civil War, the Union Army set up barracks in Elmira. In 1864, one of those barracks was turned into a prison camp for Confederate soldiers. The prison was poorly built and desperately overcrowded; thousands of prisoners died within a year.

Samuel Clemens, a.k.a. Mark Twain, spent more than 20 summers in Elmira. His wife, Olivia Langdon, grew up in the area and Twain wrote many of his masterpieces—including *Tom Sawyer* and *The Adventures of Huckleberry Finn*—while at the Langdon family farm.

Most of Elmira is north of the Chemung River. Exiting off Route 17 onto Route 352W (Church St.) will take you into the heart of the city. Route 14N runs past Elmira College and Woodlawn Cemetery (off West Woodlawn Ave.).

In July and August, hour-long **trolley tours**

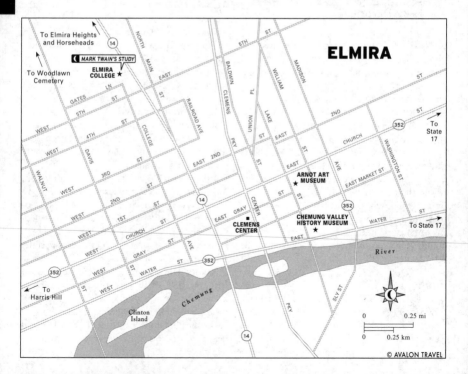

(Chemung County Chamber of Commerce, 607/734-5137 or 800/627-5892) of Elmira's historical attractions are offered.

SIGHTS
◖ Mark Twain's Study

The story of Mark Twain and Olivia Langdon began in 1867 when Twain fell in love with her after viewing her portrait, shown to him by a friend as they were crossing the Atlantic. Upon his return to the United States, Twain immediately set up a meeting with Olivia. At first, she was not at all impressed. He was a rough-and-tumble self-made man; she was a refined young woman from a good family.

But Twain was stubborn. For the next two years, he visited Elmira regularly, and eventually won over the entire Langdon family. In fact, near the end of his courtship, Olivia, who was sickly and delicate, was only allowed to visit with him for five minutes a day because she became so excited.

Mark Twain's Study (1 Park Pl., 607/735-1941, May 1-Labor Day Mon.-Sat. 9am-5pm and Sun. noon-5pm, Labor Day-Oct.15 Sat. 9am-5pm and Sun. noon-5pm, free), modeled after a Mississippi steamboat pilot house, was built for Twain by his sister-in-law. Twain once described it as "the loveliest study you ever saw. It is octagonal in shape with a peaked roof, each space filled with a spacious window and it sits perched in complete isolation on the very top of an elevation that commands leagues of valleys and city and retreating ranges of blue hill." In 1952, Twain's study was moved to its current location on the campus of Elmira College, one of the earliest colleges for women. The study's interior is simple and functional. A Remington Rand sits on a desk (Twain was one of the first writers to submit a typed manuscript to a publisher) and a trunk inscribed with the name "Clemens" rests on the floor. The author's hat and pipe rest on a desk. A student guide is stationed at the study and offers details and stories about its history.

Twain fans will want to visit several other campus spots, including statues dedicated to Twain and his wife. The Center for Mark Twain Studies hosts visiting scholars and annual symposia about the author's life, work, and influence.

Woodlawn Cemetery and Mark Twain Burial Site

In **Woodlawn Cemetery** (1200 Walnut St., 607/732-0151, daily dawn-dusk), Mark Twain is buried in the Langdon family plot, along with his wife, his father-in-law, and his son-in-law, Ossip Gabrilowitsch, a noted Russian-born pianist. A 12-foot-high monument commemorates the two famous men. Many visitors to Twain's grave consider their trip a pilgrimage and leave items like coins and cigars (Twain was known to smoke up to 22 cigars a day) on his tombstone.

Adjacent to the main cemetery is the **Woodlawn National Cemetery** (1825 Davis St., 607/732-5411, daily dawn-dusk), containing the graves of the 2,963 Confederate soldiers who died in the Elmira prison. Surrounding the Confederate graves are the graves of 322 Union soldiers. When families came north to retrieve their loved ones, they saw what respect had been afforded the soldiers and many made the decision to leave them in their resting place.

Arnot Art Museum

Arnot Art Museum (235 Lake St., at W. Gray St., 607/734-3697, www.arnotartmuseum.org, Tues.-Fri. 10am-5pm, Sat. noon-5pm, adults $7, seniors and students $5, children under 18 free), in a restored 1833 neoclassical mansion, displays a fine collection of 17th- to 19th-century European and 19th- to 20th-century American paintings. At the heart of the collection are works acquired by Matthias Arnot in the late 1800s. Among them are paintings by Brueghel, Daubigny, Rousseau, and Millet, hung floor to ceiling in the old salon style.

Behind the mansion, a handsome modern wing houses both temporary exhibitions and rotating selections from the museum's Asian, Egyptian, and pre-Columbian collections.

Chemung Valley History Museum

To learn more about Elmira'a past, visit the

FINGER LAKES

© FRANCISCO COLLAZO

Mark Twain's grave at Woodlawn Cemetery in Elmira

Chemung Valley History Museum (415 E. Water St., 607/734-4167, www.chemungvalleymuseum.org, Mon.-Sat. 10am-5pm, adults $3, seniors $2, students 6-18 $1, children under 6 free). Exhibits on the Seneca, Mark Twain in Elmira, and the Civil War prison camp are featured. Trolley into Twain Country tours depart from the lobby throughout July and August. The tour is narrated by a guide.

◖ Harris Hill

Unassuming Elmira has been known as the Soaring Capital of America ever since 1930, when the first National Soaring Contest took place here. Today at **Harris Hill** (57 Soaring Hill Dr., 607/742-4213 or 607/734-0641, www.harrishillsoaring.org), you'll find **The National Soaring Museum, Harris Hill Soaring Center,** and **Harris Hill Amusement Park.** At the Soaring Museum, visitors can learn more about the history and sport of gliding, while the Soaring Center provides the opportunity to experience gliding, either through demonstrations or a gliding excursion. Visitors

who prefer to keep their feet on the ground can enjoy the rides and activities at the 27-acre amusement park, which features kiddie rides, batting cages, and go-karts. There is no admission fee; visitors pay by activity as they go along.

Wings of Eagles Discovery Center

Wings of Eagles Discovery Center (339 Daniel Zenker Dr., Horseheads, 607/358-4247, www.wingsofeagles.com, Tues.-Sat. 10am-4pm, adults $7, seniors $5.50, children 7-18 $4.50, children 6 and under free) is a 25,000-square-foot hangar where you can walk among or climb aboard a wide range of military aircraft dating from World War II to the present. On-site Wings Cafe ($9) serves soups, salads, flatbread pizzas, and sandwiches, the latter named after famous aircraft and aviators.

ACCOMMODATIONS AND CAMPING

A few miles south of Elmira lies **Newtown Battlefield State Park** (2346 Rte. 60,

607/732-6067, www.nysparks.com/parks/107, tent camping $15-21/night), where General John Sullivan won a decisive battle over a large force of Iroquois and Tories on August 19, 1779. Situated on a hilltop with wide-angled views of the Chemung Valley, the former battlefield is now a county park with hiking trails, a picnic area, and campgrounds.

Located between Elmira and Corning is **Rufus Tanner House Bed and Breakfast** (60 Sagetown Rd., Pine City, 607/732-0213, www.rufustanner.com, $130-150), a meticulously restored 1864 Greek Revival country home offering three spacious rooms with fireplaces and private baths. The B&B also has an outdoor garden and hot tub.

Elmira's Painted Lady Bed and Breakfast (520 W. Water St., 607/846-3500, www.elmiraspaintedlady.com, $170-230) is located near the Westside Historic District. Guests can't help but leave this lovely and lovingly-kept 1875 historic Victorian feeling like family due to the warmth of the excellent innkeepers who manage that perfect level of constant at-the-ready service without being obtrusive. A truly stellar and generous hot breakfast, tailored to guests' tastes, in-room fresh flowers, whirlpool soaking tubs, romantic fireplaces, the wide sitting porch, and 1880s billiard parlor where Mark Twain himself once puttered about make this a can't miss spot.

FOOD

Charlie's Café and Bakery (205 Hoffman St., 607/733-0440, www.charliescafeelmira.com) offers sandwiches, salads, soups, pastas, and Finger Lakes wine and beer in a casual but elegant dining room. Leave room for the Finger Lakes Harvest Wine Cake, a specialty of the restaurant and region. It features local ingredients, including Finger Lakes apples and, of course, Riesling.

Soup's On Café (311 College Ave., 607/398-7278, www.soupsoncafe-elmira.com, Mon.-Thurs. 10:30am-3:30pm, Fri. 10:30am-8pm, Sat. 7:30am-3:30pm, $7-10) is a great lunch stop, offering nearly a dozen homemade soups, along with wraps, sandwiches, burgers, and desserts. Wine and beer are also available.

Third-generation **Hill Top Inn Restaurant** (171 Jerusalem Hill Rd., 607/732-6728, $20) is just that and a friendly place to sit out on the large terrace and enjoy a gorgeous view of the valley below. It's just a stone's throw from the lookout where Mark Twain sat so inspired in the original location of his study. The spot is popular with locals and large loads of tourists stopping in as a midway point between Niagara and New York City. Fortunately, the establishment has the space to accommodate them all. Generous portions of items like Haystack Crab and a good-sized wine list keep the crowd happy.

FINGER LAKES

Corning

If good things come in small packages, Corning is indeed a special present waiting for visitors to unwrap. One of the most popular tourist destinations in New York State, Corning is home to two exceptional museums, Rockwell Museum of Western Art and the more widely known Corning Museum of Glass, which, contrary to popular belief, does not exhibit Pyrex measuring cups or Corningware baking pans.

Corning, current population 11,108, became a one-industry town not long after 1868, when the Flint Glass Company of Brooklyn relocated

here. The company chose Corning largely because of its strategic position on the Chemung River and Chemung Canal, which allowed for easy delivery of raw materials.

In 1875, the company began to produce specialized types of glass, such as railway signal lenses and thermometer tubing. In 1880, the light bulb division was developed in response to Edison's invention, and by the early 1930s, Corning was manufacturing 1,250,000 bulbs a day. In 1915, the company's research and development department invented Pyrex.

In the early 1970s, a fiber optics division was established.

Corning, Inc. remains a major employer in the area, but tourism is an increasingly important industry here, too.

SIGHTS
◖ Corning Museum of Glass

Billed as the world's largest museum devoted to glass, **Corning Museum of Glass** (1 Museum Way, 607/937-5371, www.cmog.org, Sept. 3-May 23 daily 9am-5pm, May 24-Sept. 2 daily 9am-8pm, adults $15, seniors and students $12.75, children under 19 free) features thousands of objects—including more than 1,000 paperweights and, of course, plenty of examples of Tiffany lampshades and windows—spanning 35 centuries. The museum's Glass Sculpture Gallery claims to be the largest display of glass in the world, showcasing more than 10,000 glass objects at a time, many dramatically displayed in darkened rooms with spotlights. The oldest objects date back to 1400 BC, the newest seen in famous designers' contributions to constantly changing installations. Among the many highlights are an iridescent vase from 10th-century Iran, an 11-foot-high Tiffany window, and a table-long glass boat cut by Baccarat in 1900. With over 40 daily shows (included in admission), glass flowers at the Corning Museum of Glass

such as the Hot Glass Show, Flameworking Demos, and a demonstration where visitors can whip up a drawing and see it created out of glass in front of their eyes by a master gaffer, visitors can observe the art of glass up close. A **combination ticket** (adults $20, seniors and students $18.25) offers admission to both the Corning Museum of Glass and the Rockwell Museum.

The massive nonprofit gift shop, **GlassMarket,** is populated by the works of individual outside artisans, as well as pieces made by museum gaffers. Museum guests can also make their own souvenirs at **The Studio,** where visitors as young as three can participate in a brief glassmaking workshop. Classes start at $12 and include an impressively sturdy and beautiful object to bring home, each tailored to visitors' preferred style and colors. Create gorgeous ornaments like colorful blooms on deceptively delicate-looking stems by pulling molten glass into flower petals. Purchase tickets for designated time slots on entry to the museum or online.

Historic Market Street

After visiting the glass museum, most visitors stroll down a wide walkway that leads to Corning's historic downtown. This 19th-century district, called Corning Gaffer District, was extensively restored following Hurricane Agnes in 1972, when the street was all but destroyed by the flooding of Chemung River.

Today, Market Street is brick sidewalks, locust trees, and one bustling shop or restaurant after another. At one end are contemporary glass studios with artisans at work, including **Vitrix Hot Glass Studio** (77 W. Market St., 607/936-8707, Mon.-Fri. 9am-8pm, Sat. 10am-8pm, Sun. noon-5pm).

◖ Rockwell Museum of Western Art

Rockwell Museum of Western Art (111 Cedar St., 607/937-5386, www.rockwellmuseum.org, late May-early Sept. daily 9am-8pm, rest of the year daily 9am-5pm, adults $8, seniors and students $7, children under 19 free) has nothing to do with Norman Rockwell and everything

FINGER LAKES

Corning's iconic tower

to do with art of the American West. Collected by Corning denizen Robert F. Rockwell, this is said to be the most comprehensive assemblage of Western art in the eastern United States. A **combination ticket** (adults $20, seniors and students $18.25) offers admission to both the Rockwell Museum and the Corning Museum of Glass.

The museum occupies the restored Old City Hall; permanent and temporary exhibits are well-curated in equally well-cared for galleries. Works by Frederic Remington, Charles M. Russell, and Albert Bierstadt hang from the walls, and Navajo rugs drape the stairwell. Exhibit cases contain Native American art and artifacts.

Rockwell was a passionate collector who once used the walls of his father's department store to exhibit his artwork, and the museum has an engaging, personal feel. The staff provides children with backpacks filled with fun, educational activities developed for each exhibit. This exceptionally family-friendly museum opened a kids' drawing

room in 2013. The museum's gift shop is small, but has a thoughtful selection of art, jewelry, and handcrafts, most of which were made by Western artists, many of whom are Native American.

Benjamin Patterson Inn Museum Complex

A half mile north of Market Street is **Benjamin Patterson Inn Museum Complex** (59 W. Pulteney St., 607/937-5281, Mon.-Fri. 10am-4pm, adults $4, seniors $3, children and students $2), peopled by guides in costume dress. Restored historic buildings include Benjamin Patterson Inn Museum, complete with a women's parlor, tap room, and ballroom and the Painted Post-Erwin Museum, housed in a former freight depot.

ACCOMMODATIONS

One of the area's most popular B&Bs, the handsome **Rosewood Inn** (134 E. 1st St., 607/962-3253, www.rosewoodinn.com, $110-185), is located close to downtown. The five guest rooms and two suites are outfitted with antiques and have private baths. Downstairs is an elegant parlor with a fireplace, where afternoon tea is served.

Hillcrest Manor (227 Cedar St., 607/936-4548, www.corninghillcrestmanor.com, $155-185), located in an 1890s Greek Revival mansion, is a showplace for the area's art, which first drew the owners to visit Corning.

FOOD

Visit **Old World Cafe and Ice Cream** (1 W. Market St., 607/936-1953, www.oldworldcafe.com, spring and fall Mon.-Sat 10am-6pm, winter Mon.-Sat. 10am-5pm, summer Mon.-Sat. 10am-9pm and Sun. noon-5pm, $8) for hearty homemade soups, sandwiches, salad, old-fashioned candy, and ice cream. If grabbing a slice is more your taste, try **Atlas Brick Oven Pizzeria** (35 E. Market St., 607/962-2626, www.atlaspizzeria.com, Mon.-Thurs. 11am-10pm, Fri.-Sat. 11am-11pm, Sun. noon-10pm, $8). In addition to pizza, Atlas sells calzones, pasta, salads, and sandwiches.

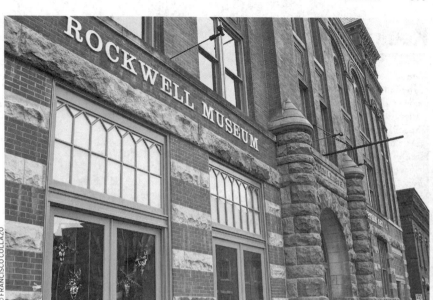

© FRANCISCO COLLAZO

the Rockwell Museum of Western Art

Locals love rustic, family-run **Spencer's** (359 E. Market St., 607/936-9196, daily 7am-10pm), popular for its homemade sticky buns and breakfast menu with only one or two options over the $5 mark.

Tiny, hidden **Bento Ya Masako** (31 E. Market St., 607/936-3659, Tues.-Fri. 11am-3pm, $9) is tucked between two jewelry shops, up a flight of stairs, and marked only by a small "Open" sign half-covering a Japanese symbol on a nondescript door. First timers might be caught off guard by the open kitchen at the top of the stairs in what looks like an apartment with two women cooking away. Just grab a seat at one of a handful of tables and prepare to be surprised. This cash-only establishment has limited hours, but offers authentic Japanese and sushi to those in the know.

Market Street Brewing Co. (63 W. Market St., 607/936-2337, www.936-beer.com, Mon.-Sat. 11:30am-10pm, Sun. noon-9pm, $18) offers something for everyone, including rooftop and biergarten dining, dishes ranging from salads to steaks, a kids' menu, and, of course, fresh brews on tap. The casually elegant **Three Birds Restaurant and Martini Bar** (73 E. Market St., 607/936-8862, www.threebirdsrestaurant.com, restaurant Mon.-Sat. 5pm-10pm, martini bar Mon.-Sat. 4pm-1am, $22) serves "progressive American fare" made with fresh local ingredients. It's also known for its popular martini bar.

The Cellar (21 W. Market St., 607/377-5552, www.corningwinebar.com, Mon.-Thurs. 5pm-9pm, Fri.-Sat. 5pm-10pm, Sun. 10:30am-3pm, $30) is an elegant wine bar and modern fusion restaurant, offering plates focused on locally-sourced ingredients.

Keuka Lake

FINGER LAKES

Gentle, Y-shaped Keuka Lake is the only one of the Finger Lakes with an irregular outline, made up of over 70 miles of curving lakeshore, scalloped with coves and bays. Its name means "canoe landing" in Iroquois.

At the southern head of Keuka Lake lies Hammondsport, site of one of the nation's first wineries, established in 1860. The small town Penn Yan occupies the lake's northern tip. Several Mennonite communities are scattered throughout the Keuka Lake region. Driving south between Penn Yan and Dundee along Routes 14A or 11, or north of Penn Yan along Routes 14A, 374, and 27, you're bound to pass a horse-and-buggy or two clip-clopping down the road. Handwritten signs advertising Mennonite quilts, furniture, or produce for sale sometimes appear by the roadside, while more permanent shops are located near Penn Yan and Dundee.

HAMMONDSPORT

Nestled between steep, verdant hills and Keuka Lake, Hammondsport is a fetching Victorian village with a lively tourist trade. At its center lies the village square, anchored by a charming white Presbyterian church. Antique shops, cafés, and restaurants line Shethar Street, the main drag. A park and two public beaches are along the lakeshore; the beach at the foot of Shethar Street is said to be the best. It is the local viticulture, though, that draws the most visitors. Tumbling down the surrounding hillsides are vineyard after vineyard, all supplying grapes for the area's 17 wineries.

Glenn Hammond Curtiss, the pioneer aviator, was born in Hammondsport in 1878. Though not as well known as the Wright brothers, Curtiss made the world's first preannounced flight on July 4, 1908 when he piloted his "June Bug" airplane over 5,090 feet just outside Hammondsport. Curtiss developed the U.S. Navy's first amphibian airplane, opened the first flying school in America, and

established the Curtiss Aeroplane Company—all in Hammondsport. During World War I, the Curtiss company manufactured the popular Curtiss Jenny airplane, which later became a favorite of barnstormers.

Great Western Winery Visitor Center

Even if you're the odd Finger Lakes visitor who isn't interested in wine, you might want to stop by the **Great Western Winery Visitor Center** (8260 Pleasant Valley Rd./County Rd. 88, 607/569-6111, www.pleasantvalleywine. com, Apr.-Dec. daily 10am-5pm, Jan.-Mar. Tues.-Sat. 10am-4pm, free, tours $5 per person), one of the largest tourist attractions in the region. The Pleasant Valley Wine Company, better known as the Great Western Winery, is one of the oldest continuous makers of wine in the United States, founded by a group of Hammondsport businessmen in 1860.

The visitor center holds exhibits that explain

AMONG THE MENNONITES

A surprisingly large number of Mennonite and Amish Mennonite communities are scattered throughout the Finger Lakes and Western New York. Some were established generations ago, but many others were set up more recently by people from Pennsylvania and Ohio who were attracted to New York by its numerous abandoned family farms.

The Mennonite religion is a Protestant sect, founded by Dutch reformer Menno Simons in Switzerland in the 1500s. The Amish are the Mennonites' most conservative branch, established in Pennsylvania in the 18th century. Both groups shun modern society and technology.

An especially large Amish population lives in Cattaraugus County in Western New York, but a growing number of Mennonites are settling in Yates, Schuyler, and Ontario Counties in the Finger Lakes. Local residents estimate that the Mennonite population in these three counties—all centered around Keuka Lake—has

increased exponentially since the late 1970s; in Yates County alone, there are more than 520 Mennonite families.

Throughout the region, you'll see Amish driving their horse and buggies, and you'll spot occasional signs advertising handmade quilts, furniture, or baskets for sale. Though not as organized as Western New York, whose Amish participate in the Amish Trail program for visitors, the Finger Lakes' Amish and Mennonite communities are still accessible to visitors. Travelers can purchase goods at Amish farms throughout the region. Good places to stop include The Windmill Farm and Craft Market and Oak Hill Bulk Foods and Cafe, both near Penn Yan.

The Amish and Mennonites dislike having their pictures taken. Please respect their wishes. Also, be aware that they do not work on Sundays, so their farms and shops will be closed on that day.

the history of the winery and the region, as well as an informative film, which is screened inside a 35,000-gallon former wine tank. A nearby working model train replicates the old Bath-Hammondsport Railroad, and a tasting room offers products for sampling. Winery tours are offered throughout the day. Take the hour-long tour through magnificent stone winery buildings, eight of which are listed on the National Register of Historic Places. The tour ends with a wine tasting.

Wine Tasting

One of the odder tales in the chronicles of Finger Lakes viticulture is that of the battle waged over the name Taylor. Walter S. Taylor, a grandson of the founder of the Taylor Wine Co., was kicked out of the company in 1970. Subsequently, he and his father Greyton began their own winery high on Bully Hill. In 1977, Coca-Cola bought the Taylor Wine Co. and sued Walter for using his family name on his own labels. The case went to court and Walter

lost, only to become a local hero. "They have my name and heritage but they didn't get my goat!" he proclaimed and flamboyantly struck out the Taylor name on all his labels. "Branded For Life, by a man that shall remain nameless without Heritage" reads the byline in his brochures. The **Wine and Grape Museum of Greyton H. Taylor** (8843 G.H. Taylor Memorial Dr., 607/868-3610, www.bullyhillvineyards.com, Wed.-Sun. 11am-5pm, free) tells little of this story. Instead, it focuses on antique winemaking equipment and the delicate, lyrical Bully Hill labels, all drawn by "Walter St. Bully." Adjacent to the museum are **Bully Hill Vineyards,** open for tastings. Also on site is Bully Hill Restaurant, offering great views of the lake.

Dr. Frank's Vinifera Wine Cellars (9749 Middle Rd., 607/868-4884, www.DrFrankWines.com, Mon.-Sat. 9am-5pm, Sun. noon-5pm, tastings free) was one of the first in the region to grow the European Vinifera grape. Dr. Frank was an immigrant from Ukraine who arrived in the Finger Lakes in 1962. Today, his family still runs the winery, best known for their multiple award-winning chardonnays and Rieslings.

A few miles beyond Dr. Frank's is **Heron Hill Winery** (9301 Rte. 76, 607/868-4241, www.heronhill.com, Mon.-Sat. 10am-5pm, Sun. noon-5pm). Opened in 1977, it specializes in chardonnays, Rieslings, and Concord grape juice for the kids. Heron Hill also operates a café in the summer. Enjoy views of the lake and the vineyards from its deck.

Glenn H. Curtiss Museum
The cavernous hangars of the former Curtiss Aeroplane Company now contain the sprawling **Glenn H. Curtiss Museum** (8419 Rte. 54, 607/569-2160, www.glennhcurtissmuseum.org, May 1-Oct. 31 Mon.-Sat. 9am-5pm and Sun. 10am-5pm, Nov. 1-Apr. 30 daily 10am-4pm, adults $8.50, seniors $7, children 7-18 $5.50), devoted to both Curtiss and the early history of aviation. About a dozen spiffy antique airplanes crowd the main hall, along with antique bicycles, motorcycles, propellers, and engines. Curtiss's first interest was the bicycle. One of his earliest planes, the Curtiss Pusher, looks just like a bike with double wings and wires attached.

A highlight of the museum is a replica of the famous "June Bug" airplane, built by volunteers in the mid-1970s. A Curtiss Jenny and delicate Curtiss Robin—resembling a giant grasshopper—stand nearby.

Accommodations
Vinehurst Inn and Suites (7988 Rte. 54, 607/569-2300, www.vinehurstinn.com, $110-160) features spacious motel rooms, many with cathedral ceilings. Suites, including three for families and three with whirlpool tubs, are also available.

Lake & Vine Bed and Breakfast (61 Lake St., 607/569-3282, www.lakeandvinebb.info, $125-150), an 1868 Queen Anne style home, offers four rooms, candlelit gourmet breakfast served with china and crystal, and many modern amenities.

Black Sheep Inn (8329 Pleasant Valley Rd., 607/569-3767, www.stayblacksheepinn.com, $155-275) is a five-room boutique inn, offering indulgent organic breakfasts utilizing local and organic products. This historic octagonal house also features an on-site spa.

About 15 miles away, in the village of Avoca, is a bit of novelty: the storybook 🄲 **Caboose Motel** (8620 Rte. 415, 607/566-2216, www.caboosemotel.net, $75). Here, you can sleep in snug, restored 1916 train cabooses outfitted with modern conveniences.

Food
In addition to its mouth-watering ice-cream treats, cozy **Crooked Lake Ice Cream Parlor** (33 Shethar St., 607/569-2405) serves a good breakfast and lunch.

As its name suggests, **The Waterfront Restaurant** (12664 W. Lake Rd., 607/868-3455, www.waterfrontkeuka.com, Mon.-Fri. 4pm-close, Sat.-Sun. noon-close, $16) offers lakeside dining. Specials are featured every night of the week. The Original Clammin' and Jammin' happens on the dock every Sunday, Memorial Day through Labor Day, with fresh steamed clams and free live music.

PENN YAN
Named for its early Pennsylvanian and Yankee settlers, Penn Yan is an attractive small town (pop. 5,131) that serves as the seat of Yates County. Its claim to fame is the world's largest pancake.

Birkett Mills
On a windowless wall of **Birkett Mills** (1 Main St., www.thebirkettmills.com), an enormous griddle is mounted alongside the words: "The annual Buckwheat Harvest Festival. Size of big griddle used to make world record pancake, Sept. 27, 1987. 28 feet, 1 inch." What more needs to be said? Established in 1797 and in continuous operation ever since, Birkett Mills is the world's largest producer of buckwheat products and maintains a small **retail shop** (163 Main St., 315/536-3311) in its offices.

FINGER LAKES

© FRANCISCO COLLAZO

vineyards at Heron Hill Winery

Oliver House Museum

Oliver House Museum (200 Main St., 315/536-7318, www.yatespast.com, Tues.-Fri. 9am-4pm, free), housed in a handsome brick building, is run by the Yates County History Center. Permanent and temporary exhibits are on display, interpreting a variety of regional historical and cultural themes.

Recreation

The proprietors of *The Esperanza Rose* (481 Mill St., Branchport, 315/595-6618, www.esperanzaboat.com), a 65-foot, 85-ton wooden cruising yacht, offer lake excursions. In addition to sightseeing trips, lunch and dinner cruises are offered. The boat departs from its dock on Mill Street in the town of Branchport, about a 10-minute drive from Penn Yan.

Events

Yates County Fair takes over Penn Yan fairgrounds in mid-July. On the Fourth of July and the Saturday before Labor Day, the shores of Keuka Lake glow with magical **Rings of Fire,** as in the days of the Seneca. The Seneca lit bonfires to celebrate the harvest; today, highway flares celebrate the holidays. For information about any of these events, contact the **Yates County Chamber of Commerce** (315/536-3111, www.yatesny.com).

Shopping

Midway between Penn Yan and Dundee is **Windmill Farm and Craft Market** (3900 Rte. 14A, 315/536-3032, www.thewindmill.com, late Apr.-mid-Dec. Sat. 8am-4:30pm), the oldest and biggest of several indoor/outdoor farm-and-crafts markets operating in the Finger Lakes. Every Saturday, from the last Saturday in April to the second Saturday in December, more than 200 local vendors set up shop in a large fairgrounds area off Route 14A. Produce, flowers, furniture, crafts, wine, antiques, and homemade food are among the goods for sale. Many Mennonite families operate booths here.

In Dundee, you'll find **Martin's Kitchen** (4898 John Green Rd., 607/243-8197), selling homemade pickles, pickled watermelon rinds, jams, apple butter, and other Mennonite specialties.

Accommodations and Food

Cozy **Fox Inn** (158 Main St., 315/536-3101, www.foxinnbandb.com, $155-180), near downtown, is an 1820s Greek Revival home with five guest rooms and a carriage house loft. Common areas include a parlor with billiards table, a sitting room with a wood-burning fireplace, and a rose garden.

Merritt Hill Manor (2756 Coates Rd., 315/536-7682, www.merritthillmanor.com, $165-189) is situated on an 18-acre estate with great views of both Keuka and Seneca Lakes. The 1822 country manor offers five guest rooms, a breezy porch, and a living room with a fireplace.

Diner aficionados will want to stop by the classic **Penn Yan Diner** (131 E. Elm St., 315/536-6004, www.pennyandiner.com, Tues.-Sat. 7am-7pm, Sun. 7am-1pm, $12), which dates back to 1925.

Canandaigua Lake

The farthest west of the major Finger Lakes, Canandaigua is also the most commercialized. Rochester is less than 30 miles away, and the lake has served as that city's summer playground since the late 1800s. At the northern end of the lake is the historic city of Canandaigua, now largely a resort town. At the southern end is the village of Naples.

Canandaigua is Iroquois for "The Chosen Place." According to legend, the Seneca people were born at the south end of the lake, on South Hill. The Creator caused the ground to open, allowing the Seneca to climb out. All went well until a giant serpent coiled itself around the base of the hill. Driven by an insatiable hunger, the snake picked off the Seneca one by one until at last a young warrior slew him with a magic arrow. The dying serpent writhed down the hill, disgorging the heads of its victims as he went; large rounded stones resembling human skulls have been found in the area. South Hill is now part of the Hi Tor Wildlife Management Area.

Also connected with the Seneca is tiny Squaw Island, located in the northern end of the lake. Many women and children escaped slaughter by hiding here during General Sullivan's 1779 campaign.

CANANDAIGUA

The city of Canandaigua has a wide, expansive feel. Busy Main Street, a four-lane thoroughfare lined with leafy trees and imposing Greek Revival buildings, runs through its center. The lake and City Pier are at the foot of Main. Tourist-oriented businesses dominate.

Following the Revolution, two New Englanders, Oliver Phelps and Nathaniel Gorham, purchased what is now Canandaigua, along with the rest of western New York, from the Native Americans. Settlers arrived in 1789, and shortly thereafter, the first land office in the United States was established near present-day Main Street.

On November 11, 1794, Seneca chiefs and General Timothy Pickering met in Canandaigua to sign what was later known as the Pickering Treaty. A document of enormous significance, the treaty granted whites the right to settle the Great Lakes Basin. An original copy of the treaty can be found in the Ontario County Historical Society Museum.

Sonnenberg Gardens and Mansion

A serene 50-acre garden estate, **Sonnenberg Gardens and Mansion** (151 Charlotte St., 585/394-4922, www.sonnenberg.org, May 1-May 26 and Sept. 3-Oct. 31 daily 9:30am-4:30pm, May 27-Sept. 2 daily 9:30am-5:30pm, adults $12, seniors $10, students 13-17 $6, children 4-12 $1, children under 4 free), sits in the heart of the bustling downtown. The Smithsonian Institution credited the place "one of the most magnificent late-Victorian gardens ever created in America," thanks to its nine formal gardens, an arboretum, a turn-of-the-20th-century greenhouse, and a massive 1887 stone mansion.

Sonnenberg (German for "Sunny Hill") was once the summer home of Mary Clark and Frederick Ferris Thompson. Thompson, whose father helped establish Chase Bank, was co-founder of the First National City Bank of New York City.

The estate's nine gardens were created by Mrs. Thompson as a memorial after her husband's death in 1899. A classic rose garden features over 4,000 rose bushes, and the Japanese Garden took seven workers six months to

create. The secluded Sub Rosa Garden contains statues of Zeus, Diana, and Apollo. The Blue & White Garden contains only blue and white flowers.

Visitors to Sonnenberg can wander freely— even the mansion is self-guided—though guided walking tours are also offered June-September. Near the entrance is an inviting café, housed in one of the greenhouses, and the huge, commercial **Finger Lakes Wine Center** (585/394-9016, May-Oct. daily 11am-4pm), selling regional wines.

Granger Homestead and Carriage Museum

The 1816 Federal-style **Granger Homestead**

and Carriage Museum (295 N. Main St., 585/394-1472, www.grangerhomestead.org, Tues., Wed., and Sun. 1pm-5pm, Thurs.-Sat. 11am-5pm, adults $6, seniors $5, students $2) once housed Gideon Granger, U.S. postmaster general under Presidents Jefferson and Madison. The home, which Granger once boasted was "unrivalled in all the nation," is especially notable for its elaborate carved moldings and mantelpieces, and for its fine original furnishings.

Dark, towering trees surround the house. Out back is a carriage museum, packed with about 50 spit-and-polish coaches, sporting carriages, sleighs, commercial wagons, and an undertaker's hearse.

Ontario County Historical Museum

To learn more about the history of Canandaigua, step into the **Ontario County Historical Museum** (55 N. Main St., 585/394-4975, www.ochs.org, Tues.-Fri. 10am-4:30pm, Sat. 11am-3pm, free, donations accepted), situated in a handsome brick building. On display is the original Six Nations' copy of the Pickering Treaty with the signatures of Iroquois leaders Red Jacket, Cornplanter, Handsome Lake, Farmer's Brother, Little Beard, and Fish Carrier. Each signed with an X. The museum also features "life masks" of Abraham Lincoln (plaster-of-Paris masks taken from a mold of his face), a small children's discovery area, and temporary exhibits.

Ontario County Courthouse

Dominating downtown Canandaigua, and indeed much of the surrounding countryside, is the bulbous dome of **Ontario County Courthouse** (27 N. Main St., at Gorham, 585/396-4200, Mon.-Fri. 8:30am-5pm). A marvelous collection of portraits hangs in the two courtrooms of this 1858 Greek Revival structure. Among them are likenesses of Red Jacket and Susan B. Anthony, who was tried here in 1873 for voting in the national election in Rochester. She was found guilty and fined $100. A boulder on the courthouse grounds

commemorates the Pickering Treaty, signed here in 1794.

New York Wine and Culinary Center

A treat for foodies, **New York Wine and Culinary Center** (800 S. Main St., 585/394-7070, www.nywcc.com, Wed.-Thurs. and Sun. 11am-6pm, Fri.-Sat. 11am-8pm) is a beautiful 20,000-square-foot facility housing a tempting boutique with food products and kitchen tools for culinary-minded visitors. The center also has a glass-walled educational theater where classes and demos can be observed and the occasional food show is filmed. There is an impressive **Tasting Center** featuring the state's finest wines, beers, and spirits in a warm wood and stone setting. At **Upstairs Bistro,** locally farmed ingredients come together in excellent meals with suggested wine and beer pairings that bring out the fullest flavors of the food. Visitors sticking around for a day or two can also sign up for a cooking class.

Live music makes weekend evenings a great time to visit for beer lovers, as a rotating selection of brews, chosen from New York's burgeoning number of craft breweries, are featured on tap (flight tasting available), as well as bottle choices from the state. New York State Charcuterie Sampler and Artisan Cheese Plate are two good choices for nibbling.

Recreation

The *Canandaigua Lady* (205 Lakeshore Dr., 585/396-7350, www.steamboatlandingresort.com, May-Oct.) is a 150-passenger paddle-wheel boat offering lunch, afternoon, and dinner cruises.

For a more active experience on the lake, **Canandaigua Sailboarding** (11 Lakeshore Dr., 585/394-8150, www.cdgasailboard.com, daily 10am-6pm) rents kayaks, stand-up paddleboards, and water-bikes. The staff also gives windsurfing lessons during the summer.

In winter, **Bristol Mountain Winter Resort** (5662 Rte. 64, 585/374-1100, www.bristolmountain.com), at 1,200-feet, claims to have the highest vertical rise between the

Adirondacks and the Rocky Mountains. Thirty-four slopes and trails represent a varied terrain, offering skiing and snowboarding opportunities for novices as well as experts. Several local hotels and bed-and-breakfast lodgings partner with the ski resort, offering free passes to Bristol Mountain with a one-night stay.

Seven miles northwest of Canandaigua is **Finger Lakes Gaming & Racetrack** (5857 Rte. 96, 585/924-3232, www.fingerlakesracetrack.com). Thoroughbred racing takes place April-November Friday-Tuesday. Also on-site are more than 1,200 gaming machines. The already ample casino expanded exponentially in late 2013 with the addition of 33,000 square feet of space, which included a new bar and restaurant, among other gaming installations.

Entertainment

During the summer, Rochester Philharmonic Orchestra performs regularly at **Constellation Brands—Marvin Sands Performing Arts Center (CMAC)** (3355 Marvin Sands Dr., 585/394-4400, www.cmacevents.com), an outdoor amphitheater with 10,000 lawn seats and 5,000 covered seats. Rock, jazz, and pop-music concerts are sometimes presented as well.

Accommodations

The Canandaigua region is home to many luxury B&Bs. One of the best is the snug, colonial-style ⟨ **1795 Acorn Inn** (4508 Rte. 64, Bristol Center, 585/229-2834, www.acorninnbb.com, $170-275), which has achieved the AAA four-diamond rating for nearly 20 years, a rarity for a B&B. Once a stagecoach stop, the inn now pampers guests with comfy canopy beds, luxurious private baths, an outdoor hot tub, and multi-course breakfasts.

The Inn on the Lake (770 S. Main St., 585/394-7800, www.theinnonthelake.com, $152-255) is a full-service hotel and conference center. Among its features are 134 nicely appointed guest rooms, many with patios or balconies; a pristine outdoor pool; saunas; and the airy, inviting restaurant, The Shore. The restaurant looks out to the lake and tiny Squaw Island. Just 20 by 50 yards, the wild, tree-covered spot where Native Americans were said to have placed their women and children for safety during skirmishes can be reached by kayak (Canandaigua Sailboarding, 585/394-8150, www.cdgasailboard.com).

Not too far away is plush 1810 **Morgan-Samuels B&B Inn** (2920 Smith Rd., 585/394-9232, www.morgansamuelsinn.com, $169-325), which also holds the coveted AAA four-diamond rating. Here, you'll have your choice of one among six guest rooms, all of which are decorated in a Victorian antique style. The inn has eight fireplaces, tennis courts, and serves gourmet breakfast by candlelight. A six-course dinner is available by request for an additional fee.

Bristol Harbour Resort (5410 Seneca Point Rd., 585/396-2200, www.bristolharbour.com, $185-495) is a 31-room, Adirondack-style resort that sits on Bristol Mountain, a perch offering spectacular lake views. The resort also has cottages and condos for rent. Golfers particularly enjoy this resort, as it has an 18-hole championship golf course designed by Robert Trent Jones. Other amenities and services include a spa, a restaurant, a private marina and beach, and a year-round hot tub.

Food

Il Posto Bistro and Wine Bar (137 S. Main St., 585/905-0535, www.ilpostobistroandwinebar.com, Tues.-Thurs. 5pm-9pm, Fri.-Sat. 5pm-10pm, $17) is a small, intimate restaurant specializing in Italian cuisine. It has a robust wine list, though few of the wines are from the area; most are from Italy and France.

The Shore (770 S. Main St., 585/394-7800, $26), located at The Inn on the Lake, offers great views of the lake and contemporary American fare.

The Office Restaurant (2574 Macedon Rd., 585/394-8787, www.ericsofficerestaurant.com, Mon.-Sat. 11am-midnight, $16) is especially worth keeping in mind if you're looking for a late night meal, as it's open until midnight. Burgers, bar fare, and heavier American entrées (think tenderloin topped with bleu cheese) are on offer here.

VICTOR

About 10 miles northwest of Canandaigua sprawls the village of Victor, worth visiting because an important Seneca village once stood here. The village was home to about 4,500 people; its palisaded granary stored hundreds of thousands of bushels of corn. All was destroyed in 1687 by a French army, led by the governor of Canada, who wanted to eliminate the Seneca as competitors in the fur trade.

Ganondagan State Historic Site

A visit to **Ganondagan State Historic Site** (1488 Rte. 444, 585/742-1690, www.ganondagan.org, May 1-Sept. 30 Tues.-Sun. 9am-5pm, Oct. Tues.-Sat. 9am-5pm, adults $3, children $2), which means "Town of Peace," begins with an interesting video that tells the story of the Seneca Nation and that of Jikohnsaseh, or Mother of Nations. Together with "The Peacemaker" and Hiawatha, Jikohnsaseh was instrumental in forging the Five Nations Confederacy; it was she who proposed that the Onondangan chief, who at first refused to join the confederacy, be appointed chairman of the Chiefs' Council. Jikohnsaseh once lived in the vicinity of Ganondagan and is believed to be buried nearby. No one searches for her grave, however, as a sign of respect.

Three trails that lead over gentle terrain past informative plaques begin just outside the visitor center. The Trail of Peace relates important moments in Seneca history. The Earth of Our Mother Trail identifies plants important to the Seneca. The Granary Trail recreates the day in 1687 that Ganondagan was destroyed, through journal entries from the French forces. There is also a replica of a 17th-century bark longhouse on site.

Food

Warfield's (3 Coulter Ln., Clifton Springs, 315/462-7184, www.warfields.com, Tues.-Sat. 11:30am-2:30pm and 5pm-9pm, $24) features seasonal "country fare" inflected with Asian and European influences, served in a dining room with a pressed tin ceiling.

Lucca Wood-Fire Bistro (90 W. Main St., Victor, 585/924-9009, www.luccawfpizza.com, Wed.-Thurs. 11:30am-8pm, Fri. 11:30am-9pm, Sat. noon-9pm, Sun. noon-7pm, $11) serves pizzas crisped to perfection in its wood-fired oven, as well as panini and salads.

PALMYRA

About 15 miles due north of Canandaigua is Palmyra, an old Erie Canal town where Joseph Smith allegedly received a set of gold tablets inscribed with the Book of Mormon from the angel Moroni. The Hill Cumorah Pageant commemorates that event every July.

Downtown Palmyra is small and compact, lined with sturdy brick buildings. A church stands at each corner of the intersection of Main Street and Route 21, a fact that once made it into *Ripley's Believe It or Not.* Just west of downtown is the graceful stone **Erie Canal Aqueduct,** off Route 31.

Three small museums run by Historic Palmyra sit side-by-side downtown. On the outskirts of town are the Hill Cumorah Visitor Center and Joseph Smith Farm, run by the Mormon Church.

Historic Palmyra

A **trail ticket** (adults $7, seniors and children $5) offers admission to all four historic Palmyra museums. **William Phelps General Store and Home Museum** (140 Market St., 315/597-6981, www.historicpalmyrany.com, May 1-Oct. 31 Tues.-Sat. 10:30am-4:30pm, Nov. 1-Apr. 30 Tues.-Thurs. 11am-4pm, adults $3, seniors and children 12-17 $2, children under 12 free) was operated by the Phelps family from the 1860s until the 1940s. The museum recreates the general store of the 1890s and is an incredible untouched place to poke around, with excellent guides leading the way back into a simpler time. Shelves feature, among other items, spices and extracts that have retained their scents.

The **Alling Coverlet Museum** (122 William St., 315/597-6981, www.historicpalmyrany.com, Mon.-Sat. 1pm-4pm, adults $3, seniors

PALMYRA

FINGER LAKES

four miles south of downtown. Most visitors are Mormons, but non-Mormons are welcome and are left more or less in peace to peruse the exhibits. A film provides a good introduction to Mormon history and beliefs, and exhibits tout the growth of the religion. There are currently about nine million Mormons worldwide, though only 1,500 live in upstate New York.

Behind the center stands Hill Cumorah, the drumlin where Joseph Smith is said to have found the gold tablets on September 22, 1827. It took him years to translate the tablets, and after he was done, he reburied them. A gold statue of the angel Moroni sits atop Hill Cumorah.

Joseph Smith Farm and Sacred Grove

Born in Vermont in 1805, Joseph Smith first came to Palmyra with his family in 1815. The Smiths were farmers, and Joseph—described by one contemporary as a "quiet, low-speaking, unlaughing" boy—lived in this simple, white clapboard house, now known as the **Joseph Smith Farm** (29 Stafford Rd., 315/597-5851, www.hillcumorah.com, Mon.-Sat. 9am-7pm, Sun. 12:30pm-7pm, free), until he was 22. He received his first vision in the **Sacred Grove** behind the house when he was only 14.

Events

The largest outdoor pageant in the United States, the **Hill Cumorah Pageant** (www.hill-cumorah.org/Pageant) commemorates Joseph Smith's visitation from the angel Moroni, which led to the founding of the Mormon religion. It's a spectacular performance with a cast and technological special effects worthy of Broadway.

Each August Palmyra hosts the **Wayne County Fair** (www.waynecountyfair.org), one of the oldest fairs in the country, having originated in 1849. Livestock displays and beauty pageants are just two of the many activities at this beloved fair.

Palmyra Canaltown Days (www.palmyra-canaltowndays.org) celebrates the town's historic connection to the Erie Canal. Held every

and children 12-17 $2, children under 12 free) houses the largest collection of handwoven coverlets in the United States. Often referred to as the American tapestry, coverlets are ornate bed coverings made out of wool, cotton, or linen.

The nearby **Palmyra Historical Museum** (132 Market St., 315/597-6981, www.historic-palmyrany.com, May 1-Oct. 31 Tues.-Sat. 10:30am-4:30pm, Nov. 1-Apr. 30 Tues.-Thurs. 11am-4pm, adults $3, seniors and children 12-17 $2, children under 12 free) occupies the former St. James Hotel. Exhibits here include 19th-century furniture, Erie Canal art and artifacts, children's toys, stern Victorian portraits, and a tour led by an expressive guide who brings the historic objects to life with animated anecdotes.

Palmyra Print Shop (140 Market St., 315/597-6981, www.historicpalmyrany.com, May 1-Oct. 31 Tues.-Sat. 10:30am-4:30pm, Nov. 1-Apr. 30 Tues.-Thurs. 11am-4pm, adults $3, seniors and children 12-17 $2, children under 12 free) features Palmyra-made printing presses and cutters with handmade type and print blocks from 1838 through 1972.

Hill Cumorah Visitor Center

A good place to learn about the Mormon religion is at the **Hill Cumorah Visitor Center** (603 Rte. 21, 315/597-5851, www.hillcumorah.com, Mon.-Sat. 9am-9pm, Sun. noon-9pm, free),

September, the festival features craft and food vendors, and draws thousands of visitors.

Accommodations

A generous breakfast and kind hosts make **Liberty House** (131 W. Main St., Palmyra, 315/597-0011, www.libertyhousebb.com, $89-99) particularly noteworthy; the affordable rates don't hurt, either. Three guest rooms are available in this beautiful Victorian home with a wrap-around porch.

Palmyra Inn (955 Canandaigua Rd., 800/426-9900, www.palmyrainn.com, $119-199) offers 60 rooms and suites, with kitchenettes in each room. Amenities include free wireless Internet access, a whirlpool tub and exercise room, and deluxe continental breakfast.

SOUTH ON ROUTES 364 AND 245

Heading south down Canandaigua's eastern shore, you'll pass through a series of picturesque valleys. At the southern end of the lake, the route skirts around South Hill and **High Tor Wildlife Management Area** (585/226-2466). Hiking trails traverse the preserve, which is also one of the few places left in New York where you can still spot Eastern bluebirds, the state bird. The main entrance to the area is off Route 245 between Middlesex and Naples.

NAPLES

Just south of Canandaigua Lake, surrounded by hills, lies Naples (pop. 2,500). A tidy village with a brisk tourist trade, Naples centers around a historic **Old Town Square**. Naples is one of the best places in the Finger Lakes to sample a sweet regional specialty: grape pie. The pies, made with dark grapes, are best during fall harvest season.

Wineries

The local grapes are used for something more than pie. **Hazlitt's Red Cat Cellars** (5712 Rte. 414, 607/546-9463, www.hazlitt1852.com) hosts wine-tastings in its wood-paneled tasting room. **Inspire Moore Winery and Vineyard** (197 N. Main St., 585/374-5970, www.

inspiremoorewinery.com) has a casual restaurant next to the winery. **Arbor Hill Grapery** (6461 Rte. 64, 583/374-2870, www.thegrapery.com) features a shop and **Brew & Brats,** a restaurant specializing in exactly what its name suggests.

Cumming Nature Center

About eight miles northwest of the village lies 900-acre **Cumming Nature Center** (6472 Gulick Rd., 585/374-6160, www.rmsc.org, Wed.-Fri. 9am-3:30pm, Sat.-Sun. 9am-4:30pm, $3), owned by the Rochester Museum and Science Center. A veritable outdoor museum, the preserve holds six miles of themed trails leading through forests and wetlands. The Conservation Trail illustrates theories of forest management; the Pioneer Trail, complete with a reconstructed homestead, teaches about the early settlers' lives. The Beaver Trail focuses on the principles of ecology, and the Iroquois Trail focuses on Native American life. A visitors' center is near the entrance.

Gannett Hill

Scenic Route 21 heads due north out of Naples to the highest point in Ontario County: Gannett Hill, 2,256 feet above sea level. Now part of Ontario County Park, the hill offers bird's-eye views of the surrounding countryside.

Entertainment

The only performing arts venue of its kind in the immediate area, **Bristol Valley Theater** (151 S. Main St., 585/374-6318, www.bvtnaples.org) is housed inside an old church. Music, theater, dance, comedy, and children's events are staged in spring, summer, and fall.

Shopping

At **Artizanns** (118 N. Main St., 585/374-6740, www.artizanns.com), more than 200 Finger Lakes artists and artisans exhibit their wares for purchase, with pottery, jewelry, photography, paintings, metalwork, and much more on display.

Food

The historic 1895 **Little Italy** (111 S. Main St., 585/374-6641, www.napleslittlealy.info, Tues.-Sat. 4pm-9pm, Sun. 4pm-8pm, $17) specializes in traditional Italian fare. On Saturdays, live music is often presented in the hotel's rathskeller downstairs.

Brew & Brats (6461 Rte. 64, 585/374-2870, www.brewandbrats.com, Fri.-Sun. noon-9pm, $7) specializes in local craft brews and nearly 10 kinds of bratwurst. Non-drinkers can enjoy non-alcoholic slushies made of locally-made grape juice or root beer. Saturday nights feature live music.

Rochester

Rochester (pop. 210,532) straddles the Genesee River gorge just south of Lake Ontario and north of the Erie Canal. New York's third-largest city, Rochester has traditionally been known for its corporate high-tech industries, with Eastman Kodak, Xerox, and Bausch & Lomb being the biggest. Many major educational and cultural institutions are based here as well, including the Eastman School of Music, Rochester Philharmonic, National Museum of Play at The Strong, and International Museum of Photography at the George Eastman House.

Established in 1803, Rochester became America's first boomtown with the opening of the Erie Canal, increasing its population 13-fold between 1825 and 1845. During the mid-1800s, Rochester was a hotbed of radical thought and social activism. Frederick Douglass, the escaped slave and abolitionist, settled in Rochester in 1847 and published his newspaper, *The Northern Star,* here for 17 years. One of his close associates was Susan B. Anthony, who was arrested in 1872 for daring to vote in a national election.

In 1881, a quiet young bank clerk named George Eastman patented and produced the world's first rollable film, an invention that changed Rochester forever. By the turn of the century, Eastman Kodak was Rochester's largest employer, and Eastman was a generous philanthropist. During his lifetime, he gave away over $100 million (more than $1 billion in today's economy) mainly to schools, parks, the University of Rochester, and local hospitals. "I want to make Rochester the best city in which to live and work." He succeeded: For much of

the 20th century, Rochester was famed for its prosperity.

In more recent decades, the city has been forced to reinvent itself. As Eastman Kodak and other major employers have downsized or shuttered completely, laying off thousands of employees, Rochester's population has learned to take nothing for granted. The city has traded its identity as a company town for one characterized by local businesses and smaller firms. Rochester today is home to dozens of thriving but relatively unknown computer software, telecommunications, and medical equipment companies. Downtown Rochester is experiencing something of a renaissance, and many of the city's suburbs remain prosperous.

Famous Rochesterians include musicians Cab Calloway, Mitch Miller, and Chuck Mangione. Jamaican-born Garth Fagan, the dancer, choreographer, and theater director best known for his choreography of the Broadway hit *The Lion King,* has lived in Rochester since 1970 and continues to headquarter his world-renowned eponymous dance troupe in the city.

Orientation

Downtown Rochester is encircled by I-490, sometimes called the Inner Loop. Main Street runs east-west through the center of downtown, flanked by a mix of historic buildings and modern glass-sheathed skyscrapers. Clinton Avenue runs north-south. At the corner of Main Street and Clinton Avenue sprawls the 1962 **Midtown Plaza,** the oldest downtown shopping mall in the country. At the corner of Main Street and South Avenue stand the **Rochester Riverside**

FINGER LAKES

DOWNTOWN ROCHESTER

© AVALON TRAVEL

Convention Center. Just west of South Street is the Genesee River. Graceful **Eastman Theatre,** with its rounded facade, is tucked onto Gibbs Street near Main Street, while the stunning Art Deco **Times Square Building** towers one block off Main Street at the intersection of Exchange Boulevard and Broad Street.

Major thoroughfares fanning out from I-490 include East Avenue, Park Avenue, Monroe Avenue (Route 31), and Mt. Hope Avenue (Route 15). I-90 runs just south of the city. Lake Ontario lies about eight miles north of the downtown.

The genteel southeastern quadrant of Rochester boasts four major museums, the University of Rochester, Mount Hope Cemetery, and Highland Park. Expansive **East Avenue,** peppered with stately mansions, gardens, and churches, runs through its center. Parallel to East Avenue runs **Park Avenue,** known for its classy boutiques, restaurants, and outdoor cafés. South of Park Avenue lies **Monroe Avenue,** a major commercial artery that's also one of the city's more eclectic neighborhoods. It's a haven for students, artists, performers, and activists. Most of the activity is centered between I-490 and Goodman Street.

You'll find several parking garages downtown, on or just off Main Street. Street parking is generally available elsewhere in the city. Downtown sights are within walking distance of each other and the major museums in southeast Rochester.

SIGHTS
High Falls and Brown's Race

Walk a few blocks north of Main Street and you'll see an enormous gaping gorge that rips right through the heart of the city, providing spectacular views. Brown's Race sits at the edge of wide, semi-circular, 96-foot-high High Falls. Cupping the falls to both sides, but especially to the east, are jagged brown walls streaked with dull red. A **pedestrian bridge** crosses the river just south of the falls.

Brown's Race is made up of four interconnected brick buildings that once contained water-powered mills. Extensively renovated in the early 1990s, it now features shops and restaurants. The word "race" refers to the diverted raceways that once harnessed the power of the falls.

◖ National Museum of Play

The **National Museum of Play** (1 Manhattan Sq., 585/263-2700, www.museumofplay.org, Mon.-Thurs. 10am-5pm, Fri.-Sat. 10am-8pm, Sun. noon-5pm, children over 2 and adults $13, children under 2 free) is one of the largest children's museums in the country, with 150,000 square feet of exhibits. The National Toy Hall of Fame features new and historic versions of classic toys. Main interactive exhibits include Sesame Street, a kid-sized supermarket, and a 1918 carousel.

Before her death in 1969, the museum's founder, Margaret Woodbury Strong, the daughter of wealthy parents, had amassed more than 300,000 objects, some of which she began collecting as a child. Often, during her family's many trips abroad, she was given a large shopping bag at the start of each day and told she could shop until she filled it.

Strong's many passions included fans, parasols, Asian artifacts and art, dolls, dollhouses, miniatures, toys, marbles, canes, paperweights, glass, pottery, samplers, figurines, kitchen equipment, and costumes. Her doll collection, numbering 27,000, is especially impressive. Many of these items remain on display.

Memorial Art Gallery

Connected with the University of Rochester, **Memorial Art Gallery** (500 University Ave., 585/276-8900, www.mag.rochester.edu, Wed.-Sun. 11am-5pm, Thurs. 11am-9pm, adults $12, seniors $8, students and children 6-18 $5) is a small gem, containing a little bit of everything, from pre-Columbian sculpture and ancient Chinese ceramics to American folk art and late-20th-century painting. The gallery owns more than 9,500 objects in all, spanning 5,000 years. A dozen or so temporary exhibitions are staged each year. In the center of the gallery is an enclosed, sky-lit sculpture garden filled with works by Henry Moore and Albert Paley, a Rochesterian.

Rochester Museum and Science Center

Like many other top science museums, **Rochester Museum and Science Center** (657 East Ave., 585/271-4320, www.rmsc.org, Mon.-Sat. 9am-5pm, Sun. 11am-5pm, adults $13, seniors and students $12, children 3-18 $11) houses plenty of fossils, dioramas, exhibits on flora and fauna, and prehistoric beasts.

What makes the place really unusual, however, is **At the Western Door,** a powerful exhibit about the Seneca Nation. The exhibit examines Seneca life from pre-European contact in the 1550s to the present. Separate sections, brimming with artifacts, focus on such subjects as the fur trade, the Iroquois Confederacy, the Sullivan campaign, and the sad history of broken treaties. As late as 1960, the Allegheny Senecas lost one-third of their reservation when it was flooded to create Kinzua Dam.

State-of-the-art **Strasenburgh Planetarium** (sky shows $6-7) is also at the museum.

George Eastman House

Just east of the Rochester Museum and Science Center is the grand, 50-room **George Eastman House** (900 East Ave., 585/271-3361, www.eastmanhouse.org, Tues.-Sat. 10am-5pm, Sun. 11am-5pm, adults $12, seniors $10, students $5, children 12 and under free), where Eastman Kodak founder George Eastman lived alone with his mother for much of his life. The Georgian mansion contains all the finest furnishings of its day, including Persian rugs, oil paintings, and carved mahogany furniture polished to a high gleam. But what makes the place interesting is the information and ephemera related to Eastman himself.

Born in 1854, Eastman left school at age 13 to help support his family. He worked first as a messenger boy, earning $3 a week, then as an accountant. He began taking photographs at age 23 while on vacation and started searching for an easier way to develop negatives. He

spent three years experimenting in his mother's kitchen. By 1880, Eastman had invented a dry plate coating machine, the genesis of his Eastman Kodak Company.

Eastman's passions included music, fresh flowers, wild game hunting, and philanthropy. One year, he gave a free camera to every child in America who was turning 13. Then, at age 78, suffering from an irreversible spinal disease, he committed suicide in his bedroom. His suicide note read: "To my friends; My work is done—why wait?"

Adjoining the mansion is the **International Museum of Photography,** a modern museum holding a fascinating collection of antique cameras and photographic equipment, along with two theaters and four galleries. First-rate exhibits by artists such as Ansel Adams and Henri Cartier-Bresson are presented.

Stone-Tolan House Museum

Continuing to the far eastern end of East Avenue, you'll come to the oldest structure in Rochester, the 1792 **Stone-Tolan House Museum** (2370 East Ave., 585/546-7029, www.landmarksociety.org, Mar.-Dec. Fri.-Sat. noon-3pm, adults $5, children $2). A handsome, rustic building with wide floorboards, large fireplaces, and an orchard out back, the house was once both the Stone family home and a popular tavern. It is now owned by the Landmark Society of Western New York.

Highland Park

In 1888, Frederick Law Olmsted designed Highland Park, a planned arboretum bounded by Mt. Hope, Highland, and Elm Avenues and Goodman Street. One of the city's biggest celebrations, the Lilac Festival, takes place here every May, when the park's 1,200 lilac bushes bloom.

But lilacs are just the beginning. From early spring through late fall, Highland offers a riotous delight of Japanese maples, sweet-smelling magnolias, dazzling spring bulbs, delicate wildflowers, and 700 varieties of rhododendrons, azaleas, and mountain laurel.

In the center of the park reigns the 1911

Lamberton Conservatory (180 Reservoir Ave., 585/753-7270, daily 10am-4pm, adults $3, seniors and children $2). A tropical forest grows under the main dome, while other rooms contain orchid collections, banana trees, cacti, and house plants. Across from the conservatory is the 1898 **Frederick Douglass statue,** the first public statue erected to honor an African American.

Mount Hope Cemetery

From the corner of Mt. Hope and Elmwood Avenues extends extravagant **Mount Hope Cemetery** (entrance at 1133 Mt. Hope Ave.), a landscaped oasis of green strewn with knobby hills, ancient trees, marble tombs, and elaborate mausoleums. One of the oldest cemeteries in the country, established in 1838, Mt. Hope contains the graves of every Rochesterian who was anyone, including Frederick Douglass and Susan B. Anthony.

An 1874 neo-Romanesque gatehouse marks the cemetery entrance, while just inside are a Gothic chapel and a white Moorish gazebo. The Douglass grave is off East Avenue near the northern end of the cemetery; the Anthony grave is off Indian Trail Avenue at the far northern end.

Maps to the cemetery are available at the Rochester Convention and Visitors Bureau. **Friends of Mt. Hope Cemetery** (585/461-3494, www.fomh.org) offers guided walking tours on Saturdays in the spring, summer, and fall.

Susan B. Anthony House

In a quiet, somewhat run-down neighborhood west of downtown stands the narrow, red-brick **Susan B. Anthony House** (17 Madison St., off W. Main St., 585/235-6124, www.susanbanthonyhouse.org, Tues.-Sun. 11am-5pm, adults $10, seniors $8, students and children $5) that once belonged to the women's rights advocate. Simply furnished in the style of the late 1800s, the house contains much Anthony memorabilia, including her typewriters, clothes, letters, photos, and stuffed Victorian furniture.

Anthony, born in Massachusetts in 1820, lived in this house from 1866 until her death in 1906. It was here where she was arrested for voting in 1872, and here that she met and planned with fellow reformers Elizabeth Cady Stanton and Frederick Douglass. Together with Elizabeth Cady Stanton and Matilda Gage, Anthony wrote her *History of Woman Suffrage* in the third-floor attic, a wonderful hideaway now once again strewn with her books and papers.

Seneca Park Zoo

North of the downtown, along the Genesee River, runs the long, skinny **Seneca Park Zoo** (2222 St. Paul St., 585/336-7200, www.senecaparkzoo.org, Nov. 1-Mar. 31 daily 10am-3pm, Apr. 1-Oct. 31 daily 10am-4pm, rates vary seasonally, adults $9-11, seniors $8-10, children 3-11 $6-8). About 500 animals from nearly 200 species live in the zoo, including polar bears, a Siberian tiger, and reindeer. Don't miss the aviary, where brightly colored tropical birds fly about freely. Younger kids will enjoy the barnyard petting area.

Ontario Beach Park

When in downtown Rochester, it's easy to forget that Lake Ontario is less than 15 minutes away. But indeed, north of the city along Lake Avenue, you'll soon find a land of wide open spaces, beaches, and parks.

Just before reaching the lake, you'll pass the 1822 **Charlotte-Genesee Lighthouse** (70 Lighthouse St., 585/621-6179, www.geneseelighthouse.org, hours vary seasonally, adults $3, children under 17 free), now a small museum with exhibits tracing the history of lighthouses and lake transportation. Originally, the lighthouse stood on the lakeshore, but sand deposits have moved it inland.

Ontario Beach Park (Lake and Beach Aves., 585/753-5887) is a 0.5-mile-long beach with an aging Art Deco bathhouse and weathered fishing pier illuminated on summer nights. Around the turn of the century, the park was the "Coney Island of the West," attracting tens of thousands of Rochesterians to its elephant shows, water slides, and beachfront

FINGER LAKES

hotels. Harking back to those heady days is the park's still-operating 1905 **Dentzel menagerie carousel,** one of the oldest carousels in the United States. Stop by the locally famous **Abbott's Custard** (www.abbottscustard. com), at the park's entrance, for sweet, creamy ice-cream.

Seabreeze Amusement Park
From Ontario Beach Park, travel east about five miles along Lake Shore Boulevard to reach **Seabreeze Amusement Park** (4600 Culver Rd., 585/323-1900, www.seabreeze. com, June-Aug. daily 11am-8pm, May weekends). First established in 1879, the park has over 75 rides and attractions, including a water park. It's also the home of the oldest continuously operating roller coaster in the United States, the **Jack Rabbit,** which opened in 1920.

An unlimited Ride & Slide Pass is $27.99 for those 48 inches and taller and $22.99 for those under 48 inches. A Spectator Pass allows access to the grounds, but no rides, and costs $11.99. Tickets are several dollars cheaper if bought in advance on the park's website.

RECREATION
The 49-passenger *Sam Patch* (585/662-5748, www.samandmary.org, May-Oct.), a replica packet boat, offers sightseeing and specialty cruises, as does the historic wooden boat, *Mary Jemison.*

ENTERTAINMENT
Classical Music
The renowned **Rochester Philharmonic Orchestra** (585/454-7311, www.rpo.org) performs at the Eastman Theatre October-May. One of the world's premier music schools, **Eastman School of Music** (26 Gibbs St., 585/274-1000, www.esm.rochester.edu) stages over 700 performances annually by students, faculty, and guest artists. **Hochstein School of Music and Dance** (50 N. Plymouth Ave., 585/454-4596, www.hochstein.org) hosts the Rochester Chamber Orchestra and classical music concerts.

Theater
Rochester's resident professional theater, **Geva Theatre** (75 Woodbury Blvd., 585/232-4382, www.gevatheatre.org) stages nearly a dozen productions annually. It's housed in a historic brick-and-limestone building that was once the Naval Armory. **Downstairs Cabaret Theatre** (20 Windsor St., 585-325-4370, www.downstairscabaret.org) produces popular comedies and musicals.

Rochester Broadway Theatre League (885 Main St., 585/325-7760, www.rbtl.org) presents touring Broadway shows and concerts, while **Rochester Contemporary Art Center** (137 East Ave., 585/461-2222, www.rochester-contemporary.org) is the place to go for performance art and avant-garde theater.

Live Music and Nightlife
The best music listings are published by *City Newspaper* (www.rochestercitynewspaper. com), a free alternative weekly. One of the biggest and most active music clubs in the city is **Water Street Music Hall** (204 N. Water St., 585/325-5600, www.waterstreetmusic.com). Regional and national acts play blues, rock, funk, and industrial.

California Brew Haus (402 W. Ridge Rd., 585/621-1480) presents a good dose of Southern rock in a space that is the longest, continuously operated rock and roll bar in the city.

Rochester International Jazz Festival (downtown Rochester, www.rochesterjazz. com) is a massive event each June, held over the course of more than a week, featuring more than 300 concerts and 1,200 performers in nearly 20 different venues, all within walking distance of downtown's East End Cultural District. Options to attend include approximately 80 free performances, 40 headliner shows, over 180 club pass concerts, and dozens of late-night, no-cover charge jam sessions.

ACCOMMODATIONS
There are a handful of great places to stay, all in downtown Rochester. In a city of nearly all chain hotels, **Inn on Broadway** (26 Broadway, 585/232-3595, www.innonbroadway.com,

$169-199) is a boutique hotel housed in the historic 1929 University Club of Rochester. Luxury rooms include polished hardwood floors and natural stone bathrooms with extra touches like multi-headed showers, whirlpool tubs, Keurig coffeemakers, and gas fireplaces. Complimentary continental breakfast is served in elegant Tournedos, a restaurant whose lunch and dinner menus feature in-house dry-aged beef, seafood flown in daily from Hawaii, and a wine list with over 550 selections.

The **East Avenue Inn & Suites** (384 East Ave., 585/325-5010, www.eastaveinn.com, $129-169), fresh off a 2012-2013 renovation, transformed from a cheap and basic hotel to a boutique property where Wi-Fi, parking, and breakfast are all free.

One of the loveliest bed-and-breakfasts in Rochester is **Dartmouth House** (215 Dartmouth St., 585/271-7872, www.dartmouthhouse.com, $109-209), a spacious English Tudor home with a fireplace, window seats, very knowledgeable hosts, and four guest rooms equipped with private baths. The bed-and-breakfast is within easy walking distance of several museums and many cafés and shops.

Another good bed-and-breakfast choice is romantic **Edward Harris House Inn** (35 Argyle St., 585/473-9752, www.edwardharrishouse.com, $169-189), with nice touches like fresh flowers, robes and towel warmers, sunflower showerheads, all organic and natural breakfasts, and welcome snack baskets.

Just outside Rochester, **Woodcliff Hotel and Spa** (199 Woodcliff Dr., Fairport, 585/381-4000, www.woodcliffhotelspa.com, $156-540), is a perfect home base for exploring the surrounding area's attractions, including small canal towns like Fairport. The room decor runs the gamut from Art Deco to Southwestern to Asian. The expansive property has spa and a 9-hole golf course, as well as an on-site restaurant.

FOOD

For a quick lunch, visit **DiBella's Old Fashioned Submarines** (620 Jefferson Rd.,

585/475-1831, www.dibellas.com, Mon.-Sat. 10am-9pm, Sun. 11am-7pm, $10), serving hot and cold subs on hand-shaped rolls since 1918. Another good lunch spot is **Orange Glory Café** (240 East Ave., 585/232-7340, www.orangeglorycafe.com, Mon.-Fri. 11am-3pm, $8), which offers tasty homemade organic dishes, gourmet sandwiches, and cookies. Head to this little eatery early for the best selection.

In the heart of downtown, **Dinosaur Bar-B-Que** (99 Court St., 585/325-7090, www.dinosaurbarbque.com, Mon.-Wed. 11am-11pm, Thurs. 11am-midnight, Fri.-Sat. 11am-1am, Sun. noon-10pm, $12) offers great ribs and Cajun food, along with live blues on weekends. Romantic **Tapas 177 Lounge** (177 St. Paul St., 585/262-2090, www.tapas177.com, $16) is a very popular spot, serving an eclectic menu by candlelight. The lounge also features a wide variety of martinis, salsa lessons, and live music on the weekends.

The spirits of generations of brewers permeate the cavernous **Genesee Brew House** (25 Cataract St., 585/263-9200, www.geneseebeer.com, 11am-9pm Mon.-Wed., 11am-10pm Thurs.-Sat., noon-9:00pm Sun.), one of the country's oldest, continuously operating breweries. Expect typical American brew pub fare like burgers and wings, served alongside Genesee's own brews. A guest tap features other local beers.

Nestled into the East End entertainment district is popular **2 Vine** (24 Winthrop St., 585/454-6020, www.2vine.com, Mon.-Thurs. 11:30am-10pm, Fri. 11:30am-11pm, Sat. 5pm-11pm, $26), serving lots of fresh seafood flown in daily, fresh local produce, and homemade pastries.

For a simple salad or tofu burger, step into no-frills **Aladdin's Natural Eatery** (646 Monroe Ave., 585/442-5000, www.myaladdins.com, $8). On Clinton Avenue, parallel to Monroe, is **Highland Park Diner** (960 S. Clinton Ave., 585/461-5040, www.highland-park-diner.com, Mon.-Thurs. and Sat. 7am-9pm, Fri. 7am-10pm, Sun. 7am-8pm, $10), a classic 1948 Art Deco Orleans diner.

On Jefferson Road, you'll find **Raj Mahal**

(368 Jefferson Rd., 585/730-7360, www.rajmahalrestaurant.com, $14), known for its tandoori and vegetarian dishes and fresh breads.

VICINITY OF ROCHESTER
Pittsford
To the immediate southeast of the city, the canal town of Pittsford offers unique shops and cafés, some inhabiting historic buildings. The town's **Lock 32** (585/328-3960, www.geneseewaterways.org, hours and prices vary seasonally) offers whitewater kayaking in the spillway. Live music also rocks the locks, with a **Summer Concert Series** (Port of Pittsford Park, 22 N. Main Street, www.townofpittsford.org, free), **Positively Pittsford** (Main St. and Church St., www.townofpittsford.org, free), and **Pittsford Celebrates** (www.townofpittsford.org, free), all filled with family entertainment and the occasional fireworks display.

Bushnell's Basin, a charming spot to dock just outside of the village, is home to one of Rochester's landmark restaurants, **Richardson's Canal House** (1474 Marsh Rd., 585/248-5000, www.richardsonscanalhouse.net, Mon.-Sat. 5pm-10pm, $28), a restored 1818 Erie Canal tavern with its own secluded garden. Elegant and highly acclaimed, the restaurant serves French country and American regional fare by candlelight.

Along the banks of the canal, **Coal Tower** (9 Schoen Pl., 585/381-7866, www.villagecoaltower.com, hours vary seasonally) serves burgers and sandwiches.

Macedon
Macedon's **Mid-Lakes Erie Macedon Landing** is the home marina to **Mid-Lakes Navigation** (315/685-8500, www.midlakesnav.com), where you can learn to drive one of the gleaming wooden canal boats that await visitors who come to relive a bit of history. These simple-to-pilot boats can be driven by anyone with a few lessons.

Nearby **Long Acre Farms** (1342 Eddy Rd., 315/986-4202, www.longacrefarms.com), a family farm with a Scandinavian jumping pillow (for all ages), gemstone panning, and the Amazing Maize Maze, attracts visitors. The town's annual, mid-September **Lumberjack Festival** (Macedon Center Fireman's Field, Rte. 31 and Canandaigua Rd., 315/986-3732, www.macedoncenterfire.org) lets even amateurs unleash their inner Paul Bunyan with log rolling and team greased pole climbing.

Fairport
The bustling, canal-side community of Fairport can be explored with bicycle rentals from **RV&E** (40 N. Main St., 585/388-1350, www.rvebike.com) or kayak rentals from **Erie Canal Boat Company** (7 Lift Bridge Ln., 585/748-2628, www.eriecanalboatcompany.com). For a more in depth look at life on the canal, join an overnight excursion, which includes kayak rental, food, and an overnight campsite with sleeping gear. Paddling adventures with itineraries for up to 10 days are also available.

With any luck, a boater will need the **Lift Bridge** triggered, the only one of its kind on the canal system. With no angle the same, the irregularly constructed bridge once largely stayed raised in a crooked slant at its top 15-foot height to allow for the high volume of traffic on the canal below. A pedestrian bridge was created to accommodate foot traffic in this raised position. Current times see more road traffic, so the opposite is true and the bridge is raised from its usual six-foot-above-the-water level only when a boat needs to pass.

Red Bird Market (130 Village Landing, 585/377-5050, www.redbirdmarket.com) is a good morning pre-paddle pit stop for baked goods and coffee. Afternoon cool downs can be had at **Donnelly's Public House** (1 Water St., 585/377-5450, www.donnellysph.com), an excellent pub with 33 taps and good pub food.

GENESEE COUNTRY VILLAGE AND MUSEUM

Twenty miles southwest of Rochester, world-class **Genesee Country Village and Museum** (1410 Flint Hill Rd., Mumford, 585/538-6822, www.gcv.org, hours vary seasonally, adults $15.50, seniors and students $12.50, children ages 4-16 $9.50) consists of more than 40 meticulously restored and furnished 19th-century buildings laid out around a village square, depicting life of three different historic periods. Among the buildings are an early land office, two-story log cabin, fly-tier's shop, octagonal house, Greek Revival mansion, Italianate mansion, bookshop, small-scale farm, blacksmith's shop, doctor's office, and pharmacy. Gravel walkways lead between the buildings; guides in period dress cook, spin, weave, and demonstrate other folk arts of the pre-industrial age.

Near the entrance are a Carriage Museum and **The John L. Wehle Art Gallery,** which houses a world-class collection of wildlife and sporting art spanning four centuries of work by such artists as Audubon and Remington. An extensive renovation completed in 2012 also debuted a new exhibit: the Susan Greene Historic Clothing Collection, a remarkably intact representation of period clothing, unique for its pieces that represent both the working class (whose clothing was so well-worn that it rarely survived to be able to be exhibited) and the upper class.

Another delightful curiosity on the grounds is *The Intrepid,* a replica Civil War-era helium balloon. Its basket occasionally holds passengers, who soar up to 300 feet over the Genesee grounds.

An heirloom garden provides blooms and seeds to be used in the village. To the north is a 175-acre **Nature Center,** networked with three miles of hiking and nature trails.

Little Finger Lakes

West of the six major Finger Lakes extend what are known as the little Finger Lakes: Honeoye (pronounced Honey-oy), Canadice, Hemlock, and Conesus. Honeoye sports a village of the same name at its northern end, and Conesus—closest to Rochester—is crowded with summer homes. Canadice and Hemlock, which serve as reservoirs for Rochester, remain largely undeveloped and comprise Hemlock/Canadice State Forest. Set in deep, wooded valleys with no towns nearby, these two Finger Lakes are totally undeveloped. As a state forest, they and their surroundings will remain "forever green." Fishing, boating, and hiking can be enjoyed in the area.

HONEOYE

At the southwestern end of Honeoye lies the largely undeveloped **Harriet Hollister Spencer State Recreation Area** (Canadice Hill Rd./Rte. 37, 585/335-8111, www.nysparks.com/parks/164/details.aspx). Set on Canadice Hill, the park offers great views of the lake and, on a clear day, the Rochester skyline.

Another quirky stop outside Honeoye is the unusual **Wizard of Clay** (7851 Rte. 20A, Bloomfield, 585/229-2980, www.wizardofclay.com), where the Kozlowski potters use 100,000 pounds of clay each year, hand-throwing the family's functional creations. The workshop is open to tour and see each stage of the process, even that of the unique patented Bristoleaf collection, made by pressing locally collected leaves into the soft clay before firing, leaving the imprints to be glazed for a final vase or picture frame. A densely pinned map on the wall shows the hometowns of thousands of visitors.

Accommodations and Food

The area offers several good lodging options including **Little Lakes Inn and Healing Center** (4646 County Rd. 37, Honeoye,

585/229-5557, www.littlelakesinn.com, $135-165), an Italianate style inn with five suites and an on-site "healing center," which offers traditional spa treatments alongside more mystical-sounding therapies.

Abner Adams House (2 Howard Ave., Bloomfield, 585/657-4681, www.abneradamshouse.com, $159-179) is a sturdy brick home built in 1810, featuring high ceilings and wood floors. All three guest rooms have fireplaces.

The Holloway House (29 State St., Bloomfield, 585/657-7120, www.thehollowayhouse.com, Tues.-Fri. 11:30am-2pm and 5pm-9pm, Sat. 5pm-9pm, Sun. 11:30am-7:30pm) is a fine dining restaurant located in a colonial home built in 1808. American favorites include roast duck and broiled lamb chops.

LETCHWORTH STATE PARK

Along the Genesee River at the far western edge of the Finger Lakes plunges one of the most magnificent sights in the state: 17-mile-long Letchworth Gorge, now part of **Letchworth State Park** (1 Letchworth State Park, Castile, 585/493-3600, camping reservations 800/456-2267, www.nysparks.com/parks/79, daily 6am-11pm, $8 parking). Dubbed the "Grand Canyon of the East," the gorge is flanked by dark gray cliffs rising nearly 600 feet. Dense, thicketed forest grows all around and at the center of it all sparkle three thundering waterfalls. Excellent hiking and snowshoeing are available through the wild terrain.

Much of the Letchworth Gorge was purchased by industrialist William P. Letchworth in 1859. A conservationist and humanitarian, Letchworth bought the gorge both for his own personal use and to save the falls from becoming Rochester's hydroelectric plant. Before his death in 1910, he deeded the gorge to the people of New York to be used as a permanent park.

One main road runs through the park alongside the gorge, affording scenic views. Recreational facilities include over 25 hiking trails ranging from 0.5 to 7 miles in length, two swimming pools, 82 cabins, and a 270-site campground.

The park can be entered from Mt. Morris (off Rte. 36), Portageville (off Rtes. 19A or 436), or Castile (off Rte. 19A); Portageville entrances are closed in winter.

Letchworth Museum

At the southern end of the park stands the rambling **Letchworth Museum** (585/493-2760, May-Oct. daily 10am-5pm) with exhibits on the Seneca, William Letchworth, and the gorge's natural history. Note especially the exhibits relating to Mary Jemison, the "white woman of the Genesee."

The daughter of Irish immigrants, Jemison was taken prisoner by the Seneca at the age of 15 and lived the rest of her life among them. She married first a Delaware warrior and then, following his death, a Seneca chief; she bore seven children, and became a Seneca leader in her own right. Under the Big Tree Treaty of 1797, she was granted close to 18,000 acres along the Genesee River. Eventually, however, Jemison was moved to the Buffalo Creek Reservation with the rest of her people, where she died at the age of 91.

Letchworth moved Jemison's remains to the gorge in 1910 when her grave was in danger of being destroyed, and today, the **Mary Jemison Grave** stands on a hill behind the museum. Also on the hill is the **Council House** in which the last Iroquois council on the Genesee River was held on October 1, 1872. In attendance were the grandchildren of Red Jacket, Joseph Brant, and Mary Jemison; and William Letchworth and Millard Fillmore.

Accommodations and Food

At the southern end of the park, across from the Letchworth Museum is the **Glen Iris Inn** (inside Letchworth State Park, 585/493-2622, www.glenirisinn.com, breakfast, lunch, and dinner, $18), a favorite lunch spot. The inn's bustling restaurant, flanked by picture windows, specializes in gourmet salads prepared tableside, seafood, and veal. The stately, yellow-and-white (**Glen Iris Inn** (inside Letchworth State Park, 585/493-2622, www.glenirisinn.com, $95-120) sits in a large flat field overlooking the 107-foot Middle Falls. Once the home of William Letchworth, the Victorian mansion is now a modernized inn with 16 comfortable guest rooms, a library with a good collection of regional books, and a gift shop.

For a serene, scenic splurge, check availability for the signature **Cherry Suite at the Glen Iris Inn** (inside Letchworth State Park, 585/493-2622, www.glenirisinn.com, $210),

which features patterned hardwood floors, a whirlpool tub, and a balcony overlooking the incredible middle falls. The balcony of the Cherry Suite, perched above the glass-walled restaurant, is a coveted spot of passersby. Four-bedroom **The Stone House** (585/493-2622, $350 for up to 8 people) is another option rented by Letchworth State Park, situated across from Inspiration Point overlook.

The Thousand Islands

An hour or two from the northeastern part of the Finger Lakes is the Thousand Islands-Seaway region, accessible by I-81. In point of fact, there are 1,864 islands here, ranging in size from a few square feet to 22 miles long. Some support nothing more than a lone tree; one is home to Boldt Castle, a haunting Gothic presence near Alexandria Bay that is the region's premier visitor attraction.

Though the term "Thousand Islands" is often used to describe the large area reaching from Oswego in the south to Akwesasne in the north to Adirondack Park in the east, the islands themselves are clustered only in the center, between Cape Vincent and Alexandria Bay. Much of the rest of the region supports farms or endless unbroken acres of low-growing forests, rivers, and lakes.

Prior to the arrival of Europeans, the Thousand Islands were inhabited by the Iroquois, who called the region Manitonna, or Garden of the Great Spirit. The first white man to enter the region was Jacques Cartier, who sailed down the St. Lawrence in 1635 and allegedly exclaimed, *"Les milles isles!"* Later, the region bore the brunt of much of the War of 1812. Handsome stone fortifications still stand in Sackets Harbor and Oswego, where major battles were fought. The wealthy discovered the beauty of the Thousand Islands in the 1870s and soon built magnificent summer homes on private islands. Grand hotels went up on the shore as well, and huge steamboats plied the waters.

All this opulence ended with the Depression, but evidence of it remains.

Most of the Thousand Islands' attractions lie along the Seaway Trail, which hugs the shores of the St. Lawrence and Lake Ontario. From the trail, views of the river and its bypassing boat traffic are outstanding. Enormous tankers and cargo vessels slide by, on their way between the Atlantic Ocean and the Great Lakes. The 1959 completion of the St. Lawrence Seaway—a series of connecting channels and locks—turned the river into the longest navigable inland water passage in the world. It stretches over 2,300 miles.

New York and Canada share the islands. Canada's oldest national park east of the Rockies, Thousand Islands National Park, is here, where the Canadian Shield mountain range connects across the river with New York's Adirondack Mountains. As a result, the region attracts as many Canadian visitors as American visitors. The Thousand Islands International Bridge (an extension of I-81) crosses over the St. Lawrence River near Alexandria Bay; the Prescott-Ogdensburg Bridge connects the two cities, and the Seaway International Bridge spans the river near Massena.

OSWEGO

The small city of Oswego (pop. 18,142) sits at the southwestern end of the region, just north of the Finger Lakes. Straddling the mouth of the Oswego River and overlooking Lake Ontario, Oswego operated as an important fort

THE SEAWAY TRAIL

The Seaway Trail is a 518-mile scenic highway that parallels New York's northern coastline along the St. Lawrence River, Lake Ontario, the Niagara River, and Lake Erie. Marked by green-and-white route markers, as well as brown-and-white War of 1812 signs, it is the longest national recreational trail in the United States.

In the Thousand Islands region, the Seaway Trail runs from Oswego in the south to Akwesasne in the north along Routes 104, 3, 180, 12 E, and 37. More parks and beaches are located along this section of the trail than anywhere else in New York State. In total, the Thousand Islands region boasts 45 New York and Canadian state parks; two of the largest are Wellesley Island and Robert Moses.

Seaway Trail, Inc. (401 W. Main St., Sackets Harbor, 315/646-1000, www.seawaytrail. com) publishes a free annual magazine, available in most regional tourism offices, and helpful touring guides. Among them are *Seaway Trail Bicycling*, which outlines some of the region's excellent bike routes, and *Seaway Trail Lighthouses*. Their website is a rich resource, with detailed maps available for download.

and trading post throughout the 1700s. During the American Revolution, Oswego served as a haven for Loyalists fleeing the Mohawk Valley, and remained in British hands until 1796. Named the first freshwater port in the United States in 1799, Oswego protected the supply route to the naval base at nearby Sackets Harbor during the War of 1812.

Today, Oswego continues to function as a Great Lakes port and is a major sport-fishing center.

Fort Ontario State Historic Site

Fort Ontario State Historic Site (1 E. 4th St., 315/343-4711, www.nysparks.com/historic-sites/20, July 1-Sept. 2 daily 10am-4:30pm, hours vary off-season, adults $4, seniors and students $3, children 12 and under free) continues to stand sentinel over Lake Ontario, nearly 200 years after it was built. Originally built by the British in 1755, the site was attacked and rebuilt four times, with the present-day fort constructed between 1839 and 1844.

During World War II, Fort Ontario served as a sort of emergency refugee center/internment camp for victims of the Holocaust. The only one of its kind for European refugees in the country, the center invited 874 Jews and 73 Catholics to relocate here, but upon arrival, the refugees were placed in a fenced-in compound and told not to leave. The shocked refugees were interned for a total of 18 months.

Today, Fort Ontario has been restored to its 1867-72 appearance. Costumed guides interpret the lives of soldiers and civilians who once lived here.

H. Lee White Marine Museum

The delightful **H. Lee White Marine Museum** (1 W. 1st St. at West First St. Pier, 315/342-0480, www.hleewhitemarinemuseum.com, Sept.-June daily 1pm-5pm, July-Aug. daily 10am-5pm, adults $7, children 13-17 $3, children 12 and under free) is a sprawling, hodgepodge affair filled with everything from archaeological artifacts to mounted fish. One exhibit focuses on Lake Ontario shipwrecks; another on the city's once-thriving shipbuilding industry; a third on the legendary "monsters" of the lake; and a fourth on the region's strong abolitionist history. Most everything in the museum has been donated, which gives it a folksy appeal. Outside, a World War II tugboat and a derrick barge invite exploration.

Richardson-Bates House Museum

Built in the late 1860s, **Richardson-Bates House Museum** (135 E. 3rd St., 315/343-1342, www.rbhousemuseum.org, Apr.-Dec. Thurs.-Sat 1pm-5pm, Jan.-Mar. by appointment,

OSWEGO

Lake Ontario

FORT
ONTARIO

★ H LEE WHITE
MARINE MUSEUM

WRIGHT'S
LANDING

LAKE RD

E SENECA ST

W SECOND ST

W FIRST ST

E THIRD ST

E FOURTH ST

E CAYUGA ST

E SECOND ST

E FIRST ST

ST

E BRIDGE ST

0   0.25 mi

W SENECA ST

O s w e g o

0   0.25 km

W CAYUGA ST

Washington
Square

E ONEIDA ST

R i v e r

W BRIDGE ST

RICHARDSON-BATES
★   MUSEUM

W ONEIDA ST

→ To State College and
Niagara Power

E UTICA ST

W UTICA ST

© AVALON TRAVEL

adults $5, seniors and students $3, children 6-12 $2, children under 6 free) is a regal Italianate mansion still equipped with 95 percent of its original furnishings. The five plush period rooms downstairs are arranged according to photographs taken around 1890, while upstairs, succinct exhibits explain the history of Oswego County. The museum is run by the Oswego County Historical Society.

Camping
Selkirk Shores State Park (7101 Rte. 3, 315/298-5737, reservations 800/456-2267, www.nysparks.com/parks/84) is on the lakeshore about 15 miles northeast of Oswego.

It has a beach, hiking trails, and a 148-site campground.

Food
The ever popular **Rudy's Lakeside Drive-in** (78 Rte. 89, 315/343-2671, www.rudyshot. com), a quarter-mile west of the State University of New York (SUNY) College at Oswego, has been serving up fish and chips and fried scallops and clams since 1946.

EN ROUTE TO SACKETS HARBOR
The **Seaway Trail** (Rte. 104 to Rte. 3) heads north out of Oswego to Selkirk Shores State

Park and the mouth of the Salmon River. Take a two-mile detour east on Route 13 along the river to reach the Salmon Capital of **Pulaski,** where almost everything caters to anglers.

Continue another five miles east on Route 13 to reach Altmar, where the **New York State Salmon River Fish Hatchery** (2133 Rte. 22, Altmar, 315/298-5051, www.dec.ny.gov/outdoor/21663.html, Apr. 1-Nov. 30 daily 8:30am-3:30pm, free). Over three million fish are raised here each year, including chinook and coho salmon and brown, rainbow, and steelhead trout.

From the mouth of the Salmon River, Seaway Trail continues north along the shores of Lake Ontario. It bypasses several more parks and then bumps into deep blue **Henderson Harbor,** a perfectly shaped semicircle ringed with historic homes, vacation cottages, marinas, and ship-shape small boats.

About a mile southeast of Henderson Harbor is the hamlet of **Henderson,** where Confederate general Stonewall Jackson came for medical treatment for a stomach ailment before the Civil War. Part of his cure was to walk between the hamlet and the harbor daily.

SACKETS HARBOR

About 45 miles north of Oswego, or 8 miles west of Watertown, lies picturesque Sackets Harbor. Built on a bluff overlooking Lake Ontario, Sackets Harbor is peppered with handsome limestone buildings that date back to the early 1800s. Though now primarily a resort village, Sackets Harbor remains for the most part undiscovered, which helps account for its charm.

During the War of 1812, Sackets Harbor dominated American naval and military activity. A large fleet was constructed in its shipyard and thousands of soldiers were housed in the barracks built on its shores. Heavy fighting between British and American troops took place on the bluffs.

The former shipyard and adjoining battlefield is now Sackets Harbor's foremost visitor attraction. It is located at the end of a short Main Street lined with cheery shops, cafés,

and historic buildings; more historic buildings flank quiet, tree-shaded Broad Street.

Sackets Harbor Battlefield State Historic Site

The silent and all-but-deserted **Sackets Harbor Battlefield State Historic Site** (foot of Main and Washington Sts., 315/646-3634, www.sacketsharborbattlefield.org, grounds: daily dawn-dusk, buildings: May 24-June 30 Wed.-Sat. 10am-5pm, summer Mon.-Sat. 10am-5pm and Sun. 1pm-5pm, adults $3, seniors and students $2, children 12 and under free) was once the site of intense fighting between American and British troops. Monuments and plaques commemorating the events are strewn here and there, but for the most part, the battlefield remains an idyllic park, set atop a lush green bluff with glorious lake views. The **Battle of Sackets Harbor** is reenacted here every July.

Adjoining the battlefield is the partially restored Navy Yard, enclosed by a white picket fence. Built in the 1850s to replace the thriving shipyard once situated here, the yard contains a restored commandant's house and a museum showcasing exhibits on the War of 1812.

Madison Barracks

A mile or two east of the village center stand the former barracks, now known as **Madison Barracks** (85 Worth Rd., 315/646-3374, www.madisonbarracks.com), a converted complex holding apartments, restaurants, and a small inn. Visitors are welcome to explore the barracks' bucolic grounds, encompassing a parade ground, polo lawn, stone tower, officers' row, and military burial ground. Pick up walking-tour brochures in the management office just inside the main gate.

Augustus Sacket Mansion

Housed in the handsome 1803 **Augustus Sacket Mansion** (301 W. Main St.) is **Sackets Harbor Visitors Center** (315/646-2321, www.sacketsharborny.com, hours vary seasonally, free), which contains three rooms of exhibits and an informative introductory video on the area.

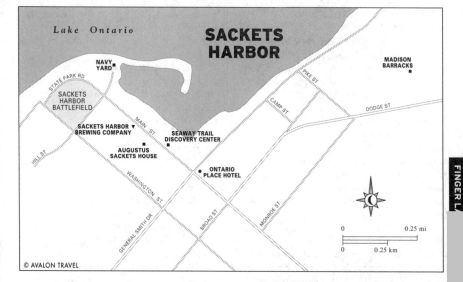

Seaway Trail Discovery Center

One block away from the visitors center is the **Seaway Trail Discovery Center** (401 W. Main St., 315/646-1000, www.seawaytrail.com, hours vary seasonally, adults $4, seniors $3, children $2), housed in the old Union Hotel, which was built in 1817. Here, you'll find nine rooms of exhibits and lots of free literature on the historic trail.

Accommodations

In the heart of the village, three-story **Ontario Place Hotel** (103 General Smith Dr., 315/646-8000, www.ontarioplacehotel.com, $90-165) offers 28 spacious rooms and 10 suites with whirlpool tubs.

Also in the center of town, **Jacob Brewster House B&B** (107 S. Broad St., 315/646-4663, www.jacobbrewsterbandb.com, $100-125) is a renovated 1815 New England-style Georgian house with four guest rooms. Each has a private bathroom, a fireplace, and free Wi-Fi.

Food

❰ Sackets Harbor Brewing Company (212 W. Main St., 315/646-2739, www. sacketsharborbrewpub.com, daily 11:30am-10pm, $25) is located in a refurbished railroad station in the heart of the village. Its historic location inspires the names of many of its brews, including War of 1812 Amber Ale and Grant's Golden Ale. On the dining room menu, find everything from fresh fish to pot pies; a pub menu is also available.

WATERTOWN

One of the few towns in the Thousand Islands whose population has increased in recent years (just over 27,000), Watertown is named for the numerous falls of the Black River. Its proximity to so many waterways was, in large part, responsible for its industrial prosperity, a prosperity that was so robust that the town was said to have the most millionaires—at least per capita—in the United States at the beginning of the 20th century. That wealth helped Watertown develop infrastructure and architecture that were particularly remarkable given its size. It is the smallest town to have a park designed by Frederick Law Olmsted, Thompson Park, which is the location of The New York State Zoo.

The New York State Zoo at Thompson Park

Nearly a century old, **The New York State Zoo** (1 Thompson Park, 315/782-6180, www.nyszoo.org, Mar.-Oct. daily 10am-5pm, Nov.-Feb. Sat.-Sun. 10am-4pm, adults $8, seniors $6, children 4-12 $5, children under 4 free) is a 32-acre park that focuses on species that are native to New York. Some of the species are common, while others are rare, threatened, or endangered. Among them, expect to see bears, eagles, and wolverines. The zoo has a particularly strong educational and family program, so if you're coming with kids, be sure to see what activities are planned during your visit.

Recreation

If you're keen to get out on the river to run the rapids, **Adirondack River Outfitters** (140 Newell St., 800/525-7238, www.aroadventures.com, May-Oct.) will take you on a Black River whitewater excursion. Expect 14 rapids ranging from Class II to Class IV.

Accommodations and Food

As Watertown's oldest restaurant, **The Crystal Restaurant** (87 Public Square, 315/782-9938, www.thecrystalrestaurant.com, Tues.-Sun. 7am-10pm) is an institution. Little has been done over the years to modernize the restaurant: the decor, the menu, and even the prices have refused to conform to trends. Service is generally excellent, which is one reason to visit. Another is the restaurant's contribution to cocktail culture: The Tom and Jerry, a Christmas holiday eggnog drink, wasn't invented here, but many locals claim it was perfected here. It's served only from Black Friday through New Year's Day.

Most lodging options in and immediately around Watertown are chain hotels, offering basic, reliable rooms and amenities.

CAPE VINCENT

Situated on a windswept spit of land at the mouth of the St. Lawrence River is Cape Vincent, "home of the gamey black bass" ("gamey" as in "feisty"). Cape Vincent has few tourist attractions, but it's a pretty village to drive through, with historic homes along Broadway.

The area's first European settlers were French, a fact that is celebrated every July on **French Heritage Day**. Real Street was once the location of "Cup and Saucer House," built in 1818 by Napoleon's chief of police, Count Real, in the hopes that the emperor could be rescued from the island of St. Helena. The building burned to the ground in 1867.

Sights

Cape Vincent Historical Museum (174 James St., 315/654-3094, July-Aug. Mon.-Sat. 10am-4pm, Sun. noon-4pm, free), in the heart of the village, showcases historical artifacts and a delightful collection of tiny figures created out of scrap metal by local farmer Richard Merchant. Not far from the museum is **New York State Department of Environmental Conservation's Research Station and Aquarium** (541 Broadway, 315/654-2147, May-Oct. daily 9am-4pm, free), housing several hundred local fish.

It's also worth driving out to the 1854 **Tibbetts Point Lighthouse** (33439 County Rte. 6, 315/654-3450, www.hiusa.org/cape-vincent), several miles west of the village on the very tip of the cape. The lighthouse is not open for touring—it's now a youth hostel—but the drive along the shore road (Route 6) is outstanding.

Horne's Ferry

Cape Vincent is the only community left in New York State with a ferry to Canada crossing the St. Lawrence River. **Horne's Ferry** (855/442-2262, www.hornesferry.com, $15 for car and driver, one-way, $2 per extra passenger) operates in May-October and it takes 10 minutes to cross the river on the ferry.

Accommodations and Food

Two blocks from the water, **Aubrey's Inn** (126 S. James St., 315/654-3754, www.aubreysinn.com, daily from 7am) offers inexpensive, generous portions at breakfast, lunch, and dinner.

For historic lodging, **Tibbetts Point Lighthouse** (33439 County Rte. 6, 315/654-3450, www.hiusa.org/capevincent, July 1-Sept. 15, $25 per night in dorms) is a Hosteling International property offering 21 dormitory-style beds in single-sex rooms; family rooms also are available.

The boxy, brick **Roxy Hotel** (Broadway and Market St., 315/654-2456, www.theroxy-hotel.com, $80) has operated continuously since 1894, with a brief break for renovations in 2011. Downstairs, an Irish pub offers beer and food; upstairs are 10 simple but adequate guest rooms.

CLAYTON

One of the most interesting villages along the St. Lawrence, Clayton contains four museums and the Thousand Islands Inn, where Thousand Island salad dressing was invented. The town spreads along the riverfront, with lots of park benches ideal for watching the swift current slide by. All along Riverside Drive stand sturdy brick storefronts, built in the late 1800s. An exception to the functional brick retail spaces is **Simon Johnston House,** a clapboard Italianate home with a widow's walk and decorative eaves, located at the corner of Riverside Drive and Merrick Street.

Settled in 1822, Clayton soon developed into a major shipbuilding center and steamboat port. The St. Lawrence skiff, known for its sleekness and beauty, was first constructed here by Xavier Colon in 1868, and the 900-passenger *St. Lawrence,* the largest steamboat ever made, was built in the 1890s. During World War I, the Clayton shipyards produced submarine chasers and pontoon boats.

Tourists began frequenting Clayton in the late 1800s. Most came to fish and boat, and they stayed in huge wooden hotels—which have since burned down—along the waterfront. During Clayton's heyday, five express trains arrived here daily from New York City, and one hotel was equipped with a direct line to the New York Stock Exchange. Some

vacationers even came during the winter, to ice-fish and watch the horse races run on the frozen St. Lawrence River.

Walking tour maps of the town are available at **Clayton Chamber of Commerce** (517 Riverside Dr., 315/686-3771, www.1000islands-clayton.com, July-Sept. daily 9am-5pm, Oct.-June Mon.-Fri. 9am-4pm).

Antique Boat Museum

Appropriately enough, Clayton has the finest collection of antique wooden boats in America. Among them are canoes, sailboats, launches, race boats, runabouts, and, of course, the famed *St. Lawrence* skiff. The gleaming boats, most built of highly polished woods and brass, are housed at the **Antique Boat Museum** (750 Mary St., 315/686-4104, www.abm.org, hours and admission vary seasonally) in a former lumberyard on the edge of town. There are over 300 vessels in all, spread out over eight buildings, along with a boatbuilding shop, almost 300 inboard and outboard motors, and thousands of nautical artifacts. The museum also contains extensive historical exhibits.

Thousand Islands Museum

Inside the eclectic **Thousand Islands Museum** (312 James St., 315/686-5794, www.timuseum. org, hours vary seasonally, donations accepted), you'll find the Muskie Hall of Fame, devoted to the region's most prized fish, and an enormous collection of hand-carved decoys, a popular North Country folk art. According to the exhibit, one riverman claims to have carved over 1,000 decoys, another about 5,000. Also on-site are recreated turn-of-the-century storefronts, including a general store, millinery shop, law office, and old country kitchen.

Thousand Islands Arts Center

The **Thousand Islands Arts Center** (314 John St., 315/686-4123, www.tiartscenter.org, Mon.-Fri. 9am-5pm, Sat. 10am-4pm) began its life as the Handweaving Museum, but its name, mission, collection, and schedule of events and workshops expanded in 2009 to reflect a more diverse range of arts. Handwoven

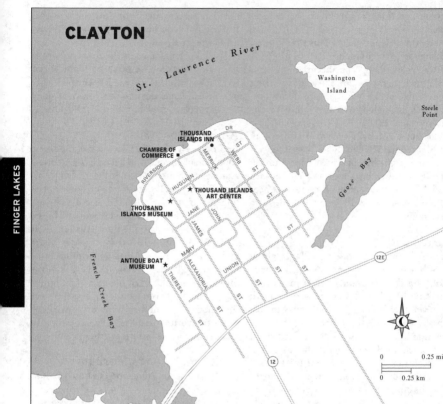

American textiles are still a specialty here, but photographs and other arts are exhibited and taught here as well.

Events

One of the region's most popular events, sponsored by the Antique Boat Museum, is the resplendent **Antique Boat Show and Auction** (315/686-3771), held every August for nearly 50 years. The **Decoy and Wildlife Art Show** (315/686-3771), attracting over 200 exhibitors, is held in the Clayton Arena in mid-July.

Accommodations and Camping

The 1897 **☾ Thousand Islands Inn** (335 Riverside Dr., 315/686-3030, www.1000-islands.com/inn, $85-170) is the last of the great old hotels that once lined Clayton. Significantly smaller than it was in its heyday, it offers 13 modern guest rooms, some overlooking the river. The historic restaurant where Thousand Island dressing was invented is downstairs.

Campsites are available at 165-site **Cedar Point State Park** (36661 Cedar Point State Park Dr., 315/654-2522, reservations 800/456-2267, www.nysparks.com/parks/21) and at three island campgrounds accessible only by boat.

Vacationing onboard houseboats is a popular activity in the Thousand Islands, and numerous houseboat-rental companies once lined the New York side of the St. Lawrence. Today, visitors who want to rent a houseboat will have to cross to the Canadian side, as insurance costs have made houseboat rentals cost-prohibitive for U.S. companies. No boating experience is necessary to rent a houseboat, as instruction is provided. Reservations should be made well in advance.

Food

At **Thousands Islands Inn** (355 Riverside Dr., 315/686-3030, $22), you'll find a comfortable, old-fashioned restaurant serving everything from steak and fish to pasta. For sale are bottles of "Original Thousand Island Salad Dressing," created here in the early 1900s by Sophia LaLonde.

Koffee Kove (220 James St., 315/686-2472, daily 6am-8pm) is known for its chili and homemade breads.

The chef-owned **Clipper Inn** (126 State St., 315/686-3842, www.clipperinn.com, Wed.-Sun. 5pm-close, $22) is a local favorite, serving lots of seafood in an upscale yet casual setting.

ALEXANDRIA BAY

About 10 miles northeast of Clayton is Alexandria Bay, a busy tourist village where you'll find all sorts of 1950s-era attractions, including miniature golf courses, junior speedways, kitschy souvenir shops, and mom-and-pop motels.

But for all its summertime hustle and bustle, Alexandria Bay has a permanent population of just 1,116 and a laid-back, down-home charm. The village centers around its waterfront, where a few narrow streets are crowded with tiny shops and restaurants. Teenagers strut their stuff in front of an amusement arcade, while twentysomethings exchange glances outside a boisterous bar.

Alexandria Bay was a popular tourist resort and steamboat stop throughout the late 1800s and early 1900s. Millionaires built second homes on the islands across from the village, while hotels went up along the shore.

Today, Alexandria Bay is the main port for touring the Thousand Islands. Excursion boats dock at weathered piers at both ends of the village. For more information on the area, stop into the **Alexandria Bay Chamber of Commerce** (7 Market St., 315/482-9531, www.visitalexbay.org, daily 9am-5pm, with extended hours in July-Aug.).

Boldt Castle

Looming over Heart Island, across from Alexandria Bay, is a 127-room replica of a Rhineland castle. **Boldt Castle** (Heart Island, 315/482-2501, www.boldtcastle.com, hours vary seasonally, adults $11, children 6-12 $7, plus the cost of the boat ride over) was built by George Boldt, who came to the United States from Prussia in the 1860s. The son of poor parents, Boldt had tremendous industry and skill, and eventually became the most successful hotel magnate in the country. Both the Waldorf Astoria in New York City and the Bellevue Stratford in Philadelphia were his.

Boldt was deeply in love with his wife, Louise, and built the castle around the turn of the 20th century as a symbol of his love for her. The castle was to be their summer home, and he employed the finest craftspeople, instructing them to embellish the building with hearts wherever they could. Boldt even had the island reshaped into the form of a heart.

Then in 1904, when the castle was 80 percent complete, Louise passed away. Boldt sent a telegram to the construction crew to stop work immediately, and never set foot on the island again. The castle was abandoned and allowed to deteriorate.

Finally, in 1977, the Thousand Islands Bridge Authority bought Boldt Castle, partially rehabilitated it, and introduced it to the tourist trade. Today, hundreds of visitors traipse through it daily, but all the activity in the world can't erase the castle's haunted, wildly romantic feel. In the former ballroom, exhibits explain the castle's history.

A shuttle boat operates from the castle to the **Boldt Yacht House,** perched on a separate island nearby. Completed before Louise's death, the boathouse contains three original

FINGER LAKES

spit-and-polish boats and restored living quarters furnished with handsome antiques.

Excursion Boats

The only way to reach Boldt Island, as well as the other 1,800-plus islands in the St. Lawrence River, is by boat. Several boat companies offer tours, including **Uncle Sam's Boat Tours** (315/482-2611, www.usboattours.com), whose huge replica paddle boats dock at the eastern end of James Street. Uncle Sam's features an hourly **shuttle service** (adults $8, children 4-12 $4.50) to Boldt Castle that allows visitors to stay as long as they like, as well as various sightseeing and dining cruises.

Cornwall Brothers Store and Museum

Evidence of Alexandria Bay's early 20th-century heyday can be found at **Cornwall Brothers Store and Museum** (36 Market St., 315/482-4586, www.alexandriahistorical.com, May-Sept. days vary 9am-5pm). Originally owned by the town's founder, Azariah Walton, the building is now part museum, part recreated general store. Up front, choose from a nice selection of penny candy, vintage postcards, handicrafts, and books; in the back are historic photographs and artifacts.

Wellesley Island State Park

To reach Wellesley Island and **Wellesley Island State Park** (44927 Cross Island Rd., Fineview, 315/482-2722, www.nysparks.com/parks/52, $8 parking) you must travel over the **Thousand Islands International Bridge,** a slim suspension expanse that seems to lead straight up into the sky. Built in 1938, the bridge extends over five spans and stretches seven miles.

At the end of the first span lies the 2,636-acre state park, featuring hiking trails, swimming beaches, a campground, nine-hole golf course, playground, and great views of the river. Covering 600 acres of the park is the **Minna Anthony Common Nature Center** (44927 Cross Island Rd., 315/482-2479, daily 10am-4pm, extended hours in summer, free), which includes both a museum and a wildlife

sanctuary laced with trails. Live fish and reptiles, mounted birds, and an observation beehive are in the museum.

Thousand Island Park

South of the state park, at the very tip of Wellesley Island, lies **Thousand Island Park** (Wellesley Island, 315/482-2576, www.tiparkcorp.com), a quiet community filled with hundreds of wooden Victorian homes painted in luscious ice-cream pastels. Ornate carvings, shingled roofs, porches, turrets, and gables abound.

On the National Register of Historic Places, the park is largely privately owned but visitors are welcome. The community has its own movie theater, post office, library, and playground.

Accommodations and Camping

Campsites are available at the 73-site **Grass Point State Park** (42247 Grassy Point Rd., 315/686-4472, reservations 800/456-2267, www.nysparks.com/parks/139) and the 434-site **Wellesley Island State Park** (Wellesley Island, 315/482-2722, reservations 800/456-2267, www.nysparks.com/parks/52).

Capt. Thomson's (45 James St., 315/482-9961, www.captthomsons.com, $79-139) contains 68 standard rooms, some with balconies overlooking the river. **Hart House Inn Bed and Breakfast** (21979 Club Rd., 315/482-5683, www.harthouseinn.com, $95-325) served as the 1000 Island Golf Club and now offers peaceful guest rooms with fireplaces, whirlpools, and canopy beds, along with a hearty local breakfast.

◖ **Riveredge Resort** (17 Holland St., 315/482-9917, www.riveredge.com, $72-198) features views of the river and Boldt Castle. The hotel's rooms and suites are spacious and well-appointed; on-site are a health spa, indoor and outdoor pools, and a restaurant and lounge.

The sleek **Bonnie Castle** (31 Holland St., 315/482-4511, www.bonniecastle.com, $180-290 d) is the region's largest resort, equipped with 129 rooms and suites, a conference center, private beach, swimming pools, tennis courts, nightclub, miniature golf courses, and restaurants.

Food
Numerous casual restaurants can be found on James and Market Streets downtown. Among them is lively **Dockside Pub** (17 Market St., 315/482-9849), serving sandwiches, soups, and pizza in a setting near the water.

Hidden waterfront hot spot **Foxy's** (18187 Reed Point Rd., Fishers Landing, between Clayton and Alexandria Bay, 315/686-3781) is a small family-run eatery with great lobster bisque and an even better view of the sunset.

Historic **Admiral's Inn** (20 James St., 315/482-4469, $16) features a comfortable bar to one side, several cheery dining rooms to the other. Sandwiches and salads are offered at lunch, while dinner entrées include prime rib and fresh seafood.

The best restaurant in town is **Jacques Cartier Dining Room** (17 Holland St., 315/482-9917, www.riveredge.com, $32) in the Riveredge Resort. On the menu is creative American and French cuisine. The dining room offers fine views of Boldt Castle.

OGDENSBURG
The oldest settlement in northern New York, established in 1749, Ogdensburg is a busy port and industrial town at the juncture of the Oswegatchie and St. Lawrence Rivers. Downtown, **Greenbelt Riverfront Park** runs along the St. Lawrence, dotted with historical plaques that detail the War of 1812 Battle of Ogdensburg. A few blocks south of the park is the town's foremost visitor attraction: the Frederic Remington Art Museum.

Frederic Remington Art Museum
Artist Frederic Remington (1861-1909), best known for his paintings and bronzes of the American West, was born in the northernmost reaches of New York State. In his youth he made a total of 18 trips out West, collecting information and taking photographs that he would later use in his studio in New Rochelle,

NY, to create his masterpieces. Remington never lived in Ogdensburg, but was born and is buried in nearby Canton. His wife moved to Ogdensburg after his death.

Housed in an imposing 1810 mansion, **Frederic Remington Art Museum** (303 Washington St., 315/393-2425, www.fredericremington.org, May 15-Oct. 15 Mon.-Sat. 10am-5pm and Sun. 1pm-5pm, Oct. 16-May 14 Wed.-Sat. 11am-5pm and Sun. 1pm-5pm, adults $9, students and seniors $8, children under 15 $2-7) contains the largest single Remington collection in the United States. On display are scores of oil paintings, watercolors, drawings, illustrations, and bronzes, including many small and relatively unknown gems. One room is filled with watercolors depicting the Adirondacks, another with a reproduction of Remington's studio. The most valuable Remingtons are kept in a locked gallery that is only open during guided tours, scheduled regularly throughout the day.

CANTON
About 20 miles east of Ogdensburg lies Canton, artist Frederic Remington's birthplace. Settled by Vermonters in the early 1800s, Canton today is a busy small town (pop. 6,669), best known as the home of St. Lawrence University.

TAUNY Center and North Country Folkstore
It's worth a detour to Canton to visit **TAUNY Center and North Country Folkstore** (53 Main St., 315/386-4289, www.tauny.org, Tues.-Fri. 10am-5pm, Sat. 10am-4pm, donation), a unique arts gallery and gift shop located in a historic downtown building. North Country Folkstore offers buyable art made through traditional practices in the region. TAUNY (Traditional Arts in Upstate New York) Center exhibits detail specific elements of local life, and a portrait gallery of North Country Heritage Award winners rounds out the facility, which also offers hands-on demonstrations and lectures by skilled artisans. Exhibits in the past have highlighted such subjects as St. Lawrence River fishing arts,

THERE ARE A THOUSAND STORIES IN THE THOUSAND ISLANDS

The 1,864 islands of the Thousand Islands laze in the deep blue St. Lawrence River like a "drunken doodle made by an addled cartographer," as one observer once said. Each and every one tells a story.

- The largest of the islands is **Wolfe Island.** The smallest is Tom Thumb. The only artificial island, **Longue Vue Island,** was formed by filling in the area between two shoals. As the story goes, Longue Vue was created by a doting husband who wanted to build a summer home for his wife. When he couldn't find a single island that suited her, he had one built, and then added a luxurious mansion atop it. His wife then ran off with another man.

- Devil's Oven on **Devil's Island** was the 1838 refuge of Canadian patriot Bill Johnston. After an aborted attempt to wrest Canada from the British Empire, Johnston hid out in the cave for nearly a year before surrendering to the authorities. He was later pardoned and appointed a lighthouse keeper.

- The **Price is Right Island** was given away in 1964 by Bill Cullen on *The Price is Right* TV game show. **Deer Island** is owned by the Skull and Bones Society of Yale University.

Abbie Hoffman lived incognito–under the name Barry Freed–on **Wellesley Island** after jumping bail on cocaine charges in 1974.

- **Florence Island,** Arthur Godfrey's isle, was given to him as a gift by the Thousand Islands Bridge Authority in return for free advertising. Godfrey sang the song "Florence on the St. Lawrence."

- **Grindstone Island** was the site of the last existing one-room schoolhouse in New York State, in use until 1989.

- **Ash Island** has its own private railroad line running from the boathouse to the main house on the cliff.

- George Pullman of Pullman Car fame once owned **Pullman Island** and played frequent host to President Ulysses S. Grant.

- **Calumet Island** was once the property of Charles Emery, president of the American Tobacco Company.

- **Picton Island** was owned by M. Heineman, originator of Buster Brown Shoes.

- **Oppawaka Island** was owned by J.H. Heinz of Heinz 57 fame.

Mohawk tourist arts, quilts and quilting bees, and Old Order Amish crafts. Thoughtfully laid out displays offer plenty of background information and photographs.

The gallery is also a good place to find out about folk arts events. Storytelling still thrives in the North Country, and there are occasional traditional music concerts and dance fests in the area.

Silas Wright Museum

Run by the St. Lawrence County Historical Association, the columned Greek Revival **Silas Wright Museum** (3 E. Main St., 315/386-8133, Tues.-Thurs. and Sat. noon-4pm, Fri. noon-8pm, donations welcome) once belonged to U.S. senator and New York governor Silas

Wright. Regarded as an honest and intelligent man, Wright was so respected by his neighbors that he won his first election to the state senate in 1823 by 199 votes to one; legend has it that he himself cast the one dissenting vote. The first floor of the house has been restored to its 1830-50 period appearance, while upstairs are local history exhibits. St. Lawrence County is one of the largest and least populated counties east of the Mississippi.

MASSENA

The main reason to make a stop in the small industrial city of Massena is to get a good look at the giant **St. Lawrence Seaway,** which connects the Atlantic Ocean with the Great Lakes. A joint project of the United States and

Canada, the Seaway can accommodate ships up to 730 feet long and 76 feet wide. The public works project was formally dedicated on June 26, 1959 by Queen Elizabeth II and President Eisenhower.

Dwight D. Eisenhower Lock

Atop the long, spare **Dwight D. Eisenhower Lock** (Barnhart Island Rd., off Rte. 37, 315/764-3200) is a viewing deck from which you can watch ships being raised or lowered 42 feet as they pass through the Seaway. The process takes about 10 minutes and displaces 22 million gallons of water. Ships pass through regularly, except in the winter when the St. Lawrence freezes over, but the viewing deck is only open June-September. Below the lock, a small **interpretive center** (315/769-2049, June-Sept. daily 9am-9pm) offers exhibits and a short film.

Robert Moses State Park and Campground

Adjoining the Power Project, **Robert Moses State Park** (19 Robinson Bay Rd., 315/769-8663, camping reservations 800/456-2267, www.nysparks.com/parks/51) is spread across the mainland and Barnhart Island. It is accessible through a tunnel beneath Eisenhower Lock and includes a swimming beach, bathhouse, boat rentals, picnic tables, playground, and great views of the river. The park also offers a 212-site campground.

AKWESASNE

At the confluence of the St. Regis and St. Lawrence Rivers lies the St. Regis Indian Reservation, or Akwesasne (the name means

"Where the Ruffed Grouse Drums"). Gas stations selling tax-free gasoline, and mock tepees selling souvenirs line the roadsides. Signs along Route 37 include: This Is Indian Land; Private Property; No FBI, IRS, or Other Agencies.

Akwesasne is home to about 12,000 residents. The reservation straddles the St. Lawrence Seaway and the United States/Canadian border, and includes several islands.

In Hogansburg, about 10 miles east of Massena, is the large and well laid out **Akwesasne Museum** (321 Rte. 37, 518/358-2240 or 518/358-2461, www.akwesasneculturalcenter.org, hours vary seasonally, adults $2, children 5-16 $1), housed in a big brown building that's also home to the Akwesasne Cultural Center and Library. The museum covers an entire floor and contains an outstanding collection of medicine masks, wampum belts, lacrosse sticks, carved cradle boards, water drums, Bibles written in the Mohawk language, beadwork, quillwork, modern artwork, historical photographs, and basketry.

Especially striking are the photography and basket exhibits. The photographs date back to the 1920s and depict a prosperous, pre-Depression Mohawk community bustling with shiny cars, sturdy baby prams, women in white dresses, and men in hats. The basket exhibit contains everything from a wedding basket, which looks just like a cake, to a thimble basket.

East of the museum is **Akwesasne Mohawk Casino** (873 Rte. 37, 877/99-CASINO, www.mohawkcasino.com, daily 24 hours). Opened in spring 1999, the casino offers blackjack, craps, and roulette tables, and hundreds of video lottery terminals.

Information and Services

The **Finger Lakes Tourism Alliance** (309 Lake St., Penn Yan, 315/536-7488, www.fingerlakes. org) is a good central information source for the entire region.

Contact **Finger Lakes Wine Country**

Tourism Marketing Association (1 W. Market St., Corning, 607/936-0706, www.fingerlakeswinecountry.com) for information about grape-growing regions around Keuka, Seneca, and Cayuga Lakes. Each of the lakes also has

FINGER LAKES

a "wine trail" website: www.keukawinetrail.com, www.senecalakewine.com, and www.cayugawinetrail.com.

Contact **The Landmark Society of Western New York** (585/546-7029, www.landmarksociety.org) for walking tours in Rochester. For self-guided tours, download maps on their website.

Several B&B registries operate in the Finger Lakes. Among them are **Finger Lakes B&B Association** (www.flbba.org), **B&B Association of Greater Ithaca** (800/806-4406, www.bbithaca.com), and B&B's of Skaneateles (www.bbskaneateles.com).

Many counties, cities, and towns have their own visitor information centers. Most are open Monday-Friday 9am-5pm.

- **Greater Syracuse Convention and Visitors Bureau** (572 S. Salina St., Syracuse, 315/470-1910, www.visitsyracuse.org)

- **Skaneateles Area Chamber of Commerce** (22 Jordan St., Skaneateles, 315/685-0552, www.skaneateles.com)

- **Cayuga County Office of Tourism** (131 Genesee St., Auburn, 800/499-9615, www.tourcayuga.com)

- **Seneca County Chamber of Commerce** (2020 Rtes. 5 and 20 W., Seneca Falls, 800/732-1848, www.fingerlakescentral.com)

- **Ithaca/Tompkins County Convention and Visitors Bureau** (904 E. Shore Dr., Ithaca, 607/272-1313, www.visitithaca.com)

- **Geneva Area Chamber of Commerce** (1 Franklin Sq., Geneva, 315/789-1776, www.genevany.com)

- **Finger Lakes Visitors Connection** (25 Gorham St., Canandaigua, 877/386-4669, www.visitfingerlakes.com)

- **Clifton Springs Chamber of Commerce** (2 E. Main St., Clifton Springs, 315/462-8200, www.cliftonspringschamber.com)

- **Victor Chamber of Commerce** (37 E. Main St., Victor, 585/742-1476, www.victorchamber.com)

- **Phelps Chamber of Commerce** (116 Main St., Phelps, 315/548-5481, www.phelpsny.com)

- **Steuben County Conference & Visitors Bureau** (1 W. Market St., Ste. 201, Corning, 607/936-6544, www.corningfingerlakes.com)

- **Corning Area Chamber of Commerce** (1 W. Market St., Corning, 607/936-4686, www.corningny.com)

- **Canandaigua Chamber of Commerce** (113 S. Main St., Canandaigua, 585/394-4400, www.canandaiguachamber.com)

- **Cortland County Convention and Visitors' Bureau** (37 Church St., Cortland, 607/753-8463, www.experiencecortland.com)

- **Wayne County Tourism** (9 Pearl St., Lyons, 800/527-6510, www.waynecountytourism.com)

- **Watkins Glen Area Chamber of Commerce** (214 N. Franklin St., Watkins Glen, 607/535-4300, www.watkinsglenchamber.com)

- **VisitRochester** (45 East Ave., Ste. 400, 585/279-8300, www.visitrochester.com)

- **Thousand Islands Regional Tourism Development Corporation** (Box 709 Wellesley Island, 315/482-2520, www.visit1000islands.com)

Getting There and Around

Syracuse Hancock International Airport (www.syrairport.org) is serviced by **AirCanada** (888/247-2262), **Allegiant** (702/505-8888), **American Airlines** (800/433-7300), **Delta** (800/221-1212), **JetBlue** (800/538-2583), **United** (800/241-6522), and **USAirways** (800/428-4322). Delta, United, and USAirways also service **Ithaca Tompkins Regional Airport** (www.flyithaca.com). Allegiant, Delta, and USAirways fly into and out of **Elmira-Corning Regional Airport** (www.ecairport.com). AirCanada, American Airlines, Delta, JetBlue, **Southwest** (800/435-9792), United, and USAirways service **Greater Rochester International Airport** (www2.monroecounty.gov/airport-index.php).

A taxi ride from any of these airports to their respective downtowns costs $20-30.

Amtrak (800/872-7245, www.amtrak.com) travels to Syracuse and Rochester. **Greyhound** (800/231-2222, www.greyhound.com) and **New York State Trailways** (800/295-5555 or 800/776-7548) provide bus service throughout the region.

By far the best way to explore the Finger Lakes and Thousand Islands is by car.

FINGER LAKES

BUFFALO AND THE NIAGARA REGION

Western New York looks and feels different from the rest of the state, shaped not only by distinct geographical features (proximity to two of the Great Lakes) and geological forces (glacial activity), but also by different historical influences and developments.

The region was first inhabited by Seneca Indians, who called the region the "Western Door." European settlers eventually made their way here, taking advantage of the boomtown opportunities that followed the Erie Canal's completion, as well as ample parcels of land that were—and remain—perfect for farming.

Western New York's two primary destinations are Buffalo and Niagara Falls, situated about 20 miles apart along the Niagara River, across from Canada. At Buffalo's southwestern edge lies Lake Erie, while Lake Ontario presides north of Niagara Falls; both attract serious anglers keen to fish the Great Lakes.

Buffalo is the area's population center and New York's second largest city. Seriously depressed following the decline of its steel industry in the 1970s, it still faces economic challenges, but it is in the midst of a surprising rejuvenation, with renovated waterfront and theater districts. To the north, south, and east of Buffalo extends especially fertile farm country, supporting Concord grapes, apples, and a variety of produce. The Erie Canal snakes through this land, passing a number of towns still rich with history.

Niagara Falls has long been regarded as one of the world's great natural wonders. As far back as 1678, missionary Father Louis Hennepin wrote, "Betwixt the Lake Ontario

HIGHLIGHTS

◖ Canalside District: Buffalo's revitalized waterfront buzzes with festivals, live music concerts, recreation options, and a naval and military park (page 421).

◖ Niagara Falls State Park: The famed waterfalls spanning the U.S.-Canada border are among the most visited attraction in New York for a reason: Their magnitude and intensity incite wonder. Amp up the excitement by sailing into the mist on a boat tour (page 433).

◖ Erie Canal Cruise: Rent a canal boat or let someone take the helm and explore historic towns along the canal. Landlubbers can take advantage of the nearly 400-mile-long multiuse Erie Canalway Trail (page 443).

◖ Ellicottville: The "Aspen of the East" is a compact community with lots of year-round recreational opportunities, including skiing, snowboarding, mountain biking, golfing, climbing, zip-line, and adventure obstacle courses (page 446).

◖ Amish Trail: Get a glimpse of the way of life in Old Order Amish communities. Along the way, you can purchase handmade toys, furniture, and other traditional goods made of wood, metal, and even alpaca wool (page 447).

LOOK FOR ◖ TO FIND RECOMMENDED SIGHTS, ACTIVITIES, DINING, AND LODGING.

and Erie, there is a vast and prodigious Cadence of Water.... The Universe does not afford its Parallel." Standing before Niagara Falls, you'll probably agree with Father Hennepin: The spectacular natural wonder really has no equal. The thundering sound of a massive volume of water cascading over three distinct falls—American, Bridal Veil, and Horseshoe Falls—will leave a lasting impression whether you choose to experience them from an observation deck, from an excursion boat, or via guided walking tour.

Most visitors to western New York include only these two destinations on their itineraries, but the region's people and attractions beg for more attention. The Amish Trail makes a

relatively closed culture accessible to visitors. Historic lighthouses and hotels punctuate the Erie shoreline. Ski resorts and year-round outdoor recreation are the draws in places like Findley Lake and Ellicottville. And in a seemingly endless number of charming small towns, both transplants and families who have lived here for generations are coaxing Main Streets back to life.

PLANNING YOUR TIME

Visitors can make an easy one-week loop through this region. Spend a full day or two in Buffalo before heading north to Niagara Falls, where you'll want to budget another day to see the Falls and the park and center for which it

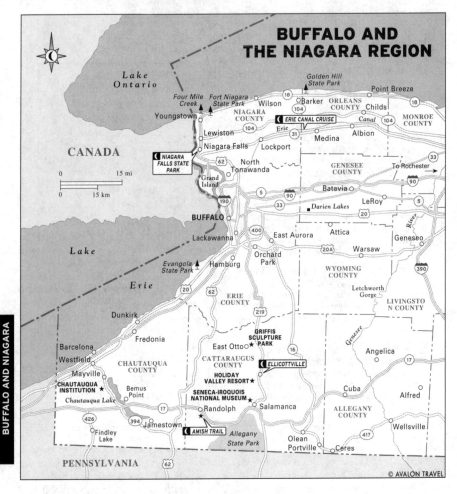

BUFFALO AND THE NIAGARA REGION

is named. Continuing north along Route 18, you'll drive through a series of small towns and attractions that sit along Niagara River, including Lewiston, Youngstown, Fort Niagara State Park, Wilson, and Barker, all of which can be visited in a day. Lewiston makes a good home base; its Barton Hill Hotel and Spa sits right above the Niagara River.

After visiting these small towns, head south on Route 219, taking one or two days to explore the Amish Trail and nearby attractions, including the Sky High Climbing Forest and

Aerial Adventure Park at Holiday Valley in Ellicottville. Holiday Valley has a variety of comfortable accommodations and on-site restaurants.

From there, head west on I-86 toward Jamestown, birthplace of beloved comedian Lucille Ball and home to a museum established in her honor. Continue on to Bemus Point and Chautauqua; followed by Findley Lake, known for its skiing and outdoor recreation; and Barcelona and Dunkirk, both with historic lighthouses. These towns are all clustered along Routes 430 and 394, two roads that form a ring around Chautauqua Lake and make for a pleasant drive. All of these towns along the lake can be visited in one or two days, depending on how much time you want to spend at the famed Chautauqua Institution or at picturesque Bemus Point. Rambling Hotel Lenhart in Bemus Point is a lovely place to stay, and that town also has several excellent restaurants. When you're ready to head back to Buffalo, continue north on I-90 from Dunkirk.

Buffalo

Visiting Buffalo is like visiting an overgrown small town. People talk to strangers here and point to recent civic improvements with enormous, and quite justified, pride. After several decades of economic decline, Buffalo's comeback is palpable, and it's attracting artists, do-it-yourselfers, and entrepreneurs who have defected from more expensive parts of the state to establish themselves here, where starting up is easier and the sense of community is often stronger.

Once the domain of the Iroquois, the Buffalo area was visited sporadically by French explorers in the 18th century. The origins of its name are disputed, but by 1832, Buffalo was incorporated as a city. The city's position between the Great Lakes and the canal made it thrive as a watery crossroads for commerce. Shortly after its incorporation, warehouses sprang up along the waterfront and thousands of immigrants, most from Ireland and Germany, arrived, helping fill the demand for laborers. By 1845, the city also boasted a stove factory, nail factory, cabinet factory, bell foundry, and numerous other plants producing such products as mirrors, picture frames, and bathtubs. One of the railways, completed in 1873, connected Buffalo with the anthracite coal fields of Pennsylvania. That coal, together with Lake Superior iron ore and the newly developed Bessemer process, allowed for large-scale production of steel. More immigrants, this time from Poland and Italy, poured in; the newly rich built lavish mansions along Delaware Avenue.

By 1900, Buffalo was ready to show off its wealth and sophistication to the world. What better way to do so than to host the 1901 Pan-American Exposition? The expo covered 350 acres, attracted eight million visitors, and featured everything from columned temples to the latest scientific inventions. The glamorous event was tragically marred, however, by the assassination of President William McKinley, who was shot at the expo on September 6, 1901 by anarchist Leon Czolgosz. Following McKinley's death, Theodore Roosevelt was sworn into office as president in Buffalo. Today, you can visit the house where his swearing in occurred.

Buffalo reached its industrial zenith shortly after World War II. Relative prosperity continued, however, until the early 1970s, when newer, more efficient steel plants abroad caused a major shakedown of the steel industry. Buffalo's steel plants closed, the region's economy declined, and its population ebbed. During the 1980s, smaller manufacturing, finance, and advanced technology companies opened and flourished. In 1989, the U.S.-Canada Free Trade Agreement was signed and Buffalo became a center for American companies looking to expand into Canada. Today, Buffalo owes much of its economic base to that agreement.

Currently, revitalization is being driven by the arts, as new cultural organizations and institutions plant roots here. Visitors will find plenty to see and do, from open-air bus tours of the city's diverse and iconic architecture to unique, under-the-radar museums and attractions.

Orientation

Buffalo is a large city, and each of its

© AVALON TRAVEL

neighborhoods has something distinct—whether in vibe or attractions (or both)—to recommend it.

The **Canalside District,** as its name suggests, sits along Buffalo's portion of the Erie Canal, and is a waterfront neighborhood that has only recently been revitalized. Here, you'll find attractions where you can learn more about Buffalo's marine and industrial history, and if you're keen to experience the water yourself, you can kayak or take a boat ride. Canalside is also home to Buffalo's pro hockey team, the Sabres, who play at First Niagara Center, a sports complex ringed by a growing number of hotels and restaurants.

Downtown is home to some of Buffalo's loveliest buildings, many of which are significant to American architectural history. Downtown makes an excellent home base for visitors, with plenty of hotels and restaurants; in good weather, this neighborhood is easy to navigate on foot.

Buffalo's **Theater District** has a number of venues where live performances of all types—from American favorites to Irish classics—are staged. Many of these theaters are found on Main Street.

The neighborhoods of **Allentown** and **Elmwood Village** are hot spots for independent businesses, including boutiques, bookstores, and cafés and restaurants. You can also find fantastic art galleries and live music venues in these two neighborhoods.

Buffalo's **Museum District** is a leafy, peaceful neighborhood with large, inviting museums housing world-class collections. Two standouts are Albright-Knox and Burchfield-Penney.

Named for the Frederick Law Olmsted-designed Delaware Park, **Parkside** is the neighborhood where you'll find two top attractions: Buffalo's zoo and Frank Lloyd Wright's Darwin D. Martin House Complex. The neighborhood is best explored by car, with exception of the park, which calls for on-foot exploration.

Once the ethnic enclave of Polish and German immigrants, **The East Side** is particularly notable for a number of large, beautiful churches.

South Buffalo is home to several pretty outdoor spaces, including Cazenovia Park and Tifft Nature Preserve.

SIGHTS
◖ Canalside District

One of Buffalo's most ambitious civic projects in recent years is the $295 million **Canalside District** (www.canalsidebuffalo.com). The former western terminus of the Erie Canal, largely abandoned for years, has been spruced up considerably, turning a disused section of the city into a multiuse recreational area where more than 800 free events are held every year. In summer months, the area is buzzing with live music concerts, outdoor yoga classes, and kayak launches. A hockey complex and hotels round out the offerings.

Also part of this neighborhood is **Erie Basin Marina,** where hundreds of pleasure boats dock. One side of the marina features a pleasant park; on the other side, several restaurants overlook Lake Erie. At the end of the dock is an **observation tower** (716/842 4141, May-Oct. daily 8am-10pm).

Buffalo and Erie County Naval and Military Park (1 Naval Park Cove, foot of Pearl and Main Sts., 716/847-1773, www.buffalonavalpark.org, Apr.-Oct. daily 10am-5pm, Nov. Sat.-Sun. 10am-4pm, adults $10, seniors and children 6-16 $6) is also part of the Canalside neighborhood. The six-acre maritime park is dedicated to all branches of the armed forces.

Most of the exhibits, however, have to do with the U.S. Navy; three decommissioned ships are berthed here. Largest among them is the USS *Little Rock,* a 610-foot-long guided missile cruiser outfitted much the way it was in the 1960s when 1,400 men lived onboard. Next door slumbers USS *Croaker,* a compact submarine that sank 11 Japanese vessels during World War II. Also seeing action in World War II was USS *The Sullivans,* a destroyer named after five brothers from Waterloo, Iowa, who died in 1942 when a Japanese torpedo sank their ship. Shamrocks on the destroyer's smokestacks pay tribute to the brothers' Irish heritage.

BUFFALO AND NIAGARA

Downtown

NIAGARA SQUARE

Niagara Square centers around **McKinley Monument,** designed by architects Carrere and Hastings. The monument honors President William McKinley, who was assassinated in Buffalo while attending the 1901 Pan-American Exposition. Another significant structure on Niagara Square is the monumental Art Deco **Buffalo City Hall** (65 Niagara Square, 716/851-4200), erected in 1929. The hall's front entrance is lined with eight Corinthian columns three stories high; inside are vast, vaulted ceilings covered with sculpted figures and paintings depicting local history. An **observation deck** (716/851-4200, Mon.-Fri. 9am-4pm, free) on the 28th floor provides great views.

Old County Hall (92 Franklin St., 716/852-2356, Mon.-Fri. 9am-5pm) is where President Grover Cleveland got his start, first as a lawyer and then as mayor of Buffalo. Designed in the high Victorian Romanesque style, the 1870s building has a lavish lobby done up in marble and bronze.

Another block south, at the corner of Franklin and Church Streets, stands **Guaranty Building** (28 Church St., 716/848-1335, tours available by appointment), also known as the Prudential Building. Designed by Louis H. Sullivan in 1894, the 12-story terra-cotta-clad skyscraper is covered with elaborate ornamentation repeated on the elevators and mosaic ceilings indoors.

One block east, at the corner of Church and Pearl Streets, is **St. Paul's Episcopal Cathedral** (128 Pearl St., 716/855-0900, open to the public daily 9am-5pm). Designed by Richard Upjohn in the 1880s, the brown sandstone church features a front central tower topped with a tall, delicate spire.

Straddling both Downtown and the Theater District are Main Street and Buffalo Place. In the late 1970s, downtown Main Street—semi-abandoned for years thanks to urban flight—was transformed into a pedestrian thoroughfare named Buffalo Place. A sleek, above-ground section of the Metro Rail was built through its center, and business began returning downtown. Today, the pedestrian thoroughfare is being reverted to accommodate car traffic, but downtown is thriving.

Entering Buffalo Place from Church Street, you'll spot **Ellicott Square Building** (295 Main St.) on the southeast corner. When completed in 1896, this block-wide edifice was the world's largest commercial office building.

Two long blocks north, at Huron Street, is **M&T Bank Gold Dome Building** (Main St. at North Division, 716/852-2356), whose rotunda features some of the finest murals in Buffalo. On the north side is a scene depicting the city's harbor in the 1940s; the east side shows the Seneca, headed by Red Jacket.

Theater District

The restored Theater District is a 20-block area extending west as far as Delaware Avenue and north to Tupper Street. At least a half-dozen theaters and cabarets operate here, along with restaurants, galleries, and shops. Along Chippewa Street is **Chippewa District,** known for nightclubs.

Buffalo has an impressive theater history, which began in the mid-1800s, thanks to traffic along the Erie Canal. Dozens of theaters catering to travelers sprang up almost overnight; by the turn of the 20th century, Buffalo was one of the country's foremost drama centers. Actress Katherine Cornell, songwriter Harold Arlen, and choreographer Michael Bennett are among the many stars whose careers were launched in Buffalo.

The centerpiece of the district is **Shea's Performing Arts Center** (646 Main St., 716/847-1410, tours 716/829-1166, www.sheas. org), an opulent 1926 movie palace filled with marble and gilt. Saved at the last moment from the wrecking ball in 1975, Shea's is nearly fully restored and tours are given of the space.

To find out more about what's happening in the city arts-wise, pick up a copy of *ArtVoice* (www.artvoice.com), a free weekly publication.

Allentown

Allentown, the nation's second-largest historic

district, is just northwest of the Theater District. Streets here are lined with one Victorian structure after another, with all styles represented. Many of the homes have been converted into restaurants, art galleries, boutiques, and antique shops.

Allentown is roughly bounded by Main Street to the east, Edward Street to the south, North Street to the north, and Cottage and Pennsylvania Streets to the west. Allen Street and Virginia Street run through its center.

Among the district's foremost architectural treasures are the typically middle-class **Tifft Houses** (Allen St. between Park and Irving Pl.); the extravagant **Williams-Butler Mansion** (672 Delaware Ave.), now housing the Jacobs Executive Development Center; and **Wilcox Mansion** (now the Theodore Roosevelt Inaugural Site, 641 Delaware Ave.). Samuel Clemens, a.k.a. Mark Twain, once lived at 472 Delaware Avenue, and F. Scott Fitzgerald spent part of his childhood at 29 Irving Place.

THEODORE ROOSEVELT INAUGURAL NATIONAL HISTORIC SITE

Theodore Roosevelt was formally inaugurated in the stately Wilcox Mansion, now the **Theodore Roosevelt Inaugural National Historic Site** (641 Delaware Ave., 716/884-0095, www.trsite.org, tours hourly Mon.-Fri. 9:30am-3:30pm, Sat.-Sun. 12:30pm-3:30pm, adults $10, seniors and students $7, children 6-18 $5), in 1901 after the assassination of President McKinley. "It is a dreadful thing to come into the Presidency this way," wrote the pragmatic Roosevelt shortly after the event, "but it would be far worse to be morbid about it. Here is the task, and I have got to do it to the best of my ability; and that is all there is about it."

Once owned by prominent lawyer Ansley Wilcox, the 1838 house is now run by the National Park Service. The library where Roosevelt was sworn in has been fully restored.

Take a tour of the Theodore Roosevelt Inaugural National Historic Site.

BUFFALO'S PRESERVATION MOVEMENT

Twenty years ago–or even a decade ago–people betting on a bright future for Buffalo comprised a minority. Buffalo, New York State's second most populous city, was once the state's titan of industry and manufacturing. But the cumulative effects of the decline of canal and rail transport and the trend of moving American jobs offshore contributed to a sharp decline in Buffalo's fortune and a period of ambiguity about its future.

The mass exodus of traditional manufacturing businesses in the latter part of the 20th century left Buffalo with one of the highest vacant property rates in the country, and as businesses disappeared, so did jobs. Many of the newly unemployed left Buffalo, compounding the problems of abandoned property.

That would be a problem for any city–unoccupied buildings attract vandals and other social ills–but for Buffalo, it almost constituted a tragedy. The city is an architecture-lover's trove; the 20th century's most illustrious architects all designed buildings for Buffalo and more than 80 of the city's buildings are listed on the National Register of Historic Places. Many also have National Historic Landmark status. What makes the collection particularly interesting is that the structures represent a vast range of styles, from Art Deco to Victorian, and take an equally vast number of forms, from family homes to mental hospitals to skyscrapers. Losing any of the city's iconic buildings would be a loss not just for Buffalo, but for architectural history. As *New York Times* architecture critic Nicolai Ouroussoff wrote in 2008, "Buffalo is home to some of the greatest American architecture of the late 19th and early 20th centuries...[having] shaped one of the grandest early visions of the democratic American city." The city, he wrote, "was founded on a rich tradition of architectural experimentation...among the first to break with European traditions.... "

Fortunately, a passionate group of preservationists, some with unlikely backgrounds, stepped up to save Buffalo's landmarks, fighting everywhere from newspaper columns to courts in an effort to preserve iconic buildings. Today, Buffalo is one of the country's most exciting–if not *the* most exciting–city to learn about historic preservation and enjoy American architecture's diversity. Here are some particularly interesting preservation projects, and a couple ways to see preservation in action:

· **Babeville** (341 Delaware Ave., 716/852-3835, www.babevillebuffalo.com): Babeville, the nerve center for Buffalo native and

Museum District

Many of Buffalo's museums are clustered about four or five miles north of downtown, near Delaware Park. To get here, take Delaware Avenue, a wide thoroughfare lined with mansions, most once owned by wealthy families and now home to law firms and the like.

ALBRIGHT-KNOX ART GALLERY

The centerpiece of Buffalo's art scene, the airy, low-slung **Albright-Knox Art Gallery** (1285 Elmwood Ave., 716/882-8700, www.albright-knox.org, Tues.-Sun. 10am-5pm, adults $12, seniors and students 13-18 $8, children 6-12 $5, children under 5 free) is known around the world for its superb collection of contemporary art. Albright-Knox was the first museum in the United States to purchase works by Picasso and Matisse, and the first anywhere to present a major exhibition of photography, in 1910.

All major American and European artists of the past 50 years are well represented, including van Gogh, Gauguin, Pollock, Miró, and Mondrian. The museum also presents 10 first-rate temporary exhibits each year and houses a solid general collection that spans the history of art. The Gallery Shop includes an extensive selection of art books.

THE BUFFALO HISTORY MUSEUM

The Buffalo History Museum (1 Museum Ct., 716/873-9644, Tues. and Thurs.-Sat. 10am-5pm, Wed. 10am-8pm, Sun. noon-5pm, adults $7, seniors and students $5, children 7-12

folk rocker Ani DiFranco's music empire, is located in what was once Asbury United Methodist Church, built in 1876. Her offices are on an upper floor of the church, which she bought in 1999. A gorgeous event space (available to rent) occupies the former nave, and HallWalls, a contemporary art gallery, shares the same floor. The church basement has been converted into 9th Ward, an intimate live music venue.

· **Buffalo State Hospital** (400 Forest Ave.): This Revivalist Romanesque building was the only hospital designed by 19th-century architect H. H. Richardson; it is also notable because its grounds were designed by foremost landscape architect Frederick Law Olmsted. The impressive, imposing building, which wouldn't look out of place in a Gothic film, served as Buffalo's psychiatric center until the 1970s and was used for administration purposes until the mid-1990s. One of the most impressive fights for preservation was waged over this large property, which is currently being renovated. When completed, the former mental hospital will be a hotel and event center.

· **Frank Lloyd Wright's Martin House Complex** (125 Jewett Parkway, 716/856-3858, www.darwinmartinhouse.org): Martin House is one of several structures in Buffalo designed by Frank Lloyd Wright; scholars consider this residence one of Wright's finest works. It has been undergoing an extensive restoration since 1996, but remains open to the public for tours year-round.

· **OpenAir Buffalo** (716/854-3749, www. openairbuffalo.org): Buffalo preservationist Tim Tielman leads a variety of preservation-focused tours on his OpenAir Buffalo bus. His first-hand experience saving some of the city's most important buildings makes for a lively, informative tour.

· **Silo City Rocks** (105 Childs St., 716/228-9153, www.silocityrocks.com): While all of Buffalo's waterfront redevelopment is impressive, having transformed a veritable wasteland into attractive and usable recreational space for locals and visitors, Silo City Rocks is the city's most ambitious indie waterfront renovation project to date. A trio of young entrepreneurs has repurposed Buffalo's grain elevators into a multiuse recreation center that boasts the tallest artificially constructed climbing wall in the country.

Tours of the city's extraordinary architecture are offered by **Preservation Buffalo Niagara** (716/884-3138, www.cfb.bfn.org).

$2.50) is located within the only remaining permanent building from the 1901 Pan-American Exposition. Inspired by the Parthenon, the lovely structure once housed the New York State pavilion. In addition to temporary exhibits, the museum features two unusual permanent exhibits: Bflo. Made! showcases virtually every product ever produced in the Buffalo region, from Pierce-Arrow cars and General Mills cereal to pacemakers and kazoos; Neighbors: The People of Erie County focuses on the area's vibrant ethnic history, from the Poles of the east side to the Irish of south Buffalo.

BURCHFIELD-PENNEY ART CENTER
Also near the Albright-Knox is **Burchfield-Penney Art Center** (1300 Elmwood Ave., 716/878-6011, www.burchfieldpenney.org, Tues.-Wed. and Fri.-Sat. 10am-5pm, Thurs. 10am-9pm, Sun. 1pm-5pm, adults $10, seniors $8, children $5). Spread out over a few galleries, the center is a low-key affair dedicated primarily to Charles E. Burchfield, one of the 20th century's finest watercolorists. Originally from Iowa, Burchfield spent most of his life living and teaching in Buffalo. He was fascinated by Buffalo's streets and by patterns of fire and sound, which he depicted in a mystical, expressionist style.

The center owns the world's largest collection of Burchfield works, exhibited on a rotating basis. Works by other contemporary Western New York artists are also exhibited.

Art lovers might also be interested in

visiting the **Charles E. Burchfield Nature & Art Center** (2201 Union Rd., 716/677-4843, www.burchfieldnac.org, Mon.-Fri. 10am-4pm, Sun. 1pm-4pm, free) in nearby West Seneca, where Burchfield once lived. The center offers an exhibition area, nature trails, a meditation garden, and sculpture garden.

Parkside

Buffalo State College, the Albright-Knox, and The Buffalo History Museum all sit on the western edge of **Delaware Park**, a glorious, 350-acre expanse of green designed and laid out by Frederick Law Olmsted in the 1870s. Olmsted, who also designed Central Park in New York City, created an extensive park system throughout Buffalo that includes Front, Martin Luther King, Jr., Cazenovia, and South Parks.

In the heart of the park, **Buffalo Zoo** (300 Parkside Ave., 716/837-3900, www.buffalozoo.org, Sept.-June daily 10am-4pm, July 1-Aug. 31 daily 10am-5pm, adults $10.50, seniors and students $8.50, children 2-14 $7.50, parking $4) is one of the oldest zoos in the country, founded around the turn of the 20th century.

The Parkside neighborhood also includes Hertel Avenue, a vibrant shopping district for antiques, home decor, and clothing, and Buffalo's Little Italy, as well as Frank Lloyd Wright's Martin House Complex.

FRANK LLOYD WRIGHT'S MARTIN HOUSE COMPLEX

To the east of Delaware Park stands **Martin House Complex** (175 Jewett Pkwy., 716/856-3858, www.darwinmartinhouse.org, tours available). Dating to 1904, it's one of Frank Lloyd Wright's most important works. The long, horizontal building with its wide porches and few enclosed spaces is characteristic of the architect's early Prairie style. The pergola, carriage house, and conservatory have been brought back to life due to an inspirational restoration, much of it completed through the help of volunteers with a love of the master architect's work.

The **Eleanor and Wilson Greatbatch Pavilion,** designed by architect Toshiko Mori, functions as the welcome center and starting point for all tours of the Martin House. Check out the special tour packages, such as a combo tour of the multiple Wright structures in Buffalo.

BUFFALO MUSEUM OF SCIENCE

The four-story **Buffalo Museum of Science** (1020 Humboldt Pkwy., 716/896-5200, www.sciencebuff.org, Sun.-Wed. 9am-5pm, Thurs.-Sat. 9am-9pm, adults $9, seniors $8, students and children 2-17 $7) is kid-friendly, with lots of interactive exhibits about the natural world. Three permanent exhibits provide information and insight into the ecology, geology, and archaeology of Western New York.

BROADWAY MARKET

Though no longer the dynamic marketplace it once was, this Old World landmark, **Broadway Market** (999 Broadway, 716/893-0705, www.broadwaymarket.org, Mon.-Sat. 8am-5pm), founded in 1888 in the heart of Buffalo's Polish neighborhood, still sells fresh ethnic foods. Over 40 vendors hawk everything from homemade soups and potato dumplings to chickens' and pigs' heads.

South Buffalo

BUFFALO AND ERIE COUNTY BOTANICAL GARDENS

A pristine white conservatory, **Buffalo and Erie County Botanical Gardens** (2655 South Park Ave., 716/827-1584, www.buffalogardens.com, daily 10am-5pm, adults $7, seniors and students $6, children 3-12 $4, under 3 free) sits in Frederick Law Olmsted's South Park, all domes, semicircular windows, and sheets of glass. Designed by famed greenhouse architectural firm of Lord and Burnham in the 1890s, the conservatory is actually 12 small connected greenhouses. Each specializes in a different plant variety—bromeliads, orchids, cacti, fruit trees—with a pale-green glass dome crowded with palms dominating the center.

Buffalo offers many examples of fine architecture.

TIFFT NATURE PRESERVE

The 264-acre **Tifft Nature Preserve** (1200 Fuhrmann Blvd., 716/825-6397, daily dawn-dusk, free), administered by the Buffalo Museum of Science, is a peaceful area containing a 75-acre cattail marsh, a lake, several ponds, and five miles of easy hiking trails.

ENTERTAINMENT
Performing Arts

Renowned **Buffalo Philharmonic Orchestra** (716/885-5000, www.bpo.org) performs in **Kleinhans Music Hall** (3 Symphony Circle, 716/883-3560). The hall, designed by Eliel and Eero Saarinen, is one of the nation's best for acoustics.

Shea's Performing Arts Center (646 Main St., 716/847-1410, www.sheas.org) is a historic 1926 theater resembling a European opera house. Shows range from Broadway productions to opera and dance.

Theater District venues include 100-seat **Alleyway Theatre** (1 Curtain Up Alley, 716/852-2600, www.alleyway.com), **The Irish Classical Theatre Company** (625 Main St., 716/853-1380, www.irishclassical.com), **710 Main Theatre** (710 Main St., 716/847-0850, www.sheas.org), and **Towne Ballroom** (681 Main St., 716/852-3900, www.townballroom.com).

Just west of the Theater District is **Ujima Theatre Company** (545 Elmwood Ave., 716/883-0380, www.ujimatheatre.org), dedicated to works of African Americans and Third World artists. The nonprofit **African American Cultural Center** (350 Masten Ave., 716/884-2013, www.africancultural.org) presents drama and other events in its Paul Robeson Theatre.

On D'Youville Square, northwest of downtown, is **Kavinoky Theatre** (320 Porter Ave., 716/829-7668, www.kavinokytheatre.com), a beautifully restored 250-seat Victorian theater.

Nightlife

The best sources for information about Buffalo's music and nightlife are the Thursday edition of the **Buffalo News** (www.buffalonews.com) and **ArtVoice** (www.artvoice.com), a free weekly arts publication. An ever-shifting array of nightclubs operate in the **Chippewa District,** along Chippewa Street downtown. Lively, upscale bars can be found on **Elmwood Avenue** near Buffalo State College.

A must stop for jazz lovers is **Colored Musicians Club** (145 Broadway, 716/855-9383, www.coloredmusiciansclub.org, hours vary seasonally), a laid-back joint that was once the local union for black musicians. Take a look at the excellent museum on the ground floor. The **Anchor Bar** (1047 Main St., 716/883-1134, www.anchorbar.com, Mon.-Thurs. 11am-10pm, Fri. 11am-midnight, Sat. noon-midnight, Sun. noon-10pm) in Allentown also presents jazz on a regular basis.

One of the oldest and best-known clubs in the city is laid-back **Nietzsche's** (248 Allen St., 716/886-8539,www.nietzsches.com, daily noon-4am), offering rock, country, reggae, blues, and folk. Live music is on the calendar every night.

EVENTS

Buffalo loves festivals. Favorites include **Allentown Art Festival** (716/881-4269, www.allentownartfestival.com) in early June, showcasing work by over 400 artists and artisans. In mid-June the **Juneteenth Festival** (716/891-8801, www.juneteenthofbuffalo.com) takes place in Martin Luther King, Jr. Park.

A newer addition to Buffalo's festival roster is **Garden Walk Buffalo** (www.gardenwalkbuffalo.com), America's largest free garden walk, featuring about 400 private gardens open to view over the last weekend in July. Started as a neighborhood beautification project, the idea evolved and spread to the entire city; visitors can take organized garden walks, visit private homes' "open gardens," and take gardening workshops.

One of the nation's largest outdoor food fests is **Taste of Buffalo** (www.tasteofbuffalo.com), held in mid-July. Another food-focused festival is the **National Buffalo Wing Festival** (www.buffalowing.com), which celebrates Buffalo's contribution to pop food culture. Typically, it's held at the end of August.

For more information on these and other festivals, contact **Visit Buffalo Niagara** (716/852-2356, www.visitbuffaloniagara.com).

SPORTS AND RECREATION
Spectator Sports
The **Buffalo Bisons** (1 James D. Griffin Plaza, 716/846-2000, www.milb.com, Apr.-Sept.), a AAA team for the Toronto Blue Jays, play downtown at Coca-Cola Field. Tickets are generally available.

The National Football League **Buffalo Bills** (1 Bills Dr., Orchard Park, 716/648-1800, www.buffalobills.com, Sept.-Jan.) play at Ralph Wilson Stadium. Tickets are available for most games, especially if you order a few weeks in advance.

The National Hockey League **Buffalo Sabres** (foot of Main St., 716/855-4100, www.sabres.com, Sept.-Apr.) play at First Niagara Center in Canalside. Tickets are generally available.

Boating
Buffalo Harbor Cruises (Erie Basin Marina, 716/856-6696, www.buffaloharborcruises.com, adults $16, children $11) offer sightseeing tours such as Historic Buffalo River; River, Lock, and Canal; and Buffalo Landmark Tours. Boats leave from Erie Basin Marina. Other cruise offerings include **Queen City Ferry** (www.queencityferry.com), **Spirit of Buffalo** (www.spiritofbuffalo.com), **Seven Seas Sailing** (www.sevenseassailing.com), and **Grand Lady Cruises** (www.grandlady.com).

BFLO Harbor Kayak (1 Naval Park Cove, 716/228-9153, www.bfloharborkayak.com) rents boats and offers lessons for novices and tours for paddlers with some experience. The outfitter also rents boards for stand-up paddleboarding.

ACCOMMODATIONS
To the east of downtown, in the suburb of Clarence (known for its many antiques stores) is acclaimed **Asa Ransom House** (10529 Main St., 716/759-2315, www.asaransom.com, $120-170, with breakfast). The 1853 inn features 10

spacious and lovely guest rooms and an excellent restaurant (Sun. and Tues.-Thurs. dinner, $18) serving American fare by reservation.

A team of butlers awaits at ◖ **The Mansion on Delaware Avenue** (414 Delaware Ave., 716/886-3300, www.mansionondelaware. com, $195-240) to offer complimentary touches like ushering you to your room after whipping up a welcome cocktail of your choice; shoeshine and pressing service; evening turndown service complete with home-made cookies; chauffeuring to and from local hot spots and eateries; or if the pull of the hotel makes a night in a temptation, they will arrange an order from any local restaurant, preparing a table either in your room or in the hotel's billiard room. European breakfast, a two-hour cocktail hour, whirlpool baths with multi-head showers, and spa amenities all add to the good value.

The **Hotel @ The Lafayette** (391 Washington St., 716/853-1505, www.thehotel-lafayette.com) is a centrally located downtown hotel, near many of the city's lovely, iconic skyscrapers. Though the lobby and hallways are dark, the hotel's large, comfortable rooms are filled with natural light. An upscale restaurant on-site gets rave reviews.

FOOD

Thanks to its diverse population, Buffalo has many inexpensive ethnic restaurants. The city is also the birthplace of two odd food specialties. One is Buffalo chicken wings: spicy wings served mild, medium, or hot, with celery sticks and blue cheese dressing, invented at Anchor Bar. The other Buffalo-unique nosh is the beef-on-'weck sandwich: thinly sliced roast beef piled high on fresh kimmelweck rolls sprinkled with pretzel salt and caraway seeds.

Downtown

In the Theater District, **Bijou Grille** (643 Main St., 716/847-1512, www.bijougrille.com, Mon. 11am-3pm, Tues.-Sun. 11am-11pm, $14), a California-style bistro, is a popular choice.

For fine French fare, try **Rue Franklin** (341 Franklin St., 716/852-4416,www.ruefranklin.

com, Tues.-Sat. 5:30pm-10pm, $22), Buffalo's oldest—and some say best—French restaurant, housed in an elegant brick townhouse.

Seafood has pride of place on the menu at **Mike A** (391 Washington St., 716/253-6453, www.mikealafayette.com, Mon.-Tues. 5pm-10pm, Wed.-Thurs. 11:30am-2:30pm and 5pm-10pm, Fri. 11:30am-2:30pm and 5pm-11pm, Sat. 5pm-11pm, $25) an upscale restaurant at Hotel @ The Lafayette.

Try Buffalo's famous beef-on-'weck sandwich, along with a beer flight, at **Pearl Street Grill and Brewery** (76 Pearl St., 716/856-2337, www.pearlstreetgrill.com, Mon.-Sat. 11am-close, Sun. noon-close, $16).

Other downtown options include sushi at **SeaBar** (475 Ellicott St., 716/332-2928, www.seabarsushi.com, Mon.-Thurs. 11:30am-2:30pm and 4:30pm-9:30pm, Fri. 11:30am-2:30pm and 4:30pm-10:30pm, Sat. 4:30pm-10:30pm, $16) and steak at **Buffalo Chophouse** (282 Franklin St., 716/842-6900, www.buffalochophouse.com, dinner, $44).

Allentown

Famed Buffalo institution the ◖ **Anchor Bar** (1047 Main St., 716/886-8920, Mon.-Thurs. 11am-10pm, Fri. 11am-midnight, Sat. noon-midnight, Sun. noon-10pm, $12) is the friendly Italian restaurant where Buffalo chicken wings were invented in 1964 by Teressa Bellissimo, mother of the late owner Dominic Bellissimo. Live jazz is often featured on weekends.

Famed locally for its chicken souvlaki, Greek-American **Towne Restaurant** (186 Allen St., 716/884-5128, www.thetowne.net, daily) has been open 23 hours a day (closed 6am-7am for cleaning) for the past 30-plus years.

Other Allentown picks are contemporary Italian spot **Tempo** (581 Delaware Ave., 716/885-1594, www.tempobuffalo.com, Mon.-Sat. 5pm-11pm, $16) and **Allen Street Hardware Café** (716/882-8843, www.allen-streethardware.com, daily 5pm-10pm, $12), which serves upscale comfort food.

Elmwood Village

Dozens of trendy eateries operate along

© FRANCISCO COLLAZO

Pearl Street Grill and Brewery

Elmwood Avenue north of downtown. Among them is **Toro** (492 Elmwood Ave., 716/886-9452, www.torotapasbar.com, Tues.-Sat. 5pm-11pm, Sun. 5pm-10pm, average tapa $12), the place to go for tasty tapas.

Frequent winner of the local People's Choice award is **Hutch's** (1375 Delaware Ave., 716/885-0074, www.hutchsrestaurant.com, Mon.-Thurs. 5pm-10pm, Fri.-Sat. 5pm-midnight, Sun. 4pm-9pm, $22), a casual, bustling southwestern/Cajun bistro serving everything from rib-eye steak rubbed with garlic to grilled tuna.

GETTING AROUND

Downtown Buffalo centers on Niagara Square and Buffalo Place. The **MetroRail** (716/855-7300, www.metro.nfta.com) runs along Main Street from the Buffalo River to the University at Buffalo South Campus. The system is above ground and free along Buffalo Place (Main St. south of Tupper St.); below ground, the fare starts at $2, is zoned, and can be complicated, but the $5 unlimited day pass is a good option. Tickets may be purchased from vending machines at all stations. Most downtown sites are within walking distance of each other. The downtown area has many parking lots. Elsewhere, street parking is usually available.

Vicinity of Buffalo

EAST AURORA

Along Route 20A southeast of Buffalo is East Aurora, an idyllic village surrounded by hilly dairy country. East Aurora was once home to President Millard Fillmore, and to Elbert Hubbard, a former soap salesman turned charismatic leader of the Arts and Crafts movement. "Conformists die, but heretics live forever," Hubbard was fond of saying. "Weep not peeling other people's onions."

Hubbard was the founder of an idealistic crafts community, the Roycrofters, whose **Roycroft Campus** (31 S. Grove St., 716/655-0261, www.roycroftcampuscorporation.com) still stands at the corner of Main and Grove Streets. Now a National Historic Landmark District, the 14-building complex still houses a number of artisans' workshops, along with gift shops, offices, a small museum, and Roycroft Inn.

At the heart of the campus, **Roycroft Shops** (31 S. Grove St., 716/655-0571) sells arts and crafts of Roycroft design. Out back is **Roycroft Potters** (37 S. Grove St., 716/652-7422). Down the street is the **Elbert Hubbard-Roycroft Museum** (363 Oakwood Ave., 716/652-4735, June-Oct. Wed. and Sat.-Sun. 1pm-4pm), which documents the community's history. Nearby is **Roycroft Inn** (40 S. Grove St., 716/652-5552, www.roycroftinn.com).

Another must-stop is **Vidler's 5 & 10** (676-694 Main St., 716/652-0481, www.vidlers5and10.com, Mon.-Thurs. 9am-6pm., Fri. 9am-9pm, Sat. 9am-6pm, Sun. 11am-5pm). A spiffy red-and-white awning flaps out front; inside are creaky wooden floors and display cases from the 1920s selling old-fashioned *stuff*, including penny candy, wooden animals, marbles, magic cards, Buster Brown socks, mousetraps, lace, and ribbon. Almost everything costs under $1.

Just off Main Street is the 1826 **Millard and Abigail Fillmore House** (24 Shearer Ave., 716/652-4735, June-Oct. Wed. and Sat.-Sun. 1pm-4pm, adults $10, children 13-18 $5, children under 13 free), built by the future U.S. president with his own hands in 1826. Fillmore was then a young lawyer fresh off the farm.

Accommodations and Food

The handsome 1905 **◖ Roycroft Inn** (40 S. Grove St., East Aurora, 716/652-5552, www.roycroftinn.com, $195-350 d) is a one-of-a-kind place, filled with all original or reproduction Roycroft furnishings—mostly heavy, beautifully designed pieces in oak. All 28 suites have at least one sleeping area, a sitting area, and a whirlpool tub, while the common rooms feature fireplaces, rich wood paneling, and Roycraft lamps. The inn's **restaurant** (average entrée $26) serves innovative American cuisine with a continental touch.

Just outside East Aurora sprawls **Old Orchard** (2095 Blakely Corners Rd., 716/652-4664, www.tyromanello.com, hours vary seasonally, $20), a historic farmhouse and former hunting lodge dating back to 1901, with large stone fireplaces. The menu features American/continental fare.

To the southwest of East Aurora is **Colden Lakes** (9504 Heath Rd., Colden, 716/941-5530, www.coldenlakes.com), offering 140 campsites and some cabins. To the southeast is **Sleepy Hollow Lake** (13800 Siehl Rd., Akron, 585/542-4336, www.sleepyhollowlakeresort.com, $28), offering 200 campsites.

Locals love **Rick's on Main** (687 Main St., 716/652-1253, www.rickonmain.com, Mon.-Sat. lunch and dinner), which has plenty of surf and turf options. A favorite menu item is the restaurant's soup sampler, which includes small cups of three of its signature soups.

EDEN

As the self-proclaimed "Garden Spot of New York State," Eden, just about 30 miles south of Buffalo on Route 62, is a pristine small town surrounded by farm country. The main attraction here is the **Original American Kazoo Company: Museum, Gift Shop, Factory** (8703 S. Main St., 716/992-3960, www.edenkazoo.com, Tues.-Thurs. 10am-5pm, Fri. 10am-7pm, Sat. 10am-5pm). Established in 1916, the Original is now the only metal kazoo factory in the world. The company paid $5,000 for its first kazoo patent and still manufactures kazoos the way it always has, using die presses and sheet metal. On display is a wooden kazoo, similar to its African prototype, and liquor-bottle-shaped kazoos made to celebrate the end of Prohibition. The record for the most kazoos ever played at one time was set in Rochester on January 2, 1986, when 54,500 kazoo-ists performed.

Another attraction worth visiting in Eden is **The Asa Warren House** (2795 E. Church St., 716/992-3954), a house built in 1815 that served as a station on the Underground Railroad. Today, the house is a museum and tours are available by appointment.

GRAND ISLAND

Just north of Buffalo is Grand Island, the country's largest freshwater island. About five square miles larger than Manhattan, Grand Island was once intended to be a refuge for persecuted Jews and was also considered as a possible site for the United Nations; both plans were eventually discarded. Today, the island serves an entirely different purpose. Primarily a suburban community, Grand Island is also home to **Martin's Fantasy Island** (2400 Grand Island Blvd., 716/773-7591, www.martinsfantasyisland.com, hours vary seasonally, adults $25.95, seniors $17.95, children under 48 inches tall $20.95), an 80-acre theme park with thrill rides, live entertainment, and a petting zoo.

NORTH TONAWANDA

In the sprawling industrial city of North Tonawanda, directly across the river from Grand Island, is the old **Herschell Carrousel Factory** (180 Thompson St., 716/693-1885, www.carrouselmuseum.org, hours vary seasonally, adults $6, seniors $5, children 2-16 $3). In its heyday in the 1920s and '30s, the plant produced over 50 carousels a year. Until 1928, all featured animals were carved entirely of wood; after 1928, the magical creatures were half-wood and half-aluminum.

Now both an informal museum and a workshop, the old factory contains a major exhibit on Allan Herschell, an expert woodcarver who was once the best-known carousel maker in the United States. Also on display are hand-carved animals dating back to the early 1900s and new carved animals in various states of completion. Adults as well as kids are invited to ride the working 1916 carousel that spins out back.

A landscaped Heritage Trail connects the museum with other locales of interest, such as the tiny **Railroad Museum** (111 Oliver St., North Tonawanda, 716/694-9588, adults $2, children under 12 free) and the performing arts center of **Riviera Theatre** (67 Webster St., North Tonawanda,716/692-2413, www.riviera-theatre.org) near Gateway City.

Whimsical restaurant **◖ Old Man River** (375 Niagara St., Tonawanda, 716/693-5558, www.oldmanriverwny.com, hours vary seasonally, $10) sports a whale on its roof and washing machine fountains. On the menu is everything from Sahlen's hot dogs, a Buffalo specialty, to sweet potato French fries. Almost as quirky, and serving a similar menu, is **Mississippi Mudds** (313 Niagara St., Tonawanda, 716/694-0787, www.mississippimuddswny.com, hours vary seasonally, $10).

STATE PARKS

Just north of Niagara Falls, following Route 18, you'll come across three state parks between the towns of Youngstown and Barker. **Four Mile Creek** (1055 Lake Rd., Youngstown, 716/745-3802), **Evangola** (10191 Old Lake Shore Rd., Irving, 716/549-1802) and **Golden Hill** (9691 Lower Lake Rd., Barker, 716/795-3885) offer a chance to mix a little nature into your road trip. Reserve pre-set **campsites** (www.contentment-canvascottages.com, $60 for one-tent sites, $90 for two-tent sites, weekly rates available) with all of the necessities for a comfortable night in the woods, along with additional non-essential gear from an à la carte menu.

Niagara Falls

The name Niagara Falls refers to both the famed waterfalls and the city where they are located. The city is nondescript, surrounded by industrial plants and humming electrical wires; the Robert Moses Niagara Power Plant provides electricity for much of the northeastern United States. But the falls...ah, well, the falls. Despite the tourists, hoopla, and clichés, the falls are a sight to be seen. Stand in front of that white wall of water and you'll catch your breath. Guaranteed.

The falls began forming about 12,000 years ago at the end of the Ice Age. As the last glaciers melted away, huge torrents of water channeled along what is now the Niagara River, tumbling over the Niagara Escarpment. The water began eating away at the escarpment and the falls slowly moved upstream. Today, the falls cascade seven miles from their original location through a canyon known as Niagara Gorge.

Located along Niagara River between the United States and Canada, Niagara Falls are actually three falls: American and Bridal Veil Falls on the New York side, and Horseshoe Falls on the Ontario side. The thundering water is on its way from four of the Great Lakes—Superior, Michigan, Huron, and Erie—to the fifth, Ontario.

Orientation

The city of Niagara Falls has a compact downtown, which, while less commercialized than the Canadian side of the falls, is not without its tourist traps, including Seneca Niagara Casino. If the flash and dazzle of casino lights make you dizzy, stop by **Niagara Tourism and Convention Corporation's Visitor Center** (10 Rainbow Blvd., 716/282-8992, www.niagara-usa.com, June 1-Sept.15 daily 9am-7pm, Sept. 16-May 31 daily 9am-5pm) to get oriented to the small city's other sites of interest. The staff can provide free maps and assist with booking tours.

◖ NIAGARA FALLS STATE PARK

The falls and their accompanying attractions, which include an interactive visitors' center and aquarium, are located on the western edge of the city in **Niagara Falls State Park** (off Robert Moses Pkwy., 716/278-1796, www.niagarafallsstatepark.com, parking $8-10)). Established in 1885, it is America's oldest state park. The falls, which had been "remote as the moon" for most of the 18th-century according to Canadian writer Pierre Berton, had by the turn of the century become a notorious tourist trap.

In the mid-1800s, the land surrounding Niagara Falls was privately owned and visitors who wanted to see the waterfalls had to pay clever entrepreneurs, like Augustus Porter, a fee to glimpse the mighty wonder. One traveler of the day griped, "I know of no place where one is so constantly pestered, where hackmen so incessantly worry you when you want to be at peace, where you are so dogged over every inch of ground you tread."

By the end of the 19th-century, Niagara Falls would become no less of a tourist attraction, but it *would* become more accessible and the area around it more groomed, thanks to artist Frederick Church, landscape architect Frederick Law Olmsted, and the "Free Niagara" movement, established around 1870. For 15 years, the movement's proponents lobbied heavily to establish a park at the falls. Political opposition was enormous, but in 1885, Governor David Hill finally signed an appropriations bill that marked the beginning not only of Niagara Park, but also of the entire New York State Park System.

Today, Niagara Falls State Park receives millions of visitors a year. People come from all over the world to stroll through the park, enjoy the gardens, and, of course, see the falls. Visitors can also board a trolley that makes stops at key sites throughout the park. Maid of the Mist and Cave of the Winds tours operate from the park; for visitors who don't want to get quite so close to the watery action, excellent views of the falls can be had from the park's observation deck.

There are two main entrances to the park. One is at Prospect Point, the other at Goat Island.

Prospect Point

Prospect Point is the best place to view the falls on the New York side. The point sits at the edge of the American Falls' 1,100-foot brink, where you can look straight down into the foamy, turbulent waters. Rainbows often form in the cataract's mist.

The **Visitor Center** (716/278-1796, daily 8am-6pm, with extended hours in summer, free) can also be accessed via Prospect Point; here, visitors can get information about the falls and the park's attractions.

Niagara Falls Scenic Trolleys (daily 9am-6pm, with extended hours in summer, adults $2, children 6-12 $1) depart from behind the Visitor Center and travel throughout the park, stopping at all points of interest. Riders can hop on and off at their leisure.

American Falls is one of the three waterfalls that comprise Niagara Falls.

Niagara Falls Observation Tower ($1 per person) is just beyond the Visitor Center; it features dramatic, panoramic views of all three waterfalls from an open-air platform that extends over Niagara Gorge.

The tower's elevators also travel down to the foot of the falls, where *Maid of the Mist* (716/284-8897, www.maidofthemist.com, May-Oct. daily 9am-6pm, adults $15.50, children 6-12 $9) boats dock. Visitors are given rain slickers before being herded onto sturdy wooden vessels, which head straight into the bases of the falls, passing almost close enough to touch. Spray stings, boats rock, and water thunders all around. A tourist attraction since 1846, *Maid of the Mist* is still the best way to experience the falls.

Goat Island

The other access point for Niagara Falls State Park is quieter Goat Island, a wooded flatland often overlooked by visitors. With Bridal Veil and American Falls on one side and Horseshoe Falls on the other, the island provides a very different view of the cataracts than Prospect Point. **Cave of the Winds tours** (716/278-1730, May-Oct. daily 9am-7pm, weather permitting, adults $11, children 6-12 $8) lead visitors along drenched wooden walkways to the base of Bridal Veil Falls. Thankfully, rain slickers are included in the ticket price.

Goat Island is flanked by several smaller islands, including **Three Sisters Islands,** surrounded on all sides by swift, white-capped waters. Step out onto these specks of land and you'll feel as if you're part of the river itself and about to be swept over the curved edge of the falls.

Niagara Gorge Discovery Center

Perched on the edge of Niagara Gorge, at the northern end of the park, **Niagara Gorge Discovery Center** (716/278-1070, guided walking tours 716/745-7848, daily 9am-5pm, with extended hours in summer, adults $3, children 6-12 $2) is dedicated to the geological history of the falls. Highlights include a

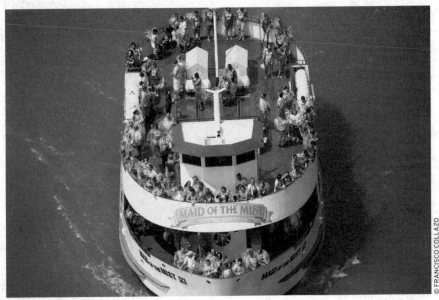

© FRANCISCO COLLAZO

Maid of the Mist **tour**

multimedia show on the gorge's formation and fossil and mineral exhibits. A footpath leads from the museum deep into the gorge; explore on your own or take a guided walking tour with a park naturalist. Hikes vary in length and difficulty.

Tours

Two of the most popular falls tours are offered by concessioners operating out of Niagara Falls State Park. *Maid of the Mist* (716/284-8897, www.maidofthemist.com, May-Oct. daily 9am-6pm, adults $15.50, children 6-12 $9) is a boat tour with close-up views of the falls; **Cave of the Winds** (716/278-1730, May-Oct. daily 9am-7pm, weather permitting, adults $11, children 6-12 $8) is a walking tour that takes visitors into the "stormy mist zone" behind Bridal Veil Falls. Visitors who purchase a "Discovery Pass" at **Niagara Tourism and Convention Corporation's Visitor Center** (10 Rainbow Blvd., 716/282-8992, www.niagara-usa.com, June 1-Sept.15 daily 9am-7pm, Sept. 16-May 31 daily 9am-5pm) or in the state park can take both tours at a discount.

Other tour options include **Gray Line of Niagara Falls** (716/285-2113, www.grayline-niagarafalls.com) and **Bedore Tours** (716/696-3200, www.bedoretours.com). For a different perspective on the falls, **Rainbow Air** (454 Main St., 716/284-2800, www.rainbowairinc.com) is available for helicopter tours.

THE CANADIAN SIDE: NIAGARA FALLS, ONTARIO

Niagara's most spectacular cataract is Horseshoe Falls, best viewed from **Queen Victoria Park** (905/356-2241) over the Canadian border in Ontario. Though slightly shorter than American Falls—176 feet as opposed to 184—Horseshoe Falls boasts a much wider brink (2,200 feet) and handles about 90 percent of the river's volume of flow.

Considerably more built up than the American side, the Canadian side is also both more stylish and more commercial. **Rainbow Bridge,** near Prospect Point, crosses over the

© FRANCISCO COLLAZO

the Canadian side of Niagara Falls

border into Queen Victoria Park. Proof of citizenship such as a driver's license or birth certificate is required to cross the border. Once on the other side, a People Mover bus operates between all points of interest.

A high point of a visit to the Canadian side is the **Journey Behind the Falls** (enter at Table Rock Welcome Centre, 6650 Niagara Pkwy., 905/354-1551, June-Sept. daily 9am-11pm, Oct.-May daily 9am-5pm, adults $10 plus tax Canadian, children 6-12 $6 plus tax Canadian). Out come the big yellow slickers again, followed by a walk *behind* Horseshoe Falls.

Along nearby Clinton Hill stands one kitsch museum after another: **Tussaud's Wax Works** (4983 Clifton Hill, 905/374-6601); **Ripley's Believe It or Not** (4960 Clifton Hill, 905/356-2238); and **Guinness Museum of World Records** (4943 Clifton Hill, 905/357-4330). A good restaurant offering buffet-style dining and superb views revolves atop the **Skylon Tower** (5200 Robinson Rd., 905/356-2651).

Those traveling with kids or fans of thrill rides might consider the **Great Wolf Lodge** (866/945-9653, www.greatwolf.com/niagara, $180-240), just over the border and minutes from the impressive Horseshoe Falls. The Lodge has good rooms and suites in a Northwood's theme, a full-service spa, two adults-only whirlpools (one, a year-round outdoor offering with indoor water entrance), wave pool, lazy river, and six giant grownup-sized tube or raft rides, including a water rollercoaster. For children, there is a nightly cookies and milk bedtime story told next to the animal-covered clock tower in the lobby.

For more information, contact the **Niagara Falls, Canada Visitors and Convention Bureau** (5433 Victoria Ave., 905/356-6061 or 800/563-2557, Mon.-Fri. 9am-5pm).

DOWNTOWN NIAGARA FALLS, NEW YORK
Seneca Niagara Casino
Seneca Niagara Casino & Hotel (310 4th St., 716/299-1100, www.senecaniagaracasino.com, 24 hours a day) looms large as downtown's

THE UNDERGROUND RAILROAD

From the early 1800s to the Civil War's end in 1865, the Buffalo-Niagara corridor, a collection of towns along the U.S.-Canada border, served as the last stop on the Underground Railroad for slaves traveling north toward freedom. Though few records were kept, it is estimated that as many as 30,000 people may have passed through the area on their way to Canada.

Today, there are several places where visitors can learn more about the region's role in the Underground Railroad:

- **Freedom Crossing at The Castellani Art Museum of Niagara University** (5795 Lewiston Rd., Lewiston): This permanent exhibit of slavery and abolition-era ephemera (including authentic shackles) is the contemporary art museum's only concession to history; it's also a concise introduction to the Buffalo-Niagara region's geographical and socio-political positions in the abolition movement.

- **Freedom Crossing Monument** (Lewiston Landing Park, Water St., Lewiston): This moving sculpture, crafted by local artist Susan Geissler, depicts a dramatic moment in the pursuit of freedom: Lewiston's Underground Railroad station master, Josiah Tryon, is handing a baby to its fugitive mother.

- **Michigan Street Baptist Church** (511 Michigan Ave., Buffalo): This small, modest church, built in 1845, hosted many of the abolition movement's luminaries, including Frederick Douglass, W.E.B. DuBois, and Booker T. Washington, and functioned as a station on the Underground Railroad. Though hours are irregular, visitors who happen to get lucky will be treated to a rich oral history narrated by clergy.

- **St. John's AME Church** (917 Garden Ave., Niagara Falls): St. John's was one of the first African American churches founded in Niagara County. Fugitive slaves could see the beckoning lights of Canada and freedom from the church's hillside location.

- **Thomas Root Home** (3106 Upper Mountain Rd., Pekin): Located midway between Niagara Falls and Lockport, the former Root home contains a trapdoor leading to a 5-by-10-foot cellar. Here "volumes bound in black," as the coded messages once read, spent the night before being driven to the border, hidden beneath piles of vegetables. The house is now privately owned, but the station is set amidst a small row of pine trees accessible to the public.

tallest building. Fresh from a $26 million renovation, the casino holds about 4,000 slot machines, plenty of games tables, and theater venues where pop stars and comedians perform. There are also a nightclub and several restaurants on site.

Niagara Falls Culinary Institute

Niagara Falls Culinary Institute (28 Old Falls St., 716/210-2525, www.nfculinary.org, hours vary seasonally) opened in the fall of 2012 in a former shopping mall. Students in Niagara Community College's culinary arts, hospitality, and restaurant management programs take classes and fulfill their internships in the center, which houses a bakery, deli, and fine dining restaurant, all open to the public. The Institute also operates a wine boutique specializing in New York State wines, and the country's only Barnes and Noble dedicated to food-themed titles.

Accommodations

Niagara Falls' most affordable accommodations are at **Hosteling International's Red Lounge Niagara** (723 3rd St., 716/286-0707, www.redloungeniagara.com, dorm beds $28/ night). Dorm rooms are equipped with six or eight beds. Laundry facilities are available and Wi-Fi is free.

B&B options in the area include **Hillcrest Inn** (1 Hillcrest St., 716/278-9676, www.hillcrestniagara.com, $119-165), which has four guest rooms. A full, hot breakfast, served on the sun porch overlooking the river or in the Asian-themed dining room, is included.

Hotel Giacomo (222 First St., 716/299-0200, www.thegiacomo.com, $120-249) is a 39-room luxury boutique hotel in a historic Art Deco high-rise. Breakfast and valet parking are included.

The Seneca Nation of Indians is one of six nations that comprise the Iroquois Confederacy, which supports its communities with a variety of cultural and economic efforts. One of these is **Seneca Niagara Casino & Hotel** (310 4th St., 716/299-1100, www.seneca-niagaracasino.com, $195-400). The property also offers a full service spa in a modern, showy 26-floor, 600+ room casino hotel, with all the benefits and drawbacks that might entail.

If you prefer roughing it, the Niagara region has several excellent campgrounds, including **Golden Hill State Park** (9691 Lower Loake Rd., Barker, 716/795-3885), on Lake Ontario's shore. The small campground has tent sites and trails for hiking and biking.

Food

The 2012 opening of **Niagara Falls Culinary Institute** (28 Old Falls St., 716/210-2525, www.nfculinary.org) was a boon for the downtown's struggling restaurant scene, where uninspired, mediocre menus were once the norm. Within the Institute's complex are café-bakery **La Patisserie** (716/210-2587, hours vary seasonally), **Old Falls Street Deli** (716/210-2525, hours vary seasonally), and the full-service, fine dining option, **Savor** (716/210-2580, hours vary seasonally). Savor has a large, open kitchen where staff, including supervised culinary students, can be seen preparing meals; an advance reservation for the restaurant's chef's table can be made for groups of six or more.

The spectacular view of Horseshoe Falls is the main reason to eat at casual **❨ Top of the Falls Restaurant** (Terrapin Point, Goat Island, 716/278-0340, hours vary seasonally, $17), which serves contemporary American cuisine, including lots of fish and pasta dishes, as well as salads, soups, and sandwiches. If you haven't yet tried the local specialty beef-on-'weck sandwich, you can do so here. For burgers, there's the requisite tourist joint, **Hard Rock Café** (333 Prospect Ave., 716/282-0007, daily 11am-midnight), where you can also pick up your "Hard Rock Cafe Niagara Falls" T-shirt.

North of Niagara Falls

WHIRLPOOL STATE PARK

Heading north of Niagara Falls on Robert Moses Parkway, you'll pass **Whirlpool State Park** (Robert Moses Pkwy., 716/284-4691, www.nysparks.com/parks/105, open year-round, free), offering great views of a giant, swirling whirlpool, and **Devil's Hole State Park** (Robert Moses Pkwy., 716/284-5778, www.nysparks.com/parks/42, open year-round), situated along the Niagara River's lower rapids. Both parks feature hiking trails.

NIAGARA POWER PROJECT'S POWER VISTA

North of the parks reigns the immense **Niagara Power Project** (5777 Lewiston Rd., 866/697-2386, www.nypa.gov/vc/niagara.htm, daily 9am-5pm, free), one of the largest hydro-electric plants in the world. During the tourist season, about half of Niagara River's water power (or 100,000 of 202,000 cubic feet) is diverted away from the falls for the production of electricity here and in Canada; at other times, that ratio rises to 75 percent.

The plant's visitors' center does an excellent job explaining the principles of hydro-electric power through hands-on exhibits and computer games. Also on-site are exhibits on Niagara Falls, past and present. Enjoy outstanding views of Niagara Gorge from the plant's observation deck.

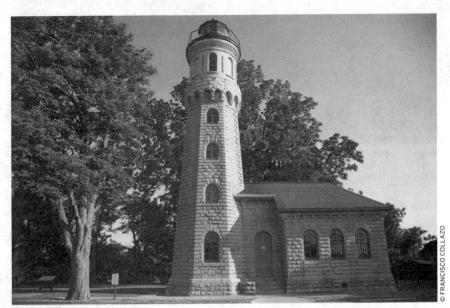

© FRANCISCO COLLAZO

Old Fort Niagara

CASTELLANI ART MUSEUM

Niagara University is home to **Castellani Art Museum** (5795 Lewiston Rd., 716/286-8200, www.castellaniartmuseum.org, Tues.-Sat. 11am-5pm, Sun. 1pm-5pm, free). Dedicated in 1990, the museum's roomy galleries house work by contemporary artists, including big names like David Hockney, Charles Burchfield, Alexander Calder, Willem de Kooning, Cindy Sherman, and Nam June Paik. The museum's strong Folk Arts Program sponsors temporary exhibits on such subjects as Polish-American Easter traditions, African American gospel traditions, and Halloween. Visitors can also learn about the region's role in the Underground Railroad through the permanent exhibit "Freedom Crossing," which features photos and artifacts from the abolition era.

LEWISTON AND VICINITY

Continue north of the power project about four miles to Lewiston. It's here where Niagara Falls originated thousands of years before glacial melt carved Niagara Gorge. It's here where the first significant battle of the War of 1812 was staged. And it's here where fleeing slaves made their final stop on the Underground Railroad before crossing the Niagara River and finding freedom in Canada. For more information on the history of the village, visit the **Historical Association of Lewiston** (469 Plain St., 716/754-4214, www.historiclewiston.org).

Freedom Crossing Monument

Local sculptor Susan Geissler created the **Freedom Crossing Monument** (Lewiston Landing Park, Water St.), drawing inspiration from real-life Underground Railroad station master Josiah Tryon, a Lewiston native, and from the children's book *Freedom Crossing*. The moving artwork shows Tryon handing a fugitive slave's child to its mother after Tryon ferried the freedom-seeking pair across Niagara River. Look carefully to find messages and clues engraved on the figures; these tell more of the Freedom Crossing story. You'll notice quotes, Bible passages, and other cryptic engravings on each figure. The numbers on

BUILDING THE ERIE CANAL

Flour merchant Jesse Hawley was one of the first New Yorkers to articulate a vision for what would become the Erie Canal. Hawley, who had gone broke spending money to transport his goods across the state, wrote 14 newspaper essays promoting a canal from his debtor's prison cell. When President Jefferson first heard of the plan, he said, "It is a splendid project and may be executed a century hence...but it is little short of madness to think of it at this day." Not every politician shared Jefferson's skepticism; when the essays came to the attention of DeWitt Clinton, he became an enthusiastic promoter of the canal and was swept into the New York governor's office in 1817 on a pro-canal platform.

Work on the canal began that very year. An engineering marvel of its day, the canal was built almost entirely by shovel and pick-ax, by men who had no engineering experience. Many of the canal builders were recent Irish immigrants earning 80 cents an hour. They started in Rome, where light soil ensured rapid progress. In 1819, the first 15-mile-long section of canal opened between Rome and Utica. Progress was slow, though; it would take another six years before the canal was completed, prompt-ing naysayers to dub the canal "Clinton's Ditch" and "Clinton's Folly."

Work was grueling and often dangerous. Close to 1,000 men died of malaria while running the canal through Montezuma Swamp. Others died while constructing locks through the Niagara Escarpment—a solid wall of rock rising 565 feet above sea level.

When the canal was finally finished in 1825, it was 363 miles long, 40 feet wide, and 4 feet deep. A towpath for mules and drivers who pulled the barges before the advent of steam power ran alongside the canal.

The astonishing success of the Erie Canal sparked a canal-building craze, and between 1823 and 1828, several important lateral canals opened, including the Champlain, Oswego, and Cayuga-Seneca. The canals were enlarged three times over the years to accommodate larger boats, but by the 1950s, New York's canal system was all but obsolete when enormous St. Lawrence Seaway was completed.

For more information on cruising or biking along the canal, contact **New York State Canal Corporation** (518/471-5016, www.canals.ny.gov).

Tryon, for instance, are the GPS coordinates of his gravesite.

Artpark

The only state park in the United States devoted to visual and performing arts, **Artpark** (450 S. 4th St., 716/754-4375, www.artpark.net, daily 8am-dusk, parking $5-10, events free-$7) occupies 150 acres on Lewiston's southern edge. All sorts of events are staged during summer, including concerts, storytelling, acrobatics, and theater and dance workshops. Other park features include hiking trails; the 2,400-seat **Mainstage Theater,** which hosts national acts; and a burial mound dating back over 2,000 years to a time when the area was inhabited by Hopewell Indians. Thirty feet long by 20 feet wide, the mound is listed on the National Register of Historic Places.

Accommodations and Food

Lewiston isn't large, so lodging and food options aren't abundant; however, its location between Buffalo and Niagara Falls and its small-town, non-touristy vibe make the village a nice spot to overnight when you're exploring the Buffalo-Niagara area.

Barton Hill Hotel and Spa (100 Center St., 716/754-9070, www.bartonhillhotel.com, $143-224) is a comfortable boutique hotel right near the waterfront, a three-minute walk to both Freedom Crossing Monument and adjacent restaurant and scoop shop, **The Silo** (115 N. Water St., 716/754-9680, www.lewistonsilo.com, May-Sept., hours vary seasonally, $10). At The Silo, humble fare like burgers, fish and chicken sandwiches, and fries is complemented by excellent, close-up views of Niagara River. Save room for ice cream, which is served from the window of the caboose parked permanently next to the silo.

OLD FORT NIAGARA

Even if you have no interest in military history, it's worth continuing a few miles north of Lewiston to Youngstown and **Old Fort Niagara** (off Robert Moses Pkwy., 716/745-7611, www. oldfortniagara.org, Sept.-June daily 9am-5pm, July-Aug. daily 9am-7pm, adults $12, seniors $11, children 6-12 $8). Strategically located at the mouth of the Niagara River, where it controlled access to the Great Lakes, the fort is a strikingly handsome place with commanding views of Lake Ontario.

Fort Niagara was established by the French in 1726 (though their first post founded here, Fort Conti, was established in 1679), taken over by the British in 1759, turned over to Americans by treaty in 1796, recaptured by the British in 1813, and finally returned to American control in 1815. After these wartime transfers of power, Fort Niagara served as a peace-time border post and remained occupied by the U.S. military until 1963. Its oldest standing structure is the 1726 French Castle, a rectangular stone edifice equipped with a bakery, guardhouse, living quarters, and chapel.

During summer, visitors can witness daily military musters and fife-and-drum drills. **Fort Niagara State Park** (716/745-7273, www. nysparks.com/parks/175, $8 vehicle entry fee), with easy hiking trails, playgrounds, and swimming pools, surrounds the fort.

WILSON AND BARKER

The towns of Wilson and Barker are a short drive east of Old Fort Niagara. Both are located on the shore of Lake Ontario in Niagara County. The towns are an ideal side jaunt for visitors interested in New York State's ever-growing craft beer and cider culture. Along the way, keep an eye open for some excellent examples of cobblestone houses, a unique form of architecture once popular in this part of the state. **Woodcock Brothers Brewery** (638 Lake St., Wilson, 716/333-4000, www. woodcockbrothersbrewery.com, Mon.-Thurs.

© AVALON TRAVEL

noon-10pm, Fri.-Sat. noon-11pm, Sun. noon-8pm) is the county's first brewery, housed in the old Wilson Cold Storage facility, where apples grown in the region were held before shipping. The cavernous interior of the on-site restaurant delights lovers of vintage design, as the owners preserved many original elements of the century-old building. Pizza from a wood-fired oven is the specialty here.

The first—and so far, only—hard cider producer in Niagara County is **BlackBird Cider Works** (8503 Lower Lake Rd., Barker, 716/795-3580, www.blackbirdciders.com, Fri. noon-6pm, Sat. 10am-6pm, Sun. noon-6pm), which has a small and inviting tasting room right on the edge of the cidery's orchard. On weekends, staff offers $3 and $5 tastings of ciders.

LOCKPORT

Just south of Wilson is the Erie Canal town of Lockport. Nearby, **Lockport Canal Museum** (80 Richmond Ave. at Locks 34 and 35, 716/434-3140, May-Oct. daily 9am-5pm) documents the area's canal history, with photos from 1812 to the present. Down the street, **Lockport Cave and Underground Boat Ride**

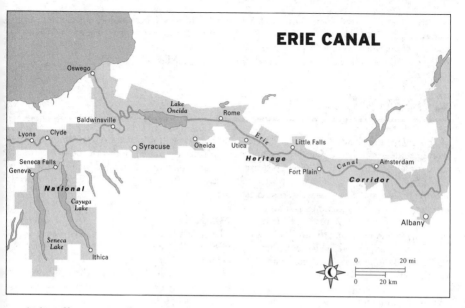

ERIE CANAL

Oswego
Lake Oneida
Rome
Baldwinsville
Lyons
Clyde
Syracuse
Oneida
Utica
Little Falls
Seneca Falls
Geneva
Erie
Heritage
Fort Plain
Amsterdam
Canal
Corridor
National
Cayuga Lake
Albany
Seneca Lake
Ithica

0   20 mi
0   20 km

(ticket office at 5 Gooding St., 716/438-0174, www.lockportcave.com, hours vary seasonally, adults $12, children $7) takes visitors through five flights of locks, industrial ruins, and a 2,430-foot-long tunnel blasted out of solid rock in the late 1850s.

Other area sites of interest include the art, education, and recreation facility, **Kenan Center** (433 Locust St., 716/433-2617, www.kenancenter.org, free); **Erie Canal Discovery Center** (24 Church St., 716/439-0431, www.niagarahistory.org/discovery-center, adults $6, children under 13 $4), which presents interactive exhibits highlighting the role Lockport played in opening the canal; and **Arrowhead Spring Vineyards** (4746 Town Line Rd., 716/434-8030, www.arrowheadspring.com), which has a tasting room with friendly, knowledgeable staff.

◖ Erie Canal Cruise

The construction of the Erie Canal catapulted New York into the industrial age; an explosion of trade between the East and Midwest occurred after its completion in 1825. Facilitating trade and transport, the canal's tolls had more than paid for the entire cost of its $7.7 million construction less than a decade after it opened. Pre-Erie Canal, New York City was the nation's fifth largest seaport, behind Boston, Baltimore, Philadelphia, and New Orleans. Fifteen years after the canal's opening, New York was America's busiest port, moving tonnages greater than those of Boston, Baltimore, and New Orleans combined.

With the exception of Binghamton and Elmira, every major city in New York falls along the trade route established by the Erie Canal. While currently less than 100 commercial barges ply the waters between Buffalo and Albany each year, approximately 75 percent of the state's population still lives along corridors created by the canals and the Hudson River.

Today, the New York State Canal System primarily serves as a low-key, relatively unknown tourist attraction for boaters, bikers, and daytrippers. Two-hour cruises of the canal, highlighted by a trip through Locks 34 and 35, are offered by **Lockport Locks & Erie Canal Cruises** (210 Market St., 716/433-6155, www.lockportlocks.com, May-Oct., adults $17.50, children 4-10 $9). Macedon's Mid-Lakes Erie

Macedon Landing is the home marina to **Mid-Lakes Navigation** (315/685-8500, www.mid-lakesnav.com), where you can learn to drive one of the gleaming wooden canal boats and relive a bit of history. These easy-to-pilot boats can be driven by anyone with a few lessons. Guided multi-day tours are also available for those leery of taking the helm.

Orleans County

If you enjoy rural landscapes, unique architecture, and occasional stops at farm stands, a drive through Orleans County, east of Niagara, might be a fine way to spend a day in western New York. It's one of the flattest and quietest areas in the state, and agriculture is the number one industry here; enormous fruit and vegetable farms spread out along the area's highways and byways. Route 104, which cuts through the center of the county, is peppered with pick-your-own farms.

Albion, the county capital, and Medina, the main commercial center, are small historic villages along the Erie Canal. To the north are Lake Ontario and Point Breeze, a harbor known for its world-class salmon fishing. Orleans County is also the best place in the state to learn about cobblestone architecture, a building style that is all but unique to New York.

MEDINA

The main attraction in Medina is its wide, old-fashioned Main Street, flanked by mid-19th-century buildings. Many were built of local red sandstone and still house thriving small businesses such as bakeries, variety stores, and clothing shops.

St. John's Episcopal Church (200 E. Center St., 585/798-3219) once listed in *Ripley's*

COBBLESTONE HOUSES

Handsome houses built of smooth rounded stones small enough to hold in one hand can be found across western New York. Of the approximately 1,200 cobblestone houses in North America, 800 are in New York State, with a good concentration along Route 104 (Ridge Rd.) in Orleans and Monroe Counties.

Cobblestone masonry is an ancient form of construction dating back to Roman times; it can be found in parts of England, Italy, and France. New York's tradition of cobblestone masonry began after the construction of the Erie Canal. Masons from Ireland and England who worked on the canal settled in the area, where they found abundant building material on hand.

There are two kinds of cobblestone houses: those made of rough ice-laid cobbles and those made of polished water-laid cobbles. The ice-laid variety can be found in glacially-formed "drumlin" areas between Rochester and Syracuse, while the water-laid variety—built of stones tumbled in Lake Ontario's waters—are found west of Rochester.

Many of New York's cobblestone houses were built between 1825 and 1860 in the Greek and Gothic Revival styles. Some featured meticulous patterns, such as herringbone or striped designs. By the late 1860s, cobblestone houses had become too expensive for the industrial age and the art died out.

Believe It or Not as "the church in the middle of the street," sits on East Center Street, just east of Main Street. At the north end of Main Street you'll find the Erie Canal and a boat basin in which canal boats once turned around. While driving through town, be sure to look up when on **Culvert Road,** where the road crosses *beneath* the canal.

The **Medina Railroad Museum** (530 West Ave., 585/798-6106, www.railroadmuseum. net, Tues.-Sun. 11am-5pm, adults $7, seniors $6, children 2-17 $4), a century-old New York Central freight depot, houses an interactive exhibit based on HO scale trains. Admission is included with any of the many themed railroad trips aboard a 1947 vintage Budd passenger coach. Fall foliage, winery excursions, and family-friendly Polar Express trips depart from the museum (fares vary by tour).

ALBION

Farther east along the Erie Canal lies quiet Albion, centered around a 34-building **Historic Courthouse District** (Rte. 98 off Rte. 31). The handsome 1858 **Orleans County Courthouse** (3 S. Main St., 585/589-4457), Greek Revival in style, sports a silver dome visible for miles around and an old-fashioned courtroom crowded with polished wooden pews.

Another interesting stop is the elongated 1904 **Pullman Memorial Universalist Church** (10 E. Park St. at Rte. 98, 585/589-7181). The old English Gothic edifice was built by the manufacturer of railroad sleeping cars, George M. Pullman, who grew up in Albion before moving to Chicago and becoming a millionaire.

One of the county's best restaurants is **Tillman's Village Inn** (14369 Ridge Rd., Albion, 585/589-9151, www.tillmansvillage-inn.com, daily lunch and dinner, $17). Built in 1824, this former stagecoach stop turned inn and restaurant serves sandwiches and salads for lunch, and meat and fish entrées for dinner.

CHILDS

If you were to speed through Childs, you likely wouldn't see anything worth stopping for. Slow down, though, and you might notice something that put Childs on the map: its cobblestone structures, whose unique architectural style also earned the town a listing on the National Register of Historic Places. The **Cobblestone Society Museum** (14393 Rte. 104, at Route 98, 585/589-9013, June-Sept. Tues.-Sat. 11am-5pm and Sun. 1pm-5pm, Sept.-Oct. Sun. 1pm-5pm, adults $8, seniors

BUFFALO AND NIAGARA

$6, children 5 and up $3) is housed in the basement of one of the oldest and best preserved of New York's 25 cobblestone churches, dating back to 1834. Simple exhibits explain the masonry's history and technique, while upstairs is an intimate sanctuary lined with wood. Next door stand two more cobblestone buildings—an 1849 schoolhouse and an 1840 house filled with Victorian-era furnishings. Also on-site are reconstructed blacksmith and print shops.

POINT BREEZE

Directly north of Childs on the shores of Lake Ontario is Point Breeze, centered around a busy marina. **County Marine Park** (Rte. 98 at Point Breeze Rd., Kent 585/682-3641, www.orleanscountytourism.com/recreation-leisure/ocmp, Apr. 15-Nov. 1 daily 7am-10pm) is a good spot to have a picnic. For easy hiking and biking, head a few miles west of Point Breeze to **Lakeside Beach State Park** (Rte. 18 Waterport, 585/682-4888, www.nysparks.com, daily 6am-11pm, $6 per vehicle).

South of Buffalo

The counties south of Buffalo—Cattaraugus, Allegany, and Chautauqua—are full of fascinating small towns that are overlooked by most travelers. While many of these towns and villages don't have headline attractions, they all have spots full of authentic local charm and residents who are thrilled to share their little piece of paradise with you. It's not uncommon, for instance, for someone to take a break from his or her work to show you a hidden historical treasure, to tell you a tale of the town's colorful characters, or to sit with you for a spell at his or her favorite watering hole.

The best way to experience these counties and their towns is by adding a few days to your road trip of the Buffalo-Niagara region. Well-maintained state roads cut through and across these three counties, offering lots of lovely vistas along the way.

CATTARAUGUS COUNTY

Cattaraugus County is also known as the "Enchanted Mountains" region. A road trip affirms the aptness of the moniker. Departing from Buffalo on Route 219 South, you'll enter Cattaraugus, and can take Route 242 to reach Ellicottville, one of western New York's principal ski destinations and a good place to eat and overnight. Along the way, there are plenty of other things to see and do.

Griffis Sculpture Park

Leave Buffalo on Route 219 South. Once you enter Cattaraugus County, you'll head west a few miles to the town of Otto, where **Griffis Sculpture Park** (6902 Mill Valley Rd., East Otto, 716/667-2808, www.griffispark.org, May-Oct. daily dawn-dusk, adults $5, seniors and students $3, children 12 and under free) awaits. The 400-acre spread is an outdoor home to more than 225 monumental works of art, ranging from the quirky 20-foot figures from Larry Griffis Jr., the park's founder, to works from regional and international artists and changing exhibits in a lovely natural setting.

C Ellicottville

From Otto, head back to Route 219 South and take that all the way to Ellicottville and its Holiday Valley Resort. Often called the Aspen of the East, this area is known for its winter sports, especially skiing.

The best place to base yourself in Ellicottville is **Holiday Valley** (6557 Holiday Valley Rd., 800/323-0020, www.holidayvalley.com), the region's premier ski and snowboard resort. It has 58 slopes and 13 lifts. During the rest of the year, people come to Holiday Valley for its **Sky High Climbing Forest and Aerial Adventure Park,** which features zip lines and obstacle courses ranging in difficulty. There's also an 18-hole golf course and 4 miles of on-resort mountain biking trails that connect to 35 miles of linked single track running through a state forest. Holiday Valley has a number of lodging options, from standard hotel rooms to three-bedroom condominiums, a spa and several indoor and outdoor pools, and an on-site restaurant, **John Harvard's Brew House,** which serves pastas and American comfort food. **Ellicottville Brewing Company** (28A Monroe St., 716/699-2537, www.ellicottville-brewing.com, daily 11:30am-2am, $16) is a pub located inside what was once a mill and carpentry shop on the town's main strip. Burgers, seafood, steaks, and, of course, beer, are on the menu here. During summer, the pub offers outdoor dining in its beer garden.

If you prefer staying in more intimate accommodations, a good option is **The Jefferson Inn** (3 Jefferson St., 716/699-5869, www.thejeffersoninn.com, $89-229), a Victorian bed-and-breakfast with four standard rooms and one suite. All have a private bath, free Wi-Fi, and access to the outdoor hot tub.

【 Amish Trail

From Ellicottville, it's just a short jaunt to the south on Route 242 to the town of Randolph, the heart of New York's Amish Trail.

Western New York's Amish population is an Old Order community, upholding traditional, conservative values and family-centered life where traditional gender roles prevail. The Old Order Amish live without electricity, phones, and cars, and make their living farming and making handicrafts, furniture, quilts, iron, leather, woodwork, and jams.

Cattaraugus County has worked closely with the Amish over the past decade to create an "Amish Trail," along which visitors can get a glimpse of Amish life and purchase handmade Amish goods. Stopping at a few spots on the trail makes for a good half-day tour as you make your way to Bemus Point in neighboring Chautauqua County. A map of the **Amish Trail** (800/331-0543, www.amishtrail.com) is available at stops along the trail and can be downloaded from the website.

Visitors to the Amish Trail should realize that most of the participating businesses are run out of community members' homes rather than storefronts and many have no formal names. Amish businesses are not open on Sundays and credit cards are not accepted; transactions are cash only. Also, it is considered inappropriate to take photos of Amish people.

Many of the businesses along the Amish Trail are scattered around the county, rather than clustered in a single area; however, one place where visitors can see and purchase a few different types of goods is on Pope Road in the town of Randolph, just off Route 242. Here, you'll find **Hill Top Toy Shop** (11369 Pope Rd., no phone or website), which evokes yesteryear with handmade wooden toys like mini Amish buggies and wagons loaded with alphabet blocks. **A Slice of Heaven Alpacas and Simply Natural Alpaca Gift Shop** (11144 Pope Rd., Randolph, 716/358-5242, www.asliceofheavenalpacas.com) sells soft sweaters, scarves, hats, and socks made of alpaca wool. Between these two businesses is an unnamed **metalworking shop** (just below Hill Top Toy Shop), where light fixtures, hand-hammered hinges, wine racks, and sundries made of iron are all on sale.

Sprague's Maple Farms

If you're in Cattaraugus County during maple sugaring season (typically early spring), it's worth a short detour—especially at breakfast time—to **Sprague's Maple Farms** (1048 Rte. 305, 716/933-6637, www.spraguesmaplefarms.com, Sun.-Thurs. 8am-8pm, Fri.-Sat. 8am-9pm, $14), located in the town of Portville in the southeastern corner of the county and sitting almost right on the New York-Pennsylvania state line.

Visitors to Sprague's Maple Farms may be surprised to see so many people in what seems like the middle of nowhere. For locals and travelers in the know, Sprague's is an obligatory stop. Though this massive maple syrup producer hosts visitors for all sorts of seasonal events, including tapping and sugaring demonstrations, its restaurant is a year-round draw. Not surprisingly, maple dominates the menu and breakfast is served all day, every day.

Surprisingly, you'll learn that maple's a lot like bacon: it tastes good in practically everything.

ALLEGANY COUNTY

No matter how you spell it (you'll see Allegany and Allegheny), Allegany County is a small but lovely rural county in southwestern New York, easily worked into a week-long road trip. If the attractions described here seem of interest to you, just take a day to tack this onto your itinerary before proceeding to Chautauqua County. Take I-86 east to one of Allegany's first towns, Cuba, before moving to the southwestern corner of the county to visit the tiny town of Ceres.

Cuba

No one in Cuba seems to have the definitive answer to the question about the origins of their town's name, the novelty of which is unique only to visitors. If you have a question about cheese, though, most anyone would be happy to answer it. The town is famous—at least in western New York—for its cheese, specifically that made and sold by the family-owned and operated **Cuba Cheese Shoppe** (53 Genesee St., 585/968-3949, www.cubacheese.com). Stop by their shop and sample your way around the store, which also sells kitchen gadgets. Pose with the life-sized cow outside the shop or take a picture of the mural on the side of the building for a lasting memory of your trip to Cuba...New York.

Another interesting attraction in this blink-and-you'll-miss-it small town is **Palmer Opera House,** a restoration work-in-progress on Cuba's main street. For more than five years, a local couple has devoted most of their time and money to a hands-on, top-to-bottom, inside-out preservation project purely out of passion for this historic opera house. When finished, the opera house will host a new era of musical and other creative performances. Until then, visitors can drop by for a peek at preservation in progress.

Ceres

Due south of Cuba is the equally small town of Ceres, which sits right on the New York-Pennsylvania border. It's most notable for one of the more unique accommodations in the area, **Oz's Homestay, The Alternative Fly Inn Bed and Breakfast** (296 Falkner Rd., 716/378-2211, www.ozhomestay-huntinglodge.com, $119-139). Everything about Oz's is out of the ordinary: The B&B is in a 100-year-old barn and furniture is handmade from reclaimed wood by co-owner Ash Easdon-Smith. But what is perhaps most unusual are some of the amenities. Pilots can arrange for private fly-ins on the Easdon-Smiths' turf landing strip, and all guests can take a skydiving lesson with the couple, who have a skydiving center on property.

CHAUTAUQUA COUNTY

After leaving Allegany or Cattaraugus County, head west on I-86 toward Jamestown, one of the larger burgs in Chautauqua County.

THE CANALWAY TRAIL

The Canalway Trail is a network of more than 365 miles of existing multiuse, recreational trails across upstate New York. Major segments follow remnants of the historic original canals of the early 1800s that have since been replaced with the working canal systems of today. **Erie Canal Heritage Trail** (518/434-1583, cycling maps available) connects with trails throughout New York State, providing one of the country's most extensive trail networks.

The canal system also offers excellent biking and walking. The **Erie Canalway Trail** (www.eriecanalway.org), a work in progress, is a nearly 400-mile-long, multiuse trail that, upon completion, will be the longest in the United States. Walking, running, hiking, cycling, and cross-country skiing are all allowed on the trail; some sections are paved and are safe for rollerblading.

Dominated by Chautauqua Lake, this county features the famed intellectual-cultural retreat, the Chautauqua Institution, and a number of picturesque small towns that sit along Chautauqua Lake and Lake Erie.

Jamestown

Jamestown is best known as the birthplace of Lucille Ball, who went on to great fame as a comedian in *I Love Lucy.* Fans can visit the **Lucy-Desi Museum and the Desilu Playhouse** (2-10 West Third St., 716/484-0800, www.lucy-desi.com, Mon.-Sat. 10am-5pm, Sun. 11am-4pm, adults $15, seniors $14, children $10), where Lucy memorabilia abounds.

Lucy isn't the only famous figure born in Jamestown. The **Roger Tory Peterson Institute of Natural History** (311 Curtis St., 716/665-2473, www.rtpi.org, Tues.-Sat. 10am-4pm, Sun. 1pm-5pm, adults $6, children $4) is a nature center and museum intended to further the legacy of 20th-century naturalist Roger Tory Peterson, renowned for his Peterson Field Guides. Exhibits and events are designed to foster curiosity about and appreciation for the natural world. If you want to overnight in the region, carry on to Bemus Point, home to historic Hotel Lenhart and several good restaurants.

Bemus Point

A few miles northwest of Jamestown is Bemus Point, which enjoys pride of place on the eastern shore of Chautauqua Lake. The town is small but charming, especially in summer, when the Bemus Bay Pops Concert Series breathes life back into seasonal Bemus Point. Lawn chairs line the shore while local and national acts perform as the sun sets behind them. Those who aren't lucky enough to score seats can eavesdrop while having dinner at **The Italian Fisherman** (61 Lakeside Dr., 716/386-7000, www.italianfisherman.com, mid-June-mid-Sept. daily 4:30pm-close, $22), an excellent lakefront restaurant with ample outdoor seating (boaters can even pull right up to a lower level dock and anchor).

Visitors who are so taken by the town

that they want to spend the night should try for a room at historic **Hotel Lenhart** (20-22 Lakeside Dr., 716/386-2715, www.hotellenhart.com, Memorial Day-Labor Day, $80-170), which feels like your grandma's rambling summer home...if she had a rambling summer home and a family to fill it up. Kids play games in the downstairs parlor and run barefoot on the front lawn while adults sip on cocktails from the hotel's Lamplighter Room and enjoy the sunset from their rocking chairs on the front porch.

Chautauqua Institution

Leave Bemus Point by crossing the bridge over Chautauqua Lake; on the other side lies the county's best known attraction. Since 1874, **Chautauqua Institution** (1 Ames Ave., Chautauqua, 800/836-2787, www.ciweb.org) has been operating as an "educational experiment in out-of-school, vacation learning" for adults, attracting luminaries from many fields, including the arts, science, politics, and philosophy. Located on spectacular, serene grounds on the shore of Chautauqua Lake, the Institution is primarily active for just nine weeks each summer, hosting more than 100,000 visitors who attend one or more of the 2,200 events on campus. The grounds also feature a restaurant and lodging at **The Athenaeum Hotel** (www.athenaeum-hotel.com).

Findley Lake

Due west of Chautauqua Institution, just off I-86, is Findley Lake. In winter, Findley Lake is a ski town. In summer, life centers around the lake, where boaters, water skiers, and kids who fly into the lake from ropes tied to sturdy tree branches all enjoy the water. There are two main lodging options: **Peek'n Peak** (1405 Olde Rd., 716/355-4141, www.pknpk.com, $149-354), a large resort that's popular with families, and **Blue Heron Inn and Restaurant** (10412 Main St., 716/769-7852, www.theblueheroninn.com), a bed-and-breakfast right across the street from the lake and a two-minute walk from the small downtown's shops. Both properties have restaurants on-site.

Westfield

From Findley Lake, take Route 5 north to Barcelona, first making a stop in Westfield. If the vineyards you pass on the way to Barcelona look different from typical wine country vines, there's a good reason: Most of the vines in Westfield are for Concord grapes, which grow differently from wine grapes. Learn why at **Grape Discovery Center** (8305 West Main Rd., Westfield, 716/326-2003, www.concordgrapebelt.org), where facts about the oldest (more than 150 years) and largest Concord-grape growing region in the world abound.

Barcelona and Dunkirk

Given its location on the shore of massive Lake Erie, it's hardly surprising that Route 5 is dotted with some spectacular lighthouses. Two of the most historic lighthouses are in Barcelona and Dunkirk. **Barcelona Lighthouse** was the first lighthouse in the United States to be powered by natural gas, but it didn't serve as a lighthouse for long. Built in 1829, it was decommissioned just 30 years later. Though it's now a private residence, it makes for a lovely photo and is easily seen from the road on Route 5.

Several miles to the north is **Dunkirk Historic Lighthouse** (1 Lighthouse Point Dr., 716/366-5050, www.dunkirklighthouse.com, hours vary seasonally, adults $8, children $3), which is open to the public. Not only can you ascend to the top for an unobstructed view of Lake Erie's vastness, but you can also learn what it was like to be a lighthouse keeper. The keeper's house, filled with memorabilia and period furniture and ephemera, is part of the tour. The upper floor of the house is also a military museum.

Information and Services

For general information on Buffalo, contact **Visit Buffalo Niagara** (617 Main St., Suite 200, Buffalo, 800/283-3256, www.visitbuffaloniagara.com). For general information on Niagara Falls, contact **Niagara Tourism and Convention Corporation** (10 Rainbow Blvd., 716/282-8992, www.niagara-usa.com), which operates an official tourist information center (June 1-Sept.15 daily 9am-7pm, Sept. 16-May 31 daily 9am-5pm).

Several counties also operate their own tourism offices.

- **Allegany County Office of Tourism and Culture** (800/836-1869, www.discoveralleganycounty.com)

- **Cattaraugus County Tourism** (303 Court St., Little Valley, 800/331-0543, www.enchantedmountains.com)

- **Chautauqua County Visitors Bureau** (716/357-4569, www.tourchautauqua.com)

- **Orleans County Tourism** (14016 Rte. 31, Albion, 800/724-0314, www.countytourism.com)

Getting There and Around

The region's largest airport is **Buffalo Niagara International Airport** (4200 Genesee St., 716/630-6000, www.buffaloairport.com), which is served by **AirTran** (800/247-8726), **American Airlines** (800/433-7300), **Delta** (800/221-1212), **JetBlue** (800/538-2583), **Southwest** (800/435-9792), **United** (800/241-6522), and **USAirways** (800/428-4322).

Buffalo Super Shuttle (716/498-8700, www.buffalosupershuttle.com) offers service from the airport to Buffalo and Niagara Falls. **Niagara Frontier Transportation Authority** ("Metro" to locals) (716/855-7211, www. metro.nfta.com) provides local bus and rail service, including transport to and from the airport.

Amtrak (800/872-7245, www.amtrak.com), **Greyhound** (800/231-2222, www.greyhound. com), and **Trailways of New York** (800/776-7548, www.trailwaysny.com) all serve Buffalo and Niagara Falls. Many smaller towns are serviced by Greyhound and **Coach USA** (www. coachusa.com). The best way to explore the region, however, is by car. Major car rental chains have rental desks at Buffalo Niagara International Airport.

BACKGROUND

The Land

Geography has shaped the development of New York State more than any other single factor. Though bordered on the north, south, and east by mountains, lakes, and rivers, the state's central position between the Atlantic and the Great Lakes, along with its flat western terrain, made it a major thoroughfare for early settlers heading west. Highways were established through the Mohawk River basin and Finger Lakes in the late 1700s, followed in 1825 by the Erie Canal. The canal was largely responsible for New York's rise to prominence, and by 1900, four out of five New Yorkers were living along either the Hudson River or the Erie Canal.

Though New York ranks only 30th among the states in terms of area, it is one of the largest states east of the Mississippi and is extremely diverse geographically. Mountains, plateaus, lowlands, forests, swamps, lakes, rivers, gorges, and beaches can all be found in the state, which was formed mainly during the last Ice Age, when a continental ice sheet up to two miles thick covered almost all of what is now New York. Today, most of the state is comprised of farmland, abandoned farmland, or semi-wilderness. While 85 percent of New York's population may be urban, 85 percent of its land is rural.

© FRANCISCO COLLAZO

Watkins Glen State Park

New York is bounded to the north by the St. Lawrence River and Lake Ontario, to the east by Lake Champlain and the Taconic Mountains, to the southeast by the Atlantic Ocean, to the south by the Delaware River and Allegheny Plateau, and to the west by Lake Erie and the Niagara River. The state's highest point is Mount Marcy (5,344 ft.) in the Adirondack region; its lowest is the Atlantic coastline.

The Hudson River, which originates at Lake Tear of the Clouds atop Mount Marcy, flows north-south through the eastern end of the state. Running east-west through the center of the state is the Mohawk River, whose headwaters are in Oneida County, near Rome. Other important rivers include the Genesee and Oswego, which flow northward into Lake Ontario; and the Delaware, Susquehanna, and Allegheny, which drain the state's southern and western portions.

CLIMATE

Late spring, early summer, and early fall are the best times to visit New York City and much of the upstate. At these times, temperatures generally hover in the 70s, and you're more likely to wake up to one of the state's precious cloudless days. Midsummers in New York City and much of upstate tend to be hot and humid; winters are overcast, wet, and cold. Summer is the best time, however, to visit the more highly elevated regions of the Catskills and Adirondacks.

Average July temperatures range from 64°F in the Adirondacks to 77°F in New York City; average January temperatures range from 14°F in the Adirondacks to 33°F on Long Island. The coldest winters occur in the central Adirondacks and St. Lawrence River Valley, where temperatures often drop below -10°F.

Annual precipitation in the state is 32-45 inches, with the Catskills, Long Island, and Tug Hill (upstate, between Lake Ontario and the Adirondacks) receiving the most rainfall.

FLORA AND FAUNA

Over half of New York State is blanketed with forests, in which over 150 kinds of trees grow.

© FRANCISCO COLLAZO

grape vines in wine country

Among the state's most common wildflowers are buttercups, violets, daisies, black-eyed Susans, devil's paintbrush, wild roses, and Queen Anne's lace. Bright specks of alpine flora can be found high on the Adirondack peaks, while woodland flora such as dewdrops and Jack-in-the-pulpits flourish in the forests. Hundreds of species of shrubs, herbs, grasses, ferns, mosses, and lichens also abound throughout the state.

ENVIRONMENTAL ISSUES

As elsewhere in the northeast United States, New York's great outdoors has been badly affected by industrial contamination. Chemical run-off from factories, intermittent oil spills, and shrinking space for solid waste are all problems that have affected the state in recent decades.

Despite those problems, there's plenty of good news to celebrate. Most of New York's rivers flow significantly cleaner today than they did 30 years ago. Back then, the Hudson, St. Lawrence, and Niagara Rivers were heavily polluted with PCBs, petrochemicals, and pesticides. The Clean Water Act of 1972, along with other state laws, and organizations such as Riverkeeper have helped reduce pollution significantly. And, of course, general improvements in social consciousness with respect to the reduce-reuse-recycle ethic have had a positive impact, too.

Among them are a few southern species, such as the tulip tree and sweetgum, and far more northern species, such as beech, sugar maple, red maple, hickory, ash, cherry, birch, various oaks, white pine, spruce, balsam fir, and hemlock. In the Adirondacks and Catskills, evergreens predominate, while elsewhere in the state, hardwoods are more numerous.

History and Government

HISTORY
Early Peoples

When Europeans first arrived in what is now New York State, they found it inhabited by two major tribes. The Algonquins lived near the Atlantic coast and along the Hudson River Valley, while in upstate dwelled the five tribes of the Iroquois: the Mohawk, Oneida, Onondaga, Cayuga, and Seneca. That New York of yore was a land of great abundance, filled with verdant forests and meadows,

ice-blue rivers, lakes and streams, plump fish and game.

Within a century after the arrival of whites, the Algonquin population was decimated, due largely to virulent European diseases such as measles and smallpox. The Iroquois, however, thrived during initial contact. First the Dutch, and then the French and British enlisted their help in the profitable fur trade, cultivating their friendship through gifts and the selling of firearms. During the French and Indian War, the

THE NATIVE AMERICAN CONFEDERACY OF SIX NATIONS

Before the arrival of European settlers, Algonquin and Iroquois tribes lived freely in New York. The Algonquin resided in the south and along the Hudson River Valley, while the Iroquois spread out across the north.

The Iroquois were actually a confederacy of five tribes—the Mohawk, Oneida, Onondaga, Cayuga, and Seneca—who had banded together around 1570 to form the Iroquois League, an advanced confederacy with social laws and government institutions designed to promote peace among its members. Fifty sachems, chosen from the village chiefs, governed the confederacy, and each nation had one vote. A sixth nation, the Tuscarora, joined the Confederacy in 1722.

The Iroquois survived through hunting, fishing, and the planting of the "Three Sisters"—corn, beans, and squash. Records were kept through storytelling and the weaving of elaborate wampum belts. Each of the Iroquois tribes was divided into matrilineal clans that took their names from birds and animals. Clans lived in longhouses comprised of 50-60 families, and all clan members were considered part of one family. Women selected clan chiefs.

The men responsible for founding the confederacy were a Huron, now known as the Peacemaker, and Hiawatha, an Onondaga chief. The two traveled from tribe to tribe for months, convincing their people to lay down arms and embrace the Great Law of Peace. The Law gave equal voice to each tribe, guaranteed freedom of speech, set up a system for impeachment of corrupt chiefs, and outlined an amendment procedure.

Sound familiar? It's because the Great Law served as one of the models for the U.S. Constitution. No firm textual evidence exists, but several framers of the Constitution met frequently with the Iroquois after the Revolution, and Benjamin Franklin in particular expressed a wish to use their system as a model. In 1988, Congress passed a resolution acknowledging this Native American contribution to the U.S. Constitution.

Today, approximately 40,000 Native Americans live in New York State. About 35 percent reside on reservations, while the rest live in large urban areas, most notably Brooklyn. Eight Iroquois communities are located upstate, ranging in size from the 30,469-acre Allegany Reservation (Seneca) to the 5,700-acre Tuscarora Reservation.

Iroquois-British alliance against the French was instrumental in allowing England to gain control over North America.

The Iroquois did not fare so well during the American Revolution. Once again allying themselves with the British, they became the object of a ruthless 1779 campaign waged by American generals Clinton and Sullivan. By the time the campaign was over, the Iroquois nation was in ruins. Thousands fled to Canada; others were resettled onto reservations.

European Settlement

In 1524, the first European, Giovanni da Verrazano, arrived in what is now New York State by sailing into New York Harbor. However, due to a sudden "violent contrary wind [that] blew in from the sea and forced us to return to our ship," Verrazano never set foot in New York.

In 1609, Samuel de Champlain sailed south from Canada to explore the lake that now bears his name. That same year, Englishman Henry Hudson made the first of two voyages aimed at finding a northwest passage to the Orient. Backed by the Dutch West India Company, he sailed into New York harbor and ventured halfway up the Hudson River before abandoning his quest and returning home. The following year, he returned as captain of a British ship. This time he sailed into Hudson Bay, where the ship became icebound. Starving and doubting their captain's navigational abilities, the crew mutinied. They cast Hudson, his son, and several others adrift in a small boat, never to be seen again.

Though unsuccessful in his search for a northwest passage, Hudson was instrumental in drawing Europeans to the New World. His reports described the area's abundant natural resources, including a wealth of beaver and mink. In 1624, a group of Dutch merchants established Fort Orange, New York's first European settlement. Situated at present-day Albany, the fort served primarily as an outpost for the fur trade.

One year later, the Dutch established a similar outpost, Fort Amsterdam, at the foot of Manhattan Island. In 1626, Peter Minuit was appointed the colony's first governor. Almost immediately, he purchased Manhattan Island from the Algonquins for trinkets worth about $24. The Algonquins considered it a good deal at the time. Having a different sense of ownership than did the Dutch, they thought they were selling only the right to use land, not the land itself.

Unlike the dour religious colonizers of New England, the Dutch traders proved to be a fun-loving bunch who had to be constantly reminded by their governors not to play tennis when they should be working and not to drink on Sunday when they should be listening to sermons. Both men and women smoked, and as one observer of the day noted, "All drink here from the moment they are able to lick a spoon."

The last and most flamboyant of New Amsterdam's Dutch governors was Peter Stuyvesant, in power from 1647 to 1664. Nicknamed "Old Peg Leg," due to a leg lost in battle, Stuyvesant was an arrogant, quick-tempered man with a puritanical streak. He ordered the taverns closed on Sundays and tried to prevent a group of Portuguese Jews from settling in the colony, an action for which he was swiftly reprimanded by his bosses back in Amsterdam.

For all his failings, however, Stuyvesant was responsible for turning New Amsterdam into a semblance of a town. He straightened streets, repaired fences, and established a night watch. And he was one of the few Dutch colonists who

wanted to fight off the English. The rest of the colony didn't much care; the English, who had by this time established a strong presence in New England, had promised New Amsterdam residents that if they surrendered, their lives would go on as before. That was just fine with the Dutch merchants. As long as they were making money, it made no difference to them who governed the colony.

Enter and Exit the British

The British took over New Amsterdam in 1664, renaming the colony New York after the Duke of York, who was later crowned King James II. The Dutch system of government was replaced with the British one, but for most colonists, life went on as before. The colony remained predominantly Dutch until the end of the century and continued to prosper and grow, with New York City reaching a population of 25,000 in 1750. In the New World, only Philadelphia was bigger.

For the colonists of African heritage, however, life under British rule became increasingly difficult. The slave trade was encouraged and a slave market was set up on Wall Street. Some black families who had owned land under the Dutch had their property confiscated; others lost it after passage of a 1712 law prohibiting blacks from inheriting land.

The land-use system in upstate New York also continued much as it had before. The Dutch had used the patroon system, whereby an individual was given a large tract of land in return for bringing over at least 50 settlers to work that land. The English established a similar landlord-tenant arrangement whereby a few men were given enormous manor estates, which they then rented out in parcels to poor farmers. In some parts of the Hudson Valley and Catskills, remnants of this feudal-like system remained in effect until the 1840s.

By the time of the Revolutionary War, New York City had reached a population of 25,000. Albany and Kingston were thriving as river ports, and several smaller settlements, including Saratoga and Fort Stanwix, had been established as far north as Lake Champlain and as far west as Rome. Manor estates lined the Hudson River, and Long Island was peppered with productive farm communities.

When rumblings of revolution began, New York took a pro-Tory stance at first. Merchants and manor landlords intent on making money wanted nothing to do with war. "What is the reason that New York must continue to embarrass the Continent?" queried John Adams. As tensions escalated, however, New Yorkers changed their position and, after 1753, supported the Revolution wholeheartedly.

No state bore the brunt of the war more than New York. The earliest battles were fought in New York City—which remained in British hands throughout the war—and many of the later ones took place upstate. The Americans were badly defeated by the British at Oriskany, near Rome, in 1777. The British were unexpectedly defeated by the Americans at Saratoga, also in 1777. Benedict Arnold plotted to betray the Continental Army at West Point in 1780. General Washington declared victory over the British in Newburgh in 1781.

In 1789, Washington was inaugurated as the first president of the United States in Federal Hall on Wall Street, New York City. The city served as the nation's capital until 1790, when the federal government transferred to Philadelphia.

Rise to Power

New York made a rapid recovery after the war. Upstate, settlers poured into the Mohawk River Valley and the Finger Lakes region. Many of the new settlers were Yankees, tired of eking out marginal livings on rocky New England soils. Attracted to New York's fertile farmland, they brought with them their strong work ethic, Protestant religion, and austere architectural styles, many examples of which still stand.

Settlers also poured into New York City. Between 1790 and 1830, the city gradually transformed itself from one of many important colonial centers into the largest and wealthiest metropolis in the new republic.

The factors leading to New York's ascendancy were many, but probably the most important was the opening of the Erie Canal in 1825. The hand-dug canal, stretching from the Hudson River to Lake Erie, established a water route to the West, thereby reducing the cost of transporting goods by a whopping 90 percent. Hundreds of thousands of small boats were soon plying the new route, carrying cargo to New York City for transfer onto oceangoing vessels. By 1834, the canal's tolls had more than paid for the entire cost of its $7.7 million construction. New York Harbor became one of the world's busiest ports, with grain elevators and warehouses sprouting up all along the docks.

The Erie Canal was the making of New York. It transformed New York City from one of many important colonial centers into the largest metropolis in the New World, and gave rise to virtually every other major city in the state, including Syracuse, Rochester, and Buffalo.

About the same time, New York established the country's first regularly scheduled transatlantic shipping service. Previously, ships had sailed only when their holds were full. This innovation gave the metropolis a competitive edge for decades to come.

Manhattan's famous grid street system was established in 1811. All of the island that had not yet been settled was scored into 12 major avenues—each 100 feet wide—and 155 consecutively numbered streets. Most of the streets were 60 feet wide, but those that intersected the already established Broadway when it crossed an avenue were 100 feet wide. Later, when the subway system was built, stops were placed along many of the wider streets.

In 1842, New York opened the Croton Aqueduct Water System, then the world's largest water system. The $12 million project dammed the Croton River, 40 miles upstate, and brought water into the city through a series of reservoirs and aqueducts. New York thus became one of the first cities in the world to supply all its citizens—even the poorest—with clean, fresh water. As a result, outbreaks of cholera and other epidemic diseases were drastically reduced. Today, New York still has one of the world's best water systems.

Slavery and Civil War

Slavery had been a fact of life in New York since 1626, when 11 African slaves were brought to New Amsterdam and forced to work as servants and craftspeople. Before the Revolution, New York had the largest number of slaves of any colony north of Maryland. Later, as a state conducting lucrative business with the cotton-growing South, New York often turned a blind eye to the cruelties of the "curious institution." In fact, New York was one of the last Northern states to abolish slavery, only doing so in 1827.

Despite this dismal beginning, New York played a critical role in the anti-slavery movement before and during the Civil War. Many of the country's most ardent abolitionists, including William Seward, Frederick Douglass, Gerrit Smith, and Martin Van Buren, lived upstate, and the Finger Lakes region was regarded as a hotbed of anti-slavery sentiment. Gerrit Smith and John Brown established a farm for escaped slaves near Lake Placid in 1849, and Underground Railroad stations dotted the state, especially along the Niagara frontier. When escaped slave William "Jerry" McHenry was arrested by federal marshals in Syracuse in 1851, he was promptly rescued by vigilante abolitionists. That rescue, which challenged the Fugitive Slave Act of 1850, was one of the early precipitating events of the Civil War.

The pre-Civil War years also witnessed the influx of the first great wave of immigrants that swept into New York City between the mid-1800s and the 1920s. From 1840 to 1855, over three million Irish and Germans arrived. Many of the Irish were escaping the potato famines; many of the Germans, the failed Revolution of 1848.

When the Civil War began, New York officially supported the Union. But the citizenry remained divided. The city's newest immigrants resented having to fight to free slaves, who might then come north and compete for jobs. In 1863, this deep-rooted discontent led to the Draft Riots, in which 2,000 people were injured or killed.

About 500,000 New Yorkers served in the war, and about 50,000 were killed. The state also contributed much in the way of supplies and weapons.

After the war, infamous William Marcy "Boss" Tweed rose to power in New York City. A tough street fighter, Tweed was America's first "political boss." He never held mayoral office, but he controlled the city from behind the scenes through the Democratic machine known as Tammany Hall. During Tweed's corrupt reign, from 1866 to 1871, he and his cronies pocketed as much as $200 million from padded or fraudulent city expenditures and tax improprieties. Eventually indicted, Tweed died in a Ludlow Street jail not far from his birthplace.

The Late 1800s

The Civil War put a temporary dent in New York's economy, but by the 1880s, it was back in full force. Corporations all over the state doubled, tripled, or even quadrupled in size, with a corresponding explosion of activity in commerce, transportation, banking, and, especially, manufacturing.

New York City was in its full glory. In 1892, 1,265 millionaires lived either in the city or its suburbs. In 1895, the city housed nearly 300 companies worth over one million dollars—more than the next six largest cities combined. In 1898, New York annexed Brooklyn, Queens, Staten Island, and the Bronx, thereby increasing its area from 23 to 301 square miles.

The rich and the powerful flocked to New York City from all over the country, and the social elite were soon defined as the "Four Hundred"—the maximum number of guests who could squeeze into Mrs. Astor's 5th Avenue ballroom. Investment bankers such as J. P. Morgan and August Belmont became household names, as did leaders of commerce and industry such as John D. Rockefeller, Andrew Carnegie, and F. W. Woolworth.

New York City became the nation's cultural capital as well. Theaters sprang up along Broadway, and the Metropolitan Museum of Art and Metropolitan Opera opened their doors in 1880 and 1890, respectively. Walt Whitman sang the city's praises in poems such as "Leaves of Grass" and "Crossing Brooklyn Ferry," and Henry James and Edith Wharton reported on the lives of the upper crust in *Washington Square* and *The Age of Innocence.*

But the years surrounding the turn of the century also had a darker side. Between 1880 and 1919, a new wave of more than 17 million immigrants, this time mainly from southern and eastern Europe, swept into New York City. Many settled in the Lower East Side, where they worked miserable, low-paying jobs in the garment industry. Overcrowding became a serious problem; by 1900, more than two-thirds of the city's residents were squeezed into some 80,000 tenements in Manhattan and Brooklyn. The Lower East Side had a population density of 209,000 people per square mile, equal to that of today's Mumbai.

Immigrants who settled upstate to work the region's many burgeoning factories suffered as well. Often illiterate and unable to speak fluent English, they were subject to exploitation, poor health and housing conditions, pollution, and increasing crime.

The larger the cities grew, the greater the need for improved transportation. Horsecars gave way to streetcars, and by 1900, nearly every city upstate had a streetcar system.

In 1904, Manhattan opened its first subway, long after London (1863) and shortly after Boston (1897). But New York's subway system would soon be distinguished for both its enormous size and its technological innovations. Within a year after opening, New York's subway—then just a single line running up Park Avenue, across 42nd Street, and up Broadway—was carrying over 600,000 passengers per day. By 1937, the city boasted over 700 miles of track handling 4.2 million passengers per day. Today, the subway system still has about 700 miles of track, and handles an average of 5.4 million passengers every weekday.

Reform, Depression, and War

At the beginning of the 20th century, New York was the most powerful state in the United States. Two-thirds of the nation's leading corporations were headquartered in New York City, and the state produced one-sixth of the gross national product. Ex-New York governor Theodore Roosevelt had just succeeded President William McKinley—assassinated in Buffalo in 1898—to the White House.

The Progressive Era in politics began to peak about a decade later, following the 1911 Triangle Shirtwaist factory fire that took the lives of 146 workers in Greenwich Village. Many progressive reforms were propelled through the state legislature by Democrat Al Smith, who later became one of New York's greatest governors. A self-educated man, born poor on the Lower East Side, Smith helped create dozens of monumental labor, safety, education, and housing bills.

After World War I, the United States emerged as a world power, and nowhere was this newfound status more evident than in dazzling New York City. Business and manufacturing flourished. The Jazz Age arrived and liquor flowed. F. Scott Fitzgerald came to town, and Jimmy Walker was elected mayor. A dandified gentleman with a taste for the good life, Walker spent most of his time visiting nightclubs, sporting halls, and showgirls. Thanks to his late-night carousing, he rarely appeared at City Hall before 3pm, if at all. "No civilized man," he once said, "goes to bed the same day he wakes up."

Strict new federal immigration laws of 1921 and 1924 slowed the influx of foreigners into New York to a trickle, but Harlem boomed as black Southerners fleeing poverty took refuge in the city. In 1910, Manhattan was home to about 60,000 blacks; by 1930, that number had tripled. Harlem became the center for African American culture, with the Harlem Renaissance attracting writers and intellectuals such as Langston Hughes and W. E. B. DuBois, and jazz clubs and theaters attracting the likes of Duke Ellington and Chick Webb.

The Great Depression of 1929 hit New York State especially hard. By 1932 industrial production upstate had fallen by one-third, bread lines filled city blocks, and New York City banks shut down and reopened as soup kitchens. Scores of shantytowns called the naval and military park in Buffalo's Canalside District

© FRANCISCO COLLAZO

"Hoovervilles" dotted Central Park and other city parks upstate.

Enter Franklin Delano Roosevelt. In 1930, as governor of New York, he devised a five-point program to help the state cope with the economic disaster. In 1932, elected president of the United States, he applied and expanded his New York program into the national New Deal. New Yorkers went back to work on public works projects ranging from transportation to housing. Many were projects envisioned and developed by Robert Moses, the autocratic "master builder" largely responsible for the shape of modern-day New York.

However, like the rest of the nation, New York's greatest boon to post-Depression recovery was World War II. Overnight, the state's factories and shipyards thrived anew, producing arms, uniforms, and other items for the war effort.

During the war, Columbia University at 116th Street and Broadway was the site of a nuclear experiment conducted by Dr. Robert Oppenheimer. Code-named "The Manhattan Project," the experiment led to the creation of the world's first atomic bomb, dropped on Japan in August 1945.

Post-War Decline and New York City's Recovery

Despite prosperity brought to New York by World War II, the state reached its economic peak relative to the rest of the country around 1940. Thereafter, certain trends already in effect began to undermine both New York and the entire Northeast. These trends would not become visible for many years, but they were there, slowly eating away.

In 1880, 16 percent of all U.S. production workers lived in the New York metropolitan area. By 1900, that figure had fallen to 14 percent, and by 1990, it had fallen to 4 percent. Between 1956 and 1985, the New York City region lost over 600,000 industrial jobs; upstate lost hundreds of thousands more. Some companies left the region due to demographic shifts toward the South and West, others due to technological changes that allowed them to decentralize. Still others fled from the rising cost of doing business in New York.

In 1959 Nelson A. Rockefeller was elected governor of New York. An ambitious man with grand visions, Rockefeller greatly expanded the state university system and built Albany's impressive, futuristic Empire State Plaza. By the time Rockefeller left office in 1973, however, the state budget had grown 400 percent from its 1959 level and state debt had increased 14 times over.

During this same period, New York's once-thriving port also declined. The advent of container ships, which require large dockside cranes for loading, spelled its death. New York's old shipyards simply did not have the space needed to maneuver the cranes.

With these economic shifts came considerable social unrest. Urban race riots and anti-war demonstrations rocked the state. In 1969 the Woodstock Music and Arts Festival drew young people from all over the country to a dairy farm in the Catskills. Between 1950 and 1970, over one million families left New York City in the "Great White Flight." In 1971, a deadly uprising at Attica prison left 43 inmates and guards dead.

On the up side, New York City's cultural scene was thriving. The Guggenheim Museum opened in 1959, followed by Lincoln Center in the mid-1960s. Broadway was producing one great hit after another, including *My Fair Lady* and *West Side Story*. "Culture had become a commodity," wrote historian Harold Syrett, "and New Yorkers were its largest producers. Most other Americans had to be content with being consumers."

Things finally came to a head in New York City in 1975. Cultural attractions aside, the city was all but bankrupt. Banks shut off credit, and the city, in desperation, turned to the federal government for help. The famous *Daily News* headline "Ford to City: Drop Dead" caustically summed up Washington's stony response.

The city was temporarily rescued by the Municipal Assistance Corporation, put together by financier Felix Rohatyn and Governor Hugh Carey to issue city bonds and thereby borrow money. Washington was impressed enough by this effort to finally extend the city a short-term loan of $2.5 billion.

The city's recovery was further aided in 1978 by the election of Mayor Ed Koch. A one-time liberal from the Bronx via Greenwich Village, Koch helped set the city back on track through budget cuts and austerity programs. Brash, shrewd, and outspoken, Koch managed to play the city's various interest groups off one another to the general public's advantage, winning the respect of many New Yorkers in the process. Much of the 1980s construction boom, which included Trump Tower and the World Financial Center, was attributed to his efforts. Unfortunately, so was the city's steadily increasing homeless population.

Upstate, however, the economic picture remained gloomy. More jobs were lost throughout the 1970s and again in the early 1990s as companies moved from the Northeast to the South and West. Many New Yorkers blamed these industrial losses on the state's steep tax rate—among the highest in the nation—but the truth was, and is, that no amount of tax cuts can make New York the state it once was. The emergence of the Pacific Rim, the shift in the nation's demographics, and the rise of a global economy have irrevocably altered New York's economic position.

The 21st Century

At the end of the 1990s, while much of upstate languished, New York City was riding the crest of the bull stock market. Dozens of new businesses, restaurants, bars, and shops were opening up daily, on even the most depressed of blocks. Rents were skyrocketing and streets teemed with well-dressed twentysomethings earning salaries their grandparents never even dreamed of.

In addition, New York was—and is—benefiting from the energy and spirit of yet another enormous influx of immigrants. Many had been steadily arriving since the easing of immigration quotas in 1965; others have come since the end of the Cold War, or following political upheaval in their home countries. Some

90,000 documented immigrants enter the city each year; one out of every three New Yorkers is foreign-born.

Then came the recession, and the September 11 terrorist attack on the World Trade Center that killed about 2,700 innocent people in a morning that will be forever seared into New York's sense of itself. In a few short moments, the city was plunged into death, devastation, and unspeakable horror.

But even as New Yorkers reeled with grief and fear, they also rose to meet the crisis. In one of the city's finest hours, thousands of citizens quickly pulled themselves together to volunteer their time, donate their money, and keep each others' spirits up, while Mayor Rudy Giuliani became a national hero for his leadership. The attacks unified the city in a way never before seen in modern times.

Giuliani was unable to run for mayor again in 2001 due to the city's term-limits law. Michael Bloomberg, a billionaire businessman, succeeded Giuliani. Bloomberg quickly set about dealing with the aftermath of the attacks and reaching out to some of the minority groups that Giuliani shunned. Though regularly criticized for his impatience and occasional tactless speech, as well as his tendency to introduce and champion causes that many citizens saw as invasive (such as the so-called "soda ban"), Bloomberg was reelected to a second term in 2005. Then, in a highly controversial move, Bloomberg led a successful campaign to change the term-limits law and ended up serving a third term as mayor, arguing that the continuity he represented and market astuteness he possessed were needed to shepherd the city through the global financial crisis.

The Bloomberg era ended in November 2013 with the landslide win of Bill de Blasio, a Brooklyn Democrat. Previously a councilman and the City's public advocate, he was viewed by many voters as a populist candidate who, along with his multiracial family (his wife is African American, their children are biracial), more accurately reflects the face of diverse New York than his predecessors.

New York State's Capitol building

© FRANCISCO COLLAZO

GOVERNMENT

New York's state government is led by an exceptionally strong governor with power over hundreds of appointments, and a legislature comprised of a 62-member Senate and 150-member Assembly. Members of both houses are elected for two-year terms, and each house has standing committees concerned with public policy issues. The governor also appoints non-legislative commissions to investigate such problems as education aid and welfare administration. The state's finances are overseen by an independently elected comptroller.

On a local level, New York is divided into 62 counties that are further subdivided into towns. The towns, which function as townships do elsewhere, contain cities and villages, most governed by a mayor and a council.

ESSENTIALS

Getting There and Around

GETTING THERE
Air

Most major U.S. airlines and many foreign carriers offer regularly scheduled flights into New York City's **La Guardia** (LGA, Elmhurst, Queens, 718/533-3400, www.panynj.gov/airports), **John F. Kennedy** (JFK, Jamaica, Queens, 718/244-4444, www.panynj.gov/airports), or **Newark Liberty International** (EWR, Newark, NJ, 973/961-6000, www.panynj.gov/airports) airports. Several major U.S. airlines also fly to other cities in the state, including **Albany** (ALB, 737 Albany Shaker Rd., Albany, 518/242-2200, www.albanyairport.com), **Rochester** (ROC, 1200 Brooks Ave., Rochester, 585/753-7000, www2.monroecounty.gov), **Islip** (ISP, 100 Arrivals Ave., Ronkonkoma, Long Island, 631/467-3300, www.macarthurairport.com), and **Buffalo** (BUF, 4200 Genesee St., Buffalo, 716/630-6000, www.buffaloairport.com).

Train

Amtrak (800/872-7245, www.amtrak.com) has several north-south and east-west routes running through New York State. Its Empire State service runs from New York City's Penn Station in the east to Niagara Falls in the west, making stops in Albany, Syracuse, Rochester, and Buffalo

© DREAMSTIME.COM

along the way. Amtrak also has the Adirondack, which runs from New York City to Montréal, stopping in Albany, and the Ethan Allen, which runs from New York City to Albany and onward to Rutland, Vermont. Amtrak's trains also depart Penn Station for other major cities in the northeast and mid-Atlantic, including Boston, Philadelphia, and Washington, D.C.

Metro-North (212/532-4900, www.mta. info/mnr), a commuter railroad, offers service between New York City's Grand Central Terminal and the Hudson Valley region, while **Long Island Rail Road** (718/217-5477, www. lirr.org) offers service between New York City's Penn Station and Long Island.

Bus

Greyhound (800/231-2222, www.greyhound. com) offers regular bus service to major cities and popular tourist destinations throughout the state. **Adirondack-Pine Hill Trailways** and **New York Trailways** also service major cities, as well as a variety of rural areas; the two Trailways

(800/776-7548, www.trailways.com) are branches of the same company. **Peter Pan Bus Company** (800/343-9999, www.peterpanbus.com) operates between New York City and a number of northeastern towns and cities, as do a number of budget-minded bus services, including **BOLT Bus** (877/265-8287, www.boltbus.com) and **megabus** (877/462-6342, www.us.megabus.com).

GETTING AROUND

Though New York City is best explored by foot, subway, bus, and taxi, upstate New York is better suited to travel by car. Outside New York City, public transportation is limited and infrequent.

I-87 is the principal highway running south-north from New York City to Canada. I-90 is the main highway running east-west, from Massachusetts and Albany to Buffalo.

The statewide speed limit for open highway driving is 65 miles per hour. Speed limits for cities, towns, villages, and smaller roads are considerably slower. It is against the law to

© FRANCISCO COLLAZO

Open Air Buffalo tour bus

drive without using seat belts in the driver and front passenger seats and all passengers under the age of 16 must be buckled in. Children eight and under must be in an approved car seat or booster seat. Unless otherwise noted by signage, a right turn on red is permitted almost everywhere except New York City. Throughout the entire state, it is illegal to talk or text on a mobile device while driving. For a full list of road rules and driver safety information, visit www.safeny.ny.gov.

If renting a car, try to do so outside Manhattan. Rates are typically lower at airports, in outer boroughs, and elsewhere in the state. Major car rental companies operating in New York State include **Avis** (800/352-7900), **Budget** (800/404-8033), **Hertz** (800/654-3131), and **National** (800/468-3334).

Accommodations

CAMPING
Excellent campgrounds are located in most of New York's 179 **state parks** (reservations 800/456-2267, www.nysparks.com). For $12-25 a night, campers are provided with a tent site, table, fire ring, running water, flush toilets, and hot showers; RV hookups are extra. Some of the campgrounds also offer cabins, cottages, or lean-tos. Some parks offer gear (lanterns, bikes, kayaks) for rent piecemeal. Only a handful of campgrounds remain open through the winter.

YOUTH HOSTELS AND YMCAS
Hosteling International-American Youth Hostels (AYH, 240/650-2100, www.hiusa. org) offer clean accommodations for people of all ages. A hostel usually consists of dormitory rooms, a kitchen, and a common room. Sometimes, hostels have private rooms available for families. Hosteling International facilities are located in New York City, Syracuse, Niagara Falls, and Cape Vincent. Overnight rates are $25-55 per person.

You must be a member to stay at many AYH hostels. Annual membership fees are adults $28, seniors $18, and youths under 18 free. Membership cards are usually sold on-site or through the **national office** (240/650-2100). They can also be purchased online (www.hiusa. org). Reservations at all AYH hostels should be made well in advance. Keep in mind that the Syracuse, Niagara Falls, and Cape Vincent hostels are seasonal.

The **Young Men's Christian Association** (YMCA) offers inexpensive, but not always clean, accommodations at six locations in New York City and several other urban areas throughout the state. For information on New York's YMCAs, which are co-ed, contact **YMCA of Greater New York** (212/630-9600, www.ymcanyc.org) or visit the website of **The Alliance of New York State YMCAs** (www.ymcanys.org).

MOTELS AND HOTELS
Motels and hotels offering anywhere from 6 to more than 200 rooms abound in New York State. Some are independent operations; others belong to nationwide chains and provide an especially good choice for families or travelers looking for affordable accommodations. Among the many chains are **Four Points Sheraton** (www.fourpoints.com), **Holiday Inn** (www.ihg.com), **Marriott** (www.marriott.com), and **Wyndham** (www.wyndham.com).

BED-AND-BREAKFASTS
B&Bs are a popular lodging option in New York State, especially in the Hudson Valley, Cooperstown, Finger Lakes, Saratoga Springs, Rochester, Ithaca, and eastern Long Island. Many are expensive and cater more to city folk looking for pampering than to budget travelers. Keep in mind, too, that rates vary considerably depending upon the season.

Check the I Love NY website (www.iloveny.com) for a list of B&B accommodations throughout the state.

© FRANCISCO COLLAZO

Resorts like the Holiday Valley Resort in Ellicottville are one option for accommodations.

Tips for Travelers

WHAT TO TAKE

Visitors to New York City will want to bring comfortable walking shoes, casual clothes, and a few items of sophisticated attire for evenings out. Since much of New York State is humid during the summer, with temperatures in the 80s and 90s, bring plenty of short-sleeved shirts. In fall and spring, you'll need a jacket, long-sleeved shirts and pants, and rain gear. In the winter, dress for cold winds and snow. A pair of sturdy shoes or sneakers come in handy for casual exploring. Insect repellent is a must, and sunscreen is essential in summer.

VISITOR INFORMATION

Council on International Educational Exchange (207/553-4000, www.ciee.org) provides information on low-cost travel and work-study programs in the United States, including New York State, for international students and professionals.

Help for disabled travelers is available through **Society for Accessible Travel and Hospitality** (212/447-7284, www.sath.org), a nationwide, nonprofit membership organization that collects data on travel facilities around the country.

New York State residents with disabilities should apply for the **Access Pass** (518/474-2324, www.nysparks.com), which provides free entry to most state parks and recreation areas.

The **Golden Park Program** provides New York State residents age 62 or older with free entry to state parks and recreation areas any weekday, excluding holidays. Simply present your current driver's license or non-driver's identification card at the entrance.

Similarly, the National Park Service (NPS) issues **Senior Passes** to people 62 years or older for national historic sites and parks. Senior Passes are $10 and are good for a lifetime. They provide free admission to parks and offer up to 50 percent off certain NPS amenity, facility, and service fees. Senior Passes replace Golden Access and Golden Age Passports, which are no longer sold. If you have one of these, however, the NPS will continue to honor it. For more information, visit the National Park Service website (www.nps.gov).

Anyone over age 50 is eligible to join **AARP** (888/687-2276, www.aarp.org), which provides its members with hotel, airfare, car rental, and sightseeing discounts. **Road Scholar** (800/454-5768, www.roadscholar.org) offers educational tour packages in New York City and State for travelers who are interested in lifelong learning. Once aimed at budget travelers age 60 and older, the Road Scholar programs now have no minimum age limit, though they still tend to attract adults between the ages of 55 and 75.

HEALTH AND SAFETY
City Safety
Though crime is no longer the problem it was before the era of Mayor Rudy Giuliani, it remains a concern in the Big Apple and other New York cities. Wherever you go, stay alert and use common sense. Carry only small amounts of cash; ignore hustlers and con artists; keep a tight hold on your purse and camera; label and lock your luggage; lock your car; and avoid lonely and unlit stretches, especially after dark.

Outdoor Safety
Before heading into forests and semi-wilderness areas of New York State, be sure you know where you're going and what you're doing. Check with park officials and other knowledgeable outdoorspeople about trail conditions, weather, water sources, and fire danger. Be sure your equipment is functioning properly, and don't head out alone. If you're an outdoors novice, accompany someone with more experience.

Basic gear for day hikes includes a small knapsack, hat, sunscreen, lip balm, compass, whistle, insect repellent, multipurpose knife, good hiking boots, layered clothing, food, and an ample water supply. For longer or more demanding hikes, bring a butane lighter or waterproof matches, nylon rope, first-aid kit, "space blanket," extra socks and shoelaces, and a waterproof poncho or large plastic bag.

Lyme Disease
Anyone who spends time outdoors in New York should be aware of the symptoms of Lyme disease. The bacterium that causes the disease is carried by deer ticks, which are found in brush, meadows, forests, and even lawns. In early stages, the disease is easily treatable with antibiotics, but if left unattended, it can lead to serious neurological, heart, and joint problems.

Many—*but not all*—of those infected develop a red circular rash around the bite location within three days to one month. The rash usually begins with a small red dot that expands to a diameter of 1-5 inches. The expanded rash may feature a bright red border and a hard, pale center.

The rash is usually accompanied by flu-like symptoms. These include fatigue, nausea, vomiting, diarrhea, muscle and joint pain, stiff neck, swollen lymph glands, headaches, fevers, chills, sore throat, dry cough, dizziness, sensitivity to the sun, and chest, ear, or back pain.

Lyme disease was first identified in Old Lyme, Connecticut, in 1975, and quickly spread throughout New England. More than 95,000 cases have been documented in New York State since Lyme became reportable in 1986. If you suspect you have Lyme disease, contact your doctor immediately.

Wear light-colored clothing to spot ticks easily, and long pants and long-sleeved shirts to discourage them. Tuck pants cuffs into socks, and use an insect repellent with a 25-30 percent DEET content around clothing openings and on exposed skin.

Use gloves and tweezers to remove ticks; grasp the tick's head parts as close to your skin as possible and apply slow, steady traction. Wash your hands and the bitten area afterward. Do not attempt to remove ticks by burning them or coating them with anything like nail polish remover or petroleum jelly. If you remove a tick before it has been attached for more than 24 hours, you greatly reduce your risk of infection.

Ticks do not jump, but usually crawl upward until they find exposed skin. Their favorite spots are the back of the neck, scalp, armpits, groin area, and the backs of knees. Not all bites result in illness.

If you plan to spend much time outdoors in New York State, you may want to read additional tips on the Centers for Disease Control website (www.cdc.gov/lyme). At present, no vaccine is available for Lyme disease; it was discontinued in 2002 due to insufficient demand.

Information and Services

VISAS AND OFFICIALDOM

Most foreign visitors entering the United States are required to carry a current passport, visa, and proof they intend to leave (typically in the form of a return plane ticket). It's also wise to carry proof of citizenship, such as a driver's license or birth certificate.

Since 9/11, the process of obtaining a U.S. visa has become more difficult and lengthy. Apply early to avoid disappointment. For information about how to apply or how to extend an existing visa, visit the website of the U.S. Department of State (www.travel.state.gov/visa).

To replace a passport lost while in the United States, contact your country's nearest embassy or consulate; many consulates are located in New York City; a full list of these can be found on the city's website (www.nyc.gov/html/ia/html/affairs/consular.shtml).

Visitors to the United States do not need inoculations unless they are coming from an area known to be suffering from an epidemic such as cholera or yellow fever. Visitors with medical conditions requiring treatment with narcotics or the use of drug paraphernalia such as syringes must carry a valid, signed physician's prescription.

BUSINESS HOURS AND MONEY

Standard business hours in New York are Monday-Friday 9am-5pm. Banks are usually open Monday-Friday 9am-5pm, with some branches open Saturday 9am-1pm or 3pm. Most banks offer 24-hour ATMs.

Most shops are open Monday-Saturday from 9am or 10am to 5pm or 6pm. In New York City, Sunday afternoon and evening hours are also common, and many grocery stores and delis remain open 24/7. The state sales tax is 4 percent, with counties imposing an additional 3-5 percent.

With the exception of some inexpensive motels, restaurants, and shops, credit cards are accepted almost everywhere in the state, and are mandatory for renting cars and most sports equipment.

MEASUREMENTS, MAIL, AND AREA CODES

Like the rest of the United States, New York still eschews the metric system. See the U.S.-Metric Conversion Chart in the back of this book. New York lies within the Eastern Standard Time zone. Daylight saving time, which sets the clocks one hour ahead, goes into effect from the first Sunday in April to the last Sunday in October.

Normal post office hours are Monday-Friday 9am-5pm and Saturday 9am-noon.

New York State uses an ever-proliferating number of area codes. To obtain a number from directory services, dial 411.

MAPS AND TOURIST INFORMATION

The best source for general information on New York State is the official tourism department, the **New York State Division of Tourism** (800/225-5697, www.iloveny.com). It publishes a free *I*

Love New York guide that's updated annually, as well as an official state map and a wide variety of brochures on specific regions, attractions, and interests. For an updated calendar of events staged throughout the state, including New York City, call 800/225-5697. Most regions, cities, and towns also staff their own tourism offices and visitors' centers. These are listed at the end of each region's chapter in this book.

For a free basic guide to New York's state parks, including hiking and camping information, contact **New York State Parks** (518/474-0456, www.nysparks.com).

Excellent maps of New York State are published by the **American Automobile Association** (AAA, 1415 Kellum Pl., Garden City, NY, 516/746-7730, www.ny.aaa.com). The AAA maps are available for free to members at any local AAA office.

Rand McNally (www.store.randmc-nally.com) publishes excellent street maps of Manhattan, as well as a subway map, a Brooklyn map, and street maps for Buffalo, Niagara Falls, Syracuse, and Long Island. The **DeLorme Mapping Company** (www.shop.delorme.com) publishes the excellent, large-format print version of its *New York State Atlas & Gazetteer.*

RESOURCES

Suggested Reading

NEW YORK CITY
Fiction

Auster, Paul. *The New York Trilogy: City of Glass, Ghosts, the Locked Room*. New York, NY: Penguin Books, 1994. Dark humor, suspense, mind games, and film noir in a modern classic about New York City.

Capote, Truman. *Breakfast at Tiffany's*. New York, NY: Vintage, 1993. The moving story of a glamorous madcap adrift on the Upper East Side in the 1950s.

Ellison, Ralph. *Invisible Man*. New York, NY: Vintage, 1995. The classic 1952 novel follows a nameless protagonist from his home in the Deep South to the basements of Harlem. A masterpiece of African American literature that chronicles effects of bigotry on victims and perpetrators alike.

Finney, Jack. *Time and Again*. New York, NY: Simon & Schuster, 1970. A cult classic that time-travels back and forth between the present and the 1880s, when New York was little more than an overgrown small town.

Hamill, Pete. *Forever*. New York, NY: Back Bay Books, 2003. A lark through history (helped by a bit of suspension of belief at times) following Irish-Jewish Cormac O'Connor from 1741 Ireland to New York where he becomes cursed, and blessed, to live "forever" so long as he never leaves the island of Manhattan.

Hijuelos, Oscar. *The Mambo Kings Play Songs of Love*. New York, NY: Perennial Classics, 2000. A rich, deeply resonant novel that recreates the world of immigrant Cuban musicians living in New York post-World War II.

James, Henry. *Washington Square*. New York, NY: Modern Library, 2000. One of James's shorter and more accessible novels, and an engrossing tale of the manners and mores of upper-crust 19th-century New York.

McInerney, Jay. *Bright Lights, Big City*. New York, NY: Vintage Contemporaries, 1984. A young man immerses himself in the excesses of 1980s New York—the clubs, the drugs, the after-hour hot spots—until he is brought to an abrupt reckoning.

Paley, Grace. *Enormous Changes at the Last Minute*. New York, NY: Farrar, Straus and Giroux, 1985. Quirky, funny, sad, combative, vulnerable Paley, who grew up in immigrant New York in the 1920s and '30s, captures the soul of New York in one of her best story collections.

Parker, Dorothy. *The Portable Dorothy Parker*. New York, NY: Penguin Books, 1991. Poems, stories, articles, and reviews by that most quotable of *New Yorker* writers.

Wharton, Edith. *The Age of Innocence*. New York, NY: Modern Library, 1999. The first book written by a woman to win the Pulitzer

Prize is a subtle, elegant portrait of desire and betrayal in moneyed Old New York. Among Wharton's other books set in the city are *The House of Mirth, A Backward Glance,* and *Old New York.*

Nonfiction

Caro, Robert A. *The Power Broker: Robert Moses and the Fall of New York.* New York, NY: Vintage, 1975. Much more than a biography, this Pulitzer Prize-winning tome tells the fascinating and often scandalous story behind the shaping of 20th-century New York. Though over 1,000 pages, the book is a compelling page-turner.

Editors of *New York Magazine. My First New York: Early Adventures in the Big City.* New York, NY: Ecco, 2010. Everyone who visits or lives in New York City has a "my first time" story; this anthology compiles the stories of notable New Yorkers, including Nora Ephron, Liza Minnelli, and Diane Von Furstenberg.

Fitzpatrick, Kevin C. *A Journey into Dorothy Parker's New York.* New York, NY: Roaring Forties Press, 2005. A biographical guide to Dorothy Parker's favorite bars, salons, homes, and offices using archival personal photographs to illustrate her fascinating life and her love of 1920-30s New York City.

Grimes, William. *Appetite City: A Culinary History of New York.* New York, NY: North Point Press, 2009. The former *New York Times* food critic makes readers hungry not only for the city's iconic foods, but also for bygone chapters of New York City's history.

Gross, Michael. *Rogues' Gallery: The Secret Story of the Lust, Lies, Greed, and Betrayals That Made the Metropolitan Museum of Art.* New York, NY: Broadway, 2009. Worthy of a fiction thriller, this fascinating history of the backstory of the Met Museum is really

a history of turn-of-the-century New York's robber baron-philanthropists.

Johnson, James Weldon. *Black Manhattan.* New York, NY: Da Capo Press, 1991. First published in 1930, this classic work paints one of the earliest portraits of lives of African Americans in New York City. Much more than a history, the book also illuminates the Harlem Renaissance, of which Johnson was a part.

Kazin, Alfred. *A Walker in the City.* New York, NY: Harvest/HBJ, 1969. This is the perambulatory memoir of a distinguished literary critic who grew up in immigrant Brownsville. Kazin's sojourns into other neighborhoods and boroughs exposed him to new worlds.

Magnum Photographers, with introduction by David Halberstam. *New York September 11.* New York, NY: powerHouse Books, 2001. A moving tribute to the city, its emergency workers, the World Trade Center, and victims of the terrorist attack.

Mitchell, Joseph. *Up in the Old Hotel.* New York, NY: Vintage, 1993. A reprint of four classics penned by the deadpan *New Yorker* chronicler of city life. "McSorley's Wonderful Salon," "Old Mr. Flood," "The Bottom of the Harbor," and "Joe Gould's Secret" are included.

Sante, Luc. *Low Life.* New York, NY: Farrar, Straus, and Giroux, 2003. A highly original and literate book that delves into the underbelly—opium dens, brothels, sweatshops—of old New York.

Thomas, Piri. *Down These Mean Streets.* New York, NY: Vintage, 1997. This 1967 memoir by the famed writer of Cuban-Puerto Rican descent, who lived in El Barrio, tells of the neighborhood's challenges and dangers, including gangs and drugs.

Poetry

Among the many poets who have written extensively on New York City are Djuna Barnes, Hart Crane, Allen Ginsberg, Victor Hernández Cruz, Langston Hughes, Frank O'Hara, and Walt Whitman.

Specialty Guides

Federal Writers' Project. *The WPA Guide to New York City*. New York, NY: New Press, 1995. First published in 1939 and since reissued, the classic guidebook remains remarkably on target. It provides long and evocative descriptions of everything from long-gone Ebbets Field to the then-new Empire State Building.

Frank, Gerry. *Gerry Frank's Where to Find It, Buy It, Eat It in New York*. Portland, OR: Gerry's Frankly Speaking, 2011. A monumental, nearly 600-page, reference manual on where to find everything from bridal gowns to massage therapists.

White, Norval, and Elliot Willensky, eds. *AIA Guide to New York City*. Three Rivers, MI: Three Rivers Press, 2000. The most important and entertaining book on New York architecture, organized as a series of walking tours. An urban classic, with over 2,000 photos and 100 maps.

BEYOND NEW YORK CITY
Fiction and Memoir

Banks, Russell. *The Sweet Hereafter*. New York, NY: Perennial, 1992. A horrific school-bus accident in Sam Dent, New York, results in the deaths of 14 children. Banks writes compassionately of how the small town responds and somehow moves beyond grief to redemption.

Dobyns, Stephen. *Saratoga Haunting*. New York, NY: Viking Press, 1993. Low-key detective Charlie Bradshaw, operating in the summer horse-racing capital of America, reopens two cases he thought he had solved 20 years earlier. The seventh of poet Dobyns's Charlie Bradshaw books; all are set in Saratoga.

Dreiser, Theodore. *An American Tragedy*. New York, NY: Signet Classics, 2000. The classic book on the dark side of the American Dream, set largely in the Adirondacks and central New York.

Fitzgerald, F. Scott. *The Great Gatsby*. New York, NY: Scribner, 1995. One of the finest works of 20th-century literature takes place largely on the north shore of Long Island.

Gardner, John. *The Sunlight Dialogues*. New York, NY: Random House, 1972. A grand and complex portrait of America in the 1960s, set in the small, agricultural town of Batavia, New York.

Irving, Washington. *Rip Van Winkle and the Legend of Sleepy Hollow*. Tarrytown, NY: Sleepy Hollow Press, 1980. The first American literary writer of note tells tales of the Headless Horseman galloping through Sleepy Hollow and Rip Van Winkle awakening from his 20-year sleep.

Kennedy, William. *Billy Phelan's Greatest Game*. New York, NY: Penguin Books, 1982. The second, and arguably best, of Kennedy's triumvirate of novels set in underworld Albany chronicles the fall and redemption of a small-time hustler. The other two books in the cycle are *Legs* and *Ironweed*.

Oates, Joyce Carol. *Bellefleur*. New York, NY: Plume Books, 1991. The complex and opulent tale of six generations of Bellefleurs, a wealthy and notorious family who live in a region much like the Adirondacks. Other Oates novels set upstate are *A Bloodsmoor Romance* and *Mysteries of Winterthurn*.

Luper, Eric. *Bug Boy*. New York, NY: Farrar, Straus, and Giroux, 2009. Jack "Shabby" Walsh, an apprentice jockey at Saratoga

Race Track in 1934, introduces readers to the fascinating and hard-edged world of horse-racing and the reality of Saratoga life in the Depression.

Wilson, Edmund. *Upstate: Records and Recollections of Northern New York.* Syracuse, NY: Syracuse University Press, 1990. One of the rare books that examines the character of upstate New York, where Wilson and his family summered for generations. The first third of the book, covering various aspects of New York history, is especially astute; the rest is diary entries.

Zabor, Rafi. *The Bear Comes Home.* New York, NY: W.W. Norton, 1998. In this winner of the PEN-Faulkner Award, an intellectual, sax-playing bear, well versed in literature, jazz, and philosophy, fights to find his place in the world. A comic gem, with great insights into what it means to be an artist, set largely in New York City and Woodstock/Bearsville, New York.

Outdoor Guides
Card, Skip. *Moon Take a Hike New York City.* Berkeley, CA. Avalon Travel, 2012. This trail guide leads you turn by turn through hikes within two hours of Manhattan.

McMartin, Barbara. *50 Hikes in the Adirondacks.* Woodstock, VT: Countryman Press, 2003. Though this book could use an update, most of the region's top trails and detailed maps can be found in this edition.

New York-New Jersey Trail Conference, Inc. *New York Walk Book.* Mahwah, NJ: New York-New Jersey Trail Conference, 2001. This updated "hiker's Bible" reflects the many changes that have occurred in the region since the book was first published in 1923. Some of the old trails are gone, of course, but a surprising number of new areas have also opened up, thanks largely to the public acquisition of land. The book also features excellent sections on the history, geology, flora, and fauna of the regions immediately surrounding New York City.

Wadsworth, Bruce. *An Adirondack Sampler: Day Hikes for All Seasons.* Lake George, NY: Adirondack Mountain Club, 1996. An excellent guide for beginning hikers and those new to the Adirondacks. Fifty hikes are recommended.

Internet Resources

GENERAL TRAVEL
The Official New York State Tourism Website
www.iloveny.com
This official site is packed with information on all regions of the state. Recreational areas, accommodations listings, suggested itineraries, activities and events calendars, road maps, and state facts—they're all here.

RECREATION AND THE OUTDOORS
Adirondack Mountain Club
www.adk.org
Visit this site for detailed information on outdoor activities in the Adirondacks. All topics from camping and hiking to educational seminars are covered; books, maps, and gear can be ordered from the site as well.

America's Byways
www.byways.org
This is a U.S. Department of Transportation site that offers descriptions and maps of the country's most scenic back roads. Three New York State byways are highlighted: Great Lakes Seaway Trail, Lakes to Locks Byway, and Mohawk Towpath Byway.

New York State Department of Environmental Conservation
www.dec.ny.gov

This is a first-stop site for information on hiking, canoeing, camping, and other outdoor activities throughout the state. News articles on environmental issues and special events listings are also included.

New York State Office of Parks, Recreation, and Historic Preservation
www.nysparks.com

Each state park and historic site has its own extensive page on this informative site. Search by region or by activity for information about facilities, features, and fees.

NEW YORK CITY
NYC & Company
www.gonyc.com

At the official website of New York City's convention and visitors bureau, you can book a hotel, learn about attractions and special events, check the weather, search out the perfect restaurant, and create your own itinerary. It makes an excellent first stop for Big Apple visitors.

New York City Government
www.nyc.gov

On the city's official government website, find information about local laws and government departments, including the Taxi and Limousine Commission, New York Police Department, and many others. The site also has an event listings page.

LONG ISLAND
Long Island Convention and Visitors Bureau and Sports Commission
www.discoverlongisland.com

Run by Long Island Convention and Visitors Bureau and Sports Commission, this site covers cultural attractions, recreation, golf courses, restaurants, shopping malls, and more. Information on hotels and special events is also included.

THE HUDSON VALLEY AND CATSKILLS
Albany County Convention and Visitors Bureau
www.albany.org

Visitors to Albany might want to check out this official tourism site, with things to do, places to stay, and events listings.

Catskill Region
www.visitthecatskills.com

This official tourism site covers the four counties of the Catskills. Category listings include lodging, camping, attractions, and activities.

Hudson Valley Tourism
www.travelhudsonvalley.com

This official tourism site provides information about accommodations, dining, events, and a "see and do" section about local outdoor and cultural attractions.

Saratoga County Chamber of Commerce
www.saratoga.org

Here you'll find information on where to stay, eat, and play in the horse-racing capital of New York. If you're visiting in the fall, it also has a useful fall foliage report to keep you informed about peak leaf peeping times.

THE ADIRONDACKS
Adirondack Regional Tourism Council
www.visitadirondacks.com

To help plan your trip to the North Country, visit this site run by the Adirondacks Regional Tourism Council. A "trip planner" feature can assist you in setting up a personalized itinerary and you can download free travel guides.

THE FINGER LAKES AND THE THOUSAND ISLANDS-SEAWAY
Finger Lakes Tourism Alliance
www.fingerlakes.org

Visitors to the Finger Lakes will want to check out this site, run by the Finger Lakes Tourism Alliance. In addition to information on attractions, lodging, and restaurants, the site also recommends special interest itineraries concentrating on subjects such as nature, art, and history.

1000 Islands International Tourism Council
www.visit1000islands.com
Everything you wanted to know about the Thousand Islands, from where to stay or play golf to "1000 Things to Do." The "Communities" section offers profiles about each town and its attractions.

BUFFALO AND THE NIAGARA REGION
Buffalo Niagara Convention and Visitors Bureau
www.visitbuffaloniagara.com
Run by the Buffalo Niagara Convention and Visitors Bureau, this site covers attractions, hotels, restaurants, and events in western New York's two biggest cities. Information on regional driving tours and special packages is also included.

Niagara USA
www.niagara-usa.com
This site, managed by Niagara USA, maintains an up-to-date events calendar and provides all the usual visitor information, including things to do and places to stay.

Index

List of Maps

MAP SYMBOLS

▭▭▭	Expressway	**◖**	Highlight	✗	Airfield	⚲	Golf Course
▬▬▬	Primary Road	○	City/Town	✈	Airport	**P**	Parking Area
▭▭▭	Secondary Road	◉	State Capital	▲	Mountain	▰	Archaeological Site
▭ ▭ ▭	Unpaved Road	⊛	National Capital	✦	Unique Natural Feature	▮	Church
- - - -	Trail	★	Point of Interest	⚲	Waterfall	▮	Gas Station
⋯⋯⋯	Ferry	•	Accommodation	⚲		⬭	Glacier
▬▬▬	Railroad	▼	Restaurant/Bar	▲	Park ·	▰	Mangrove
▬▬▬	Pedestrian Walkway	▪	Other Location	▣	Trailhead	▱	Reef
▥▥▥	Stairs	△	Campground	✗	Skiing Area	▰	Swamp

CONVERSION TABLES

°C = (°F - 32) / 1.8
°F = (°C x 1.8) + 32
1 inch = 2.54 centimeters (cm)
1 foot = 0.304 meters (m)
1 yard = 0.914 meters
1 mile = 1.6093 kilometers (km)
1 km = 0.6214 miles
1 fathom = 1.8288 m
1 chain = 20.1168 m
1 furlong = 201.168 m
1 acre = 0.4047 hectares
1 sq km = 100 hectares
1 sq mile = 2.59 square km
1 ounce = 28.35 grams
1 pound = 0.4536 kilograms
1 short ton = 0.90718 metric ton
1 short ton = 2,000 pounds
1 long ton = 1.016 metric tons
1 long ton = 2,240 pounds
1 metric ton = 1,000 kilograms
1 quart = 0.94635 liters
1 US gallon = 3.7854 liters
1 Imperial gallon = 4.5459 liters
1 nautical mile = 1.852 km

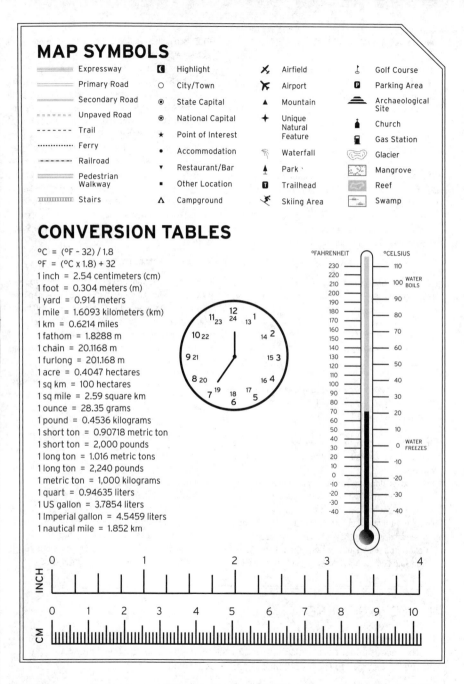

MOON NEW YORK STATE

Avalon Travel
a member of the Perseus Books Group
1700 Fourth Street
Berkeley, CA 94710, USA
www.moon.com

Editor: Kevin McLain
Series Manager: Kathryn Ettinger
Copy Editor: Naomi Adler Dancis
Graphics and Production Coordinator: Lucie Ericksen
Cover Design: Faceout Studios, Charles Brock
Moon Logo: Tim McGrath
Map Editor: Mike Morgenfeld
Cartographer: Stephanie Poulain
Proofreader: Mindy Cooper
Indexer: Greg Jewett

ISBN: 978-1-61238-520-4
ISSN: 1542-6068

Printing History
1st Edition – 1997
6th Edition – July 2014
5 4 3 2 1

Front cover photo: waterfalls in Fillmore Glen State Park, New York © Shobeir Ansari/Getty Images
Title page photo: Lake Placid © dreamstime.com
Other front matter photos: pg 4: Manhattan skyline © dreamstime.com; pg. 5: the Niagara River © Francisco Collazo; pg. 6 top-left: Watkins Glen State Park © Francisco Collazo; top-right: spring in New York City © Francisco Collazo; bottom: hiker at the Adirondacks © cotesebastien/istockphoto.com; page 7 top: "I Love NY" street art by Nick Walker © Francisco Collazo; bottom-left: Brooklyn Bridge © Milo DeMartile; bottom-right: architecture in Buffalo, NY © Francisco Collazo; page 8: Time Square, NYC © dreamstime.com; page 9 top: Central park in Autumn © dreamstime.com; bottom-left: walking tour of Niagara Falls © Francisco Collazo; bottom-right: waterfall in New York's Finger Lakes region © dreamstime.com; page 11, 12, 14, 20, 22 and 24: © Francisco Collazo; page 16: photo courtesy of CMOG; page 17: © Andrew Kazmierski/123RF; page 18 left: © Songquan Deng/123RF; page 18 right: © Lucie Ericksen; page 23: © dreamstime.com;
Back cover photo: horse, the Catskills © beklaus/iStock.com

Printed in Canada by Friesens

KEEPING CURRENT

If you have a favorite gem you'd like to see included in the next edition, or see anything that needs updating, clarification, or correction, please drop us a line. Send your comments via email to feedback@moon.com, or use the address above.